2A

America Reads

EDYTHE DANIEL
Associate Professor of Education, Supervisor of Off-Campus Student Teaching of Secondary English and Speech, Wisconsin State University, Platteville. Formerly teacher of English and Speech, Lincoln Junior High School, Kenosha, Wisconsin

EDMUND J. FARRELL
Assistant Executive Secretary, National Council of Teachers of English. Formerly Supervisor of Secondary English, University of California, Berkeley; formerly English Department Chairman, James Lick High School, San Jose, California

ALFRED H. GROMMON
Professor of Education and English, Stanford University. Formerly teacher of English and department head, Ithaca High School, Ithaca, New York. Editor, The Education of Teachers of English for American Schools and Colleges, National Council of Teachers of English

OLIVE STAFFORD NILES
Consultant in Reading, State Department of Education, Hartford, Connecticut; Lecturer, American International College, Springfield, Massachusetts; formerly Director of Reading, Public Schools of Springfield

ROBERT C. POOLEY
Formerly Professor of English, University of Wisconsin; and Director, Wisconsin English-Language Arts Curriculum Project. First Chairman of the Board of Trustees of the Research Foundation of the National Council of Teachers of English. First Recipient of the W. Wilbur Hatfield Award for extraordinary contributions to the teaching of English

COUNTERPOINT
in literature

EDYTHE DANIEL

EDMUND J. FARRELL

ALFRED H. GROMMON

OLIVE STAFFORD NILES

ROBERT C. POOLEY

SCOTT, FORESMAN AND COMPANY
Editorial Offices: Glenview, Illinois

Regional Sales Offices: Palo Alto, California ·
Tucker, Georgia · Glenview, Illinois ·
Oakland, New Jersey · Dallas, Texas

COUNTERPOINT in literature

COVER Artwork by George Ortman, 1965, courtesy of "The Great Ideas of Western Man Series of Container Corporation of America"

ILLUSTRATIONS by Franz Altschuler, 104–105, 121, 131, 137, 173, 191; Robert Amft, 249, 264, 278–279, 536, 547; Robert Blechman, 146; Bernarda Bryson, 199, 202; Shelley Canton, 568; Bernard D'Andrea, 104–105, 121; Herb Danska, 56–57, 466–467, 476, 489, 494, 499, 511, 518, 528; Dave Dumo, 261; John Everds, 295; Mary Flammang, 215; Elmer Jacobs, 41, 48–49, 403, 413; Herb Kane, 304–305, 315, 323; Carl Kock, 25, 386; Joan Landis, 345; Robert J. Lee, 216, 221; Pat Lenihan, 229; Sally Linn, 546; Charles Mikolaycak, 4, 12–13; Roy Moody, 538; Susan Perl, 81, 93; Bill Peterson, 274, 280, 281; Albert John Pucci, 153, 328; Phil Renaud, 432, 445, 451, 456, 460; Leslie Robin, 396–397; George Roth, 61; Fred Steffen, 167, 372–373, 382; George Suyeoka, 65, 73, 356–357, 424–425, 542, 549, 551, 553, 557, 559, 561, 564, 567; Phero Thomas, 442–443; Justin Wager, 289; Jerome Walker, 363; Dave Wylie, 251, 253, 540

PHOTOGRAPHY by Franz Altschuler, 241, 243; Robert Amft, 195; George Olexy, 143; John Van Dorn, 125

PICTURE CREDITS: Courtesy of American Heritage Publishing Co., Inc., 531; Robert Amft, 215; A. N. P. Foto, Amsterdam, 506; Antikensammlungen, Munich (photo by Hartwig Koppermann), 420; Antikensammlungen, Munich (courtesy Hirmer Verlag), 421; Courtesy Atheneum Publishers, 462; Jerry Bauer–Pix, 222; European Pictures Service, 145, 401; Photo by Alfred Eisenstaedt, 340; Courtesy Farrar, Straus and Giroux (photo by Rollie McKenna), 96; Courtesy LIFE Magazine (photo by George Rodger), 532; Courtesy Little, Brown and Co., 207; Musée du Louvre, Paris (photo by Erich Lessing–Magnum), 420; Photo by Muybridge, Animal Locomotion 1885–87 (courtesy Radio Times Hulton), 266–267; Courtesy George and Helen Papashvily, 333; Courtesy Paramount Pictures, 307; Courtesy of Gordon Parks, 340, 341, 342, 343; Pix, 505; Courtesy Raymond V. Schoder S. J., 419, 422, 423, 463; The Times, London, 431; Courtesy of the Trustees of the British Museum, 238–239; UPI, 349, 532; Courtesy of the Viking Press (photos by W. Suschitzky), 38, 39; Wide World, 415

The authors and editors of *Counterpoint in Literature* wish to acknowledge the important contributions to this anthology made by a group of wise and dedicated teachers and administrators. They suggested areas of study appropriate to students at this age level; they tried out materials in classrooms; they assessed the effect of various selections on students; and they sent us thoughtful analyses of why a given piece was, or was not, suitable for inclusion in a junior-high-school anthology. The students also helped in commenting with candor and perception on the selections they were asked to read.

Mr. Edward Bringhurst, Thomas Williams Junior High School,
    Cheltenham Township Schools, Elkins Park, Pennsylvania
Mr. William E. Dunkum, Garfield Junior High School,
    Berkeley, California
Miss Virginia Evans, Governor Mifflin Junior High School,
    Shillington, Pennsylvania
Miss Mildred A. Franz, Highland Junior High School,
    Louisville, Kentucky
Mrs. Ellyn Geller, Hughes High School,
    Cincinnati, Ohio
Mrs. Dorothy Johnson, Northlawn School,
    Streator, Illinois
Mrs. Naomi Madgett, Northwestern High School,
    Detroit, Michigan
Mrs. Florence Meaghan, Franklin Junior High School,
    Cedar Rapids, Iowa
Mrs. Marie Miller, Emma J. Woerner Junior High School,
    Louisville, Kentucky
Mrs. Mary Ellen Murphy, Monroe Junior High School,
    Mason City, Iowa
Sister Rose Bernard SCN, Saint Agnes School,
    Louisville, Kentucky
Mrs. Olga-Marie Schultz, Lincoln School,
    Spring Valley, Illinois
Mrs. Elizabeth Spirduso, Oakland Park School,
    Streator, Illinois
Miss Marcia Sweeney, River Forest Junior High School,
    River Forest, Illinois
Miss Catherine Zehe, Alexander Hamilton Junior High School,
    Cleveland, Ohio

Unit

Encounter

INTRODUCTION PAGE 2

CONTENTS

Unit 2

Two Generations

Unit 3

Values

INTRODUCTION PAGE 164

Unit **4**

Poetry

INTRODUCTION PAGE 236

Unit

The American Romance

INTRODUCTION PAGE 286

Unit **6**

The Well-Told Tale

INTRODUCTION PAGE 354

Unit

Heroes
of
Olympus

INTRODUCTION PAGE 418 | Roger Lancelyn Green

Unit 8

The
Diary of
Anne Frank

INTRODUCTION PAGE 466

Frances Goodrich and Albert Hackett

Supplementary Articles

Handbook of Literary Terms

Composition Guide

1

What makes a person decide
    to risk his life
    for a friend, a principle, an adventure?
Why do some people take the unpopular stand?
What do you say to the challenger when you're
    proud, young,
    and the odds are against you?
These are problems to meet,
    consider, discuss, in

Encounter

See
PLOT
Handbook
of Literary
Terms
page 553

"Fighting is against my principles, which
makes it necessary for me to fight you."
How do events cause this man of peace to
become, for a short time, a man of violence?

A Man of Peace

Lawrence Williams

I READ in the paper the other day about the death of a man I used to know—not on the obituary page among the peaceful ends, but on the front page, where deaths of violence are reported. This man, Ramon de Parma, had been assassinated during an abortive three-day revolution in his native Latin-American country—a country which had better not have a name, because this story isn't meant to grind any political axes.

De Parma, it said in the newspaper story, had been a colonel in the army in his country. The army, I gathered, together with an aristocratic, strongly antidemocratic clique, had a good deal to do with running things down there, and not everybody liked it that way. One man in particular who didn't like it had shot Colonel de Parma through the head while he was having breakfast on the terrace of his home overlooking a beautiful bay.

The piece said De Parma was thirty-six. I would have thought he was a couple of years older than that, but it doesn't make any difference.

The point is, I used to know this De Parma, and the story got me to thinking about him again. Right away I remembered swords and a sort of duel De Parma had been involved in. The memory, together with the news item, made me think of what used to be called "poetic justice"[1] in stories. Poetic justice is out of fashion in stories these days but it seemed to me, all the same, that it would have been more "poetic" if De Parma had been run through with a saber down there in his revolution instead of being shot. I'll try to show you what I mean by

---

Reprinted by permission of the author.
1. poetic justice, an outcome of a situation in which vice is punished and virtue is rewarded, usually in a manner appropriate to the situation.

telling you what I remembered about him.

Back in the years before the war, the parents of American schoolboys used to send for a circular from the École Internationale,[2] a boys' boarding school in Lake Geneva in Switzerland. In the circular, listed under the school's curriculum, they used to read: Escrime[3] (optional) — Maître d'escrime,[4] M.[5] Claude Lafleur. After they had got out their French-English dictionaries and learned that escrime meant "fencing," the parents, and particularly the mothers, were apt to look vaguely upset. The word struck an unfamiliar, sort of medieval, note. Americans can find dozens of ways to fight and dozens of weapons to fight with, but a rapier rests uneasily in our hands.

The mothers needn't have worried. Monsieur Claude Lafleur, the fencing master, had about as sinister designs on the wholesome natures of their sons as a flower has on a bee.

I saw Lafleur for the first time after I'd been at the school about a week. He was striding across the gravel courtyard of the old chateau which was now the school. I didn't know who he was — I was one of those unlucky ones protected from the alien notion of swordplay — but I don't think anybody could have seen him once without looking again.

He was in his early fifties then, I suppose, lean and wiry and about middle sized. He wore a little pointed dark imperial and a waxed mustache, and there was a genially diabolical upcurve to his eyebrows. He had on a black Homburg hat, buff linen spats, and a slightly seedy black overcoat with a white rose in the buttonhole. He wore the coat thrown across his shoulders like a cape and he carried a Malacca cane, which rumor later assured me was a sword cane.

He strode across the courtyard to-ward the gymnasium, jauntily swinging his stick, and disappeared around a corner. I sneaked into the gym that day to see what went on there, and afterward rushed off to my room to explain to my mother in a letter all about why fencing was an absolutely indispensable part of my education.

I was twelve, and while I didn't know anything about anything useful, I knew all about the everyday advantages of bang-up swordsmanship from reading all the Dumas and Sabatini[6] books I could get hold of. In my mind I had already been the fourth musketeer for some time, and Lafleur looked like an answer to a dream.

I must have done quite a selling job in my letter home because I managed to get back a kind of dubious okay — wedged in between wistful panegyrics to tennis and soccer.

The school provided the equipment, and there I was in the gymnasium a half hour ahead of time the next Friday. Lafleur made his entrance exactly on the hour, dressed in slim black trousers and a spotless white canvas fencing jacket with a scarlet heart embroidered on it. His mask was tucked under his left arm, his foil held loosely in his right hand.

"Messieurs," he said, and snapped his foil up in front of his face, then let it swing gracefully downward and outward toward his right side as he bowed from the waist.

We were a polyglot crew he was addressing so elegantly. There were about fifteen of us, ranging in age between eleven and nineteen, from

---

2. **École** (ā kôl′) **Internationale** (ĕN ter na syō nal′), International School. [French]
3. **Escrime** (e skrim′), fencing. [French]
4. **Maître d'escrime** (me′trə de skrim′), fencing master. [French]
5. **M.,** monsieur (mə syœ′), French for Mr. or Sir. *Messieurs* (mes′ərz; French mā syœ′) is the plural form.
6. **Dumas** (dü mä′ or dü′mä) **and Sabatini** (säb′ə tē′nē), writers of adventure stories including many about swashbuckling swordsmen. Dumas wrote *The Three Musketeers* and Sabatini wrote *Scaramouche*.

everywhere under the sun. Three or four of us were Americans, the others were French, Spanish, Dutch, Czech, South American, Greek, English, Cuban, everything—there was even one Egyptian kid. Language wasn't —or wasn't supposed to be—any barrier between us. French was the language of the school and we were meant to speak it twenty-four hours a day under threat of fairly severe punishment.

A few of us, myself included, made a stab at returning Lafleur's fancy salute, but even I know most of us loused it up pretty much. Only one of us didn't. He was a boy I'd never seen before, a tall, athletically built young Latin of eighteen or nineteen, with a startlingly handsome dark face and beautiful teeth. He imitated Lafleur's salute exactly, or almost exactly. It had equal precision and equal grace but it contained an element of mockery in the depth of the bow, in the almost girlish delicacy with which the weapon was handled, which subtly changed the courtesy to a discourtesy.

Lafleur seemed to see only the signs of a practiced hand. He smiled appreciatively and went up to the young man, who apparently was a newcomer to the class, too, because Lafleur asked him his name.

"De Parma, monsieur," he said. He stood very straight, speaking distinctly. "Don Ramon Jesus Sebastian Miguel de Parma y Malaga."

"You seem to have some knowledge of your weapon, Monsieur de Parma."

"On my eighth birthday my father engaged a private fencing master for me, monsieur," De Parma said. "I have studied with him ever since." De Parma's French was very good, almost completely unaccented by his native tongue.

Lafleur's eyes brightened with pleasure. "When you were eight," he said. "Ah, that's the time to begin— when the foil is heavy. Your fencing master, was he a Frenchman?"

"French, monsieur, like yourself."

"They are certainly among the finest," Lafleur said, smiling, "but you mistake me. I am Swiss."

De Parma bowed his head slightly in acknowledgment, and Lafleur returned to the front of his class.

"Your attention, messieurs," he said. "I must run the risk of wearying our friend De Parma by speaking about fundamental things to those of you who are less experienced than he. First of all, we should agree about why you are here. A sword is a weapon. Yet in these days, you will say, surely men no longer need to defend themselves with a sword. Just so. You are right. Then why, you will ask me, should modern young men waste several hours a week learning skill in the art of swordsmanship?"

Lafleur paused and looked at each of us as though somebody had really asked his question. Nobody said anything. De Parma stood listening silently with the trace of a smile on his face.

"You will perhaps see that I have answered my own question," Lafleur continued. "I have said the art of swordsmanship. If you will permit the prejudiced declaration of a man who has studied it humbly for fifty years, it is the noblest in the noble company of arts."

As he talked, his face gradually grew solemn, his voice more intense, and you could see that it was his heart talking—making a statement of his own faith.

"I would be the last man alive," he went on, "to speak meanly of the art of Mozart or of Michelangelo or of

Shakespeare or of Pavlova.[7] I cannot presume to speak of them at all with any authority because I am too ignorant. I can only be awed into reverent silence by their greatness. But of the art of swordsmanship I know the very little a lifetime can teach. And, for me, because I have learned just enough to understand how little I know, it is capable of being the most profound art that civilization has yet produced. Why, you ask, should young men study this thing? Ask instead why a man should train his voice to sing or his fingers to play on a violin. But, in the end, is the mastery of a fine art worth the trouble? I can only say to you that I deeply believe that it is. To understand with humility how near to perfection human beings dare to reach is worth any trouble. I believe that a man who understands this will be a better man than he was. And surely, messieurs, that is the object of life."

His creed stated, Lafleur began to act on it. It was amazing to watch the enthusiasm and concentrated care he put into teaching a bunch of kids, not one in a hundred of whom, he must have known, would ever become even a competent swordsman. He put us in an *en garde*[8] position, then walked down the line. He finally got to me. It was perfectly clear that I didn't know my foil from my elbow, but he had an additional jolt in store for me.

He looked down at me for a while, thoughtfully. I was gripping my foil like a life line and glaring threateningly at the opposite wall. Finally he touched his imperial with the hilt of his foil and said, "I see you are left-handed, young man. That can be an advantage to a skilled swordsman——"

"Yes, monsieur."

"Although a disadvantage to a beginner." He looked at my stance, and then, rather apologetically: "I would not say you seem to be cut out for—ah, you should perhaps consider, my young friend—being left-handed in fencing is sometimes considered a serious disadvantage. There are many fine sports provided here at the school—tennis, rowing, soccer. . . ."

He sounded just like my mother. I guess my face must have shown he had cut my heart out and stamped on it. I couldn't answer. If you're left-handed, you're left-handed. I'm afraid I couldn't keep my lip still, looking back at him.

He didn't even hesitate. "Well, well," he said briskly, "no need to decide at once. We will see. Perhaps hard work can turn your left-handedness into an advantage."

After he had pulled me back to life again, he examined my stance gravely. Finally, in a gentle voice, he said, "You do not mean to chop wood, I suppose?"

"No, monsieur."

"Then grasp your foil lightly so that you may use it. Like this." He demonstrated. "Hold your weapon always as you would hold a captive bird," he said, "so that it cannot escape you, but so you will not crush it."

Lafleur moved on till he got to De Parma. "And you, monsieur, I need not tell you how to hold your weapon," he said, smiling. "Perhaps you would care to show me some parries. Shall we try *seconde, tierce, quarte*, and *septime*?[9] In that order, eh?"

De Parma nodded slightly and put himself on guard. "Thrust, monsieur."

---

7. Mozart (mō′tsärt) **or of Michelangelo** (mī′kl an′jə lō) **or of Shakespeare or of Pavlova** (päv′lō və), famous artists in the fields of (respectively) music, sculpture, drama, and ballet.
8. en garde (äN gard), on guard, the position taken before fencers begin combat. [*French*]
9. seconde, tierce, quarte, and septime, different stances or positions in fencing. [*French*]

Then I saw Lafleur in action for the first time, and in that instant he became my hero, superseding all my cape-and-buskin[10] braves at one swoop. I would have died for him. He had whatever it is the few people have who can do something better than most people. Authority, I guess, sureness, poise, confidence. Anyway, Lafleur had it.

The moment he raised his foil, you could tell. Each movement had a purpose, and there were no movements without purpose. If you don't know much about fencing, maybe all good fencers look pretty much alike. But they're not. There can be as many different styles as there are men, and Lafleur's was perfect.

"*Seconde,* monsieur," Lafleur said, and made the thrust. De Parma executed the second parry expertly. "Excellent, excellent, your hand is strong. Now, *tierce.*"

Together they went through the four commonest thrusts and parries, Lafleur commenting with pleasure as they went. "Nice, very nice. Fingernails down, elbow close to the body. Up, up a little. *Quarte.* The wrist bent exactly so. Ah, lovely!"

De Parma was good. He lacked some of Lafleur's grace, but he was extremely skillful and young and strong and agile as a cat. He was absolutely out of the class of anybody else in the room, even the few good ones. As he parried Lafleur's thrusts, I noticed that he was smiling a little, smiling with the faintest edge of condescension, as though he were doing what he was doing to humor a clever child.

With the final thrust, Lafleur said, "No riposte, if you please. I congratulate you." He started to drop his foil to his side.

But De Parma did riposte. He returned with a quick lunge, darted his foil under Lafleur's from the side (called technically a *flanconade*), snapped his wrist hard, and sent the fencing master's foil clattering across the wooden floor of the gymnasium. Then he touched Lafleur's heart carefully with the end of his blade.

"Your bird has flown away, monsieur," he said.

Somebody snickered.

"I asked you not to riposte," Lafleur said, looking at him. "I dropped my guard."

"I must have misunderstood. I offer a hundred pardons, monsieur." De Parma still had the half smile on his face. He walked over and picked up Lafleur's foil and returned it to him with his mocking, too-elegant bow. "The fencing master's sword," he said.

Lafleur took it, silently, a mixture of bewilderment and chagrin on his face, and a few moments later dismissed the class.

As the weeks went on, it became more obvious that I was a hopeless prospect as a fencer. The harder I worked, the worse I got. And I did work desperately hard. Lafleur never gave up. He seemed to respect my devotion to his art—left-handedness, ineptness, and all. Given that, he could embrace a hopeless cause with enthusiasm. His patience was unbelievable. The worse I got, the more I loved him. For me, there was nothing he couldn't do.

I took to following him around, lying in wait for him behind trees. One day, after class, he caught me peering at him. He beckoned to me.

"You would like to walk a little, Mitchell?" he said.

I fell in beside him blissfully, and we walked on toward the village of

---

10. **cape-and-buskin.** Famous swordsmen in novels traditionally wore capes and buskins—boots which were worn to calf or knee.

Brisac. I wanted to tell him I was going to work harder to overcome being such a terrible parrier, but he asked me a question. He asked me what part of the United States I was from. I told him New Jersey. Then he asked a lot of questions, like what political party did my parents belong to and did we have a good senator. He knew a lot about America.

I was trying to get the conversation around to fencing again, when he said, "I think we have found the best way to live in this world, have we not, Mitchell—in our two republics, our two democracies, yours and mine? Your new one and my old one."

"Oh, ours isn't new," I said. "It's old—since 1776."

"Well, yes. I only meant relatively new," Lafleur said pleasantly. Then he added, with a touch of quiet pride in his voice. "Switzerland, you see, is the oldest democracy on the earth. We Swiss chose to rule ourselves in 1499. It's not perfect, of course, but the principle seems to be the one that works the best. In Switzerland, for example, we have not been involved in a war for almost a hundred and fifty years." He made a flourish with his sword cane and pointed with it to a little stone cottage. "My home," he said. "I hope you will want to have a cup of tea with us, Mitchell."

I said I would like to.

When we got inside, it struck me for the first time that perhaps Lafleur didn't have an easy time making ends meet as a fencing master. While he was officially a member of the school faculty, he held only two classes a week there and was no doubt paid accordingly less. He had two other classes in the middle of the week at a girls' school up the lake at Lausanne, and that was it. I don't mean that there was anything dilapidated about the Lafleurs' place. It was immensely, almost frighteningly, clean, the way a lot of Swiss houses are, but it was very small, and there were the little signs of worn things made to stretch beyond their normal life span.

Madame Lafleur, a short, jolly, healthy-looking woman, met us at the door, and led us into her parlor.

"I have brought a young man, my dear," Lafleur said, "One of my pupils, who will have tea with us. His name is Mitchell."

"Mitchell," repeated Madame Lafleur, beaming at me interestedly, as though she didn't have many visitors. "I know that you are an American. My husband likes very much to collect Americans." She went after the tea.

"My wife, too, is a democrat," Lafleur said, smiling after her. He motioned me to a chair. "And my daughter—but here is my daughter."

A girl had come into the parlor and stood just inside the door. Lafleur's face lighted up with wonder and love, although he tried not to let it show so much. The girl was about sixteen, the most beautiful girl I'd ever seen. She had a lovely oval face with great big dark eyes and unbelievable skin. Her rich, chestnut-colored hair fell to her shoulders.

"Come in, Claudine," Lafleur said, "and meet my young friend, Mitchell. Perhaps he will let you practice your English on him."

She came up to me and held out her hand, smiling a little shyly. "Ow deu you deu, Meetchelle?" she said. "Ow air yeu?"

"Fine, thank you," I said. I started to tremble. I'd never seen anything like Claudine, and so I fell in love with her.

She sat down with us and we talked for a while—rather Lafleur talked most, Claudine a little, and I sat in dumb contentment. It didn't make much difference what they talked about; I was content. Out of politeness, Lafleur slipped into English too – a lot better English than his daughter's – and showed me the little prizes of his domestic life. He let me handle an épée and a light saber which had been given to him years before by a famous French fencing master, and he took me to the window and showed me the best points of his little garden, neat and bright as a Persian carpet.

Claudine sat there, smiling at us. Whenever she said anything, Lafleur tried desperately to look as though what she'd said wasn't the cleverest thing he'd ever heard. He loved her as much as I did. It was a peaceful scene, and I must say Lafleur – this gentle, middle-aged man who made his living with a sword – seemed a man of peace, sitting there in his home, waiting for his tea. I must say, too, that this picture of Lafleur was vaguely disappointing to me.

This artist business was all very well up to a point, but for my hero who, I was convinced, could match rapiers with anybody on earth, to be primarily a man of peace struck me as an awful waste. I didn't admire him less; I just thought he was misguided.

Presently Lafleur got up. "Entertain our guest for a few moments, Claudine," he said. "I'll help your mother in the kitchen. You should speak English. Mitchell will help you."

He went out, and Claudine prepared to be a hostess. "My Eenglees ees so – so formidable," she said, smiling across at me.

"Oh, no. It's as good as my French," I said. It wasn't true, but love will make you say anything.

"Yeu air a great fencair, I suppose?" I took a quick look at the kitchen door. "Well, naturally, I'm not as good as your father," I said. No one could deny that that was true.

Claudine looked at the door, then back at me with a new expression. She lowered her voice, not much, but enough to show me she was going to say something particular. She spoke casually, but in French again. "Tell me, do you know a student named De Parma?"

I nodded, badly disappointed.

"You like him, Meetchelle?"

"He's all right, I guess, I don't know him very well. He's a senior."

"I know." Claudine's face flushed suddenly, and for a moment she looked flustered and very young. "Do the others like him, do you think?"

"I guess some of them like him and some don't. He's a pretty good fencer," I said dismally.

"And my father, does he like him?"

"Who am I to like?" Lafleur asked with a smile, coming back into the room. He was carrying a tea tray. "Some friend of ours, Mitchell?"

I wasn't exactly sure why I hesitated, but I didn't answer him. It was Claudine who came out with it.

"Meetchelle was just telling me about a pupil of yours, Papa," she said, phrasing things pretty loosely it seemed to me. "His name is De Parma – a good fencer, Meetchelle says."

Lafleur stiffened. "De Parma," he repeated quietly. "Yes, he is a good fencer, a very expert fencer for so young a man." He looked suddenly at his daughter. "Claudine, you do not know De Parma?"

"I've only happened to meet him a few times in the village with the other boys, Papa," she said. "On Saturdays sometimes, when the boys come to town."

"But – but you do not know him – especially?"

Claudine didn't look quite at her father. "Oh, we have only spoken once or twice on the street, Papa. He asked me once, I think, to show him the way to the boat landing, nothing more."

Lafleur looked at her, just stood looking at her for a long time, as though he'd forgotten where he was. There was in his face something which I couldn't come close to really understanding then. I could only recognize it and wonder at it. It was fear—plain, naked, and paralyzing.

After a while Lafleur set down the tray, and his wife came in, and although nobody said any more about De Parma, the afternoon was no good any more. . . .

The school term hadn't got very far along before De Parma's personality made itself felt around the place in an increasingly wide range. Somehow, nobody could just feel neutral about him. It was characteristic of De Parma that he made absolutely no effort to make friends; yet there gathered about him a clique of passionate partisans. It wasn't a big clique numerically—maybe ten or twelve boys —and it didn't seem to have any particular national aspects. There were a couple of De Parma's countrymen in it, but then there were also a boy from Michigan and an Albanian and a German baron.

Whatever they all had in common seemed to crystallize in a devotion to De Parma's attitude toward the world in general. They followed him around like a sovereign's court, eager for his favor and apparently immune to his insult. Most of them joined Lafleur's fencing class in order to watch their idol where he so plainly excelled.

On the other side were the rest of us, numerically superior but with no rallying point other than a shared opinion that De Parma was an impos-

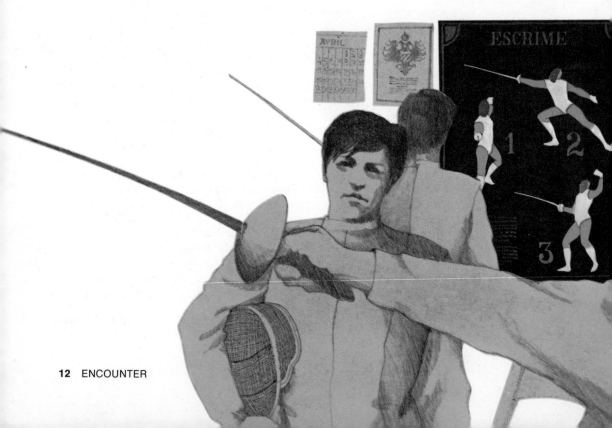

sible, arrogant louse who regarded us all as scum. It's funny, but when you know somebody regards you as an inferior, you can hate him and wish he were dead and all that, but you somehow partake of a little of his belief yourself. Maybe you don't actually believe you're his inferior, but you wish he would hate you actively so you could hate him back on an even footing. As it was, a lot of us went around hating De Parma rather unsatisfactorily because we knew all our best hate was beneath his contempt.

Then at fencing class one day, I knew right away that Lafleur had found out that Claudine was seeing De Parma. I suppose they'd had a scene about it at home. Lafleur was absent-minded and distracted as I'd never seen him, and to De Parma he was cold, ice cold.

He went through the motions of teaching, but you could tell in every-

thing he did that he was sick with worry—and behind it was fear. That's what got me, that he should be afraid. What was there to be afraid of? To me it was simple. Challenge De Parma to a duel and maybe not kill him exactly but show him up in front of everyone for the louse he was. I couldn't understand Lafleur at all; how he could love his daughter so, and freedom and decency, and let somebody like De Parma walk all over him? I ached with the courage I feared he didn't have.

Lafleur left immediately after class, forgetting his customary fancy salute. Some of us hung around the gymnasium afterward, including most of the De Parma clique. They often held a sort of extra session with De Parma in charge. He'd let them slash away at him for a while, playing with them, only parrying their uncomplicated lunges, then suddenly let them

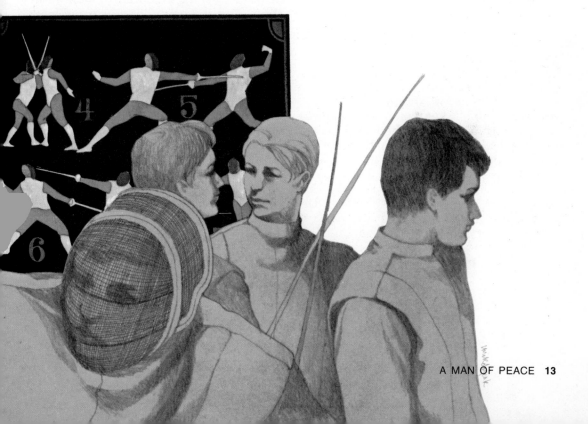

have it—and hard, too. A quick riposte to the heart, the button of his foil exactly on its target, the foil itself bent halfway back on itself from the force of the lunge. That can hurt, you know. Then he'd laugh at them. They seemed to love it.

But this time, De Parma, as he polished off one after the other of his clique, was doing what was meant to be an imitation of Lafleur. It was a vicious parody, and the clique delighted in it. As he danced expertly around one boy, he was saying, "No, no, monsieur, you must not thrust so hard! Remember that the thing you hold in your hand is not a sword. It only looks like a sword to you. It is really a little bird. You are not practicing fighting, monsieur. No! This is a peaceful nation. You are practicing ornithology." As a sort of accent on the last syllable, he lunged through to the boy's heart.

He minced up to another one and made a deep court bow. "Shall we dance, monsieur?" he said. "I mean fence. Ah, well, to me it's all one; dancing, fencing—what's the difference? Art, art." He parried a couple of thrusts, pointing out his toes as though he were doing a minuet.

"You know, my daughter dances," he went on. "She has been dancing lately with a fellow named De Parma, a bad, bad fellow. I've forbidden her to see him, you know. Of course, if she should see him anyhow, I don't know what I'll do because, the truth is, I'm scared to death of this fellow De Parma. If I should make him angry, he might try to hurt me or even take my sword away from me—like this." In a movement so quick your eye could hardly follow it, De Parma's foil darted in from the side and out again, and the other fellow stood there with nothing in his hand.

After the clique's laughter had died down, I managed to make myself heard. "That's a lie, De Parma!" I hollered at him. "He's not afraid of you and he could beat you fencing left-handed if he wanted to!"

De Parma spun around when I first called him a liar; then he saw it was me and he started walking slowly toward me, his foil still in his hand.

I got set to run, but he said, "Wait a minute, you. I'm not going to hurt you. I just want you to deliver a message for me, little trained American. Listen."

He turned back to his clique for a second, and they quieted down at once.

"Tell the fencing master," he said slowly, so that nobody would miss it, "that De Parma would like to meet him in a match, a match without time limit—to a finish. Tell him I suggest next Friday afternoon, here in the gymnasium. If he refuses, we will all understand, won't we?" He turned around to the clique again, looking at them significantly. They grinned back at him.

I went right to Lafleur's, half elated and half worried over what I'd started, but he wasn't there. His wife told me he'd already left on the train for Lausanne for his classes the next day. So I didn't see him until Thursday evening. By that time everybody in the place knew about De Parma's challenge. I found Lafleur down on his hands and knees in his little garden, fussing absently with some bulbs. He couldn't believe I was serious.

"But, Mitchell, a challenge?" he said. "It's too absurd. I am an instructor; De Parma is my pupil. We cannot fight, fight a match. It would be—be ridiculous. The school doesn't want its instructors fighting matches with the boys. No, no."

"But everybody expects it now,

monsieur," I said. "They'll all think——" *His Belief*

"Why should they expect it?" Lafleur demanded hotly. "I have told you all a hundred times that I am a fencing master, an artist, not a duelist. I am a peaceful man, not a warrior. Fighting is stupid; it solves nothing."

After he'd said this, Lafleur bent down at once to his flower bed without looking at me. A new idea—really a brand-new idea—occurred to me.

"You could beat De Parma, all right," I said. "You could beat him without any trouble, couldn't you?"

He jabbed into the flower bed with a trowel. The back of his neck and the one cheek I could see turned red. "That has nothing to do with it!" he said irritably. "It is a matter of principle."

I began to have a tight, sick feeling in my stomach. He poked apologetically in the dirt for a while. Then he said quietly, staring into the bed, "I think you should try to understand—if you are not still too young to understand—that my living, my family's food and their safety depend upon my being a fencing master. I'm not such a young man, Mitchell. I must try to earn—to keep the respect of my students and of the school. I cannot afford to risk, for something that is against my principles. . . ." He let the sentence dangle and looked up at me, his face pitifully eager.

I couldn't make myself look right at him. "But they'll say you're afraid of him!" I shouted. "If I tell them you won't fight De Parma, they'll say he won, they'll say he's better! He'll say if he wants to see Claudine you won't dare stop him!"

"Mitchell!" He rapped out my name like an explosion, but he still couldn't entirely wipe the confusion off his face. He started shouting back, letting the trowel shake out of his hand, "Let them say I'm afraid! I don't care what they say, you understand? You should never have started this, never, never! You don't know what you're doing. You don't have to tell them anything. I'll tell them myself. Do you understand me?"

I could feel the hot, bitter choking in my throat, and I knew I was going to cry, so I just ran out of the yard.

The De Parma clique sent a delegation to my room in the dormitory that night to get Lafleur's answer. The spokesman was the boy from Michigan, I remember, and he spoke to me in English, which was forbidden. For some reason, that seemed to make it more serious to both of us.

"How should I know what he's going to do?" I said nastily. "Why should he tell me? He's going to answer De Parma himself in class tomorrow."

They didn't think that was a very good answer, but there wasn't anything much they could do about it.

I felt cheated and deserted. I had made Lafleur invincible, and he was invincible. It was an exquisitely bitter lesson that taught me absolutely nothing.

At five minutes before two the next afternoon, Lafleur strode across the gravel courtyard toward the gymnasium, as usual. There was a fresh white rose in the buttonhole of his seedy-looking black overcoat, and he swung his sword cane as jauntily as ever. This was to be, his manner said to us all, just any old day like a hundred others. Nothing special about today.

He changed promptly into his immaculate fencing clothes and came into the gym on the dot of two. On three sides of the gymnasium were shallow banks of seats. Usually during fencing class they were empty.

Today about fifty kids were jammed into them, looking sheepish and expectant, and very quiet for fifty kids. There was no possible way for Lafleur to ignore them.

He saluted us as usual. "Messieurs," he said, with the stylish flourish of his foil. We flourished back. "For some reason, our little class seems unusually popular today. Although I don't understand it, I confess I'm flattered by it." He turned toward the mob, speaking lightly. "I think, all the same, it's only fair to warn our fencing enthusiasts that practicing the art of fencing, like practicing scales on a piano, can be tiresome for the observer. But, of course, you are all welcome to watch if it amuses you."

The boys in the bleachers only gawked at him, as though they hadn't quite understood what he'd said. Lafleur turned back to us busily. "Now, then, in a line, if you please. Just as usual. A straight line, here in front of me. Quickly, please."

He planned to bluff it out. I couldn't believe it, couldn't believe that even he thought he would get away with it. He made a gallant try. He walked down the line, where we all stood in the second position, criticizing, complimenting. I took a quick look around for De Parma. He had stationed himself at the extreme end of the line, where he stood erect, with the point of his foil on the floor in front of him, both hands resting on its hilt. He waited with an expression of infinite patience.

Lafleur reached him at last, as he had to. "Now, Monsieur de Parma," he said briskly, "in *seconde*, if you please."

De Parma didn't move. "I have asked you a question, monsieur," he said. He looked directly into Lafleur's face with his beautiful, sadist's eyes.

"Will you be good enough to answer it?"

"A question?" Lafleur tinkered busily with his foil. "Oh, you mean that nonsense about some sort of match? It's out of the question, of course. In *seconde*, if you——"

"You refuse my offer, then?"

"It's not a question of refusing or accepting an offer, as you call it," Lafleur said steadily. "This is a class. I am an instructor, you are my pupil. I——"

De Parma's voice cut in like steel cutting butter. "But you do refuse?"

Lafleur got very red in the face. For the first time in all the months I had watched him so closely, he looked awkward, standing there facing De Parma.

"You're putting me in a very unfair position," he said finally.

From the De Parma clique, and even from some of the seats, there came a quiet sound as he said this, a muttering, miscellaneous sound of derision that swelled and died in a moment.

Lafleur's face grew tight. He didn't turn around to where the sound had come from. "You have created a ludicrous situation, Monsieur de Parma," he said, trying to keep his voice calm. "You had no right to lead others to expect that I would——"

"I took it to be my right," De Parma interrupted, watching him, smiling with careful insolence, "as a gentleman and as the son of a gentleman. Perhaps I was wrong in assuming that you would recognize——"

"I am your instructor!" Lafleur shouted. The fact that he had to shout it seemed to make the statement irrelevant.

De Parma still stood like a statue, with his hands resting on the hilt of his foil. "Then you want me to accept your refusal?" he said softly, gently.

Lafleur looked quickly around the room with the expression of a man trapped in a burning building. "Anything of the sort would be—would be against my principles."

"Ah yes, your principles," De Parma repeated solemnly, but with his mocking laugh behind his voice.

The derisive sound started to grow again, and Lafleur leaped desperately in to stop it.

"However," he said quickly, "however, if you think it would instruct our visitors to watch us exchange a few conventional exercises, I have no objection. Just as you choose. Parry in *seconde*, if you will."

De Parma smiled with the barest flicker of a glance toward his clique, and said nothing. They put on their masks and assumed their positions. Lafleur thrust methodically; De Parma parried.

"Once again," said Lafleur, in his businesslike, instructor's voice. "Your blade a little higher, if you please. That's better. Again. Much better. Your left arm is well placed now. Again."

Suddenly De Parma returned in a different position. Lafleur just managed to deflect the thrust from his heart.

He swallowed. "And that we call *quarte*, or the fourth position," he said, trying to make his voice sound like a man giving a lecture. "It is useful——"

De Parma switched again. His foil ticked Lafleur's sleeve.

"*Octave*, or the eighth position, which you have just seen, is less common," Lafleur said, clinging to his crumbling ledge. "For purposes of assault, octave is ——"

"Octave seems also more difficult to parry among the Swiss," De Parma interrupted, an open taunt in his voice now. "Perhaps the same is true of *sixte*." He lunged viciously as he spoke. Lafleur barely turned the lunge aside.

"Your wrist bent a trifle more, monsieur. Your—your left palm——"

"It may be that the cows and the cheese in this country," De Parma continued, talking louder, pressing in more quickly, "keep the people too full to fight. Or is it that so much peace has made them forget how to fight? Does too much peace take away courage, or does it make fear?"

Lafleur only clamped his jaws tight together. A couple of stifled, unpleasant sniggers came out of the quiet.

Then, as Lafleur defended himself, I could see that his harassed eyes behind his wire mask were flicking hurriedly from face to face around the gymnasium. I didn't understand what he was about, but mechanically my glance darted after his.

Every face in the room was a tense mask of concentration. But, beyond the common excitement, some faces—some few faces even outside of De Parma's clique—had in them an overlay of cruelty, a kind of merciless blood-cry for conquest of the weak by the strong. The faces were like a reproduction of De Parma's own—an insidiously spreading reproduction. They gave me an icy, wet feeling on my back, the faces watching Lafleur.

Then, very suddenly, everything changed. Lafleur jerked his eyes away from the faces and took two long fast strides backward out of range and dropped his foil. He took off his mask, and his face was deathly white. He stood stiff as a ramrod, his black eyes staring like gleaming lumps of coal. The foil in his right hand quivered just a little.

"We hold our foils for very different reasons, Monsieur de Parma," he said, very quietly. "I do not like your reason. I don't like it when I find it in you or in things larger than you. I am an artist and a peaceful man, but you despise peace. Fighting is against my principles, which makes it necessary for me to fight you. Unmask, if you please."

De Parma snapped off his mask and spun it across the gymnasium floor. He had a wild look, a crazily cunning look about him now. He grinned around at his clique for a second and then fell on guard. "At the fencing master's convenience," he said.

Lafleur raised his foil with precision. Its tip, still quivering slightly, was the only outward sign of what he was feeling, but he was an entirely different man from the one I had known. Somehow he'd thrown everything out of himself but one thing. There wasn't an ounce of fear in him now. I gloried in him—and was aware of a jarring sense of danger for him. "Begin," he said.

Their blades reaped and hissed together. The sound, with the stamp of their feet and their heavy breathing, filled the gymnasium. Nearly half a minute passed, in which they felt their way, feinting, groping, testing, each weighing the other's anger through the touch of his hand.

I'd expected De Parma to charge in with the brazenness he showed in everything else. But he was holding back, circling round and round Lafleur, constantly changing his guard and his ground, never advancing. It was Lafleur's face that finally told me what De Parma was up to. He knew Lafleur was spotting him thirty years and he meant to make use of every one of them. He had counted on those years, as I had not.

After three minutes, anybody could see that his tactics were working. Lafleur's face was already washed with sweat. His shoulders heaved very rapidly. But there was no change in the perfect rhythm of his style. He was the fencing master still, a part of him still conscious of the beauty of his art. Watching him, holding in my breath, it occurred to me suddenly that Lafleur had probably never before in his life really thought of a fencing foil as a weapon of combat.

At least he seemed to realize that he must carry the fight to De Parma, or beat himself. He realized it late, and as though the discovery surprised him. He was the better fencer and he knew it, but he had let precious minutes pare away his advantage.

Now he opened his guard, almost carelessly, it seemed, offering a tempting target. De Parma bit, lunged forward violently and nearly lost his balance when his foil touched nothing. Lafluer's riposte came like lightning in two thrusts—one a feint, the other meant to go home—but De Parma was back on his left foot in time to judge the second one for what it was. He slashed out at it with the edge of his blade and touched it in time to move it a few inches before it landed. It caught the top of his shoulder and licked over it.

An expectant gasp went up in the place.

But instead of rushing in for a kill, Lafleur began to give ground. I couldn't understand what had happened to him. It was infuriating. He was letting himself be forced back and back, half step by half step. De Parma pushed forward eagerly now, trying by sheer speed and energy to get past Lafleur's expert guard. There was a tremendous waste of motion in De Parma's attacks and a lack of economy in his recoveries, but you could see that his stamina would allow him these luxuries.

Together they moved halfway across the gymnasium, Lafleur backing, De Parma advancing. They reached the wall. Lafleur felt for it and touched it with his heel. Then, suddenly, he made three dazzling flank attacks from the right. De Parma side-stepped each one, and when they had passed, he saw that he and Lafleur had changed places. Instead of pursuing, De Parma saw now that he had been led. He stood with his back to the wall, and Lafleur stood in front of him, his feet planted in a peculiarly stationary position.

De Parma's face tightened with rage, and he burst out at Lafleur with a furious assault, attacking from all sides, agile and swift, breathing through his mouth, his lips drawn back away from his teeth.

Lafleur stood his ground, the air around him full of the darting tongues of De Parma's foil, parrying thrust after thrust. He worked like a machine. There was certainly not much left of him as a man, as the dapper, gentle fencing master. It made you want to cry. He looked a hundred years old. He couldn't breathe any more, but only panted like an exhausted dog, making a little gasping sound as he gulped in each mouthful of precious air. His imperial and his jaunty mustache had drooped, and the sweat that dropped from them splotched and smeared across his canvas jacket. His face was the color of putty.

And still he fought on, twisting, darting, plunging, the experience of a devoted lifetime making him the master of his weapon. From first to last he made no movement, half dead as he was, that hadn't in it the memory of the expert's grace. No matter where or how fast or how often or in what sequence De Parma thrust, Lafleur's foil seemed always to be

there an instant before, parrying, parrying. De Parma was like a maniac, slashing, charging, near the edge of control. His temper snapped, with a kind of guttural, growling sound in his throat, and he began to make mistakes.

You could tell it was nearly over then.

The more wildly De Parma lunged, the more easily Lafleur deflected his foil. With a sudden rush, De Parma, trying to finish it, made a huge thrust, lunging far forward from the waist, grunting with the effort. Like a striking snake, Lafleur's blade whipped under, parrying in *prime*, and, while De Parma was trying to get on guard again, darted upward and bent into a semicircle on De Parma's scarlet heart.

Seven minutes had passed since they had begun.

De Parma threw his foil down on the floor. We all began to shout like crazy people.

Lafleur turned and marched unsteadily off the floor toward his dressing room, using his foil every third step, the way an old man uses a cane.

On Tuesday Lafleur came to his fencing class on the dot of two. I don't know what we expected, but he looked no different from the way he had always looked — neither better nor worse, but exactly the same. He had a fresh flower in his buttonhole; his mustache and imperial were spruce and jaunty again; his walk was springy. When he saw that the size of his class had almost doubled since the last one, he only smiled his grave smile. De Parma wasn't there, nor were many of his clique.

Lafleur formed us in a line as he always did. It took a minute to realize that everything was to be just as it had always been. He had fought for a moment like an inspired demon because he had felt he had to fight, but nothing had changed him. He was the same man before, the same man after. He would always be Lafleur the fencing master, instructor in a classic art.

He moved slowly down the line of his pupils, going about his real business in the world, smiling a little, his head cocked critically, his voice encouraging, warm with interest. "Elbow in, close to the waist. Better, that's better. Now, again. Excellent. Lightly, Mitchell, always lightly. Don't crush it. Hold your weapon always as you would hold a captive bird. . . ."

That's about all, I guess. Except that De Parma never came back to the class, and after Christmas we heard he had transferred to another school.

The last time I saw Lafleur was at the very end of the spring term the next year. He asked me to come to his house one afternoon, and it turned out to be a sort of engagement party for Claudine. She looked wonderfully beautiful and happy. She was going to marry a nice-looking young fellow, a Swiss, a chemist I think he was, at one of the chocolate factories near Vevey.

Lafleur was having a great time at the party, passing around plates of cakes and listening to people praise his daughter, and taking me, and everybody who would go, out to the garden. He was anxious to see that everybody was having a good time.

De Parma, as I told you I saw in the newspaper, was shot through the head by a democratic revolutionary while he was having breakfast on his terrace the other day. It would have been more poetic if it had been a sword, but I suppose you can't expect everything to come out just so, even in a story.

∗

Discussion

1. (a) What are some of the things which are important to Lafleur? (b) What are some of De Parma's personal qualities? (c) Why is it appropriate that Lafleur is a Swiss and De Parma a South American?
2. (a) Why does the boy choose Lafleur for his hero? (b) Does the boy understand Lafleur's views and attitudes? Explain.
3. (a) Why does De Parma challenge the fencing master to a duel? (b) Why does Lafleur refuse the challenge? (c) At what point in the story does Lafleur finally agree to the duel? Why does he agree?
4. What attitudes toward oneself and toward society are involved in the duel between Lafleur and De Parma?
5. (a) What event causes the narrator to recall the duel between Lafleur and De Parma? (b) Why does the narrator feel it would have been "poetic justice" if De Parma had been killed with a sword rather than a gun?
6. Has the narrator as an adult come to understand and appreciate Lafleur's views and attitudes? Explain.
7. (a) Do you think Lafleur was right in refusing to fight De Parma? Why or why not? (b) Do you think he was right in finally agreeing to the duel? Explain.
8. (a) What is the major conflict in this story? (b) Does the conflict proceed logically from the events of the story? Explain. (c) Could the conflict have had different results? (d) Why do you think the author ended the story the way he did?

An Author Explains His Story

In response to your question about the
writing of "A Man Of Peace," I'll try to tell you what
I remember, but it was a pretty long time ago. However,
unlike most of the fiction I've written, there was
an element of autobiography in that particular story,
so I can remember the writing of it more easily than most.

When I was a boy of grade-school age I
spent two years in a famous old school in Switzerland,
much like the one described in the story. The students
came from everywhere in the world and included a smattering of royalty, some with countries to rule over, some
without. And there was just such a fencing instructor as
Lafleur. (If fencing classes in a boarding school
sound esoteric, I may add that we also had "lessons" in
hand-kissing and in the judging of French wines.) Anyhow,
Lafleur was my idol -- I suppose I am the kid in the
story -- and I wanted to be just like him. To this
day I still can't fence, but I'm glad I knew him.

Also the South American boy was based
on a real person. Actually, he was a German baron, but
this was written a few years after the war and we'd all
had a bellyfull of German villains in the movies, so
I suppose that's why I made him a Latin. In any case,
this boy (I can't remember what I called him and I haven't
got a copy of the story with me) was every bit as arrogant
and sadistic as the character in the story. And he did,
in fact, issue what amounted to a challenge to a duel
to Lafleur, with the same results as written.

continued

Now -- and this is probably the only thing of interest to your students of short stories -- that sequence of events is just that, not a story. Anyhow, not a good story. The events in themselves are fairly dramatic, to be sure, but they don't mean anything in particular. An obstreperous kid gets his comeuppance. So what? A dinner-party anecdote maybe, a story, no. I had to invent circumstances that would give a more universal meaning and importance to Lafleur's victory. Have more at stake than just an old man putting down an arrogant student. Make the victory not just the surface one, but a victory of one social philosophy over another, of one way of life over another. Hence the implied Democracy-versus-Totalitarian theme. Stick that in and the characters are really fighting about something. Stick that in and an anecdotal sequence of real events become a short story. Otherwise, why write it?

Well, enough of that. As to biographical material, there isn't much to tell that would interest students. I have published stories and novelettes and serials in a wild variety of magazines from The Saturday Evening Post to The New Yorker, had two novels published, a play in London and have written altogether too many episodes for some of the comedy series on television. Maybe the kids will remember "Dobie Gillis." I hope not. Other than that, I spent the first ten years of my working life as an actor, on Broadway and in Hollywood. In fact, if your students choose to stay up very late at night -- and have nothing better to do -- they can still see some old movies I made. I very seriously advise against the experiment, and strictly follow my own advice.

Sincerely,

Lawrence Williams

Lawrence Williams

At fifteen, a boy encounters a dream
and makes a decision.

Fifteen | *William Stafford*

South of the Bridge on Seventeenth
I found back of the willows one summer
day a motorcycle with engine running
as it lay on its side, ticking over
5 slowly in the high grass. I was fifteen.

I admired all that pulsing gleam, the
shiny flanks, the demure headlights
fringed where it lay; I led it gently
to the road and stood with that
10 companion, ready and friendly. I was fifteen.

We could find the end of a road, meet
the sky on out Seventeenth. I thought about
hills, and patting the handle got back a
confident opinion. On the bridge we indulged
15 a forward feeling, a tremble. I was fifteen.

Thinking, back farther in the grass I found
the owner, just coming to, where he had flipped
over the rail. He had blood on his hand, was pale—
I helped him walk to his machine. He ran his hand
20 over it, called me good man, roared away.

I stood there, fifteen.

From THE RESCUED YEAR by William Stafford. Copyright © 1964 by William E. Stafford. Reprinted by permission of Harper & Row, Publishers, Inc.

Discussion

1. Summarize what the boy does in each stanza of the poem.
2. Why do you think his age is given so much importance?

The Author

William Edgar Stafford has been a teacher of English at various colleges in the United States. He is also a contributor of poems and articles to magazines, and the author of several full-length books. Mr. Stafford's *Traveling Through the Dark* won the National Book Award for Poetry in 1962.

What sort of job is collecting wild animals?
Does it bring to mind elephant guns,
pith helmets,
narrow escapes from tigers
and boa constrictors?
Compare Durrell's
experience capturing an anteater
in British Guiana with your ideas
about hunting wild animals.

After the *Anteater*

Gerald Durrell

TO CAPTURE a giant anteater had been one of our main objectives in going to the Rupununi,[1] for we had heard that they were much easier to catch in the grassland than in the forests of Guiana. For three days after our arrival at Karanambo we did nothing but talk and think about anteaters, until eventually McTurk promised to see what he could do. One morning just after breakfast a short, squat Amerindian[2] materialized in front of the house in the disconcertingly silent way these people do. He had a bronze, Mongolian-looking face, and his dark slitlike eyes were saved from being crafty by the shy twinkle in them. He was dressed quite simply in the remains of a shirt and pants, and on his sleek black head was perched an absurd pixie hat constructed out of what once had been velvet. To anyone who had been expecting a fierce warrior, clad in a vivid feather headdress and daubed with tribal signs of clay, he would have been a great disappointment. As it

From THREE TICKETS TO ADVENTURE by Gerald M. Durrell. Copyright 1954 by Gerald M. Durrell. Reprinted by permission of The Viking Press, Inc., and Rupert Hart-Davis Limited.

1. **Rupununi** (rü′pù nü′nē), one of the nine divisions of the South American country of British Guiana. It is located in the interior of the country and named for the Rupununi River, which runs through it.
2. **Amerindian,** a member of one of the native peoples of America. The word is a blend of two words, *American* and *Indian.*

was, he had an air of dour confidence about him, which I found comforting.

"This is Francis," said McTurk, waving at the apparition. "I think he knows where you might find an anteater."

We could not have greeted Francis more delightedly if he had known the whereabouts of a large reef of gold. And we discovered after some questioning that Francis *had* known where an anteater was, having seen one some three days before, but whether it was still there or not was another matter. McTurk suggested that Francis should go and see, and, if the creature was still hanging around, he would come and fetch us and we would have a try at catching it. Francis smiled shyly and agreed to the plan. He went off and returned the next morning to say that he had been successful. He had found where the anteater was living, and was willing to lead us there the next day.

"How are we to reach the place?" I asked McTurk.

"On horses, of course," he answered. "It's no use going in the jeep; you'll have to crisscross about the savanna a good bit, and the jeep's no use for that sort of thing."

I turned to Bob. "Can you ride?" I inquired hopefully.

"Well, I've been *on* a horse, if that's what you mean," said Bob cautiously, and then hastily added, "only a very quiet one, of course."

"If we have nice docile mounts I expect we can manage," I said to McTurk.

"Oh, I'll pick you out a pair of quiet animals," said McTurk, and he went off with Francis to arrange the details. Later he told us that we were to meet Francis and the horses the following morning at a spot about two miles away. From there we were to strike out into the unknown.

The grassland was a lovely golden green in the first rays of the sun when we set off, bumping our way in the jeep towards the distant line of trees that was the place of rendezvous. The sky was a delicate jay's-wing blue, and high about us two minute hawks circled slowly, searching the vast grassland for their breakfast. Dragonflies, vivid as fireworks, shot across the swerving nose of the jeep, and the warm wind of our progress stirred and tumbled the fawn dust of the track into a swirling cloud behind us. McTurk, holding the steering wheel negligently with one hand and using the other to cram his hat more firmly on his head, leaned across and began to tell me something, shouting to make himself heard above the roar of the engine and the wind.

"This Indian—Francis. Thought I'd warn you—apt to be a bit queer. Gets excited—sort of fits, I think. Says the world turns round inside his head. No reason why today—thought I'd warn you. Quite harmless, of course."

"Are you sure he's harmless?" I roared back, aware of a sinking feeling in the pit of my stomach.

"Oh, quite harmless, definitely."

"What's all this?" Bob asked from the back seat.

"McTurk says Francis has fits," I said soothingly.

"Has what?" shouted Bob.

"Fits."

"*Fits?*"

"Yes, you know—goes a bit queer in the head sometimes. But McTurk says he's quite harmless."

"My lord!" said Bob sepulchrally, lying back in his seat and closing his eyes, an expression of extreme martyrdom on his face.

We reached the trees, and there, squatting on the ground, was Francis, his pixie hat tilted at a rakish angle. Behind him stood the horses in a dejected half-circle, heads drooping and reins dangling. They were clad in high-pommelled and extremely uncomfortable-looking saddles. We extricated ourselves from the jeep and greeted Francis with slightly strained joviality. McTurk wished us good hunting, turned the jeep, and started off with a roar that sent all the horses onto their hind legs, stirrups and bits jangling. Francis calmed them somewhat and led them forward for our inspection. We gazed at our mounts, and they gazed back with equal suspicion.

"Which one are you going to have?" I asked Bob.

"I don't suppose it'll make much difference," he said, "but I'll have the brown one with the cast in its eye."

That left me with a large grey that appeared to have a good deal of mule in its make-up. I addressed it in what I hoped was a cheerful voice and stepped up to its side, whereupon it waltzed sideways and showed the whites of its eyes.

"Good boy," I crooned huskily, trying to get my foot into the stirrup.

"It's not a he, it's a she," said Bob helpfully.

I at last managed to hoist myself onto my mount's bony back, and I gathered up the reins hastily. Bob's beast seemed more tractable, letting him get mounted before showing any signs of restiveness. Once he was planted in the saddle, however, it proceeded to walk backwards, quite slowly but with grim determination, and would, I think, have gone on until it reached the Brazilian border if its progress had not been halted by a large prickly bush. It stopped dead and refused to move.

By this time Francis had mounted his grim black horse and was jogging off down the path, so with an effort I pulled my mount over and followed him. Bob's cries of encouragement to his steed grew faint in the distance. We rounded a corner, and he became lost to view. Presently he caught up with us, his horse cleverly executing a movement that was a cross between a walk and a trot, while Bob jolted in the saddle, red in the face, clutching in one hand a large twig with which he belaboured the creature's backside whenever he could spare a hand to do so. I reined in and watched his progress with interest.

"How does it feel?" I inquired as he passed.

He gave me an awful look. "It — would — be — all right," he replied, speaking between jolts, "if — he — would — only move — properly."

"Wait a second," I said helpfully, "and I'll come up behind and give him a slap."

From behind, Bob and his steed looked as though they were performing an intricate Latin rumba. I kicked my mount into a trot, and as I drew level with the waggling rump of the animal in front I gathered up my reins and leaned over to give it a slap. Up till then my horse's actions had been exemplary, but now she decided that I was making a sly and dastardly attack on her for no reason at all, so she gathered herself into a bunch and leaped forward with the alacrity of a grasshopper. I had a quick glimpse of Bob's surprised face, and then we were shooting down the path towards Francis. As we drew level with him he turned in his saddle and grinned broadly. He chirruped to his horse, flapped the reins on its neck, and before I realized what was happening we were galloping neck and neck down the path, Francis uttering strange guttural yelps to his mount to encourage it to further efforts.

"Francis!" I yelled. "This is not a race! I'm trying to stop—*stop!*"

The idea slowly took root in our guide's mind, and a look of acute disappointment spread over his face. Reluctantly he drew in his horse, and to my infinite relief mine also slowed down. We stopped and waited until Bob danced up on his animal, and then I worked out a new arrangement. Francis was to lead, Bob was to follow him, and I was to bring up the rear and thus keep Bob's steed up to the mark. So, at a gentle walk, we continued on our way.

The sun was now very hot, and the savanna stretched away before us, shimmering in its rays—mile upon mile of grassland, green, gold, and brown, and in the distance, it seemed at the very rim of the world, a line of humpbacked mountains of pale greeny-blue. There was no life to be seen on this ocean of grass; the only moving things were ourselves and our shadows. For over two hours we rode through the knee-high grass, led by Francis, who was slouching at ease in his saddle, his hat over his eyes, apparently asleep. The monotony of the view and the hot sun made us sleepy, and we followed our guide's example and dozed.

Suddenly I opened my eyes and found to my surprise that the flat savanna had produced a hollow, a great oval crater with gently sloping sides. In the centre was a reed-fringed lake, its banks covered with a scattering of stunted bushes. As we skirted the lake everything seemed suddenly to come to life: a small cayman slid into the smooth waters with hardly a ripple; ten jabiru storks marched solemnly along the farther shore, gazing down their long beaks in a meditative way; the bushes were full of tiny birds, twittering and fluttering.

"Bob, wake up and enjoy the fauna," I suggested. He peered sleepily from under the brim of his hat, said, "Um," as intelligently as he could, and went back to sleep again.

Two emerald-green lizards darted across the path between my horse's slowly plodding hoofs, so intent on each other that they never noticed us. A diminutive kingfisher dropped from a branch into the lake and flew up to its perch again with something in its beak. Gold and black dragon-flies zoomed about the reeds and hovered over the tiny pink orchids that bloomed like a mist over the swampy ground. On a battered tree stump sat a pair of black vultures; they watched us with a macabre hopefulness that was far from reassuring in view of our guide's mental condition. We rode past the lake and headed once more across the grassland, and the twittering of the birds faded and died behind us. Then there was only the steady swish of our horses' legs pushing through the grass. I went to sleep.

I was awakened by my horse's ambling to a standstill. I found that Francis had also awakened and was sitting on his horse, surveying the area like a battered Napoleon. In front of us the land lay flat as a chessboard; on our left the ground rose gently, the slope covered with great clumps of grass and stunted bushes. I rode up alongside our guide and looked at him inquiringly. He waved a brown hand and gestured at the country. I presumed that we had arrived at anteater territory.

"What is it?" Bob asked.

"I think this is where he saw the anteater."

Francis, we had been assured, could speak English, and now was the great moment when he was to give us the details of the chase. Looking me squarely in the eye, he proceeded to utter a series of sounds which, for sheer incomprehensibility, I have rarely heard equalled. He repeated them twice while I listened carefully, but still I could not make out a single word that seemed at all familiar. I turned to Bob, who had been easing himself painfully up and down in the saddle and taking no part in this exchange.

"Didn't you say you could speak an Indian dialect?"

"Well, yes. But those were Indians in Paraguay, and I don't think it's anything like Munchi."

"Can you remember any?"

"Yes, I think so. Just a smattering."

"Well, have a shot at trying to understand what Francis is saying."

"Isn't he speaking English?" asked Bob in surprise.

"For all I can make of it he might be speaking Patagonian. Go on, Francis, say it again."

Francis, with a long-suffering air, repeated his little speech. Bob listened carefully, with a frown on his face. "No," he said at last, "I can't make anything of it. It's certainly not English."

We looked at Francis, and he looked pityingly back at us. Soon, however, an idea occurred to him, and with many gestures and shrill cries he at last managed to explain what he was getting at. This was the place where he had seen the anteater. Somewhere in this area it was probably asleep—here he folded his hands against his cheek, closed his eyes, and uttered loud snores. We were to spread out into a line and beat through the undergrowth making as much noise as possible.

So we spread out at thirty-yard intervals and urged our steeds through the long grass with loud cries and yodellings. Francis, away on my right, was giving a very fair imitation of a pack of hounds in full cry, while on my left I could hear Bob singing snatches of "Loch Lomond," interspersed with shrill screeches of "Shoo!"—a combination guaranteed to flush any anteater. Thus we progressed for about half a mile, until my throat was sore with shouting and I was beginning to wonder if there really had been an anteater there, or if, indeed, there were any anteaters in Guiana at all. My cries lost their first rich quality and became more like the depressed cawing of a lone crow.

Suddenly Francis uttered a piercing and triumphant cry, and I could see a dark shape bobbing through the long grass in front of his horse. I turned my steed and rode towards it as fast as I could, yelling to Bob as I did so. My horse staggered wildly over the tussocks of grass and the deep heat cracks in the soil as I urged her on. The dark shape burst from the cover of the long grass and started off across a comparatively grassless plain at a rolling gallop, and I saw that it was indeed an anteater, and a bigger one than any I had seen in captivity. It travelled across the plain at remarkable speed, its great icicle-shaped head swinging from side to side, and its shaggy tail streaming out behind it like a pennant. Francis was in hot pursuit, uncoiling his lasso as he rode, and cheering his horse on with wild, staccato cries. I had by now extricated my horse from the long grass, and I headed her towards the anteater, but no sooner did she catch sight of our quarry than she decided she did not like it and turned and made off in the opposite direction with speed and determination. It took all my strength to turn her, for her mouth was like a bucket, but eventually I managed to gain a certain control over her. Even so, we approached the fray in a circular and crablike fashion. I was just in time to see Francis gallop alongside the anteater, and, after whirling his lasso, drop it over the beast's head. It was a bad throw, for the noose slipped right over the anteater's head, and the animal simply cantered straight through it, swerved wildly, and headed back towards the long grass. Francis was forced to pause, haul in his rope, and recoil it, and meanwhile the quarry was heading at full speed for thick undergrowth, in which it would be impossible for Francis to use his lasso. Urging my reluctant mount forward, I succeeded in heading the anteater off, and steering it back onto the plain, and by keeping my horse at a brisk canter I found I could stay alongside the animal.

The anteater galloped on over the plain, hissing and snorting down its long nose, its stunted little legs thumping on the sunbaked earth. Francis caught us up again, spun his rope round two or three times, and dropped it neatly over the animal's forequarters, pulling the noose tight as it reached the anteater's waist. He was off his horse in a second, and, hanging grimly to the rope, was dragged across the grass by the enraged anteater. I asked Bob to hold the horses, and joined Francis on the end of the rope. The anteater had incredible strength in its thick bow legs and shaggy body, and the two of us had all we could do to bring it to a standstill. Francis, the sweat pouring down his face, peered around; then he uttered a grunt and pointed behind me. Looking round, I saw a small tree growing about a hundred yards away, the only one for miles. Gasping and panting, we managed to chivvy the anteater towards it. When we at

length arrived at the tree we succeeded in getting another loop of rope round the angry animal's body, and then we proceeded to tie the loose end to the trunk of the tree. Just as we were tying the last knot Francis looked up into the branches and gave a warning yelp. Looking up, I saw about two feet above my head a wasps' nest the size of a football, with the entire colony clinging to the outside and looking extremely irritated, to say the least. The anteater's struggles were making the small tree sway as though struck by a hurricane, and the movement was not appreciated by the wasps. Francis and I backed away silently and hurriedly. At our retreat the anteater decided to have a short rest before getting down to the stern work of removing the ropes. The tree stopped swaying, and the wasps settled down again.

We made our way back to where Bob was holding the horses and unpacked the various items we had brought with us to capture the anteater: two large sacks, a ball of thick twine, and some lengths of stout cord. Armed with these and a murderous-looking jackknife belonging to Francis, we again approached the tree. We were just in time to see the anteater shake itself free of the last loop of rope and waddle off across the savanna. I was only too pleased to leave Francis to disentangle his lasso from the wasp-infested tree, while I pursued the quarry on foot, rapidly tying a slipknot in a piece of cord as I ran. I dashed up alongside the creature and flung my makeshift lasso at its head. I missed. I tried again, with the same result. This went on for some time, until the anteater became a trifle tired of my attentions. It suddenly skidded to a standstill, turned, and rose up on its hind legs, facing me. I also halted, and examined it warily, particularly the great six-inch claws with which its front feet were armed. It snuffled at me, quivering its long nose, its tiny boot-button eyes daring me to come a step nearer. I walked round it in a circumspect manner, and it revolved also, keeping its claws well to the fore. I made a rather half-hearted attempt to throw the noose over its head, but it greeted this with such a violent waving of claws and enraged, snuffling hisses that I desisted and waited for Francis to bring his lasso. I made a mental note that seeing an animal behind bars in a well-regulated zoo is quite a different matter from trying to catch one with a short length of cord. In the distance I could see Francis still trying to disentangle his lasso from the tree without bringing the wasps down about his ears.

The anteater sat down on its tail and proceeded solemnly to brush bits of grass off its nose with its large curved claws. I had noticed that each time it hissed or snuffled a stream of saliva dribbled from its mouth and hung in long, glutinous strands like a thick spiderweb. As the beast galloped across the plain this sticky saliva trailed on the ground and collected bits of grass and twig. Each time the anteater tossed its head in anger these strands of saliva and their debris were flapped onto its nose and shoulders, where they stuck like glue. Now it had come to the conclusion that this armistice was an ideal moment for a quick wash and brush-up. Having cleaned its long grey nose to its satisfaction, it then rubbed its shoulders on the grass to free them from the adhesive saliva. Then it rose to its feet, gave an absurdly doglike shake, and plodded off towards the long grass as slowly and calmly as though such things as human beings with lassos

had never entered its life. At this moment Francis joined me, out of breath but unstung, carrying his rope. We started after the anteater, which was still shuffling along in a slow, nonchalant way. Hearing our approach, it sat down again and watched us in a resigned fashion. With two of us, it was at a distinct disadvantage, and while I attracted its attention Francis crept up behind it, threw the noose over its shoulders, and pulled it tight round its waist. The anteater was off again in a moment, dashing across the grass and dragging us with it. For half an hour we struggled back and forth across the savanna, but at last we succeeded in getting so many ropes around the beast that it could not move. Then we thrust it, trussed up and immobile as a Christmas turkey, into the largest sack and sat down to have a much needed cigarette, feeling rather pleased with ourselves.

But then another snag developed. The horses were unanimous in their disapproval when we tried to hoist the sackful of anteater onto their backs. Their alarm was increased by the anteater, which uttered loud and prolonged hisses every time we staggered up to the horses with it. We made several attempts, but had to give up, for the horses showed every symptom of a collective nervous breakdown. After a good deal of thought Francis indicated that the only way out of the difficulty was for me to lead his horse while he followed, carrying the anteater on his back. I was a bit doubtful whether he would succeed, as the sack was extremely heavy and we were a good eight or nine miles from Karanambo. But I helped him to get the sack onto his back, and we set off. Francis struggled along bravely, the sweat pouring off him, his burden making things as difficult as possible by wriggling violently. The heat of the afternoon sun was intense, and there was no breeze to fan the brow of our anteater carrier. He began to mutter to himself. Soon he was lagging fifty yards behind.

We progressed a tortuous half mile, and Bob turned round to have a look. "What's the matter with Francis?" he asked in astonishment.

Turning round, I saw that our guide had put the anteater down and was walking round and round it, talking to it violently and waving his arms.

"I have a horrible feeling that the world's turning round on him," I said.

"*What?*"

"That's what he says happens when he has a fit."

"Good lord!" said Bob, really startled. "I hope you know the way back from here."

"No, I don't. Anyway, hang on to his horse a second, and I'll go back and see what's happening."

I cantered back to where Francis was having his long conversation with the anteater. My arrival did not interrupt him; he did not even look up. From the expression on his face and his wild gesticulations I gathered that he was going into the subject of the anteater's ancestors with all the thoroughness allowed by the Munchi dialect. The object of his abuse was gazing up at him unmoved, blowing a few gentle bubbles from its nose. Presently, having exhausted his vocabulary, Francis stopped talking and looked at me sorrowfully.

"What's the matter, Francis?" I asked soothingly and rather fatuously, since it was perfectly obvious what was the matter. Francis drew a deep breath and then let forth a torrent of speech at me. I listened carefully, but all I could understand was the oft-repeated word *draftball*, which, whatever it meant, struck me as having nothing whatsoever to do with the matter in hand. After some considerable time I gathered that what Francis wanted us to do was this: someone was to stay with the anteater while the other two rode to the outstation—a distant speck on the horizon he pointed out to me—to procure this very necessary item, a draftball. Hoping we would find someone at the outstation who had a greater command of English, I agreed to the suggestion and helped him carry the anteater into the shade of some nearby bushes. Then I rode back to explain to Bob.

"You'll have to stay here with the anteater while Francis and I ride back to the outstation for a draftball," I said.

"A draughtboard?" asked Bob in amazement. "What the devil for?"

"Not a draughtboard, a draftball," I corrected airily.

"And what is a draftball?"

"I haven't the faintest idea. Some form of transport, I imagine."

"Is this your idea, or did Francis think it up?"

"Francis. He seems to think it's the only way."

"Yes, but what *is* a draftball?"

"My dear chap, I'm no linguist; some form of cart, I think. Anyway there will be other people at the outstation, and I can enlist their aid."

"By which time I shall have died of thirst or been disembowelled by the anteater," said Bob bitterly. "What a wonderful idea."

"Nonsense, the anteater's perfectly safe in his sack, and I'll bring you a drink from the outstation."

"If you reach the outstation. For all you know, Francis, in his present mental condition, might take you on a four-day jaunt over the Brazilian border. Oh, well, I suppose I shall have to sacrifice myself once again for the sake of your collecting."

As I rode off with Francis, Bob shouted after us, "I should like to point out that I came to Guiana to *paint*, not play nursemaid to a blasted anteater—*and don't forget that drink!*"

I prefer not to remember the ride to the outstation. Francis made his horse go like the wind, and mine, obviously under the impression that we were going home for good, followed suit. It seemed as if we rode forever, but at last I heard dogs barking, and we galloped in at a gate and drew up in front of a long, low white house in a manner I have rarely seen equalled outside a Western film. I half expected a sign informing me that we had arrived at the Gold Dust Saloon. A delightful old Amerindian appeared and greeted me in Spanish. I grinned stupidly and followed him into the blessed cool and shade of the house. Two wild-looking youths and a handsome girl were seated on the low wall of the room; one of the youths was engaged in splitting up a stick of sugar cane and dropping the bits to three naked infants who sprawled on the floor. I seated myself on a low wooden form, and presently the girl brought me a most welcome cup of coffee, and while I drank it the old man conducted a long conversation with me in a mixture of English and very inferior Spanish. Presently Francis reappeared and led me outside to a field, where grazed a large and very obvious bull.

"Draftball," said Francis, pointing.

I went inside and had more coffee while the bull was being saddled, and then, before mounting my horse again, I got the old man to give me a bottle of water for Bob. We said good-bye, mounted our steeds, and rode through the gate.

"Where's the draft-bull?" I asked Francis.

He pointed. I saw the bull cantering heavily over the savanna, and perched on his back was a woman who later proved to be Francis' wife, her long dark hair flowing in the wind, looking from that distance not unlike a brunette Lady Godiva.[3]

By taking a short cut across the savanna we arrived back well in advance of the bull. We found things in chaos. The anteater had freed both its front legs by some gigantic effort and had then ripped open the sack and crawled half out of it. When we arrived it was dashing round in a circle wearing the sack on its hindquarters like an ill-fitting pair of shorts, with Bob in hot pursuit. After recapturing the beast and pushing it into a new sack, I soothed Bob by producing the bottle of water, and after this lukewarm refreshment he recovered enough to tell me what had happened since we left him. As soon as we were out of sight his horse, which he had thought was securely tied to a small bush, had wandered off and refused to be caught for some time. Bob pursued it over the savanna, mouthing endearments, and eventually succeeded in catching it. When he got back he found that the anteater had broken out of the sack and was trying to undo the ropes. Hot and angry, Bob forced it back into the sack, only to find that the horse had wandered off again. This apparently went on for a long time; at one point the monotony was relieved slightly by the arrival of a herd of longhorned cattle that stood around

---

3. **Lady Godiva**, wife of an English nobleman who lived in the eleventh century. According to legend she rode naked through the town of Coventry to win relief for the people from a burdensome tax. Her body was hidden from view by her long blond hair.

watching Bob's efforts in a supercilious and slightly belligerent way. Bob said he would not have minded their presence so much if bulls had not seemed so predominant in the herd. Eventually they drifted off, and Bob was making yet another sortie after the anteater when we appeared.

"The world," he said, "was just starting to turn round on me when you all arrived."

Just at that moment Francis' wife appeared, galloping across the grass on the bull, and Bob watched her approach with bulging eyes. "What is *that*?" he asked in tones of awe. "Can you see it too?"

"That, my dear fellow, is the draft-ball, procured at considerable expense to rescue us."

Bob lay back in the grass and closed his eyes. "I've seen quite enough of bulls today to last me a lifetime," he said. "I refuse to help you load the anteater onto that creature. I shall lie here until you have been gored to death, and then I'll ride quietly home."

So Francis, his wife, and I loaded the snorting anteater onto the bull's broad and stoical back. Then we levered our aching bodies onto the horses again and set off on the long trail back to Karanambo. The sun hung for a brief moment over the distant rim of mountains, flooding the savanna with a glorious green twilight, and then it was dark. In the gloom the burrowing owls called softly to one another, and as we passed the lake a pair of white egrets skimmed its surface like shooting stars. We were dead tired and aching in every limb. Our horses stumbled frequently, nearly sending us over their heads. The stars came out, and still we plodded on over the endless grass, not knowing in which direction we were travelling and not caring very much. A pale chip of moon rose, silvering the grass and making the draft-bull look huge and misshapen in its light, like some great, heavy-breathing, prehistoric monster moving across the gloom of a newly formed world. I dozed uncomfortably, jogging back and forth in my saddle. Occasionally Bob's horse stumbled, and I heard him curse fluently as the jerk stabbed the pommel of the saddle into his long-suffering abdomen.

Presently I noticed a pale light flickering through some trees ahead of us, vanishing and reappearing like a will-o'-the-wisp. It was very small and wan in comparison to the gigantic stars that seemed to hang only a few feet above our heads.

"Bob," I called, "I think those are the lights of the jeep."

"Praise the Lord!" said Bob fervently. "If you only knew how I long to get off this saddle!"

The lights of the jeep grew brighter and we could hear the throb of its engine. It rounded the trees, bathing us in the cold beam of its headlights, and the horses bobbed and bucked, but in a very tired and dispirited manner. We dismounted and hobbled towards the car.

"What luck?" asked McTurk from the gloom.

"We got a big male," I replied with a certain amount of vanity.

"And we've had a *lovely* day," said Bob.

McTurk chuckled. We sat down and had a smoke, and presently the prehistoric monster staggered into the glare of the headlights, and we unloaded the anteater from his back. The precious creature was then placed in the jeep on a bed of sacks, and we scrambled in beside it, having turned our horses loose on the savanna to find their way back to the outstation.

The anteater awoke suddenly as the jeep started, and began to thrash about. I held its long nose in a firm grip, for I knew that a bang on the metal sides of the jeep would kill it as surely as a bullet would.

"Where are you going to keep it?" asked McTurk.

The thought had not occurred to me before. I realized suddenly that we had no cages and no wood to make them. Moreover, we could not obtain any. But it would take more than this sobering thought to destroy my delight in having captured the anteater.

"We'll have to tether it somehow," I said airily.

McTurk grunted.

When we got back to the house we unloaded the beast and unwound the yards of rope and sacking that enveloped it. Then, with McTurk's aid, we fashioned a rope harness and placed it round the anteater's shoulders. To this was attached a long piece of rope, which we tied to a shade tree in the compound. Beyond giving the animal a drink of water I did nothing for it that night, for I wanted to get it onto a substitute food straight away, and I felt it would be more likely to eat if it was really hungry.

Getting an animal onto a substitute food is one of the most difficult and worrying jobs a collector has to face. It is necessary when you obtain a creature, such as the anteater, that has a very restricted diet in the wild state — it might be a certain kind of leaf or fruit, a particular kind of fish, or something equally tricky. Only very rarely can this diet be supplied when the animal reaches England, and the collector's job is to teach his specimen to eat something else, something that *can* be supplied by the zoo to which the animal is going. So you have to concoct a palatable substitute food that the creature will eat, enjoy, and thrive on. With some beasts it is a very difficult job, this changing over of diets, for you stand the risk of the substitute's disagreeing with the creature and making it ill. If this happens you may lose it. Some beasts are very stubborn and go on refusing the substitute until, in despair, you are forced to let them go. Others fall on the substitute the first time it is offered and feed off it greedily. Sometimes you get this contradictory attitude in two members of the same species.

The substitute for the anteater consisted of three pints of milk with two raw eggs and a pound or so of finely minced raw beef mixed in, the whole thing being topped off with three drops of codliver oil. I prepared this mixture early the next morning, and when it was ready I broke open the nearest termites' nest and scattered a thick layer of these creatures on the surface of the milk. Then I carried the bowl out to the anteater.

He was lying curled up on his side under the tree, completely covered by his tail, which was spread over him like an enormous ostrich feather. It hid his body and nose from view, and from a distance it made him look like a pile of grey grass. When you see these animals in the zoo, you never realize how useful their great tails are. On the open savanna, curled up between two tussocks of grass, its tail spread over it like an umbrella, the anteater is sheltered from all but the very worst weather.

When the animal heard me approaching he snorted in alarm, whipped back his tail, and rose onto his hind legs, ready to do battle. I put the bowl down in front of him, offered up a brief prayer that he would not be difficult, and retreated to watch. He shambled over to the bowl and sniffed loudly round the rim. Then he plunged the tip of his nose into the milk, and his long grey snake-like tongue began to whip in and out of the mixture. He did not pause once until he had emptied the bowl, and I stood and watched him with incredulous delight.

Anteaters belong to a group of animals that do not possess teeth; instead they are furnished with sticky saliva and a long tongue with which to pick up their food—a tongue that acts on the principle of flypaper. So each time the anteater whipped his tongue back into his mouth it carried with it a certain amount of egg, milk, and chopped meat. Even by this laborious method it did not take him long to clean up the mixture, and when he had finished he sniffed around the bowl for some time to make sure he had not overlooked any. Then he lay down, curled himself up, spread his tail over himself like a tent, and sank into a contented sleep. From that moment on he was little or no trouble to look after.

Some weeks later, when we were back in Georgetown,[4] we got a mate for Amos, as we called him. A pair of slim, well-dressed East Indians[5] arrived one morning in a sleek new car and asked us if we wanted a *barim* (the local name for the giant anteater). When we replied that we certainly did, they calmly opened the trunk of the car, and inside, tied up with masses of rope, was a full-grown female anteater. As a conjuring trick this was considerably more impressive than producing a rabbit out of a hat. However, the creature was exhausted and had several nasty cuts on her body and legs; we were a bit doubtful whether she would survive. But after some first aid to her wounds, and a long

drink, she revived enough to attack us all in a very determined manner, and we thought she was well enough to be introduced to Amos.

Amos was living in a spacious pen under trees. When we opened the door of his pen and introduced the pointed nose of his bride-to-be, he greeted her with such an ungentlemanly display of hissings, snufflings, and waving of claws that we hastily removed her to safety. Then we divided Amos' pen with a row of stakes and put the female next door to him. They could see and smell each other through this division, and we hoped that constant sniffing would bring about a more tender feeling on the part of Amos.

The first day the female worried us by refusing the substitute food completely. She would not even sample it. The next day I had an idea, and I pushed Amos' feeding bowl right up against the dividing fence at breakfast time. As soon as the female saw—and heard—him eating his meal she went across to investigate. Obviously Amos was enjoying whatever it was, so she poked her long tongue through the bars and into his bowl. Within ten minutes they had finished the food. Every day after that we were treated to the touching sight of Amos and his wife-to-be, separated by bars, feeding lovingly out of the same bowl. Eventually she learned to eat out of her own dish, but she always preferred to feed with Amos if she could.

When I landed Amos and his wife at Liverpool and saw them driven off to the zoo they were destined for, I felt considerable pride at having landed them safely, for anteaters are not the easiest of creatures to keep in captivity.

4. *Georgetown*, capital of British Guiana.
5. *East Indians*. A large per cent of the population of British Guiana is made up of people from India, who are referred to as East Indians.

Discussion

1. Gerald Durrell has said, "There has been quite a bit written about the collecting of wild animals and most of it gives a very untrue picture. You do not spend your time on a trip risking death twenty times a day. . . . Naturally, doing this sort of work, you are bound to run certain risks, but they have been greatly exaggerated."[1] **(a)** In your opinion, does Durrell run any risks in this episode? If so, what are they? **(b)** What does Durrell consider one of the animal collector's most difficult jobs? **(c)** Summarize Durrell's character and personality.

2. In describing his adventures Durrell makes much use of contrast between what is expected and what actually happens. For example, he tells about the start of the ride when Bob expects his horse to go forward and it goes backward instead. Explain how Durrell uses contrast to describe **(a)** his first impression of Francis; **(b)** his efforts to help Bob's horse go faster; **(c)** Francis' conversation with the anteater (page 32). What effect do descriptions such as these have?

3. Reviewers have said that Durrell often describes the human-like behavior of animals. Find examples of this in "After the Anteater."

[1]From THE OVERLOADED ARK by Gerald M. Durrell. Copyright 1953 by Gerald M. Durrell. Reprinted by permission of The Viking Press, Inc. and Faber & Faber Ltd.

Word Study

Three aids can help you understand words you don't know:

CONTEXT — the setting in which the word appears; that is, other words or ideas in the sentence, paragraph, or selection.

STRUCTURE — the arrangement and meaning of parts of words.

DICTIONARY

Many times you can figure out the meaning of a word from its context. Context clues can help you in several different ways.

The *knots* loosened and the boat drifted out to sea

The ship's speed was twelve *knots*.

What is the meaning of *knot* in each of these sentences?

Many familiar words have more than one meaning. You can decide which meaning is intended only by seeing or hearing the word in context.

Context can also help you define words which are unfamiliar to you. For example, you may not know the meaning of the word *calabash*.

I placed the *calabash* on the table.

What is a *calabash*? Is it a living thing or an object? The sentence does not provide many context clues. You know only that a *calabash* is something small enough to be on a table.

She placed the yarn-filled *calabash* on the table.

This sentence provides more context clues. You now know that a *calabash* is a container which can hold yarn. For more exact information you would have to go to a dictionary.

Using context as an aid, select the definition of the italicized word in the following sentences from the definitions given after each sentence. If you think there are not enough context clues to enable you to define the word, choose answer **(d)**.

1. Because Bob was not an experienced rider, he asked for a *docile* mount, one that he could manage easily. **(a)** attractive **(b)** lively **(c)** obedient **(d)** insufficient context clues

2. Durrell's horse had trouble maintaining his footing among the *tussocks*. **(a)** tangled undergrowth **(b)** rocks **(c)** tufts of grass **(d)** insufficient context clues

3. Because they were busy chasing the anteater, the men had no time to enjoy the birds, reptiles, and other *fauna* of the region. **(a)** plants **(b)** animal life **(c)** anteaters **(d)** insufficient context clues

4. The men chased and finally captured their four-footed *quarry*. **(a)** hunter **(b)** man **(c)** prey **(d)** insufficient context clues

5. Because Durrell and Bob could not understand Francis' words, they had to interpret his facial expressions and the *gesticulations* he made with his hands and arms. **(a)** statements **(b)** movements **(c)** objects **(d)** insufficient context clues

Durrell's Island Zoo

As a small boy in India, Gerald Durrell had a great interest in animals and a desire someday to open his own zoo. His dream has come true, for he and his wife, Jacquie, now house about six hundred animals of various kinds in their private zoo on Jersey Island in the English Channel. Durrell's zoo is no ordinary one, for he tries to keep the animals as tame as possible and always ready to show to visitors. Also, Durrell tries to get animals that other zoos do not have; he is particularly interested in preserving specimens of rare and almost extinct animals before man's destruction of their natural environment wipes out the species.

Expeditions to collect animals for his own as well as other zoos have taken Gerald Durrell to the remotest regions of Africa, South America, Australia, and Southeast Asia. He has written much about these expeditions and about his experiences with animals. Some of his most popular books are *Three Tickets to Adventure*, from which "After the Anteater" is taken, *The Overloaded Ark*, and *Island Zoo*.

Hairy Armadillo

Guiana Dragon

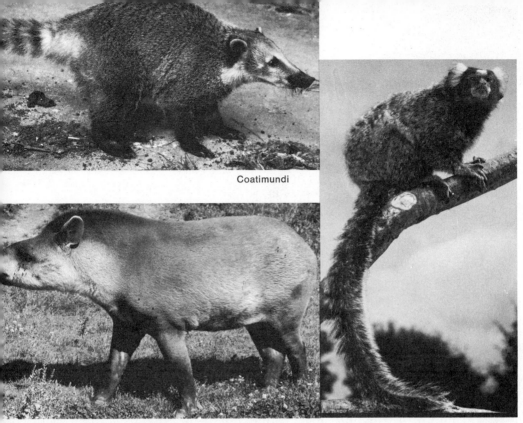

Coatimundi

Tapir

White-eared Marmoset

Mandrill

Slender Loris

See
SETTING
Handbook
of Literary
Terms
page 564

"The mountain, to all of us,
was no longer a mere giant of ice;
it had become a living thing, an enemy,
watching us, waiting for us, hostile,
relentless." What role does such a
setting play in the various conflicts in
this story of mountain climbing?

TOP MAN

James Ramsey Ullman

THE GORGE BENT. The walls fell suddenly away and we came out on the edge of a bleak, boulder-strewn valley. And there it was.

Osborn saw it first. He had been leading the column, threading his way slowly among the huge rock masses of the gorge's mouth. Then he came to the first flat, bare place and stopped. He neither pointed nor cried out, but every man behind him knew instantly what it was. The long file sprang taut, like a jerked rope. As swiftly as we could, but in complete silence, we came out into the open ground where Osborn stood, and raised our eyes with his. In the records of the Indian Topographical Survey it says:

Kalpurtha: a mountain in the Himalayas, altitude 28,900 ft. The highest peak in British India and fourth highest in the world. Also known as K3. A Tertiary formation of sedimentary limestone——

There were men among us who had spent months of their lives—in some cases, years—reading, thinking, planning about what now lay before us, but at that moment statistics and geology, knowledge, thought and plans, were as remote and forgotten as the faraway western cities from which we had come. We were men bereft of everything but eyes, everything but the single, electric perception: There it was!

Before us the valley stretched away into miles of rocky desolation. To right and left it was bounded by low ridges which, as the eye followed them, slowly mounted and drew closer together until the valley was no longer a valley at all, but a narrowing, rising corridor between the cliffs. What happened then I can describe only as a single, stupendous crash of music. At the end of the corridor and above it—so far above it that it shut out half the sky—hung the blinding white mass of K3.

It was like the many pictures I had seen, and at the same time utterly unlike them. The shape was there, and the familiar distinguishing features—the sweeping skirt of glaciers; the monstrous vertical prec-

ipices of the face and the jagged ice line of the east ridge; finally the symmetrical summit pyramid that transfixed the sky. But whereas in the pictures the mountain had always seemed unreal—a dream image of cloud, snow and crystal—it was now no longer an image at all. It was a mass, solid, imminent, appalling. We were still too far away to see the windy whipping of its snow plumes or to hear the cannonading of its avalanches, but in that sudden silent moment every man of us was for the first time aware of it, not as a picture in his mind but as a thing, an antagonist. For all its twenty-eight thousand feet of lofty grandeur, it seemed, somehow, less to tower than to crouch—a white-hooded giant, secret and remote, but living. Living and on guard.

I turned my eyes from the dazzling glare and looked at my companions. Osborn still stood a little in front of the others. He was absolutely motionless, his young face tense and shining, his eyes devouring the mountain as a lover's might devour the face of his beloved. One could feel in the very set of his body the overwhelming desire that swelled in him to act, to come to grips, to conquer. A little behind him were ranged the other white men of the expedition: Randolph, our leader, Wittmer and Johns, Doctor Schlapp and Bixler. All were still, their eyes cast upward. Off to one side a little stood Nace, the Englishman, the only one among us who was not staring at K3 for the first time. He had been the last to come up out of the gorge and stood now with arms folded on his chest, squinting at the great peak he had known so long and fought so tirelessly and fiercely. His lean British face, under its mask of stubble and windburn, was expressionless.

His lips were a colorless line, and his eyes seemed almost shut. Behind the sahibs ranged the porters, bent over their staffs, their brown, seamed faces straining upward from beneath their loads.

For a long while no one spoke or moved. The only sounds between earth and sky were the soft hiss of our breathing and the pounding of our hearts.

Through the long afternoon we wound slowly between the great boulders of the valley and at sundown pitched camp in the bed of a dried-up stream. The porters ate their rations in silence, wrapped themselves in their blankets and fell asleep under the stars. The rest of us, as was our custom, sat close about the fire that blazed in the circle of tents, discussing the events of the day and the plans for the next. It was a flawlessly clear Himalayan night and K3 tiered up into the blackness like a monstrous sentinel lighted from within. There was no wind, but a great tide of cold air crept down the valley from the ice fields above, penetrating our clothing, pressing gently against the canvas of the tents.

"Another night or two and we'll be needing the sleeping bags," commented Randolph.

Osborn nodded. "We could use them tonight, would be my guess."

Randolph turned to Nace. "What do you say, Martin?"

The Englishman puffed at his pipe a moment. "Rather think it might be better to wait," he said at last.

"Wait? Why?" Osborn jerked his head up.

"Well, it gets pretty nippy high up, you know. I've seen it thirty below at twenty-five thousand on the east ridge. Longer we wait for the bags, better acclimated we'll get."

Osborn snorted. "A lot of good

being acclimated will do if we have frozen feet."

"Easy, Paul, easy," cautioned Randolph. "It seems to me Martin's right."

Osborn bit his lip, but said nothing. The other men entered the conversation, and soon it had veered to other matters: the weather, the porters and pack animals, routes, camps and strategy—the inevitable, inexhaustible topics of the climber's world.

There were all kinds of men among the eight of us, men with a great diversity of background and interest. Sayre Randolph, whom the Alpine Club had named leader of our expedition, had for years been a well-known explorer and lecturer. Now in his middle fifties, he was no longer equal to the grueling physical demands of high climbing, but served as planner and organizer of the enterprise. Wittmer was a Seattle lawyer, who had recently made a name for himself by a series of difficult ascents in the Coast Range of British Columbia. Johns was an Alaskan, a fantastically strong, able sourdough, who had been a ranger in the U.S. Forest Service and had accompanied many famous Alaskan expeditions. Schlapp was a practicing physician from Milwaukee, Bixler a government meteorologist with a talent for photography. I, at the time, was an assistant professor of geology at an eastern university.

Finally, and preëminently, there were Osborn and Nace. I say "preëminently," because even at this time, when we had been together as a party for little more than a month, I believe all of us realized that these were the two key men of our venture. None, to my knowledge, ever expressed it in words, but the conviction was there, nevertheless, that if any of us were eventually to stand on the hitherto unconquered summit of K3, it would be one of them, or both. They were utterly dissimilar men. Osborn was twenty-three and a year out of college, a compact, buoyant mass of energy and high spirits. He seemed to be wholly unaffected by either the physical or mental hazards of mountaineering and had already, by virtue of many spectacular ascents in the Alps and Rockies, won a reputation as the most skilled and audacious of younger American climbers. Nace was in his forties—lean, taciturn, introspective. An official in the Indian Civil Service, he had explored and climbed in the Himalayas for twenty years. He had been a member of all five of the unsuccessful British expeditions to K3, and in his last attempt had attained to within five hundred feet of the summit, the highest point which any man had reached on the unconquered giant. This had been the famous tragic attempt in which his fellow climber and life-long friend, Captain Furness, had slipped and fallen ten thousand feet to his death. Nace rarely mentioned his name, but on the steel head of his ice ax were engraved the words: TO MARTIN FROM JOHN. If fate were to grant that the ax of any one of us should be planted upon the summit of K3, I hoped it would be his.

Such were the men who huddled about the fire in the deep, still cold of that Himalayan night. There were many differences among us, in temperament as well as in background. In one or two cases, notably that of Osborn and Nace, there had already been a certain amount of friction, and as the venture continued and the struggles and hardships of the actual ascent began, it would, I knew, increase. But differences were unimportant. What mattered—all that mattered—was that our purpose was one—to conquer the monster of rock and ice that now loomed above us in the night; to stand for a moment where no man, no living thing, had ever stood before. To that end we had come from half a world away, across oceans and continents to the fastnesses of inner Asia. To that end we were prepared to endure cold, exhaustion and danger, even to the very last extremity of human endurance. Why? There is no answer, and at the same time every man among us knew the answer; every man who has ever looked upon a great mountain and felt the fever in his blood to climb and conquer, knows the answer. George Leigh Mallory, greatest of mountaineers, expressed it once and for all when he was asked why he wanted to climb unconquered Everest. "I want to climb it," said Mallory, "because it's there."

Day after day we crept on and upward. The naked desolation of the valley was unrelieved by any motion, color or sound, and, as we progressed, it was like being trapped at the bottom of a deep well or in a sealed court between great skyscrapers. Soon we were thinking of the ascent of the shining mountain not only as an end in itself but as an escape.

In our nightly discussions around the fire, our conversation narrowed more and more to the immediate problems confronting us, and during them I began to realize that the tension between Osborn and Nace went deeper than I had at first surmised. There was rarely any outright argument between them—they were both far too able mountain men to disagree on fundamentals—but I saw that at almost every turn they were rubbing each other the wrong way. It was a matter of personalities chiefly. Osborn was talkative, enthusiastic, optimistic, always chafing to be up and at it, always wanting to take the short, straight line to the given point. Nace, on the other hand, was matter-of-fact, cautious, slow. He was the apostle of trial-and-error and watchful waiting. Because of his far greater experience and intimate knowledge of K3, Randolph almost invariably followed his advice, rather than Osborn's, when a difference of opinion arose. The younger man usually capitulated with good grace, but I could tell that he was irked.

During the days in the valley I had few occasions to talk privately with either of them, and only once did either mention the other in any but the most casual manner. Even then, the remarks they made seemed unimportant, and I remember them only in view of what happened later.

My conversation with Osborn occurred first. It was while we were on the march, and Osborn, who was directly behind me, came up suddenly to my side.

"You're a geologist, Frank," he began without preamble. "What do you think of Nace's theory about the ridge?"

"What theory?" I asked.

"He believes we should traverse under it from the glacier up. Says the ridge itself is too exposed."

"It looks pretty mean through the telescope."

"But it's been done before. He's done it himself. All right, it's tough —I'll admit that. But a decent climber could make it in half the time the traverse will take."

"Nace knows the traverse is longer," I said. "but he seems certain it will be much easier for us."

"Easier for him is what he means."

Osborn paused, looking moodily at the ground. "He was a great climber in his day. It's a damn shame a man can't be honest enough with himself to know when he's through." He fell silent and a moment later dropped back into his place in line.

It was that same night, I think, that I awoke to find Nace sitting up in his blanket and staring at the mountain.

"How clear it is," I whispered.

The Englishman pointed. "See the ridge?"

I nodded, my eyes fixed on the great, twisting spine of ice that climbed into the sky. I could see now, more clearly than in the blinding sunlight, its huge indentations and jagged, wind-swept pitches.

"It looks impossible," I said.

"No, it can be done. Trouble is, when you've made it, you're too done in for the summit."

"Osborn seems to think its shortness would make up for its difficulty."

Nace was silent a long moment before answering. Then for the first and only time I heard him speak the name of his dead companion. "That's what Furness thought," he said quietly. Then he lay down and wrapped himself in his blanket.

For the next two weeks the uppermost point of the valley was our home and workshop. We established our base camp as close to the mountain as we could, less than half a mile from the tongue of its lowest glacier, and plunged into the arduous tasks of preparation for the ascent. Our food and equipment were unpacked, inspected and sorted, and finally repacked in lighter loads for transportation to more advanced camps. Hours on end were spent poring over maps and charts and studying the monstrous heights above us through telescope and binoculars.

Under Nace's supervision, a thorough reconnaissance of the glacier was made and the route across it laid out; then began the backbreaking labor of moving up supplies and establishing the advance stations.

Camps I and II were set up on the glacier itself, in the most sheltered sites we could find. Camp III we built at its upper end, as near as possible to the point where the great rock spine of K3 thrust itself free of ice and began its precipitous ascent. According to our plans, this would be the advance base of operations during the climb; the camps to be established higher up, on the mountain proper, would be too small and too exposed to serve as anything more than one or two nights' shelter. The total distance between the base camp and Camp III was only fifteen miles, but the utmost daily progress of our porters was five miles, and it was essential that we should never be more than twelve hours' march from food and shelter. Hour after hour, day after day, the long file of men wound up and down among the hummocks and crevasses of the glacier, and finally the time arrived when we were ready to advance.

Leaving Doctor Schlapp in command of eight porters at the base camp, we proceeded easily and on schedule, reaching Camp I the first night, Camp II the second and the advance base the third. No men were left at Camps I and II, inasmuch as they were designed simply as caches for food and equipment; and, furthermore, we knew we would need all the man power available for the establishment of the higher camps on the mountain proper.

For more than three weeks now the weather had held perfectly, but on our first night at the advance base, as if by malignant prearrangement of Nature, we had our first taste of the supernatural fury of a high Himalayan storm. It began with great streamers of lightning that flashed about the mountain like a halo; then heavily through the weird glare snow began to fall. The wind howled about the tents with hurricane frenzy, and the wild flapping of the canvas dinned in our ears like machine-gun fire.

There was no sleep for us that night or the next. For thirty-six hours the storm raged without lull, while we huddled in the icy gloom of the tents. At last, on the third morning, it was over, and we came out into a world transformed by a twelve-foot cloak of snow. No single landmark remained as it had been before, and our supplies and equipment were in the wildest confusion. Fortunately, there had not been a single serious injury, but it was another three days before we had regained our strength and put the camp in order.

Then we waited. The storm did not return, and the sky beyond the ridges gleamed flawlessly clear, but night and day we could hear the roaring thunder of avalanches on the mountain above us. To have ventured so much as one step into that savage, vertical wilderness before the new-fallen snow froze tight would have been suicidal. We chafed or waited patiently, according to our individual temperaments, while the days dragged by.

It was late one afternoon that Osborn returned from a short reconnaissance up the ridge. His eyes were shining and his voice jubilant.

"It's tight!" he cried. "Tight as a drum! We can go!" All of us stopped whatever we were doing. His excitement leaped like an electric spark from one to another. "I went about a thousand feet, and it's sound all the

way. What do you say, Sayre? Tomorrow?"

Randolph hesitated a moment, then looked at Nace.

"Better give it another day or two," said the Englishman.

Osborn glared at him. "Why?" he challenged.

"It's generally safer to wait until——"

"Wait! Wait!" Osborn exploded. "Don't you ever think of anything but waiting? The snow's firm, I tell you!"

"It's firm down here," Nace replied quietly, "because the sun hits it only two hours a day. Up above it gets the sun twelve hours. It may not have frozen yet."

"The avalanches have stopped."

"That doesn't necessarily mean it will hold a man's weight."

"It seems to me, Martin's point ——" Randolph began.

Osborn wheeled on him. "Sure," he snapped. "I know. Martin's right. The cautious bloody English are always right. Let him have his way, and we'll be sitting here twiddling our thumbs until the mountain falls down on us." His eyes flashed to Nace. "Maybe with a little less of that bloody cautiousness, you English wouldn't have made such a mess of Everest. Maybe your pals Mallory and Furness wouldn't be dead."

"Osborn!" commanded Randolph sharply.

The youngster stared at Nace for another moment, breathing heavily. Then, abruptly, he turned away.

The next two days were clear and windless, but we still waited, following Nace's advice. There were no further brushes between him and Osborn, but an unpleasant air of restlessness and tension hung over the camp. I found myself chafing almost as impatiently as Osborn himself for the moment when we would break out of that maddening inactivity and begin the assault.

At last the day came. With the first paling of the sky, a roped file of men, bent almost double beneath heavy loads, began slowly to climb the ice slope just beneath the jagged line of the great east ridge. In accordance with prearranged plan, we proceeded in relays; this first group consisting of Nace, Johns, myself and eight porters. It was our job to ascend approximately two thousand feet in a day's climbing and establish Camp IV at the most level and sheltered site we could find. We would spend the night there and return to the advance base next day, while the second relay, consisting of Osborn, Wittmer and eight more porters, went up with their loads. This process was to continue until all necessary supplies were at Camp IV, and then the whole thing would be repeated between Camps IV and V, and V and VI. From VI, at an altitude of about 26,000 feet, the ablest and fittest men—presumably Nace and Osborn—would make the direct assault on the summit. Randolph and Bixler were to remain at the advance base throughout the operations, acting as directors and coördinators. We were under the strictest orders that any man, sahib or porter, who suffered illness or injury should be brought down immediately.

How shall I describe those next two weeks beneath the great ice ridge of K3? In a sense, there was no occurrence of importance, and at the same time everything happened that could possibly happen, short of actual disaster. We established Camp IV, came down again, went up again, came down again. Then we crept laboriously higher. The wind increased, and the air grew steadily colder and more difficult to breathe.

One morning two of the porters awoke with their feet frozen black; they had to be sent down. A short while later Johns developed an uncontrollable nosebleed and was forced to descend to a lower camp. Wittmer was suffering from splitting headaches and I from a continually dry throat. But providentially, the one enemy we feared the most in that icy, gale-lashed hell did not again attack us—no snow fell. And day by day, foot by foot, we ascended.

It is during ordeals like this that the surface trappings of a man are shed and his secret mettle laid bare. There were no shirkers or quitters among us—I had known that from the beginning—but now, with each passing day, it became more manifest which were the strongest and ablest among us. Beyond all argument, these were Osborn and Nace.

Osborn was magnificent. All the boyish impatience and moodiness which he had exhibited earlier were gone, and, now that he was at last at work in his natural element, he emerged as the peerless mountaineer he was. His energy was inexhaustible, and his speed, both on rock and ice, almost twice that of any other man in the party. He was always discovering new routes and short cuts; and there was such vigor, buoyancy and youth in everything he did that it gave heart to all the rest of us.

In contrast, Nace was slow, methodical, unspectacular. Since he and I worked in the same relay, I was with him almost constantly, and to this day I carry in my mind the clear image of the man—his tall body bent almost double against endless, shimmering slopes of ice; his lean brown face bent in utter concentration on the problem in hand, then raised searchingly to the next; the bright prong of his ax rising, falling,

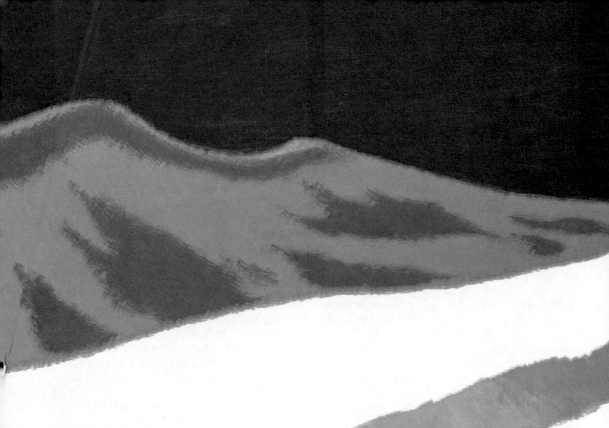

rising, falling with tireless rhythm, until the steps in the glassy incline were so wide and deep that the most clumsy of the porters could not have slipped from them had he tried. Osborn attacked the mountain, head on Nace studied it, sparred with it, wore it down. His spirit did not flap from his sleeve like a pennon; it was deep inside him, patient, indomitable.

The day came soon when I learned from him what it is to be a great mountaineer. We were making the ascent from Camp IV to V, and an almost perpendicular ice wall had made it necessary for us to come out for a few yards on the exposed crest of the ridge. There were six of us in the party, roped together, with Nace leading, myself second, and four porters bringing up the rear. The ridge at this particular point was free of snow, but razor-thin, and the

rocks were covered with a smooth glaze of ice. On either side the mountain dropped away in sheer precipices of five thousand feet.

Suddenly the last porter slipped. In what seemed to be the same instant I heard the ominous scraping of boot nails and, turning, saw a wildly gesticulating figure plunge sideways into the abyss. There was a scream as the next porter followed him. I remember trying frantically to dig into the ridge with my ax, realizing at the same time it would no more hold against the weight of the falling men than a pin stuck in a wall. Then I heard Nace shout, "Jump!" As he said it, the rope went tight about my waist, and I went hurtling after him into space on the opposite side of the ridge. After me came the nearest porter.

What happened then must have happened in five yards and a fifth

of a second. I heard myself cry out, and the glacier, a mile below, rushed up at me, spinning. Then both were blotted out in a violent spasm, as the rope jerked taut. I hung for a moment, an inert mass, feeling that my body had been cut in two; then I swung in slowly to the side of the mountain. Above me the rope lay tight and motionless across the crest of the ridge, our weight exactly counter-balancing that of the men who had fallen on the far slope.

Nace's voice came up from below. "You chaps on the other side!" he shouted. "Start climbing slowly! We're climbing too!"

In five minutes we had all re-gained the ridge. The porters and I crouched panting on the jagged rocks, our eyes closed, the sweat beading our faces in frozen drops. Nace carefully examined the rope that again hung loosely between us.

"All right, men," he said pres-ently. "Let's get on to camp for a cup of tea."

Above Camp V the whole aspect of the ascent changed. The angle of the ridge eased off, and the ice, which lower down had covered the moun-tain like a sheath, lay only in scat-tered patches between the rocks. Fresh enemies, however, instantly appeared to take the place of the old. We were now laboring at an altitude of more than 25,000 feet—well above the summits of the highest surround-ing peaks—and day and night, without protection or respite, we were buffeted by the savage fury of the wind. Worse than this was that the atmosphere had become so rarefied it could scarce-ly support life. Breathing itself was a major physical effort, and our prog-ress upward consisted of two or three painful steps, followed by a long period of rest in which our hearts pounded wildly and our burning lungs gasped for air. Each of us carried a small cylinder of oxygen in our pack, but we used it only in emergencies, and found that, though its immediate effect was salutary, it left us later even worse off than before.

But the great struggle was now mental rather than physical. The lack of air induced a lethargy of mind and spirit; confidence and the powers of thought and decision waned. The mountain, to all of us, was no longer a mere giant of rock and ice; it had become a living thing, an enemy, watching us, waiting for us, hostile, relentless.

On the fifteenth day after we had first left the advance base, we pitched Camp VI at an altitude of 26,500 feet. It was located near the uppermost extremity of the great east ridge, directly beneath the so-called shoulder of the mountain. On the far side of the shoulder the stupendous north face of K3 fell sheer to the glaciers, two miles below. Above it and to the left rose the symmetrical bulk of the summit pyramid. The topmost rocks of its highest pinnacle were clearly visible from the shoulder, and the intervening fifteen hundred feet seemed to offer no insuperable obstacles.

Camp VI, which was in reality no camp at all but a single tent, was large enough to accommodate only three men. Osborn established it with the aid of Wittmer and one porter; then, the following morning, Wittmer and the porter descended to Camp V, and Nace and I went up. It was our plan that Osborn and Nace should launch the final assault —the next day, if the weather held —with myself in support, following their progress through binoculars and going to their aid or summoning help

from below if anything went wrong. As the three of us lay in the tent that night, the summit seemed already within arm's reach, victory securely in our grasp.

And then the blow fell. With fiendishly malignant timing, which no power on earth could have made us believe was a simple accident of nature, the mountain hurled at us its last line of defense. It snowed.

For a day and a night the great flakes drove down upon us, swirling and swooping in the wind, blotting out the summit, the shoulder, everything beyond the tiny white-walled radius of our tent. At last, during the morning of the following day, it cleared. The sun came out in a thin blue sky, and the summit pyramid again appeared above us, now whitely robed in fresh snow. But still we waited. Until the snow either froze or was blown away by the wind, it would have been the rashest courting of destruction for us to have ascended a foot beyond the camp. Another day passed. And another.

By the third nightfall our nerves were at the breaking point. For hours on end we had scarcely moved or spoken, and the only sounds in all the world were the endless moaning of the wind outside and the harsh, sucking noise of our breathing. I knew that, one way or another, the end had come. Our meager food supply was running out; even with careful rationing, there was enough left for only two more days.

Presently Nace stirred in his sleeping bag and sat up. "We'll have to go down tomorrow," he said quietly.

For a moment there was silence in the tent. Then Osborn struggled to a sitting position and faced him.

"No," he said.

"There's still too much loose snow above. We can't make it."

"But it's clear. As long as we can see——"

Nace shook his head. "Too dangerous. We'll go down tomorrow and lay in a fresh supply. Then we'll try again."

"Once we go down we're licked. You know it."

Nace shrugged. "Better to be licked than——" The strain of speech was suddenly too much for him and he fell into a violent paroxysm of coughing. When it had passed, there was a long silence.

Then, suddenly, Osborn spoke again. "Look, Nace," he said, "I'm going up tomorrow."

The Englishman shook his head.

"I'm going—understand?"

For the first time since I had known him, I saw Nace's eyes flash in anger. "I'm the senior member of this group," he said. "I forbid you to go!"

With a tremendous effort, Osborn jerked himself to his feet. "You forbid me? This may be your sixth time on this mountain, and all that, but you don't own it! I know what you're up to. You haven't got it in you to make the top yourself, so you don't want anyone else to get the glory. That's it, isn't it? Isn't it?" He sat down again suddenly, gasping for breath.

Nace looked at him with level eyes. "This mountain has licked me five times," he said softly. "It killed my best friend. It means more to me to lick it than anything else in the world. Maybe I'll make it and maybe I won't. But if I do, it will be as a rational, intelligent human being, not as a damned fool throwing my life away——"

He collapsed into another fit of coughing and fell back in his sleeping bag. Osborn, too, was still. They lay there inert, panting, too exhausted for speech.

It was hours later that I awoke from dull, uneasy sleep. In the faint light I saw Nace fumbling with the flap of the tent.

"What is it?" I asked.

"Osborn. He's gone."

The words cut like a blade through my lethargy. I struggled to my feet and followed Nace from the tent.

Outside, the dawn was seeping up the eastern sky. It was very cold, but the wind had fallen and the mountain seemed to hang suspended in a vast stillness. Above us the summit pyramid climbed bleakly into space, like the last outpost of a spent lifeless planet. Raising my binoculars, I swept them over the gray waste. At first I saw nothing but rock and ice; then, suddenly, something moved.

"I've got him," I whispered.

As I spoke, the figure of Osborn sprang into clear focus against a patch of ice. He took three or four slow upward steps, stopped, went on again. I handed the glasses to Nace.

The Englishman squinted through them a moment, returned them to me and re-entered the tent. When I followed, he had already laced his boots and was pulling on his outer gloves.

"He's not far," he said. "Can't have been gone more than half an hour." He seized his ice ax and started out again.

"Wait," I said. "I'm going with you."

Nace shook his head. "Better stay here."

"I'm going with you," I said.

He said nothing further, but waited while I made ready. In a few moments we left the tent, roped up and started off.

Almost immediately we were on the shoulder and confronted with the paralyzing two-mile drop of the north face, but we negotiated the short exposed stretch without mishap and in ten minutes were working up the base of the summit pyramid. Our progress was creepingly slow. There seemed to be literally no air at all to breathe, and after almost every step we were forced to rest.

The minutes crawled into hours, and still we climbed. Presently the sun came up. Its level rays streamed across the clouds far below, and glinted from the summits of distant peaks. But, although the pinnacle of K3 soared a full five thousand feet above anything in the surrounding world, we had scarcely any sense of height. The stupendous wilderness of mountains and glaciers that spread beneath us to the horizon was flattened and remote, an unreal, insubstantial landscape seen in a dream. We had no connection with it, or it with us. All living, all awareness, purpose and will, was concentrated in the last step and the next—to put one foot before the other; to breathe; to ascend. We struggled on in silence.

I do not know how long it was since we had left the camp—it might have been two hours, it might have been six—when we suddenly sighted Osborn. We had not been able to find him again since our first glimpse through the binoculars, but now, unexpectedly and abruptly, as we came up over a jagged outcropping of rock, there he was. He was at a point, only a few yards above us, where the mountain steepened into an almost vertical wall. The smooth surface directly in front of him was obviously unclimbable, but two alternate routes were presented. To the left, a chimney cut obliquely across the wall, forbiddingly steep, but seeming to offer adequate holds.

To the right was a gentle slope of snow that curved upward and out of sight behind the rocks. As we watched, Osborn ascended to the edge of the snow, stopped and tested it with his foot; then, apparently satisfied that it would bear his weight, he stepped out on the slope.

I felt Nace's body tense. "Paul!" he cried out.

His voice was too weak and hoarse to carry. Osborn continued his ascent. Nace cupped his hands and called his name again, and this time Osborn turned. "Wait!" cried the Englishman.

Osborn stood still, watching us, as we struggled up the few yards to the edge of the snow slope. Nace's breath came in shuddering gasps, but he climbed faster than I had ever seen him climb before.

"Come back!" he called. "Come off the snow!"

"It's all right! The crust is firm!" Osborn called back.

"But it's melting! There's"—Nace paused, fighting for air—"there's nothing underneath!"

In a sudden, horrifying flash I saw what he meant. Looked at from directly below, at the point where Osborn had come to it, the slope on which he stood appeared as a harmless covering of snow over the rocks. From where we were now, however, a little to one side, it could be seen that it was in reality no covering at all, but merely a cornice or unsupported platform clinging to the side of the mountain. Below it was not rock, but ten thousand feet of blue air.

"Come back!" I cried. "Come back!"

Osborn hesitated, then took a downward step. But he never took the next. For in that same instant the snow directly in front of him disappeared. It did not seem to fall or to break away. It was just soundlessly and magically no longer there. In the spot where Osborn had been about to set his foot there was now revealed the abysmal drop of the north face of K3.

I shut my eyes, but only for a second, and when I reopened them Osborn was still, miraculously, there.

Nace was shouting, "Don't move! Don't move an inch!"

"The rope," I heard myself saying.

The Englishman shook his head. "We'd have to throw it, and the impact would be too much. Brace yourself and play it out." As he spoke, his eyes were traveling over the rocks that bordered the snow bridge. Then he moved forward.

I wedged myself into a cleft in the wall and let out the rope which extended between us. A few yards away, Osborn stood in the snow, transfixed, one foot a little in front of the other. But my eyes now were on Nace. Cautiously, but with astonishing rapidity, he edged along the rocks beside the cornice. There was a moment when his only support was an inch-wide ledge beneath his feet, another where there was nothing under his feet at all and he supported himself wholly by his elbows and hands. But he advanced steadily, and at last reached a shelf wide enough for him to turn around on. At this point he was perhaps six feet away from Osborn.

"It's wide enough here to hold both of us," he said in a quiet voice. "I'm going to reach out my ax. Don't move until you're sure you have a grip on it. When I pull, jump."

He searched the wall behind him and found a hold for his left hand. Then he slowly extended his ice ax, head foremost, until it was within two feet of Osborn's shoulder. "Grip it!" he cried suddenly.

Osborn's hands shot out and seized the ax. "Jump!"

There was a flash of steel in the sunlight and a hunched figure hurtled inward from the snow to the ledge. Simultaneously another figure hurtled out. The haft of the ax jerked suddenly from Nace's hand, and he lurched forward and downward. A violent, sickening spasm convulsed my body as the rope went taut. Then it was gone. Nace did not seem to hit the snow; he simply disappeared through it, soundlessly. In the same instant the snow itself was gone. The frayed, yellow end of broken rope spun lazily in space.

Somehow my eyes went to Osborn. He was crouched on the ledge where Nace had been a moment before, staring dully at the ax he held in his hands. Beyond his head, not two hundred feet above, the white, untrodden pinnacle of K3 stabbed the sky.

Perhaps ten minutes passed, perhaps a half hour. I closed my eyes and leaned forward motionless against the rock, my face against my arm. I neither thought nor felt; my body and mind alike were enveloped in a suffocating numbness. Through it at last came the sound of Osborn moving. Looking up, I saw he was standing beside me.

"I'm going to try to make the top," he said tonelessly.

I merely stared at him.

"Will you come?"

I shook my head slowly. Osborn hesitated a moment, then turned and began slowly climbing the steep chimney above us. Halfway up he paused, struggling for breath. Then he resumed his laborious upward progress and presently disappeared beyond the crest.

I stayed where I was, and the hours passed. The sun reached its zenith above the peak and sloped away behind it. And at last I heard above me the sound of Osborn returning. As I looked up, his figure appeared at the top of the chimney and began the descent. His clothing was in tatters, and I could tell from his movements that only the thin flame of his will stood between him and collapse. In another few minutes he was standing beside me.

"Did you get there?" I asked.

He shook his head slowly. "I couldn't make it," he answered. "I didn't have what it takes."

We roped together silently and began the descent to the camp. There is nothing more to be told of the sixth assault on K3—at least not from the experiences of the men who made it. Osborn and I reached Camp V in safety, and three days later the entire expedition gathered at the advance base. It was decided, in view of the appalling tragedy that had occurred, to make no further attempt on the summit, and we began the evacuation of the mountain.

It remained for another year and other men to reveal the epilogue.

The summer following our attempt a combined English-Swiss expedition stormed the peak successfully. After weeks of hardship and struggle, they attained the topmost pinnacle of the giant, only to find that what should have been their great moment of triumph was, instead, a moment of the bitterest disappointment. For when they came out at last upon the summit, they saw that they were not the first. An ax stood there. Its haft was embedded in rock and ice, and on its steel head were the engraved words: TO MARTIN FROM JOHN.

They were sporting men. On their return to civilization they told their story, and the name of the conqueror of K3 was made known to the world. ✻

Discussion

1. (a) Explain how the setting is a vital part of this story. (b) To portray a setting vividly, an author frequently appeals to more than one of the reader's five senses: sight, hearing, touch or feeling, taste, and smell. To what senses does Ullman appeal in his description of K3? Cite examples.

2. (a) What external conflicts are present in the story? (b) What internal conflicts are there? (c) What, in your opinion, is the most important conflict?

3. Osborn and Nace are both expert mountain climbers, but the personalities of the two men are quite different. Read the following two remarks taken from the story:

   (1) "Let's get on to camp for a cup of tea."

   (2) "Let him have his way, and we'll be sitting here chewing our nails until the mountain falls down on us."

(a) Who is speaking in the first quotation? (b) What incident occurs just before this remark? (c) What do the remark and the incident show about this man's character? (d) Who is speaking in the second quotation? (e) What is the speaker talking about? (f) What does the sentence reveal about his character?

4. There are a number of scenes memorable for their tension and suspense. Which did you find most suspenseful? Why?

5. (a) Why do you think the author titled his story "Top Man"? (b) Who do you think is the "top man" in this story? Explain.

Word Study

Recognizing the meaningful parts or structure of a word may help you understand the meaning of the whole word.

There are two main kinds of word parts:

1. word parts which carry the basic meaning of a word
2. affixes

Once you understand the meaning of the basic part of a word, you can frequently determine the meaning of the whole word. For example, the basic meaning of the word *unsmiling* is carried by the English root word *smile*. What is the basic word part in *unsinkable? unforgivable?*

Affixes (*prefixes* and *suffixes*) are word parts placed at the beginnings and ends of words. Prefixes, parts like *un-, re-, mis-,* or *pro-,* are placed at the beginning of a word and change its meaning (for example, *un*lock, *mis*step). Suffixes are parts such as *-ly, -ness,* or *-able* which are used primarily to show how the word is used in a sentence—whether it is a noun, adjective, or adverb (for example, great*ly*, break*able*).

Many English words are derived from Latin or Greek words. The English word *incredible,* for example, is derived from Latin.

prefix	Latin word	suffix
in (not)	*credere* (believe)	*ible* (that can be)

What does the word *incredible* mean? Would you probably believe someone whose story was *credible?*

While you are not expected to learn a long list of affixes and Latin and Greek words, you will find that a familiarity with some of the most common will help you in your reading and also in using these words more precisely in your speaking and writing.

Many English words are derived from the Latin word *portare,* which means "to carry" or "to bear"; for example, a *porter* is a man who carries luggage. Following is a list of affixes which can be combined with the Latin root *port* to form words.

ex-, from, out of	*-able,* that can be
im-, in	*trans-,* across
re-, again, back	

Select the word formed by *port* and an affix which best fits the context of each of the following sentences.

1. We always listen to the ten o'clock weather _____.
2. Because John travels frequently, he prefers a _____ typewriter.
3. Products which are sent out of the United States are called _____.
4. Products which are brought into this country are called _____.
5. The airplane is large enough to _____ seventy-five people.

The Author

James Ramsey Ullman, author of many books and articles about mountaineering, was not content to write about what he himself had not experienced. Born in New York in 1907, he grew up to become "more familiar with Tibet than Times Square" and traveled widely throughout the world before his death in 1971. He climbed many mountains on all continents, and in 1963 he was a member of the successful American Mount Everest Expedition.

In his early career Ullman was both a newspaper reporter and a broadway producer, and he devoted the major part of his later life to writing. Among his best known books are *The White Tower, Banner in the Sky, The Age of Mountaineering, Tiger of the Snows,* and *Americans on Everest.*

The Highwayman | *Alfred Noyes*

Part One:

The wind was a torrent of darkness among the gusty trees;
The moon was a ghostly galleon tossed upon cloudy seas;
The road was a ribbon of moonlight over the purple moor;
And the highwayman came riding—
5   Riding—riding—
The highwayman came riding, up to the old inn door.

He'd a French cocked hat on his forehead, a bunch of lace at his chin,
A coat of the claret velvet, and breeches of brown doeskin;
They fitted with never a wrinkle; his boots were up to the thigh!
10 And he rode with a jeweled twinkle,
     His pistol butts a-twinkle,
His rapier hilt a-twinkle, under the jeweled sky.

Over the cobbles he clattered and clashed in the dark inn yard;
And he tapped with his whip on the shutters, but all was locked and barred;
15 He whistled a tune to the window, and who should be waiting there
But the landlord's black-eyed daughter,
     Bess, the landlord's daughter,
Plaiting a dark red love knot into her long black hair.

And dark in the dark old inn yard a stable-wicket creaked
20 Where Tim the ostler listened; his face was white and peaked;
His eyes were hollows of madness, his hair like moldy hay,
But he loved the landlord's daughter,
    The landlord's red-lipped daughter;
Dumb as a dog he listened, and he heard the robber say—

25 "One kiss, my bonny sweetheart; I'm after a prize tonight;
But I shall be back with the yellow gold before the morning light;
Yet, if they press me sharply, and harry me through the day,
Then look for me by moonlight,
    Watch for me by moonlight,
30 I'll come to thee by moonlight, though hell should bar the way."

He rose upright in the stirrups; he scarce could reach her hand,
But she loosened her hair i' the casement! His face burned like a brand
As the black cascade of perfume came tumbling over his breast;
And he kissed its waves in the moonlight
35   (Oh, sweet black waves in the moonlight!);
Then he tugged at his rein in the moonlight, and galloped away to the West.

Part Two:

He did not come in the dawning; he did not come at noon;
And out o' the tawny sunset, before the rise o' the moon,
When the road was a gypsy's ribbon, looping the purple moor,
40 A redcoat troop came marching—
    Marching—marching—
King George's men came marching, up to the old inn door.

They said no word to the landlord; they drank his ale instead;
But they gagged his daughter and bound her to the foot of her narrow
                    bed;
45 Two of them knelt at her casement, with muskets at their side!
There was death at every window,
        And hell at one dark window,
For Bess could see, through her casement, the road that *he* would ride.

They had tied her up to attention, with many a sniggering jest;
50 They had bound a musket beside her, with the barrel beneath her breast!
"Now keep good watch!" and they kissed her.
She heard the dead man say:
Look for me by moonlight,
        Watch for me by moonlight,
55 *I'll come to thee by moonlight, though hell should bar the way!*

She twisted her hands behind her, but all the knots held good!
She writhed her hands till her fingers were wet with sweat or blood!
They stretched and strained in the darkness, and the hours crawled by like
                    years,
Till, now, on the stroke of midnight,
60   Cold on the stroke of midnight,
The tip of one finger touched it! The trigger at least was hers!

The tip of one finger touched it; she strove no more for the rest!
Up she stood, to attention, with the barrel beneath her breast.
She would not risk their hearing; she would not strive again;
65 For the road lay bare in the moonlight,
        Blank and bare in the moonlight,
And the blood of her veins in the moonlight throbbed to her love's refrain.

Tlot-tlot; tlot-tlot! Had they heard it? The horse-hoofs ringing clear;
Tlot-tlot, tlot-tlot, in the distance! Were they deaf that they did not hear?
70 Down the ribbon of moonlight, over the brow of the hill,
The highwayman came riding —
        Riding — riding —
The redcoats looked to their priming! She stood up, straight and still!

Tlot-tlot, in the frosty silence! *Tlot-tlot,* in the echoing night!
75 Nearer he came and nearer! Her face was like a light!
Her eyes grew wide for a moment; she drew one last deep breath,
Then her finger moved in the moonlight,
        Her musket shattered the moonlight,
Shattered her breast in the moonlight and warned him — with her death.

80 He turned; he spurred to the westward; he did not know who stood
Bowed, with her head o'er the musket, drenched with her own red blood!
Not till the dawn he heard it; and slowly blanched to hear
How Bess, the landlord's daughter,

The landlord's black-eyed daughter,
85 Had watched for her love in the moonlight, and died in the darkness there.

Back he spurred like a madman, shrieking a curse to the sky,
With the white road smoking behind him, and his rapier brandished high!
Blood-red were his spurs i' the golden noon; wine-red was his velvet coat,
When they shot him down on the highway,
90   Down like a dog on the highway,
And he lay in his blood on the highway, with the bunch of lace at his throat.

And still of a winter's night, they say, when the wind is in the trees,
When the moon is a ghostly galleon tossed upon cloudy seas,
When the road is a ribbon of moonlight over the purple moor,
95 *A highwayman comes riding—*
    Riding—riding—
A highwayman comes riding, up to the old inn door.

Over the cobbles he clatters and clangs in the dark inn yard;
And he taps with his whip on the shutters, but all is locked and barred;
100 *He whistles a tune to the window, and who should be waiting there*
But the landlord's black-eyed daughter,
    Bess, the landlord's daughter,
Plaiting a dark red love knot into her long black hair.

Discussion

1. Poems, too, sometimes have plots and tell stories. What are the major incidents in the plot of "The Highwayman"?
2. (a) What is the setting of the poem? **(b)** Why is this setting appropriate?
3. Why are the last two stanzas printed in italics?
4. Read Alfred Noyes' comments printed in the next two columns. What did he mean when he wrote, "The point of the poem is not that the highwayman was a highwayman, but that the heroine was a heroine"?

The Author

While still in his twenties, Alfred Noyes became a successful English poet, and he continued writing both poetry and prose throughout his life. Before his death in 1958, he wrote of "The Highwayman":

"'The Highwayman' was written on the actual scene where the Golden Farmer, Jerry Abershaw, and other highwaymen used to lie in wait for the stagecoaches, about thirty miles from London. I was only just down from Oxford at the time and had taken rooms in a little cottage on the edge of the heath, which was still as unspoiled a bit of wild country as it was in the eighteenth century. I had gone there to finish my longer poem on Sir Francis Drake, who is himself sometimes described as a great buccaneer. But one night the wind blowing through the pines and the clatter of a horse's hoofs on the roads gave me the first line of 'The Highwayman' —'The wind was a torrent of darkness among the gusty trees.'

"The poem was written in a few hours, and shortly afterwards appeared in *Blackwood's Magazine.* In the half century since that date it has been reprinted in scores of anthologies; two musical cantatas (one by a famous American composer) have been made of it; and recently a film of it has been made in Technicolor.

"I have had fun out of 'The Highwayman.' On one occasion it very nearly got me arrested. Permission had been asked for its use in a book, and I went into a small post office on the coast of Maine to telegraph that my Highwayman was entirely at the service of those concerned. The telegram was misunderstood; and the postmistress ran out at the back of the office, calling for help. I have told the whole story in my autobiography, *Two Worlds for Memory.*

"The point of the poem is not that the highwayman was a highwayman, but that the heroine was a heroine."

For a few tense moments, their encounter
with the turtle separates father and son.
What conflict arises between them
on the dark Wisconsin road?

The Turtle

George Vukelich

THEY WERE DRIVING up to fish the White Creek for German Browns and the false dawn was purpling the Wisconsin countryside when they spotted the huge humpbacked object in the middle of the sand road and Jimmy coasted the station wagon to a stop.

"Pa," he said. "Turtle. Lousy snapper."

Old Tony sat up.

"Is he dead?"

"Not yet," Jimmy said. "Not yet he isn't." He shifted into neutral and pulled the hand brake. The snapper lay large and dark green in the headlight beams, and they got out and went around to look at it closely. The turtle moved a little and left razorlike claw marks in the wet sand, and it waited.

"Probably heading for the creek," Jimmy said. "They kill trout like crazy."

They stood staring down.

"I'd run the wagon over him," Jimmy said. "Only he's too big."

He looked around and walked to the ditchway, and came back with a long finger-thick pine branch. He jabbed it into the turtle's face and the snakehead lashed out and struck like spring steel and the branch snapped like a stick of macaroni, and it all happened fast as a match flare.

"Looka that!" Tony whistled.

"You bet, Pa. I bet he goes sixty pounds. Seventy maybe."

The turtle was darting its head around now in long stretching movements.

"I think he got some branch stuck in his craw," Jimmy said. He got out a cigarette and lighted it, and flipped the match at the rock-green shell.

"I wish now I'd brought the twenty-two," he said. "The pistol."

"You going to kill him?"

"Why not?" Jimmy asked. "They kill trout, don't they?"

They stood there smoking and not talking, and looking down at the unmoving shell.

"I could use the lug wrench on him," Jimmy said. "Only I don't think it's long enough. I don't want my hands near him."

Tony didn't say anything.

"You watch him," Jimmy said. "I'll go find something in the wagon."

From *The University Review*, Vol. 24, No. 4 (Summer 1958). Reprinted by permission of the author and *New Letters* (a continuation of *The University Review*).

Slowly Tony squatted down onto his haunches and smoked and stared at the turtle. Poor Old One, he thought. You had the misfortune to be caught in the middle of a sand road, and you are very vulnerable on the sand roads, and now you are going to get the holy life beaten out of you.

The turtle stopped its stretching movements and was still. Tony looked at the full webbed feet and the nail claws and he knew the truth.

"It would be different in the water, turtle," he said. "In the water you could cut down anybody."

He thought about this snapper in the water and how it would move like a torpedo and bring down trout, and nobody would monkey with it in the water—and here it was in the middle of a sand road, vulnerable as a baby and waiting to get its brains beaten out.

He finished his cigarette and field-stripped it,[1] and got to his feet and walked to the wagon and reached into the glove compartment for the thermos of coffee. What was he getting all worked up about a turtle for? He was an old man and he was acting like a kid, and they were going up to the White for German Browns, and he was getting worked up about a God-forsaken turtle in the middle of a God-forsaken sand road. *God-forsaken.* He walked back to the turtle and hunched down and sipped at the strong black coffee and watched the old snapper watching him.

Jimmy came up to him holding the bumper jack.

"I want to play it safe," he said. "I don't think the lug wrench is long enough." He squatted beside Tony. "What do you think?"

"He waits," Tony said. "What difference what I think?"

Jimmy squinted at him.

---

1. *field-stripped it.* After finishing his cigarette, he tore it apart, probably to prevent an accidental fire.

"I can tell something's eating you. What are you thinking, Pa?"

"I am thinking this is not a brave thing."

"What?"

"This turtle—he does not have a chance."

Jimmy lit a cigarette and hefted the bumper jack. The turtle moved ever so slightly.

"You talk like an old woman. An old tired woman."

"I can understand this turtle's position."

"He doesn't have a chance?"

"That's right."

"And that bothers you?"

Tony looked into Jimmy's face.

"That is right," he said. "That bothers me."

"Well of all the dumb stupid things," Jimmy said. "What do you want me to do? Get down on all fours and fight with him?"

"No," Tony said. "Not on all fours. Not on all fours." He looked at Jimmy. "In the water. Fight this turtle in the water. That would be a brave thing, my son."

Jimmy put down the bumper jack and reached for the thermos jug and didn't say anything. He drank his coffee and smoked his cigarette, and he stared at the turtle and didn't say anything.

"You're crazy," he said finally.

"It is a thought, my son. A thought. This helpless plodding old one like a little baby in this sand road, eh? But in the water, his home . . ." Tony snapped his fingers with the suddenness of a switch blade. "In the water he could cut down anyone, anything . . . any man. Fight him in the water, Jimmy. Use your bumper jack in the water . . ."

"I think you're nuts," Jimmy said. "I think you're honest to goodness nuts."

Tony shrugged. "This does not seem fair for you, eh? To be in the water with this one." He motioned at the turtle. "This seems nuts to you. Crazy to you. Because in the water you are not a match."

"What are you trying to prove, Pa?"

"Jimmy. This turtle is putting up his life. In the road here you are putting up nothing. You have nothing to lose at all. Not a finger or a hand or your life. Nothing. You smash him with a long steel bumper jack and he cannot get to you. He has as much chance as a ripe watermelon."

"So?"

"So I want you to put up something also. You should have something to lose or it is no match."

Jimmy looked at the old man and then at the turtle.

"Any fool can smash a watermelon," Tony said. "It does not take a brave man."

"Pa. It's only a turtle. You're making a federal case."

Old Tony looked at his son. "All right," he said. "Finish your coffee now and do what you are going to do. I say nothing more. Only for the next five minutes put yourself into this turtle's place. Put yourself into his shell and watch through his eyes. And try to think what he is thinking when he sees a coward coming to kill him with a long steel bumper jack."

Jimmy got to his feet and ground out his cigarette.

"All right, Pa," he said. "All right. You win."

Tony rose slowly from his crouch.

"No," he said. "Not me. You. You win."

"But Pa, they do kill trout."

"So," Tony said. "They kill trout. Nature put them here, and they kill trout. To survive. The trout are not extinct, eh? We kill trout also, we men.

To survive? No, for sport. This old one, he takes what he needs. I do not kill him for being in nature's plan. I do not play God."

Jimmy walked to the rear of the wagon then and flung down the bumper jack and closed up the door and came back.

"Pa," he said. "Honest to goodness you got the nuttiest ideas I ever heard."

Old Tony walked around behind the snapper and gently prodded it with his boot toe, and the turtle went waddling forward across the road and toppled over the sand shoulder and disappeared in the brushy growth of the creek bank. Tony and his son climbed into the wagon and sat looking at each other. The sun was coming up strong now and the sky was cracking open like a shell and spilling reds and golds and blues, and Jimmy started the engine.

Tony put the thermos away and got out his cigarettes and stuck one in his son's mouth.

"So?" he said.

They sat smoking for a full minute watching each other, and then Jimmy released the emergency and they rolled slowly along the drying sand road and down past the huge cleansing dawn coming, and the pine forests growing tall in the rising mists, and the quickly quiet waters of the eternal creek.   ✳

Discussion

1. (a) What conflict arises between Jimmy and his father? **(b)** Explain the attitude of each character toward the turtle. Cite passages to support your answers.

2. (a) On page 62, column 2, paragraph 5 Old Tony says, "So I want you to put up something also. You should have something to lose or it is no match." What does he mean? **(b)** Do you think Old Tony is serious when he suggests that Jimmy fight the turtle in the water? Why or why not?
3. (a) Do you think Jimmy finally understands and accepts his father's attitude? Explain. **(b)** Do you think Jimmy is a coward for wanting to kill the turtle? **(c)** Do you think his father would have felt the same way when he was young?
4. Of what importance is the setting of "The Turtle"?

From the Author

"The Turtle" actually happened. We were driving up to fish the White Creek for German Browns. The false dawn was purpling the Wisconsin countryside. And we did spot the huge humpbacked object in the middle of the sand road.

Back in Madison, I set everything down on paper, as faithfully as possible. I read the first draft and felt that Old Tony was a kind of backwoods Albert Schweitzer defining the philosophy of "Reverence for Life." I then committed a cardinal sin of writing. I went back and padded. I had Old Tony discuss Albert Schweitzer. I had him mouth beautiful lines of Schweitzer's. I had him quoting Schweitzer as though they were old school chums from way back.

Mari Sandoz, my teacher at the University of Wisconsin, put a stop to all this nonsense.

"What's the point of the story?" she asked.

I told her "Reverence for Life."

"Fine," she said, "but you're preaching."

I cut the references to Albert Schweitzer, to "Reverence for Life"; I cut to the bone. Miss Sandoz read the story again.

"You're not preaching now," she smiled.

"The Turtle" has stood unchanged from that moment. If the story comes off for you, you can thank Mari Sandoz. I did.

A man who used the stage name
of Harry Houdini became famous
throughout the world for fantastic escapes
from almost every conceivable type of restraint.
However, his rise to fame was, as this account
makes clear, neither magical nor easy.

See
FACT AND FICTION
Handbook
of Literary
Terms
page 541

JAIL BREAKS

Lace Kendall

IN THE FALL OF 1898, Harry Houdini, magician and escape artist, and his wife Bess walked into the city jail in Chicago and made their way to the desk of Andy Rohan, lieutenant of the detective force and the chief of police's right-hand man.

Rohan, a heavy man with drooping red mustaches, looked up and recognized the dark-haired young man he had been introduced to by reporters some time before.

"I'd like you to meet my wife," Houdini said. "I told her you were interested in some of our adventures on the road and she's a better storyteller than I am."

Vaguely surprised, Rohan acknowledged the introduction, murmured something about being busy, and then found Bess leaning on his desk and beginning a long tale about a time when Houdini had been unable to get out of a pair of handcuffs a challenger had placed on him. "It's the only time he ever failed," Bess said. "And that was because a slug had been

placed in the lock. Nobody could have opened the lock, even with a hammer and chisel. Houdini actually wept . . ."

While she talked, Houdini strolled off, trying to look like a casual visitor merely glancing around the jail. Actually, he was making a quick study of the complicated lock system. A swift glance here, another there, a moment's close inspection of this lock and that, and he knew what he wanted to know. He had gone to great pains to arrange this secret inspection, the prelude to an exploit which he counted on to make all of Chicago gasp. Challenges to local sheriffs and police in the various towns they were passing through had been bringing gratifying results in the way of publicity. But, so far, the publicity had been confined to smaller cities. Now, if Bess could just keep the detective distracted long enough . . .

" . . . And another time," Bess was telling Rohan, "we were doing mind-reading acts together and pretending that we were in communication with departed spirits. Only, Houdini couldn't stand it. People really believed he had mystic powers, and finally he said he'd rather starve than take advantage of people's faith. So then ——"

"I'm sorry, Mrs. Houdini," Rohan interrupted, "but I'm a busy man. This jail was built for people who have official business here. I'm afraid I'll have to ask you to leave now." Even as he looked up, Houdini was standing back beside Bess.

"Of course," Houdini said. "We don't want to interfere with your work. But perhaps we'll see you again."

"Well —" Rohan said with some lack of enthusiasm.

Outside, Houdini tucked Bess's arm in his. "We're all set. Now for my date with the reporters tomorrow. You did a good job with Rohan — only, did you have to roll your eyes at him like that?"

"Why not? He's a nice man."

"He's going to be a surprised one tomorrow."

The next day Houdini gathered a number of reporters around him and announced, "If you fellows want a good news story, come down to the city jail with me. I'll let the boys down there handcuff me and lock me in a cell and then I'll get out faster than you can say 'Chicago.' "

The reporters agreed that it would be a good story if Houdini could do it. Nobody had tried the feat before. So they got a photographer and set out.

Rohan grumbled a little about the whole idea's being so much foolishness, but actually he was pleased at the presence of the reporters. Free publicity didn't hurt the jail, either, so

he finally said, "Go ahead, Houdini. We'll lock you up, all right. If you want to make a fool of yourself, that's no skin off my nose." Therewith, he ordered two of the guards to handcuff Houdini carefully and put him in one of the stoutest cells.

Rohan and the reporters had scarcely time to sit down in Rohan's office, prepared to wait indefinitely, before Houdini walked in and joined them.

Houdini's broad grin faded as the reporters shrugged. "You're not fooling anybody," one of them said. "Rohan says you were around here just yesterday, and a couple of times before. You've had plenty of time, apparently, to make wax impressions of the locks in the cells and corridor exits and have some keys manufactured. Who couldn't open a lock when he's got keys right in his pockets?"

Rohan sat smiling, hands folded over his huge belly. "Maybe your stunts make big news in the sticks, Houdini, but not in Chicago."

"All right," Houdini said coolly, "why don't you strip me of my clothes and then lock me up?"

Rohan looked at him sharply. The reporters pricked up their ears. "That sounds fair enough," Rohan agreed. "Go ahead, boys, strip him down to the skin."

They did. And when one suggested that Houdini might be concealing a key in his mouth, Houdini told them to tape his mouth shut. This was done and Houdini was led naked and manacled to a cell. His clothes were locked in another cell.

Back in the warden's office, the group sat down to wait once more. They were there less than ten minutes when Houdini strolled in, smiling and completely dressed, entering through the door that opened onto the street. He was a little breathless and, when questioned, confessed that the escape had taken him longer than it would have otherwise because he had taken time to run to his lodgings nearby and yell of his success to his wife.

The reporters, the photographer, Andy Rohan, and the small crowd that was gathering quickly, were stunned.

"It's—impossible," Rohan muttered.

The reporters rushed to their newspaper offices. The photographer snapped a picture and rushed after them.

In the morning, Houdini hurried to the newsstand. There it was—his picture and a single column several inches long telling about his feat. He bought every copy of the newspaper on the stand and ran back to show Bess.

"Look, Bess!" he yelled, almost breaking the apartment door down as he entered the room. "My picture's in the paper! I'm famous now!"

That night they celebrated with an extra-good dinner, and with a special bone for their pet terrier.

After a few days of waiting for the publicity to produce something more than clippings for their scrapbook, a representative from the Hopkins Theatre called on the Houdinis and offered them a job. It was the first time in their four years together, that they had had a chance at a first-class house. Although Bess had the flu, she got out of bed and rode with Houdini in a cab to the theatre. She was twenty-two years old and it was the first cab ride she had ever had.

The engagement at the Hopkins Theatre was a moderate success, but when it was over Houdini and Bess found themselves playing in dime museums again. Then one night at a museum in Minneapolis, Minnesota, a stranger approached Houdini and suggested that he and Bess have a cup of coffee with him in a nearby restaurant.

Without introducing himself, the man proceeded to criticize Houdini's act. "Your trunk trick and handcuff escape are fine acts—nobody can beat you with those—but you don't use the right showmanship. You've got your act all cluttered up with pigeons and guinea pigs popping out of nowhere, and a lot of hocus-pocus that only draws attention away from the big thrillers. If you'll cut out the minor magic I can use you on my circuit at sixty dollars. Maybe more, if you earn it."

"We'd like the chance," Houdini said meekly. "But—what's your name?"

"Martin Beck," the man said. "Of the Orpheum Circuit."

Houdini and Bess squeezed hands under the table. At last they were going to be in big-time vaudeville! Their dime museum and side show days were behind them.

Back at their lodgings, they sadly said good-by to the pigeons and guinea pigs. From now on, as Beck had advised, Houdini would concentrate on the "big thrillers."

The job with the Orpheum Circuit marked the real beginning of Houdini's fame as an escape artist. In one of the large West Coast cities a chief of police locked Houdini in a jail cell with four sets of handcuffs on his arms, shackles on his legs, and one leg imprisoned in an Oregon boot. The iron boot weighed fifty-five pounds and had no key, working by a combination lock. Houdini escaped with apparent ease. Astonished by this, the police chief issued a statement warning that Houdini could be one of the most dangerous criminals in the United States if he wished, and that law officers should remember what he looked like in case they ever needed to apprehend him.

It was not a flattering statement, but it proved that people were beginning to take Houdini seriously as a master of his trade.

In San Francisco, Houdini again astounded police and public. His feats at the Orpheum Theatre earned him a feature story in the *San Francisco Examiner,* June 18, 1899, with six photographs showing him extricating himself from ropes with which he had been tied to a chair.

Said the article, "Anybody who goes to the Orpheum may have a trial at lashing him to a chair with as long a rope as may be obtainable and with as many turns and twists and knots as may be devised." The article went on to quote Houdini as saying, "My offer of fifty dollars for a pair of regulation handcuffs which I cannot escape from is still open to doubting Thomases."

There were scarcely any doubting Thomases left in the city when Houdini challenged the police. The police put ten pairs of handcuffs on his arms, and then the arm-bands were handcuffed to the fetters. Houdini was so weighed down with irons and locks he could scarcely hobble into a room which had been set aside for him—a room which he had not been permitted to enter before. Even as a sergeant of detectives told reporters that it was absolutely impossible for a man so shackled to get free, Houdini walked up to the sergeant carrying all the irons in his hands.

A strait jacket was tried next, but it held Houdini no better than the iron shackles had.

Houdini's years of physical training were beginning to bring their rewards. Although he was very strong, it was not strength alone that helped him escape from restraints, but technique and ability besides. His first task, when in a strait jacket, was to try to raise his strapped, canvas-sheathed arms up in front of his body. He did this by placing one elbow on some solid foundation and, by sheer strength, forcing his arm gradually upward until he could push his head under his elbow. He then managed to undo the buckles of the straps of the cuffs with his teeth. Once his arms were free, he undid the buckles at the back of the strait jacket, even though his fingers had to work through the canvas sleeves still encasing his hands. With the back buckles open, it was comparatively simple to free himself of the jacket.

Houdini's mastery of all kinds of locks came partly from a thorough knowledge of how they operated and from his having hidden tools which he used in opening them. He made some of his picklocks from piano wire. Such a picklock was easily concealed on his body, whether in his mouth or nostrils, or glued to the sole of his foot.

According to a writer in *Variety* magazine, he was able to swallow steel bars and files of considerable size and regurgitate them when necessary. Also, he was said to be able to make his wrists and ankles bigger when shackles were applied. Most often he relied on his knowledge of lock mechanisms to free himself from handcuffs or leg irons. Some handcuffs could be made to spring open by striking the part near the hinge and keyhole on the heel of a shoe or against the floor. For some time Houdini had a plate of lead fastened inside the knee of his trousers where it would not be noticeable, and struck the handcuff against that.

Committees that tied him with rope usually used new rope, to be certain that it would not break. This was an advantage to Houdini, as knots in new rope can be untied more easily than in old, soft rope. Such challenging committees usually used a long, continuous piece of rope, which also was to Houdini's advantage, for he found it easier to get a slack in a long rope. If, when the rope was being pulled around him, the committee seemed to be doing too good a job, he would swell his muscles, slightly hunch his shoulders, and hold his arms a little away from his sides to try to insure some slack. And sometimes he had a sharp knife with a hook-shaped blade concealed in his clothing somewhere, in case a knot proved too troublesome.

Concealed picklocks or keys or knives are all part of an escape artist's trade. Houdini used such props as all other magicians did and do. It was his skill in their use, together with his daring and muscular control, that made him great.

His greatness was recognized wherever he went in the days following his first successes with the Orpheum Circuit, from San Francisco to Los Angeles, Memphis to Nashville, Kansas City to Providence. Police in numerous cities began to compete with each other for the chance to test his skill.

All the while, Houdini kept studying more difficult methods of escape. His beginning fame was only a spur to his ambition. Wherever he went, he continued to seek other performers and try to ferret out their secrets. At last he was learning to dramatize his ability so that he was becoming a real showman, but his deepest desire was to attain the highest perfection of his art of which he was capable. He spent his energies and his money extravagantly, laboring hour after hour to develop or master new feats, spending what was left from his earnings (after deducting a regular, weekly amount for his mother) on old books and curios

and anything and everything having to do with magic. Although he was now a success, he was still not earning what his tremendous skill deserved.

Nor was he getting any attention from the eastern cities, where the reputations of performers were generally made. When the Orpheum tour ended in the fall of 1899, there was still no job for him in the large cities of the East. Agents and managers were unimpressed by the twenty-five year old veteran of show business, and Houdini found himself facing the prospect of small-time halls and museums again.

"What can I do, Bess?" he repeated over and over, pacing the floor of an apartment they had rented in New York at the end of the successful tour. "What can I do to make them accept me here in the East? If I were some European magician from Paris or Berlin they'd come running to sign me up. But just because I'm an ordinary American—" He paused, snapping his fingers. "That's it, Bess! We'll go to Europe. We'll win our reputation there and then we'll come back and let them beg us to appear on their stages here! That's the answer!"

It was a big gamble, but Bess agreed that it was worth trying.

On a spring day in 1900 a small, second-class liner carrying Bess and Harry Houdini steamed out into New York harbor. The small ship shook with every reverberation of its engines and rocked about even in the mild swell of the bay. Houdini, standing at the ship's rail, watching the skyline of New York recede, felt his eyes glaze. A beginning nausea rose in his stomach.

When the ship reached the ocean the swells began to rock it in earnest. Green in the face, Houdini went staggering toward his cabin and flung himself on the berth.

The cabin was hot and stuffy. For the next two days Bess sat fanning Houdini, putting cold cloths on his head, forcing him to sip lemon juice, constantly trying to assuage his seasickness. On the third day Houdini became delirious.

The ship's doctor shook his head and said, "You'll have to tie him to his berth. He might do something rash in his delirium."

Bess felt an hysterical desire to laugh. Tie Houdini down so he couldn't escape from his berth! Soberly, she managed to answer, "Yes, I'll try."

Mostly, she relied on verbal persuasion, sitting by, holding his hand, restraining him when he reared up on his elbow crying out in a nightmare. But she could not stay by his side every minute. When she went to have her meals in the dining room she took the bed sheets and bound Houdini to the berth, making certain that the knots were tied underneath the bed where he could not get at them.

The worst point of the voyage was reached when Houdini muttered deliriously that he was going to throw himself into the sea. "I'll get out!" he proclaimed, wild-eyed. "Packing case — chains — I'll get out, even under the sea. Just let me jump in. Let me get up!"

"Harry, darling," Bess pleaded, "you're sick. You must try to lie still. Just lie still."

Her nerves frayed, almost sick from exhaustion herself, she got a life preserver from the steward and strapped it on Houdini just in case he should throw himself over the rail when she was not near to prevent him.

Once, when he was free of his delirium, but still miserably ill, she said, "Oh, Harry, I wonder if it's worth it." Anxiety drilled through her. What if this were a fool's chase? What if London and Paris and Berlin should be as cold to them as New York had been? She trembled at the thought of being in a foreign land without money, without friends.

London with its gray towers and bridges was as indifferent to Houdini and Bess as New York had been. As he walked the unfamiliar streets — Drury Lane, Charing Cross Road, the Strand — seeing one theatrical agent after another, Houdini's optimism flagged. But he kept going. He could not give up.

His spirits were at a low ebb the day that he met a young theatrical agent named Harry Day, but Day was impressed by Houdini and arranged an interview for him with C. Dunas Slater, manager of the fine Alhambra Theatre.

Houdini went through some of his tricks for Slater, and then looked hopefully at him. "So you claim you can escape from any kind of irons, do you?" Slater asked skeptically.

"Yes, sir." Houdini pushed his press clippings in front of the manager again, pointing out the news stories of his escapes from handcuffs and jail cells in the States. "I'll let anybody challenge me."

"Including Scotland Yard?"

Houdini's expression of confidence did not change at the mention of that famous police organization. "Yes."

"Of course, the Yard men may not be as co-operative as the sheriffs back in your country," Slater said slyly.

"Co-operative?"

"I've heard of men bribing police and wardens."

Houdini flushed. "You've never heard it about me, and never will. How soon can we go to Scotland Yard?"

"Right now," Slater answered and

reached for the phone. He made the arrangements and the group set out.

Houdini and Bess held hands in the carriage as it rattled over the cobblestones toward Scotland Yard's headquarters on the Thames. Harry Day looked nervous, obviously afraid that he had gone too far in recommending the cocky young American beside him.

At the Yard's headquarters, Superintendent Melville laughed openly at the idea of anyone's escaping from Yard handcuffs. "However," he said, "if Mr. Slater wants to have a bit of sport at your expense, young man, I'll oblige him." He pulled open a drawer and took out a pair of shiny new bracelets connected by heavy links. "This is the kind of jewelry we put on young Yankees who get into trouble over here. And you'll be in trouble once I fasten these on you." He led Houdini to a large, upright beam that was a building support. "Put your arms around this pillar, lad."

Houdini did as he was told and the superintendent locked the cuffs to Houdini's wrists.

Superintendent Melville turned, smiling, to Slater and the others. "We may as well go and sit down for a couple of hours. When he's had his fill I'll go back and set him free."

Bess gave Houdini an anxious glance as she followed the men away from the pillar.

"Just a minute!" Houdini called out. "I'll go with you."

Melville turned.

"This is the way Yankees got out of handcuffs," Houdini said. The cuffs clattered to the floor and he stepped away from the pillar.

Melville's smile faded. Slater's eyes popped. Harry Day rubbed his hands together as if he saw a clear and dazzling road leading into his own future.

"You're hired," Slater said. "Come back to my office and I'll sign you up for two weeks."

On the way back to the office, Day whispered, "When that's over, I'll get you another engagement, Houdini. I'd be happy to be your agent from now on."

"Fine," Houdini said, and turned his attention to Bess, who was smiling up at him radiantly.

Back at the office, Slater got busy at once ordering press releases and handbills advertising Houdini's forthcoming appearance at his theatre. "I'll leave the word 'marvel' out of the publicity," he told the Houdinis. "London's had so many fake marvels that the public won't swallow any more. And just to make sure, and to get the reporters on our side, I'm going to arrange a special showing for you before the press. Some of the reporters have played a big part in exposing frauds."

Although Slater didn't say so in so many words, Houdini realized that the manager still suspected trickery.

When Houdini gave his special performance before members of the press who had come prepared to "expose" him, even to bringing along an ancient slave iron from which they were certain he could not escape – but from which he did escape in less than three minutes – he won Slater's confidence entirely. The reporters admitted frankly that they did not know how he performed his feats but that they were satisfied there was no fakery about it.

Jubilant, Bess said when they were alone, "You've won them all over now, Harry!"

"No, I still have to win the English public. My big performance is still ahead."

Looking at him, Bess realized that Houdini was truly nervous, more so than she had ever known him to be before.

On the night of the opening performance Houdini paced back and forth in the wings of the Alhambra, waiting for his cue to walk onto the stage. Bess paced with him, dressed in the page boy costume she wore as his assistant. When the orchestra struck up a loud march, his signal to go on, Bess pressed his hand and whispered, "Good luck," before taking her place behind him.

The stagelights gleamed against Houdini's eyes as he stepped from the wings and walked to the center of the stage. Bess followed. Beyond the lights were row on row of men and women, vague shapes in the dimness of the big theatre.

Carefully, slowly, Houdini began his introduction. "Ladies and gentlemen of the audience, it is my privilege tonight to try to demonstrate to you——"

A voice rang out. A man leaped upon the stage. "You are an imposter, a fraud!" the stranger cried. He turned and faced the audience, pointing at Houdini, claiming the center of the stage for himself. "I am the Great Cirnoc, the original Handcuff King. This man is a fake. You owe it to your self-respect not to be duped by him."

Houdini stared helplessly, completely unable to cope with the wild turn of events. His mouth worked soundlessly and he even backed away before the stranger's accusing finger. Bess was equally dumfounded. They found themselves standing almost offstage like two culprits who had invaded a forbidden palace.

"Furthermore," Cirnoc shouted, "this man is not even an American! He has never been in the United States."

"Just a moment," another voice said, speaking from the audience, a calm and cultivated voice that carried authority. "I happen to know that Mr. Houdini is an American. I am an American, too, and my name is Chauncey M. Depew. I saw the young man in question perform a handcuff act several years ago in my country."

Houdini looked at Bess. Senator Depew, the great orator and railroad magnate! Houdini's courage came back in a rush. "Get the Bean Giant," he whispered to Bess. "We'll take care of the Great Cirnoc!"

Bess ran off stage, and returned with the giant handcuff that had been named for its inventor, a Captain Bean of Boston. The captain had offered five hundred dollars to anybody who could discover the secret of its lock, a lock made to resist any key. Houdini had been the first and only man to solve the mystery.

Now Houdini walked over to Cirnoc and said loudly, so that all could hear, "Perhaps it's time for you to prove your credentials as the Handcuff King." He held the cuffs out. "I'll give you five hundred dollars if you can free yourself from these manacles."

Cirnoc drew back haughtily. "Since this is your show, let's see you get out of them first."

Houdini obliged, asking Cirnoc to lock the cuffs on him. Then he disappeared into the small cabinet which kept his methods secret from the audience and from other magicians. Almost at once he stepped out again, free of the cuffs.

"Your turn," Houdini said to Cirnoc with a smile, and locked the handcuffs on the other man's wrists. "In case you have trouble, here's a key."

Cirnoc retired reluctantly to the cabinet as the audience applauded Houdini's show of sportsmanship.

Houdini, completely self-possessed now, ordered the orchestra to play.

The orchestra played bar after bar, page after page. There were chuckles in the audience as Cirnoc did not appear. The chuckles grew to laughter. Finally, in the midst of the laughter, the Great Cirnoc emerged from the cabinet. Sweating and red-faced, with rage and humiliation distorting his features, he held out his handcuffed wrists and forced himself to ask Houdini to free him.

The Alhambra Theatre echoed with applause as Houdini removed the handcuffs and, bowing, accepted the ovation that swept away all fear or doubt. The English public was his.

Everywhere, in England and on the Continent, going from one triumph to another, Houdini's first act on reaching a new city was to challenge the police to confine him. Time after time he escaped from the most intricate shackles the police could devise. Houdini's reputation spread across Europe, and he was soon earning a thousand dollars or more a week. After many long months on the road Bess had begun to speak wistfully of returning home, but Houdini was not yet ready to try his luck back in America. "Bess, I want to go to Russia. Day is writing to the authorities there. Maybe I can perform before the Tsar himself."

Getting into Russia, Houdini found, was not quite as simple as getting out of a nailed packing case. Passports had to be obtained. Long questionnaires had to be filled out. There was the Russian language to be learned — or at least enough of it so that Houdini could make his stage speeches in Russian. This was a custom he practiced in all countries he visited.

When Houdini and Bess and their assistants finally crossed the Russian border in May, 1903, one of the first things Houdini did was to ask the manager of the theatre where he was to appear to listen to the speech he had prepared in Russian.

The manager listened with a look of growing distress. When Houdini had finished, the manager cried, "If you perform your stunts the way you talk Russian we are ruined! What you're speaking is Polish — and that's forbidden here!"

Crestfallen, Houdini went to work to learn the speech all over again. Walking around Moscow, he practiced the speech aloud as he went, reciting in Russian that he was the handcuff king and the greatest of jail breakers and that no prison could hold him. He was congratulating himself on his mastery of the speech when a small army of policemen surrounded him, handcuffed him, and rushed him off to prison as a maniac.

Back at the hotel where the Houdinis were staying, Bess waited for Houdini to appear for dinner. Dinnertime came and no Houdini. Alarmed, Bess called the theatre manager. The manager, in turn, called the police. Yes, said the police, they had a Mr. Houdini locked up. He was a madman.

Bess and the manager hurried to the prison. There sat Houdini, securely locked in a cell with a band of guards watching over him.

"I thought you could get out of any jail," the manager taunted.

"I've been busy concentrating on my speech," Houdini replied with a weak smile.

It was the only cell that ever held Houdini and it took a few serious explanations by Bess and the manager to make him a free man again. ✱

Discussion

1. **(a)** According to this account what methods did Houdini use to make his escapes? **(b)** What was the most important aspect of his preparations for these escapes? **(c)** How did he learn his methods?

2. On the basis of the article you have just read, would you agree with this statement? Explain. "While there may have been a lot of showmanship in Houdini's acts, there was nothing of the supernatural or magical—everything was carefully planned and carefully executed."

3. **(a)** What indications can you find that this account is based largely on fact? Locate relevant passages and details. **(b)** Can you find any places in this account where the author *may* have added imagined but appropriate details to highlight an episode? **(c)** Which parts of this account seem most dramatic? **(d)** Which parts seem most ironic?

4. Does this article lead you to believe that Houdini was a man who was considerate of others? that he was a dedicated, hard-working man? that he was generally unsure of himself? that he had a sense of humor? Explain your responses.

5. This account ends with Houdini in Russia, his European tour still not completed. Does anything in this article lead you to believe that Houdini was headed for a successful career? What facts outside this article can you find to support your answer?

Word Study

When neither context nor structure gives you clues to the meaning of a word, you will need to consult a dictionary.

Besides definitions and a key to the pronunciation of words, dictionaries provide etymologies (word origins), biographical information on historical figures, geographical facts, common abbreviations, technical terms, and facts about language usage.

Using your Glossary, answer the following questions.

1. In what year was Harry Houdini born?

2. "If you'll cut out the minor magic I can use you on my circuit . . ." What is the meaning of *circuit* in this sentence?

3. From what language is the word delirium taken?

4. Explain the relationship of the original meaning of *delirium* to its present meaning.

5. What is the meaning of the expression "big time"? Is it considered formal usage, informal usage, or slang?

The Author

The story of a young Wisconsin boy-magician, Erich Weiss, who later was to become the world's greatest escape artist, is told in a warm, personalized study called *Houdini: Master of Escape*, from which our selection is taken. The author, Lace Kendall, was born, raised, and educated in Minnesota. Her real name is Adrien Stoutenburg, but she uses several pseudonyms as well. When not writing, she is an amateur artist and sculptor who also likes to play the piano, guitar, and harmonica.

Unit 1 Review

1. The following selections are classified as short stories, a type of fiction: "A Man of Peace," "Top Man," and "The Turtle." (a) Which of these stories contain factual elements? (b) What effect do such elements have on the stories?

2. Practically all important types of conflict occur in one or another of the selections in this unit. From the selections, cite examples which involve (a) man against man; (b) man against society; (c) man against nature; (d) internal conflict.

3. A good writer is careful to select only those details and incidents which are important to his story. Why is each of the following details important to the story in which it appears?

(a) De Parma's being a South American ("A Man of Peace")

(b) Claudine's interest in De Parma ("A Man of Peace")

(c) Lafleur's interest in gardening ("A Man of Peace")

(d) an ice ax inscribed: TO MARTIN FROM JOHN ("Top Man")

(e) a near-fatal accident involving Nace and five other men ("Top Man")

(f) a bumper jack ("The Turtle")

4. (a) In which of the selections in this unit do you consider the setting to be of major importance? Give reasons for your answers. (b) Could any of the stories take place in other settings? Explain.

5. (a) Why do you think this unit is entitled "Encounter"? (b) Think of other titles which might be equally appropriate.

6. Before this anthology was published, various groups of eighth-grade students were asked to read "A Man of Peace" and to write a statement explaining what the story is about. Here are some of their statements:

1. This story is about a peaceful man who enjoyed the art of fencing but when pushed too far he will stick up for his rights and fight.
2. This story is about a man who has courage and a boy who has pride.
3. This story shows that fighting can't settle all things.
4. This story is about courage and fear and feeling.
5. This story is about a master of his art who believes so strongly in his ideal of non-violence that he finally takes part in a duel to uphold his statements.

(a) Which of the statements do you think best explains the meaning of the story? Be prepared to defend your choice. (b) Write similar statements about three of the other selections in this unit.

SUGGESTED READING

ADAMSON, JOY, *Born Free*. (Pantheon *Bantam) Elsa, an orphaned lioness, is raised as a pet in the African household of Mrs. Adamson and her husband. Though the Adamsons love Elsa dearly, they realize that they must train her to return to her natural habitat. A sequel, *Living Free* (Harcourt *Macfadden), continues Elsa's story as she returns to natural life in the African bush, mates, rears a family, and all along maintains a bond of friendship with the Adamsons. Both books are illustrated with absorbing photographs.

COOPER, JAMES FENIMORE, *The Last of the Mohicans*. (Scribner *Washington Square) Good readers will find plenty of conflict and action in this classic historical novel of frontier and Indian life.

CORBETT, JAMES E., *Jungle Lore*. (Oxford) The author narrates fascinating stories about wild animals and about his boyhood adventures in the Indian jungles.

DONOVAN, ROBERT J., *PT 109, John F. Kennedy in World War II.* (McGraw *Fawcett) A well-written, factual account of Kennedy's role in the war, this carefully documented biography is illustrated with many photographs.

DUMAS, ALEXANDRE, *The Count of Monte Cristo.* (Grosset *McGraw) In this story of nineteenth-century Europe, Edmund Dante, a young sailor, attempts to avenge the wrongs done to him. *The Three Musketeers* (Dodd *Pyramid) is a still unexcelled story of brilliant swordplay and swift action at the court of Louis XIII.

DURRELL, GERALD M., *Island Zoo.* (Macrae) Here is an illustrated view of Durrell's private zoo. *The Overloaded Ark* (Viking *Ballantine) relates the story of a six-month collecting expedition for English zoos.

GUARESCHI, GIOVANNI, *The Little World of Don Camillo.* (Farrar *Pocket Books) This enjoyable novel reveals the sometimes amusing, sometimes pathetic struggle between a village priest and a communist village mayor, one of his wayward flock. Cartoonlike drawings enhance the story.

HEYERDAHL, THOR, *Kon-Tiki.* (Rand *Pocket Books) With five companions, the author built a raft and sailed off on a 4300-mile journey across the Pacific. This is a vivid and exciting tale of true adventure.

LONDON, JACK, *The Sea Wolf.* (Macmillan *Houghton) A ruthless tramp-steamer captain receives an unexpected passenger on the high seas, and becomes an instrument for good in spite of his brutality. *The Call of the Wild* (Macmillan *Airmont) is the story of the dog, Buck, that after the death of the one man he had learned to love and respect, breaks away from civilization and becomes the leader of a pack of Alaskan wolves.

MAXWELL, GAVIN, *Ring of Bright Water.* (Dutton *Fawcett) Mijbel and Edal, the author's pet otters, hold the spotlight in this account of life on the coast of Scotland.

MOWAT, FARLEY, *Never Cry Wolf.* (Little *Dell) In this illuminating book, Mr. Mowat tells about his experiences in the subarctic Barren Lands of Canada, where he was sent to study the behavior of wolves.

SABATINI, RAFAEL, *Captain Blood, His Odyssey.* (Houghton) This exciting romance is woven around the Irishman Peter Blood, soldier, country doctor, slave, pirate, and Governor of Jamaica. *Scaramouche* (Houghton) is a romantic novel about an adventurous strolling player in the early years of the French Revolution.

SANDOZ, MARI, *Winter Thunder.* (Westminster, originally appeared in the *Saturday Evening Post* as "The Lost School Bus") This suspenseful tale relates how a young teacher saved seven children stranded by a severe blizzard.

STEVENSON, ROBERT LOUIS, *Kidnapped.* (Scribner *Dell) A young Scot has romantic adventures on sea and land shortly after the uprising in support of Prince Charlie in 1745. In *Treasure Island* (Scribner *Dell), a delightful yarn of buried gold, pirates, and mutiny is woven around a brave cabin boy and the villainous Long John Silver.

TARKINGTON, BOOTH, *Monsieur Beaucaire.* (Doubleday) This story of adventure and mystery involves romantic ladies and dueling French gentlemen.

TUNIS, JOHN R., *Silence Over Dunkerque.* (Morrow *Berkley) This stirring book concerns one of the most astonishing feats of World War II: the evacuation of some 350,000 English and French soldiers from the coast of France just as they seemed doomed to destruction.

ULLMAN, JAMES RAMSEY, *Banner in the Sky.* (Lippincott *Pocket Books, entitled *Third Man on the Mountain*) A boy climbs the greatest mountain in Switzerland and conquers himself as well.

WHITE, WILLIAM L., *They Were Expendable.* (Harcourt *Harbrace) The author relates the heroic and tragic adventure of a PT boat squadron in the Philippines in World War II. His information came from four officers, who were all that survived.

*paperback

2

How does youth learn
  —courage
  —tolerance
  —self-respect
  —responsibility
  —and reverence for life?
What are the emotional bonds that link
  —a boy and his father
  —a boy and his mother
  —a young child and an older friend?
How does a young person deal with
  —an overprotective father
  —or a scheming friend?
What happens when young people
come in conflict with adult standards?
These are the problems between

Two
Generations

Picasso
1905

See
CHARACTERIZATION
Handbook
of Literary
Terms
page 537

Emily Vanderpool and Virgil Meade share a remarkable ability for getting into trouble! Pay particular attention to the methods of characterization Jean Stafford has used to create these individuals.

the SCARLET letter

Jean Stafford

I KNEW from the beginning that Virgil Meade was crazy, but I didn't know he was a crook until it was too late and he had got me into a fine how-do-you-do that might have altered the whole course of my life. I mean I might have killed him and either gone to the gallows or spent the rest of my natural days in the pen.

Virgil unofficially became my fellow when he put a big valentine in the box for me. At first I was sorely affronted because it was a very insulting comic one he had made himself — when you opened it up, there was the outline of a huge foot on each page and underneath it said, "All policemen have big feet but Emily Vanderpool's got them beat." Moreover, he had signed it so there would be no doubt in my mind who was trying to hurt my feelings. I couldn't decide whether to write him a poison pen letter beginning "Dear (oh yeah?) Four-Eyes" or to beat him on the head with an Indian club. But then I discovered that he had written "S.W.A.K." on the back of the envelope and I knew what that stood for because my sister Stella, who was popular and was therefore up on codes and slang, had told me, "Sealed With a Kiss." Ordi-

narily such mushiness would have made me go ahead and write the letter or take out after him with the Indian club; but it so happened that at that particular time I didn't have a friend to my name, having fought with everyone I knew, and the painful truth was that Virgil's valentine was positively the only one I got that year except for a dinky little paper-doily thing, all bumpy with homemade paste, from my baby sister, Tess. And besides being all alone in the world, I was a good deal impressed by Virgil because he was as clever as a monkey on the parallel bars (the way he skinned the cat was *something*), and I had heard that at the age of eleven he already had a wisdom tooth, a rumor that seemed somehow the more likely because his father was a dentist. And so, on second thought, although he had insulted me and although he wore glasses (a stigma far more damning than the biggest clodhoppers in the world), I decided that he was better than nobody and I looked across the room at him. He was staring moodily out the window at the

icicles, cracking his knuckles to the tune of "Shave and a Haircut." To attract his attention I cracked mine in harmony, and he turned around and smiled at me. He had a nice smile, rather crooked and wry, and I liked his pert pug nose and the way his shiny black hair came to a neat widow's peak in the exact middle of his forehead.

We kept up our antiphony for about a minute and then Miss Holderness heard us and looked up from the valentine box she had been grubbing in. Her snappish brown eyes went darting around the room as, in her ever irascible voice, she cried, "Valentine's Day or no Valentine's Day, I decidedly will not tolerate any levity in this class. Who is making that barbarous noise?" She pushed up the paper cuffs that protected the sleeves of her tan challis dress and glared. There was one of those weighty, stifling silences in which everyone held his breath, everyone feeling accused and everyone feeling guilty. Finally, unable to single out any faces that looked more blameworthy than any others, she had to give up with the threat, "If there is ever again any knuckle-cracking in this class, the miscreant will go straight to Mr. Colby for his or her punishment. I have reiterated *ad infinitum*[1] that levity is out of place in the sixth grade." (Miss Holderness abhorred children and she loved hard words. Once, after making me sing a scale by myself, she put her fingers in her ears and she said, "I have never heard such cacophony. Try it again, Emily, and this time endeavor not to agonize my Eustachian tube." To get even with her I read the dictionary that night and the next day asked her what "palimpsest" meant, but she outsmarted me by congratulating me on my intellectual curiosity and asking me to go to the Unabridged and read the definition out loud to the class. Everyone, including Miss Holderness, was baffled.) Virgil and I looked at each other again and grinned, and when Miss Holderness had bent her head once more to the valentine box he stuck out his tongue and thumbed his nose. This demoralized everybody in his immediate vicinity and a general giggle began like a gale. Luckily, all the valentines had been handed out and the bell rang and Miss Holderness dismissed us with a look of hatred. A humorist, especially an antiteacher one, enjoys great prestige in grammar school, and the more I thought about it, the more I was sure I would realize considerable benefit in being associated with Virgil. My own status was at present so low, by reason of my many quarrels, that I could not possibly elevate it by myself and very quickly I began to look on Virgil as the savior who would raise me from my ignominy. Little did I dream that that wily boy had a long-range plan to ruin me.

As we were putting on our galoshes, Virgil asked if he could walk me home, thereby proving that his intentions were serious. I shrugged my shoulders and said, "Suit yourself. It's a free country." I may have sounded nonchalant, but actually I was already afire with that puzzling, unnamable feeling that had preceded each of my betrothals since the age of five (I was a roughneck, fond of Indian wrestling and addicted to swearing, but I was vulnerable to love and the lacunae between my romances were melancholy); my throat and eyes were hot, my stomach was uneasy, my brains tick-tocked like an Ingersoll[2]

---

1. *ad infinitum* (ad in'fə nī'təm), a Latin phrase meaning "without limit."
2. *Ingersoll*, a one-dollar watch.

and some of my bones felt as if they were coming loose. As we were leaving the schoolyard, a two-legged rat, a former friend of mine—in fact, he was Virgil's predecessor, with whom once upon a time I had planned to grow old gracefully—Dicky Scott, saw us and yelled, "Red and yella, kiss your fella! You'll be sorry, Specs! Vanderloop-the-loop's a dizzy old doughhead!" Virgil put his books and his lunch box down on the stone wall and before you could say "Knife" he had made a good hard snowball and caught Dicky on the chin, surprising him so that he just stood there gaping and making no attempt to retaliate. Several other children who had witnessed the episode called, "Atta-boy, Meade!" and "You tell 'em, partner!" Nobody had anything against Dicky—it was simply that in our savage society it was de rigueur[3] to applaud whoever cast the first stone. I was gratified that my honor had been so swiftly and brilliantly defended and I seemed to sense that my stock was going up among the spectators. Indeed, Ruby Miller, who had not spoken to me for two weeks after an altercation over the ownership of a roller-skate key (it belonged to her but I was too proud to admit it when I found that out), came up and said, "Will you come to my birthday party on the twenty-first of July? I'm going to wear silk stockings."

Virgil and I walked home in total silence. Sometimes, in unspoken agreement, we walked stiff-legged; sometimes we left the cleared path and scuffed through the snow up to our knees. In the last block we broad-jumped from crack to crack in the sidewalk. Nobody was home at my house and I was glad of that because I wanted our first interview to be conducted without any interference from Mother (who had some crazy idea

that kids liked to be asked such questions as "Have your folks taken up the new contract bridge[4] that's all the rage?" or "What does your mother think about taking off the interurban and running buses to Denver[5]?") or from Jack and Stella, who loved to tease me about my suitors. I made some sandwiches for Virgil and me of peanut butter and piccalilli and mayonnaise and Virgil said it was better than eating a fried chicken dinner. I told him to go on—this was the standard after-school sandwich in every house in Adams I'd ever been in—but he said he'd never eaten one before and he asked if he could have another. "Pardon me for living, girl, but can I have seconds?" He used this expression, "Pardon me for living," to precede almost everything he said, and although I didn't know exactly what it meant, it sounded sporty and I filed it away to spring on my family as soon as I could. When we had eaten we went into the living room and Virgil told me some riddles and jokes he had learned from his father, who was in great demand as the end man for minstrel shows at the B.P.O.E.[6] One riddle was "What's black and white and red all over?" and the answer was not "A newspaper" but "A blushing zebra." Another was "Why is the Statue of Liberty's hand eleven inches long?" The answer was that if it were twelve inches it would be a foot. He taught me several Mr. Tambo-Mr. Bones dialogues[7] and we decided that when it got warmer we would put on a show in his father's garage. His

---

3. de rigueur (də rē goer'), a French phrase meaning "absolutely required."
4. contract bridge, a card game for four players played with fifty-two cards.
5. Denver, Colorado. The story takes place in a Colorado town. All references to mountains, slopes, and ridges concern the Rockies.
6. B.P.O.E., Benevolent and Protective Order of the Elks, a national men's club.
7. Mr. Tambo-Mr. Bones dialogues, dialogues common at minstrel shows.

father, he said, had the latest thing in make-up kits—grease paint, false noses, funny whiskers.

Then we talked about what we were going to do when we grew up; it was a romantic coincidence that I was going to be an organist in a movie house and Virgil was going to be an usher, and we both planned to follow our calling in a big city, Omaha, perhaps, or Chicago. Virgil and I had a great deal in common; we both walked in our sleep and had often waked up just before we fell out of the window or down the stairs; both of us loved puzzles and card games and the two things in the world we really detested were Sunday school (Virgil said in so many words that he didn't believe in God) and geography homework.

"Down with the blankety-blank principal exports of the Malay Archipelago," said this articulate and forthright boy. "Gutta-percha—don't make me laugh."

"Tell the class all you know about the Hottentots," I said, imitating Miss Holderness, and Virgil got up and stood on his head, putting his feet against the wall. Upside down he said, "The Hottentots eat gutta-percha out of the gutta-percha nose bags and they teach their grandmothers how to suck eggs."

Reddie, the dog, came padding in and looked at Virgil for a long time and then he yawned and padded out again. After that, Muff, the cat, came in to give Virgil the once-over. Virgil righted himself and waved his hands madly at Muff, who walked out of the room slowly, twitching her tail with disgust. Virgil said, "If there's one thing I can't stand it's to have an animal rubberneck at me. Especially cows. Pardon me for living, if a cow rubbernecks at me, I sock it right on the snoot," and he went on to tell me how he showed who was boss when he

went to visit at his uncle's ranch on the western slope. There was a cow named Hildy that he had pasted in the beezer more than once and there was also a gawking billy goat that he had given a good lesson to. I was thrilled to think of this brave gladiator striding through pastures walloping cows that gave him the eye and when he said, "I'm about the only man in this town that can make those mangy old burros of Mr. Hodge's turn off their headlights," I was bowled over with admiration and I exclaimed, "Boy, you're the only man *I* ever heard of that can do it." Virgil promised that some day soon he would take me up to Mr. Hodge's ratty shack on the mesa and show me how he could make the little donkeys "see stars instead of yours truly." The fact was that I dearly loved those little animals, Pearl and Princess, and whenever Jack and I got a quarter saved up we hired them from Mr. Hodge and rode them all over town. And here, out of blinding rapture, I was accepting an invitation to watch Virgil mistreat them.

He made a general survey of the living room. He picked the Bible up off the library table and said, "Phooey," and then he began to examine the Civil War saber that had belonged to a bounty-jumping relative[8] on my mother's side. He unsheathed it and hefted it and he said thoughtfully, "This may come in handy sometime."

After a pause he said, "Pardon me for living, girl, can I have another one of those keen sandwiches?" While he ate it Reddie came out to the kitchen to watch him with his big heartbroken hungry eyes and Virgil slapped him on the nose. "You heard me, you good-for-nothing scalawag,"

8. **bounty-jumping relative.** During the Civil War, many men entered military service only to receive the money (bounty) that was offered to recruits. A bounty-jumper deserted as soon as he got his bounty.

he said. "Don't you look at me and my sandwich with your googly-googly eyes." Reddie, the meekest thing in the world, looked as if he were going to cry, and when I, disloyal to my nice old dog because I was in love with this bloodthirsty swashbuckler, laughed, he cringed and slunk out of the room, and for the rest of the afternoon he lay under the china closet in the dining room with his head between his paws.

Virgil pardoned himself for living again and again asked for a sandwich. When he was finally satisfied and we went back to the living room he told me a sad story that explained why he was so hungry. He said that at home they had nothing to eat but doughnuts. His mother made about a million of them on Sunday, enough to last a week, and every day they had doughnuts with maple sirup for breakfast. These she called "doughnut waffles"; for supper she put ketchup on them and called them "doughnut meatballs" or "doughnut roast." "Doughnut surprise" had canned salmon and peas in the doughnut hole and it was awful. At one of the sanitariums in our town the food was all made of cereal; the cranky old valetudinarians ate things like "Grape Nut cutlet" and "Corn Flake loaf," a bill of fare that never ceased to amaze and sadden my mother, who occasionally had lunch there with a friend of my grandmother's. So I got the idea that Mrs. Meade was some sort of invalid and I thought it was cruelly unfair that everybody in her family willy-nilly had to follow her diet. But after a while I realized that Virgil was only telling lies because he went on to say that the reason they only had doughnuts was that his mother had bats in the belfry and spent all her time, when she should have been cooking for her growing children, collecting cold cream jars in the alleys and on the dump. She caught the bats in her belfry in the cold cream jars, screwed the lids down tight and sent them by post to her nutty twin sister in Boise who was named Aunt Dandelion. Aunt Dandelion! Did he really think I was dumb enough to believe a name like that?

This is what I mean about Virgil being crazy. One time he told me that he had been kidnaped by a runaway convict from Canon City named Ben the Red Beard. The desperado, who had murdered hundreds and permanently crippled many more with his six-shooter, handcuffed Virgil and took him up to a shack in the mountains and kept him there for three days. On the third night, after the man was asleep, Virgil managed to crawl over to the grocery supplies and he ate three big onions; then he crawled back to the cot where Ben the Red Beard was snoring away and breathed into his face until the kidnaper, undone by the fumes, took off the handcuffs and Virgil was free. He had walked all the way home in the dark, a distance of twenty-two miles, and it was seventeen below zero. When I asked him why his family hadn't sent out a posse for him, he said, "I go away for three or four days at a time by myself without telling them and they don't mind—I mean, if they did mind, I'd tell them where to get off. I go deer hunting, you see. Last year, I got an eight-point buck up by the glacier but I gave it away to some bootleggers I know. And now and then I hop a rattler and go down to Denver and hang around Larimer Street playing pool for two or three days."

Virgil left long before anyone came home, but there were traces of him everywhere. When he had stood on his head he had left two precise footprints on the white wall; his voracity had done away with most of the bread and all of the peanut butter; Reddie was still grieving and Mother, thinking he was sick, wanted to call the vet. Naturally I couldn't take the blame for all these things and had to let the cat out of the bag. When I told Mother why Reddie was so woebegone, she was at first too shocked to speak and then she said, "Emily, no good will ever come of this friendship, you mark my words." Would that I had! I tried to make up with Reddie but Jack snarled, "You stay away from him," and Stella, weeping, implored Mother to send me away, anywhere, so that she would never again have to lay eyes on a dastardly tormentor of man's best friend.

I was chastened, but I had no intention of giving up Virgil and thereafter we had our sandwiches at his house. They were usually made of peanut butter, mayonnaise and piccalilli — I never saw a single doughnut in his house and the smells in his mother's kitchen were perfectly delicious. I had been right about one thing: though my family might deplore my new alliance, the other kids looked on it with envy because Virgil and I were always whispering and passing notes in school and we refused to play or even talk with anyone else. Dicky Scott one day offered me an arrowhead and I haughtily refused — I might have accepted it but I happened to know, because Dicky himself had one time unwisely told me, that it was spurious.

Virgil and I were together every afternoon except on ballet day. Sometimes we coasted and sometimes we made lists (of kinds of automobiles, of three-letter words, of the movies we had seen), but usually we just sat in his father's den and talked. I loved this dark and crowded room that smelled of cigars and furniture polish, and I wished that my own father had a room of his own. The walls were hung with all sorts of documents in frames, diplomas, certificates of membership in dental and social and religious societies; there was a serape with a bird and a snake on it; there was a tomahawk, a collection of minerals, an Indian headdress that Virgil said had once belonged to King Philip.[9] On the roll-top desk, whose pigeonholes were so stuffed that nothing could ever be inserted in any of them, there was an enormous typewriter that had eight banks, three for the upper-case letters, three for the lower and two for the characters. When we used it, as we often did (wrote our names, wrote "Down with Miss Holderness"), it sounded like a small tractor and its bell was like one on a trolley car. Here, seated in leather armchairs, we were continually eyed by Virgil's dog, a His Master's Voice dog,[10] who lay on a deerskin rug. We discussed our many projects. For one thing, we planned to make a trip in the summer with a wagon and horses up to a mine where Virgil knew that a lot of pieces of eight[11] were buried; this involved making lists of what we would take and we wrote out a long order to Montgomery Ward — Virgil said the money would turn up somehow. Then there was the minstrel show we were going to put on and we had to rehearse our acts.

More immediately, though, what we talked about was a plan we had to draw up a petition against geography homework, which was really ruining our lives and the lives of everybody

9. **King Philip,** a seventeenth-century king of the Wampanoag Indians who fought the settlers in New England. The English named him Philip.
10. **a His Master's Voice dog,** a dog like the large white dog used in advertising for Victor records. The dog was always pictured listening at an old Victrola horn, beneath which was printed the slogan, "His Master's Voice."
11. **pieces of eight,** Spanish gold pieces.

else in the sixth grade. At least three thousand years ago Miss Holderness had gone around the world with some other old maids and she never stopped bragging about rice paddies and rickshas and the Yangtze and Big Ben.[12] She was forever passing around pale brown picture post cards that showed camels, Norwegian fisheries and the Victoria and Albert Museum; she showed us a little bottle with water from the Jordan and an ordinary pebble she had picked up in the neighborhood of the Taj Mahal.[13] Every blessed night of the world we had to get something by heart—the chief rivers of Asia, the capitals of the Isles of Greece, European mountain ranges, famous monuments in Rome—and the next day she would either give us a paper test or would single out some poor kid to recite, and it seemed to Virgil and me that the poor kid was always one of us. We had to make relief maps with salt and flour and each Friday afternoon during the last period, when we were all wild with fidgets, she made us draw a map of the United States from memory; to this day I don't know whether Delaware is on the left-hand side of Maryland or the right, and I can never find room for Vermont. Talk about a one-track mind.

One Friday afternoon she told us that by Monday we would have to know all the counties of England, and Virgil and I decided that this was the limit and the time had come for us to act. I had intended to depart from custom that afternoon and go straight home, because that morning at Assembly I had won a school letter for collateral reading and I wanted to sew it on the sleeve of my middy right away, but Virgil said, "Pardon me for living, girl, haven't you got any class spirit? Do you know that this geography junk may keep us in the sixth

grade for eighty-nine years?" He said we had no time to lose, that everybody was now so mad at Holderness (hadn't I heard the whole room groan?) that we'd have no trouble getting signatures for our petition. We must draw it up this afternoon and then spend tomorrow going from door to door getting people to sign. "In *ink*," said Virgil. "This has gotta be official with no ifs and buts about it." And so, ever his slave, I went along home with him.

I want to say something about that afternoon that isn't related to the Mutiny of the Sixth Grade of Carlyle Hill but will show you the kind of looniness Virgil was capable of. His mother wasn't home that day so Virgil made the sandwiches. He couldn't find the peanut butter but he said for me not to look and he would make a surprise. I'll say he made a surprise. He made those sandwiches of Campbell's vegetable soup and I'm not kidding. I was eating this stuff and I couldn't tell for the life of me what it was; it didn't taste bad but it *felt* funny, so I surreptitiously turned my back and lifted up the top slice of bread and there I saw a lima bean. And then I saw the empty can on the drainboard.

After the soup sandwiches and after one game of Shasta Sam, we got down to work in the den. Among Dr. Meade's framed testimonials there was a bounty land grant awarded to Virgil's Great-Uncle Harry, who had fought at Murfreesboro.[14] It was signed by Abraham Lincoln, and Vir-

12. **Yangtze and Big Ben.** The Yangtze is the longest river in China. Big Ben is a huge bell in the clock tower of the Parliament building in London, England.
13. **Victoria and Albert Museum . . . Taj Mahal.** The museum is a widely known art museum in London, England. The Jordan is a river flowing between Israel and Jordan. The Taj Mahal is a white marble mausoleum in central India.
14. **bounty land grant . . . Murfreesboro.** The government awarded a gift of land to Virgil's uncle, who had fought in an important Civil War battle in Murfreesboro, Tennessee.

gil, taking it down and handing it to me, said it was worth several million dollars. (If all the things in the Meades' house had had the value Virgil assigned to them, Dr. Meade could have retired and bought the Teapot Dome.[15]) We would use it, said Virgil, as the model for our petition because it had a high and mighty tone and high and mighty was what we were going to be from now on. Virgil typed while I dictated, paraphrasing the land grant. It was uphill work because every key stuck and the *s* wouldn't budge at all so that had to be filled in later with ink. But when we were finished we were pleased with the results, although there were mistakes abounding. The petition (more properly, the declaration) read:

HTE SIXTH GRADEO%F CRa-
LYLE HILL
SCHOOL OF ADAMS
TO?ALLT
TO ALL TI WHOM THESE
PRESENTS SHALL COME 1/4
GREETING WHEREAS, in
persuace of the act of
Ggeography Ha Enemys,
approved March 2, 1926, entitled
aN Act to Stop Geography
Homewoork, the undersigned
people will not do any more
Geograph HomeWork because it
is not fair to give t so much of it.

We left a space for the signatures and then:

NOW NOW YE, that there is
there3fore granted by the
Surveyor Genersl of this class
unto the said undersigned the
privelege tto have and to hold, of
NO MORE Geography
HOMEWORK AND TO their
heirs the privelege above
described with the
apuurtenances therefo.

WHEREOF I,   , have caused these letters to be made patent and affixed my signature thereto.

Abraham Lincoln's name was after the "WHEREOF I" and we debated what to write there. We thought it would look wrong to say "WHEREOF WE" and sign both our names and at last Virgil gallantly said that my name should be there because I now had a school letter and this gave me a status he didn't have. He said I should be the one, too, to hand it to Miss Holderness and he suggested that on Monday morning I carry Mother's Civil War saber to school, not to intimidate Miss Holderness but to carry out the motif of the Civil War. He rather regretfully rejected King Philip's headdress as an anachronism.

He said, "Boy, oh, boy, can I see old Prune Face when you march into the room with the sword and say, 'Madam, allow me to present these presents,' and you hand her this!"

A flicker of trepidation entered my infatuated mind and I said, "What if she sends me to Mr. Colby and I get expelled?"

"She'd have to send the whole class—everybody's name will be there. Pardon me for living, girl, you're not by any chance getting cold feet? Because if you are—well, you know how I feel about cowards. I wouldn't be seen at a dogfight with a coward."

I blushed and hastily said that of course I wasn't getting cold feet, what was there to get cold feet about—as he had said, if anybody had to go to Mr. Colby, we'd all have to go. Anyhow, Holderness wouldn't have any right to punish us since we were protected by freedom of speech. Reassured that I was stout-hearted, Virgil

15. *Teapot Dome,* rich oil lands in Wyoming. During the administration of President Harding, the Secretary of the Interior was convicted of taking a hundred-thousand-dollar bribe to turn the reserve over to private interests.

smiled his crooked smile and began to tinker with the petition, putting in the absent *s*'s and filling in the *o*'s. When he had finished he handed me the scratchy pen and said, "Here, put your John Hancock[16] here on the dotted line." When I had signed—the pen went through the paper a couple of times and a big blob of ink floated like a rain cloud over my surname—I was both scared and proud and had a stomach sensation that was half pleasant and half terrible. I was by no means sure that freedom of speech would cover our action; I was by no means sure that a petition of this sort was not against the law, and to distract my thought from the possible consequences of our daring I took my red felt *C* out of my book bag and held it up to my sleeve.

Virgil said, "Listen, Emily, you know what? Why don't you sew it on someplace else? Someplace different? So you'll be different from the common herd?"

"Like on my back?" I asked. "You mean like an athlete?"

"No, I was thinking of like on your sock."

"My *sock*!" I yelled. "Have you gone cuckoo?" But I rather liked the idea and I placed the letter experimentally on the outside of my right leg about in the middle of my shank. The bright red looked very striking against my navy blue knee-length sock, sort of like a cattle brand.

"Higher," said Virgil critically. "Yeah, right there. Hey, that's the pig's wings."

"Well, I don' know . . ." I began doubtfully, for on reconsideration it seemed to me that the letter would be more conspicuous on my sleeve. But Virgil said, "I double dare you," and that, of course, was that; I went home and blanket-stitched the scarlet letter on my sock. That evening

when I went into the dining room and my family saw what I had done, they all began to fuss at me. My mother, who was active in the P.T.A., said, "Why, Emily, do you think that's a nice thing to do when Miss Holderness was so nice to give you that letter?"

"Miss Holderness was so nice! What did that dopey old goop have to do with it?" I demanded. "I suppose she read all those books and wrote all those reports. I'll have you know I *earned* this letter. And anyhow the *school* gave it to me."

"Well, then, the school was nice," said Mother, missing the point as usual. "Oh, Emily, why must you forever and a day be so contrary?"

"Because she's a scurvy rapscallion black sheep," said Jack, who had barely spoken to me since Virgil had upset Reddie.

"Baa, baa, black sheep, Emily's a black sheep," chanted copycat Tess and began to bubble her milk.

"Shut up, you little wart hog," I said to her and she did, terrified.

"Miss Holderness is not a dopey old goop," said Stella, who was sanctimonious and stood up for authority of all kinds. "She's a lady which is something you're never going to be in a thousand million years."

"Lady! Who wants to be a *lady*?" I said. "You make me sick." I made a sound of intense nausea and then I said, "Hasten, Jason, bring the basin. Ulp! Too late! Bring the mop!"

My father put down his napkin and faced me with his chin outthrust. "Now you listen to me, Emily Vanderpool. I've had just about enough of your shenanigans. I will not have bad language at my supper table and I will not have wrangling, do you hear me? I'm a hard-working man

---

16. *your John Hancock,* slang for "your signature." John Hancock was the first signer of the Declaration of Independence.

and when I come home at night, I'm tired and I want peace and quiet instead of this eternal confounded trouble you're always stirring up."

The unfairness of his attack brought tears to my eyes. Had anyone in the history of the world ever been so lamentably misunderstood? My voice was quivery as I said, "I didn't start it. Everybody started picking on *me* about my own personal property, damn it to hell!"

"What did I say about bad language?" he shouted, rising menacingly from his chair.

The devil at that moment made a conquest of my tongue and, blue in the face with fury, my eyes screwed shut, my fists clenched, I delivered a malediction in the roughest billingsgate imaginable, vilifying everyone at the table, all the teachers at Carlyle Hill, my uncles and aunts and cousins, my father's best friend, Judge Bay. The reaction was the same as it always was to one of my tantrums: appalled, fascinated, dead silence. When I was finished Jack, awed, said, "Yippi-ki-yi! That was a humdinger of a one!" I threw my glass of water in his face and stamped out of the room.

That was the last that was said at home about my school letter and when Stella came into the room we shared, she was at pains not to cross the chalk line I had drawn down the middle of the floor and not to speak to me; if she had uttered one word, on any subject whatsoever, I would have beaten the hide off her.

The next day a blizzard somewhat hampered Virgil and me in our house-to-house canvass. Most people were at home because the wind made it uncomfortable coasting weather, and though this meant that they were easy to find (and so bored that they were delighted to see us), it also meant

that there were a lot of nosy mothers around, asking questions and trying to distract us from our mission by inviting us to make popcorn or taffy. We had very little respect for the intelligence of these snoops, but we didn't want to run the risk of having some one of them call up Miss Holderness and spill the beans, and so we had to dally in a number of houses and pretend we had just come to pay a social call. We got stuck in Valerie Bemis' house for nearly an hour while her mother showed views of Yellowstone and the Grand Canyon through a stereopticon.

To our considerable surprise and disappointment, we found that several of our classmates were partisans of Miss Holderness (Estelle Powell, for instance, said she loved our teacher because she smelled so wonderful), and we found, furthermore, that the phobia for geography homework was not, after all, universal. Indeed, six or seven stick-in-the-muds said they liked it better than anything else and they refused to sign the petition. Ruby Miller admitted that she agreed with us, but she had already learned the English counties and didn't want them to go to waste, so she too refused to sign. This schism disturbed us, but all the same, at the end of the day, we had a majority of seventeen names. It was dark by the time we left the last house and the street lights had come on. Under a light beside a mailbox we paused in the whirling snow and Virgil solemnly put the petition in a long envelope, solemnly handed it to me and solemnly said, "Pardon me for living, girl, but this will probably get us into the Hall of Fame. Good luck." And with this he started off in the direction of his house, his dramatic shadow long and lean beside him.

When the sixth grade got into line on Monday morning there was an undercurrent of great excitement and everybody was looking at me; there were gasps from those who caught sight of the honor badge on my leg; there were uneasy whispers about my Civil War saber, which was imperfectly hidden under my coat. Someone murmured in my ear, "Scratch out my name, Emily, please?" and someone else said, "Looky, if you're going to kill her, I don't want to have anything to do with it." I glared fiercely but I didn't feel fierce; I felt foolish and scared because Virgil Meade was nowhere to be seen.

The soft exclamations of incredulity and fear continued as we marched into the building and hung up our wraps, and even after we had said, "Good morning, Miss Holderness," and had sat down, there was still a faint buzzing and thrumming like noises in the grass on a summer day.

"Quiet, please!" said Miss Holderness and clapped her hands smartly. "What is the meaning of this deafening pandemonium?"

There was immediate silence and then Johnny Thatcher, who had not signed the petition, held up his hand and giggled and said, "Emily has something to show you, teacher."

"I see Emily's sword," said Miss Holderness. I had tried to put it under my desk but it stuck out into the aisles on each side. "And I think we will simply ignore it. We do not know why she brought it to school and we do not care to know."

Johnny Thatcher said, "No, I don't mean that. She's got something else to show you. Something about geography homework."

"Very well, Emily," said the teacher, snapping her fingers and snapping her eyes. "Show me what it is. We cannot spend the entire day on the subject of Emily Vanderpool's tricks to attract attention to herself. Come along, Emily, quickly, quickly!"

"I haven't got anything," I stammered.

"You have too," said Johnny.

Everyone began to babble at once and Miss Holderness angrily rapped her desk with her ruler. "I have a good mind to punish everyone in this class," she said. "Emily, I want you to show me whatever this is at once."

Reluctant, furious, I stumbled up to the desk and put the petition down in front of her. She gave me a black look and then she opened the envelope; as she read, moving her lips, her color rose until she looked like an apple.

"So!" she cried. "So Miss Emily Vanderpool is now known as 'the surveyor-general of this class.' I was not aware that elections had been held and she had been voted into office."

Everyone tittered.

"I . . ." I began, but Miss Holderness held up her hand for silence.

"Now let me see," she said and began checking the names on the petition against those in the class book. There was a pause and every heart beat wildly. Then she said, "Ruby, Estelle, Homer, Johnny, Marjorie and Virgil—these are the children who are still loyal to Carlyle Hill Grade School and have not kowtowed to this self-styled surveyor-general. Children, I congratulate you."

"Virgil!" I cried. "But Virgil . . ." Then, because I did not want to be a tattletale, even against that foxy fourflusher, I held my peace.

"What about Virgil?" asked Miss

Holderness. "I am sorry that Virgil is absent today, for I would like him to know how deeply I appreciate his refusing to affix his signature to this outrageous scrap of paper. Shame on you, Emily Vanderpool, shame on you!"

She looked me up and down with revulsion as if I were a reptile or a skunk and suddenly she saw the school letter on my sock. She gaped, speechless, and then said, "Ruby, I shall leave you in charge of the class. Emily and I have some business to transact in Mr. Colby's office."

That was a long last mile[17] I walked. I thought sadly and enviously of all the children behind the closed doors who would continue their lives of ease and respectability while I was working on a mason gang at the reform school. All my sensations were intense: the smell of cedar shavings was stronger than ever and the smell of wet Mackinaws and overshoes (overshoes are made of gutta-percha, I thought sorrowfully, homesick for the principal exports of the Malay Archipelago), and the sounds of teachers' voices and the thud of feet and balls in the gym below and the piping squeals from the kindergarten room were like a loud song of farewell to me. Miss Holderness' hand, grasping my arm, was a cruel metal claw.

Mr. Colby was an asthmatic old man with a purple-veined nose and a sorrel toupee. He had very short legs but he had strong, broad shoulders and sitting behind his magisterial desk he looked like a giant. His two bluebell blue eyes were on quite different levels, giving him a quizzical and half-amused look as if he were trying to figure out a joke he didn't entirely understand. He was playing with a sharp letter opener when we came into his office, flicking the point with his index finger as he made half-revolutions in his swivel chair. He invited Miss Holderness to sit down and with the letter opener indicated the place where I was to stand, directly in front of his desk. Several times in the course of my teacher's indignant recital of my felonies he swiveled himself completely around so that his back was to us and he coughed and wheezed—it sounded like strangled laughter. When he leaned over his desk to look at my shameful leg he had such a seizure that he had to bury his face in his handkerchief, and when he read the petition I thought he was going to explode. After the case against me had been stated, Mr. Colby told Miss Holderness to go back to her class and said that he would deal with me himself.

"Now, Emily," he said when she was gone, "there is no doubt about the gravity of your misdemeanors . . . incidentally, why did you bring a sword to school?"

"Well, it's a Civil War one and Vir . . . I mean it's a Civil War one and since the petition was a Civil War thing . . ."

"A Civil War thing? What sort of thing?"

"Just a thing. I don't know what you call it. But where my name is is really Abraham Lincoln's name."

He wheeled his chair around again and he wheezed for quite some time. "The name of Emily Vanderpool has been substituted for that of Honest Abe," he said at length. "The case grows stranger. I confess to a certain amount of confusion. I can't seem to see the tie-in with the sword, the petition, and your putting your school letter on your stocking, a gesture tantamount, as Miss Holder-

17. *last mile*, the walk of a condemned person to the place of execution.

ness so aptly put it, to dragging the Star-Spangled Banner in the dirt. Can you help me out?"

Mr. Colby's voice, though firm, was kind and his funny eyes were sweet and though my legs were buckling and my heart thundered, I longed to tell him the whole truth. But naturally I could not without involving Virgil and I said only, as mad murderers often do, "I don't know why I did it."

He picked up the petition again and this time I thought he was really going to fly apart. He threw back his head so far I thought his toupee would surely fall off and he coughed and wheezed and gurgled fearsomely. "You'll be the death of me!" he howled and I thought I really would be. He groped, blinded with tears, for a bottle of pills and a carafe of water, and when he had dosed himself and straightened his vest and put on a pair of severe spectacles he gave me a sober lecture on the value of geography and the sin of insubordination, the inadvisability of carrying arms, the folly of arrogating power, the extreme impropriety of wearing an honor badge on the leg. Finally he told me to go back to my room and apologize to Miss Holderness and then to go home for the rest of the day and explain to my mother exactly why I was in disgrace. When I had closed the door behind me I heard him having another attack and I knew that it would be the gallows for me if he died.

For the next two weeks I was in double dishonor. Miss Holderness made me stay after school every day and write lists of rivers and cities and principal exports. I had to go home immediately thereafter and stay in my room with the door closed until suppertime. Jack and Stella did not speak one word to me. During those weeks I was not allowed to wear my letter even in its proper place. The sixth grade got more geography homework than ever and consequently I was sent to Coventry by all my classmates.[18] I crept around like a sick dog and wished I were dead.

At first the namby-pamby boobs in my grade took Virgil's side against me even though they knew good and well that I could have got him in Dutch too if I had snitched. They all knew, of course, that he had been just as responsible for the petition as I, but they did not know that he had put me up to sewing the *C* on my sock and it was this act of insolence to dear old Carlyle Hill that they regarded as my cardinal crime. For the two weeks of my quarantine Virgil enjoyed an immense, ill-gotten popularity, and I heard, with mixed feelings, that he was practically engaged to Ruby Miller. I did not deign to recognize his existence.

And then, on the very day I was first allowed to wear my letter, silly Virgil tipped his hand. Ruby Miller told me during lunch hour. At morning recess she and he had been swapping bird cards out of Arm and Hammer Baking Soda boxes as I passed by. Ruby saw that I was wearing my letter again and asked Virgil why he thought I had done that awful thing. Ruby said, "Who would *think* of doing a thing like that?" and Virgil had said, "I'll tell you somebody who wouldn't and that's Vanderloop-the-loop—she's too dumb. *I* told her to sew it on her leg."

The news spread rapidly, whispered during Palmer Method,[19] written on notes in Current Events, and by the end of the afternoon session I

18. *I was sent to Conventry by all my classmates.* I was ignored by all my classmates.
19. *Palmer Method,* a method of handwriting.

was in and Virgil was out. People came up to me singly and in groups to congratulate me on my nobility; some of them shook my hand. I accepted their acclaim with a wan and martyred smile, thanked them for their many invitations to visit their houses but said that I had to go home because I was reading the Bible.

I remained aloof only that one day and the next day plunged into a social whirl. Virgil, as it was fitting, was totally ostracized. In time I took pity on him; indeed, some months later, we again became boon companions, but I saw to it that he never hoodwinked me again: I ruled him with an iron glove and after he had made one slip he never made another.

The slip was this. We were walking home one day in the spring and he picked a leaf off a lilac bush. He said to me, "If you can divide this exactly in half, I'll give you a quarter." What could be easier than dividing a lilac leaf? The midrib is clear and the flesh is crisp, and I accomplished the feat in a second. "O.K., where's my quarter?" I said, and Virgil, tearing one of the halves of the leaf in two, handed me a piece. "Here's your quarter," he said and doubled up with laughter. I simply looked at him and then I turned and walked away. He came running after me, begging for mercy, reminding me of all the good times we'd had together. I marched on for two blocks, ignoring him, but then, at a vacant lot, I stopped, climbed up on top of a boulder and told him to kneel on the ground. Then, like Moses on Mount Sinai,[20] I laid down the law, and ever after that Virgil Meade was the most tractable boon companion I had. ✳

20. *like Moses on Mount Sinai.* Moses was on Mount Sinai when God gave him the Ten Commandments. [Exodus 20:2–17; Deuteronomy 5:6–22]

Discussion

1. (a) Why does Emily Vanderpool look to Virgil Meade for friendship? (b) How do Emily's feelings for Virgil affect her behavior? (c) Why doesn't Emily tell the truth about Virgil's role in writing the petition and in selecting the place she wears her letter? (d) How does Emily's relationship to Virgil change by the end of the story?

2. The passages below are taken from the story. After reading each one, answer the following questions: (a) Who is being characterized? (b) What do you learn about this character? (c) What method or methods of characterization are used?

1. . . . was an asthmatic old man with a purple-veined nose and a sorrel toupee. He had very short legs but he had strong, broad shoulders and sitting behind his magisterial desk he looked like a giant. His two bluebell blue eyes were on quite different levels, giving him a quizzical and half-amused look as if he were trying to figure out a joke he didn't entirely understand.

2. "Because she's a scurvy rapscallion black sheep," said Jack, . . .

3. "I'm about the only man in this town that can make those mangy old burros of Mr. Hodge's turn off their headlights."

4. "Valentine's Day or no Valentine's Day, I decidedly will not tolerate any levity in this class. Who is making that barbarous noise?"

5. I thought sadly and enviously of all the children behind the closed doors who would continue their lives of ease and respectability while I was working on a mason gang at the reform school.

6. The devil at that moment made a conquest of my tongue and, blue in the face with fury, my eyes screwed shut, my fists clenched, I delivered a malediction in the roughest billingsgate imaginable, vilifying everyone at the table, all the teachers at Carlyle Hill, my uncles and aunts and cousins, my father's best friend, Judge Bay.

7. "Miss Holderness is not a dopey old goop," said. . . . . , who was sanctimonious and stood up for authority of all kinds. "She's a lady which is something you're never going to be in a thousand million years." (How many persons does this passage characterize?)

3. Jean Stafford has used many different means to create humor in "The Scarlet Letter." Pick out two or three humorous places

in the story, read them aloud, and explain what makes each of them funny.

4. Often an author creates suspense by hinting at what may happen later on in the story. Find examples of sentences which suggest that Emily is going to get into trouble.

5. (a) The date on the petition is March 2, 1926, but there are many other details which tell us that the time setting of the story is sometime in the past. Find as many of these details as you can. **(b)** Is the time setting important? Explain.

6. (a) How does the fact that Emily tells the story limit what we know about the other characters? **(b)** How would the story differ if Virgil had told it? **(c)** What changes would there be if Miss Holderness were the narrator?

Word Study

Whenever in your reading you come upon a word which is unfamiliar to you, you will have to decide how to unlock its meaning. You may use the context in which the word appears, the structure of the word, the dictionary, or a combination of these methods.

Read each of the following sentences, noting especially the italicized words. Then answer the questions which follow each sentence. Be prepared to explain which method or methods you used to determine the meaning of the word. You may refer to your Glossary.

1. Smith and Johnson are common *surnames*.

The word *surname* means **(a)** last name **(b)** first name **(c)** aristocratic title.

2. The man was wearing a red *serape*.

What is a *serape*? How many syllables does the word have?

3. The Davis Expressway has been closed to *interurban* traffic.

What is the base word in *interurban*? What is the prefix? What does *interurban* mean?

4. Larry spent the rest of the evening in his room thinking about his *misdemeanors*.

What does the word *demeanor* mean? What does *misdemeanor* mean?

5. The mother *chastened* her small son for playing with matches.

The word *chastened* might mean **(a)** praised **(b)** ridiculed **(c)** punished. Does the word *chasten* have exactly the same meaning as **a, b,** or **c**? Explain.

The Author

As the daughter of a writer, Jean Stafford grew up in a literary atmosphere. Most of her childhood was spent in Colorado, where many of her short stories, including "The Scarlet Letter," take place. She taught at Stephens College in Columbia, Missouri, but now devotes herself full time to writing. A diligent worker, she spends a great deal of time on her articles, stories, and novels, doing much rewriting. Miss Stafford once described herself and her work in an interview: "I'm a rather slow person, in that experience has to sink in for years and years before I can use it. . . . I have to let impressions and experiences age within me until they become integrated into my whole life and perceptions before I can use them as material for fiction."[1] Ten of Miss Stafford's short stories are collected in *Children Are Bored on Sunday;* her longer works include *Boston Adventure* and *The Catherine Wheel.*

1. Reprinted by permission from the April 1951 issue of the *Wilson Library Bulletin.* Copyright 1951 by The H. W. Wilson Company.

Who has to learn the
first lesson: father or daughter?

First Lesson

Phyllis McGinley

The thing to remember about fathers is, they're men.
A girl has to keep it in mind.
They are dragon-seekers, bent on improbable rescues.
Scratch any father, you find
5 Someone chock-full of qualms and romantic terrors,
Believing change is a threat—
Like your first shoes with heels on, like your first bicycle
It took such months to get.

Walk in strange woods, they warn you about the snakes there.
10 Climb, and they fear you'll fall.
Books, angular boys, or swimming in deep water—
Fathers mistrust them all.
Men are the worriers. It is difficult for them
To learn what they must learn:
15 How you have a journey to take and very likely,
For a while, will not return.

From TIMES THREE by Phyllis McGinley. Copyright © 1959 by Phyllis McGinley. Originally appeared in *The New Yorker*. Reprinted by permission of The Viking Press, Inc., New York, and Martin Secker & Warburg Ltd., London.

Discussion

1. (a) Who is the speaker in this poem? **(b)** Whose "first lesson" is the speaker talking about?
2. (a) Why are the terrors of the fathers called "romantic"? **(b)** What are some of the things fathers rescue their daughters from?
3. (a) What kind of "journey" does the speaker refer to in line 15? **(b)** What comment on the relationship between fathers and daughters is made in lines 15–16?

The Author

Phyllis McGinley worked as a teacher, a writer for an advertising agency, and a magazine staff writer before coming into her own as poet and author. She is particularly noted for her poetry, which is often inspired by her children. A characteristic of her writing is that it is often witty while carrying a serious undertone. "I've always read poetry," she once said. "I read it for enjoyment, for delight, to get drunk on. . . ."[1] In 1961, her volume of poetry *Times Three* won the Pulitzer Prize.

Besides poetry, Phyllis McGinley has written essays *(Sixpence in Her Shoe)*, a film narration, and the lyrics for a Broadway revue. She says that her ambition is to write a musical comedy in the tradition of Gilbert and Sullivan.

---

1. From CONTEMPORARY AUTHORS. Reprinted by permission of Gale Research Company.

See
POINT OF VIEW
Handbook
of Literary
Terms
page 558

"Please God, I don't want a high grade,
all I want is to pass. . . . I don't want
to pass this exam for myself only. I mean,
it means a lot to my family. My father
will be very disappointed if I flunk the exam. . . ."

The boy who says these words is caught in a dilemma. How does the point of view used in this story help you understand why P. S. makes the choices he does?

so much
unfairness
of things

C. D. B. Bryan

THE VIRGINIA PREPARATORY SCHOOL lies just off the Shirley Highway between Washington, D.C., and Richmond. It is a small Southern school with dull-red brick dormitories and classroom buildings, quiet old school buildings with quiet old Southern names—Page House, Stuart Hall, Randolph Hall, Breckinridge, Pinckney, and Coulter. The high brick wall that surrounds the school is known as the Breastworks, and the shallow pond behind the football field is the Crater. V.P.S. is an old school, with an old school's traditions. A Virginia Department of Conservation sign commemorates the use of the school by Union troops as a military hospital in 1861, and every October the school celebrates "Liberation Day," in honor of the day in 1866 when the school reopened.

Graduates of the Virginia Preparatory School who have not returned for some years are shocked by the glass-and-steel apartment houses and cinderblock ramblers that have sprung up around the school grounds, but once they have driven along the Breastworks and passed through the ornate wrought-iron East Gate, they see, with satisfaction, that the school has not changed. Neither have its customs. For example, new boys, or "toads," still must obey the Toad Code. They must be courteous to old boys and faculty. They must know the school song and cheers by the end of the second week. They must know the names of all members of the faculty and the varsity football team. They must hold doors open for old boys and see that old boys are served first in the dining room. And they must "run relay"—meaning that they have to wake up the old boys in the morning when they wish to be wakened and see that they are not disturbed when they wish to sleep.

Philip Sadler Wilkinson was fourteen; he was an old boy. The new boy shook him lightly. "Mr. Wilkinson? Mr. Wilkinson? It's five-thirty, sir. You asked me to wake you up!"

Next year the new boy would be permitted to call Philip Sadler Wilkinson "P.S.," like the others. He watched P.S. stretch, turn over, and go back to sleep. "Sir? Hey! Wake up!"

P.S. rolled out of his metal cot, rubbed his eyes, felt around the top of his desk for his glasses, put them on, and looked at the new boy.

"Toad?"

"Yes, sir?"

"What is the date?"

"Thursday, the seventh of June."

"How much longer do we have until the end of the school year?"

"Seven days, twenty-three hours, and"—the new boy looked at his wristwatch—"and thirteen minutes, sir."

P.S. smiled. "Are you sure?"

"No, sir."

"Ah-hah! Ah-HAH! Toad, assume the position."

The new boy locked his knees and bent over and grabbed his ankles.

"What is a 'toad,' toad?" P.S. asked.

"Sir, a toad is a loathsome warty creature who eats insects and worms, sir. A toad is the lowest form of amphibian. A toad is despicable."

"Well, well, now, straighten those knees, toad." P.S. looked at the new boy and saw that his face was turning red with strain. "Toad, are you in pain?"

"No, sir," the new boy lied.

"Then you may straighten up."

The new boy massaged his calves. "Honest to Pete, P.S., you're a sadist."

"No, no, wait till next year.

You'll be pulling the same thing on some toad yourself. I had it done to me, you had it done to you. And did I detect you calling me by my rightful name?"

The new boy smiled.

"Ah, you toads will never learn. Assume the position."

The new boy started to bend over again.

"Oh, hell, go away," P.S. said. The new boy started out of the door and P.S. called him back. "Hey, toad? You gonna kill the Latin exam?"

"I hope so."

"How do you conjugate the verb 'to spit'?"

"*Exspuo, exspuere, exspui——*"

"Heck, no!" P.S. laughed. "It's *spitto, spittere, ach tui, splattus!*"

The new boy groaned and left the room.

P.S. looked at his watch. It was twenty minutes to six. He could hear the new boy waking up the boy in the next room. P.S. picked up his water glass and toothbrush and tiptoed down the corridor. He stopped at Charlie Merritt's room and knocked softly.

"Who is it?"

"It's me, Charlie."

"Oh, hey, P.S. Come on in."

P.S. pushed aside the curtain of the cubicle. Charlie was sitting at his desk, studying.

"Morning," P.S. whispered.

"Morning."

"Studying the Latin?"

"Yep."

"You know how to conjugate the verb 'to spit'?"

"Yep," Charlie said. "*Spitto, spittere, ach——*"

"O.K., O.K.!" P.S. laughed. "You gonna kill the exam?"

"I hope so. You think you'll pass it?"

"Doubt it. I haven't passed one

yet." P.S. looked over at Charlie's bureau. "Say, Charlie? Can I borrow your toothpaste? I'm out."

"Sure, but roll it from the bottom of the tube, will you?"

P.S. picked up the toothpaste and went down the hall to the bathroom. Mabrey, the head monitor, was shaving. P.S. watched him in the mirror.

"You must have had a porcupine for a father," P.S. said. "You've got the heaviest beard in school."

Mabrey began to shave the length of his neck.

"Wilkinson, you're about as funny as a rubber crutch."

"Cut your throat! Cut your throat!" P.S. began to dance around behind Mabrey, sprinkling voodoo potions on the top of the older student's head. "Monkey dust! Monkey dust! Oh, black Pizzoola! Great Kubla of the Ancient Curse! Make this bad man cut his throat!"

Mabrey cursed and a small red stain began to seep through the lather on his throat. "P.S., will you *get out of here!*"

P.S. stared, eyes wide open, at the broadening stain. "My gosh! Hey! It worked!"

Mabrey undid the towel from around his waist and snapped P.S.'s skinny behind. P.S. yelped and jumped away. "Hey, Mr. Mabrey, sir? Hey, Mabrey? I'm sorry, I really am. I didn't know it would work."

"What would work?"

"My voodoo curse. I didn't know it would make you cut yourself."

"For heaven's sake, P.S., what're you talking about? I cut a pimple. Will you leave me alone before I throw you out of a closed window?"

P.S. was quiet for a moment. Then he moved over to the washbasin next to Mabrey and looked at himself in the mirror. He ran his fingers through his light-brown hair and pushed his glasses higher on his nose. "Hey, Mabrey? Do you think I'm fresh? I mean, I have great respect for you—you being the head monitor and all. I mean it. Sometimes I worry. I mean, do you think I'm too fresh?"

Mabrey finished rinsing his face. "P.S., kid," he said as he dried himself, "you're all right. You're a nice guy. And I'm willing to bet that if you could only learn to throw a baseball from center field to second base overhand, you might turn out to be a pretty fair little baseball player."

"*Overhand!* Whaddya mean 'overhand'? They call me 'Deadeye Wilkinson.'" P.S. wound up with an imaginary baseball and threw it as hard as he could. Then he pantomimed being the second baseman. He crouched and caught the incoming baseball at his knees and thrust his hand down to tag out the runner. "Safe!" he shouted. "I mean, out! Out! Out!"

"Too late," Mabrey said, and laughed. "An umpire never changes his decision."

"I meant out," P.S. said.

Mabrey disappeared down the hall.

P.S. brushed his teeth, being careful to squeeze the toothpaste from the bottom of the tube. He looked at himself in the mirror and chanted, *"Fuero, fueris, fuerit, fuerimus, fueritis, fuerint[1]!"* He examined his upper lip and was disappointed. He wished that he didn't have such a young face. He wished he had a heavy beard, like Mabrey. He washed his face, wet his hair down, and walked back into Charlie's room. Charlie was P.S.'s best friend. He was very short. The other boys kidded him about being an engineer for Lionel

trains. P.S. was very tall and thin, and he had not yet grown into his height. At fourteen he was already six feet tall, and he had a tendency to stoop to compensate. He and Charlie were known as Mutt and Jeff. When P.S. entered the room, Charlie was curled up on his bed studying his Latin notes. He didn't look up until P.S. dropped the toothpaste tube on his pillow.

"Rolled from the bottom," P.S. said.

"Hey, how do you expect to pass your Latin exam if you don't study? I heard you and Mabrey clowning around in the can."

"If I don't study!" P.S. said. "Do you know how long I've studied for this exam? Two years! If I flunk it again this year, I get to keep the trophy."

"What trophy?"

"For Pete's sake, I don't know what trophy. But I'll get something, for sure. I've spent the last two weeks practically doing nothing but studying Latin. I recopied all my notes. I underlined practically the whole book. And I memorized all the irregular verbs. Come on, come on, ask me anything. Gosh, if I don't pass it this year, I've had it. Come on, ask me anything."

"O.K., what's the word for 'ridge'?"

"The word for 'ridge'?" P.S. stalled.

"Yep."

P.S. thought for a moment. "Look, I don't know. Make it two out of three."

"The word for 'ridge' is *iugum.*" Charlie looked at his notes. "O.K., two out of three. What's the word for 'crowd'? And 'troop,' as in 'a troop of cavalry'?"

---

1. *"Fuero, . . . fuerint!"* P. S. is conjugating one tense of the Latin verb "to be."

"The word for 'crowd' is *turba, turbae*. . . . What was the other one?"

" 'Troop of cavalry.' "

" 'Cavalry' is *equitatus*. . . . I don't know. What is 'troop'?"

" 'Troop' is *turma*." Charlie laughed. "Well, you got one out of three."

"Did I get partial credit for the 'cavalry'?"

"Nope."

"I hope Dr. Fairfax is more lenient than you are."

"He won't be," Charlie said.

"If I flunk the Latin exam again this year . . ."

"How come you flunked it last year?"

"How come anybody flunks an exam? I didn't know the answers. Boy, Charlie, I don't know what I'm going to do with you. If you weren't such a nice guy and lend me your toothpaste and things like that all the time, I'd probably feed you to the—to the what's-their-name fish. Those fish who eat people in South America all the time."

"Well, since you don't know what to do with me, as a start why don't you let me study?"

"Sure. Sure, O.K. . . . O.K., be a grind. See if I care."

P.S. walked back to his cubicle and pulled his Ullman and Henry *Latin II* from his unpainted bookcase. First he studied the irregular verbs in the back of the book. Then he went over his vocabulary list. He concentrated for as long as he could; then he leaned out of his window to look at the shadows of the trees directly below, dropped a penny out of the window to see if a squirrel would pick it up, checked his window sill to see if the cookie crumbs he had left for the mockingbird were still there. He turned back to his Latin book and leafed through the Fores-

tier illustrations of Roman soldiers. He picked up the picture his father had given him last Christmas. Within the frame were four small round photographs of Wilkinsons in uniform. There was his father as an infantry major during the Second World War, his grandfather as a captain in the field artillery during the First World War, his great-great-grandfather as a corporal in a soft gray Confederate uniform, and a great-great-great-great something or other in a dark uniform with a lot of bright buttons. P.S. didn't know who the last picture was of. He imagined it to be somebody from the Revolutionary War. P.S. had seen the oil portrait the photograph had been taken from hanging in the hall-way of his grandfather's house. P.S. had the long, thin nose of the other Wilkinsons in the pictures, but he still had the round cheeks of youth and the perfect eyebrows. He was the fifteenth of his family to attend the Virginia Preparatory School. Among the buildings at V.P.S. there was a Wilkinson Memorial Library and a Sadler Gymnasium. When P.S. was packing to begin his first year at the school, his father had said, "Son, when your great-grandfather went off to V.P.S., his father gave him a dozen silk handkerchiefs and a pair of warm gloves. When your grandfather went off to V.P.S., his father gave him a dozen silk handkerchiefs and a pair of warm gloves. When I went off to V.P.S., your grandfather gave me a dozen silk handkerchiefs and a pair of warm gloves. And now here are a dozen silk handkerchiefs and a pair of warm gloves for you."

P.S. looked at the brightly patterned Liberty-silk handkerchiefs[2] and the fuzzy red mittens. No thirteen-year-old ever wore red

2. *Liberty-silk handkerchiefs,* handkerchiefs from Liberty and Company, a well-known firm in London, England.

mittens, except girls, and particularly not fuzzy red mittens. And P.S. knew he would never dare to wear the silk handkerchiefs.

"Well, thank you very much, Dad," he had said.

"That's all right, son."

P.S. left the red mittens behind when he went away to V.P.S. He used two of the silk handkerchiefs to cover the top of his bureau and bookcase, gave one other away to a girl, and hid the rest beneath his underwear on the second shelf of his bureau. His father had done very well at the school; he had been a senior monitor, editor-in-chief of the yearbook, and a distance runner in winter and spring track. P.S. hoped he would do as well, but he knew he had disappointed his father so far. When he flunked the Latin examination last year and tried to explain to his father that he just could not do Latin, he could see the disbelief in his father's eyes. "Good Lord, son, you just didn't study. 'Can't do Latin,' what nonsense!" But P.S. knew that studying had nothing to do with it. His father said that no Wilkinson had ever flunked at V.P.S.; P.S. was the first. His father was not the kind to lose his temper. P.S. wished he were. When P.S. had done something wrong, his father would just look at him and smile sadly and shake his head. The boy had never felt particularly close to his father. He had never been able to talk to or with his father. He had found the best means of getting along with his father was to keep out of his way. He had given up their ever sharing anything. He had no illusions about leading a calendar-picture life with his father—canoeing or hunting together. He could remember trying to get his father to play catch with him and how his father would always say, "Not now, son, not now." But

there were certain occasions that his father felt should be shared with P.S. These were the proper father-son occasions that made P.S. feel like some sort of ornament. There would be Father's Day, or the big football game of the season. P.S. would be told to order two tickets, and the afternoon of the game he and his father would watch the first half together. His father remembered all of the cheers and was shocked when P.S. didn't remember some of the words to the school song. At the half, his father would disappear to talk to his friends and P.S. would be left alone to watch the overcoats or umbrellas. After the game, P.S. would wander back to the field house, where the alumni tables were set up. He would locate his father and stand next to him until his father introduced him to the persons he was talking to. Then his father would say, "Run along, son. I'll meet you back in your room." So P.S. would go back to his room and wait for his father to come by. The boy would straighten up the bed, dust the bureau, and sweep the floor. And then after a long wait his father would come in and sit down. "Well, how are you, son?" the conversation would always start. And P.S. would answer, "Fine, thank you, sir." His father would look around the room and remark about its not being large enough to swing a cat in, then there would be two or three anecdotes about the times when he was a boy at V.P.S., and then he would look at his watch and say, "Well, I guess I'd better be pushing off." His father would ask him if there was anything he needed, and P.S. would say that he didn't think there was anything. His father would give him a five-dollar bill and drive away. And P.S., with enormous relief, would go look

for Charlie. "Did you and your dad have a good time?" Charlie would ask. "Sure," P.S. would say. And that would end the conversation.

P.S. knew that his father loved him, but he also knew better than to expect any sign of affection. Affection always seemed to embarrass his father. P.S. remembered his first year at school, when his father had first come up to see him. He had been very happy to see his father, and when they were saying goodbye P.S. stepped forward as usual to kiss him and his father drew away. P.S. always made it a point now to shake hands with his father. And at fourteen respect and obedience had taken the place of love.

P.S. picked up his Latin notes and went over the translations he had completed. He wished he knew what questions would be asked. In last year's exam there were questions from all over the book, and it made the exam very difficult to study for, if they were going to do that. He pictured himself handing in the finished examination to Dr. Fairfax and saying, "Sir? Wilkinsons do not flunk. Please grade my exam accordingly."

P.S. looked at his wristwatch. The dining hall would begin serving breakfast in fifteen minutes. He made his bed and put on a clean pair of khakis and a button-down shirt. He slipped into his old white bucks and broke a lace tying them, and pulled out the shorter piece and threaded what was left through the next eyelet up, as the older boys did. He tidied up his room for inspection, picked up his notes, and went back to Charlie's room. Charlie was sweeping the dust into the hall. The new boy on duty that day would be responsible for sweeping the halls and emptying all trash bas-

kets. P.S. entered and sat down on the bed.

"For Pete's sake, P.S.! I just made the bed!"

"O.K., O.K., I'll straighten it up when I leave." P.S. ran his fingers across the desk top. "Merritt, two demerits—dust. . . . Hey, the exam's at ten-thirty, isn't it?"

"Yep. If you flunk Latin again, will they make you go to summer school?"

"Probably. I really think it's archaic the way they make you pass Latin to get out of this place."

"Boy, I sure hope I pass it," Charlie said.

"You will. You will. You're the brain in the class."

"Come on, let's go to chow."

"That's what I've been waiting for, my good buddy, my good friend, old pal of mine." P.S. jumped off the bed, scooped up his notebook, and started out of the room.

"Hey!" Charlie said. "What about the bed?"

At eight o'clock chapel, P.S. knelt in the pew and prayed: "Dear God, I pray that I pass my Latin exam this morning. . . . If I can pass this exam, then I'll do anything you want me to do. . . . God, please. If I don't pass this exam, I've really had it. . . . *They must have made these pews for midgets; I never fit in them right. . . . How am I ever going to get out to Colorado this summer unless I pass that exam? . . .* Please God, I don't want a high grade, all I want is to pass . . . and you don't have to help me on the others. . . . I don't want to pass this exam for myself only. I mean, it means a lot to my family. My father will be very disappointed if I flunk the exam. . . . *I wonder if Charlie will be able to go out to Colorado with me. . . .* God bless Mom, God bless Dad, God bless

Grandpa Sadler and Grandma Sadler, God bless Grandpa Wilkinson and Granny Wilkinson, God bless all my relatives I haven't mentioned. . . . Amen. And . . . and, God, please, please help me to pass this exam."

At ten-fifteen, P.S. and Charlie fell in step and walked over to Randolph Hall, where the examination was to be held.

"Well, if we don't know it now, we never will," Charlie said.

"Even if I did know it now, I wouldn't know it tomorrow." P.S. reached into his pants pocket and pulled out his lucky exam tie. It was a stained and unraveled blue knit. As they walked up the path, he was careful to tie the tie backwards, the wide end next to his shirt, the seam facing out. Then he checked his watch pocket to see that his lucky silver dollar was there.

"What's the Latin for 'then'?" Charlie asked.

"'*Tum*,'" P.S. answered. "Tums for your tummy."

"What's the word for 'thence,' or 'from there'?"

"*Inde*." P.S. began to sing: "*Inde* evening *byde* moonlight you could *hearde*—"

"For Pete's sake, P.S.!" Charlie laughed.

"You don't like my singing?"

"Not much."

"You know? I'm thinking of joining the choir and glee club next year. You know why? They've got a couple of dances next fall. One with St. Catherine's and another with St. Tim's. You wanta try out with me?"

"I don't know. I can't sing."

"Who's gonna sing?" P.S. grabbed Charlie's arm and growled, "Baby, I'm no singer, I'm a lover!"

"Lover? Who says you're a lover?"

"Ask me no questions and I'll tell you no lies."

P.S. and Charlie walked up the worn wooden steps of Randolph Hall to the third-floor study hall, where the Latin examination was to be given. They both were in the upper study hall, since they were underclassmen still. P.S.'s desk was in the back corner of the study hall, against the wall. He sat down and brushed the dust off the top of his desk with his palm. Someone had traced a hand into the wood. Others had traced and retraced the hand and deepened the grooves. They had added fingernails and rings. P.S. had added a Marlboro tattoo.[3] He lifted the desk top and, searching for his pencil sharpener, saw that he had some more Latin translations in his desk. He read them through quickly and decided it was too late to learn anything from them. He pulled out his pencil sharpener and closed his desk. The study hall was filling with boys, who took their places at their desks and called back and forth to each other in their slow Southern voices. It was a long, narrow room with high windows on either side, and the walls were painted a dirty yellow. Between the windows were framed engravings of Roman ruins and Southern generals. The large fluorescent lights above the desks buzzed and blinked into life. A dark, curly-haired boy sat down in the desk next to P.S. and began to empty his pockets of pencils and pens.

"Hey, Jumbo," P.S. said. "You gonna kill the exam?"

"I hope so. If I can get a good grade on it, then I don't have to worry so much about my math exam tomorrow."

"Well, if we don't know it now we never will."

"You're right."

Jumbo had played second-string

---

3. *Marlboro tattoo.* A tattoo on the back of a man's hand was the advertising symbol of Marlboro cigarettes.

tackle on the varsity this year. He was expected to be first-string next year, and by his final year, the coaches thought, he might become All-Virginia High School tackle. Jumbo was a sincere, not very bright student who came from a farm in Virginia and wanted to be a farmer when he finished college. P.S. had sat next to Jumbo all year, but they had never become particularly close friends. Jumbo lived in a different dormitory and had a tendency to stick with the other members of the football team. But P.S. liked him, and Jumbo was really the only member of the football team that he knew at all.

P.S. looked up at the engraving of General Robert E. Lee and his horse, Traveller. He glanced over at Jumbo. Jumbo was cleaning his fingernails with the tip of his automatic pencil.

"Well, good luck," P.S. said.

"Good luck to you."

"I'll need it."

P.S. stood up and looked for Charlie. "Hey! Hey, Charlie?"

Charlie turned around. "Yeah?"

"*Piggo, piggere, squeely, gruntum!*"

"For Pete's sake, P.S.!"

"Hey, P.S.?" someone shouted. "You gonna flunk it again this year?"

"No, no, I don't think so," P.S. answered in mock seriousness. "In point of fact, as the good Dr. Fairfax would say—in point of fact, I might just come out with the highest grade in class. After all, I'm such a brain."

The noise in the study hall suddenly stopped; Dr. Fairfax had entered. The Latin instructor walked to the back of the study hall, where P.S. was sitting.

"And what was all that about, Wilkinson?"

"Sir, I was telling the others how I'm the brain in your class."

"Indeed?" Dr. Fairfax asked.

"Yes, sir. But I was only kidding."

"Indeed," the Latin instructor said, and the other students laughed.

Dr. Fairfax was a large man with a lean, aesthetic face, which he tried to hide with a military mustache. He had taught at the Virginia Preparatory School since 1919. P.S.'s father had had Dr. Fairfax for a Latin instructor. When P.S. read *Goodbye, Mr. Chips,*[4] he had kept thinking of Dr. Fairfax. The Latin instructor wore the same suit and vest all winter. They were always immaculate. The first day of spring was marked by Dr. Fairfax's appearance in a white linen suit, which he always wore with a small blue bachelor's-button. Before a study hall last spring, someone had placed an alarm clock set to go off during the middle of study hall in one of the tall wastepaper baskets at the rear of the room. The student had then emptied all of the pencil sharpeners and several ink bottles into the basket and covered all this with crumpled-up pad paper. When the alarm clock went off, Dr. Fairfax strode down the aisle and reached into the wastepaper basket for the clock. When he lifted it out, the sleeve of his white linen jacket was covered with ink and pencil shavings. There was a stunned silence in the study hall as Dr. Fairfax looked at his sleeve. And then Dr. Fairfax began to laugh. The old man sat down on one of the desk tops and laughed and laughed, until finally the students had enough nerve to join him. The next day, he appeared in the same linen suit, but it was absolutely clean. Nobody was given demerits or punished in any manner. Dr. Fairfax was P.S.'s favorite instructor. P.S. watched him separate the examination papers and blue

4. *Goodbye, Mr. Chips,* a novel by James Hilton. Mr. Chips is an old and beloved teacher in a private school for boys.

books[5] into neat piles at the proctor's desk. Dr. Fairfax looked up at the electric clock over the study-hall door and then at his thin gold pocket watch. He cleared his throat. "Good morning, gentlemen."

"GOOD MORNING, SIR!" the students shouted.

"Gentlemen, there will be no talking during the examination. In the two hours given you, you will have ample time to complete all of the necessary work. When the bell sounds signifying the end of the examination, you will cease work immediately. In point of fact, anyone found working after the bell will be looked upon most unfavorably. When you receive your examinations, make certain that the print is legible. Make sure that you place your names on each of your blue books. If you have any difficulty reading the examination, hold your hand above your head and you will be given a fresh copy. The tops of your desks should be cleared of all notes, papers, and books. Are there any questions? . . . If not, will Baylor and you, Grandy, and . . . and Merritt . . . will the three of you please pass out the examinations."

P.S. watched Charlie get up and walk over to the desk.

Dr. Fairfax reached into his breast pocket and pulled out a pair of steel-rimmed spectacles. He looked out across the room. "We are nearing the end of the school year," he said. "Examinations always seem to cause students an undue amount of concern. I assure you, I can well remember when I was a student at V.P.S. In point of fact, I was not so very different from some of you——"

The instructor was interrupted by a rasping Bronx cheer.[6] He looked quickly over in the direction of the sound. "Travers, was that you?"

"No, sir."

"Brandon, was that you?"

The student hesitated, then answered, "Yes, sir."

"Brandon, I consider that marked disrespect, and it will cost you ten demerits."

"Aww, sir——"

"Fifteen." Dr. Fairfax cleared his throat again. "Now, if I may continue? . . . Good. There are a few important things to remember when taking an examination. First, do not get upset when you cannot at once answer all of the questions. The examination is designed——"

P.S. stopped listening. Charlie was walking down the aisle toward him.

"Hey, Charlie," he whispered, "give me an easy one."

"There will be no favoritism on my part."

"How does it look?"

"Tough."

"Merritt and Wilkinson?" Dr. Fairfax said. "That last little bit of conversation will cost you each five demerits."

The Latin instructor looked up at the electric clock again. "When you receive your examinations, you may begin. Are there any questions? . . . If not, gentlemen, it might be well for us to remember this ancient Latin proverb: 'Abusus non tollit usum.'" Dr. Fairfax waited for the laugh. There was none. He cleared his throat again. "Perhaps . . . perhaps we had better ask the class brain what the proverb means. Wilkinson?"

P.S. stood up. "'Abusus non tollit usum,' sir?"

"That's right."

"Something like 'Abuse does not tolerate the use,' sir?"

---

5. *blue books*, blue-covered booklets of blank paper in which tests are to be written.
6. *Bronx cheer*, slang for a sound of contempt made by trilling the tongue between the protruded lips.

"What does the verb *tollo, tollere, sustuli, sublatus* mean?"

"To take away, sir."

"That's right. The proverb, then, is 'Abuse does not take away the use,' or, in the context I was referring to, just because you gentlemen cannot do Latin properly does not mean that it should not be done at all."

"Yes, sir," P.S. said, and he sat down.

Dr. Fairfax unfolded his newspaper, and P.S. began to read the examination. He picked up his pencil and printed in large letters on the cover of his blue book:

PHILIP SADLER WILKINSON
LATIN EXAMINATION
LATIN II – DR. FAIRFAX
VIRGINIA PREPARATORY
SCHOOL
7 JUNE 1962 – BOOK ONE (1)

Then he put down his pencil, stretched, and began to work.

P.S. read the examination carefully. He saw that he would be able to do very little of it from memory, and felt the first surge of panic moisten his palms. He tried to translate the first Latin-to-English passage. He remembered that it fell on the right-hand side of the page in his Ullman and Henry, opposite the picture of the Roman galley. The picture was a still taken from the silent-movie version of *Ben-Hur*.[7] He recognized some of the verbs, more of the nouns, and finally he began to be able to translate. It was about the Veneti ships, which were more efficient than the Roman galleys because they had high prows and flat keels. He translated the entire passage, put down his pencil, and stretched again.

An hour later P.S. knew he was in trouble. The first translation and the vocabulary section were the only parts of the exam he had been able to do without too much difficulty. He was able to give the rule and examples for the datives of agent and possession. The English-to-Latin sentences were the most difficult. He had been able to do only one of those. For the question, "How do you determine the tense of the infinitive in indirect statement?" he wrote, "You can determine the tense by the construction of the sentence and by the word endings," and hoped he might get some credit. The two Latin-to-English passages counted twenty points apiece. If he could only do that second translation, he stood a chance of passing the examination. He recognized the adverb *inde*, but saw that it didn't help him very much. The examination was halfway over. He tried to count how many points he had made so far on the examination. He thought he might have somewhere between fifty and fifty-five. Passing was seventy. If he could just translate that second passage, he would have the points he needed to pass. Dr. Fairfax never scaled the grades.[8] P.S. had heard that one year the Latin instructor had flunked everybody but two.

He glanced over at Jumbo. Then he looked back down at his own examination and swore under his breath. Jumbo looked over at him and smiled. P.S. pantomimed that he could not answer the questions, and Jumbo smiled again. P.S. slid his glasses off and rubbed his eyes. He fought down the panic, wiped his hands on his pants legs, and looked at the passage again. He couldn't make any sense out of the blur of the words. He squinted, looked at them, put on his glasses again, and knew that he was in trouble.

---

7. ***Ben Hur,*** a novel by Lew Wallace about the life of Christ.

8. **scaled the grades,** distributed the grades according to a planned percentage of A's, B's, etc.

He leaned over his desk and closed his eyes. *Dear God, please help me on this examination . . . please, God, please . . . I must pass this examination.* He opened his eyes and looked carefully around to see if anyone had seen him praying. The others were all working hard on the examination. P.S. looked up again at the engraving on the wall above his desk. Beneath the portrait was the caption "Soon after the close of the War Between the States, General Robert E. Lee became the head of a school for young men. General Lee made this statement when he met with his students for the first time: 'We have but one rule in this school, and that is that every student must be a gentleman.'" *They left out that other rule,* P.S. thought. *They left out the one that says you have to have Latin to graduate! Or is that part of being a gentleman, too?*

He read the Latin-to-English passage through twice, then he read it through backwards. He knew he had seen the passage before. He even remembered seeing it recently. But where? He knew that the passage dealt with the difficulties the Romans were having in fortifying their positions, but there were so many technical words in it that he could not get more than five of the twenty points from the translation, and he needed at least fifteen to pass. . . . He was going to flunk. *But I can't flunk! I can't flunk! I've got to pass!*

P.S. knew if he flunked he wouldn't be able to face his father. No matter what excuse P.S. gave, his father would not believe he hadn't loafed all term.

He looked at the passage and tried to remember where he had seen it. And then his mouth went dry. He felt the flush burn into the back of his neck and spread to his cheeks. He swallowed hard. *The translation's in my desk! . . . It's in my desk! Oh, God! . . . It's the translation on the top of the stack in my desk . . . in my desk!*

All he would have to do would be to slip the translation out of his desk, copy it, put it away, and he would pass the examination. All of his worries would be over. His father would be happy that he passed the examination. He wouldn't have to go to summer school. He and Charlie could go out to Colorado together to work on that dude ranch. He would be through with Latin forever. His Latin grade would never pull his average down again. Everything would be all right. Everything would be fine. All he would have to do would be to copy that one paragraph. Everyone cheated. Maybe not at V.P.S. But in other schools they bragged about it. . . . Everyone cheated in one way or another. Why should that one passage ruin everything? Who cared what problems the Romans had!

P.S. glanced over at Jumbo. Jumbo was chewing on his pencil eraser as he worked on the examination. Dr. Fairfax was still reading his newspaper. P.S. felt his heart beat faster. It began beating so hard that he was certain Jumbo could hear it. P.S. gently raised his desk top and pretended to feel around for a pencil. He let his blue book slide halfway off his desk so it leaned in his lap. Then he slid the translation under his blue book and slid the blue book and notes back onto his desk. He was certain that everyone had seen him—that everyone knew he was about to cheat. He slowly raised his eyes to look at Dr. Fairfax, who went on reading. P.S. covered part of the notes with his examination and began to copy the rest into his blue book. He could feel the heat in his cheeks, the dryness in his mouth. *Dear God . . . God, please don't let them catch me! . . . Please!*

He changed the smooth translation into a rough one as he copied, so that it would match his other translations.

From these things the army was taught the nature of the place and how the slope of the hill and the necessity of the time demanded more than one plan and order for the art of war. Different legions, some in one part, others in another, fought the enemy. And the view was obstructed by very thick hedges. Sure support could not be placed, nor could it be seen what work would be necessary in which part, nor could all the commands be administered by one man. Therefore, against so much unfairness of things, various consequences ensued.

He put down his pencil and looked around the study hall. No one was watching. P.S. carefully slid the translation back into his desk. He looked to see if the translation had given him any words that might help him on the rest of the examination. His heart was still beating wildly in his chest, and his hands shook. He licked his lips and concentrated on behaving normally. *It's over. . . . It's over. . . . I've cheated, but it's all over and no one said anything!*

He began to relax.

Fifteen minutes later Dr. Fairfax stood up at his desk, looked at the electric clock, then down at his pocket watch. He cleared his throat and said, "Stop!"

Several students groaned. The rest gathered up their pencils and pens.

"Make certain you have written out the pledge in full and signed it," Dr. Fairfax said.

P.S. felt the physical pain of fear again. He opened his blue book and wrote, "I pledge on my honor as a gentleman that I have neither given nor received unauthorized assistance on this examination." He hesitated; then he signed his name.

"Place your examination inside your blue book," Dr. Fairfax continued. "Make certain that you put your name on your blue book. . . . Baylor? If you and, uh, Ferguson and Showalter will be good enough to pick up the examinations, the rest of you may go. And, um, gentlemen, your grades will be posted on the front door of my office no sooner than forty-eight hours from now. In point of fact, any attempt to solicit your grade any sooner than that will result in bad temper on my part and greater severity in the marking of papers. Are there any questions? . . . If not, gentlemen, dismissed."

The students stood up and stretched. An immediate, excited hum of voices filled the study hall. P.S. looked down at his exam paper. He slid it into his blue book and left it on his desk.

Charlie was waiting at the door of the study hall.

"Well, P.S., how'd the brain do?"

"You know it's bad luck to talk about an exam before the grades are posted."

"I know. I'm just asking how you think you did."

"I don't know," P.S. said.

"Well, well, I mean, do you think you passed?"

"I don't know!"

"Whooey!" Charlie whistled. "And you called *me* a grump!"

They walked down the stairs together. At the bottom, Charlie asked P.S. if he was going to go to lunch.

"No, I don't think so," P.S. said. "I'm not feeling so well. I think I'll lie down for a while. I'll see ya."

"Sure," Charlie said. "See ya."

In his cubicle in Memorial Hall, P.S. took off his lucky exam tie. He put his silver dollar back onto his bookcase. He reached inside the hollow copy of *Gulliver's Travels* for the pack of cigarettes he kept there. Then he walked down the corridor to the bathroom, stepped into one of the stalls, and locked the door. He lit the cigarette and leaned his forehead against the cool green marble divider. He was sick with fear and dread. *It's over! It's all over!* he said, trying to calm himself. He did not like the new knowledge he had of himself. He was a cheater. He rolled his forehead back and forth against the stone, pressing his forehead into it, hurting himself. P.S. had broken the Honor Code of the school, and he was scared.

I shouldn't have cheated! What if someone had seen me! I shouldn't have cheated! . . . Maybe somebody did see me. . . . Maybe Dr. Fairfax will know I cheated when he sees my exam. . . . Maybe somebody will check my desk after the exam and find the copy of the translation. . . . I cheated! . . . Stupid, damned fool. . . . What if somebody finds out! . . . Maybe I should turn myself in. . . . I wonder if they'd kick me out if I turned myself in. . . . It would prove that I really am honest, I just made a mistake, that's all. . . . I'll tell them I couldn't help it. . . . Maybe they'll just give me a reprimand.

But P.S. knew that if he turned himself in, they would still tell his parents he had cheated, so what good would that do? His father would be just as angry. Even more so, since Wilkinsons don't cheat, either. P.S. knew how ashamed his father would make him feel. His father would have

to tell others that P.S. had cheated. It was a part of the Southern tradition. "My son has disgraced me. It is better that you hear it from me than somebody else." His father would do something like that. And having other people know he had cheated would be too much shame to bear. And even if he did turn himself in, the school would make him take another exam. . . . And he'd flunk that one, too. . . . He knew it. . . . *Oh, God, what am I going to do?*

If he didn't turn himself in and no one had seen him, then who would know? He would never cheat again. If he could just get away with it this one time. Then everything would be O.K. Nobody need ever know—except himself. And P.S. knew he would never be able to forget that he had cheated. Maybe if he turned himself in, it would be better in the long run. *What long run? What the hell kind of long run will I have if I turn myself in? Everybody in the school will know I cheated, no matter whether I turn myself in or not. . . . They won't remember me for turning myself in. . . . They'll remember that I cheated in the first place. . . .*

P.S. wanted to cry, but he couldn't. He dropped the cigarette into the toilet and flushed it down. Then he went over to the sink and rinsed his mouth out. He had some chewing gum in his room; that would cover the smell of his smoking. He looked at himself in the mirror. He couldn't see any change since this morning, and yet he felt so different. He looked at his eyes to see if there were lines under them now. *What shall I do?* he asked his reflection. *What the hell shall I do?* He turned on the cold water and rinsed his face. He dried himself on a towel someone had left behind, and walked back down the corridor to his room. He brushed aside the curtain, entered the cubicle, and stopped, frozen with fear. Mabrey, the head monitor, was sitting on P.S.'s bed.

"Wilkinson," Mabrey said, "would you mind coming with me?"

He called me Wilkinson, not P.S. . . . not P.S.! "Where do you want to go?"

"Just outside for a few minutes."

"What about?"

Mabrey got up from the bed. "Come on, P.S."

"What . . . what do you want me for?"

"We want to talk to you."

We! WE! P.S. picked up his jacket and started to put it on.

"You won't need your jacket," Mabrey said.

"It doesn't matter, I'll wear it anyway."

P.S. followed Mabrey out of the dormitory. *I didn't have a chance to turn myself in*, he thought. *I didn't have a chance to choose. . . .*

"You think you'll make the varsity baseball team next year?" Mabrey asked.

"I don't know," P.S. said. *What is he talking about baseball for?*

The new boy who had wakened P.S. passed them on the walk. He said hello to both Mabrey and P.S. He received no answer, and shrugged.

Mabrey and P.S. took the path to the headmaster's office. P.S. could feel the enormous weight of the fear building up inside him again. Mabrey opened the door for P.S. and ushered him into the headmaster's waiting room. Nelson, a pale, fat-faced senior, was sitting there alone. He was the secretary of the Honor Committee. P.S. had always hated him. The other members of the Honor Committee were Mabrey, the vice-president; Linus Hendricks, the president; Mr. Seaton, the head-

master; and Dr. Fairfax, who served as faculty adviser. Mabrey motioned that P.S. was to sit down in the chair facing the others—the only straight-backed wooden chair in the room. Every now and then Nelson would look up at P.S. and shake his head. The door to the headmaster's office opened and Mr. Seaton came out, followed by Linus Hendricks, Dr. Fairfax, and—*My God, what is Jumbo doing here! Don't tell me he cheated, too! He was sitting right next to me!* Jumbo walked out of the room without looking at P.S.

Linus Hendricks waited for the others to seat themselves, then he sat down himself and faced P.S. "Well, P.S., I imagine you know why you're here."

P.S. looked at Hendricks. Hendricks was the captain of the football team. He and Mabrey were the two most important undergraduates in the school.

"Well, P.S.?" Hendricks repeated.

"Yes, sir," P.S. said.

He could feel them all staring at him. He looked down at his hands folded in his lap. He could see clearly every line in his thumb knuckle. He could see the dirt caught under the corner of his fingernail, and the small blue vein running across the knuckle.

He looked up at Dr. Fairfax. He wanted to tell him not to worry. He wanted to tell him that he was sorry, so very sorry.

The headmaster, Mr. Seaton, was a young man. He had just become the headmaster of V.P.S. this year. He liked the students, and the students liked him. He was prematurely bald, and smiled a lot. He had a very young and pretty wife, and some of the students were in love with her and fought to sit at her table in the dining room. Mr. Seaton liked to play tennis. He would play the students and bet his dessert that he would win. And most of the time he would lose, and the students were enormously pleased to see the headmaster of the school have to get up from the table and pay his bets. Mr. Seaton would walk very quickly across the dining hall, his bald head bent to hide his smile. He would swoop up to a table, drop the dessert, and depart, like a bombing airplane. P.S. could tell that the headmaster was distressed he had cheated.

Linus Hendricks crossed his legs and sank back into the deep leather armchair. Mabrey and Nelson leaned forward as though they were going to charge P.S.

"P.S.," Hendricks said, "you're here this afternoon because the Honor Committee has reason to suspect that you may have cheated on the Latin exam this morning. We must ask you whether or not this is true."

P.S. raised his head and looked at Hendricks. Hendricks was wearing a bright striped tie. P.S. concentrated on the stripes. Thick black, thin white, medium green, thin white, and thick black.

"P.S., did you, or did you not, cheat on the Latin examination?"

P.S. nodded.

"Yes or no, P.S.?" Hendricks asked.

P.S. no longer felt anything. He was numb with misery. "Yes," he said, in a small, tired voice. "Yes, I cheated on the examination. But I was going to turn myself in. I was going to turn myself in. I swear I was."

"If you were going to turn yourself in, why didn't you?" Nelson asked.

"I couldn't. . . . I couldn't yet. . . ." P.S. looked at Dr. Fairfax. "I'm sorry, sir. I'm terribly sorry. . . ." P.S. began to cry. "I'm so ashamed. . . ." P.S. tried to stop crying. He couldn't. The tears stung his eyes. One tear slipped

into the inside of his glasses and puddled across the bottom of the lens. He reached into his back pocket for a handkerchief, but he had forgotten to bring one. He started to pull out his shirttail, and decided he'd better not. He wiped his face with the side of his hand.

Mr. Seaton walked over to P.S. and gave him his handkerchief. The headmaster rested his hand on P.S.'s shoulder. "Why, P.S.? Why did you cheat?"

P.S. couldn't answer.

"P.S., you were the last boy I expected this of. Why did you feel you had to cheat on this exam?"

"I don't know, sir."

"But, P.S., you must have had some reason."

Nelson said, "Answer the headmaster when he's asking you a question, Wilkinson."

P.S. looked up at him with such loathing that Nelson looked away.

Mr. Seaton crouched down next to P.S. "You must have been aware of the penalty for cheating."

P.S. nodded.

"Then why, in heaven's name, did you risk expulsion just to pass the examination?"

"Sir—sir, I flunked Latin last year, sir. I knew I'd flunk it this year, too. I—I knew I couldn't pass a Latin exam ever."

"But why did you *cheat*?"

"Because . . . because, sir, I had to pass the exam."

The headmaster ran his hand across his forehead. "P.S., I'm not trying to trick you, I'm only trying to understand why you did this thing. Why did you bring the notes into the exam with you?"

"Sir, Mr. Seaton, I didn't bring the notes in, they were in my desk. If they hadn't been, I wouldn't be here. I didn't want to cheat. I didn't mean to cheat. I—It was just the only way I could pass the exam."

Nelson rested his pudgy arms on the sides of his leather armchair and looked at the headmaster and then back to P.S. Then he said, "Wilkinson, you have been in V.P.S. for two years. You must be familiar, I imagine, with the Honor Code. In fact, in your study hall there is a small wooden plaque above the proctor's desk. On it are carved the four points of the Honor Code: 'I will not lie. I will not steal. I will not cheat. I will report anyone I see doing so.' You are familiar with them, aren't you?"

"Of course I'm familiar with them," P.S. said impatiently.

"Why did you think you were so much better than everyone else that you could ignore it?"

"I don't think I'm better than everyone else, Nelson," P.S. said.

"Well, you sure aren't! The others don't cheat." Nelson sat back again, very satisfied with himself.

Dr. Fairfax came from behind the chairs and stood next to P.S. "Unless you hold your tongue, Nelson—unless you hold your tongue, I shall personally escort you out of here."

"But, sir," Nelson whined. "I'm only trying to—"

"SHUT UP!" Dr. Fairfax roared. He returned to the back of the room.

Mr. Seaton spoke again. "P.S., if you had flunked this exam, you would have been able to take another. Perhaps you would have passed the reëxamination. Most boys do."

"I wouldn't have, sir," P.S. said. "I just cannot do Latin. You could have given me fifty examinations, sir. And I don't mean any disrespect, but I would have flunked all fifty of them."

Mabrey asked the headmaster if he could speak, then he turned to P.S. "P.S., we—all of us have been tempted at some time or another to cheat. All of us have either resisted that temptation or, perhaps, we were lucky enough to get away with it. I think that what we want to know is what *made* you cheat. Just having to pass the exam isn't enough. I know you, P.S. I may know you better than anyone else in the room, because I've shared the same floor in the dorm with you for this year. And we were on the same floor when you were a toad. You're not the kind who cheats unless he has a damn good——" Mabrey glanced over at the headmaster. "Excuse me, sir. I didn't mean to swear."

The headmaster nodded and indicated that Mabrey was to continue.

"What I mean is this, P.S. I know you don't care how high your grade is, just so long as you keep out of trouble. . . . You're one of the most popular boys in your class. Everybody likes you. Why would you throw all of this over, just to pass a Latin exam?"

"I don't know. I don't know. . . . I had to pass the exam. If I flunked it again, my father would kill me."

"What do you mean he would kill you?" Mr. Seaton asked.

"Oh, nothing, sir. I mean—I don't mean he would hurt me. He would just—Oh, I don't know how to explain it to you. If I flunked the exam again, he'd just make me feel so, I don't know . . . ashamed . . . so terrible. I just couldn't take it again."

There was a moment of silence in the room. P.S. began to cry again. He could tell the headmaster still didn't understand why he had cheated. He looked down at his hands again. With his index finger he traced the veins that crossed the back of his hand. He looked over at the wooden arm of his straight-backed chair. He could see the little drops of moisture where his hand had squeezed the arm of the chair. He could make out every grain of wood, every worn spot. He took off his glasses and rubbed his eyes. He tried taking deep breaths, but each time his breath would be choked off.

Hendricks cleared his throat and recrossed his legs. "P.S.," he said, "we have your examination here. You signed your name to the pledge at the end of the exam. You swore on your honor that you had not cheated." Hendricks paused. P.S. knew what he was driving at.

"If I hadn't signed my name to the pledge, you would have known I had cheated right away," P.S. explained. "I didn't want to break my honor again. I was going to turn myself in, honest I was."

"You didn't, though," Nelson said.

"I would have!" P.S. said. But he still wasn't sure whether he would have or not. He knew he never would be certain.

"So, we've got you on lying and cheating," Nelson said. "How do we know you haven't stolen, too?"

Dr. Fairfax grabbed the lapels of Nelson's jacket, pulled him out of the chair, and pushed him out of the room. The old man closed the door and leaned against it. He wiped his brow and said, "Mr. Seaton, sir, I trust you won't find fault with my actions. That young Nelson has a tendency to bother me. In point of fact, he irritates me intensely."

P.S. looked gratefully at Dr. Fairfax. The old man smiled sadly. Mabrey was talking quietly to Hendricks. Mr. Seaton sat down in Nelson's chair and turned to P.S. "I know this is a difficult question. Would you—would you have turned Jumbo in had you seen him cheating?"

P.S. felt the blood drain from his face. *So Jumbo turned me in! . . . Jumbo saw me! . . . Sitting next to me all year! . . . Jumbo turned me in! Why?*

He looked up at the others. They were all waiting for his answer. He had the most curious feeling of aloofness, of coldness. If he said yes, that he would have turned Jumbo in, it would be a lie, and he knew it. If he answered yes, it would please the headmaster, though. Because it would mean that P.S. still had faith in the school system. If he said no, he wouldn't have turned Jumbo in, it would be as good as admitting that he would not obey the fourth part of the Honor Code—"I will report anyone I see doing so." He waited a moment and then answered, "I don't know. I don't know whether I would have turned Jumbo in or not."

"Thank you very much, P.S.," the headmaster said.

P.S. could tell that Mr. Seaton was disappointed in his answer.

"Gentlemen, do you have any further questions you would like to ask Wilkinson?"

"Nothing, sir," Hendricks answered.

The headmaster looked over at Dr. Fairfax, who shook his head. "Well, then, P.S., if you don't mind, we'd like you to sit in my office until we call for you."

P.S. got up and started for the door.

"Have you had any lunch?" Dr. Fairfax asked.

"No, sir. But I'm not very hungry."

"I'll have Mrs. Burdick bring in some milk and cookies."

"Thank you, sir."

The door opened and P.S. stood up as Mr. Seaton walked over to his desk and eased himself into the swivel chair. P.S. had been sitting alone in the headmaster's office for several hours.

"Sit down, please," the headmaster said. He picked up a wooden pencil and began to roll it back and forth between his palms. P.S. could hear the click of the pencil as it rolled across the headmaster's ring. Mr. Seaton laid the pencil aside and rubbed his cheek. His hand moved up the side of his face and began to massage his temple. Then he looked up at P.S. and said, "The Honor Committee has decided that you must leave the school. The penalty for cheating at V.P.S. is immediate expulsion. There cannot be any exceptions."

P.S. took a deep breath and pushed himself back into the soft leather seat. Then he dropped his hands into his lap and slumped. He was beyond crying; there was nothing left to cry about.

"We were able to reach your father before he left Washington, and he is waiting for you in the other room," Mr. Seaton said. "I've asked him to wait outside for a few minutes, because I want to speak to you alone. I want you to understand why the school had to make the decision to expel you. The school—this school—is only as good as its honor system. And the honor system is only as good as the students who live by it."

P.S. cleared his throat and looked down at his fingernails. He wished the headmaster wouldn't talk about it. He knew why the school had to expel him. It was done. It was over with. What good would it do to talk about it?

"The honor system, since it is based on mutual trust and confidence, no doubt makes it easier for some students to cheat," the headmaster said. "I am not so naïve as to believe that there aren't any boys who cheat here. Unfortunately, our honor system makes it easy for them to do so. These boys have not been caught. Perhaps they will never be caught. But I feel that it was far better for you to have been caught right away, P.S., because you are not a cheater. Notice that I

said you *are* not a cheater instead of you *were* not a cheater. . . . Yes, you cheated this one time. I do not need to ask whether you cheated before. I know you haven't. I know also that you will not cheat again. I was frankly stunned when I heard that you had cheated on Dr. Fairfax's examination. You were the last boy I would have expected to cheat. I am still not entirely satisfied by the reasons you gave for cheating. I suppose a person never is. Maybe it is impossible to give reasons for such an act." Mr. Seaton began massaging his temple again. "P.S., the most difficult thing that you must try to understand is that Jumbo did the right thing. Jumbo was correct in turning you in."

P.S. stiffened in the chair. "Yes, sir," he said.

"If no one reported infractions, we would have no Honor Code. The Code would be obeyed only when it was convenient to obey it. It would be given lip service. The whole system would break down. The school would become just another private school, instead of the respected and loved institution it now is. Put yourself in Jumbo's shoes for a moment. You and Jumbo are friends—*believe me*, you are friends. If you had heard what Jumbo said about you in here, and how it hurt him to turn you in, you would know what a good friend Jumbo is. You have been expelled for cheating. You will not be here next fall. But Jumbo will be. Jumbo will stay on at V.P.S., and the other students will know that he was the one who turned you in. When I asked you whether you would have turned Jumbo in, you said that you didn't know. You and I both know from your answer that you wouldn't have turned Jumbo in. Perhaps the schoolboy code is still stronger in you than the Honor Code. Many students feel stronger about the schoolboy code than the Honor Code. No one likes to turn in a friend. A lot of boys who don't know any better, a lot of your friends, will never forgive Jumbo. It will be plenty tough for him. Just as it is rough on anybody who does his duty. I think—I honestly think that Jumbo has done you a favor. I'm not going to suggest that you be grateful to him. Not yet. That would be as ridiculous as my saying something as trite as 'Someday you will be able to look back on this and laugh.' . . . P.S., you will never be able to look back on this and laugh. But you may be able to understand." The headmaster looked at his wristwatch and then said, "I'm going to leave you alone with your father for a few minutes; then I suggest you go back to your room and pack. The other students won't be back in the dormitories yet, so you can be alone." He got up from behind the desk. P.S. rose also. He looked down at the milk and cookies Mrs. Burdick had left him. There was half a glass of milk and three cookies left.

The headmaster looked at P.S. for a moment and then he said, "I'm sorry you have been expelled, P.S. You were a good student here. One of the most popular boys in your class. You will leave behind a great many good friends."

"Thank you, sir," P.S. said.

"I'll see you before you and your father leave?"

"Yes, sir."

The headmaster walked into the waiting room. P.S. could hear Dr. Fairfax talking, and then his father. The door closed, and P.S. sat down to wait for his father. He could feel the fear building up inside him again. He did not know what to say to his father. What could he say? He sipped the last of the milk as the door opened. P.S. put down the glass and stood up.

Stewart Wilkinson closed the door behind him and looked at his son. He wanted to hold the boy and comfort him, but Phil looked so solid, so strong, standing there. Why isn't he crying, he wondered, and then he told himself that he wouldn't have cried either; that the boy had had plenty of time to cry; that he would never cry in front of his father again. He tried to think of something to say. He knew that he often was clumsy in his relations with Phil, and said the wrong thing, and he wondered whether he had been that sensitive at his son's age. He looked down at the plate of cookies and the empty milk glass.

"Where did you get the milk and cookies, son?"

"Mrs. Burdick brought them to me, sir."

He never calls me "Dad" now, Stewart Wilkinson said to himself. Always "sir." . . . My own son calls me "sir." . . .

"Did you thank her?"

"Yes, sir."

Stewart Wilkinson walked over to the couch next to his son and sat down. The boy remained standing.

"Phil, son, sit down, please."

"Yes, sir."

Looking at his son, Stewart Wilkinson could not understand why they had grown apart during the last few years. He had always remained close to his father. Why wasn't it the same between him and the boy who sat so stiff beside him, so still in spite of the horror he must have gone through during the past few hours?

"I'm sorry, sir."

"Yes . . . yes, son, I know you are. . . . I'm terribly sorry myself. Sorry for you. . . . Mr. Seaton told me another boy turned you in, is that right?"

P.S. nodded.

"He also told me that he believes you would have turned yourself in had you been given enough time."

"I don't know whether I would have or not. I never had the chance to find out."

"I think you would have. I think you would have."

He waited for his son to say something; then, realizing there was nothing the boy could say, he spoke again. "I was talking to Dr. Fairfax outside—you knew he was my Latin teacher, too?"

"Yes, sir."

"We always used to be able to tell when the first day of spring came, because Dr. Fairfax put on his white linen suit."

"Yes, sir."

"At any rate, that man thinks very highly of you, Phil. He is very upset that you had to be expelled. I hope you will speak to him before we go. He's a good man to have on your side."

"I want to speak to him."

"Phil . . . Phil . . ." Stewart Wilkinson thought for a minute. He wanted so desperately what he said to be the right thing to say. "Phil, I know that I am partly responsible for what has happened. I must have in some way pressured you into it. I wanted your marks to be high. I wanted you to get the best education that you could. V.P.S. isn't the best school in the country, but it's a very fine one. It's a school that has meant a lot to our family. But that doesn't matter so much. I mean, that part of it is all over with. I'm sorry that you cheated, because I know you're not the cheating kind. I'm also sorry because you are going to have to face the family and get it over with. This is going to be tough. But they'll all understand. I doubt that there is any of us who has never cheated in one way or another. But it will make them very proud of you if you can go see them and look them in the eye."

He picked up one of the cookies and began to bite little pieces out of the edge. Then he shook his head sadly, in the gesture P.S. knew so well. "Ah, son, it's so terrible that you have to learn these lessons when you are young. I know that you don't want me to feel sorry for you, but I can't help it. I'm not angry with you. I'm a little disappointed, perhaps, but I can understand it, I think. I suppose I must appear as an ogre to you at times. But Phil, I—If I'm tough with you, it's just because I'm trying to help you. Maybe I'm too tough." Stewart Wilkinson looked over at his son. He saw that the boy was watching him. He felt a little embarrassed to have revealed so much of himself before his son. But he knew they were alike. He knew that Phil was really his son. They already spoke alike, already laughed at the same sort of things, appreciated the same things. Their tastes were pretty much the same. He knew that, if anything, he was too much like the boy to be able to help him. And also that the problem was the boy's own, and that he would resent his father's interfering.

"Phil, I'll go speak with Mr. Seaton for a little while, and then I'll come on over and help you pack. If you'd like, I'll pack for you and you can sit in the car."

"No, that's all right, sir, I'll pack. I mean, most of the stuff is packed up already. I'll meet you over there."

Stewart Wilkinson rose with his son. Again he wanted to hold the boy, to show him how much he loved him.

"I'll be through packing in a few minutes. I'll meet you in my room," P.S. said.

"Fine, son."

Together they carried the footlocker down the staircase of Memorial Hall. P.S. stopped at the door, balanced the footlocker with one hand, then pulled the heavy door open. The door swung back before they could get through. Stewart Wilkinson stumbled and P.S. said, "I'm sorry."

They carried the footlocker across the small patch of lawn between the front of Memorial Hall and the main drive and slid the footlocker into the back of the station wagon.

"How much more is there, son?"

"A couple of small boxes, some books, and a couple of pictures."

Stewart Wilkinson pulled a silk handkerchief out of his back pocket and wiped his brow. "You think we can get all of them in one more trip?"

"I think so, sir. At least, we can try."

They turned back toward the dormitory. Stewart Wilkinson rested his hand on his son's shoulder as they walked back across the lawn. "Phil, Mr. Seaton told me that he thinks he might be able to get you into Hotchkiss. How does that sound to you?"

"It's a funny name for a school."

"Hotchkiss, funny? Why?"

"I don't know, it just sounds funny."

"Well, do you think you'd like to go there?"

"Sure. I mean I don't know. I haven't given it much thought."

Stewart Wilkinson laughed. "I guess you haven't."

The boy looked worriedly at his father for a moment. He wondered whether his father was making fun of him. And then he saw the humor in his remark and laughed too.

They brought the last of the boxes down from the room and slid them into the car and closed the tailgate.

"Did you get a chance to talk to Dr. Fairfax?"

"Yes, sir. He came by the room while I was packing."

"What did he say?"

"I don't know. I mean he was sorry I was going and all that, but he said I'd get along fine anywhere and that it wasn't the end of the world."

"Did he say 'in point of fact'?"

"Yeah." P.S. laughed. "He said, 'Well, boy, you'll do all right. In point of fact, you have nothing to worry about.' I really like old Doc Fairfax."

They went around the side of the car and climbed in.

"Anything you've forgotten? Books out of the library, equipment in the gym? Anybody special you want to see before we go home?"

"No, Dad, thanks, that's all—Hey, wait a minute, could you, Dad?" P.S. got out of the car. "It's Charlie—Charlie Merritt. I'd like to say goodbye to him."

"Sure, son, take your time."

The two boys spoke together for a moment, standing in the road; then they shook hands. Stewart Wilkinson turned off the engine and watched as the boys walked back up the road toward him. As they drew near, he got out of the station wagon.

"Dad, this is Charlie Merritt. . . . Charlie, you remember my father."

"Yes, sir. How are you, sir?"

"Fine, thank you, Charlie."

"Sir, Mr. Wilkinson, I'm sorry about P.S. getting kicked out and all."

Stewart Wilkinson nodded.

"He's just sorry because I won't be around to borrow his toothpaste any more. He likes to lend it to me because I always roll it from the top and lose the cap."

P.S. and Charlie laughed.

"Hey, P.S.?" Charlie said. "Does this mean you're not going to have to work off the five demerits Doc Fairfax gave us this morning?"

"What did you two get five demerits for?" Stewart Wilkinson asked.

"We were talking before the exam," P.S. said.

Father and son looked at each other, and then P.S. turned away. It was clear that he was thinking about the exam and his cheating again. And then the boy took a deep breath and smiled. "You know? It's funny," he said. "I mean, it seems that that exam took place so long ago. . . . Well, Charlie?" P.S. stuck out his hand and Charlie took it. "Well, I guess we'd better get going. I'll see you around, O.K.?"

"Sure, P.S.," Charlie said.

The two boys shook hands again solemnly. Then Charlie shook hands with P.S.'s father. P.S. and Stewart Wilkinson got back into the station wagon.

Charlie walked around to P.S.'s window. "Hey, P.S.! Make sure you let me hear from you this summer, O.K.?"

"Sure, Charlie. Take care of yourself."

They drove around the school drive, past the Wilkinson Memorial Library and the Sadler Gymnasium, and then they turned down the slight hill toward the Breastworks, and as they passed through the ornate, wrought-iron gate P.S. began to cry.

The Author

Courtlandt Dixon Barnes Bryan is a 1958 graduate of Yale University. Following his college career he served for two years as an army officer in Okinawa and Korea. Mr. Bryan's short stories and book reviews have appeared in several magazines including *The New Yorker* and the *New Republic*.

Discussion

1. (a) How has P. S. Wilkinson changed from the beginning to the end of the story? (b) What narrative point of view has Mr. Bryan used in telling the story? (c) How does the point of view help you to know P.S.?

2. (a) Point out the place in the second half of the story where Mr. Bryan changes the focus of his point of view. (b) On which character is the last portion of the story focused? (c) Why do you think Mr. Bryan changes the focus?

3. P.S.'s family background is important in showing the kind of boy P.S. is. Point out specific details which show (a) his home life, (b) the things which are important to his family, and (c) his relationship to his father before they meet in the headmaster's office.

4. (a) What place does the Honor Code have in the life of V.P.S.? (b) Why does P.S. break the Honor Code? (c) How well has P.S. prepared for the Latin exam? (d) How do his cheating and lying affect his attitude toward himself? (e) How does he react to the decision of the Honor Committee?

5. (a) What does P.S.'s crying at the end of the story tell you about the change in his relationship to his father? (b) What releases the tension between P.S. and his father as they are packing the car? (c) How does P.S. then address his father to show that he is beginning to realize that his father is on his side?

6. The headmaster says that perhaps the schoolboy code is stronger in P.S. than the Honor Code. (a) What does he mean by the schoolboy code? (b) Would P.S. have turned Jumbo in for cheating? Give reasons for your answer. (c) Do you think that P.S. would have turned himself in? Explain. (d) Who will suffer more, P.S. or Jumbo? Why?

7. Find the place in the story from which the title is taken. (a) What does "so much unfairness of things" mean in the Latin passage? (b) What does the phrase mean as the title of the story?

How does a boy ever understand a man so full
of contradictions as Doc Marlowe——
liar, cheat, and benefactor of the poor and ill? Notice
how James Thurber develops the complex
personality of this elderly medicine-show man.

Doc Marlowe

James Thurber

I WAS TOO YOUNG to be other than awed and puzzled by Doc Marlowe when I knew him. I was only sixteen when he died. He was sixty-seven. There was that vast difference in our ages and there was a vaster difference in our backgrounds. Doc Marlowe was a medicine-show man.[1] He had been a lot of other things, too: a circus man, the proprietor of a concession at Coney Island, a saloon-keeper; but in his fifties he had traveled around with a tent-show troupe made up of a Mexican named Chickalilli, who threw knives, and a man called Professor Jones, who played the banjo. Doc Marlowe would come out after the entertainment and harangue the crowd and sell bottles of medicine for all kinds of ailments. I found out all this about him gradually, toward the last, and after he died. When I first knew him, he represented the Wild West to me, and there was nobody I admired so much.

I met Doc Marlowe at old Mrs. Willoughby's rooming house. She had been a nurse in our family, and I used to go and visit her over weekends sometimes, for I was very fond of her. I was about eleven years old then. Doc Marlowe wore scarred leather leggings, a bright-colored bead vest that he said he got from the Indians, and a ten-gallon hat with kitchen matches stuck in the band, all the way around. He was about six feet four inches tall, with big shoulders, and a long, drooping mustache. He let his hair grow long, like General Custer's.[2] He had a wonderful collection of Indian relics and six-shooters, and he used to tell me stories

1. **medicine-show man.** A medicine show is a traveling show which uses entertainers to attract a crowd of people. Following the entertainment, the proprietor of the show sells medicines and various remedies to the audience. The tent-show troupe of which Doc Marlowe was a member is a type of medicine show.
2. **General Custer,** George Armstrong Custer (1839–1876), American general and Indian fighter. He is famous for his role in the Battle of the Little Big Horn, popularly known as Custer's Last Stand.

of his adventures in the Far West. His favorite expressions were "Hay, boy!" and "Hay, boy-gie!" which he used the way some people now use "Hot dog!" or "Doggone!" He told me once that he had killed an Indian chief named Yellow Hand in a tomahawk duel on horseback. I thought he was the greatest man I had ever seen. It wasn't until he died and his son came on from New Jersey for the funeral that I found out he had never been in the Far West in his life. He had been born in Brooklyn.

Doc Marlowe had given up the road when I knew him, but he still dealt in what he called "medicines." His stock in trade was a liniment that he had called Snake Oil when he traveled around. He changed the name to Blackhawk Liniment when he settled in Columbus. Doc didn't always sell enough of it to pay for his bed and board, and old Mrs. Willoughby would sometimes have to "trust" him for weeks at a time. She didn't mind, because his liniment had taken a bad kink out of her right limb that had bothered her for thirty years. I used to see people whom Doc had massaged with Blackhawk Liniment move arms and legs that they hadn't been able to move before he "treated" them. His patients were day laborers, wives of streetcar conductors, and people like that. Sometimes they would shout and weep after Doc had massaged them, and several got up and walked around who hadn't been able to walk before. One man hadn't turned his head to either side for seven years before Doc soused him with Blackhawk. In half an hour he could move his head as easily as I could move mine. "Glory be to God!" he shouted. "It's the secret qualities in the ointment, my friend," Doc Marlowe told him, suavely. He always called the liniment ointment.

News of his miracles got around by word of mouth among the poorer classes of town—he was not able to reach the better people (the "tony folks," he called them)—but there was never a big enough sale to give Doc a steady income. For one thing, people thought there was more magic in Doc's touch than in his liniment, and, for another, the ingredients of Blackhawk cost so much that his profits were not very great. I know, because I used to go to the wholesale chemical company once in a while for him and buy his supplies. Everything that went into the liniment was standard and expensive (and well-known, not secret). A man at the company told me he didn't see how Doc could make much money on it at thirty-five cents a bottle. But even when he was very low in funds Doc never cut out any of the ingredients or substituted cheaper ones. Mrs. Willoughby had suggested it to him once, she told me, when she was helping him "put up a batch," and he had got mad. "He puts a heap of store by that liniment being right up to the mark," she said.

Doc added to his small earnings, I discovered, by money he made gambling. He used to win quite a few dollars on Saturday nights at Freck's saloon, playing poker with the marketmen and the railroaders who dropped in there. It wasn't for several years that I found out Doc cheated. I had never heard about marked cards until he told me about them and showed me his. It was one rainy afternoon, after he had played seven-up with Mrs. Willoughby and old Mr. Peiffer, another roomer of hers. They had played for small stakes (Doc wouldn't play cards unless there was some money up, and Mrs. Willoughby wouldn't play if very much was up). Only twenty or thirty cents had changed hands in the end. Doc had won it all. I remember my astonishment and indignation when it dawned on me that Doc had used the marked cards in playing the old lady and the old man. "You didn't cheat *them*, did you?" I asked him. "Jimmy, my boy," he told me, "the man that calls the turn wins the money." His eyes twinkled and he seemed to enjoy my anger. I was outraged, but I was helpless. I knew I could never tell Mrs. Willoughby about how Doc had cheated her at seven-up. I liked her, but I liked him, too. Once he had given me a whole dollar to buy fireworks with on the Fourth of July.

I remember once, when I was staying at Mrs. Willoughby's, Doc Marlowe was roused out of bed in the middle of the night by a poor woman who was frantic because her little girl was sick. This woman had had the sciatica driven out of her by his liniment, she reminded Doc. He placed her then. She had never been able to pay him a cent for his liniment or his "treatments," and he had given her a great many. He got up and dressed, and went over to her house. The child had colic, I suppose. Doc couldn't have had any idea what was the matter, but he sopped on liniment; he sopped on a whole bottle. When he came back home, two hours later, he said he had "relieved the distress." The little girl had gone to sleep and was all right the next day, whether on account of Doc Marlowe or in spite of him I don't know. "I want to thank you, Doctor," said the mother, tremulously, when she called on him that afternoon. He gave her another bottle of liniment, and he didn't charge her for it or for his "professional call." He used to massage, and give liniment to, a lot of sufferers who were too poor to pay. Mrs. Willoughby told him once that he was too generous and too easily taken in. Doc laughed— and winked at me, with the twinkle in his eye that he had had when he told me how he had cheated the old lady at cards.

Once I went for a walk with him out Town Street on a Saturday afternoon. It was a warm day, and after a while I said I wanted a soda. Well, he said, he didn't care if he took something himself. We went into a drugstore, and I ordered a chocolate soda and he had a lemon phosphate. When we had finished, he said, "Jimmy, my son, I'll match you to see who pays for the drinks." He handed me a quarter and told me to toss the quarter and he would call the turn. He called heads and won. I paid for the drinks. It left me with a dime.

I was fifteen when Doc got out his pamphlets, as he called them. He had eased the misery of the wife of a small-time printer and the grateful man had given him a special price on two thousand advertising pamphlets. There was very little in them about Blackhawk Liniment. They were mostly about Doc himself and his "Life in the Far West." He had gone out to Franklin Park one day with a photographer—another of his numerous friends—and there the photographer took dozens of pictures of Doc, a lariat in one hand, a six-shooter in the other. I had gone along. When the pamphlets came out, there were the pictures of Doc, peering around trees, crouching behind bushes, whirling the lariat, aiming the gun. "Dr. H. M. Marlowe Hunting Indians" was one of the captions. "Dr. H. M. Marlowe after Hoss-Thieves" was another one. He was very proud of the pamphlets and always had a sheaf with him.

He would pass them out to people on the street.

Two years before he died Doc got hold of an ancient, wheezy Cadillac somewhere. He aimed to start traveling around again, he said, but he never did, because the old automobile was so worn out it wouldn't hold up for more than a mile or so. It was about this time that a man named Hardman and his wife came to stay at Mrs. Willoughby's. They were farm people from around Lancaster who had sold their place. They got to like Doc because he was so jolly, they said, and they enjoyed his stories. He treated Mrs. Hardman for an old complaint in the small of her back and wouldn't take any money for it. They thought he was a fine gentleman. Then there came a day when they announced that they were going out to St. Louis, where they had a son. They talked some of settling in St. Louis. Doc Marlowe told them they ought to buy a nice auto cheap and drive out, instead of going by train—it wouldn't cost much and they could see the country, give themselves a treat. Now, he knew where they could pick up just such a car.

Of course, he finally sold them the decrepit Cadillac—it had been stored away somewhere in the back of a garage whose owner kept it there for nothing because Doc had relieved his mother of a distress in the groins, as Doc explained it. I don't know just how the garage man doctored up the car, but he did. It actually chugged along pretty steadily when Doc took the Hardmans out for a trial spin. He told them he hated to part with it, but he finally let them have it for a hundred dollars. I knew, of course, and so did Doc, that it couldn't last many miles.

Doc got a letter from the Hard-mans in St. Louis ten days later. They had had to abandon the old junk pile in West Jefferson, some fifteen miles out of Columbus. Doc read the letter aloud to me, peering over his glasses, his eyes twinkling, every now and then punctuating the lines with "Hay, boy!" and "Hay, boy-gie!" "I just want you to know, Dr. Marlowe," he read, "what I think of low-life swindlers like you [Hay, boy!] and that it will be a long day before I put my trust in a two-faced lyer and imposture again [Hay, boy-gie!]. The garrage man in W. Jefferson told us your old rattle-trap had been doctored up just to fool us. It was a low down dirty trick as no swine would play on any man [Hay, boy!]." Far from being disturbed by the letter, Doc Marlowe was plainly amused. He took off his glasses after he finished it and laughed, his hand to his brow and his eyes closed. I was pretty mad, because I had liked the Hardmans, and because they had liked him. Doc Marlowe put the letter carefully back into its envelope and tucked it away in his inside coat pocket, as if it were something precious. Then he picked up a pack of cards and began to lay out a solitaire hand. "Want to set in a little seven-up game, Jimmy?" he asked me. I was furious. "Not with a cheater like you!" I shouted, and stamped out of the room, slamming the door. I could hear him chuckling to himself behind me.

The last time I saw Doc Marlowe was just a few days before he died. I didn't know anything about death, but I knew that he was dying when I saw him. His voice was very faint and his face was drawn; they told me he had a lot of pain. When I got ready to leave the room, he asked me to bring him a tin box that was on his bureau. I got it and handed it to him. He poked around in it for a while with unsteady fingers and finally found what he wanted. He handed it to me. It was a quarter, or rather it looked like a quarter, but it had heads on both sides. "Never let the other fella call the turn, Jimmy, my boy," said Doc, with a shadow of his old twinkle and the echo of his old chuckle. I still have the two-headed quarter. For a long time I didn't like to think about it, or about Doc Marlowe, but I do now. ✳

Discussion

1. (a) Why does the boy admire Doc Marlowe? **(b)** What qualities of Doc Marlowe does the boy dislike? To support your answers, cite passages which reveal Doc Marlowe's admirable qualities and those which show him in less favorable lights.
2. (a) Why does Doc Marlowe, just before he dies, give the boy a quarter? **(b)** Reread the last sentence of the selection. Why do you think the narrator's attitude toward Doc Marlowe has changed?
3. (a) What methods does Thurber use to characterize Doc Marlowe? **(b)** Do you think the author's portrayal is true to life? Why or why not?
4. (a) Why do you think the author chose the first person narrative point of view to tell his story? **(b)** How would the story differ if it had been told by Doc Marlowe? by Mrs. Willoughby?

Word Study

Words, like people, have histories. The English words you use originate from many different sources, among them Latin, Greek, French, and German. Study of word origins is called *etymology*.

In your Glossary, look up the word *imposture*. What is the origin of the word *imposture*? What does LL mean?

Copy each of the following words on a sheet of paper. Opposite each word, indicate the language (or languages) from which the word is derived. Refer to a dictionary for the etymologies of these words.

bead	*garage*	*saloon*
cheat	*groin*	*swindler*
colic	*kink*	*swine*
funds	*lariat*	

The Author

If we are to take as truth all the stories from his "autobiography," *My Life and Hard Times*, James Thurber (1894–1964) must have led a rather bizarre life as a child in Columbus, Ohio. We get a picture of such events as the night the bed fell on his father and the night the ghost got into the house. There is also a portrait of his mother as a woman whose great fear was that the Victrola would blow up. This unusual childhood seems to have influenced Thurber's adult life, for he is said to have lived in reverse, vacationing in the country in winter, sleeping during the day and working at night, although it is also said that, as time passed, Mrs. Thurber succeeded in changing his schedule into a more normal one. He was noted for his changing moods, absentmindedness, and an inability to concentrate.

Thurber began to write at the age of ten (*Horse Sandusky, The Intrepid Boy Scout*) and to draw at fourteen. He was an endless reviser, having been known to rewrite a single piece as many as twenty-five times. In contrast to his careful writing techniques, his famous pencil-line drawings of dogs, men, and women were always done hurriedly. He wrote and illustrated about two dozen books and turned out numerous essays and sketches. Among his most famous works are *The Male Animal* (a Broadway play), and *A Thurber Carnival* (a collection of short pieces which includes "The Secret Life of Walter Mitty").

He was only seven; she was sixty-something. They were distant cousins who had only each other. As he grew older, Buddy would recall Christmas and his unusual friend. Notice how the author's use of imagery makes vivid this memory.

See
IMAGERY
Handbook
of Literary
Terms
page 549

A CHRISTMAS MEMORY

Truman Capote

IMAGINE A MORNING in late November. A coming of winter morning more than twenty years ago. Consider the kitchen of a spreading old house in a country town. A great black stove is its main feature; but there is also a big round table and a fireplace with two rocking chairs placed in front of it. Just today the fireplace commenced its seasonal roar.

A woman with shorn white hair is standing at the kitchen window. She is wearing tennis shoes and a shapeless gray sweater over a summery calico dress. She is small and sprightly, like a bantam hen; but, due to a long youthful illness, her shoulders are pitifully hunched. Her face is remarkable—not unlike Lincoln's, craggy like that, and tinted by sun and wind; but it is delicate too, finely boned, and her eyes are sherry-colored and timid. "Oh my," she exclaims, her breath smoking the windowpane, "it's fruit-cake weather!"

The person to whom she is speaking is myself. I am seven; she is sixty-something. We are cousins, very distant ones, and we have lived together—well, as long as I can remember. Other people inhabit the house, relatives; and though they have power over us, and frequently make us cry, we are not, on the whole, too much aware of them. We are each other's best friend. She calls me Buddy, in memory of a boy who was formerly her best friend. The other Buddy died in the 1880's, when she was still a child. She is still a child.

"I knew it before I got out of bed," she says, turning away from the window with a purposeful excitement in her eyes. "The courthouse bell sounded so cold and clear. And there were no birds singing; they've gone to warmer country, yes indeed. Oh, Buddy, stop stuffing biscuit and fetch our buggy. Help me find my hat. We've thirty cakes to bake."

It's always the same: a morning arrives in November, and my friend, as though officially inaugurating the Christmas time of year that exhilarates her imagination and fuels the blaze of her heart, announces: "It's fruitcake weather! Fetch our buggy. Help me find my hat."

The hat is found, a straw cartwheel corsaged with velvet roses out-of-doors has faded: it once belonged to a more fashionable relative. Together, we guide our buggy, a dilapidated baby carriage, out to the garden and into a grove of pecan trees. The buggy is mine; that is, it was bought for me when I was born. It is made of wicker, rather unraveled, and the wheels wobble like a drunkard's legs. But it is a faithful object; springtimes, we take it to the woods and fill it with flowers, herbs, wild fern for our porch pots; in the summer, we pile it with picnic paraphernalia and sugar-cane fishing poles and roll it down to the edge of a creek; it has its winter uses, too: as a truck for hauling firewood from the yard to the kitchen, as a warm bed for Queenie, our tough little orange and white rat terrier who has survived distemper and two rattlesnake bites. Queenie is trotting beside it now.

Three hours later we are back in the kitchen hulling a heaping buggy-load of windfall pecans. Our backs hurt from gathering them: how hard they were to find (the main crop having been shaken off the trees and sold by the orchard's owners, who are not us) among the concealing leaves, the frosted, deceiving grass. Caarackle! A cheery crunch, scraps of miniature thunder sound as the shells collapse and the golden mound of sweet oily ivory meat mounts in the milk-glass bowl. Queenie begs to taste, and now and again my friend sneaks her a mite, though insisting we deprive ourselves. "We mustn't, Buddy. If we start, we won't stop. And there's scarcely enough as there is. For thirty cakes." The kitchen is growing dark. Dusk turns the window into a mirror: our reflections mingle with the rising moon as we work by the fireside in the firelight. At last, when the moon is quite high, we toss the final hull into the fire and, with joined sighs, watch it catch flame. The buggy is empty, the bowl is brimful.

We eat our supper (cold biscuits, bacon, blackberry jam) and discuss tomorrow. Tomorrow the kind of work I like best begins: buying. Cherries and citron, ginger and vanilla and canned Hawaiian pineapple, rinds and raisins and walnuts and whiskey and oh, so much flour, butter, so many eggs, spices, flavorings: why, we'll need a pony to pull the buggy home.

But before these purchases can be made, there is the question of money. Neither of us has any. Except for skinflint sums persons in the house occasionally provide (a dime is considered very big money); or what we earn ourselves from various activities: holding rummage sales, selling buckets of hand-picked blackberries, jars of homemade jam and apple jelly and peach preserves, rounding up flowers for funerals and weddings. Once we won seventy-ninth prize, five dollars, in a national football contest. Not that we know a fool thing about football. It's just that we enter any contest we hear about: at the moment our hopes are centered on the fifty-thousand-dollar Grand Prize being offered to name a new brand of coffee (we suggested "A.M."; and, after some hesitation, for my friend thought it perhaps sacrilegious, the slogan "A.M.! Amen!"). To tell the truth, our only *really* profitable enterprise was the Fun and Freak Museum we conducted in a back-yard woodshed two summers ago. The Fun was a stereopticon with slide views of Washington and New York lent us by a relative who had been to those places (she was furious when she discovered why we'd borrowed it); the Freak was a three-legged biddy chicken hatched by one of our own hens. Everybody hereabouts wanted to see that biddy: we charged grownups a nickel, kids two cents. And took in a good twenty dollars before the museum shut down due to the decease of the main attraction.

But one way and another we do each year accumulate Christmas savings, a Fruitcake Fund. These moneys we keep hidden in an ancient bead purse under a loose board under the floor under a chamber pot under my friend's bed. The purse is seldom removed from this safe location except to make a deposit, or, as happens every Saturday, a withdrawal; for on Saturdays I am allowed ten cents to go to the picture show. My friend has never been to a picture show, nor does she intend to: "I'd rather hear you tell the story, Buddy. That way I can imagine it more. Besides, a person my age shouldn't squander their eyes. When the Lord comes, let me see him clear." In addition to never having seen a movie, she has never: eaten in a restaurant, traveled more than five miles from home, received or sent a telegram, read anything except funny papers and the Bible, worn cosmetics, cursed, wished someone harm, told a lie on purpose, let a hungry dog go hungry. Here are a few things she has done, does do: killed with a hoe the biggest rattlesnake ever seen in this county (sixteen rattles), dip snuff (secretly), tame hummingbirds (just try it) till they balance on her finger,

tell ghost stories (we both believe in ghosts) so tingling they chill you in July, talk to herself, take walks in the rain, grow the prettiest japonicas in town, know the recipe for every sort of old-time Indian cure, including a magical wart-remover.

Now, with supper finished, we retire to the room in a faraway part of the house where my friend sleeps in a scrap-quilt-covered iron bed painted rose pink, her favorite color. Silently, wallowing in the pleasures of conspiracy, we take the bead purse from its secret place and spill its contents on the scrap quilt. Dollar bills, tightly rolled and green as May buds. Somber fifty-cent pieces, heavy enough to weight a dead man's eyes. Lovely dimes, the liveliest coin, the one that really jingles. Nickels and quarters, worn smooth as creek pebbles. But mostly a hateful heap of bitter-odored pennies. Last summer others in the house contracted to pay us a penny for every twenty-five flies we killed. Oh, the carnage of August: the flies that flew to heaven! Yet it was not work in which we took pride. And, as we sit counting pennies, it is as though we were back tabulating dead flies. Neither of us has a head for figures; we count slowly, lose track, start again. According to her calculations, we have $12.73. According to mine, exactly $13. "I do hope you're wrong, Buddy. We can't mess around with thirteen. The cakes will fall. Or put somebody in the cemetery. Why, I wouldn't dream of getting out of bed on the thirteenth." This is true: she always spends thirteenths in bed. So, to be on the safe side, we subtract a penny and toss it out the window.

Of the ingredients that go into our fruitcakes, whiskey is the most expensive, as well as the hardest to obtain: state laws forbid its sale. But everybody knows you can buy a bottle from Mr. Haha Jones. And the next day, having completed our more prosaic shopping, we set out for Mr. Haha's business address, a "sinful" (to quote public opinion) fish-fry and dancing café down by the river. We've been there before, and on the same errand; but in previous years our dealings have been with Haha's wife, an iodine-dark Indian woman with brassy peroxided hair and a dead-tired disposition. Actually, we've never laid eyes on her husband, though we've heard that he's an Indian too. A giant with razor scars across his cheeks. They call him Haha because he's so gloomy, a man who never laughs. As we approach his café (a large log cabin festooned inside and out with chains of garish-gay naked lightbulbs and standing by the river's muddy edge under the shade of river trees where moss drifts through the branches like gray mist) our steps slow down. Even Queenie stops prancing and sticks close by. People have been murdered in Haha's café. Cut to pieces. Hit on the head. There's a case coming up in court next month. Naturally these goings-on happen at night when the colored lights cast crazy patterns and the Victrola wails. In the daytime Haha's is shabby and deserted. I knock at the door, Queenie barks, my friend calls: "Mrs. Haha, ma'am? Anyone to home?"

Footsteps. The door opens. Our hearts overturn. It's Mr. Haha Jones himself! And he *is* a giant; he *does* have scars; he *doesn't* smile. No, he glowers at us through Satan-tilted eyes and demands to know: "What you want with Haha?"

For a moment we are too paralyzed to tell. Presently my friend half-finds her voice, a whispery voice at best: "If you please, Mr. Haha, we'd like a quart of your finest whiskey."

His eyes tilt more. Would you believe it? Haha is smiling! Laughing, too. "Which one of you is a drinkin' man?"

"It's for making fruitcakes, Mr. Haha. Cooking."

This sobers him. He frowns. "That's no way to waste good whiskey." Nevertheless, he retreats into the shadowed café and seconds later appears carrying a bottle of daisy yellow unlabeled liquor. He demonstrates its sparkle in the sunlight and says: "Two dollars."

We pay him with nickels and dimes and pennies. Suddenly, jangling the coins in his hand like a fistful of dice, his face softens. "Tell you what," he proposes, pouring the money back into our bead purse, "just send me one of them fruitcakes instead."

"Well," my friend remarks on our way home, "there's a lovely man. We'll put an extra cup of raisins in *his* cake."

The black stove, stoked with coal and firewood, glows like a lighted pumpkin. Eggbeaters whirl, spoons spin round in bowls of butter and sugar, vanilla sweetens the air, ginger spices it; melting, nose-tingling odors saturate the kitchen, suffuse the house, drift out to the world on puffs of chimney smoke. In four days our work is done. Thirty-one cakes, dampened with whiskey, bask on window sills and shelves.

Who are they for?

Friends. Not necessarily neighbor friends: indeed, the larger share are intended for persons we've met maybe once, perhaps not at all. People who've struck our fancy. Like President Roosevelt. Like the Reverend and Mrs. J. C. Lucey, Baptist missionaries to Borneo who lectured here last winter. Or the little knife grinder who comes through town twice a year. Or Abner Packer, the driver of the six o'clock bus from Mobile, who exchanges waves with us every day as he passes in a dust-cloud whoosh. Or the young Wistons, a California couple whose car one afternoon broke down outside the house and who spent a pleasant hour chatting with us on the porch (young Mr. Wiston snapped our picture, the only one we've ever had taken). Is it because my friend is shy with everyone *except* strangers that these strangers, and merest acquaintances, seem to us our truest friends? I think yes. Also, the scrapbooks we keep of thank-you's on White House stationery, time-to-time communications from California and Borneo, the knife grinder's penny post cards, make us feel connected to eventful worlds beyond the kitchen with its view of a sky that stops.

Now a nude December fig branch grates against the window. The kitchen is empty, the cakes are gone; yesterday we carted the last of them to the post office, where the cost of stamps turned our purse inside out. We're broke. That rather depresses me, but my friend insists on celebrating—with two inches of whiskey left in Haha's bottle. Queenie has a spoonful in a bowl of coffee (she likes her coffee chicory-flavored and strong). The rest we divide between a pair of jelly glasses. We're both quite awed at the prospect of drinking straight whiskey; the taste of it brings screwed-up expressions and sour shudders. But by and by we begin to sing, the two of us singing different songs simultaneously. I don't know the words to mine, just: *Come on along, come on along, to the dark-town strutters' ball.* But I can dance: that's what I mean to be, a tap dancer

in the movies. My dancing shadow rollicks on the walls; our voices rock the chinaware; we giggle: as if unseen hands were tickling us. Queenie rolls on her back, her paws plow the air, something like a grin stretches her black lips. Inside myself, I feel warm and sparky as those crumbling logs, carefree as the wind in the chimney. My friend waltzes round the stove, the hem of her poor calico skirt pinched between her fingers as though it were a party dress: *Show me the way to go home*, she sings, her tennis shoes squeaking on the floor. *Show me the way to go home.*

Enter: two relatives. Very angry. Potent with eyes that scold, tongues that scald. Listen to what they have to say, the words tumbling together into a wrathful tune: "A child of seven! whiskey on his breath! are you out of your mind? feeding a child of seven! must be loony! road to ruination! remember Cousin Kate? Uncle Charlie? Uncle Charlie's brother-in-law? shame! scandal! humiliation! kneel, pray, beg the Lord!"

Queenie sneaks under the stove. My friend gazes at her shoes, her chin quivers, she lifts her skirt and blows her nose and runs to her room. Long after the town has gone to sleep and the house is silent except for the chimings of clocks and the sputter of fading fires, she is weeping into a pillow already as wet as a widow's handkerchief.

"Don't cry," I say, sitting at the bottom of her bed and shivering despite my flannel nightgown that smells of last winter's cough syrup, "don't cry," I beg, teasing her toes, tickling her feet, "you're too old for that."

"It's because," she hiccups, "I *am* too old. Old and funny."

"Not funny. Fun. More fun than

anybody. Listen. If you don't stop crying you'll be so tired tomorrow we can't go cut a tree."

She straightens up. Queenie jumps on the bed (where Queenie is not allowed) to lick her cheeks. "I know where we'll find pretty trees, Buddy. And holly, too. With berries big as your eyes. It's way off in the woods. Farther than we've ever been. Papa used to bring us Christmas trees from there: carry them on his shoulder. That's fifty years ago. Well, now: I can't wait for morning."

Morning. Frozen rime lusters the grass; the sun, round as an orange and orange as hot-weather moons, balances on the horizon, burnishes the silvered winter woods. A wild turkey calls. A renegade hog grunts in the undergrowth. Soon, by the edge of knee-deep, rapid-running water, we have to abandon the buggy. Queenie wades the stream first, paddles across barking complaints at the swiftness of the current, the pneumonia-making coldness of it. We follow, holding our shoes and equipment (a hatchet, a burlap sack) above our heads. A mile more: of chastising thorns, burs and briers that catch at our clothes; of rusty pine needles brilliant with gaudy fungus and molted feathers. Here, there, a flash, a flutter, an ecstasy of shrillings remind us that not all the birds have flown south. Always, the path unwinds through lemony sun pools and pitch vine tunnels. Another creek to cross: a disturbed armada of speckled trout froths the water round us, and frogs the size of plates practice belly flops; beaver workmen are building a dam. On the farther shore, Queenie shakes herself and trembles. My friend shivers, too: not with cold but enthusiasm. One of her hat's ragged roses sheds a petal as she lifts her head and inhales the pine-heavy air. "We're almost there; can you smell it, Buddy?" she says, as though we were approaching an ocean.

And, indeed, it is a kind of ocean. Scented acres of holiday trees, prickly-leafed holly. Red berries shiny as Chinese bells: Black crows swoop upon them screaming. Having stuffed our burlap sacks with enough greenery and crimson to garland a dozen windows, we set about choosing a tree. "It should be," muses my friend, "twice as tall as a boy. So a boy can't steal the star." The one we pick is twice as tall as me. A brave handsome brute that survives thirty hatchet strokes before it keels with a creaking, rending cry. Lugging it like a kill, we commence the long trek out. Every few yards we abandon the struggle, sit down and pant. But we have the strength of triumphant huntsmen; that and the tree's virile, icy perfume revive us, goad us on. Many compliments accompany our sunset return along the red clay road to town; but my friend is sly and noncommittal when passers-by praise the treasure perched on our buggy: what a fine tree and where did it come from? "Yonderways," she murmurs vaguely. Once a car stops and the rich mill owner's lazy wife leans out and whines: "Giveya two-bits cash for that ol' tree." Ordinarily my friend is afraid of saying no; but on this occasion she promptly shakes her head: "We wouldn't take a dollar." The mill owner's wife persists. "A dollar, my foot! Fifty cents. That's my last offer. Goodness, woman, you can get another one." In answer, my friend gently reflects: "I doubt it. There's never two of anything."

Home: Queenie slumps by the fire and sleeps till tomorrow, snoring loud as a human.

A trunk in the attic contains: a shoebox of ermine tails (off the opera cape of a curious lady who once rented

a room in the house), coils of frazzled tinsel gone gold with age, one silver star, a brief rope of dilapidated, undoubtedly dangerous candy-like light bulbs. Excellent decorations, as far as they go, which isn't far enough: my friend wants our tree to blaze "like a Baptist window," droop with weighty snows of ornament. But we can't afford the made-in-Japan splendors at the five-and-dime. So we do what we've always done: sit for days at the kitchen table with scissors and crayons and stacks of colored paper. I make sketches and my friend cuts them out: lots of cats, fish too (because they're easy to draw), some apples, some watermelons, a few winged angels devised from saved-up sheets of Hershey-bar tin foil. We use safety pins to attach these creations to the tree; as a final touch, we sprinkle the branches with shredded cotton (picked in August for this purpose). My friend, surveying the effect, clasps her hands together. "Now honest, Buddy. Doesn't it look good enough to eat?" Queenie tries to eat an angel.

After weaving and ribboning holly wreaths for all the front windows, our next project is the fashioning of family gifts. Tie-dye scarves for the ladies, for the men a home-brewed lemon and licorice and aspirin syrup to be taken "at the first Symptoms of a Cold and after Hunting." But when it comes time for making each other's gifts, my friend and I separate to work secretly. I would like to buy her a pearl-handled knife, a radio, a whole pound of chocolate-covered cherries (we tasted some once, and she always swears: "I could live on them, Buddy, Lord yes I could—and that's not taking His name in vain"). Instead, I am building her a kite. She would like to give me a bicycle (she's said so on several million occasions: "If only I could, Buddy. It's bad enough in life to do without

something *you* want; but confound it, what gets my goat is not being able to give somebody something you want *them* to have. Only one of these days I will, Buddy. Locate you a bike. Don't ask how. Steal it, maybe"). Instead, I'm fairly certain that she is building me a kite—the same as last year, and the year before: the year before that we exchanged slingshots. All of which is fine by me. For we are champion kite-fliers who study the wind like sailors; my friend, more accomplished than I, can get a kite aloft when there isn't enough breeze to carry clouds.

Christmas Eve afternoon we scrape together a nickel and go to the butcher's to buy Queenie's traditional gift, a good gnawable beef bone. The bone, wrapped in funny paper, is placed high in the tree near the silver star. Queenie knows it's there. She squats at the foot of the tree staring up in a trance of greed: when bedtime arrives she refuses to budge. Her excitement is equaled by my own. I kick the covers and turn my pillow as though it were a scorching summer's night. Somewhere a rooster crows: falsely, for the sun is still on the other side of the world.

"Buddy, are you awake?" It is my friend, calling from her room, which is next to mine; and an instant later she is sitting on my bed holding a candle. "Well, I can't sleep a hoot," she declares. "My mind's jumping like a jack rabbit. Buddy, do you think Mrs. Roosevelt will serve our cake at dinner?" We huddle in the bed, and she squeezes my hand I-love-you. "Seems like your hand used to be so much smaller. I guess I hate to see you grow up. When you're grown up, will we still be friends?" I say always. "But I feel so bad, Buddy. I wanted so bad to give you a bike. I tried to sell my cameo Papa gave me. Buddy"—she hesitates, as though embarrassed—"I made you another kite." Then I confess that I made her one, too; and we laugh. The candle burns too short to hold. Out it goes, exposing the starlight, the stars spinning at the window like a visible caroling that slowly, slowly daybreak silences. Possibly we doze; but the beginnings of dawn splash us like cold water: we're up, wide-eyed and wandering while we wait for others to waken. Quite deliberately my friend drops a kettle on the kitchen floor. I tap-dance in front of closed doors. One by one the household emerges, looking as though they'd like to kill us both; but it's Christmas, so they can't. First, a gorgeous breakfast: just everything you can imagine—from flapjacks and fried squirrel to hominy grits and honey-in-the-comb. Which puts everyone in a good humor except my friend and I. Frankly, we're so impatient to get at the presents we can't eat a mouthful.

Well, I'm disappointed. Who wouldn't be? With socks, a Sunday school shirt, some handkerchiefs, a hand-me-down sweater and a year's subscription to a religious magazine for children. *The Little Shepherd.* It makes me boil. It really does.

My friend has a better haul. A sack of Satsumas,[1] that's her best present. She is proudest, however, of a white wool shawl knitted by her married sister. But she *says* her favorite gift is the kite I built her. And it *is* very beautiful; though not as beautiful as the one she made me, which is blue and scattered with gold and green Good Conduct stars; moreover, my name is painted on it, "Buddy."

"Buddy, the wind is blowing."

The wind is blowing, and nothing will do till we've run to a pasture below the house where Queenie has scooted to bury her bone (and where, a winter hence, Queenie will be buried, too). There, plunging through the healthy waist-high grass, we unreel our kites, feel them twitching at the string like sky fish as they swim into the wind. Satisfied, sunwarmed, we sprawl in the grass and peel Satsumas and watch our kites cavort. Soon I forget the socks and hand-me-down sweater. I'm as happy as if we'd already won the fifty-thousand-dollar Grand Prize in that coffee-naming contest.

"My, how foolish I am!" my friend cries, suddenly alert, like a woman remembering too late she has biscuits in the oven. "You know what I've always thought?" she asks in a tone of discovery, and not smiling at me but a point beyond. "I've always thought a body would have to be sick and dying before they saw the Lord. And I imagined that when He came it would be like looking at the Baptist window: pretty as colored glass with the sun pouring through, such a shine you don't know it's getting dark. And it's been a comfort: to think of that shine taking away all the spooky feeling. But I'll wager it never happens. I'll wager at the very end a body realizes the Lord has already shown Himself. That things as they are"—her hand circles in a gesture that gathers clouds and kites and grass and Queenie pawing earth over her bone—"just what they've always seen, was seeing Him. As for me, I could leave the world with today in my eyes."

This is our last Christmas together.

Life separates us. Those who Know Best decide that I belong in a military school. And so follows a miserable succession of bugle-blowing prisons, grim reveille-ridden summer camps. I have a new home too. But it doesn't count. Home is where my friend is, and there I never go.

1. *Satsumas*, a type of orange.

And there she remains, puttering around the kitchen. Alone with Queenie. Then alone. ("Buddy dear," she writes in her wild hard-to-read script, "yesterday Jim Macy's horse kicked Queenie bad. Be thankful she didn't feel much. I wrapped her in a Fine Linen sheet and rode her in the buggy down to Simpson's pasture where she can be with all her Bones. . . .") For a few Novembers she continues to bake her fruitcakes single-handed; not as many, but some: and, of course, she always sends me "the best of the batch." Also, in every letter she encloses a dime wadded in toilet paper: "See a picture show and write me the story." But gradually in her letters she tends to confuse me with her other friend, the Buddy who died in the 1880's; more and more thirteenths are not the only days she stays in bed: a morning arrives in November, a leafless birdless coming of winter morning, when she cannot rouse herself to exclaim: "Oh my, it's fruitcake weather!"

And when that happens, I know it. A message saying so merely confirms a piece of news some secret vein had already received, severing from me an irreplaceable part of myself, letting it loose like a kite on a broken string. That is why, walking across a school campus on this particular December morning, I keep searching the sky. As if I expected to see, rather like hearts, a lost pair of kites hurrying toward heaven.   ✱

Discussion

1. (a) When and where does this story take place? (b) What elements of the setting are important?
2. (a) How do Buddy and the old woman feel toward one another? (b) How are they different from the rest of the household? (c)

Point out passages which you think are particularly effective in showing their friendship.
3. (a) Review the passage in which Buddy lists the things his friend has and has not done (page 133, column 1, paragraph 1). What is unusual about this list? (b) What characteristics does his friend display? (c) How do you feel toward her? Why?
4. The first sentence of "A Christmas Memory" asks you to "imagine a morning in late November," and throughout the selection Truman Capote uses vivid sensory imagery. Pick one scene in which you think the images are particularly good; then (a) point out the senses to which they appeal, and (b) explain how they help you to become involved in the scene.
5. (a) From what narrative point of view is this story told? (b) How would the story be different if told from the point of view of the old woman? (c) How would it differ if told by one of the other members of the household?
6. This story deals with a series of rather unimportant events. Why did they make such a lasting impression on the child? Recall similar incidents in your own life that seemed trivial but that were not.

The Author

Truman Capote began writing when still a child; in fact, in school nothing *but* writing interested him. After publishing many stories in local newspapers, he wrote his first major prize-winning story at the age of nineteen. Since then he has written numerous stories and novels ranging in scope from nightmarish tragedy to light comedy. Much of his writing reflects his Southern background.

Mr. Capote is recognized as a very particular writer, one who spends an unusual amount of time rewriting in order to say something in exactly the right way. Among his best-known works are *Other Voices, Other Rooms; The Grass Harp; The Muses Are Heard;* and *Breakfast at Tiffany's,* which was made into a popular motion picture. In 1965 he published *In Cold Blood,* a factual account of a Kansas murder case.

A young boy is forced to recognize the finality of death. What does he learn from his experience?

the kitten

Richard Wright

IN MEMPHIS we lived in a one-story brick tenement. The stone buildings and the concrete pavements looked bleak and hostile to me. The absence of green, growing things made the city seem dead. Living space for the four of us—my mother, my brother, my father, and me—was a kitchen and a bedroom. In the front and rear were paved areas in which my brother and I could play, but for days I was afraid to go into the strange city streets alone.

It was in this tenement that the personality of my father first came fully into the orbit of my concern. He worked as a night porter in a Beale Street drugstore and he became important and forbidding to me only when I learned that I could not make noise when he was asleep in the daytime. He was the lawgiver in our family and I never laughed in his presence. I used to lurk timidly in the kitchen doorway and watch his huge body sitting slumped at the table. I stared at him with awe as he gulped his beer from a tin bucket, as he ate long and heavily, sighed, belched, closed his eyes to nod on a stuffed belly. He was quite fat and his bloated stomach always lapped over his belt. He was always a stranger to me, always somehow alien and remote.

One morning my brother and I, while playing in the rear of our flat, found a stray kitten that set up a loud, persistent meowing. We fed it some scraps of food and gave it water, but it still meowed. My father, clad in his underwear, stumbled sleepily to the back door and demanded that we keep quiet. We told him that it was the kitten that was making the noise and he ordered us to drive it away. We tried to make the kitten leave, but it would not budge. My father took a hand.

"Scat!" he shouted.

The scrawny kitten lingered, brushing itself against our legs, and meowing plaintively.

"Kill that damn thing!" my father exploded. "Do anything, but get it away from here!"

He went inside, grumbling. I resented his shouting and it irked me that I could never make him feel my resentment. How could I hit back at him? Oh, yes. . . . He had said to kill the kitten and I would kill it! I knew that he had not really meant for me to kill the kitten, but my deep hate of him urged me toward a literal acceptance of his word.

"He said for us to kill the kitten," I told my brother.

"He didn't mean it," my brother said.

"He did, and I'm going to kill 'im."

"Then he *will* howl," my brother said.

"He can't howl if he's dead," I said.

"He didn't really say kill 'im," my brother protested.

"He did!" I said. "And you heard him!"

My brother ran away in fright. I found a piece of rope, made a noose, slipped it about the kitten's neck, pulled it over a nail, then jerked the animal clear of the ground. It gasped, slobbered, spun, doubled, clawed the air frantically; finally its mouth gaped and its pink-white tongue shot out stiffly. I tied the rope to a nail and went to find my brother. He was crouching behind a corner of the building.

"I killed 'im," I whispered.

"You did bad," my brother said.

"Now Papa can sleep," I said, deeply satisfied.

"He didn't mean for you to kill 'im," my brother said.

"Then why did he *tell* me to do it?" I demanded.

My brother could not answer; he stared fearfully at the dangling kitten.

"That kitten's going to get you," he warned me.

"That kitten can't even breathe now," I said.

"I'm going to tell," my brother said, running into the house.

I waited, resolving to defend myself with my father's rash words, anticipating my enjoyment in repeating them to him even though I knew that he had spoken them in anger. My mother hurried toward me, drying her hands upon her apron. She stopped and paled when she saw the kitten suspended from the rope.

"What in God's name have you done?" she asked.

"The kitten was making noise and Papa said to kill it," I explained.

"You little fool!" she said. "Your father's going to beat you for this!"

"But he told me to kill it," I said.

"You shut your mouth!"

She grabbed my hand and dragged me to my father's bedside and told him what I had done.

"You know better than that!" my father stormed.

"You told me to kill 'im," I said.

"I told you to drive him away," he said.

"You told me to kill 'im," I countered positively.

"You get out of my eyes before I smack you down!" my father bellowed in disgust, then turned over in bed.

I had had my first triumph over my father. I had made him believe that I had taken his words literally. He could not punish me now without risking his authority. I was happy because I had at last found a way to throw my criticism of him into his face. I had made him feel that, if he whipped me for killing the kitten, I would never give serious weight to his words again. I had made him know that I felt he was cruel and I had done it without his punishing me.

But my mother, being more imaginative, retaliated with an assault upon my sensibilities that crushed me with the moral horror involved in taking a life. All that afternoon she directed toward me calculated words that spawned in my mind a horde of invisible demons bent upon exacting vengeance for what I had done. As evening drew near, anxiety filled me and I was afraid to go into an empty room alone.

"You owe a debt you can never pay," my mother said.

"I'm sorry," I mumbled.

"Being sorry can't make that kitten live again," she said.

Then, just before I was to go to bed, she uttered a paralyzing injunction: she ordered me to go out into the dark, dig a grave, and bury the kitten.

"No!" I screamed, feeling that if I went out of doors some evil spirit would whisk me away.

"Get out there and bury that poor kitten," she ordered.

"I'm scared!"

"And wasn't that kitten scared when you put that rope around its neck?" she asked.

"But it was only a kitten," I explained.

"But it was alive," she said. "Can you make it live again?"

"But Papa said to kill it," I said, trying to shift the moral blame upon my father.

My mother whacked me across my mouth with the flat palm of her hand.

"You stop that lying! You knew what he meant!"

"I didn't!" I bawled.

She shoved a tiny spade into my hands.

"Go out there and dig a hole and bury that kitten!"

I stumbled out into the black night, sobbing, my legs wobbly from fear. Though I knew that I had killed the kitten, my mother's words had made it live again in my mind. What would that kitten do to me when I touched it? Would it claw at my eyes? As I groped toward the dead kitten, my mother lingered behind me, unseen in the dark, her disembodied voice egging me on.

"Mama, come and stand by me," I begged.

"You didn't stand by that kitten, so why should I stand by you?" she asked tauntingly from the menacing darkness.

"I can't touch it," I whimpered, feeling that the kitten was staring at me with reproachful eyes.

"Untie it!" she ordered.

Shuddering, I fumbled at the rope and the kitten dropped to the pavement with a thud that echoed in my mind for many days and nights. Then, obeying my mother's floating voice, I hunted for a spot of earth, dug a shallow hole, and buried the stiff kitten; as I handled its cold body my skin prickled. When I had completed the burial, I sighed and started back to the flat, but my mother caught hold of my hand and led me again to the kitten's grave.

"Shut your eyes and repeat after me," she said.

I closed my eyes tightly, my hand clinging to hers.

"Dear God, our Father, forgive me, for I knew not what I was doing. . . ."

"Dear God, our Father, forgive me, for I knew not what I was doing," I repeated.

"And spare my poor life, even though I did not spare the life of the kitten. . . ."

"And spare my poor life, even though I did not spare the life of the kitten," I repeated.

"And while I sleep tonight, do not snatch the breath of life from me . . ."

I opened my mouth but no words came. My mind was frozen with horror. I pictured myself gasping for breath and dying in my sleep. I broke away from my mother and ran into the night, crying, shaking with dread.

"No," I sobbed.

My mother called to me many times, but I would not go to her.

"Well, I suppose you've learned your lesson," she said at last.

Contrite, I went to bed, hoping that I would never see another kitten. ✱

Discussion

1. (a) What is the boy's attitude toward his father? **(b)** Why does he feel this way?

2. (a) What does the boy hope to accomplish by killing the kitten? **(b)** How does he defend his action?

3. (a) How does the father react to the boy's killing the kitten? **(b)** What effect does the father's reaction have on the boy?

4. (a) What does the mother force the boy to do? **(b)** What do you think the mother was trying to teach the boy? **(c)** Does she accomplish her purpose? Explain. **(d)** Do you think the mother did the right thing? Give reasons for your answer.

5. Give several alternate titles for this selection and explain why each might be appropriate.

Word Study

A *compound word* is a word made up of two words which combine their meanings to form a new word. The words *bedroom* and *drugstore,* for example, are compound words.

Combine the words in the first column with those in the second column to form compound words. Explain the meaning of the new word, and ways in which the meanings of the separate words are contained in the compound.

common	*guard*
dug	*wealth*
keep	*sake*
life	*paste*
quarter	*back*
rain	*coat*
tooth	*out*

The Author

Richard Wright (1908–1960), one of the most prominent black American writers of the first half of the twentieth century, was born on a Mississippi plantation. When his father deserted the family, his mother made an effort to keep the children together; but she was stricken with paralysis, and young Richard spent his childhood living with various relatives, none of whom took particular interest in him or his education. At fifteen he struck out on his own, going to Memphis where he worked as a porter and as a messenger. He became interested in reading, but as the library at that time was segregated, he had to get books through a white co-worker. As a result of his reading, he developed the urge to write. After years of supporting himself at odd jobs all over the United States, Richard Wright finally arrived in Chicago, where he began publishing poetry, articles, and stories, including his famous *Native Son.*

Laurie's mother became worried that Charles
might be a bad influence on her son.
But just who was Charles?

See
INFERENCE
Handbook
of Literary
Terms
page 550

CHARLES

Shirley Jackson

THE DAY MY SON Laurie started kindergarten he renounced corduroy overalls with bibs and began wearing blue jeans with a belt. I watched him go off the first morning with the older girl next door, seeing clearly that an era of my life was ended, my sweet-voiced nursery-school tot replaced by a long-trousered, swaggering character who forgot to stop at the corner and wave good-bye to me.

He came home the same way, the front door slamming open, his hat on the floor, and the voice suddenly become raucous shouting, "Isn't anybody *here?*"

At lunch he spoke insolently to his father, spilled his baby sister's milk, and remarked that his teacher said we were not to take the name of the Lord in vain.

"How *was* school today?" I asked, elaborately casual.

"All right," he said.

"Did you learn anything?" his father asked.

Laurie regarded his father coldly. "I didn't learn nothing," he said.

"Anything," I said. "Didn't learn anything."

"The teacher spanked a boy, though," Laurie said, addressing his bread and butter. "For being fresh," he added, with his mouth full.

"What did he do?" I asked. "Who was it?"

Laurie thought. "It was Charles," he said. "He was fresh. The teacher spanked him and made him stand in a corner. He was awfully fresh."

"What did he do?" I asked again, but Laurie slid off his chair, took a cookie, and left, while his father was still saying, "See here, young man."

The next day Laurie remarked at lunch, as soon as he sat down, "Well, Charles was bad again today." He grinned enormously and said, "Today Charles hit the teacher."

"Good heavens," I said, mindful of the Lord's name. "I suppose he got spanked again?"

"He sure did," Laurie said. "Look up," he said to his father.

"What?" his father said, looking up.

"Look down," Laurie said. "Look at my thumb. Gee, you're dumb." He began to laugh insanely.

"Why did Charles hit the teacher?" I asked quickly.

"Because she tried to make him color with red crayons," Laurie said. "Charles wanted to color with green crayons so he hit the teacher and she spanked him and said nobody play with Charles but everybody did."

The third day—it was Wednesday of the first week—Charles bounced a see-saw on the head of a little girl and made her bleed, and the teacher made him stay inside all during recess. Thursday Charles had to stand in a corner during story-time because he kept pounding his feet on the floor. Friday Charles was deprived of blackboard privileges because he threw chalk.

On Saturday I remarked to my husband, "Do you think kindergarten is too unsettling for Laurie? All this toughness and bad grammar, and this Charles boy sounds like such a bad influence."

"It'll be all right," my husband said reassuringly. "Bound to be people like Charles in the world. Might as well meet them now as later."

On Monday Laurie came home late, full of news. "Charles," he shouted as he came up the hill; I was waiting anxiously on the front steps. "Charles," Laurie yelled all the way up the hill, "Charles was bad again."

"Come right in," I said, as soon as he came close enough. "Lunch is waiting."

"You know what Charles did?" he demanded, following me through the door. "Charles yelled so in school they sent a boy in from first grade to tell the teacher she had to make Charles keep quiet, and so Charles had to stay after school. And so all the children stayed to watch him."

"What did he do?" I asked.

"He just sat there," Laurie said, climbing into his chair at the table. "Hi, Pop, y'old dust mop."

"Charles had to stay after school today," I told my husband. "Everyone stayed with him."

"What does this Charles look like?" my husband asked Laurie. "What's his other name?"

"He's bigger than me," Laurie said. "And he doesn't have any rubbers and he doesn't ever wear a jacket."

Monday night was the first Parent-Teachers meeting, and only the fact that the baby had a cold kept me from going; I wanted passionately to meet Charles' mother. On Tuesday Laurie remarked suddenly, "Our teacher had a friend come to see her in school today."

"Charles's mother?" my husband and I asked simultaneously.

"Naaah," Laurie said scornfully. "It was a man who came and made us do exercises, we had to touch our toes. Look." He climbed down from his chair and squatted down and touched his toes. "Like this," he said. He got solemnly back into his chair and said, picking up his fork, "Charles didn't even *do* exercises."

"That's fine," I said heartily.

"Didn't Charles want to do the exercises?"

"Naaah," Laurie said. "Charles was so fresh to the teacher's friend he wasn't *let* do exercises."

"Fresh again," I said.

"He kicked the teacher's friend," Laurie said. "The teacher's friend told Charles to touch his toes like I just did and Charles kicked him."

"What are they going to do about Charles, do you suppose?" Laurie's father asked him.

Laurie shrugged elaborately. "Throw him out of school, I guess," he said.

Wednesday and Thursday were routine; Charles yelled during story hour and hit a boy in the stomach and made him cry. On Friday Charles stayed after school again and so did all the other children.

With the third week of kindergarten Charles was an institution in our family; the baby was being a Charles when he filled his wagon full of mud and pulled it through the kitchen; even my husband, when he caught his elbow in the telephone cord and pulled telephone, ashtray, and a bowl of flowers off the table, said, after the first minute, "Looks like Charles."

During the third and fourth weeks it looked like a reformation in Charles; Laurie reported grimly at lunch on Thursday of the third week, "Charles was so good today the teacher gave him an apple."

"What?" I said, and my husband added warily, "You mean Charles?"

"Charles," Laurie said. "He gave the crayons around and he picked up the books afterward and the teacher said he was her helper."

"What happened?" I asked incredulously.

"He was her helper, that's all," Laurie said, and shrugged.

"Can this be true, about Charles?"

I asked my husband that night. "Can something like this happen?"

"Wait and see," my husband said cynically. "When you've got a Charles to deal with, this may mean he's only plotting."

He seemed to be wrong. For over a week Charles was the teacher's helper; each day he handed things out and he picked things up; no one had to stay after school.

"The PTA meeting's next week again," I told my husband one evening. "I'm going to find Charles's mother there."

"Ask her what happened to Charles," my husband said. "I'd like to know."

"I'd like to know myself," I said.

On Friday of that week things were back to normal. "You know what Charles did today?" Laurie demanded at the lunch table, in a voice slightly awed. "He told a little girl to say a word and she said it and the teacher washed her mouth out with soap and Charles laughed."

"What word?" his father asked unwisely, and Laurie said, "I'll have to whisper it to you, it's so bad." He got down off his chair and went around to his father. His father bent his head down and Laurie whispered joyfully. His father's eyes widened.

"Did Charles tell the little girl to say *that?*" he asked respectfully.

"She said it *twice,*" Laurie said. "Charles told her to say it *twice.*"

"What happened to Charles?" my husband asked.

"Nothing," Laurie said. "He was passing out the crayons."

Monday morning Charles abandoned the little girl and said the evil word himself three or four times, getting his mouth washed out with soap each time. He also threw chalk.

My husband came to the door with me that evening as I set out for the PTA meeting. "Invite her over for a cup of tea after the meeting," he said. "I want to get a look at her."

"If only she's there," I said prayerfully.

"She'll be there," my husband said. "I don't see how they could hold a PTA meeting without Charles's mother."

At the meeting I sat restlessly, scanning each comfortable matronly face, trying to determine which one hid the secret of Charles. None of them looked to me haggard enough. No one stood up in the meeting and apologized for the way her son had been acting. No one mentioned Charles.

After the meeting I identified and sought out Laurie's kindergarten teacher. She had a plate with a cup of tea and a piece of chocolate cake; I had a plate with a cup of tea and a piece of marshmallow cake. We maneuvered up to one another cautiously, and smiled.

"I've been so anxious to meet you," I said. "I'm Laurie's mother."

"We're all so interested in Laurie," she said.

"Well, he certainly likes kindergarten," I said. "He talks about it all the time."

"We had a little trouble adjusting, the first week or so," she said primly, "but now he's a fine little helper. With occasional lapses, of course."

"Laurie usually adjusts very quickly," I said. "I suppose this time it's Charles's influence."

"Charles?"

"Yes," I said, laughing, "you must have your hands full in that kindergarten, with Charles."

"Charles?" she said. "We don't have any Charles in the kindergarten." ✱

Discussion

1. (a) What changes in Laurie's behavior take place at the beginning of the story? (b) How does Laurie treat his father after his first morning at school? (c) Does Laurie's behavior toward his parents improve as time goes on? (d) What similarities do you find between Laurie's behavior at home and the acts that Charles is reported to have done at school? (e) Is there anything in Laurie's actions at the beginning of the story that might help you understand his teacher's comments at the end of the story? (f) What inferences can you draw about Laurie's activities from his teacher's last statement? (g) Is there any irony in the closing scene of the story? What kind? What circumstances have created it?

2. (a) From whose point of view is this story told? (b) What does this person think of Laurie, as revealed by her thoughts or comments? (c) How does Laurie's father react to his behavior? (d) What do both parents think about Charles? (e) From what you know of children of Laurie's age, are his actions believable? (f) On the basis of this story, what kind of parents do you think Laurie's mother and father are? Too strict, too easy-going? Too suspicious, too trusting?

3. (a) What kind of person do you think Laurie might grow up to be? (b) With a different set of parents in what ways might his growth and development be different? Characterize different parents and specify the changes you think might occur in Laurie.

The Author

Laurie, the child in "Charles," is indeed modelled on a real person—the first of four children born to Shirley Jackson and her husband. The story appears, among other places, in a collection of Jackson's stories, *Life Among the Savages*, which she once called "a disrespectful memoir of my children."

About her own life Jackson usually had little to say beyond the fact that she disliked writing about herself or her work. When pressed for autobiographical statements she usually gave only a bare outline of the facts: her birthdate—1919 in San Francisco—her marriage in 1940, and a long list of published stories, essays and novels which earned her wide recognition before her death in 1965.

"Nothing might have gone wrong except for the coming of spring. . . . But the spring came," bringing with it a chain of events which test the understanding between a boy and his father.

the
colt

Wallace Stegner

IT WAS the swift coming of spring that let things happen. It was spring, and the opening of the roads, that took his father out of town. It was spring that clogged the river with floodwater and ice pans, sent the dogs racing in wild aimless packs, ripped the railroad bridge out and scattered it down the river for exuberant townspeople to fish out piecemeal. It was spring that drove the whole town to the river bank with pike poles, and coffeepots and boxes of sandwiches for an impromptu picnic, lifting their sober responsibilities out of them and making them whoop blessings on the C.P.R.[1] for a winter's firewood. Nothing might have gone wrong except for the coming of spring. Some of the neighbors might have noticed and let them know; Bruce might not have forgotten; his mother might have remembered and sent him out again after dark.

But the spring came, and the ice went out, and that night Bruce went to bed drunk and exhausted with excitement. In the restless sleep just before waking he dreamed of wolves and wild hunts, but when he awoke finally he realized that he had not been dreaming the noise. The window, wide open for the first time in months, let in a shivery draught of fresh, damp air, and he heard the faint yelping far down in the bend of the river.

He dressed and went downstairs, crowding his bottom into the warm oven, not because he was cold but because it had been a ritual for so long that not even the sight of the sun outside could convince him it wasn't necessary. The dogs were still yapping; he heard them through the open door.

"What's the matter with all the pooches?" he said. "Where's Spot?"

"He's out with them," his mother said. "They've probably got a porcu-

1. *C. P. R.*, the Canadian Pacific Railroad.

pine treed. Dogs go crazy in the spring."

"It's dog days they go crazy."

"They go crazy in the spring, too." She hummed a little as she set the table. "You'd better go feed the horses. Breakfast won't be for ten minutes. And see if Daisy is all right."

Bruce stood perfectly still in the middle of the kitchen. "Oh, my gosh!" he said. "I left Daisy picketed out all night!"

His mother's head jerked around. "Where?"

"Down in the bend."

"Where those dogs are?"

"Yes," he said, sick and afraid. "Maybe she's had her colt."

"She shouldn't for two or three days," his mother said. But just looking at her he knew that it might be bad, that there was something to be afraid of. In another moment they were both out the door, both running.

But it couldn't be Daisy they were barking at, he thought as he raced around Chance's barn. He'd picketed her higher up, not clear down in the U where the dogs were. His eyes swept the brown, wet, close-cropped meadow, the edge of the brush where the river ran close under the north bench. The mare wasn't there! He opened his mouth and half turned, running, to shout at his mother coming behind him, and then sprinted for the deep curve of the bend.

As soon as he rounded the little clump of brush that fringed the cutbank behind Chance's he saw them. The mare stood planted, a bay spot against the grey brush, and in front of her, on the ground, was another smaller spot. Six or eight dogs were leaping around, barking, sitting. Even at that distance he recognized Spot and the Chapmans' Airedale.

He shouted and pumped on. At a gravelly patch he stooped and clawed and straightened, still running, with a handful of pebbles. In one pausing, straddling, aiming motion he let fly a rock at the distant pack. It fell far short, but they turned their heads, sat on their haunches and let out defiant short barks. Their tongues lolled as if they had run far.

Bruce yelled and threw again, one eye on the dogs and the other on the chestnut colt in front of the mare's feet. The mare's ears were back, and as he ran, Bruce saw the colt's head bob up and down. It was all right then. The colt was alive. He slowed and came up quietly. Never move fast or speak loud around an animal, Pa said.

The colt struggled again, raised its head with white eyeballs rolling, spraddled its white-stockinged legs and tried to stand. "Easy, boy," Bruce said. "Take it easy, old fella." His mother arrived, getting her breath, her hair half down, and he turned to her gleefully. "It's all right, Ma. They didn't hurt anything. Isn't he a beauty, Ma?"

He stroked Daisy's nose. She was heaving, her ears pricking forward and back; her flanks were lathered, and she trembled. Patting her gently, he watched the colt, sitting now like a dog on its haunches, and his happiness that nothing had really been hurt bubbled out of him. "Lookit, Ma," he said. "He's got four white socks. Can I call him Socks, Ma? He sure is a nice colt, isn't he? Aren't you, Socks, old boy?" He reached down to touch the chestnut's forelock, and the colt struggled, pulling away.

Then Bruce saw his mother's face. It was quiet, too quiet. She hadn't answered a word to all his jabber. Instead she knelt down, about ten feet from the squatting colt, and stared at it. The boy's eyes followed hers. There was something funny about. . . .

"Ma!" he said. "What's the matter with its front feet?"

He left Daisy's head and came around, staring. The colt's pasterns looked bent—*were* bent, so that they flattened clear to the ground under its weight. Frightened by Bruce's movement, the chestnut flopped and floundered to its feet, pressing close to its mother. As it walked, Bruce saw, flat on its fetlocks, its hooves sticking out in front like a movie comedian's too-large shoes.

Bruce's mother pressed her lips together, shaking her head. She moved so gently that she got her hand on the colt's poll, and he bobbed against the pleasant scratching. "You poor broken-legged thing," she said with tears in her eyes. "You poor little friendly ruined thing!"

Still quietly, she turned toward the dogs, and for the first time in his life Bruce heard her curse. Quietly, almost in a whisper, she cursed them as they sat with hanging tongues just out of reach.

To Bruce, standing with trembling lip, she said, "Go get Jim Enich. Tell him to bring a wagon. And don't cry. It's not your fault."

His mouth tightened; a sob jerked in his chest. He bit his lip and drew his face down tight to keep from crying, but his eyes filled and ran over.

"It is too my fault!" he said, and turned and ran.

Later, as they came in the wagon up along the cutbank, the colt tied down in the wagon box with his head sometimes lifting, sometimes bumping on the boards, the mare trotting after with chuckling vibrations of solicitude in her throat, Bruce leaned far over and tried to touch the colt's haunch.

"Gee whiz!" he said. "Poor old Socks."

His mother's arm was around him

keeping him from leaning over too far. He didn't watch where they were until he heard his mother say in surprise and relief, "Why, there's Pa!"

Instantly he was terrified. He had forgotten and left Daisy staked out all night. It was his fault, the whole thing. He slid back into the seat and crouched between Enich and his mother, watching from that narrow space like a gopher from its hole. He saw the Ford against the barn and his father's big body leaning into it pulling out gunny sacks and straw. There was mud all over the car, mud on his father's pants. He crouched deeper into his crevice and watched his father's face while his mother was telling what had happened.

Then Pa and Jim Enich lifted and slid the colt down to the ground, and Pa stooped to feel its fetlocks. His face was still, red from windburn, and his big square hands were muddy. After a long examination he straightened up.

"Would've been a nice colt," he said. "Damn a pack of mangy mongrels, anyway." He brushed his pants and looked at Bruce's mother. "How come Daisy was out?"

"I told Brucie to take her out. The barn seems so cramped for her, and I thought it would do her good to stretch her legs. And then the ice went out, and the bridge with it, and there was a lot of excitement. . . ." She spoke very fast, and in her voice Bruce heard the echo of his own fear and guilt. She was trying to protect him, but in his mind he knew he was to blame.

"I didn't mean to leave her out, Pa," he said. His voice squeaked, and he swallowed. "I was going to bring her in before supper, only when the bridge. . . ."

His father's somber eyes rested on him, and he stopped. But his father didn't fly into a rage. He just seemed tired. He looked at the colt and then at Enich. "Total loss?" he said.

Enich had a leathery, withered face, with two deep creases from beside his nose to the corners of his mouth. A brown mole hid in the left one, and it emerged and disappeared as he chewed a dry grass stem. "Hide," he said.

Bruce closed his dry mouth, swallowed. "Pa!" he said. "It won't have to be shot, will it?"

"What else can you do with it?" his father said. "A crippled horse is no good. It's just plain mercy to shoot it."

"Give it to me, Pa. I'll keep it lying down and heal it up."

"Yeah," his father said, without sarcasm and without mirth. "You could keep it lying down about one hour."

Bruce's mother came up next to him, as if the two of them were standing against the others. "Jim," she said quickly, "isn't there some kind of brace you could put on it? I remember my dad had a horse once that broke a leg below the knee, and he saved it that way."

"Not much chance," Enich said. "Both legs, like that." He plucked a weed and stripped the dry branches from the stalk. "You can't make a horse understand he has to keep still."

"But wouldn't it be worth trying?" she said. "Children's bones heal so fast, I should think a colt's would too."

"I don't know. There's an outside chance, maybe."

"Bo," she said to her husband, "why don't we try it? It seems such a shame, a lovely colt like that."

"I know it's a shame!" he said. "I don't like shooting colts any better than you do. But I never saw a broken-legged colt get well. It'd just be a lot of worry and trouble, and then you'd have to shoot it finally anyway."

"Please," she said. She nodded at him slightly, and then the eyes of both were on Bruce. He felt the tears coming up again, and turned to grope for the colt's ears. It tried to struggle to its feet, and Enich put his foot on its neck. The mare chuckled anxiously.

"How much this hobble brace kind of thing cost?" the father said finally. Bruce turned again, his mouth open with hope.

"Two-three dollars, is all," Enich said.

"You think it's got a chance?"

"One in a thousand, maybe."

"All right. Let's go see Mac-Donald."

"Oh, good!" Bruce's mother said, and put her arm around him tight.

"I don't know whether it's good or not," the father said. "We might wish we never did it." To Bruce he said, "It's your responsibility. You got to take complete care of it."

"I will!" Bruce said. He took his hand out of his pocket and rubbed below his eye with his knuckles. "I'll take care of it every day."

Big with contrition and shame and gratitude and the sudden sense of immense responsibility, he watched his father and Enich start for the house to get a tape measure. When they were thirty feet away he said loudly, "Thanks, Pa. Thanks an awful lot."

His father half-turned, said something to Enich. Bruce stooped to stroke the colt, looked at his mother, started to laugh and felt it turn horribly into a sob. When he turned away so that his mother wouldn't notice he saw his dog Spot looking inquiringly around the corner of the barn. Spot took three or four tentative steps and paused, wagging his tail. Very slowly (never speak loud or move fast around an animal) the boy bent and found a good-sized stone. He straightened casually, brought his arm back, and threw with all his might. The rock caught Spot squarely in the ribs. He yiped, tucked his tail, and scuttled around the barn, and Bruce chased him, throwing clods and stones and gravel, yelling, "Get out! Go on, get out of here or I'll kick you apart. Get out! Go on!"

So all that spring, while the world dried in the sun and the willows emerged from the floodwater and the mud left by the freshet hardened and caked among their roots, and the grass of the meadow greened and the river brush grew misty with tiny leaves and the dandelions spread yellow along the flats, Bruce tended his colt. While the other boys roamed the bench hills with .22's looking for gophers or rabbits or sage hens, he anxiously superintended the colt's nursing and watched it learn to nibble the grass. While his gang built a darkly secret hideout in the deep brush beyond Hazards', he was currying and brushing and trimming the chestnut mane. When packs of boys ran hare and hounds through the town and around the river's slow bends, he perched on the front porch with his slingshot and a can full of small round stones, waiting for stray dogs to appear. He waged a holy war on the dogs until they learned to detour widely around his house, and he never did completely forgive his own dog, Spot. His whole life was wrapped up in the hobbled, leg-ironed chestnut colt with the slow-motion lunging walk and the affectionate nibbling lips.

Every week or so Enich, who was now working out of town at the Half Diamond Bar, rode in and stopped. Always, with that expressionless quiet that was terrible to the boy, he stood and looked the colt over, bent to feel pastern and fetlock, stood back to watch the plunging walk when the boy held out a handful of grass. His ex-

pression said nothing; whatever he thought was hidden back of his leathery face as the dark mole was hidden in the crease beside his mouth. Bruce found himself watching that mole sometimes, as if revelation might lie there. But when he pressed Enich to tell him, when he said, "He's getting better, isn't he? He walks better, doesn't he, Mr. Enich? His ankles don't bend so much, do they?" the wrangler gave him little encouragement.

"Let him be a while. He's growin', sure enough. Maybe give him another month."

May passed. The river was slow and clear again, and some of the boys were already swimming. School was almost over. And still Bruce paid attention to nothing but Socks. He willed so strongly that the colt should get well that he grew furious even at Daisy when she sometimes wouldn't let the colt suck as much as he wanted. He took a butcher knife and cut the long tender grass in the fence corners, where Socks could not reach, and fed it to his pet by the handful. He trained him to nuzzle for sugar-lumps in his pockets. And back in his mind was a fear: In the middle of June they would be going out to the homestead again, and if Socks weren't well by that time he might not be able to go.

"Pa," he said, a week before they planned to leave. "How much of a load are we going to have, going out to the homestead?"

"I don't know, wagonful, I suppose. Why?"

"I just wondered." He ran his fingers in a walking motion along the round edge of the dining table, and strayed into the other room. If they had a wagonload, then there was no way Socks could be loaded in and taken along. And he couldn't walk thirty miles. He'd get left behind before they got up on the bench, hobbling along like the little crippled boy in the Pied Piper, and they'd look back and see him trying to run, trying to keep up.

That picture was so painful that he cried over it in bed that night. But in the morning he dared to ask his father if they couldn't take Socks along to the farm. His father turned on him eyes as sober as Jim Enich's, and when he spoke it was with a kind of tired impatience. "How can he go? He couldn't walk it."

"But I want him to go, Pa!"

"Brucie," his mother said, "don't get your hopes up. You know we'd do it if we could, if it was possible."

"But, Ma. . . ."

His father said, "What you want us to do, haul a broken-legged colt thirty miles?"

"He'd be well by the end of the summer, and he could walk back."

"Look," his father said. "Why can't you make up your mind to it? He isn't getting well. He isn't going to get well."

"He is too getting well!" Bruce shouted. He half stood up at the table, and his father looked at his mother and shrugged.

"Please, Bo," she said.

"Well, he's got to make up his mind to it sometime," he said.

Jim Enich's wagon pulled up on Saturday morning, and Bruce was out the door before his father could rise from his chair. "Hi, Mr. Enich," he said.

"Hello, Bub. How's your pony?"

"He's fine," Bruce said. "I think he's got a lot better since you saw him last."

"Uh-huh." Enich wrapped the lines around the whipstock and climbed down. "Tell me you're leaving next week."

"Yes," Bruce said. "Socks is in the back."

When they got into the back yard Bruce's father was there with his hands behind his back, studying the colt as it hobbled around. He looked at Enich. "What do you think?" he said. "The kid here thinks his colt can walk out to the homestead."

"Uh-huh," Enich said. "Well, I wouldn't say that." He inspected the chestnut, scratched between his ears. Socks bobbed, and snuffed at his pockets. "Kid's made quite a pet of him."

Bruce's father grunted. "That's just the damned trouble."

"I didn't think he could walk out," Bruce said. "I thought we could take him in the wagon, and then he'd be well enough to walk back in the fall."

"Uh," Enich said. "Let's take his braces off for a minute."

He unbuckled the triple straps on each leg, pulled the braces off, and stood back. The colt stood almost as flat on his fetlocks as he had the morning he was born. Even Bruce, watching with his whole mind tight and apprehensive, could see that. Enich shook his head.

"You see, Bruce?" his father said. "It's too bad, but he isn't getting better. You'll have to make up your mind. . . ."

"He will get better though!" Bruce said. "It just takes a long time, is all." He looked at his father's face, at Enich's, and neither one had any hope in it. But when Bruce opened his mouth to say something else his father's eyebrows drew down in sudden, unaccountable anger, and his hand made an impatient sawing motion in the air.

"We shouldn't have tried this in the first place," he said. "It just tangles everything up." He patted his coat pockets, felt in his vest. "Run in and get me a couple cigars."

Bruce hesitated, his eyes on Enich. "Run!" his father said harshly.

Reluctantly he released the colt's halter rope and started for the house. At the door he looked back, and his father and Enich were talking together, so low that their words didn't carry to where he stood. He saw his father shake his head, and Enich bend to pluck a grass stem. They were both against him; they both were sure Socks would never get well. Well, he would! There was some way.

He found the cigars, came out, watched them both light up. Disappointment was a sickness in him, and mixed with the disappointment was a question. When he could stand their silence no more, he burst out with it. "But what are we going to *do*? He's got to have some place to stay."

"Look, kiddo." His father sat down on a sawhorse and took him by the arm. His face was serious and his voice gentle. "We can't take him out there. He isn't well enough to walk, and we can't haul him. So Jim here has offered to buy him. He'll give you three dollars for him, and when you come back, if you want, you might be able to buy him back. That is, if he's well. It'll be better to leave him with Jim."

"Well . . ." Bruce studied the mole on Enich's cheek. "Can you get him better by fall, Mr. Enich?"

"I wouldn't expect it," Enich said. "He ain't got much of a show."

"If anybody can get him better, Jim can," his father said. "How's that deal sound to you?"

"Maybe when I come back he'll be all off his braces and running around like a house afire," Bruce said. "Maybe next time I see him I can ride him." The mole disappeared as Enich tongued his cigar.

"Well, all right then," Bruce said, bothered by their stony-eyed silence. "But I sure hate to leave you behind, Socks, old boy."

"It's the best way all around," his father said. He talked fast, as if he were in a hurry. "Can you take him along now?"

"Oh, gee!" Bruce said. "Today?"

"Come on," his father said. "Let's get it over with."

Bruce stood by while they trussed the colt and hoisted him into the wagon box, and when Jim climbed in he cried out, "Hey, we forgot to put his hobbles back on." Jim and his father looked at each other. His father shrugged. "All right," he said, and started putting the braces back on the trussed front legs. "He might hurt himself if they weren't on," Bruce said. He leaned over the endgate, stroking the white-blazed face, and as the wagon pulled away he stood with tears in his eyes and the three dollars in his hand, watching the terrified straining of the colt's neck, the bony head raised above the endgate and one white eye rolling.

Five days later, in the sunslanting, dew-wet spring morning, they stood for the last time that summer on the front porch, the loaded wagon against the front fence. The father tossed the key in his hand and kicked the doorjamb. "Well, good-bye, Old Paint," he said. "See you in the fall."

As they went to the wagon Bruce sang loudly,

Good-bye, Old Paint, I'm leavin' Cheyenne,
I'm leavin' Cheyenne, I'm goin' to Montana,
Good-bye, Old Paint, I'm leavin' Cheyenne.

"Turn it off," his father said. "You want to wake up the whole town?" He boosted Bruce into the back end, where he squirmed and wiggled his way neck-deep into the luggage. His mother, turning to see how he was settled, laughed at him. "You look like a baby owl in a nest," she said.

His father turned and winked at him. "Open your mouth and I'll drop in a mouse."

It was good to be leaving; the thought of the homestead was exciting. If he could have taken Socks along it would have been perfect, but he had to admit, looking around at the jammed wagon box, that there sure wasn't any room for him. He continued to sing softly as they rocked out into the road and turned east toward MacKenna's house, where they were leaving the keys.

At the low, slough-like spot that had become the town's dump ground the road split, leaving the dump like an island in the middle. The boy sniffed at the old familiar smells of rust and tar paper and ashes and refuse. He had collected a lot of old iron and tea lead and bottles and broken machinery and clocks, and once a perfectly good amber-headed cane, in that old dump ground. His father turned up the right fork, and as they passed the central part of the dump the wind, coming in from the northeast, brought a rotten, unbearable stench across them.

"Pee-you!" his mother said, and held her nose. Bruce echoed her. "Pee-you! Pee-you-willy!" He clamped his nose shut and pretended to fall dead.

"Guess I better get to windward of that coming back," said his father.

They woke MacKenna up and left the key and started back. The things they passed were very sharp and clear to the boy. He was seeing them for the last time all summer. He noticed things he had never noticed so clearly before: how the hills came down into the river from the north like three folds in a blanket, how the stovepipe on the Chinaman's shack east of town had a little conical hat on it. He chanted at the things he saw.

"Good-bye, old Chinaman. Good-bye, old Frenchman River. Good-bye, old dump ground, good-bye."

"Hold your noses," his father said. He eased the wagon into the other fork around the dump. "Somebody sure dumped something rotten."

He stared ahead, bending a little, and Bruce heard him swear. He slapped the reins on the team till they trotted. "What?" the mother said. Bruce, half rising to see what caused the speed, saw her lips go flat over her teeth, and a look on her face like the woman he had seen in the traveling dentist's chair, when the dentist dug a living nerve out of her tooth and then got down on his knees to hunt for it, and she sat there half raised in her seat, her face lifted.

"For gosh sakes," he said. And then he saw.

He screamed at them. "Ma, it's Socks! Stop, Pa! It's Socks!"

His father drove grimly ahead, not turning, not speaking, and his mother shook her head without looking around. He screamed again, but neither of them turned. And when he dug down into the load, burrowing in and shaking with long smothered sobs, they still said nothing.

So they left town, and as they wound up the dugway to the south bench there was not a word among them except his father's low, "I thought he was going to take it out of town." None of them looked back at the view they had always admired, the flat river bottom green with spring, its village snuggled in the loops of river. Bruce's eyes, pressed against the coats and blankets under him until his sight was a red haze, could still see through it the bloated, skinned body of the colt, the chestnut hair left a little way above the hooves, the iron braces still on the broken front legs. ✳

Discussion

1. (**a**) To what extent are Bruce's parents and outside factors responsible for the colt's condition? (**b**) Why does Bruce feel he is to blame? (**c**) How does this affect his attitudes and actions?

2. (**a**) How does the mother feel about keeping the colt? (**b**) What is the father's attitude toward the colt's condition? (**c**) Why does the father allow Bruce to keep the colt?

3. (**a**) Why does Bruce sell the colt to Enich? (**b**) Does the father know what Enich plans to do with the colt? Explain. (**c**) Do you think the father did the right thing? Give reasons for your answer. (**d**) Is the father responsible for Bruce's seeing the colt's carcass? Explain.

4. (**a**) Reread the handbook article on characterization (page 537). What methods of characterization does the author use in this story? (**b**) Do you think the characters seem true to life? Explain.

5. What elements of setting are important to events in this story?

6. Wallace Stegner gives the background for his story, "The Colt," in his letter in column 2 of this page. (**a**) Which events in the story actually happened? (**b**) What fictional elements did Mr. Stegner add? (**c**) Do you feel that the author improved the story by including fictional elements? Explain.

Word Study

A *synonym* is a word which has approximately the same meaning as another word. The word *small,* for example, is a synonym for *little.*

From the list of words below, choose the word which is most nearly synonymous with the italicized word in each sentence in the next column. You may refer to your Glossary if necessary.

concern	gloomy
crack	unwilling
direct	worried

1. His mother's face was *somber* as she looked at the crippled colt.

2. Bruce eagerly agreed to *superintend* the colt's care and feeding.

3. Bruce watched the colt's progress with *solicitude.*

4. Bruce fed the colt with tender shoots of grass which he plucked from a small *crevice* in the corner of the corral.

5. Bruce was *apprehensive* whenever Enich examined the colt.

6. Bruce was *reluctant* to leave the colt with Enich.

From the Author

With particular respect to "The Colt," I must admit that the events of the story, though not the matrix within which I embedded them when I included the story as part of the novel *The Big Rock Candy Mountain,* are pretty much from life. I had such a colt, I got my father to make braces for his pasterns, I spent a lot of time one spring trying to make him well. And I did find his body on the dump when I got back from the summer out on the homestead. As you will see at once, I modified the events slightly to keep the time span shorter; and in the novel, I involved this episode with some other fictional episodes that dealt with the character and actions of the boy's father. But those modifications and that "surround" of other actions didn't modify too much either the simple line of this story, or the feeling I had when it happened. It was not only a lost quest, of a sort—an urgent attempt that failed—but it was also the loss of a creature I had grown intensely fond of, and it involved a sort of betrayal, since my parents had tried to spare me by lying about what they had done with the colt. I thought he was out on a ranch down the river. So it all came on me with a big destructive shock when I found out.

Sometimes a minor incident takes on a
meaning much greater than itself.

The Secret Heart

Robert P. Tristram Coffin

Across the years he could recall
His father one way best of all.

In the stillest hour of night
The boy awakened to a light.

5 Half in dreams, he saw his sire
With his great hands full of fire.

The man had struck a match to see
If his son slept peacefully.

He held his palms each side the spark
10 His love had kindled in the dark.

His two hands were curved apart
In the semblance of a heart.

He wore, it seemed to his small son,
A bare heart on his hidden one,

15 A heart that gave out such a glow
No son awake could bear to know.

It showed a look upon a face
Too tender for the day to trace.

One instant, it lit all about,
20 And then the secret heart went out.

But it shone long enough for one
To know that hands held up the sun.

Discussion

1. (a) What do the father's hands look like to the boy? **(b)** What does this shape represent?
2. (a) What does the father's night visit mean to the son? **(b)** Why do you think this incident made such a lasting impression on the boy?

The Author

Robert P. Tristram Coffin (1892–1955) once said that he was "a New Englander by birth, by bringing up, by spirit"; and much of his writing reflects his love for New England and its people. Coffin was born in Brunswick, Maine, and grew up on a "saltwater farm." Following his graduation from Bowdoin College, he went to England where he studied at Oxford. Later he taught English at several American colleges in addition to pursuing his career as a writer. Though he is most famous as a poet, Coffin is the author of an autobiography, essays, novels, historical reports, and literary criticism. His volume of poetry *Strange Holiness* was awarded the Pulitzer Prize in 1936.

Unit 2 Review

1. In this unit you have explored different relationships between generations. You have seen that in some cases, the relationship is one of understanding, while in other cases it is one of misunderstanding and distrust. In some selections, the relationship between generations undergoes a change.

Divide a sheet of paper into four columns. Across the top of your paper, write the following headings: **Selection, Understanding, Misunderstanding,** and **Change.** In column one, list the titles of the selections in this unit. Opposite each selection, place a check mark to indicate whether the selection reveals understanding or misunderstanding between generations and whether the selection shows a change in the relationship. Be prepared to explain why you think the relationship is one of understanding or misunderstanding. For each selection checked in column 4, be prepared to explain what the change is and what has caused it.

2. Choose the one selection which you think best displays what a relationship between generations ought to be and explain your choice.

3. Reviewing the unit as a whole, what inferences can you make about relationships between generations? What conclusions can you draw to help you understand people who are older than you are?

4. Which of the fictional characters in this unit seems most real to you? How do the narrative point of view and the methods of characterization which the author has used make this character seem real?

SUGGESTED READING

ALLEN, MERRITT P., *Johnny Reb.* (McKay) Because of his devotion to a man who has befriended him, a South Carolina boy grows from a raw recruit to a stanch Civil War cavalryman.

BELL, MARGARET, *Watch for a Tall White Sail.* (Morrow *Grosset) Alaska in 1887 provides the background for this story of sixteen-year-old Florence Monroe, who experiences hardship and tragedy but finally finds happiness in the tall white sail. *Ride Out the Storm* (Morrow) is the story of Lisbeth Craig's uprooting from her home in Alaska, and her embarkation on a new and frightening life in boarding school.

BENARY-ISBERT, MARGOT, *The Long Way Home.* (Harcourt) Following World War II, Cristoph, a thirteen-year-old orphan, is brought by a G.I. from Germany to America. This book tells about the friendship and understanding they share.

CAUDILL, REBECCA, *Tree of Freedom.* (Viking) Opportunities to serve their country in the Revolution come to Stephanie and her brother, both of whom disagree with Pappy's wartime views.

CLEARY, BEVERLY, *Fifteen.* (Morrow) This story focuses on the joys and worries common to a fifteen-year-old. Warmth and humor make Jane Purdy's experiences thoroughly enjoyable reading.

CRONIN, A. J., *The Green Years.* (Little) Robert Shannon is orphaned at seven and taken to live with his grandparents. With the help of an eccentric great-grandfather he overcomes difficulties and finds himself on his way to becoming a doctor.

DE TREVIÑO, ELIZABETH BORTON, *I, Juan de Parejo.* (Farrar) During the seventeenth century in the Spanish court, the painter Velázquez inherits Juan, a Negro slave, who becomes his master's friend.

ELLSBERG, EDWARD, *"I have just begun to fight!"* (Dodd) The exciting career of John Paul Jones, naval hero, is told through the adventures of Tom Folger, a boy who shares the adventures of Jones' life.

FITZHUGH, LOUISE, *Harriet, the Spy*. (Harper) Harriet, a sixth-grader determined to grow up to be a writer, records her observations in a comical, caustic way. Only Ole Golly, her nursemaid, really understands her.

FORBES, ESTHER, *Johnny Tremain*. (Houghton *Riverside) Colonial Boston in pre-Revolutionary War days provides the background for this exciting story of a young apprentice who gains insight and courage from the silversmith, Paul Revere.

GALLICO, PAUL, *The Snow Goose*. (Knopf) This beautifully written tale concerns a lonely, hunchbacked painter, a little girl, and a wild goose driven by a storm to the coast of England during World War II.

GUNTHER, JOHN, *Death Be Not Proud*. (Harper *Pyramid) The inspiring courage of young Johnny Gunther sees him through the last fifteen months of life. His story is simply told by his father.

KIPLING, RUDYARD, *Captains Courageous*. (Doubleday *Dell) The pampered son of a millionaire is saved from drowning by the crew of a New England fishing boat and forced to share the labor on board.

MOODY, RALPH, *Little Britches*. (Norton) In a fine father-son tale of ranch life about fifty years ago, Ralph Moody tells how he helped to establish the family on a barren Colorado homestead.

O'HARA, MARY, *My Friend Flicka*. (Lippincott) Ken receives a colt from his father, but only after intervention by a mother who understands her son's adolescent behavior.

PERSON, TOM, *The Land and the Water*. (Farrar) Two sons of a displaced Latvian family help their father escape exploitation in the Mississippi Delta region. The story shows the awareness of the younger generation to opportunities in a new culture.

RAWLINGS, MARJORIE K., *The Yearling*. (**Scribner) A pet deer and the problems he brings force Jody to sacrifice what he loves best.

SAROYAN, WILLIAM, *The Human Comedy*. (Harcourt) In this warm tale of a boy growing up, Saroyan combines humor, tragedy, and love.

STOLZ, MARY, *Ready or Not*. (**Harper) Sixteen-year-old Morgan Conner must deal with everyday matters and difficult circumstances when she takes over the household following the death of her mother.

STUART, JESSE, *God's Oddling, The Story of Mick Stuart, My Father*. (McGraw) Jesse Stuart writes of his father, who could neither read nor write anything but his own name, but who was a man to be respected and loved.

TARKINGTON, BOOTH, *Penrod, His Complete Story*. (Doubleday) This book deals with the matchless Penrod and his companions, who stir up fun for themselves and trouble for their enemies and elders.

THURBER, JAMES, *My Life and Hard Times*. (Harper *Bantam) Here is a collection of amusing incidents, illustrated with Thurber's satirical drawings. Included are "The Night the Bed Fell," "The Night the Ghost Got In," "The Dog That Bit People," and others.

WOJIECHOWSKA, MAIA, *Shadow of a Bull*. (Atheneum) Manolo's father, the great bullfighter, is dead, and everyone awaits the boy's coming of age—everyone except Manolo, who fears his first fight.

*paperback
**hardcover and paperback

3

What are the individual's
responsibilities
    to himself,
    to society,
    to future generations?
What causes an individual
    to steal,
    to kill,
    to dedicate his life to an ideal?
Every man must make
    choices,
    decisions,
    judgments.
What he thinks, feels, does, reveal his

Values

PETER BLUME, "THE ROCK," THE ART INSTITUTE OF CHICAGO

See
THEME
Handbook
of Literary
Terms
page 566

For centuries before the flight of the
Wright brothers, man had dreamed of being
able to fly. What meaning for twentieth-
century man may be found in this story of
a flying machine in ancient China?

The Flying Machine

Ray Bradbury

IN THE YEAR A.D. 400, the Emperor
Yuan held his throne by the Great
Wall of China, and the land was green
with rain, readying itself toward the
harvest, at peace, the people in his
dominion neither too happy nor too
sad.

Early on the morning of the first
day of the first week of the second
month of the new year, the Emperor
Yuan was sipping tea and fanning
himself against a warm breeze when a
servant ran across the scarlet and
blue garden tiles, calling, "Oh, Emperor, Emperor, a miracle!"

"Yes," said the Emperor, "the air
is sweet this morning."

"No, no, a miracle!" said the servant, bowing quickly.

"And this tea is good in my mouth,
surely that is a miracle."

"No, no, Your Excellency."

"Let me guess then—the sun has
risen and a new day is upon us. Or the
sea is blue. That now is the finest of
all miracles."

"Excellency, a man is flying!"

"What?" The Emperor stopped
his fan.

"I saw him in the air, a man flying
with wings. I heard a voice call out of
the sky, and when I looked up, there
he was, a dragon in the heavens with
a man in its mouth, a dragon of paper
and bamboo, colored like the sun and
the grass."

"It is early," said the Emperor,
"and you have just wakened from
a dream."

"It is early, but I have seen what
I have seen! Come, and you will see
it too."

"Sit down with me here," said the
Emperor. "Drink some tea. It must be
a strange thing, if it is true, to see a

man fly. You must have time to think of it, even as I must have time to prepare myself for the sight."

They drank tea.

"Please," said the servant at last, "or he will be gone."

The Emperor rose thoughtfully. "Now you may show me what you have seen."

They walked into a garden, across a meadow of grass, over a small bridge, through a grove of trees, and up a tiny hill.

"There!" said the servant.

The Emperor looked into the sky.

And in the sky, laughing so high that you could hardly hear him laugh, was a man; and the man was clothed in bright papers and reeds to make wings and a beautiful yellow tail, and he was soaring all about like the largest bird in a universe of birds, like a new dragon in a land of ancient dragons.

The man called down to them from high in the cool winds of morning, "I fly, I fly!"

The servant waved to him. "Yes, yes!"

The Emperor Yuan did not move. Instead he looked at the Great Wall of China now taking shape out of the farthest mist in the green hills, that splendid snake of stones which writhed with majesty across the entire land. That wonderful wall which had protected them for a timeless time from enemy hordes and preserved peace for years without number. He saw the town, nestled to itself by a river and a road and a hill, beginning to waken.

"Tell me," he said to his servant, "has anyone else seen this flying man?"

"I am the only one, Excellency," said the servant, smiling at the sky, waving.

The Emperor watched the heav-ens another minute and then said, "Call him down to me."

"Ho, come down, come down! The Emperor wishes to see you!" called the servant, hands cupped to his shouting mouth.

The Emperor glanced in all directions while the flying man soared down the morning wind. He saw a farmer, early in his fields, watching the sky, and he noted where the farmer stood.

The flying man alit with a rustle of paper and a creak of bamboo reeds. He came proudly to the Emperor, clumsy in his rig, at last bowing before the old man.

"What have you done?" demanded the Emperor.

"I have flown in the sky, Your Excellency," replied the man.

"What have you done?" said the Emperor again.

"I have just told you!" cried the flier.

"You have told me nothing at all." The Emperor reached out a thin hand to touch the pretty paper and the birdlike keel of the apparatus. It smelled cool, of the wind.

"Is it not beautiful, Excellency?"

"Yes, too beautiful."

"It is the only one in the world!" smiled the man. "And I am the inventor."

"The only one in the world?"

"I swear it!"

"Who else knows of this?"

"No one. Not even my wife, who would think me mad with the sun. She thought I was making a kite. I rose in the night and walked to the cliffs far away. And when the morning breezes blew and the sun rose, I gathered my courage, Excellency, and leaped from the cliff. I flew! But my wife does not know of it."

"Well for her, then," said the Emperor. "Come along."

They walked back to the great house. The sun was full in the sky now, and the smell of the grass was refreshing. The Emperor, the servant, and the flier paused within the huge garden.

The Emperor clapped his hands. "Ho, guards!"

The guards came running.

"Hold this man."

The guards seized the flier.

"Call the executioner," said the Emperor.

"What's this!" cried the flier, bewildered. "What have I done?" He began to weep, so that the beautiful paper apparatus rustled.

"Here is the man who has made a certain machine," said the Emperor, "and yet asks us what he has created. He does not know himself. It is only necessary that he create, without knowing why he has done so, or what this thing will do."

The executioner came running with a sharp silver ax. He stood with his naked, large-muscled arms ready, his face covered with a serene white mask.

"One moment," said the Emperor. He turned to a nearby table upon which sat a machine that he himself had created. The Emperor took a tiny golden key from his own neck. He fitted this key to the tiny, delicate machine and wound it up. Then he set the machine going.

The machine was a garden of metal and jewels. Set in motion, birds sang in tiny metal trees, wolves walked through miniature forests, and tiny people ran in and out of sun and shadow, fanning themselves with miniature fans, listening to the tiny emerald birds, and standing by impossibly small but tinkling fountains.

"Is it not beautiful?" said the Emperor. "If you asked me what I have done here, I could answer you well. I have made birds sing, I have made forests murmur, I have set people to walking in this woodland, enjoying the leaves and shadows and songs. That is what I have done."

"But, oh, Emperor!" pleaded the flier, on his knees, the tears pouring down his face. "I have done a similar thing! I have found beauty. I have flown on the morning wind. I have looked down on all the sleeping houses and gardens. I have smelled the sea and even seen it, beyond the hills, from my high place. And I have soared like a bird; oh, I cannot say how beautiful it is up there, in the sky, with the wind about me, the wind blowing me here like a feather, there like a fan, the way the sky smells in the morning! And how free one feels! *That* is beautiful, Emperor, that is beautiful, too!"

"Yes," said the Emperor sadly, "I know it must be true. For I felt my heart move with you in the air and I wondered: What is it like? How does it feel? How do the distant pools look from so high? And how my houses and servants? Like ants? And how the distant towns not yet awake?"

"Then spare me!"

"But there are times," said the Emperor, more sadly still, "when one must lose a little beauty if one is to keep what little beauty one already has. I do not fear you, yourself, but I fear another man."

"What man?"

"Some other man who, seeing you, will build a thing of bright papers and bamboo like this. But the other man will have an evil face and an evil heart, and the beauty will be gone. It is this man I fear."

"Why? Why?"

"Who is to say that someday just such a man, in just such an apparatus of paper and reed, might not fly in the sky and drop huge stones upon the Great Wall of China?" said the Emperor.

No one moved or said a word.

"Off with his head," said the Emperor.

The executioner whirled his silver ax.

"Burn the kite and the inventor's body and bury their ashes together," said the Emperor.

The servants retreated to obey.

The Emperor turned to his hand-servant, who had seen the man flying. "Hold your tongue. It was all a dream, a most sorrowful and beautiful dream. And that farmer in the distant field who saw, tell him it would pay him to consider it only a vision. If ever the word passes around, you and the farmer die within the hour."

"You are merciful, Emperor."

"No, not merciful," said the old man. Beyond the garden wall he saw the guards burning the beautiful machine of paper and reeds that smelled of the morning wind. He saw the dark smoke climb into the sky. "No, only very much bewildered and afraid." He saw the guards digging a tiny pit wherein to bury the ashes. "What is the life of one man against those of a million others? I must take solace from that thought."

He took the key from its chain about his neck and once more wound up the beautiful miniature garden. He stood looking out across the land at the Great Wall, the peaceful town, the green fields, the rivers and streams. He sighed. The tiny garden whirred its hidden and delicate machinery and set itself in motion; tiny people walked in forests, tiny foxes loped through sun-speckled glades in beautiful shining pelts, and among the tiny trees flew little bits of high song and bright blue and yellow color flying, flying, flying in that small sky.

"Oh," said the Emperor, closing his eyes, "look at the birds, look at the birds!" ✱

Discussion

1. Choose the phrase that best describes the setting at the opening of the story: (**a**) a troubled and war-like period; (**b**) a time of famine and poverty; (**c**) a time of peace and security.

2. What kind of man is the Emperor? Cite passages which reveal his characteristics.

3. What does the Wall of China represent to the Emperor?

4. When the Emperor asks the flyer, "What have you done?" he really means:

(**a**) "What wonders have you seen from the sky?"

(**b**) "For what purpose will your invention be used?"

(**c**) "How did you create such a marvelous invention?"

5. (**a**) What does the Emperor's invention have in common with the flyer's invention? (**b**) What, according to the Emperor, is the difference between the two inventions?

6. Why does the Emperor have the man killed?

7. Read Ray Bradbury's letter on page 171. (**a**) What conflict of values occurs in "The Flying Machine"? (**b**) Does the author believe that one set of values is superior to the other? Explain. (**c**) What other situations can you think of which have a similar conflict of values?

8. What is the theme of this story?

Ray Bradbury
Comments
On
"The Flying Machine"

      I have always been fascinated at the plight of men and their machines. Wishing to extend our senses or abilities by building mechanical eyes, ears, or brains, we often discover, ironically, we have limited ourselves in other directions, and on occasion caused our own destruction. This does not mean we should give up machines at all; it only means we must be excited by the challenge of finding ways to build better machines that by their very shape and function induce us toward the ideal of humanity. All machines are amoral, neither bad nor good. But some, by their very function, are like that lovely high electric tower all boys like to shinny up when walking in the country; they are tempted toward electrocution by a device that gives power and light.

      THE FLYING MACHINE is the result of my having come across a mention somewhere, about 15 years ago, that an actual emperor in China, back around the 12th century or perhaps somewhat earlier, had beheaded a man for inventing wings. Taking this small mention, I emotionalized my own emperor and my own version of a man who might have invented such fine wings.

      As will be noted, I did not throw my weight on either side. I wanted to fly with the man in the cool morning light and laugh with happiness above the world. But I could easily understand the emperor's fear which caused him to delay the invention of wings by a few centuries by the use of the headsman's ax. Both men are at the same time wrong and right. The flying man is too innocent, and the emperor perhaps, too knowing of the world's evil. The perfect man, one would suppose, would be a rare combination of innocence and knowledge of evil, who could build and use machines to good purpose in the world we all dream for and desire.

      THE FLYING MACHINE is a sad story because, for that moment in history, the dream was shattered and the desire buried deep. I wept for both men; the one who had to die, and the one who had to go on living with the knowledge of that death.

Ray Bradbury

Charlie Gordon had the unique opportunity of living in two worlds. In which was he happier? Had he been given a choice, which would he have chosen?

FLOWERS FOR ALGERNON

Daniel Keyes

progris riport 1—martch 5, 1965

Dr. Strauss says I shud rite down what I think and every thing that happins to me from now on. I dont know why but he says its importint so they will see if they will use me. I hope they use me. Miss Kinnian says maybe they can make me smart. I want to be smart. My name is Charlie Gordon. I am 37 years old. I have nuthing more to rite now so I will close for today.

progris riport 2—martch 6

I had a test today. I think I faled it. And I think maybe now they wont use me. What happind is a nice young man was in the room and he had some white cards and ink spilled all over them. He sed Charlie what do yo see on this card. I was very skared even tho I had my rabits foot in my pockit because when I was a kid I always faled tests in school and I spilled ink to.

I told him I saw a inkblot. He said yes and it made me feel good. I thot that was all but when I got up to go he said Charlie we are not thru yet. Then I dont remember so good but he wantid me to say what was in the ink. I dint see nuthing in the ink but he said there was picturs there other pepul saw some picturs. I couldnt see any picturs. I reely tryed. I held the card close up and then far away. Then I said if I had my glases I coud see better I usally only ware my glases in the movies or TV but I said they are in the closit in the hall. I got them. Then I said let me see that card agen I bet Ill find it now.

I tryed hard but I only saw the ink. I told him maybe I need new glases. He rote something down on a

paper and I got skared of faling the test. I told him it was a very nice ink-blot with littel points all around the edges. He looked very sad so that wasnt it. I said please let me try agen. Ill get it in a few minits becaus Im not so fast somtimes. Im a slow reeder too in Miss Kinnians class for slow adults but I'm trying very hard.

He gave me a chance with another card that had 2 kinds of ink spilled on it red and blue.

He was very nice and talked slow like Miss Kinnian does and he ex-planed it to me that it was a *raw shok.*[1] He said pepul see things in the ink. I said show me where. He said think. I told him I think a inkblot but that wasn't rite eather. He said what does it remind you—pretend something. I closed my eyes for a long time to pretend. I told him I pretend a fown-tan pen with ink leeking all over a table cloth.

I dont think I passed the *raw shok* test

progris riport 3 — martch 7

Dr Strauss and Dr Nemur say it dont matter about the inkblots. They said that maybe they will still use me. I said Miss Kinnian never gave me tests like that one only spelling and reading. They said Miss Kinnian told that I was her bestist pupil in the adult nite school becaus I tryed the hardist and I reely wantid to lern. They said how come you went to the adult nite scool all by yourself Charlie. How did you find it. I said I asked pepul and sumbody told me where I shud go to lern to read and spell good. They said why did you want to. I told them becaus all my life I wantid to be smart and not dumb. But its very hard to be smart. They said you know it will probly be tempirery. I said yes. Miss Kinnian told me. I dont care if it herts.

Later I had more crazy tests to-day. The nice lady who gave it to me told me the name and I asked her how do you spellit so I can rite it my progris riport. THEMATIC APPER-CEPTION TEST.[2] I dont know the frist 2 words but I know what *test* means. You got to pass it or you get bad marks. This test lookd easy becaus I coud see the picturs. Only this time she dint want me to tell her the pic-turs. That mixd me up. She said make up storys about the pepul in the picturs.

I told her how can you tell storys about pepul you never met. I said why shud I make up lies. I never tell lies any more becaus I always get caut.

She told me this test and the other one the raw-shok was for getting personality. I laffed so hard. I said how can you get that thing from inkblots and fotos. She got sore and put her picturs away. I don't care. It was sily. I gess I faled that test too.

Later some men in white coats took me to a difernt part of the hospitil and gave me a game to play. It was like a race with a white mouse. They called the mouse Algernon. Algernon was in a box with a lot of twists and turns like all kinds of walls and they gave me a pencil and paper with lines and lots of boxes. On one side it said START and on the other end it said FINISH. They said it was *amazed*[3] and that Algernon and me had the same *amazed* to do. I dint see how we could have the same *amazed* if Algernon had a box and I had a paper but I dint say nothing. Anyway there wasnt time because the race started.

One of the men had a watch he was trying to hide so I wouldnt see it

1. *raw shok,* Rorschach (rôr'shäk) test, a psychological test used to measure personality traits and general intel-ligence.
2. *Thematic Apperception Test,* another psychological test.
3. *amazed,* a maze, a network of paths through which one must find his way.

so I tryed not to look and that made me nervus.

Anyway that test made me feel worser than all the others because they did it over 10 times with different *amazeds* and Algernon won everytime. I dint know that mice were so smart. Maybe thats because Algernon is a white mouse. Maybe white mice are smarter than other mice.

progris riport 4 — Mar 8

Their going to use me! Im so exited I can hardly write. Dr Nemur and Dr Strauss had a argament about it first. Dr Nemur was in the office when Dr Strauss brot me in. Dr Nemur was worryed about using me but Dr Strauss told him Miss Kinnian rekemmended me the best from all the people who she was teaching. I like Miss Kinnian becaus shes a very smart teacher. And she said Charlie your going to have a second chance. If you volenteer for this experament you mite get smart. They dont know if it will be perminint but theirs a chance. Thats why I said ok even when I was scared because she said it was an operashun. She said dont be scared Charlie you done so much with so little I think you deserv it most of all.

So I got scaird when Dr. Nemur and Dr. Strauss argud about it. Dr. Strauss said I had something that was very good. He said I had a good *motor-vation*. I never even knew I had that. I felt proud when he said that not every body with an eye-q of 68[4] had that thing. I dont know what it is or where I got it but he said Algernon had it too. Algernons *motor-vation* is the cheese they put in his box. But it cant be that because I didn't eat any cheese this week.

Then he told Dr Nemur something I dint understand so while they were talking I wrote down some of the words.

He said Dr. Nemur I know Charlie is not what you had in mind as the first of your new brede of intelek** (coudnt get the word) superman. But most people of his low ment** are host** and uncoop** they are usually dull apath** and hard to reach. He has a good natcher hes intristed and eager to please.

Dr Nemur said remember he will be the first human beeng ever to have his intellijence tripled by surgicle meens.

Dr. Strauss said exakly. Look at how well hes lerned to read and write for his low mentel age its as grate an acheve** as you and I lerning einstines therey of **vity without help. That shows the inteness motor-vation. Its comparat** a tremen** achev** I say we use Charlie.

I dint get all the words but it sounded like Dr Strauss was on my side and like the other one wasnt.

Then Dr Nemur nodded he said all right maybe your right. We will use Charlie. When he said that I got so exited I jumped up and shook his hand for being so good to me. I told him thank you doc you wont be sorry for giving me a second chance. And I mean it like I told him. After the operashun Im gonna try to be smart. Im gonna try awful hard.

progris riport 5 — Mar 10

Im skared. Lots of the nurses and the people who gave me the tests came to bring me candy and wish me luck. I hope I have luck. I got my rabits foot and my lucky penny. Only a black cat crossed me when I was comming to the hospitil. Dr Strauss says dont be supersitis Charlie this is science. Anyway Im keeping my rabits foot with me.

I asked Dr Strauss if Ill beat Algernon in the race after the oper-

---

4. *eye-q of 68.* An average I.Q. is 100.

ashun and he said maybe. If the operashun works Ill show that mouse I can be as smart as he is. Maybe smarter. Then Ill be abel to read better and spell the words good and know lots of things and be like other people. I want to be smart like other people. If it works perminint they will make everybody smart all over the wurld.

They dint give me anything to eat this morning. I dont know what that eating has to do with getting smart. Im very hungry and Dr. Nemur took away my box of candy. That Dr Nemur is a grouch. Dr Strauss says I can have it back after the operashun. You cant eat befor a operashun. . .

progress report 6 — Mar 15
The operashun dint hurt. He did it while I was sleeping. They took off the bandijis from my head today so I can make a PROGRESS REPORT. Dr. Nemur who looked at some of my other ones says I spell PROGRESS wrong and told me how to spell it and REPORT too. I got to try and remember that.

I have a very bad memary for spelling. Dr. Strauss says its ok to tell about all the things that happin to me but he says I should tell more about what I feel and what I think. When I told him I dont know how to think he said try. All the time when the bandijis were on my eyes I tryed to think. Nothing happened. I dont know what to think about. Maybe if I ask him he will tell me how I can think now that Im suppose to get smart. What do smart people think about. Fancy things I suppose. I wish I knew some fancy things alredy.

progress report 7 — mar 19
Nothing is happining. I had lots of tests and different kinds of races with Algernon. I hate that mouse. He always beats me. Dr. Strauss said I got to play those games. And he said some time I got to take those tests over again. Those inkblots are stupid. And those pictures are stupid too. I like to draw a picture of a man and a woman but I wont make up lies about people.

I got a headache from trying to think so much. I thot Dr Strauss was my frend but he dont help me. He dont tell me what to think or when Ill get smart. Miss Kinnian dint come to see me. I think writing these progress reports are stupid too.

progress report 8 — Mar 23
Im going back to work at the factory. They said it was better I shud go back to work but I cant tell anyone what the operashun was for and I have to come to the hospitil for an hour evry night after work. They are gonna pay me mony every month for learning to be smart.

Im glad Im going back to work because I miss my job and all my frends and all the fun we have there.

Dr Strauss says I shud keep writing things down but I dont have to do it every day just when I think of something or something speshul happins. He says dont get discoridged because it takes time and it happins slow. He says it took a long time with Algernon before he got 3 times smarter than he was before. Thats why Algernon beats me all the time because he had that operashun too. That makes me feel better. I coud probly do that *amazed* faster than a reglar mouse. Maybe some day Ill beat him. That would be something. So far Algernon looks smart perminent.

Mar 25 (I dont have to write PROGRESS REPORT on top any more just when I hand it in once a week for Dr Nemur. I just have to put the date on. That saves time)
We had a lot of fun at the factery

today. Joe Carp said hey look where Charlie had his operashun what did they do Charlie put some brains in. I was going to tell him but I remembered Dr Strauss said no. Then Frank Reilly said what did you do Charlie forget your key and open your door the hard way. That made me laff. Their really my friends and they like me.

Sometimes somebody will say hey look at Joe or Frank or George he really pulled a Charlie Gordon. I dont know why they say that but they always laff. This morning Amos Borg who is the 4 man at Donnegans used my name when he shouted at Ernie the office boy. Ernie lost a packige. He said Ernie what are you trying to be a Charlie Gordon. I dont understand why he said that.

Mar 28. Dr. Strauss came to my room tonight to see why I dint come in like I was suppose to. I told him I dont like to race with Algernon any more. He said I dont have to for a while but I shud come in. He had a present for me. I thot it was a little television but it wasnt. He said I got to turn it on when I go to sleep. I said your kidding why shud I turn it on when Im going to sleep. Who ever herd of a thing like that. But he said if I want to get smart I got to do what he says. I told him I dint think I was going to get smart and he puts his hand on my sholder and said Charlie you dont know it yet but your getting smarter all the time. You wont notice for a while. I think he was just being nice to make me feel good because I dont look any smarter.

Oh yes I almost forgot. I asked him when I can go back to the class at Miss Kinnians school. He said I wont go their. He said that soon Miss Kinnian will come to the hospitil to start and teach me speshul.

Mar 29 That crazy TV kept up all night. How can I sleep with something yelling crazy things all night in my ears. And the nutty pictures. Wow. I don't know what it says when Im up so how am I going to know when Im sleeping.

Dr Strauss says its ok. He says my brains are lerning when I sleep and that will help me when Miss Kinnian starts my lessons in the hospitl (only I found out it isn't a hospitil its a labatory.) I think its all crazy. If you can get smart when your sleeping why do people go to school. That thing I don't think will work. I use to watch the late show and the late late show on TV all the time and it never made me smart. Maybe you have to sleep while you watch it.

progress report 9 – April 3
Dr Strauss showed me how to keep the TV turned low so now I can sleep. I don't hear a thing. And I still dont understand what it says. A few times I play it over in the morning to find out what I lerned when I was sleeping and I don't think so. Miss Kinnian says Maybe its another langwidge. But most times it sounds american. It talks faster than even Miss Gold who was my teacher in 6 grade.

I told Dr. Strauss what good is it to get smart in my sleep. I want to be smart when Im awake. He says its the same thing and I have two minds. Theres the *subconscious* and the *conscious* (thats how you spell it). And one dont tell the other one what its doing. They dont even talk to each other. Thats why I dream. And boy have I been having crazy dreams. Wow. Ever since that night TV. The late late late show. I forgot to ask him if it was only me or if everybody had those two minds.

(I just looked up the word in the dictionary Dr Strauss gave me. The word is *subconscious. adj. Of the nature of mental operations not yet present in consciousness; as, subconscious conflict of desires.)* There's more but I still dont know what it means. This isnt a very good dictionary for dumb people like me.

Anyway the headache is from the party. My friends from the factery Joe Carp and Frank Reilly invited me to go to Muggsys Saloon for some drinks. I don't like to drink but they said we will have lots of fun. I had a good time.

Joe Carp said I shoud show the girls how I mop out the toilet in the factory and he got me a mop. I showed them and everyone laffed when I told that Mr. Donnegan said I was the best janiter he ever had because I like my job and do it good and never miss a day except for my operashun.

I said Miss Kinnian always said Charlie be proud of your job because you do it good.

Everybody laffed and we had a good time and they gave me lots of drinks and Joe said Charlie is a card when hes potted. I dont know what that means but everybody likes me and we have fun. I cant wait to be smart like my best friends Joe Carp and Frank Reilly.

I dont remember how the party was over but I think I went out to buy a newspaper and coffe for Joe and Frank and when I came back there was no one their. I looked for them all over till late. Then I dont remember so good but I think I got sleepy or sick. A nice cop brot me back home Thats what my landlady Mrs Flynn says.

But I got a headache and a big lump on my head. I think maybe I fell but Joe Carp says it was the cop they beat up drunks some times. I don't think so. Miss Kinnian says cops are to help people. Anyway I got a bad headache and Im sick and hurt all over. I dont think Ill drink anymore.

April 6 I beat Algernon! I dint even know I beat him until Burt the tester told me. Then the second time I lost because I got so exited I fell off the chair before I finished. But after that I beat him 8 more times. I must be getting smart to beat a smart mouse like Algernon. But I don't *feel* smarter.

I wanted to race Algernon some more but Burt said thats enough for one day. They let me hold him for a minit. Hes not so bad. Hes soft like a ball of cotton. He blinks and when he opens his eyes their black and pink on the eges.

I said can I feed him because I felt bad to beat him and I wanted to be nice and make friends. Burt said no Algernon is a very specshul mouse with an operashun like mine, and he was the first of all the animals to stay smart so long. He told me Algernon is so smart that every day he has to solve a test to get his food. Its a thing like a lock on a door that changes every time Algernon goes in to eat so he has to lern something new to get his food. That made me sad because if he couldn't lern he woud be hungry.

I don't think its right to make you pass a test to eat. How would Dr Nemur like it to have to pass a test every time he wants to eat. I think Ill be friends with Algernon.

April 9 Tonight after work Miss Kinnian was at the laboratory. She looked like she was glad to see me but scared. I told her dont worry Miss Kinnian Im not smart yet and she laffed. She said I have confidence in you Charlie the way you struggled so hard to read and right better than all the others. At werst you will have it for a littel wile and your doing somthing for science.

We are reading a very hard book.

Its called *Robinson Crusoe* about a man who gets merooned on a dessert Iland. Hes smart and figers out all kinds of things so he can have a house and food and hes a good swimmer. Only I feel sorry because hes all alone and has no frends. But I think their must be somebody else on the iland because theres a picture with his funny umbrella looking at footprints. I hope he gets a frend and not be lonly.

April 10 Miss Kinnian teaches me to spell better. She says look at a word and close your eyes and say it over and over until you remember. I have lots of truble with *through* that you say *threw* and *enough* and *tough* that you dont say *enew* and *tew*. You got to say *enuff* and *tuff*. Thats how I use to write it before I started to get smart. Im confused but Miss Kinnian says theres no reason in spelling.

Apr 14 Finished *Robinson Crusoe*. I want to find out more about what happens to him but Miss Kinnian says thats all there is. *Why.*

Apr 15 Miss Kinnian says Im lerning fast. She read some of the Progress Reports and she looked at me kind of funny. She says Im a fine person and Ill show them all. I asked her why. She said never mind but I shouldnt feel bad if I find out everybody isnt nice like I think. She said for a person who god gave so little to you done more then a lot of people with brains they never even used. I said all my friends are smart people but there good. They like me and they never did anything that wasnt nice. Then she got something in her eye and she had to run out to the ladys room.

Apr 16 Today, I lerned, the *comma,* this is a comma (,) a period, with a tail,

Miss Kinnian, says its important, because, it makes writing, better, she said, somebody, coud lose, a lot of money, if a comma, isnt, in the, right place, I dont have, any money, and I dont see, how a comma, keeps you, from losing it,

Apr 17 I used the comma wrong. Its punctuation. Miss Kinnian told me to look up long words in the dictionary to lern to spell them. I said whats the difference if you can read it anyway. She said its part of your education so now on Ill look up all the words Im not sure how to spell. It takes a long time to write that way but I only have to look up once and after that I get it right.

You got to mix them up, she showed? me" how. to mix! them (and now; I can! mix up all kinds" of punctuation, in! my writing? There, are lots! of rules? to lern; but Im gettin'g them in my head.

One thing I like about, Dear Miss Kinnian: (thats the way it goes in a business letter if I ever go into business) is she, always gives me' a reason" when—I ask. She's a gen'ius! I wish I cou'd be smart" like, her; (Puncuation, is; fun!)

April 18 What a dope I am! I didn't even understand what she was talking about. I read the grammar book last night and it explanes the whole thing. Then I saw it was the same way as Miss Kinnian was trying to tell me, but I didn't get it.

Miss Kinnian said that the TV working in my sleep helped out. She and I reached a plateau. Thats a flat hill.

After I figured out how punctuation worked, I read over all my old Progress Reports from the beginning. Boy, did I have crazy spelling and punctuation! I told Miss Kinnian I ought to go over the pages and fix all the mistakes but she said, "No, Charlie, Dr. Nemur wants them just as they are. That's why he let you keep them after they were photostated, to see your own progress. You're coming along fast, Charlie."

That made me feel good. After the lesson I went down and played with Algernon. We don't race any more.

April 20 I feel sick inside. Not sick like for a doctor, but inside my chest it feels empty like getting punched and a heartburn at the same time. I wasn't going to write about it, but I guess I got to, because its important. Today was the first time I ever stayed home from work.

Last night Joe Carp and Frank Reilly invited me to a party. There were lots of girls and some men from the factory. I remembered how sick I got last time I drank too much, so I told Joe I didn't want anything to drink. He gave me a plain coke instead.

We had a lot of fun for a while. Joe said I should dance with Ellen and she would teach me the steps. I fell a few times and I couldn't understand why because no one else was dancing besides Ellen and me. And all the time I was tripping because somebody's foot was always sticking out.

Then when I got up I saw the look on Joe's face and it gave me a funny feeling in my stomach. "He's a scream," one of the girls said. Everybody was laughing.

"Look at him. He's blushing. Charlie is blushing."

"Hey, Ellen, what'd you do to Charlie? I never saw him act like that before."

I didn't know what to do or where to turn. Everyone was looking at me and laughing and I felt naked. I wanted to hide. I ran outside and I threw up. Then I walked home. It's a funny thing I never knew that Joe and Frank and the others liked to have me around all the time to make fun of me.

Now I know what it means when they say "to pull a Charlie Gordon."

I'm ashamed.

progress report 11

April 21 Still didn't go into the factory. I told Mrs. Flynn my landlady to call and tell Mr. Donnegan I was sick. Mrs. Flynn looks at me very funny lately like she's scared.

I think it's a good thing about finding out how everybody laughs at me. I thought about it a lot. It's because I'm so dumb and I don't even know when I'm doing something dumb. People think it's funny when a dumb person can't do things the same way they can.

Anyway, now I know I'm getting smarter every day. I know punctuation and I can spell good. I like to look up all the hard words in the dictionary and I remember them. I'm reading a lot now, and Miss Kinnian says I read very fast. Sometimes I even understand what I'm reading about, and it stays in my mind. There are times when I can close my eyes and think of a page and it all comes back like a picture.

Besides history, geography and arithmetic, Miss Kinnian said I should start to learn foreign languages. Dr. Strauss gave me some more tapes to play while I sleep. I still don't understand how that conscious and unconscious mind works, but Dr. Strauss says not to worry yet. He asked me to promise that when I start learning college subjects next week I wouldn't read any books on psychology— that is, until he gives me permission.

I feel a lot better today, but I guess I'm still a little angry that all the time people were laughing and making fun of me because I wasn't so smart. When I become intelligent like Dr. Strauss says, with three times my I.Q. of 68, then maybe I'll be like everyone else and people will like me.

I'm not sure what an I.Q. is. Dr. Nemur said it was something that measured how intelligent you were—like a scale in the drugstore weighs pounds. But Dr. Strauss had a big argument with him and said an I.Q. didn't weigh intelligence at all. He said an I.Q. showed how much intelligence you could get, like the numbers on the outside of a measuring cup. You still had to fill the cup up with stuff.

Then when I asked Burt, who gives me my intelligence tests and works with Algernon, he said that both of them were wrong (only I had to promise not to tell them he said so). Burt says that the I.Q. measures a lot of different things including some of the things you learned already, and it really isn't any good at all.

So I still don't know what I.Q. is except that mine is going to be over 200 soon. I didn't want to say anything, but I don't see how if they don't know *what* it is, or *where* it is—I don't see how they know *how much* of it you've got.

Dr. Nemur says I have to take a *Rorschach Test* tomorrow. I wonder what *that* is.

April 22 I found out what a Rorschach is. It's the test I took before the operation—the one with the inkblots on the pieces of cardboard.

I was scared to death of those inkblots. I knew the man was going to ask me to find the pictures and I knew I couldn't. I was thinking to myself, if only there was some way of knowing what kind of pictures were hidden there. Maybe there weren't any pictures at all. Maybe it was just a trick to see if I was dumb enough to look for something that wasn't there. Just thinking about that made me sore at him.

"All right, Charlie," he said, "you've seen these cards before, remember?"

"Of course I remember."

The way I said it, he knew I was angry, and he looked surprised. "Yes, of course. Now I want you to look at this. What might this be? What do you see on this card? People see all sorts of things in these inkblots. Tell me what it might be for you—what it makes you think of."

I was shocked. That wasn't what I had expected him to say. "You mean there are no pictures hidden in those inkblots?"

He frowned and took off his glasses. "What?"

"Pictures. Hidden in the inkblots. Last time you told me everyone could see them and you wanted me to find them too."

He explained to me that the last time he had used almost the exact same words he was using now. I didn't believe it, and I still have the suspicion that he misled me at the time just for the fun of it. Unless—I don't know any more—could I have been *that* feeble-minded?

We went through the cards slowly. One looked like a pair of bats tugging at something. Another one looked like two men fencing with swords. I imagined all sorts of things. I guess I got carried away. But I didn't trust him any more, and I kept turning them around, even looking on the back to see if there was anything there I was supposed to catch. While he was making his notes, I peeked out of the corner of my eye to read it. But it was all in code that looked like this:

WF+A DdF−Ad orig. WF−A
SF+obj

The test still doesn't make sense to me. It seems to me that anyone could make up lies about things that they didn't really imagine? Maybe I'll understand it when Dr. Strauss lets me read up on psychology.

April 25 I figured out a new way to line up the machines in the factory, and Mr. Donnegan says it will save him ten thousand dollars a year in labor and increased production. He gave me a $25 bonus.

I wanted to take Joe Carp and Frank Reilly out to lunch to celebrate, but Joe said he had to buy some things for his wife, and Frank said he was meeting his cousin for lunch. I guess it'll take a little time for them to get used to the changes in me. Everybody seems to be frightened of me. When I went over to Amos Borg and tapped him, he jumped up in the air.

People don't talk to me much any more or kid around the way they used to. It makes the job kind of lonely.

April 27 I got up the nerve today to ask Miss Kinnian to have dinner with me tomorrow night to celebrate my bonus.

At first she wasn't sure it was right, but I asked Dr. Strauss and he said it was okay. Dr. Strauss and Dr. Nemur don't seem to be getting along so well. They're arguing all the time. This evening I heard them shouting. Dr. Nemur was saying that it was *his* experiment and *his* research, and Dr. Strauss shouted back that he contributed just as much, because he found me through Miss Kinnian and he performed the operation. Dr. Strauss said that someday thousands of neurosurgeons might be using his technique all over the world.

Dr. Nemur wanted to publish the results of the experiment at the end of this month. Dr. Strauss wanted to wait a while to be sure. Dr. Strauss said Dr. Nemur was more interested in the Chair of Psychology at Princeton[5] than he was in the experiment. Dr. Nemur said Dr. Strauss was nothing but an opportunist trying to ride to glory on *his* coattails.

When I left afterwards, I found myself trembling. I don't know why for sure, but it was as if I'd seen both men clearly for the first time. I remember hearing Burt say Dr. Nemur had a shrew of a wife who was pushing him all the time to get things published so he could become famous. Burt said that the dream of her life was to have a big-shot husband.

April 28 I don't understand why I never noticed how beautiful Miss Kinnian really is. She has brown eyes and feathery brown hair that comes to the top of her neck. She's only thirty-four! I think from the beginning I had the feeling that she was an unreachable genius—and very, very old. Now, every time I see her she grows younger and more lovely.

We had dinner and a long talk. When she said I was coming along so fast I'd be leaving her behind, I laughed.

"It's true, Charlie. You're already a better reader than I am. You can read a whole page at a glance while I can take in only a few lines at a time. And you remember every single thing you read. I'm lucky if I can recall the main thoughts and the general meaning."

"I don't feel intelligent. There are so many things I don't understand."

She took out a cigarette and I lit it for her. "You've got to be a *little* patient. You're accomplishing in days and weeks what it takes normal people to do in a lifetime. That's what makes

---

5. *Chair of Psychology at Princeton,* an appointment as professor of psychology at Princeton University.

it so amazing. You're like a giant sponge now, soaking things in. Facts, figures, general knowledge. And soon you'll begin to connect them, too. You'll see how different branches of learning are related. There are many levels, Charlie, like steps on a giant ladder that take you up higher and higher to see more and more of the world around you.

"I can see only a little bit of that, Charlie, and I won't go much higher than I am now, but you'll keep climbing up and up, and see more and more, and each step will open new worlds that you never even knew existed." She frowned. "I hope . . . I just hope to God——"

"What?"

"Never mind, Charles. I just hope I wasn't wrong to advise you to go into this in the first place."

I laughed. "How could that be? It worked, didn't it? Even Algernon is still smart."

We sat there silently for a while and I knew what she was thinking about as she watched me toying with the chain of my rabbit's foot and my keys. I didn't want to think of that possibility any more than elderly people want to think of death. I *knew* that this was only the beginning. I knew what she meant about levels because I'd seen some of them already. The thought of leaving her behind made me sad.

I'm in love with Miss Kinnian.

progress report 12

April 30 I've quit my job with Donnegan's Plastic Box Company. Mr. Donnegan insisted it would be better for all concerned if I left. What did I do to make them hate me so?

The first I knew of it was when Mr. Donnegan showed me the petition. Eight hundred names, everyone in the factory, except Fanny Girden.

Scanning the list quickly, I saw at once that hers was the only missing name. All the rest demanded that I be fired.

Joe Carp and Frank Reilly wouldn't talk to me about it. No one else would either, except Fanny. She was one of the few people I'd known who set her mind to something and believed it no matter what the rest of the world proved, said or did—and Fanny did not believe that I should have been fired. She had been against the petition on principle and despite the pressure and threats she'd held out.

"Which don't mean to say," she remarked, "that I don't think there's something mighty strange about you, Charlie. Them changes. I don't know. You used to be a good, dependable, ordinary man—not too bright maybe, but honest. Who knows what you done to yourself to get so smart all of a sudden. Like everybody around here's been saying, Charlie, it's not right."

"But how can you say that, Fanny? What's wrong with a man becoming intelligent and wanting to acquire knowledge and understanding of the world around him?"

She stared down at her work and I turned to leave. Without looking at me, she said: "It was evil when Eve listened to the snake and ate from the tree of knowledge. It was evil when she saw that she was naked. If not for that none of us would ever have to grow old and sick, and die."[6]

Once again, now, I have the feeling of shame burning inside me. This intelligence has driven a wedge between me and all the people I once knew and loved. Before, they laughed at me and despised me for my ignorance and dullness; now, they hate me

---

6. *"It was evil . . . die."* Fanny is referring to the Biblical story of the fall of Adam and Eve and their expulsion by God from the Garden of Eden. [Genesis 2]

for my knowledge and understanding. What in God's name do they want of me?

They've driven me out of the factory. Now I'm more alone than ever before. . . .

May 15 Dr. Strauss is very angry at me for not having written any progress reports in two weeks. He's justified because the lab is now paying me a regular salary. I told him I was too busy thinking and reading. When I pointed out that writing was such a slow process that it made me impatient with my poor handwriting, he suggested I learn to type. It's much easier to write now because I can type seventy-five words a minute. Dr. Strauss continually reminds me of the need to speak and write simply so people will be able to understand me.

I'll try to review all the things that happened to me during the last two weeks. Algernon and I were presented to the *American Psychological Association* sitting in convention with the *World Psychological Association.* We created quite a sensation. Dr. Nemur and Dr. Strauss were proud of us.

I suspect that Dr. Nemur, who is sixty—ten years older than Dr. Strauss—finds it necessary to see tangible results of his work. Undoubtedly the result of pressure by Mrs. Nemur.

Contrary to my earlier impressions of him, I realize that Dr. Nemur is not at all a genius. He has a very good mind, but it struggles under the spectre of self-doubt. He wants people to take him for a genius. Therefore it is important for him to feel that his work is accepted by the world. I believe that Dr. Nemur was afraid of further delay because he worried that someone else might make a discovery along these lines and take the credit from him.

Dr. Strauss on the other hand might be called a genius, although I feel his areas of knowledge are too limited. He was educated in the tradition of narrow specialization; the broader aspects of background were neglected far more than necessary—even for a neuro-surgeon.

I was shocked to learn the only ancient languages he could read were Latin, Greek and Hebrew, and that he knows almost nothing of mathematics beyond the elementary levels of the calculus of variations. When he admitted this to me, I found myself almost annoyed. It was as if he'd hidden this part of himself in order to deceive me, pretending—as do many people I've discovered—to be what he is not. No one I've ever known is what he appears to be on the surface.

Dr. Nemur appears to be uncomfortable around me. Sometimes when I try to talk to him, he just looks at me strangely and turns away. I was angry at first when Dr. Strauss told me I was giving Dr. Nemur an inferiority complex. I thought he was mocking me and I'm oversensitive at being made fun of.

How was I to know that a highly respected psycho-experimentalist like Nemur was unacquainted with Hindustani and Chinese? It's absurd when you consider the work that is being done in India and China today in the very field of his study.

I asked Dr. Strauss how Nemur could refute Rahajamati's attack on his method if Nemur couldn't even read them in the first place. That strange look on Strauss' face can mean only one of two things. Either he doesn't want to tell Nemur what they're saying in India, or else—and this worries me—Dr. Strauss doesn't know either. I must be careful to speak and write clearly and simply so people won't laugh.

May 18 I am very disturbed. I saw Miss Kinnian last night for the first time in over a week. I tried to avoid all discussions of intellectual concepts and to keep the conversation on a simple, everyday level, but she just stared at me blankly and asked me what I meant about the mathematical variance equivalent in Dorbermann's *Fifth Concerto.*

When I tried to explain she stopped me and laughed. I guess I got angry, but I suspect I'm approaching her on the wrong level. No matter what I try to discuss with her, I am unable to communicate. I must review Vrostadt's equations on *Levels of Semantic Progression.* I find I don't communicate with people much any more. Thank God for books and music and things I can think about. I am alone at Mrs. Flynn's boarding house most of the time and seldom speak to anyone.

May 20 I would not have noticed the new dishwasher, a boy of about sixteen, at the corner diner where I take my evening meals if not for the incident of the broken dishes.

They crashed to the floor, sending bits of white china under the tables. The boy stood there, dazed and frightened, holding the empty tray in his hand. The catcalls from the customers (the cries of "hey, there go the profits!" . . . "*Mazeltov!*"[7] . . . and "well, *he* didn't work here very long . . ." which invariably seem to follow the breaking of glass or dishware in a public restaurant) all seemed to confuse him.

When the owner came to see what the excitement was about, the boy cowered as if he expected to be struck. "All right! All right, you dope," shouted the owner, "don't just stand there! Get the broom and sweep that mess up. A broom . . . a broom, you idiot! It's in the kitchen!"

The boy saw he was not going to be punished. His frightened expression disappeared and he smiled as he came back with the broom to sweep the floor. A few of the rowdier customers kept up the remarks, amusing themselves at his expense.

"Here, sonny, over here there's a nice piece behind you . . ."

"He's not so dumb. It's easier to break 'em than wash 'em!"

As his vacant eyes moved across the crowd of onlookers, he slowly mirrored their smiles and finally broke into an uncertain grin at the joke he obviously did not understand.

I felt sick inside as I looked at his dull, vacuous smile, the wide, bright eyes of a child, uncertain but eager to please. They were laughing at him because he was mentally retarded.

And I had been laughing at him too.

Suddenly I was furious at myself and all those who were smirking at him. I jumped up and shouted, "Shut up! Leave him alone! It's not his fault he can't understand! He can't help what he is! But he's still a human being!"

The room grew silent. I cursed myself for losing control. I tried not to look at the boy as I walked out without touching my food. I felt ashamed for both of us.

How strange that people of honest feelings and sensibility, who would not take advantage of a man born without arms or eyes—how such people think nothing of abusing a man born with low intelligence. It infuriated me to think that not too long ago I had foolishly played the clown.

And I had almost forgotten. I'd hidden the picture of the old Charlie Gordon from myself because now that I was intelligent it was some-

---

7. *Mazeltov!*, a Yiddish expression meaning, in this case, "May you have better luck in the future."

thing that had to be pushed out of my mind. But today in looking at that boy, for the first time I saw what I had been. *I was just like him!*

Only a short time ago, I learned that people laughed at me. Now I can see that unknowingly I joined with them in laughing at myself. That hurts most of all.

I have often reread my progress reports and seen the illiteracy, the childish naïveté, the mind of low intelligence peering from a dark room through the keyhole at the dazzling light outside. I see that even in my dullness I knew I was inferior, and that other people had something I lacked—something denied me. In my mental blindness, I thought it was somehow connected with the ability to read and write, and I was sure that if I could get those skills I would automatically have intelligence too.

Even a feeble-minded man wants to be like other men.

A child may not know how to feed itself, or what to eat, yet it knows of hunger.

This then is what I was like. I never knew. Even with my gift of intellectual awareness, I never really knew.

This day was good for me. Seeing the past more clearly, I've decided to use my knowledge and skills to work in the field of increasing human intelligence levels. Who is better equipped for this work? Who else has lived in both worlds? These are my people. Let me use my gift to do something for them.

Tomorrow, I will discuss with Dr. Strauss how I can work in this area. I may be able to help him work out the problems of widespread use of the technique which was used on me. I have several good ideas of my own.

There is so much that might be done with this technique. If I could be made into a genius, what about thou-sands of others like myself? What fantastic levels might be achieved by using this technique on normal people? On *geniuses?*

There are so many doors to open. I am impatient to begin.

progress report 13

May 23 It happened today. Algernon bit me. I visited the lab to see him as I do occasionally, and when I took him out of his cage, he snapped at my hand. I put him back and watched him for a while. He was unusually disturbed and vicious.

May 24 Burt, who is in charge of the experimental animals, tells me that Algernon is changing. He is less coöperative; he refuses to run the maze any more; general motivation has decreased. And he hasn't been eating. Everyone is upset about what this may mean.

May 25 They've been feeding Algernon, who now refuses to work the shifting-lock problem. Everyone identifies me with Algernon. In a way we're both the first of our kind. They're all pretending that Algernon's behavior is not necessarily significant for me. But it's hard to hide the fact that some of the other animals who were used in this experiment are showing strange behavior.

Dr. Strauss and Dr. Nemur have asked me not to come to the lab any more. I know what they're thinking but I can't accept it. I am going ahead with my plans to carry their research forward. With all due respect to both these fine scientists, I am well aware of their limitations. If there is an answer, I'll have to find it out for myself. Suddenly, time has become very important to me.

May 29 I have been given a lab of

my own and permission to go ahead with the research. I'm on to something. Working day and night. I've had a cot moved into the lab. Most of my writing time is spent on the notes which I keep in a separate folder, but from time to time I feel it necessary to put down my moods and thoughts from sheer habit.

I find the *calculus of intelligence* to be a fascinating study. Here is the place for the application of all the knowledge I have acquired.

May 31 Dr. Strauss thinks I'm working too hard. Dr. Nemur says I'm trying to cram a lifetime of research and thought into a few weeks. I know I should rest, but I'm driven on by something inside that won't let me stop. I've got to find the reason for the sharp regression in Algernon. I've got to know *if* and *when* it will happen to me.

June 4
LETTER TO DR. STRAUSS (*copy*)

Dear Dr. Strauss:

Under separate cover I am sending you a copy of my report entitled, "The Algernon-Gordon Effect: A Study of Structure and Function of Increased Intelligence," which I would like to have published.

As you see, my experiments are completed. I have included in my report all of my formulae, as well as mathematical analysis in the appendix. Of course, these should be verified.

Because of its importance to both you and Dr. Nemur (and need I say to myself, too?) I have checked and rechecked my results a dozen times in the hope of finding an error. I am sorry to say the results must stand. Yet for the sake of science, I am grateful for the little bit that I here add to

the knowledge of the function of the human mind and of the laws governing the artificial increase of human intelligence.

I recall your once saying to me that an experimental *failure* or the *disproving* of a theory was as important to the advancement of learning as a success would be. I know now that this is true. I am sorry, however, that my own contribution to the field must rest upon the ashes of the work of two men I regard so highly.

Yours truly,
Charles Gordon

June 5 I must not become emotional. The facts and the results of my experiments are clear, and the more sensational aspects of my own rapid climb cannot obscure the fact that the tripling of intelligence by the surgical technique developed by Drs. Strauss and Nemur must be viewed as having little or no practical applicability (at the present time) to the increase of human intelligence.

As I review the records and data on Algernon, I see that although he is still in his physical infancy, he has regressed mentally. Motor activity is impaired; there is a general reduction of glandular activity; there is an accelerated loss of coördination.

There are also strong indications of progressive amnesia.

As will be seen by my report, these and other physical and mental deterioration syndromes can be predicted with significant results by the application of my formula.

The surgical stimulus to which we were both subjected has resulted in an intensification and acceleration of all mental processes. The unforeseen development, which I have taken the liberty of calling the *Algernon-Gordon Effect*, is the logical extension of the entire intelligence speed-up. The hypothesis here proven may be described simply in the following terms: Artificially increased intelligence deteriorates at a rate of time directly proportional to the quantity of the increase.

I feel that this, in itself, is an important discovery.

As long as I am able to write, I will continue to record my thoughts in these progress reports. It is one of my few pleasures. However, by all indications, my own mental deterioration will be very rapid.

I have already begun to notice signs of emotional instability and forgetfulness, the first symptoms of the burnout.

June 10 Deterioration progressing. I have become absent-minded. Algernon died two days ago. Dissection shows my predictions were right. His brain had decreased in weight and there was a general smoothing out of cerebral convolutions, as well as a deepening and broadening of brain fissures.[8]

I guess the same thing is or will soon be happening to me. Now that it's definite, I don't want it to happen.

I put Algernon's body in a cheese box and buried him in the back yard. I cried.

June 15 Dr. Strauss came to see me again. I wouldn't open the door and I told him to go away. I want to be left to myself. I am touchy and irritable. I feel the darkness closing in. It's hard to throw off thoughts of suicide. I keep telling myself how important this journal will be.

It's a strange sensation to pick up a book you enjoyed just a few months ago and discover you don't remember it. I remembered how great I thought John Milton was, but when I picked up *Paradise Lost* I couldn't understand it

at all. I got so angry I threw the book across the room.

I've got to try to hold on to some of it. Some of the things I've learned. Oh, God, please don't take it all away.

June 19 Sometimes, at night, I go out for a walk. Last night, I couldn't remember where I lived. A policeman took me home. I have the strange feeling that this has all happened to me before — a long time ago. I keep telling myself I'm the only person in the world who can describe what's happening to me.

June 21 Why can't I remember? I've got to fight. I lie in bed for days and I don't know who or where I am. Then it all comes back to me in a flash. Fugues of amnesia. Symptoms of senility — second childhood. I can watch them coming on. It's so cruelly logical. I learned so much and so fast. Now my mind is deteriorating rapidly. I won't let it happen. I'll fight it. I can't help thinking of the boy in the restaurant, the blank expression, the silly smile, the people laughing at him. No — please — not that again. . . .

June 22 I'm forgetting things that I learned recently. It seems to be following the classic pattern — the last things learned are the first things forgotten. Or is that the pattern? I'd better look it up again. . . .

I reread my paper on the *Algernon-Gordon Effect* and I get the strange feeling that it was written by someone else. There are parts I don't even understand.

Motor activity impaired. I keep tripping over things, and it becomes increasingly difficult to type.

---

8. *His brain . . . fissures.* There seems to be a direct relationship between intelligence and brain size, and between intelligence and the number of cerebral convolutions (folds or ridges on the surface of the brain).

June 23 I've given up using the typewriter. My coördination is bad. I feel I'm moving slower and slower. Had a terrible shock today. I picked up a copy of an article I used in my research, Krueger's *Uber psychische Ganzheit,* to see if it would help me understand what I had done. First I thought there was something wrong with my eyes. Then I realized I could no longer read German. I tested myself in other languages. All gone.

June 30 A week since I dared to write again. It's slipping away like sand through my fingers. Most of the books I have are too hard for me now. I get angry with them because I know that I read and understood them just a few weeks ago.

I keep telling myself I must keep writing these reports so that somebody will know what is happening to me. But it gets harder to form the words and remember spellings. I have to look up even simple words in the dictionary now and it makes me impatient with myself.

Dr. Strauss comes around almost every day, but I told him I wouldn't see or speak to anybody. He feels guilty. They all do. But I don't blame anyone. I knew what might happen. But how it hurts.

July 7 I don't know where the week went. Todays Sunday I know because I can see through my window people going to church. I think I stayed in bed all week but I remember Mrs. Flynn bringing food to me a few times. I keep saying over and over I've got to do something but then I forget or maybe its just easier not to do what I say I'm going to do.

I think of my mother and father a lot these days. I found a picture of them with me taken at a beach. My father has a big ball under his arm and my mother is holding me by the hand. I dont remember them the way they are in the picture. All I remember is my father drunk most of the time and arguing with mom about money.

He never shaved much and he used to scratch my face when he hugged me. My Mother said he died but Cousin Miltie said he heard his dad say that my father ran away with another woman. When I asked my mother she slapped me and said my father was dead. I dont think I ever found out the truth but I dont care much. (He said he was going to take me to see cows on a farm once but he never did. He never kept his promises. . . .)

July 10 My landlady Mrs. Flynn is very worried about me. She says the way I lay around all day and dont do anything I remind her of her son before she threw him out of the house. She said she doesn't like loafers. If Im sick its one thing, but if Im a loafer thats another thing and she won't have it. I told her I think Im sick.

I try to read a little bit every day, mostly stories, but sometimes I have to read the same thing over and over again because I don't know what it means. And its hard to write. I know I should look up all the words in the dictionary but its so hard and Im so tired all the time.

Then I got the idea that I would only use the easy words instead of the long hard ones. That saves time. I put flowers on Algernons grave about once a week. Mrs. Flynn thinks Im crazy to put flowers on a mouses grave but I told her that Algernon was special.

July 14 Its sunday again. I dont have anything to do to keep me busy now because my television set is broke and I dont have any money to get it fixed. (I think I lost this months check from the lab. I don't remember)

I get awful headaches and asperin doesnt help me much. Mrs. Flynn knows Im really sick and she feels very sorry for me. Shes a wonderful woman whenever someone is sick.

July 22 Mrs. Flynn called a strange doctor to see me. She was afraid I was going to die. I told the doctor I wasnt too sick and I only forget sometimes. He asked me did I have any friends or relatives and I said no I dont have any. I told him I had a friend called Algernon once but he was a mouse and we used to run races together. He looked at me kind of funny like he thought I was crazy. He smiled when I told him I used to be a genius. He talked to me like I was a baby and he winked at Mrs. Flynn. I got mad and chased him out because he was making fun of me the way they all used to.

July 24 I have no more money and Mrs Flynn says I got to go to work somewhere and pay the rent because I havent paid for two months. I dont know any work but the job I used to have at Donnegans Box Company. I dont want to go back because they all knew me when I was smart and maybe they'll laugh at me. But I dont know what else to do to get money.

July 25 I was looking at some of my old progress reports and its very funny but I cant read what I wrote. I can make out some of the words but they dont make sense.

Miss Kinnian came to the door but I said go away I don't want to see you. She cried and I cried too but I wouldnt let her in because I didn't want her to laugh at me. I told her I didnt like her any more. I told her I didnt want to be smart any more.

Thats not true. I still love her and I still want to be smart but I had to say that so shed go away. She gave Mrs. Flynn money to pay the rent. I dont want that. I got to get a job.

Please . . . please let me not forget how to read and write. . . .

July 27 Mr. Donnegan was very nice when I came back and asked him for my old job of janitor. First he was very suspicious but I told him what happened to me and he looked very sad and put his hand on my shoulder and said Charlie Gordon you got guts.

Everybody looked at me when I came downstairs and started working in the toilet sweeping it out like I used to. I told myself Charlie if they make fun of you dont get sore because you remember their not so smart as you once thot they were. And besides they were once your friends and if they laughted at you that doesnt meant anything because they liked you too.

One of the new men who came to work there after I went away made a nasty crack he said hey Charlie I hear your a very smart fella a real quiz kid. Say something intelligent. I felt bad but Joe Carp came over and grabbed him by the shirt and said leave him alone you lousy cracker or I'll break your neck. I didnt expect Joe to take my part so I guess hes really my friend.

Later Frank Reilly came over and said Charlie if anybody bothers you or trys to take advantage you call me or Joe and we will set em straight. I said thanks Frank and I got choked up so I had to turn around and go into the supply room so he wouldnt see me cry. Its good to have friends.

July 28 I did a dumb thing today I forgot I wasn't in Miss Kinnians class at the adult center any more like I use

to be. I went in and sat down in my old seat in the back of the room and she looked at me funny and she said Charles. I dint remember she ever called me that before only Charlie so I said hello Miss Kinnian Im redy for my lesin today only I lost my reader that we was using. She startid to cry and run out of the room and everybody looked at me and I saw they wasnt the same pepul who use to be in my class.

Then all of a suddin I remembered some things about the operashun and me getting smart and I said holy smoke I reely pulled a Charlie Gordon that time. I went away before she come back to the room.

Thats why Im going away from New York for good. I dont want to do nothing like that agen. I dont want Miss Kinnian to feel sorry for me. Evry body feels sorry at the factery and I dont want that eather so Im going someplace where nobody knows that Charlie Gordon was once a genus and now he cant even reed a book or rite good.

Im taking a cuple of books along and even if I cant reed them Ill practise hard and maybe I wont forget every thing I lerned. If I try reel hard maybe Ill be a littel bit smarter then I was before the operashun. I got my rabits foot and my luky penny and maybe they will help me.

If you ever reed this Miss Kinnian dont be sorry for me Im glad I got a second chanse to be smart becaus I lerned a lot of things that I never even new were in this world and Im grateful that I saw it all for a littel bit. I dont know why Im dumb agen or what I did wrong maybe its because I dint try hard enuff. But if I try and practis very hard maybe Ill get a littl smarter and know what all the words are. I remember a littel bit how nice I had a feeling with the blue book that has the torn cover when I red it. Thats why Im gonna keep trying to get smart so I can have that feeling agen. Its a good feeling to know things and be smart. I wish I had it rite now if I did I would sit down and reed all the time. Anyway I bet Im the first dumb person in the world who ever found out somthing importent for science. I remember I did somthing but I dont remember what. So I gess its like I did it for all the dumb pepul like me.

Goodbye Miss Kinnian and Dr. Strauss and evreybody. And P.S. please tell Dr Nemur not to be such a grouch when pepul laff at him and he would have more frends. Its easy to make frends if you let pepul laff at you. Im going to have lots of frends where I go.

P.P.S. Please if you get a chanse put some flowrs on Algernons grave in the bak yard. . . .   ✳

Discussion

1. (a) After reading *The Author* (page 193), explain how Daniel Keyes happened to create Charlie Gordon. (b) In spite of the very strange things that happen to him, Charlie seems very real to most readers. Can you explain why this is so?

2. (a) How is the form of this story different from that of any other story previously studied in this anthology? (b) Why do you suppose Daniel Keyes chose this form to tell Charlie's story?

3. What are some of Charlie's outstanding characteristics?

4. (a) How does Charlie feel immediately after the operation? (b) What first gives him hope for becoming smart? (c) How does this incident change his attitude toward Algernon?

5. Miss Kinnian, Charlie's landlady, and the factory workers all have different attitudes toward Charlie at different times in the story.

Explain how each feels about Charlie (a) before his operation, (b) as his intelligence increases, and (c) as he regresses.

6. (a) As a result of his increased ability to think, how does Charlie's view of others change? Point out specific examples. **(b)** What effect does this new knowledge of people have on Charlie? **(c)** How is his resolution to use his gift to do something for retarded people (page 186, column 1, paragraph 6), in keeping with the character he has displayed throughout the story?

7. (a) At what point in the story do you first know that Charlie is going to lose his new-found mental ability? **(b)** How do his reactions to Algernon's deterioration differ from his reactions to his own deterioration? **(c)** Why does he decide to leave town?

8. Reread the following passages and explain the clues in each that reveal Charlie's mentality at that particular time:

    (a) page 172, column 1, paragraph 1
    (b) page 177, column 2, paragraph 4
    (c) page 179, column 2, paragraph 1
    (d) page 185, column 1, paragraph 2
    (e) page 192, column 2, paragraph 1

9. (a) Is Charlie happier with an I.Q. of 68 or with one of 200+? Explain. **(b)** Had he been given a choice, which I.Q. would he have chosen? Why? **(c)** If you were to continue the story, what would you have happen to Charlie? Why?

10. Why do you think Daniel Keyes chose the title he did for this story?

Word Study

Many of Charlie Gordon's unusual spellings result from his selecting the wrong *homonyms*. Homonyms are words which sound alike but which have different spellings and different meanings. The words *to, too,* and *two* are homonyms; which of them correctly completes each sentence?

1. I am going _____ the store.
2. I asked my sister to come along _____ .
3. Mother said to buy _____ loaves of bread.

Select the homonym listed below which describes or gives information about the person or thing in each of the sentences that follow.

beach	*morning*	*serge*
beech	*mourning*	*surge*
colonel	*principal*	
kernel	*principle*	
meddle	*prophet*	
medal	*profit*	

1. This period occurs early in the day.
2. A businessman tries to make one.
3. This man heads a school.
4. You might have a suit made out of this.
5. It's found only near water.
6. This might be awarded for bravery.
7. This man is an army officer.

The Author

Daniel Keyes, born in New York in 1927, has been a merchant seaman, ship's purser, fiction editor, and teacher of English in high school and college.

Of "Flowers for Algernon" he writes: "I recall clearly the brief note in my 'idea folder' something like: 'What would happen if a person's intelligence could be increased by surgery or something like that?' But that's all it was—an idea—until more than five years later a retarded boy said to me: 'Mr. Keyes, if I try hard and become smart will they put me into a regular class and let me be like everyone else?' The impact of those words stayed with me for a long time afterwards, until one day idea fused with character and I began to write 'Flowers for Algernon.'"

Since its first publication, the short story has appeared in numerous books and magazines, has been translated into five languages, has been adapted for television under the title "The Two Worlds of Charlie Gordon," and has been purchased for the movies. A full-length, novel version of the story was published in 1966.

See
SATIRE
Handbook
of Literary
Terms
page 563

What would happen if, one day,
the machines we have created revolted and
turned against us?

Nightmare Number Three

Stephen Vincent Benét

We had expected everything but revolt
And I kind of wonder myself when they started thinking—
But there's no dice in that now.
                              I've heard fellows say
They must have planned it for years and maybe they did.
5 Looking back, you can find little incidents here and there,
Like the concrete-mixer in Jersey eating the guy
Or the roto press that printed "Fiddle-dee-dee!"
In a three-color process all over Senator Sloop,
Just as he was making a speech. The thing about that
10 Was, how could it walk upstairs? But it was upstairs,
Clicking and mumbling in the Senate Chamber.
They had to knock out the wall to take it away
And the wrecking-crew said it grinned.
                              It was only the best
Machines, of course, the superhuman machines,
15 The ones we'd built to be better than flesh and bone,
But the cars were in it, of course . . .
                              and they hunted us
Like rabbits through the cramped streets on that Bloody Monday,
The Madison Avenue buses leading the charge.
The buses were pretty bad—but I'll not forget

20 The smash of glass when the Duesenberg[1] left the show-room
And pinned three brokers to the Racquet Club steps
Or the long howl of the horns when they saw men run,
When they saw them looking for holes in the solid ground . . .

I guess they were tired of being ridden in
25 And stopped and started by pygmies for silly ends,
Of wrapping cheap cigarettes and bad chocolate bars
Collecting nickels and waving platinum hair
And letting six million people live in a town.
I guess it was that. I guess they got tired of us
And the whole smell of human hands.
30   But it was a shock
To climb sixteen flights of stairs to Art Zuckow's office
(Nobody took the elevators twice)
And find him strangled to death in a nest of telephones,
The octopus-tendrils waving over his head,
35 And a sort of quiet humming filling the air. . . .
Do they eat? . . . There was red . . . But I did not stop to look.
I don't know yet how I got to the roof in time
And it's lonely, here on the roof.
                                For a while, I thought
That window-cleaner would make it, and keep me company.
40 But they got him with his own hoist at the sixteenth floor
And dragged him in, with a squeal.
You see, they coöperate. Well, we taught them that
And it's fair enough, I suppose. You see, we built them.
We taught them to think for themselves.
45 It was bound to come. You can see it was bound to come
And it won't be so bad, in the country. I hate to think
Of the reapers, running wild in the Kansas fields,
And the transport planes like hawks on a chickenyard,
But the horses might help. We might make a deal with the
      horses.
At least, you've more chance, out there.
50   And they need us, too.
They're bound to realize that when they once calm down.
They'll need oil and spare parts and adjustments and tuning up.
Slaves? Well, in a way, you know, we were slaves before.
There won't be so much real difference—honest, there won't.
55 (I wish I hadn't looked into that beauty-parlor

---

1. *Duesenberg,* an American-made, luxury automobile.

And seen what was happening there.
But those are female machines and a bit high-strung.)
Oh, we'll settle down. We'll arrange it. We'll compromise.
It wouldn't make sense to wipe out the whole human race.
60 Why, I bet if I went to my old Plymouth now
(Of course you'd have to do it the tactful way)
And said, "Look here! Who got you the swell French horn?"
He wouldn't turn me over to those police cars;
At least I don't think he would.
                                        Oh, it's going to be jake.
65 There won't be so much real difference — honest, there won't —
And I'd go down in a minute and take my chance —
I'm a good American and I always liked them —
Except for one small detail that bothers me
And that's the food proposition. Because, you see,
70 The concrete-mixer may have made a mistake,
And it looks like just high spirits.
But, if it's got so they like the flavor . . . well . . .

Discussion

1. (a) Where physically is the narrator as he describes the events in the poem? (b) Why is the narrator afraid to leave his position?
2. (a) What happened on "Bloody Monday"? (b) What were the first indications that the machines might revolt? (c) According to the speaker, why did the machines revolt?
3. (a) Why does the speaker think the machines will not kill everyone? (b) Nevertheless, what does he fear? (c) What is the narrator's attitude toward being ruled by machines?
4. What human characteristics do the machines have? Cite specific lines which reveal these characteristics.
5. (a) What do you think the au-thor is satirizing in this poem? (b) Do you or do you not share his concern?
6. Do you think that man is responsible for the things he creates and discovers? For example, is he responsible for the use of atomic energy?

The Author

Stephen Vincent Benét developed at an early age his lifelong interest in poetry. His father, an army colonel, frequently read poetry aloud to his children, and this early influence was undoubtedly a factor in directing them toward literary careers.

At the age of thirteen, Benét won a three-dollar prize in a poetry contest and four years later published his first volume of verse. After receiving his master's degree at Yale University, Benét studied at the Sorbonne in France. While in Paris, he met his future wife, Rosemary Carr, who later collaborated with him in writing *A Book of Americans,* short poems about famous individuals. In 1926, Benét received a fellowship enabling him to write *John Brown's Body,* a long narrative poem about the Civil War, which received a Pulitzer Prize in 1929.

Among Benét's writings are radio scripts and plays, short stories, American folk tales, and poems ranging from long narratives to science fantasies. His many works dealing with America's traditions and ideals reveal Benét's love for his country and his pride in its achievements.

"The workers come like a horde of salvaging locusts, stripping a field, moving to the next, filling their boxes or crates or sacks, weighing in, collecting the bonuses offered to entice them to stay till the end of the season, and disappearing again."
What effect does a life like this have on children?

children of the harvest

Lois Phillips Hudson

ON A SUFFOCATING SUMMER DAY in 1937, the thirteenth year of drought and the seventh year of depression,[1] with our mouths, nostrils, and eyes full of the dust blowing from our bare fields, my family sold to our neighbors at auction most of the accouterments of our existence. Then we loaded what was left into a trailer my father had made and drove West to find water and survival on the Washington coast.

During the auction the two classmates with whom I had just finished the fourth grade hung about the desultory bidders giving me looks of respect and undisguised envy. They envied me not so much for the things they could imagine as for the things they couldn't—the unimaginable distance I was going and the unimaginable things along it and at the end of it.

And though we all could have imagined most of Montana well enough, how could any of us have imagined an end to the prairie's limitless sky and the giddy encroachments rising higher and higher against that sky that were the Rocky Mountains? How could we have imagined how, in burning summer, the forested profiles of the Cascades[2] could echo everywhere the shouts of white falls above us and green rivers below? Who could have imagined, once confronted with their gray expanse, that the waters of Puget Sound were not actually the

1. **depression,** the great depression in the United States which began with the stock-market crash of 1929 and left millions of people penniless.
2. **Cascades,** a mountain range in the northwestern United States. Mount Rainier is its highest peak.

Pacific, but only a minute stray squiggle of it? Who, finally, could have imagined that there were so many people in the world or that the world could offer them so hospitable a habitation?

There were so many things I could scarcely believe even when I was doing them or looking at them or eating them. We lived in a cabin on an island for a few weeks after we arrived, and it always seemed impossible to me that we could be surrounded by so much water. I spent every moment of the hour-long ferry trip from the mainland hanging over the rail gazing down at the exhilarating wake of my first boat ride. The island was exactly what any island should be—lavish green acres covered with woods and orchards and fields of berries, ringed by glistening sandy beaches richly stocked with driftwood. Once in North Dakota my aunt had brought a very small basket of black cherries to my grandfather's house, and I had made the four or five that were my share last all afternoon. I would take tiny bites of each cherry, then suck the pit and roll it around with my tongue to get the faint remaining taste, till it came out as clean and smooth as a brook-bottom pebble. But on the island I would climb into the trees with my five-year-old sister and have contests with her, seeing which of us could get the most cherries in our mouths at once. Then we would shoot the wet pits, no longer hungrily scoured of their slipperiness, at each other and at the robins who perched above us. Sometimes I would go into the fields with my mother and father and spend an hour helping pick raspberries or blackberries or loganberries or any of the other things they worked in, but there were really only two important things to do—play on the beaches and eat fruit.

It didn't occur to me that things would ever be different again, but one day early in August the last berry was picked and we took the ferry into Seattle, where we bought a big brown tent and a camp stove. We added them to our trailer load and drove back over the green-and-white Cascades, beneath the glacial sunrise face of Mount Rainier, and down into the sweaty outdoor factory that is the Yakima Valley. There the Yakima River is bled for transfusions to the millions of rows of roots, its depleted currents finally dragging themselves muddily to their relieved merger with the undiminishable Columbia. One can follow the Yakima for miles and miles and see nothing but irrigated fields and orchards—and the gaunt camps of transient laborers.

The workers come like a horde of salvaging locusts, stripping a field, moving to the next, filling their boxes or crates or sacks, weighing in, collecting the bonuses offered to entice them to stay till the end of the season, and disappearing again. They spend their repetitive days in rows of things to be picked and their sweltering nights in rows of tents and trailers. We pitched our tent beside the others, far from our pleasant island where the owners of the fields were neighbors who invited my sister and me among their cherry trees. Here the sauntering owners and their bristling foremen never smiled at those children who ran through the fields playing games, and only occasionally at those who worked beside their parents.

In North Dakota I had worked on our farm—tramping hay, driving a team of horses, fetching cows, feeding calves and chickens—but of course that had all been only my duty as a member of the family, not a way to earn money. Now I was surrounded by grownups who wanted to pay me for working, and by children my own age who were stepping up to the pay window every night with weighing tags[3] in their hands and collecting money. I saw that the time had come for me to assume a place of adult independence in the world.

I made up my mind I was going to earn a dollar all in one day. We were picking hops then, and of all the rows I have toiled my way up and down, I remember hop rows the most vividly. Trained up on their wires fifteen feet overhead, the giant vines resemble monster grape arbors hung with bunches of weird unripe fruit. A man who does not pick things for a living comes and cuts them down with a knife tied to a ten-foot pole so the people below can strip them off into sacks. Hops don't really look like any other growing thing but instead like something artificially constructed —pine cones, perhaps, with segments cleverly cut from the soft, limp, clinging leaves that lie next to the kernels of an ear of corn. A hop in your hand is like a feather, and it will almost float on a puff of air. Hops are good only for making beer, so you can't even get healthily sick of them by eating them all day long, the way you can berries or peas.

Pickers are paid by the pound, and picking is a messy business. Sometimes you run into a whole cluster that is gummy with the honeydew of hop aphids, and gray and musty with the mildew growing on the sticky stuff. Tiny red spiders rush from the green petals and flow up your arms, like more of the spots the heat makes you see.

The professionals could earn up to six dollars a day. One toothless grandmother discouraged us all by making as much as anybody in the row and at the same time never getting out of her rocking chair except to drag it behind

her from vine to vine. My father and mother each made over three dollars a day, but though I tried to work almost as long hours as they did, my pay at the end of the day would usually be somewhere between eighty and ninety cents.

Then one day in the second week of picking, when the hops were good and I stayed grimly sweating over my long gray sack hung on a child-sized frame, I knew that this was going to be the day. As the afternoon waned and I added the figures on my weight tags over and over again in my head, I could feel the excitement begin to make spasms in my stomach. That night the man at the pay window handed me a silver dollar and three pennies. He must have seen that this was a day not for paper, but for silver. The big coin, so neatly and brightly stamped, was coolly distant from the blurred mélange of piled vines and melting heat that had put it into my hand. Only its solid heaviness connected it in a businesslike way with the work it represented. For the first time in my life I truly comprehended the relationship between toil and media of exchange, and I saw how exacting and yet how satisfying were the terms of the world. Perhaps because of this insight, I did not want the significance of my dollar dimmed by the common touch of copper pettiness. I gave the vulgar pennies to my little sister, who was amazed but grateful. Then I felt even more grown-up than before, because not everybody my age was in a position to give pennies to kids.

That night I hardly slept, lying uncovered beside my sister on our mattress on the ground, sticking my hand out under the bottom of the tent to lay it on the cooling earth be-

---

3. **weighing tags.** Each tag, representing a specific amount picked, is worth a certain amount of money.

tween the clumps of dry grass. Tired as I was, I had written post cards to three people in North Dakota before going to bed. I had told my grandmother, my aunt, and my friend Doris that I had earned a dollar in one day. Then, because I did not want to sound impolitely proud of myself, and to fill up the card, I added on each one, "I'm fine and I plan to pick again tomorrow. How are you?"

I couldn't wait to get to the field the next day and earn another dollar. Back home none of my friends would have dreamed of being able to earn so much in one day. The only thing to do back there for money was to trap gophers for the bounty; and even the big kids, who ran a fairly long trap line and had the nerve to cut the longest tails in half, couldn't make more than twenty cents on a good day, with tails at two cents apiece. I earned a dollar and forty cents the next day and the day after that, and at least a dollar every day for another week, until we moved to another place of picking—a pear orchard.

By that time it was September, and most of us children from the rows of tents stood out at the gateway of the camp and waited each day for the long yellow school bus. I had never seen a school bus before, and my sister and I were shy about how to act in such a grand vehicle. We sat together, holding our lunch buckets on our knees, looking out at the trees beside the roads, trying to catch a glimpse of our mother and father on the ladders.

The school had about three times as many pupils in it as there were people in the town back in North Dakota where we used to go to buy coal and groceries. The pupils who were planning to attend this school all year were separated from those who, like me, did not know how many days or weeks we would be in that one spot. In our special classes we did a great deal of drawing and saw a number of movies. School was so luxurious in comparison with the hard work I had done in North Dakota the previous year that I wrote another post card to Doris, telling her that we never had to do fractions and that we got colored construction paper to play with almost every day. I copied a picture of a donkey with such accuracy that my teacher thought I had traced it until she held the two to the window and saw that the lines were indisputably my own. After that I got extra drawing periods and became very good at copying, which always elicited more praise than my few original compositions.

I was understandably sad when we left that school after two weeks and went to Wenatchee. For the first time, we were not in a regular camp. The previous year my father, recognizing that the crops had not brought in enough to get us through the winter, had taken the train to Wenatchee after the sparse harvest was in and picked apples for a man named Jim Baumann. Baumann wanted him back, so he let us pitch our tent on his land not far from his house. We made camp, and after supper Baumann came down to talk about the next day's arrangements. The school was not so large as the other one, and there was no school bus for us because we were only a half mile away from it. Baumann was shorthanded in the packing shed and needed my mother early in the morning. Besides, there was no reason why she should have to take us to school, because he had a daughter in my grade who could walk with us and take us to our respective rooms.

"Why, isn't that lovely!" my mother exclaimed with unwanted enthusiasm. "Now you'll have a nice lit-tle girl to play with right here and to be your friend at school."

Her excitement was rather remarkable, considering the dubious reaction she had had to everybody else I had played with since we started camping. It hadn't seemed to me that she had liked even the boy who made me a pair of stilts and taught me to walk on them. Now here she was favorably predisposed toward somebody I didn't even know. I agreed that it would be nice to have a nice little girl to play with.

The next morning my sister and I sat on the steps of the Baumanns' front porch, where Barbara's mother had told us to make ourselves at home, waiting for her to finish her breakfast. We had already been up so long that it seemed to me we must surely be late for school; I began picturing the humiliating tardy entrance into a roomful of strange faces.

Two of Barbara's friends came down the driveway to wait for her. They both wore the kind of plaid skirts I had been wondering if I could ask my mother about buying—after all, she *had* said all my dresses were too short this fall because of all the inches I'd grown in the summer. The two girls looked at us for a moment, then uncoiled shiny-handled jump ropes and commenced loudly shouting two different rhymes to accompany their jumping.

Barbara came out on the porch, greeted her friends with a disconcerting assurance, jumped down the steps past us, insinuated herself between them and clasped their hands. "I have to show these kids where the school is," she told them. Turning her head slightly she called, "Well, come if you're coming. We're going to be late." Swinging their arms together, they began to skip down the driveway.

A couple of times on the way to school they stopped and waited until we got near them; I yanked irritably on my little sister's arm and thought about how her shorter legs had been holding me back ever since she was born. I always seemed to be the one who had to drag a little kid along.

The teacher kept me standing at her desk while she called the roll and started the class on a reading assignment. When she looked up at me, I got the irrational impression that I had already managed to do something wrong. She asked where I had come from and I said "North Dakota," thinking it would be simpler than trying to tell all the places I had been in the last three months. She gave me the last seat in a row behind a boy in dirty clothes. As she passed by him she made the faintest sound of exhalation, as though she was ridding her nostrils of a disagreeable smell.

At recess a boy in a bright shirt and new cream-colored corduroy pants yelled "North Dakota, North Dakota" in a funny way as he ran past me to the ball field. The boy who sat ahead of me came up and said confidentially, "We been out all around here for two years. We come from Oklahoma. We're Okies.[4] That's what you are too, even if you didn't come from Oklahoma." I knew I could never be anything that sounded so crummy as "Okie," and I said so. "Oh, yeah!" he rejoined stiffly. I walked away before he could argue any more and went to find my sister, but the primary grades had recess at a different time, so I went and stood by the door until the period was over. That afternoon I stayed in my seat reading a history book, but the teacher, who seemed to want to go outdoors herself, said, "It's better for the room if everybody goes outside for recess." So I went out and stood around the fringes of two or three games and wondered what was funny about North Dakota. Somehow I had the feeling that it would hurt my mother if I asked her.

The last part of the day was given to a discussion period, when each of us who wanted to was given a chance to tell about an important day in his life. The important days of my classmates, all about having a part in a play or learning to ride a bike, seemed so pathetically juvenile that I was impelled to speak. I stood at my seat and told about how before we had gone to the pear orchard, which was before we had come here, I had earned a dollar all in one day in the hop fields.

From two sides of the room Barbara's friends turned to send her looks which I intercepted but found inscrutable. I had been looking at her too, watching for her reaction. A boy near me poked another and whispered in mocking awe, "A whole dollar!"

The boy ahead of me jumped suddenly to his feet, banging his leg against the desk so hard that the entire row shook. "Heck," he cried, "we just come from there, too, and I made more'n a buck and a half *every* day." He gave me a triumphant smile and sat down. Then I knew I hated that boy. That night I told my mother about how there was a mean boy just like those other mean boys at the camps and how the teacher *would* have to put me right behind him. "Well," she sighed, "just try not to pay any attention to him."

By the time I had found my sister after school, Barbara and her friends had gone. The next morning when we went to the big house she was gone, too.

After that, my sister and I walked

---

4. **Okies,** farm workers who travel from farm to farm. The term originally referred only to workers from Oklahoma, but was expanded to a derogatory term for all migrants.

together. Sometimes we would be close enough to hear Barbara's friends, who were always with her, laugh and call her "Bobby." I had never known any Barbaras before, and the name seemed full of unapproachable prestige and sophistication; it was the kind of name that could belong only to a girl who had as many dresses as Barbara Baumann had. "Bobby" was yet more awesome, as if she were as consequential as a boy. At school, if I recited in class, she acted queerly self-conscious, as though she were responsible for me—the way I often felt around my sister when she said something stupid to kids my age.

For various reasons I had that same embarrassed feeling of an enforced distasteful relationship with the boy who sat ahead of me. Once in a while somebody in the class would tease me about him or would say something about "the hop pickers." I was bitterly determined to dissociate myself from the boy, and whenever he turned around to talk to me I would pretend he was trying to copy my paper. I would put my hand over it while I kept my eyes glued to the desk and felt my face grow hot.

There were some things about the school I liked very much. We were allowed to use the library a great deal; and for the first time in my life I had access to numbers of books I hadn't already read. By reading at noon and recess I could finish a book at school every two days. I would also have a book at home that I would read in a couple of nights. One of the nice things about living in a tent was that there were hardly any household chores to do and I could read as much as I wanted.

Frosty mornings came with October, and my sister and I would try to dress under the quilts before we got up to eat our oatmeal. Leaves began to blow across the road, apples grew redder with each cold night, pickers hurried from tree to tree, filling the orchards with the soft thunder of hard round fruit rolling out of picking sacks into boxes, and packers worked faster and faster, trying to get the apples twisted up in fancy tissue and into boxes before they jammed up too thickly on the perpetually moving belts. After school my sister and I would go to the box shed behind the big house where Harry, Barbara's big brother, would be nailing boxes together for a nickel apiece. He was always glad to have company, and would let us stand at a respectful distance and watch him pound in nail after nail with two strokes—a tap to set it, then a mighty clout to send it in —three to an end, six to a side.

One afternoon, with the chill blue sky brilliant behind the orange and black Halloween cutouts on the windows, I was sitting at my desk dreamily drawing a witch in a moon when the teacher called my name. She told me that she wanted me to take all my books out of my desk and take them to the front of the room. Then she told everybody in my row to pack up his books and move one seat back. My heart banged alarmingly up in my throat and I nearly gagged from the sudden acute sensations in my viscera. In North Dakota such drastic action was taken only when an offender, after repeated warnings, had proved too incorrigible to sit anywhere except right in front of the teacher's desk. The fact that I had no idea of why I was now classified as such an incorrigible only augmented my anguish. While books, papers, and pencils fell to the floor and boys jostled each other in the aisle, I managed to sidle numbly up to the front. I sat down in my new seat, trying not to notice how shamefully close it was to the big desk facing it, and I was careful not to raise my eyes higher than the vase of zinnias standing on the corner nearest me.

When school was out I hurried to find my sister and get out of the schoolyard before seeing anybody in my class. But Barbara and her friends had beaten us to the playground entrance and they seemed to be waiting for us. Barbara said, "So now you're in the A class." She sounded impressed.

"What's the A class?" I asked.

Everybody made superior yet faintly envious giggling sounds. "Well, why did you think the teacher moved you to the front of the room, dopey? Didn't you know you were in the C class before, way in the back of the room?"

Of course I hadn't known. The Wenatchee fifth grade was bigger than my whole school had been in North Dakota, and the idea of subdivisions within a grade had never occurred to me. The subdividing for the first marking period had been done before I came to the school, and I had never, in the six weeks I'd been there, talked to anyone long enough to find out about the A, B, and C classes.

I still could not understand why that had made such a difference to Barbara and her friends. I didn't yet know that it was disgraceful and dirty to be a transient laborer and ridiculous to be from North Dakota. I thought living in a tent was more fun than living in a house. I didn't know that we were gypsies, really (how that thought would have thrilled me then!), and that we were regarded with the suspicion felt by those who plant toward those who do not plant. It didn't occur to me that we were all looked upon as one more of the untrustworthy natural phenomena, drifting here and there like mists or winds, that farmers of certain crops are resentfully forced to rely on. I didn't know that I was the only child who had camped on the Baumanns' land ever to get out of the C class. I did not know that school administrators and civic leaders held conferences to talk about the problem of transient laborers.

I only knew that for two happy days I walked to school with Barbara and her friends, played hopscotch and jump rope with them at recess, and was even invited into the house for some ginger ale—an exotic drink I had never tasted before.

Then we took down our tent and packed it in the trailer with our mattresses and stove and drove on, because the last apples were picked and sorted and boxed and shipped to the people all over the world, whoever they were, who could afford to buy them in 1937. My teacher wrote a letter for me to take to my next school. In it, she told me, she had informed my next teacher that I should be put into the A class immediately. But there wasn't any A class in my room, the new teacher explained.

By then I was traveled enough to realize that it was another special class for transients. The teacher showed us movies almost every day.

*

Discussion

1. (a) Why is the narrator's family forced to sell their North Dakota farm? (b) Where do they plan to go? (c) What do they plan to do?

2. (a) How does the narrator first react to her new life? (b) What happens to change her outlook? (c) Cite passages which effectively describe the life of a worker in the hop

fields. What specific images did you find particularly vivid? (d) Does the narrator at this time fully realize the position of her family? Explain.

3. (a) How is the first Western school different from the school in North Dakota? (b) What is the narrator's attitude toward this new school? (c) Does she know why she is treated as she is? Explain.

4. Reread page 203, column 2, paragraph 1. (a) Why is the narrator's mother so enthusiastic? (b) Why does the child fail to understand her mother's enthusiasm? (c) How do Barbara and the other students act toward the migrant child? Why? (d) When do Barbara and her friends change their attitude?

5. Reread the last four paragraphs of the story. What things has the narrator come to understand about her childhood which she did not understand when she was a child?

6. (a) Read the author's comments in the next column. How does she feel about society's attitude toward transient laborers? (b) What do you think her purpose was in writing this selection? (c) Where would you place this selection on a fact-fiction scale? (See "Fact and Fiction" page 541.) Explain your reasons for placing it where you do.

Word Study

An *antonym* is a word which means the opposite of another word. The word *big* is an antonym of *little*. What is an antonym for *cold?*

For each word listed in the column on the left, find the antonym listed in the column on the right. You may refer to your Glossary.

augment	*sadden*
commence	*fat*
dubious	*lasting*
exhilarate	*certain*
gaunt	*end*
irrational	*reasonable*
transient	*decrease*

The Author

Lois Phillips Hudson was born and reared on the prairies of the western United States. Besides teaching junior- and senior-high school, she has contributed stories to magazines and has written novels, the best-known of which is *The Bones of Plenty.*

Of her own background and its importance in "Children of the Harvest," she writes: ". . . not one school in a hundred makes any real effort to educate the children of migrant laborers. For most of the students who will ever read this story, school seems to be an all too possessive institution. They might find it hard to understand that migrant children are not welcome in ANY school! And don't think those kids take very long to find that out! My own family tramped the fruit only one season, and most of that time, as I said in the story, we were not in school . . . I sometimes wonder if even one of the many children I knew in the migrant camps even got out of high school. . . .

"I wrote the story because it was a story that had to be told. It is based on things that happened, but it has many fictional elements. Barbara, the owner's daughter, was real, but the dirty Okie boy who sat in front of me is not. Thus the story is, like almost all fiction, a . . . combination of real and imagined details and incidents."

See
TONE
Handbook
of Literary
Terms
page 567

". . . If one group's rights are infringed upon,
another group's rights are in danger."
This is a story about possibly serious issues,
but is it a serious story?

NO BOY, I'M A GIRL!

M.J. Amft

IN THE MIDDLE of junior year I became a civilian rights agitator. Not civil rights—that's no problem in our town—but civilian rights. School wasn't the army, right? They didn't own us, right? They couldn't put us in uniform. Soldiers had to wear GI clothes and GI haircuts, and polish their buttons and shoes, but this was *civilian* life, a high school in a free country, and they suspended three boys for wearing blue jeans to school. Actually they just sent them home and told them to come back wearing something else, but it was the principle of the thing that mattered to me.

I kept thinking about it all afternoon, getting madder and madder. What if those boys were so poor they didn't have anything else to wear? Are the poor to be punished? Is that Democracy? I happened to know that those particular three boys weren't poor, but what if they had been?

"It's the principle of the thing," I said. I was walking home with Allen Newman the way I always did because (for one) he lived at the end of my block and (for two) I had a hopeless crush on him. Hopeless because girls meant absolutely nothing, nothing in Allen's life. Clothes meant nothing to him either. He wore plain, conservative, utilitarian clothes that his mother ordered from a catalogue. She took his measurements and sent away for plain white shirts and plain dark wash pants. He had one lightweight windbreaker, one heavy windbreaker (both dark blue), one dark blue suit (which he never wore), one raincoat (which he never wore) and three neckties. When his shoes wore out, he went to Clark's Shoe Shop and asked for "a pair of the same." Brown moccasins. Every second Saturday he made his mother trim his hair, and he refused to wear the cologne his grandmother gave him, the after-shave lotion his aunt gave him, or the Aphrodisia I gave him. He hated perfume for men.

The reason I knew all these intimate things about Allen and the reason I gave him a Christmas present is that his mother and mine are old best-friends who are always on the telephone talking about their children.

My mother was on the phone that day when I got home. "Just be glad you don't have a daughter. Speaking of which, here she is. Good-by, Ruthie. I'll call you tomorrow. Tell Allen I'm very proud he got another A."

"That was Ruthie Newman," she said. "Allen got another A."

"I know. Listen, Mother, there's something terrible going on at our school. Allen doesn't care because he has absolutely no feeling of civic responsibility, but I think it's criminal. I'm sure it's illegal."

"Drugs!" my mother said. "Airplane glue? Or worse?"

"No, no. It's the school authorities. It's the principal, actually, Mr. Hayden. I mean he *is* the school authority. He's the one."

"Mr. Hayden is pushing drugs?!"

"Mother, will you listen? Nobody said anything about drugs. Mr. Hayden is the one saying you can't wear blue jeans to school."

"Why should I wear blue jeans to school? Much as I hate those PTA meetings, when I do go, I wear my good black suit. Where did Mr. Hayden get the idea I wanted to wear blue jeans?"

You see how it is with my mother. She's very emotional, and she jumps to conclusions. I finally managed to explain that by "you" I meant "one," or three: the three boys in the blue jeans. I didn't think any public school or any principal had the right to dictate to any student in regard to personal appearance, and I thought all parents should write a protest letter.

My mother wasn't interested and changed the subject.

"Are you going out with that ugly Roger tomorrow night?" she asked.

When I told her no, that was all

over, she was glad; but when Ralph showed up, she dragged me into the kitchen and said, "For months you dated a boy who needed a good dermatologist. Now it's a boy who needs an orthodontist. What's wrong with their parents? Where do you find these boys whose mothers neglect them? Why can't you find a nice boy whose parents take an interest in his welfare, a boy like Allen?"

Why indeed? I was willing. Meantime I didn't want to spend weekends doing chemistry experiments. That's what Allen did. He had all these smelly things in his basement which really bugged his mother. As Ruthie said, maybe daughters washed their hair so much it clogged up the drains; at least daughters didn't cause terrible smells to come up the hot-air registers. To which, of course, my mother replied that smells in the basement result in A's in chemistry, whereas hair in the drains results in nothing but a plumber's bill.

I didn't think Ralph was anything much, myself—but he was a date, he was a way to get out on Saturday nights, and he agreed with me about the blue jeans.

Monday morning every home room teacher had a mimeographed "Memo from the Principal's Office," which he read aloud and then stuck on the bulletin board:

No boy shall be allowed to wear blue jeans during school hours nor while in the school building. Unobservance of this rule shall meet with immediate suspension.

I don't think Mr. Hayden is literate. Unobservance? Is that a word? And what right had he, what right?

On the way home I fumed about it to Allen, who said there was no reason for me to get excited. Why should I concern myself over what boys couldn't wear as long as I was allowed to wear what I pleased?

"Because if one group's rights are infringed upon, another group's rights are in danger." And then I screamed and hugged him—which I did every now and then, being unable to restrain myself; he never reacted one way or the other—and said, "You've given me a great idea! I'm a girl!"

"I thought you knew that," he said.

I ignored that because I had suddenly realized the right way to protest. Not with letters and petitions, not with marches and sit-ins . . . the way to protest was to take Mr. Hayden's directive word for word, but *only* word for word. The letter killeth. Ah ha! No *boy* it said. I'm a girl.

Of course, I knew my mother wasn't going to let me wear blue jeans to school. As it was, one of her big complaints about me was my clothes. She hates colored stockings, textured stockings, fake fur, vinyl, wild colors, dots, stripes and patterns except "a nice, soft herringbone or a muted plaid." She had a running lecture on what a pretty girl I could be if I would wear a nice tweed skirt, a cashmere sweater, a string of small pearls and nylons. Fashionwise she lives in the past. I'd never get out of my own house in blue jeans. But Ruthie Newman slept late mornings, and Harry, Allen's father, left very early, so Allen was the only one up and around, and I could stuff jeans in my bookbag and change at his house. The trouble was if I told him about my plan, he might say no. So I simply asked him if he would let me use his powder room the next morning.

"I don't want to wake your mother," I said, "so I won't ring the bell. I'll just whistle through the kitchen keyhole. You'll be out there eating your cereal, and you'll hear me and let me in."

Allen eats six bowls of cold cereal every morning. He will not eat "a good, hot breakfast," which is why Ruthie sleeps late. What mother wants to torture herself watching a growing boy eat nothing but bowl after bowl of cold cereal when she would be only too glad to cook him some eggs and bacon?

Allen is shy enough so that he started to say, "Why do you want to use our—" and then gulped and blushed, which was what I was counting on.

The next morning I whistled at the keyhole. Allen let me in, looked embarrassed, and poured out another bowl of Crispy Critters, while I slipped into the powder room and my blue jeans.

As we walked along to school I said, "Don't you notice anything about me?"

Of course he hadn't. Allen never noticed anything about anybody. That was another thing that bugged Ruthie, who said he was only interested in *things*, not people, that there was something abnormal about him because he didn't seem to be aware of other people; he didn't *relate*. To which my mother said, "Be glad. Debbie is aware of other people. Debbie relates. And to whom? Stupid boys and boys with dandruff."

But as soon as I got to home room, wow. Mrs. Saunders gave me a talk on how she was a teacher, hired to teach, not to discipline. I could march right down and present myself to Mr. Hayden as *his* problem. I was really kind of scared. I'd never been sent to the principal's office, but I kept telling myself it was the principle that mattered, so the heck with the principal.

Mr. Hayden exploded. You'd have thought I was wearing a bikini. I just kept looking gee-gosh-bewildered, I'm-just-a-little-girl, and when he finally ran out of steam I said, "Gee, Mr. Hayden, sir, I sure am sorry, but your directive specifically stated 'No *boy*.' I'm a *girl*."

I stuck out my chest, which is only 32A but enough to get the idea over. Mr. Hayden closed his eyes and clenched his teeth and fists.

"And you can't send me home," I said, "because there's nobody there and I don't have a key and the temperature is below freezing, twenty-nine degrees, humidity fifty percent, barometer—"

Mr. Hayden opened everything: eyes, teeth, fists and the door to the outer office.

"Miss Nussbaum!" he screamed. "Take a memo!"

No boy and no girl, no man and no woman shall be allowed to wear blue jeans during school hours nor while in the school building. Unobservance of this rule shall meet with immediate suspension.

The next day I was a big hero with the original three blue jean boys. I hadn't even known them to talk to, but they all stopped me in the hall and told me I was the greatest and they really appreciated what I had done for them. I said I hadn't done it for them. I had done it for all free people, all civilians.

"Yesterday the armed forces, to-day the schools, tomorrow the world. It's not 1984 yet," I said, "and I'm not through fighting!"

When they asked me if I was going to wear blue jeans anyway and get suspended, I told them about my plan. It made them so happy they all introduced themselves and invited me to have a Coke at the Snackaroo. Paul, Chris and Peter. They were all quite cute, not as cute as Allen but cute enough to impress Mary Jo and Cathy,

who were in the Snackaroo and at loose ends. I'm not at all convinced that Mary Jo and Cathy really had civilian rights in their hearts, but they were more than willing to join the protest.

The next morning when I whistled Allen's keyhole he opened the door and whispered, "I didn't know you were going to be coming here every morning."

I looked at him with my Quiet Desperation look, and he said, "Uh, it's right down the hall to your left," and poured out a bowl of Alpha Bits. He still didn't notice anything until we got to school and Mrs. Saunders turned pale purple and sent Paul, Chris, Peter, Mary Jo, Cathy and me down to Mr. Hayden's office. We were all wearing light tan jeans.

"Now let me do the talking," I said, "and remember not to look defiant or sullen."

Paul, Chris and Peter—who had spent years standing in front of the mirror getting those eyebrows right *down* there, man, right in the old eye socket, cool—opened wide and grinned.

"No, no!" I said. "*Not* 'What—me worry?' Look *innocent* and bewildered." It's not easy to learn my gee-gosh look in one hurried lesson on your way to the guillotine, but they tried, and they did keep their mouths shut.

Mr. Hayden opened his, and when he had to inhale after a ten-minute rant, I quickly said, "Gee, Mr. Hayden, sir, the directive plainly says, right there in black and white, *blue*."

"Young lady," he said, "I don't know what your game is, but you're not going to win."

The new memo had to be altered several times. Its final form was:

In the school and on school grounds or property boys (unless engaged in legitimate and authorized athletics) shall wear at all times trousers or slacks or wash pants (not jeans, cowboy pants or work pants). The slacks or pants or trousers shall not be cut-off nor torn-off nor folded nor rolled up. Boys shall also wear shirts or sweaters. Girls shall wear dresses or skirts and blouses or skirts and sweaters. No other form of clothing will be tolerated.

"That about ties it up," Chris said. "Now what are you going to do?"

"I'm going to keep fighting," I said. "Civilian rights shall not perish."

That evening I asked my mother if I could wear that jumper to school, the nice, royal blue one she bought me for Christmas.

"Well, of course!" she said. "Debbie, I'd love it! I shopped all over, and it *hangs* there."

"Can I wear the shirt with the button-down collar?"

"You'll look adorable! Why, a girl with lovely—"

"You'll have to write a note, Mom. And I don't even know if that will work. You may have to get a lot of outside support. Mr. Hayden has absolutely forbidden any girl to wear anything except a dress or a skirt and blouse or sweater."

That did it. My mother leaped to the bait like a starving trout. That lovely jumper, that sweet little shirt. Was Mr. Hayden crazy? First she called Ruthie, then she called everyone else she knew in PTA. When the PTA got in on it, so did the student council and the local newspaper. Everybody had conflicting opinions. There were mothers (of daughters) demanding that all boys wear suit jackets to school; dressed like gentlemen they would act like gentlemen. Whereupon a mother screeched that her son grew six inches in six weeks and she was not going to be stuck with

a lot of expensive outgrown suit jackets. There was a compromise suggestion that all boys wear ties, but that was voted down when someone explained that it had been tried at another school and the boys wore the ties around their waists or ankles.

All boys wear ties around necks resulted in ties being wound around and around like a choker. *All boys wear ties under collars and tied.* They tied them in the back. One lady got up and said that in this temperature zone there was a problem, but no clothes meant no uniforms! No uniforms meant no war. Her family was from the South, and if there had been no boys in blue or in gray, if all had been dressed only in the skin God gave them, there would have been no war. *All* clothes were unnatural.

The controversy went on for months. When there was a memo *No girl's skirt shall be more than six inches above the kneecap*, I dutifully dragged out my ancient granny dress and shuffled off in sure anticipation of a new memo: *No girl's skirt shall be more than six inches below the kneecap.*

But my heart wasn't in it anymore. I didn't really care at all. All I really cared about was Allen. I didn't just have a crush on him. I really *liked* that Allen. He kept getting bigger and cuter every day. Those cold cereal commercials don't lie. Sugar Dots and Frosty B's were giving him muscles and rosy cheeks. Even though he spent all his time studying or doing homework or down in the basement, while his mother begged him to please, please get a little fresh air, he kept blossoming. And I was going out on Saturdays with Randy, whom I hated.

By now it was almost the end of the school year, and Mr. Hayden had washed his hands of the whole thing. His final memo was: *Anybody can wear anything. What do I care?* Mr. Hayden

was cracking up, but so was I. Every Saturday night when my mother came up and said, "He's here. He's waiting down there. In that furry vest with his skinny bare arms," I shuddered. I really wished Randy would wear a nice soft herringbone or muted plaid, something that would blend into the background so you wouldn't notice how ugly he was. He also wore a tooth-pick in the corner of his mouth. He said it kept him from smoking.

I had almost forgotten about the civilian rights fight, and so had every-body else except Mr. Hayden, a sore loser who decided to get back at me. At the last day assembly, right in front of the entire junior class, Mr. Hayden took his last shot.

"To those of you who doubted that there is a correlation between conservative dress and scholastic achievement, I would like to point out that no boys with excessively long hair and crazy shoes made the honor list. And Miss Debbie Markam, the first girl to enter these halls of learning wearing blue jeans, and who has con-sistently advocated and agitated for extremes in styles, has received a final grade of C minus in advanced algebra, which certainly keeps her out of the upper ten percent. Contrariwise the top student in the class, a boy with straight A's, has managed to maintain his fine school record under the so-called dictatorial militarism of my original directive asking for a degree of prudence and decorum in personal appearance. Allen Newman, please stand up."

And that's when Mr. Hayden lost the fight. The last thing Allen wanted to do was stand up in the assembly hall, but Mrs. Saunders kept poking and hissing at him. Mr. Hayden said, "Look at him. Our top student. And what is he wearing? Clean cut!" Everyone looked at Allen, and Allen looked at the floor. I felt Mr. Hayden had made a mistake there, but I didn't know how big a one.

On the way home Allen said, "Mr. Hayden is a boob! First of all, it was a real achievement for you to get a C minus in advanced algebra. If he knew anything about education, he would have known you have a definite math block, probably developed from incorrect teaching in the formative years. Next, no one has the right to force someone to stand up in the middle of assembly and be stared at just because he's not wearing a furry vest!"

"Well, Allen, he was really asking you to stand up because of the A's."

"That's no excuse. People have the right to be the way they want to be without being pointed out. It's the principle of the thing!"

Allen spent the summer in the country up at his grandmother's. He was killing several birds with that stone. He was growing sunflowers to prove some sort of involved thing about seed pods, number ratio and phototropism. I couldn't understand it, but whatever it was, he proved it.

He was making his grandmother deliriously happy because she's crazy about him. He was making his mother happy because he was getting a lot of fresh air and because she had the chance to clean out their basement.

I got rid of Randy and spent a dull summer baby-sitting, sitting on the beach, and trying to sit on my hair. It was everybody's ambition: hair so long you could sit on it. I never made it. By the end of August I was so bored with everybody's measuring and measuring that I had the whole works chopped off except for some thick bangs and sideburns. My mother fainted.

As she was conveniently sitting on our down-filled sofa at the time, it wasn't much of a faint, and in about two minutes she was up and on the phone with Ruthie.

A week before school started, Allen came home. Then Ruthie fainted. She called my mother, and my mother dashed over, and I dashed along with her because I couldn't believe it! Allen?

"Debbie," he said, "I like your haircut. The back of your neck is very sexy-looking."

He asked me to go to a movie with him and said he wanted to go places all week long so he could get used to people staring at him. He wanted to be in full control of his emotions when school started. He kept giving me little hugs right from the start, and by the end of the week, well, Allen was relating.

The first day of school he called for me and we walked off hand in hand. I was wearing a brown skirt and white blouse. He was wearing brown slacks and a white shirt. We both looked nice and neat, our hair clean and shiny. His was about eight inches longer than mine, hanging down below his shoulders. It was the principle of the thing. He had decided that Mr. Hayden had no scientific basis for the assumption that long hair or crazy shoes led to low marks, or that blue jeans were the cause of a continuing math block in the female.

"I intend to prove to Mr. Hayden that I can be an A student without ever getting a haircut. But I'm nervous! Stick by me, Debbie."

I was willing. Mr. Hayden was standing in the main entrance, welcoming the students. When Allen shook his hand and said, "Good morning, sir. Nice to be back," Mr. Hayden's lips started to tremble. He turned pale and his eyes rolled back, but he didn't faint. He just turned slowly away and walked into his office, a defeated man. I almost felt sorry for him except that when it comes to something as important as civilian rights you've got to be strong. After all, we only have a few years to fight before 1984.　　*

Discussion

1. (a) From whose point of view is this story told? **(b)** What impression do the speaker's words and attitudes give of her character? Locate two or three examples that support your opinion. **(c)** Do you think the speaker was at any time seriously involved in the conflicts of the story? Is the tone she uses to tell the story serious? Explain.

2. (a) Among the characters of the story which seems most satirically portrayed? **(b)** Which seems closest to some real person you know? Explain why.

3. Suppose you were in Mr. Hayden's position and had to keep the type of clothes worn in your school in line with some sort of community standards. How would you phrase the rules? Try writing a sample memo that would cover all possibilities.

4. Of the two, Allen and Debbie, which do you think would be the most stable? the most brilliant? the most creative? the best leader? Explain.

From The Author

Hair, pants, and shoes. Grown men feel threatened when boys change their styles. I have three sons, and in their lifetime "Intolerable!" has been applied to crew-cuts, to duck-tails, to sideburns and bangs, to pointy shoes, boots and sandals, to pants with legs that were too narrow, to pants with legs that were too wide. Each innovation was slowly accepted by the old and then quickly discarded by the young.

But in 1966, by golly, these kids went too far! Blue jeans? Long hair on boys? Never!

Armed with tape measures, brandishing rulers, waving dress codes, the educators waded into battle. It was Custer's last stand. I thought it was funny, and I wrote this story. My second son was a quiet, polite student who always got 100 in everything. Teachers, of course, adored him. I had fun imagining what they would do if he let his hair grow.

Now my youngest son is in high school. He wears—like everyone—long ringlets, torn jeans, ragged work shirts, falling-apart gym shoes. His principal is unshockable.

When *Seventeen* bought this story, they gave it its present title. I had called it, "It's Not 1984 Yet!" But now it almost is, and when it is my grandchildren will be in high school. Perhaps there will be no high schools, no principals, but I think there will be principles and people ready to fight for them.

See
SYMBOL
Handbook
of Literary
Terms
page 565

After being humiliated, Al Condraj
must find a way to restore his lost pride.
What connection is there between his
pride and the parsley garden? See if you
can discover what the garden symbolizes
to Al and why the author chose it
as the title of this story.

The Parsley Garden

William Saroyan

ONE DAY IN AUGUST Al Condraj was wandering through Woolworth's without a penny to spend when he saw a small hammer that was not a toy but a real hammer and he was possessed with a longing to have it. He believed it was just what he needed by which to break the monotony and with which to make something. He had gathered some first-class nails from Foley's Packing House where the boxmakers worked and where they had carelessly dropped at least fifteen cents' worth. He had gladly gone to the trouble of gathering them together because it had seemed to him that a nail, as such, was not something to be wasted. He had the nails, perhaps a half pound of them, at least two hundred of them, in a paper bag in the apple box in which he kept his junk at home.

Now, with the ten-cent hammer he believed he could make something out of box wood and the nails, although he had no idea what. Some sort of a table perhaps, or a small bench.

At any rate he took the hammer and slipped it into the pocket of his overalls, but just as he did so a man took him firmly by the arm without a word and pushed him to the back of the store into a small office. Another man, an older one, was seated behind a desk in the office, working with papers. The younger man, the one who had captured him, was excited and his forehead was covered with sweat.

"Well," he said, "here's one more of them."

The man behind the desk got to his feet and looked Al Condraj up and down.

From THE ASSYRIAN AND OTHER STORIES by William Saroyan. Reprinted by permission of the author and Laurence Pollinger Limited.

"What's *he* swiped?"

"A hammer." The young man looked at Al with hatred. "Hand it over," he said.

The boy brought the hammer out of his pocket and handed it to the young man, who said, "I ought to hit you over the head with it, that's what I ought to do."

He turned to the older man, the boss, the manager of the store, and he said, "What do you want me to do with him?"

"Leave him with me," the older man said.

The younger man stepped out of the office, and the older man sat down and went back to work. Al Condraj stood in the office fifteen minutes before the older man looked at him again.

"Well," he said.

Al didn't know what to say. The man wasn't looking at him, he was looking at the door.

Finally Al said, "I didn't mean to steal it. I just need it and I haven't got any money."

"Just because you haven't got any money doesn't mean you've got a right to steal things," the man said. "Now, does it?"

"No, sir."

"Well, what am I going to do with you? Turn you over to the police?"

Al didn't say anything, but he certainly didn't want to be turned over to the police. He hated the man, but at the same time he realized somebody else could be a lot tougher than he was being.

"If I let you go, will you promise never to steal from this store again?"

"Yes, sir."

"All right," the man said. "Go out this way and don't come back to this store until you've got some money to spend."

He opened a door to the hall that led to the alley, and Al Condraj hurried down the hall and out into the alley.

The first thing he did when he was free was laugh, but he knew he had been humiliated and he was deeply ashamed. It was not in his nature to take things that did not belong to him. He hated the young man who had caught him and he hated the manager of the store who had made him stand in silence in the office so long. He hadn't liked it at all when the young man had said he ought to hit him over the head with the hammer.

He should have had the courage to look him straight in the eye and say, "You and who else?"

Of course he *had* stolen the hammer and he had been caught, but it seemed to him he oughtn't to have been so humiliated.

After he had walked three blocks he decided he didn't want to go home just yet, so he turned around and started walking back to town. He almost believed he meant to go back and say something to the young man who had caught him. And then he wasn't sure he didn't mean to go back and steal the hammer again, and this time *not* get caught. As long as he had been made to feel like a thief anyway, the least he ought to get out of it was the hammer.

Outside the store he lost his nerve, though. He stood in the street, looking in, for at least ten minutes.

Then, crushed and confused and now bitterly ashamed of himself, first for having stolen something, then for having been caught, then for having been humiliated, then for not having guts enough to go back and do the job right, he began walking home again, his mind so troubled that he didn't greet his pal Pete Wawchek when they came face to face outside Graf's Hardware.

When he got home he was too

ashamed to go inside and examine his junk, so he had a long drink of water from the faucet in the back yard. The faucet was used by his mother to water the stuff she planted every year: okra, bell peppers, tomatoes, cucumbers, onions, garlic, mint, eggplants and parsley.

His mother called the whole business the parsley garden, and every night in the summer she would bring chairs out of the house and put them around the table she had had Ondro, the neighborhood handyman, make for her for fifteen cents, and she would sit at the table and enjoy the cool of the garden and the smell of the things she had planted and tended.

Sometimes she would even make a salad and moisten the flat old-country bread and slice some white cheese, and she and he would have supper in the parsley garden. After supper she would attach the water hose to the faucet and water her plants and the place would be cooler than ever and it would smell real good, real fresh and cool and green, all the different growing things making a green-garden smell out of themselves and the air and the water.

After the long drink of water he sat down where the parsley itself was growing and he pulled a handful of it out and slowly ate it. Then he went inside and told his mother what had happened. He even told her what he had *thought* of doing after he had been turned loose: to go back and steal the hammer again.

"I don't want you to steal," his mother said in broken English. "Here is ten cents. You go back to that man and you give him this money and you bring it home, that hammer."

"No," Al Condraj said. "I won't take your money for something I don't really need. I just thought I

ought to have a hammer, so I could make something if I felt like it. I've got a lot of nails and some box wood, but I haven't got a hammer."

"Go buy it, that hammer," his mother said.

"No," Al said.

"All right," his mother said. "Shut up."

That's what she always said when she didn't know what else to say.

Al went out and sat on the steps. His humiliation was beginning to really hurt now. He decided to wander off along the railroad tracks to Foley's because he needed to think about it some more. At Foley's he watched Johnny Gale nailing boxes for ten minutes, but Johnny was too busy to notice him or talk to him, although one day at Sunday school, two or three years ago, Johnny had greeted him and said, "How's the boy?" Johnny worked with a boxmaker's hatchet and everybody in Fresno[1] said he was the fastest boxmaker in town. He was .the closest thing to a machine any packing house ever saw. Foley himself was proud of Johnny Gale.

Al Condraj finally set out for home because he didn't want to get in the way. He didn't want somebody working hard to notice that he was being watched and maybe say to him, "Go on, beat it." He didn't want Johnny Gale to do something like that. He didn't want to invite another humiliation.

On the way home he looked for money but all he found was the usual pieces of broken glass and rusty nails, the things that were always cutting his bare feet every summer.

When he got home his mother had made a salad and set the table, so he sat down to eat, but when he put the food in his mouth he just didn't care

1. **Fresno,** a city in central California.

for it. He got up and went into the three-room house and got his apple box out of the corner of his room and went through his junk. It was all there, the same as yesterday.

He wandered off back to town and stood in front of the closed store, hating the young man who had caught him, and then he went along to the Hippodrome and looked at the display photographs from the two movies that were being shown that day.

Then he went along to the public library to have a look at all the books again, but he didn't like any of them, so he wandered around town some more, and then around half-past eight he went home and went to bed.

His mother had already gone to bed because she had to be up at five to go to work at Inderrieden's, packing figs. Some days there would be work all day, some days there would be only a half a day of it, but whatever his mother earned during the summer had to keep them the whole year.

He didn't sleep much that night because he couldn't get over what had happened, and he went over six or seven ways by which to adjust the matter. He went so far as to believe it would be necessary to kill the young man who had caught him. He also believed it would be necessary for him to steal systematically and successfully the rest of his life. It was a hot night and he couldn't sleep.

Finally, his mother got up and walked barefooted to the kitchen for a drink of water and on the way back she said to him softly, "Shut up."

When she got up at five in the morning he was out of the house, but that had happened many times before. He was a restless boy, and he kept moving all the time every summer. He was making mistakes and paying for them, and he had just tried stealing and had been caught at it and he was troubled. She fixed her breakfast, packed her lunch and hurried off to work, hoping it would be a full day.

It was a full day, and then there was overtime, and although she had no more lunch she decided to work on for the extra money, anyway. Almost all the other packers were staying on, too, and her neighbor across the alley, Leeza Ahboot, who worked beside her, said, "Let us work until the work stops; then we'll go home and fix a supper between us and eat it in your parsley garden where it's so cool. It's a hot day and there's no sense not making an extra fifty or sixty cents."

When the two women reached the garden it was almost nine o'clock, but still daylight, and she saw her son nailing pieces of box wood together, making something with a hammer. It looked like a bench. He had already watered the garden and tidied up the rest of the yard, and the place seemed very nice, and her son seemed very serious and busy. She and Leeza went straight to work for their supper, picking bell peppers and tomatoes and cucumbers and a great deal of parsley for the salad.

Then Leeza went to her house for some bread which she had baked the night before, and some white cheese, and in a few minutes they were having supper together and talking pleasantly about the successful day they had had. After supper, they made Turkish coffee over an open fire in the yard. They drank the coffee and smoked a cigarette apiece, and told one another stories about their experiences in the old country and here in Fresno, and then they looked into their cups at the grounds to see if any good fortune was indicated, and there was: health and work and supper out of doors in the summer and enough money for the rest of the year.

Al Condraj worked and overheard some of the things they said, and then Leeza went home to go to bed, and his mother said, "Where you get it, that hammer, Al?"

"I got it at the store."

"How you get it? You steal it?"

Al Condraj finished the bench and sat on it. "No," he said, "I didn't steal it."

"How you get it?"

"I worked at the store for it," Al said.

"The store where you steal it yesterday?"

"Yes."

"Who give you job?"

"The boss."

"What you do?"

"I carried different stuff to the different counters."

"Well, that's good," the woman said. "How long you work for that little hammer?"

"I worked all day," Al said. "Mr. Clemmer gave me the hammer after I'd worked one hour, but I went right on working. The fellow who caught me yesterday showed me what to do, and we worked together. We didn't talk, but at the end of the day he took me to Mr. Clemmer's office and he told Mr. Clemmer that I'd worked hard all day and ought to be paid at least a dollar."

"That's good," the woman said.

"So Mr. Clemmer put a silver dollar on his desk for me, and then the fellow who caught me yesterday told him the store needed a boy like me every day, for a dollar a day, and Mr. Clemmer said I could have the job."

"That's good," the woman said. "You can make it a little money for yourself."

"I left the dollar on Mr. Clemmer's desk," Al Condraj said, "and I told them both I didn't want the job."

"Why you say that?" the woman said. "Dollar a day for eleven-year-old boy good money. Why you not take job?"

"Because I hate the both of them," the boy said. "I would never work for people like that. I just looked at them and picked up my hammer and walked out. I came home and I made this bench."

"All right," his mother said. "Shut up."

His mother went inside and went

to bed, but Al Condraj sat on the bench he had made and smelled the parsley garden and didn't feel humiliated any more.

But nothing could stop him from hating the two men, even though he knew they hadn't done anything they shouldn't have done.　*

Discussion

1. **(a)** What kind of life do Al Condraj and his mother lead? **(b)** What sort of relationship exists between Al and his mother? **(c)** How does Mrs. Condraj react to her son's stealing?
2. In this story, Al Condraj experiences a number of emotions. **(a)** Why does he try to steal the hammer? **(b)** How could he laugh and be humiliated and ashamed at the same time (page 218, column 2, paragraph 1)? **(c)** Why does he refuse his mother's offer of ten cents to buy the hammer? **(d)** Why does he return to the store and ask for a job? **(e)** Why does he refuse the dollar and the full-time job? **(f)** Why does he hate the men?
3. **(a)** From what point of view is this story told? **(b)** After reading the biography of the author in the next column, tell why you think the author wrote his story from this point of view. **(c)** How does the point of view affect your feelings for the main character in this story?
4. **(a)** Why did Mrs. Condraj plant the parsley garden? **(b)** What place does the garden play in the lives of Al and his mother? **(c)** Reread the last two paragraphs of the story. Why is Al no longer humiliated? **(d)** What does the parsley garden symbolize? **(e)** Why do you think William Saroyan titled his story as he did?
5. Suppose the value of the object stolen had been much greater than ten cents. Would the difference in value alter the meaning of the story? Explain.

The Author

Born to Armenian parents in California in 1908, William Saroyan grew up with a passion for reading. Nevertheless, at the age of thirteen he left school to go to work. His experiences as a telegraph messenger, newsboy, farm laborer, and office clerk provided material for his many works, which include "The Daring Young Man on the Flying Trapeze," a short story which launched his literary career; *My Name is Aram,* stories about his Armenian childhood; *The Human Comedy,* a warm novel of family life; and *The Time of Your Life,* a Pulitzer Prize-winning drama.

Mr. Saroyan writes, "'The Parsley Garden' is a straight-out story, without any kind of literariness, so to put it. The stuff in it happened to me; of course, not necessarily literally, but very definitely in essence. Little things out of the past come along when a writer is working and they very nearly demand not to be ignored—I think that is how it was with 'The Parsley Garden,' which was written suddenly, unexpectedly, in New York sometime in 1949. . . . I have always wanted to see about understanding kids, because they are essentially what the human race just might be, at its best."

What values can a mother
pass on to her child?

Taught Me Purple

Evelyn Tooley Hunt

My mother taught me purple
   Although she never wore it.
Wash-gray was her circle,
   The tenement her orbit.

5 My mother taught me golden
   And held me up to see it,
Above the broken molding,
   Beyond the filthy street.

My mother reached for beauty
10   And for its lack she died,
Who knew so much of duty
   She could not teach me pride.

Discussion

1. (**a**) What kind of life did the speaker's family lead? (**b**) Which lines tell you this?
2. Colors are often used as symbols—red for danger, black for gloom, etc. (**a**) What might the colors *purple* and *golden* symbolize? What lines tell you this? (**b**) How is the mother able to teach her child about beauty even though she has not experienced it?
3. (**a**) How is the quality of pride (line 12) different from the quality of beauty? (**b**) Did the mother possess either pride or beauty? (**c**) Why was she unable to teach pride in the same way she taught beauty?
4. (**a**) What do you think the speaker means by the word *pride?* (**b**) Does the speaker feel that pride is a good quality to have? Explain.

The Author

Evelyn Tooley Hunt is a grandmother who has been writing poetry since her childhood. Though it is only within the last few years that she has been sending her poems to publishers, she has won many honors for her work. "Why do we call it *work?*" she asks. "It's fun!"
   Besides contributing numerous poems to magazines, Mrs. Hunt has compiled two volumes of her poetry, *Look Again, Adam* and *Under the Baobab Tree.*

From *Negro Digest* (February 1964). Reprinted by permission of the author.

How great a sacrifice must someone make
to help someone else discover a sense
of value in himself?

The Kid Nobody Could Handle

Kurt Vonnegut, Jr.

IT WAS SEVEN-THIRTY in the morning.
Waddling, clanking, muddy machines
were tearing a hill to pieces behind a
restaurant, and trucks were hauling
the pieces away. Inside the restaurant, dishes rattled on their shelves.
Tables quaked, and a very kind fat
man with a headful of music looked
down at the jiggling yolks of his breakfast eggs. His wife was visiting relatives out of town. He was on his own.

The kind fat man was George M.
Helmholtz, a man of forty, head of the
music department of Lincoln High
School, and director of the band. Life
had treated him well. Each year he
dreamed the same big dream. He
dreamed of leading as fine a band as
there was on the face of the earth.
And each year the dream came true.

It came true because Helmholtz
was sure that a man couldn't have a
better dream than his. Faced by this
unnerving sureness, Kiwanians, Rotarians, and Lions paid for band
uniforms that cost twice as much as
their best suits, school administrators

let Helmholtz raid the budget for expensive props, and youngsters played
their hearts out for him. When youngsters had no talent, Helmholtz made
them play on guts alone.

Everything was good about Helmholtz's life save his finances. He was
so dazzled by his big dream that he
was a child in the marketplace. Ten
years before, he had sold the hill behind the restaurant to Bert Quinn, the
restaurant owner, for one thousand
dollars. It was now apparent, even to
Helmholtz, that Helmholtz had been
had.

Quinn sat down in the booth with
the bandmaster. He was a bachelor, a
small, dark, humorless man. He
wasn't a well man. He couldn't sleep,
he couldn't stop working, he couldn't
smile warmly. He had only two moods:
one suspicious and self-pitying, the
other arrogant and boastful. The first

mood applied when he was losing money. The second mood applied when he was making it.

Quinn was in the arrogant and boastful mood when he sat down with Helmholtz. He sucked whistlingly on a toothpick, and talked of vision—his own.

"I wonder how many eyes saw the hill before I did?" said Quinn. "Thousands and thousands, I'll bet—and not one saw what I saw. How many eyes?"

"Mine, at least," said Helmholtz. All the hill had meant to him was a panting climb, free blackberries, taxes, and a place for band picnics.

"You inherit the hill from your old man, and it's nothing but a pain in the neck to you," said Quinn. "So you figure you'll stick me with it."

"I didn't figure to stick you," Helmholtz protested. "The good Lord knows the price was more than fair."

"You say that now," said Quinn gleefully. "Sure, Helmholtz, you say that now. Now you see the shopping district's got to grow. Now you see what I saw."

"Yes," said Helmholtz. "Too late, too late." He looked around for some diversion, and saw a fifteen-year-old boy coming toward him, mopping the aisle between booths.

The boy was small but with tough, stringy muscles standing out on his neck and forearms. Childhood lingered in his features, but when he paused to rest, his fingers went hopefully to the silky beginnings of sideburns and a mustache. He mopped like a robot, jerkily, brainlessly, but took pains not to splash suds over the toes of his black boots.

"So what do I do when I get the hill?" said Quinn. "I tear it down, and it's like somebody pulled down a dam. All of a sudden everybody wants to build a store where the hill was."

"Um," said Helmholtz. He smiled genially at the boy. The boy looked through him without a twitch of recognition.

"We all got something," said Quinn. "You got music; I got vision." And he smiled, for it was perfectly clear to both where the money lay. "Think big!" said Quinn. "Dream big! That's what vision is. Keep your eyes wider open than anybody else's."

"That boy," said Helmholtz, "I've seen him around school, but I never knew his name."

Quinn laughed cheerlessly. "Billy the Kid? The storm trooper? Rudolph Valentino?[1] Flash Gordon?" He called the boy. . . . "Hey, Jim! Come here a minute."

Helmholtz was appalled to see that the boy's eyes were as expressionless as oysters.

"This is my brother-in-law's kid by another marriage—before he married my sister," said Quinn. "His name's Jim Donnini, and he's from the south side of Chicago, and he's very tough."

Jim Donnini's hands tightened on the mop handle.

"How do you do?" said Helmholtz.

"Hi," said Jim emptily.

"He's living with me now," said Quinn. "He's my baby now."

"You want a lift to school, Jim?"

"Yeah, he wants a lift to school," said Quinn. "See what you make of him. He won't talk to me." He turned to Jim. "Go on, kid, wash up and shave."

Robotlike, Jim marched away.

"Where are his parents?"

"His mother's dead. His old man married my sister, walked out on her, and stuck her with him. Then the court didn't like the way she was raising him, and put him in foster homes for a while. Then they decided to get

---

1. **Rudolph Valentino** (1895–1926), silent film star and matinée idol.

him clear out of Chicago, so they stuck me with him." He shook his head. "Life's a funny thing, Helmholtz."

"Not very funny, sometimes," said Helmholtz. He pushed his eggs away.

"Like some whole new race of people coming up," said Quinn wonderingly. "Nothing like the kids we got around here. Those boots, the black jacket—and he won't talk. He won't run around with the other kids. Won't study. I don't think he can even read and write very good."

"Does he like music at all? Or drawing? Or animals?" said Helmholtz. "Does he collect anything?"

"You know what he likes?" said Quinn. "He likes to polish those boots—get off by himself and polish those boots. And when he's really in heaven is when he can get off by himself, spread comic books all around him on the floor, polish his boots, and watch television." He smiled ruefully. "Yeah, he had a collection too. And I took it away from him and threw it in the river."

"Threw it in the river?" said Helmholtz.

"Yeah," said Quinn. "Eight knives—some with blades as long as your hand."

Helmholtz paled. "Oh." A prickling sensation spread over the back of his neck. "This is a new problem at Lincoln High. I hardly know what to think about it." He swept spilled salt together in a neat little pile, just as he would have liked to sweep together his scattered thoughts. "It's a kind of sickness, isn't it? That's the way to look at it?"

"Sick?" said Quinn. He slapped the table. "You can say that again!" He tapped his chest. "And Doctor Quinn is just the man to give him what's good for what ails him."

"What's that?" said Helmholtz.

"No more talk about the poor little sick boy," said Quinn grimly. "That's all he's heard from the social workers and the juvenile court, and God knows who all. From now on, he's the no-good bum of a man. I'll ride his tail till he straightens up and flies right or winds up in the can for life. One way or the other."

"I see," said Helmholtz.

"Like listening to music?" said Helmholtz to Jim brightly, as they rode to school in Helmholtz's car.

Jim said nothing. He was stroking his mustache and sideburns, which he had not shaved off.

"Ever drum with the fingers or keep time with your feet?" said Helmholtz. He had noticed that Jim's boots were decorated with chains that had no function but to jingle as he walked.

Jim sighed with ennui.

"Or whistle?" said Helmholtz. "If you do any of those things, it's just like picking up the keys to a whole new world—a world as beautiful as any world can be."

Jim gave a soft Bronx cheer.

"There!" said Helmholtz. "You've illustrated the basic principle of the family of brass wind instruments. The glorious voice of every one of them starts with a buzz on the lips."

The seat springs of Helmholtz's old car creaked under Jim, as Jim shifted his weight. Helmholtz took this as a sign of interest, and he turned to smile in comradely fashion. But Jim had shifted his weight in order to get a cigarette from inside his tight leather jacket.

Helmholtz was too upset to comment at once. It was only at the end of the ride, as he turned into the teachers' parking lot, that he thought of something to say.

"Sometimes," said Helmholtz, "I get so lonely and disgusted, I don't see how I can stand it. I feel like doing all kinds of crazy things, just for the heck of it—things that might even be bad for me."

Jim blew a smoke ring expertly.

"And then!" said Helmholtz. He snapped his fingers and honked his horn. "And then, Jim, I remember I've got at least one tiny corner of the universe I can make just the way I want it! I can go to it and gloat over it until I'm brand-new and happy again."

"Aren't you the lucky one?" said Jim. He yawned.

"I am, for a fact," said Helmholtz. "My corner of the universe happens to be the air around my band. I can fill it with music. Mr. Beeler, in zoology, has his butterflies. Mr. Trottman, in physics, has his pendulum and tuning forks. Making sure everybody has a corner like that is about the biggest job we teachers have. I—"

The car door opened and slammed, and Jim was gone. Helmholtz stamped out Jim's cigarette and buried it under the gravel of the parking lot.

Helmholtz's first class of the morning was C Band, where beginners thumped and wheezed and tooted as best they could, and looked down the long, long, long road through B Band to A Band, the Lincoln High School Ten Square Band, the finest band in the world.

Helmholtz stepped onto the podium and raised his baton. "You are better than you think," he said. "A-one, a-two, a-three." Down came the baton.

C Band set out in its quest for beauty—set out like a rusty switch engine, with valves stuck, pipes clogged, unions leaking, bearings dry.

Helmholtz was still smiling at the end of the hour, because he'd heard in his mind the music as it was going to be someday. His throat was raw, for he had been singing with the band for the whole hour. He stepped into the hall for a drink from the fountain.

As he drank, he heard the jingling of chains. He looked up at Jim Donnini. Rivers of students flowed between classrooms, pausing in friendly eddies, flowing on again. Jim was alone. When he paused, it wasn't to greet anyone, but to polish the toes of his boots on his trousers legs. He had the air of a spy in a melodrama, missing nothing, liking nothing, looking forward to the great day when everything would be turned upside down.

"Hello, Jim," said Helmholtz. "Say, I was just thinking about you. We've got a lot of clubs and teams that meet after school. And that's a good way to get to know a lot of people."

Jim measured Helmholtz carefully with his eyes. "Maybe I don't want to know a lot of people," he said. "Ever think of that?" He set his feet down hard to make his chains jingle as he walked away.

When Helmholtz returned to the podium for a rehearsal of B Band, there was a note waiting for him, calling him to a special faculty meeting.

The meeting was about vandalism.

Someone had broken into the school and wrecked the office of Mr. Crane, head of the English Department. The poor man's treasures—books, diplomas, snapshots of England, the beginnings of eleven novels—had been ripped and crumpled, mixed, dumped and trampled, and drenched with ink.

Helmholtz was sickened. He couldn't believe it. He couldn't bring himself to think about it. It didn't become real to him until late that night, in a dream. In the dream Helmholtz saw a boy with barracuda teeth, with claws like baling hooks. The monster climbed into a window of the high school and dropped to the floor of the band rehearsal room. The monster clawed to shreds the heads of the biggest drum in the state. Helmholtz woke up howling. There was nothing to do but dress and go to the school.

At two in the morning, Helmholtz caressed the drum heads in the band rehearsal room, with the night watchman looking on. He rolled the drum back and forth on its cart, and he turned the light inside on and off, on and off. The drum was unharmed. The night watchman left to make his rounds.

The band's treasure house was safe. With the contentment of a miser counting his money, Helmholtz fondled the rest of the instruments, one by one. And then he began to polish the sousaphones. As he polished, he could hear the great horns roaring, could see them flashing in the sunlight, with the Stars and Stripes and the banner of Lincoln High going before.

"Yump-yump, tiddle-tiddle, yump-yump, tiddle-tiddle!" sang Helmholtz happily. "Yump-yump-yump, ra-a-a-a-a-a, yump-yump, yump-yump — boom!"

As he paused to choose the next number for his imaginary band to play, he heard a furtive noise in the chemistry laboratory next door. Helmholtz sneaked into the hall, jerked open the laboratory door, and flashed on the lights. Jim Donnini had a bottle of acid in either hand. He was splashing acid over the periodic table of the elements, over the blackboards covered with formulas, over the bust of Lavoisier.[2] The scene was the most repulsive thing Helmholtz could have looked upon.

Jim smiled with thin bravado.

"Get out," said Helmholtz.

"What're you gonna do?" said Jim.

"Clean up. Save what I can," said Helmholtz dazedly. He picked up a wad of cotton waste and began wiping up the acid.

"You gonna call the cops?" said Jim.

"I — I don't know," said Helmholtz. "No thoughts come. If I'd caught you hurting the bass drum, I think I would have killed you with a single blow. But I wouldn't have had any intelligent thoughts about what you were — what you thought you were doing."

"It's about time this place got set on its ear," said Jim.

"Is it?" said Helmholtz. "That must be so, if one of our students wants to murder it."

"What good is it?" said Jim.

"Not much good, I guess," said Helmholtz. "It's just the best thing human beings ever managed to do." He was helpless, talking to himself. He had a bag of tricks for making boys behave like men — tricks that played on boyish fears and dreams and loves. But here was a boy without fear, without dreams, without love.

"If you smashed up all the schools," said Helmholtz, "we wouldn't have any hope left."

"What hope?" said Jim.

"The hope that everybody will be glad he's alive," said Helmholtz. "Even you."

"That's a laugh," said Jim. "All I ever got out of this dump was a hard time. So what're you gonna do?"

"I have to do something, don't I?" said Helmholtz.

"I don't care what you do," said Jim.

"I know," said Helmholtz. "I know." He marched Jim into his tiny office off the band rehearsal room. He dialed the telephone number of the principal's home. Numbly, he waited for the bell to get the old man from his bed.

2. **Lavoisier** (lä vwä zyā'), Antoine Laurent Lavoisier (1743–1794), French chemist who discovered oxygen.

P. LENIHAN

Jim dusted his boots with a rag.

Helmholtz suddenly dropped the telephone into its cradle before the principal could answer. "Isn't there anything you care about but ripping, hacking, bending, rending, smashing, bashing?" he cried. "Anything? Anything but those boots?"

"Go on! Call up whoever you're gonna call," said Jim.

Helmholtz opened a locker and took a trumpet from it. He thrust the trumpet into Jim's arms. "There!" he said, puffing with emotion. "There's my treasure. It's the dearest thing I own. I give it to you to smash. I won't move a muscle to stop you. You can have the added pleasure of watching my heart break while you do it."

Jim looked at him oddly. He laid down the trumpet.

"Go on!" said Helmholtz. "If the world has treated you so badly, it deserves to have the trumpet smashed!"

"I—" said Jim. Helmholtz grabbed his belt, put a foot behind him, and dumped him on the floor.

Helmholtz pulled Jim's boots off and threw them into a corner. "There!" said Helmholtz savagely. He jerked the boy to his feet again and thrust the trumpet into his arms once more.

Jim Donnini was barefoot now. He had lost his socks with his boots. The boy looked down. The feet that had once seemed big black clubs were narrow as chicken wings now—bony and blue, and not quite clean.

The boy shivered, then quaked. Each quake seemed to shake something loose inside, until, at last, there was no boy left. No boy at all. Jim's head lolled, as though he waited only for death.

Helmholtz was overwhelmed by remorse. He threw his arms around the boy. "Jim! Jim—listen to me, boy!"

Jim stopped quaking.

"You know what you've got there—the trumpet?" said Helmholtz. "You know what's special about it?"

Jim only sighed.

"It belonged to John Philip Sousa!"[3] said Helmholtz. He rocked and shook Jim gently, trying to bring him back to life. "I'll trade it to you, Jim—for your boots. It's yours, Jim! John Philip Sousa's trumpet is yours! It's worth hundreds of dollars, Jim—thousands!"

Jim laid his head on Helmholtz's breast.

"It's better than boots, Jim," said Helmholtz. "You can learn to play it. You're somebody, Jim. You're the boy with John Philip Sousa's trumpet!"

Helmholtz released Jim slowly, sure the boy would topple. Jim didn't fall. He stood alone. The trumpet was still in his arms.

"I'll take you home, Jim," said Helmholtz. "Be a good boy and I won't say a word about tonight. Polish your trumpet, and learn to be a good boy."

"Can I have my boots?" said Jim dully.

"No," said Helmholtz. "I don't think they're good for you."

He drove Jim home. He opened the car windows and the air seemed to refresh the boy. He let him out at Quinn's restaurant. The soft pats of Jim's bare feet on the sidewalk echoed down the empty street. He climbed through a window, and into his bedroom behind the kitchen. And all was still.

The next morning the waddling, clanking, muddy machines were making the vision of Bert Quinn come true. They were smoothing off the place where the hill had been behind the restaurant. They were making it as level as a billiard table.

---

3. *John Philip Sousa* (1854–1932), American conductor and composer of marching band music.

Helmholtz sat in a booth again. Quinn joined him again. Jim mopped again. Jim kept his eyes down, refusing to notice Helmholtz. And he didn't seem to care when a surf of suds broke over the toes of his small and narrow brown Oxfords.

"Eating out two mornings in a row?" said Quinn. "Something wrong at home?"

"My wife's still out of town," said Helmholtz.

"While the cat's away—" said Quinn. He winked.

"When the cat's away," said Helmholtz, "this mouse gets lonesome."

Quinn leaned forward. "Is that what got you out of bed in the middle of the night, Helmholtz? Loneliness?" He jerked his head at Jim. "Kid! Go get Mr. Helmholtz his horn."

Jim raised his head, and Helmholtz saw that his eyes were oysterlike again. He marched away to get the trumpet.

Quinn now showed that he was excited and angry. "You take away his boots and give him a horn, and I'm not supposed to get curious?" he said. "I'm not supposed to start asking questions? I'm not supposed to find out you caught him taking the school apart? You'd make a lousy crook, Helmholtz. You'd leave your baton, sheet music, and your driver's license at the scene of the crime."

"I don't think about hiding clues," said Helmholtz. "I just do what I do. I was going to tell you."

Quinn's feet danced and his shoes squeaked like mice. "Yes?" he said. "Well, I've got some news for you too."

"What is that?" said Helmholtz uneasily.

"It's all over with Jim and me," said Quinn. "Last night was the payoff. I'm sending him back where he came from."

"To another string of foster homes?" said Helmholtz weakly.

"Whatever the experts figure out to do with a kid like that." Quinn sat back, exhaled noisily, and went limp with relief.

"You can't," said Helmholtz.

"I can," said Quinn.

"That will be the end of him," said Helmholtz. "He can't stand to be thrown away like that one more time."

"He can't feel anything," said Quinn. "I can't help him; I can't hurt him. Nobody can. There isn't a nerve in him."

"A bundle of scar tissue," said Helmholtz.

The bundle of scar tissue returned with the trumpet. Impassively, he laid it on the table in front of Helmholtz.

Helmholtz forced a smile. "It's yours, Jim," he said. "I gave it to you."

"Take it while you got the chance, Helmholtz," said Quinn. "He doesn't want it. All he'll do is swap it for a knife or a pack of cigarettes."

"He doesn't know what it is, yet," said Helmholtz. "It takes a while to find out."

"Is it any good?" said Quinn.

"Any good?" said Helmholtz, not believing his ears. "Any good?" He didn't see how anyone could look at the instrument and not be warmed and dazzled by it. "Any good?" he murmured. "It belonged to John Philip Sousa."

Quinn blinked stupidly. "Who?"

Helmholtz's hands fluttered on the table top like the wings of a dying bird. "Who was John Philip Sousa?" he piped. No more words came. The subject was too big for a tired man to cover. The dying bird expired and lay still.

After a long silence, Helmholtz picked up the trumpet. He kissed the cold mouthpiece and pumped the valves in a dream of a brilliant cadenza. Over the bell of the instrument, Helmholtz saw Jim Donnini's face, seemingly floating in space—all but deaf and blind. Now Helmholtz saw the futility of men and their treasures. He had thought that his greatest treasure, the trumpet, could buy a soul for Jim. The trumpet was worthless.

Deliberately, Helmholtz hammered the trumpet against the table edge. He bent it around a coat tree. He handed the wreck to Quinn.

"Ya busted it," said Quinn, amazed. "Why'dja do that? What's that prove?"

"I—I don't know," said Helmholtz. A terrible blasphemy rumbled deep in him, like the warning of a volcano. And then, irresistibly, out it came. "Life is no damn good," said Helmholtz. His face twisted as he fought back tears and shame.

Helmholtz, the mountain that walked like a man, was falling apart. Jim Donnini's eyes filled with pity and alarm. They came alive. They became human. Helmholtz had got a message through. Quinn looked at Jim, and something like hope flickered for the first time in his bitterly lonely old face.

Two weeks later, a new semester began at Lincoln High.

In the band rehearsal room, the members of the C Band were waiting for their leader—were waiting for their destinies as musicians to unfold.

Helmholtz stepped onto the podium, and rattled his baton against his music stand. "The Voices of Spring," he said. "Everybody hear that? The Voices of Spring?"

There were rustling sounds as the musicians put the music on their stands. In the pregnant silence that followed their readiness, Helmholtz glanced at Jim Donnini, who sat on the last seat of the worst trumpet section of the worst band in school.

His trumpet, John Philip Sousa's trumpet, George M. Helmholtz's trumpet, had been repaired.

"Think of it this way," said Helmholtz. "Our aim is to make the world more beautiful than it was when we came into it. It can be done. You can do it."

A small cry of despair came from Jim Donnini. It was meant to be private, but it pierced every ear with its poignancy.

"How?" said Jim.

"Love yourself," said Helmholtz, "and make your instrument sing about it. A-one, a-two, a-three." Down came his baton. ✳

Discussion

1. (a) What does the opening conversation between Helmholtz and Quinn reveal about the character of each man? **(b)** Describe Jim Donnini's appearance and actions just after he is introduced to Helmholtz. **(c)** What is Helmholtz's attitude toward Jim at this point? Quinn's? **(d)** What is Jim's attitude toward Helmholtz during the ride to school?

2. (a) What does Helmholtz do after he discovers Jim destroying the chemistry lab? **(b)** Which of Helmholtz's actions do you find most unexpected? Why? **(c)** Which of his actions seem most in keeping with his character? **(d)** What does the trumpet mean to Helmholtz at this point? to Jim?

3. (a) What kind of person does Quinn show himself to be when he discovers what Jim has done? What do his words and actions say about his values? **(b)** What do Helmholtz's actions during the confrontation in the restaurant say about his values? **(c)** Is there any observable effect on Jim?

4. (a) Does the final scene in the story hold out any hope for Jim in the future? **(b)** What might he have learned about what people value? **(c)** Do you find the ending of the story satisfying? realistic? Would you change it? How?

Word Study

From the words following each sentence below, select the word which is most nearly synonymous with the italicized word in the sentence. You may refer to your Glossary if necessary.

1. Quinn was in an *arrogant* mood.
jubilant   haughty   bashful
2. *Genially*, Helmholtz offered Jim a ride to school.
Crossly   Pleasantly   Extravagantly
3. The music teacher's conversation made Jim sigh with *ennui*.
delirium   boredom   decorum
4. Mr. Helmholtz was *appalled* at the lifeless look in Jim's eyes.
dismayed   assuaged   chastened
5. When told to return the trumpet to Helmholtz, Jim *impassively* laid the instrument on the table in front of the teacher.
wistfully   unemotionally   insolently

The Author

In the 1960's, Kurt Vonnegut emerged as one of the most widely read and influential writers of the contemporary scene. Although the ending of "The Kid Nobody Could Handle" offers a glimmer of hope for its characters, Vonnegut tends in much of his writing to emphasize despair and disillusionment. Indeed, he has described himself as "a total pessimist." Much of his writing is a reaction to his experiences in World War II, among them the destruction of Dresden, Germany by American bombers—a holocaust that Vonnegut himself lived through as a prisoner of war.

Unit **3** Review

There was a choked hush. Then, breaking the silence, came a plaintive voice from the back of the crowd: "What? *Every* Wednesday?"[1]

1. Does the anecdote have a theme? What is it?

2. What do you think the author is satirizing in this anecdote? Is he satirizing more than one thing? Explain.

[1]From the *Courier Magazine*. Reprinted by permission of Norman Kark Publications Ltd.

Part I

1. In this unit you have explored the values held by different people in various situations. What would happen in the world today if everyone had the values of (**a**) the Emperor, (**b**) Bert Quinn, (**c**) the narrator in "No Boy. I'm a Girl!" (**d**) Al Condraj?

2. Suppose that the speaker in "Nightmare Number Three," Charlie Gordon, and Dr. Nemur could observe the events which take place in "The Flying Machine." Consider the character and experiences of each. Decide whether each would sympathize with the inventor or with the Emperor. Be prepared to defend your position.

3. Explain what each object symbolizes to the people listed after it: (**a**) the flying machine to the Emperor, to the inventor; (**b**) a silver dollar to the narrator in "Children of the Harvest," to the students in Wenatchee School; (**c**) Algernon to Charlie Gordon, to Dr. Nemur.

Part II

All personnel had been summoned to listen to a most important announcement by the chairman. "Ladies and gentlemen," he said, "for some time now the board has been aware that a rumor has been circulating. It is true; on the first of next month the whole plant will change over to full automation."

Rumble, rumble, rumble went the multitude. The chairman raised his hand for silence, then went on. "Not a single person will be laid off. Wages will continue as before. Bonuses will be as usual. Holidays with pay, sick benefits, and pension schemes will go on. Every member of the firm will be expected to appear for work on Wednesday of each week. Wednesday only."

SUGGESTED READING

CLEMENS, SAMUEL, *The Adventures of Huckleberry Finn.* (Dodd *Dell) In this classic story, Huck, the waif, and Jim, an escaping slave, take refuge on a Mississippi raft. *Tom Sawyer* (Dodd *Airmont) is the story of a boy's vigorous, humorous escapades in the Missouri of the author's youth.

DICKENS, CHARLES, *Christmas Stories.* (World) This collection contains the famous "A Christmas Carol" and other favorites.

EARL, LAWRENCE, *She Loved a Wicked City.* (Dutton) Warned of frustration and failure, meeting with superstition and cruel opposition, Mary Bell, a missionary nurse, worked tirelessly to help the sick of the Chinese city of Tatung.

FELSEN, H. G., *Hot Rod.* (Dutton) Bud Crayne is proud to be thought of as the most reckless driver in Avondale. He is the idol of the younger boys, who listen to his boast that "Speed will get you anywhere."

GARRATY, JOHN A. (editor), *Quarrels That Have Shaped the Constitution.* (Harper) Far from being dull reports, these exciting cases from the files of the Supreme Court read like detective fiction, but have the virtue of being true. Good readers will appreciate the significant human values that emerge from the accounts of conflicts between interests and ideals.

GRAY, J. GLENN, *The Warriors.* (Harcourt) From his experiences in World War II, Gray, a philosopher and soldier, sets down his observations about men and war.

• HATANO, ISOKO and ICHIRO, *Mother and Son.* (Houghton) The simple inspiring courage of a Japanese boy and his mother trying to live normal lives in the abnormal war and postwar years of 1944–1948 is revealed through their letters to one another.

KENNEDY, JOHN F., *Profiles in Courage.* (**Harper) Good readers will enjoy this study of moral courage in men who faced crises. The collection includes sketches of John Quincy Adams, Daniel Webster, Sam Houston, Robert A. Taft, and others.

MARSHALL, CATHERINE, *A Man Called Peter.* (McGraw) Catherine Marshall reveals both her husband and herself in this biography of Peter Marshall, who as minister and Senate Chaplain made a remarkable impression on the religious life of the entire country.

MEANS, FLORENCE C., *Knock at the Door, Emmy.* (Houghton) At fifteen, Emmy Lou Lane is fed up with the migrant life that her father loves and her mother endures. Her longing for a permanent home is the motivation she needs to face almost insurmountable obstacles.

RICHTER, CONRAD, *The Light in the Forest.* (Knopf *Bantam) Here is a provocative story of conflicting loyalties as a white boy is returned to his parents' civilization after years of captivity by the Indians.

RIZK, SALOM, *Syrian Yankee.* (Doubleday) Through his fascinating story of how he established his claim to American citizenship and became a distinguished lecturer, Salom Rizk reveals the intense love of country which gave him the determination to become a true American.

ROOSEVELT, ELEANOR, *The Autobiography of Eleanor Roosevelt.* (Harper) This book contains the most interesting material from Mrs. Roosevelt's three previous autobiographical volumes, *This Is My Story, This I Remember,* and *On My Own.*

SPENDER, D. J., *The Jing Affair.* (Wagnalls) Here is an imaginative story of international conflict, the lives of millions at stake, with the courage and ideals of a small group the only defense against conquest and slavery.

TUNIS, JOHN R., *All-American.* (Harcourt) A boy's values are severely tested when a football star is barred from a game because of the color of his skin.

WIBBERLEY, LEONARD, *The Mouse That Roared.* (Little *Bantam) The enduring and endearing human values that evolve from a conflict of a little nation with a big nation form the substance of this hilarious, unforgettable yarn.

*paperback
**hardcover and paperback

Poetry

A poem can be many things, said many ways. It can speak softly, like a quick fluttering in the stillness, or it can speak out like a fist beating against the ear. It can concern everything from animal crackers and circuses to cruel injustice and horrible deaths. It can be a laugh, a cry, a song, a curse. It can reflect the stench of hate or the freshness of love. It can be an adventure, a sentiment, an observation, or a comment. It can be as various as all the things real and unreal that all people in this world can feel, imagine, and express.

Section 1

In the poems in this section, seven poets set down
some impressions of the world.
The subjects they observe are commonplace,
but the ways in which they view them are not.
How do these seven keen observers use words to help you
share their visions and
form visions of your own?

Prelude I

T. S. Eliot

The winter evening settles down
With smell of steak in passageways.
Six o'clock.
The burnt-out ends of smoky days.
5 And now a gusty shower wraps
The grimy scraps
Of withered leaves about your feet
And newspapers from vacant lots;
The showers beat
10 On broken blinds and chimney pots,
And at the corner of the street
A lonely cab horse steams and stamps.

And then the lighting of the lamps.

Discussion

1. **(a)** Does "Prelude I" take place in the city or the country? **(b)** Is it set in the past or the present? **(c)** What is the season? **(d)** Describe the weather.

2. **(a)** Should line 3 be read as a cry, a sigh, or a statement? Why? **(b)** To what might the poet be comparing the day's end in line 4? **(c)** Which of the following words best describes the tone lines 3 and 4 establish: tragic, unhappy, drab?

3. **(a)** Is the image the poet creates in lines 5–8 a happy or a grim one? Explain. **(b)** How would this image be altered if *grimy* were changed to *gaudy* and *withered* to *autumn*?

4. **(a)** Which images in lines 9–10 contribute to the ugliness of the scene? **(b)** How does the image in the last line differ from all the other images in the poem? **(c)** What, then, is the poet saying about beauty and ugliness?

The Author

Thomas Stearns Eliot (1888–1965), one of the most scholarly and influential poets of his time, was born in St. Louis, Missouri, but spent most of his life in England. Eliot's poetry often reflects his immense knowledge and reveals an ability to probe behind the obvious to find hidden, often more important truths. Much of his poetry, especially his early work, is concerned with the hopelessness and helplessness of life. But one group of his poems, a collection entitled *Old Possum's Book of Practical Cats*, reveals a sense of humor and a sharp wit.

THE LONELY STREET

William Carlos Williams

School is over. It is too hot
to walk at ease. At ease
in light frocks they walk the streets
to while the time away.
5 They have grown tall. They hold
pink flames in their right hands.
In white from head to foot,
with sidelong, idle look —
in yellow, floating stuff,
10 black sash and stockings —
touching their avid mouths
with pink sugar on a stick —
like a carnation each holds in her hand —
they mount the lonely street.

Discussion

1. (**a**) In what season is the poem probably set? (**b**) For whom is it "too hot/to walk at ease"? (**c**) Who does walk at ease? (**d**) Why do you think the speaker tells us "They have grown tall"?

2. (**a**) How many girls are walking on the street? (**b**) How is each one dressed? (**c**) What are they eating? (**d**) How old do they seem to be?

3. If this poem were a painting, would the painting probably be one in which the figures were sharply defined, or indefinite and slightly blurred? Explain.

4. (**a**) What reasons might the poet have had for calling this poem "The Lonely Street"? (**b**) Do you think the title is a fitting one? Why or why not?

5. Both Eliot and Williams describe street scenes. (**a**) What differences in the poets' attitudes toward their subject can you find? (**b**) Are there any similarities in their attitudes?

The Author

Dr. William Carlos Williams (1883–1963) was born, grew up, practiced medicine, wrote poetry, and died in a New Jersey town. But his poems, short stories, and novels won him an international reputation. Williams' poetry resembles conversation; his subject matter is the commonplace stuff of life stripped of unnecessary detail. His poems *seem* simple but upon examination they reveal more than their surface presents.

See
FIGURATIVE LANGUAGE
Handbook
of Literary
Terms
page 543

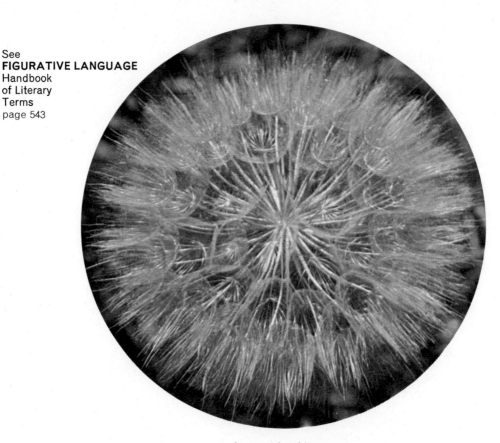

dandelions

Deborah Austin

under cover of night and rain
the troops took over.
waking to total war in beleaguered houses
over breakfast we faced the batteries
5 marshalled by wall and stone, deployed
with a master strategy no one had suspected
and now all
firing

pow   CONTINUED

10 all day, all yesterday
and all today
the barrage continued
deafening sight.
reeling now, eyes ringing from noise, from walking
15 gingerly over the mined lawns
exploded at every second
rocked back by the starshellfire
concussion of gold on green
bringing battle-fatigue
20 pow by lionface firefur pow by
goldburst shellshock pow by
whoosh   splat   splinteryellow   pow   by
pow   by   pow
tomorrow smoke drifts up
25 from the wrecked battalions,
all the ammunition, firegold fury, gone.
smoke
drifts
thistle-blown
30 over the war-zone, only

here and there, in the shade by the
peartree
pow   in the crack by the
curbstone   pow   and back of the
35 ashcan, lonely
guerrilla snipers, hoarding
their fire shrewdly
never

pow

40 surrender

Discussion

1. (a) What are the "troops" mentioned in line 2 of the poem? How do you know? (b) When do the troops appear? (c) What do they seem to be attacking? (d) Explain the comparison on which the first stanza is based. (e) What kind of figurative expression is the comparison?
2. (a) How long does the battle continue? (b) What finally stops the siege? (c) To what does "smoke" in line 24 refer? (d) What are "guerrilla snipers" (line 36)? (e) Why might these guerrilla snipers be able to outlast the regular troops?
3. (a) Find images in the poem that appeal to sight. (b) A "deafening sight" is one that has the same shocking effect on the eyes as an explosion has on the ears. What is probably meant by "eyes ringing from noise" (line 14)?
4. (a) What words help you hear the dandelions' barrage as well as see it? (b) What is the effect of the frequent "pows" and run-together words in the middle section of the poem?
5. Which of the following words best describes the tone: (a) grim; (b) whimsical; (c) happy? Explain.

A HILLSIDE THAW

Robert Frost

To think to know the country and not know
The hillside on the day the sun lets go
Ten million silver lizards out of snow!
As often as I've seen it done before
5 I can't pretend to tell the way it's done.
It looks as if some magic of the sun
Lifted the rug that bred them on the floor
And the light breaking on them made them run.
But if I thought to stop the wet stampede,
10 And caught one silver lizard by the tail,
And put my foot on one without avail,
And threw myself wet-elbowed and wet-kneed
In front of twenty others' wriggling speed ——

CONTINUED

In the confusion of them all aglitter,
15 And birds that joined in the excited fun
By doubling and redoubling song and twitter ——
I have no doubt I'd end by holding none.

It takes the moon for this. The sun's a wizard
By all I tell; but so's the moon a witch.
20 From the high west she makes a gentle cast
And suddenly, without a jerk or twitch,
She has her spell on every single lizard.
I fancied when I looked at six o'clock
The swarm still ran and scuttled just as fast.
25 The moon was waiting for her chill effect.
I looked at nine: the swarm was turned to rock
In every lifelike posture of the swarm,
Transfixed on mountain slopes almost erect.
Across each other and side by side they lay.
30 The spell that so could hold them as they were
Was wrought through trees without a breath of storm
To make a leaf, if there had been one, stir.
It was the moon's: she held them until day,
One lizard at the end of every ray.
35 The thought of my attempting such a stay!

Discussion

1. (a) What are the "Ten million silver lizards" mentioned in line 3? (b) Explain lines 6–8 in literal terms. (c) Do you think the comparisons made in the first eight lines of the poem are effective? Why or why not?
2. (a) In the first stanza, what does the speaker imagine himself doing? (b) What does he think would happen if he actually tried to do this?
3. (a) What is meant by "this" in line 18? (b) In reality, what is the moon's "spell" (line 22)?
4. (a) What actually happens in lines 26–29? (b) Explain the meaning of lines 30–32. (c) If this poem were rewritten as a weather report, how might it read?
5. (a) What impression does "Hillside Thaw" give you of the speaker? (b) Does the last line add to or detract from your impression? Explain.

The Author

Robert Frost (1874–1963) has long been considered one of America's most important poets. A man who never finished college, Frost was awarded more than twenty degrees during his lifetime. He was a favorite lecturer at such schools as Yale, Dartmouth, and Harvard, where his insights and witticisms captivated students.

Frost's works reflect a deceptively casual attitude toward life. Written in unadorned Yankee language, they are about commonplace things —stones, fences, snowfalls, trees, the seasons—dealt with in uncommon ways.

DOG AT NIGHT

Louis Untermeyer

See
RHYME
Handbook
of Literary
Terms
page 560

At first he stirs uneasily in sleep
And, since the moon does not run off, unfolds
Protesting paws. Grumbling that he must keep
Both eyes awake, he whimpers; then he scolds
5 And, rising to his feet, demands to know
The stranger's business. You who break the dark
With insolent light, who are you? Where do you go?
But nothing answers his indignant bark.
The moon ignores him, walking on as though
10 Dogs never were. Stiffened to fury now,
His small hairs stand upright, his howls come fast,
And terrible to hear is the bow-wow
That tears the night. Stirred by this bugle-blast,
The farmer's hound grows active; without pause
15 Summons her mastiff and the cur that lies
Three fields away to rally to the cause.
And the next county wakes. And miles beyond
Throats ring themselves and brassy lungs respond
With threats, entreaties, bellowings and cries,
20 Chasing the white intruder down the skies.

Discussion

1. (**a**) What disturbs the dog? (**b**) Why does it disturb him? (**c**) What makes the dog grow furious? (**d**) How does he demonstrate his anger?
2. (**a**) What effect does the dog's howling have on other dogs? (**b**) Find words that suggest the different noises made by the dogs.
3. What images in the poem appeal to your sense of hearing?
4. (**a**) How is the moon personified? (**b**) How does the personification help you understand the dog's attitude toward the moon?

5. (**a**) Chart the rhyme scheme of "Dog at Night." (**b**) Does it contain any internal rhymes?
6. (**a**) Is "Dog at Night" light or serious in tone? (**b**) Does it seem to have any purpose other than to describe the dogs' reaction to the moon? (**c**) What is the speaker's attitude toward the dogs and the task they have taken upon themselves? (**d**) Are the rhymes in keeping with the purpose of the poem and the speaker's attitude?

The Author

Louis Untermeyer's first ambition was to become a composer, but at seventeen he gave up his dream and entered his father's jewelry-manufacturing business. Twenty years later, after having written eleven books, he left the family firm to give more time to his writing. Untermeyer has been active in almost every field of literature; among his outstanding contributions are the anthologies *Modern American Poetry* and *Modern British Poetry,* both highly respected critical works.

from # Bird-Witted

Marianne Moore

With innocent wide penguin eyes, three
   large fledgling mocking-birds below
the pussy-willow tree,
   stand in a row,
5 wings touching, feebly solemn,
  till they see
      their no longer larger
      mother bringing
something which will partially
10 feed one of them.

Toward the high-keyed intermittent squeak
   of broken-carriage springs, made by
the three similar, meek-
   coated bird's-eye
15 freckled forms she comes; and when
from the beak
      of one, the still living
      beetle has dropped
out, she picks it up and puts
20 it in again.

Excerpt from "Bird-Witted," reprinted by permission of The Macmillan Company and Faber and Faber Ltd. from COLLECTED POEMS by Marianne Moore. Copyright 1941 by Marianne Moore. First published in Great Britain in 1936.

Discussion

1. (a) What type of bird is described in this poem? **(b)** What are the young birds doing? **(c)** What clues to their ages are given in the poem?
2. (a) Point out images in the poem that help you visualize the birds. **(b)** Which image describes the sounds they make?
3. What is the speaker's attitude toward the birds? How do you know?
4. Read these stanzas aloud. Why are the rhymes so unnoticeable?

The Author

Original, imaginative, thoughtful, musical—these are only a few of the terms that have been used to describe Marianne Moore (1887–1972). Miss Moore was an observer, and when she looked at any object she saw what most people never notice. It was her expressed desire to make her writing as clear and vivid as she knew how to do, and she accomplished this by filling her poems with a great many specific details. Like many modern poets, Miss Moore wrote about the common matters of life; ball games, fish, furniture, moths, and seashores are just a few of the things she chose to scrutinize.

A Bird Came Down the Walk

Emily Dickinson

A bird came down the walk:
He did not know I saw;
He bit an angle-worm in halves
And ate the fellow, raw.

5 And then he drank a dew
From a convenient grass,
And then hopped sidewise to the wall
To let a beetle pass.

He glanced with rapid eyes
10 That hurried all abroad,—
They looked like frightened beads, I thought.
He stirred his velvet head

Like one in danger; cautious,
I offered him a crumb,
15 And he unrolled his feathers
And rowed him softer home

Than oars divide the ocean,
Too silver for a seam,
Or butterflies, off banks of noon,
20 Leap, plashless, as they swim.

From THE POEMS OF EMILY DICKINSON. Published by Little, Brown & Co.

Discussion

1. At the beginning of this poem, the bird is unaware of a human presence. **(a)** What actions does it perform before it realizes it is being watched? **(b)** At what point does it become aware of the speaker? **(c)** How does it react then?

2. (a) What kind of figure of speech is used in line 11? **(b)** What picture of the bird does it give you? **(c)** For what reasons might the speaker have compared the bird's head to velvet?

3. Are *unrolled* (line 15) and *rowed* (line 16) appropriate words to describe the bird's motion? Why or why not?

4. (a) To what is the bird's flight compared in lines 16–18? **(b)** To what is it compared in lines 19–20? **(c)** In what element do butterflies "swim"? **(d)** What ideas does the metaphor "banks of noon" suggest to you? **(e)** *Plashless* is a synonym for *splashless*. Why do you think the poet used the former rather than the latter? **(f)** What qualities of the bird's flight seem to make the greatest impression on the speaker?

The Author

One of the foremost poets of America, Emily Dickinson (1830–1886) lived and died almost unknown to the world. In the seclusion of her home she spent much of her time writing poems. Only a few of her works were published during her lifetime. After her death, however, relatives, realizing the greatness of her works, made them public.

BIJOU

Vern Rutsala

Huge, perfect creatures move across the screen
to the rhythms of hidden bands.
Small, imperfect creatures slouch in plush seats
and pull crystal tears from their eyes
5 when the intellectual dog is lost
or when the nearly nice supporting player
is culled from the action by a villain arrow
while saving the blond-souled hero.
They drop their tears and look around hopefully
10 when they hear the bugle of a rescue party.
But the aisles are empty. Odorless horses
spring onto the screen below waving flags.

Discussion

1. With what common experience does this poem deal?
2. (a) Who are the "Huge, perfect creatures" (line 1) and the "Small, imperfect creatures" (line 3)? **(b)** Why do you think the poet describes them in this manner?

3. Explain the meaning of: **(a)** "crystal tears" (line 4); **(b)** "intellectual dog" (line 5); **(c)** "nearly nice supporting player" (line 6); and **(d)** "blond-souled hero" (line 8).
4. (a) Do the viewers seem to believe what is happening on

the screen? How do you know? **(b)** Does the movie end happily? Explain.
5. (a) What attitude toward his subject does the poet express in this poem? How do you know? **(b)** Do you share his attitude? Why or why not?

Strong Men, Riding Horses

LESTER AFTER THE WESTERN

Gwendolyn Brooks

Strong Men, riding horses. In the West
On a range five hundred miles. A Thousand. Reaching
From dawn to sunset. Rested blue to orange.
From hope to crying. Except that Strong Men are
5 Desert-eyed. Except that Strong Men are
Pasted to stars already. Have their cars
Beneath them. Rentless, too. Too broad of chest
To shrink when the Rough Man hails. Too flailing
To redirect the Challenger, when the challenge
10 Nicks; slams; buttonholes. Too saddled.

I am not like that. I pay rent, am addled
By illegible landlords, run, if robbers call.

What mannerisms I present, employ,
Are camouflage, and what my mouths remark
15 To word-wall off that broadness of the dark
Is pitiful.
I am not brave at all.

Discussion

1. (a) Who is supposedly the speaker in this poem? (b) Who are the Strong Men he refers to?
2. In lines 2–3, what various terms are used to describe the expanse of the range?
3. (a) What differences between himself and the Strong Men does the speaker point out in lines 4–10? (b) In the context of a Western, who would the "Rough Man" and the "Challenger" be? (c) In terms of the speaker, what might they be?
4. *Illegible* usually refers to handwriting that is hard to read. Is this definition suitable in the context of line 12? If not, what does *illegible* mean here?

5. (a) What trait does the speaker reveal by using the word *mouths* rather than *mouth* in line 14? (b) What is meant by *word-wall* (line 15)? (c) What two meanings can be attached to the word *dark* (line 15)?
6. (a) What overall impression do you get of the speaker from this poem? (b) Who is more representative of actual people —the speaker or the Strong Men? Why?
7. (a) Does the speaker share the attitude expressed in "Bi-jou"? Explain. (b) Which poet treats the subject more harshly? (c) In your opinion, are the poets being fair?

The Author

At thirteen, Gwendolyn Brooks published her first poem in a magazine called *American Childhood*. In payment she received six copies of the issue in which the poem appeared and a letter of praise from the editor. She has been writing and receiving praise ever since. One critic, for example, described her work as having a "perfection of word and phrase." In 1950, Miss Brooks was awarded the Pulitzer Prize for *Annie Allen*, a collection of poems about many subjects. In addition to writing poetry, Miss Brooks gives lectures and writes book reviews.

Lord Randal

OLD BALLAD

"O where ha you been, Lord Randal, my son?
And where ha you been, my handsome young man?"
"I ha been at the greenwood; Mother, mak my bed soon,
For I'm wearied wi huntin, and fain wad lie down."[1]

5 "An wha met ye there, Lord Randal, my son?
An wha met you there, my handsome young man?"
"O I met wi my true-love; Mother, mak my bed soon,
For I'm wearied wi huntin, and fain wad lie down."

"And what did she give you, Lord Randal, my son?
10 And what did she give you, my handsome young man?"
"Eels fried in a pan[2]; Mother, mak my bed soon,
For I'm wearied wi huntin, and fain wad lie down."

CONTINUED

---

1. **down,** to be pronounced in the Scottish manner (dün) to rhyme with *soon.*
2. **Eels fried in a pan,** a method of poisoning that appears in many of the old ballads.

"And wha gat your leavins,³ Lord Randal, my son?
And wha gat your leavins, my handsome young man?"
15 "My hawks and my hounds; Mother, mak my bed soon,
For I'm wearied wi huntin, and fain wad lie down."

"And what becam of them, Lord Randal, my son?
And what becam of them, my handsome young man?"
"They stretched their legs out an died; Mother, mak my bed soon,
20 For I'm wearied wi huntin, and fain wad lie down."

"O I fear you are poisoned, Lord Randal, my son!
I fear you are poisoned, my handsome young man!"
"O yes, I am poisoned; Mother, mak my bed soon,
For I'm sick at the heart, and I fain wad lie down."

25 "What d'ye leave to your mother, Lord Randal, my son?
What d'ye leave to your mother, my handsome young man?"
"Four and twenty milk kye⁴; Mother, mak my bed soon,
For I'm sick at the heart, and I fain wad lie down."

"What d'ye leave to your sister, Lord Randal, my son?
30 What d'ye leave to your sister, my handsome young man?"
"My gold and my silver; Mother, mak my bed soon,
For I'm sick at the heart, and I fain wad lie down."

"What d'ye leave to your brother, Lord Randal, my son?
What d'ye leave to your brother, my handsome young man?"
35 "My houses and my lands; Mother, mak my bed soon,
For I'm sick at the heart, and I fain wad lie down."

"What d'ye leave to your true-love, Lord Randal, my son?
What d'ye leave to your true-love, my handsome young man?"
"I leave her hell and fire; Mother, mak my bed soon,
40 For I'm sick at the heart, and I fain wad lie down."

---

3. *wha gat your leavins*, who ate the food you didn't eat?
4. *kye*, cows.

Discussion

1. (a) Who is speaking in the first two lines of the poem? (b) Who speaks in lines 3–4? (c) Is this pattern of conversation followed throughout the poem?
2. (a) What is the situation at the opening of "Lord Randal"? Describe the scene. (b) What has Lord Randal eaten for lunch? (c) How does the mother know her son has been poisoned?
3. How do you learn who was responsible for Lord Randal's death?
4. Tell the story of this ballad in your own words.

5. In many ballads, one or more lines in each stanza are repeated exactly as they appeared in the preceding stanza, except for the addition of some new detail. (a) Find examples of such details in "Lord Randal." (b) What is the purpose of these details?

Old Ballads

The wandering minstrels of the Middle Ages traveled throughout the British countryside singing songs in exchange for food and lodging. These songs the minstrels sang are called *ballads*. No one is certain how old the first ballads are, who their authors were, or how they came to be written. But whatever their origins, ballads were sung for hundreds of years. Different versions arose as people, moving from one town to another, forgot some of the ancient lines and substituted new ones of their own. Too, minstrels changed words, making additions and omissions at will. Centuries went by

before these ballads were written down in any permanent form.

Although ballads sprang from many sources and often underwent drastic revisions in the telling, they have certain distinctive features. First of all, the ballad is a highly dramatic story told in verse; it usually contains dialogue. The story often deals with a limited number of characters and includes only the facts needed for the telling of a single incident. Secondary details are omitted, each listener filling them in for himself. For example, someone listening to "Lord Randal" might imagine the

setting, the way the characters look, and the girl's motives in poisoning her young man.

A second feature is the elemental themes with which the ballads deal —treachery, cunning, death, love, jealousy. Very few of the old ballads are humorous; most are tragic and often deal with the sensational.

A third feature is the characteristic verse form used in most of the old ballads. The stanzas are composed of four lines, and the second and fourth lines of each stanza rhyme. Rhythm usually follows a very definite pattern.

Get Up and Bar the Door

OLD BALLAD

It fell about the Martinmas time,[1]
   And a gay time it was than,
That our gudewife had puddings[2] to mak'
   And she boil'd them in the pan.

5 The wind blew cauld frae[3] east and north
   And blew intil[4] the floor;
Quoth our gudeman to our gudewife,
   "Get up and bar the door."

"My hand is in my hussyskep,[5]
10   Gudeman, as ye may see;
An it shou'dna be barr'd this hunder year,
   It's ne'er be barr'd by me."[6]

They made a paction[7] 'tween them twa,
   They made it firm and sure,
15 That the first word whaever spak,
   Should rise and bar the door.

Than by there came twa gentlemen,
   At twelve o'clock at night,
Whan they can see na ither house,[8]
20   And at the door they light.

"Now whether is this a rich man's house,
   Or whether it is a poor?"
But ne'er a word wad ane o' them speak,[9]
   For barring of the door.

---

1. *the **Martinmas** (mär′tin məs) **time.*** The feast of St. Martin is celebrated on November 11. In Scotland this is the customary time for preparing the winter's supply of meat.
2. ***puddings.*** The goodwife made these puddings of meat. They were similar to our sausages.
3. ***cauld frae*** (kôld frā), cold from.
4. ***intil,*** onto.
5. ***hussyskep*** (hus′ĭ skep′), housekeeping duties.
6. ***An it shou'dna . . . by me,*** if it were not barred for a hundred years, it would not be barred by me.
7. ***paction,*** compact, or agreement.
8. ***na ither house,*** no other house.
9. ***wad ane o' them speak,*** would one of them (the husband or the wife) speak.

25 And first they ate the white puddings,
  And syne[10] they ate the black;
  Muckle[11] thought the gudewife to hersell,
  Yet ne'er a word she spak.

  Than ane unto the ither said,
30   "Here, man, tak ye my knife;
  Do ye tak off the auld[12] man's beard,
  And I'll kiss the gudewife."

  "But there's na water in the house,
  And what shall we do than?"
35 "What ails ye at the pudding bree[13]
  That boils into the pan?"

  O up than started our gudeman,
  An angry man was he;
  "Will ye kiss my wife before my een,[14]
40   And scaud[15] me wi' pudding bree?"

  O up than started our gudewife,
  Gied[16] three skips on the floor;
  "Gudeman, ye've spak the foremost word;
  Get up and bar the door!"

---

10. *syne* (sīn), soon.
11. *Muckle* (muk'əl), much.
12. *auld* (ôld), old.
13. *pudding bree* (brē), the water in which the puddings were boiled.
14. *een* (ēn), eyes.
15. *scaud* (skôd), scald.
16. *Gied* (gēd), gave.

Discussion

1. What causes the disagreement between the husband and wife?
2. Who is talking in lines 9–12? lines 21–22?
3. (a) What "paction" do the husband and wife make? (b) At what point is the good wife first tempted to break the silence? (c) What finally causes the husband to speak?
4. What human failing does this ballad ridicule?
5. (a) What is the tone of "Get Up and Bar the Door"? (b) From what you have learned about ballads, is this tone typical? Why or why not?
6. What additional details would people who heard this ballad sung probably imagine?

DANNY DEEVER

Rudyard Kipling

See
RHYTHM
Handbook
of Literary
Terms
page 561

"What are the bugles blowin' for?" said Files-on-Parade.[1]
"To turn you out, to turn you out," the Color-Sergeant[2] said.
"What makes you look so white, so white?" said Files-on-Parade.
"I'm dreadin' what I've got to watch," the Color-Sergeant said.
5   For they're hangin' Danny Deever, you can hear the Dead March play,
    The regiment's in 'ollow square[3]—they're hangin' him today;
    They've taken of his buttons off an' cut his stripes away,[4]
    An' they're hangin' Danny Deever in the mornin'.

  "What makes the rear-rank breathe so 'ard?" said Files-on-Parade.
10 "It's bitter cold, it's bitter cold," the Color-Sergeant said.
  "What makes that front-rank man fall down?" said Files-on-Parade.
  "A touch o' sun, a touch o' sun," the Color-Sergeant said.
    They are hangin' Danny Deever, they are marchin' of 'im round,
    They 'ave 'alted Danny Deever by 'is coffin on the ground;
15   An' 'e'll swing in 'arf a minute for a sneakin', shootin' hound—
    O they're hangin' Danny Deever in the mornin'.

  "'Is cot was right-'and cot to mine," said Files-on-Parade.
  "'E's sleepin' out an' far tonight," the Color-Sergeant said.
  "I've drunk 'is beer a score o' times," said Files-on-Parade.
20 "'E's drinkin' bitter beer alone," the Color-Sergeant said.
    They are hangin' Danny Deever, you must mark 'im to 'is place,
    For 'e shot a comrade sleepin'—you must look 'im in the face;
    Nine 'undred of 'is county an' the regiment's disgrace,
    While they're hangin' Danny Deever in the mornin'.

"Danny Deever" by Rudyard Kipling, from RUDYARD KIPLING'S VERSE: Definitive Edition (English title DEPARTMENTAL DITTIES AND BARRACK-ROOM BALLADS). Reprinted by permission of Mrs. George Bambridge; Doubleday & Company, Inc.; A. P. Watt & Son; and Methuen & Co.

1. *Files-on-Parade,* a term applied to a soldier assigned to close up the files or ranks.
2. *Color-Sergeant,* the noncommissioned officer who carries the regimental colors.
3. *regiment's . . . square.* The soldiers form the four sides of a square, here facing inwards. This is the formation used on ceremonial occasions or when a soldier is to be publicly executed.
4. *taken of his buttons off . . . away,* a custom applied to a disgraced soldier.

25 "What's that so black agin' the sun?" said Files-on-Parade.
"It's Danny fightin' 'ard for life," the Color-Sergeant said.
"What's that that whimpers over'ead?" said Files-on-Parade.
"It's Danny's soul that's passin' now," the Color-Sergeant said.
  For they're done with Danny Deever, you can 'ear the quick-step[5] play,
30 The regiment's in column, an' they're marchin' us away;
  Ho! the young recruits are shakin', an' they'll want their beer today,
  After hangin' Danny Deever in the mornin'.

---

5. *quick-step,* a lively air played after the funeral march.

Discussion

1. (a) Who is carrying on the conversation recorded in this poem? **(b)** From the conversation what do you learn about Files-on-Parade? **(c)** What kind of man does the Color-Sergeant seem to be? **(d)** Why might Kipling have designated these men by rank rather than by their proper names?
2. (a) Why is Danny Deever being hanged? **(b)** What sort of person does he seem to be? How do you know?
3. (a) Is Kipling more concerned with Deever's plight or with the effect of his death upon others? **(b)** What seems to be his opinion of the military regulations involved in Deever's execution? **(c)** Who voices Kipling's attitude—Files-on-Parade, or the Color Sergeant?
4. Does this poem merely tell a story, or does it make a comment as well? Explain.
5. "Danny Deever" is considered a *literary ballad*: a poem that shares the characteristics of the old ballads but whose author is known. In what ways does "Danny Deever" resemble the old ballads?
6. A military execution is conducted in a businesslike and unsentimental manner. After Danny is hanged, the regiment will march away from the scene of the execution in a quick step. **(a)** How is the way they march reflected in the rhythm of the poem? **(b)** Is the rhythm appropriate to the mood and action? Why or why not?

The Author

Rudyard Kipling (1865–1936) was one of the most popular writers of his time—and he remains popular still. While a schoolboy in England, he wrote his first poems. These early works, published in the school magazine, later came out in book form.

Kipling was born in 1865 in India, where his father was first an art teacher and then a museum director. When young Kipling had finished his secondary education in England, his parents gave him the choice of going on to school or returning to India. He chose the latter and rejoined his family at Lahore, India, where he became assistant editor of a newspaper. In addition to his editorial duties, he wrote poems and stories which appeared in the newspaper's columns and were later published in book form.

While still a young man, Kipling left India to travel in the United States and Europe. Eventually, he returned to England, where he spent much of his time writing. Throughout his life Kipling wrote stories and poems filled with suspense and excitement.

EIGHT O'CLOCK

A. E. Housman

He stood, and heard the steeple
    Sprinkle the quarters on the morning town.
One, two, three, four, to market-place and people
    It tossed them down.

5 Strapped, noosed, nighing his hour,
    He stood and counted them and cursed his luck;
And then the clock collected in the tower
    Its strength, and struck.

Discussion

1. Although Housman gives very little information in this poem, he implies a great deal. Reread the poem and answer these questions: (**a**) What happens in the poem? (**b**) What is the scene of the action? (**c**) Does the man repent what he has done? (**d**) What time is he to die?

2. (**a**) Do the first four lines suggest that this particular morning is different from any other? (**b**) What seems to be Housman's attitude toward his subject's death? (**c**) Compare and contrast Housman's feelings with Kipling's attitude toward the execution of Danny Deever.

3. The rhythm of this poem follows the irregular pattern of everyday speech. Is the rhythm in keeping with the speaker's attitude toward the execution?

The Author

Death and the passing of all things human are themes which run through much of A. E. Housman's poetry. Housman, a perfectionist, demanded a great deal of himself. Of the difficulty he had in composing a single stanza he said, "I wrote it thirteen times, and it was a twelve-month before I got it right." That his poetry seems simple and effortless is a tribute to his talent and labor.

Housman was a scholarly, cynical man whose views of people led him to live a solitary existence. For many years a professor of Latin in England's finest schools, he spent much of his life editing Latin classics. Yet today he is best known for fewer than one hundred poems in three small books, *A Shropshire Lad, Last Poems,* and *More Poems.*

Iguanas

David Atamian

The lizards sprawl on the sun-baked stones,
Their pearly eyes fixed on the stagnant pools
Of the slow-moving river.
Their rough-scaled skins
5 Gleam in the brilliant light
Like many colored jewels.

On cautious feet I silently approach
To see their rainbow beauty lying heaped
So carelessly,
10 When, like an iridescent sigh they disappear,
Leaving a flash of azure,
Green and purple
Over the stones and in the quivering air.

From THE NEW YORK TIMES, (January 22, 1947). © 1947 by The New York Times Company.
Reprinted by permission.

Discussion

1. (a) In what kind of a landscape do the iguanas live? List details from the poem. **(b)** What is an iguana? What would you expect one to look like?

2. (a) In what terms are the iguanas described in this poem? **(b)** What terms in particular make the iguanas seem exceptional?

3. (a) In a sentence or two summarize what happens in the poem. **(b)** What descriptive words suggest that the speaker is surprised at what he sees?

Bird in the Classroom

Colin Thiele

See
ALLITERATION
Handbook
of Literary
Terms
page 536

The students drowsed and drowned
in the teacher's ponderous monotone —
Limp bodies looping in the wordy heat,
Melted and run together, desks and flesh as one,
5 Swooning and swimming in a sea of drone.

Each one asleep, swayed and vaguely drifted
With lidding eyes and lolling, weighted heads,
Was caught on heavy waves and dimly lifted,
Sunk slowly, ears ringing, in the syrup of his sound,
10 Or borne from the room on a heaving wilderness of beds.

And then, on a sudden, a bird's cool voice
Punched out song. Crisp and spare
On the startled air,
Beak-beamed
15 Or idly tossed,
Each note gleamed
Like a bead of frost.

A bird's cool voice from a neighbor tree
With five clear calls — mere grains of sound
20 Rare and neat
Repeated twice . . .
But they sprang the heat
Like drops of ice.

Ears cocked, before the comment ran
25 Fading and chuckling where a wattle[1] stirred,
The students wondered how they could have heard
Such dreary monotones from man,
Such wisdom from a bird.

From I AM A SENSATION, ed. by Goldberg and Wright. Reprinted by permission of Rigby Limited.
1. **wattle,** Australian tree.

Discussion

1. Read lines 1–10 aloud. **(a)** What kind of effect do the sounds of the words in these lines have on you? In a sentence or two describe how they make you feel. **(b)** What repeated sounds do you find in the first ten lines? Make a short list. **(c)** Do all the sounds emphasize one general quality or feeling? If so, briefly describe it. **(d)** As presented through the sound patterns of the first two stanzas, what is the teacher's voice like?

2. Read lines 11–23 aloud. **(a)** What differences in sound and feeling can you detect? **(b)** Briefly describe the effect the sounds of these lines have on you. **(c)** What particular words or sound patterns help create this effect? **(d)** How does the bird's voice contrast with the teacher's?

3. The last stanza (lines 24–28) presents a conclusion. **(a)** State that conclusion in a sentence or two. **(b)** According to the contrasts within this poem, why might the bird's voice speak more wisely than a man's?

4. Compare the attitude of the speaker in "Iguanas" with the attitude of the speaker in "Bird in the Classroom". **(a)** How does each feel about his animal subject? **(b)** In what way is the appearance of each animal unexpected or exceptional in the speaker's experience?

The Author

When Colin Thiele (pronounced Tee-lee) writes poems about a school classroom, he is handling familiar material. After serving three years in the Royal Australian Air Force during World War II, he worked up through the educational ranks from high school teacher to college lecturer, to vice-principal, and finally to principal of a teacher's college in his home country of South Australia. He is a man who takes sheer delight in the sounds of words and uses them as here to echo a familar experience.

Owl

Edward Brathwaite

The cat-eyed owl, although so fierce
at night with kittens and with mice

in daylight may be mobbed
by flocks of little birds, and in
5 the market-place, be robbed

of all its dignity and wisdom
by children, market-women, and malingering men

who hoot at it and mocking its myopic
eye, shout "Look!
10 Look at it now, he hangs his head in

shame." This never happens to the eagle
or the nightingale.

From THE NEW YORK TIMES BOOK OF VERSE. Reprinted by permission of the author.

Discussion

1. (a) What kind of bird is the owl at night? What words or phrases in the poem indicate this? **(b)** What kind of bird is the owl by day? What words or phrases indicate this?

2. Why could the types of things that happen to the owl not happen to an eagle or a nightingale? What particular qualities is each of these two birds known for?

3. (a) Do you think the speaker in this poem is critical or sympathetic toward the owl? Why? **(b)** What seems to be the speaker's attitude toward the way people treat the owl?

The Author

Edward Brathwaite is a native West Indian, born in Barbados in 1930. He was educated in his home country and in England where he won his Ph.D. from the University of Sussex in 1968. He lived for some years in Ghana and wrote a collection of poems called *Masks* which capture the spirit and rituals of Africa in a language that combines jazz and folk rhythms with English meters.

THE
FISH

Elizabeth Bishop

I caught a tremendous fish
and held him beside the boat
half out of water, with my hook
fast in a corner of his mouth.
5 He didn't fight.
He hadn't fought at all.
He hung a grunting weight,
battered and venerable
and homely. Here and there
10 his brown skin hung in strips
like ancient wall-paper,
and its pattern of darker brown
was like wall-paper:
shapes like full-blown roses
15 stained and lost through age.
He was speckled with barnacles,
fine rosettes of lime,
and infested
with tiny white sea-lice,
20 and underneath two or three
rags of green weed hung down.
While his gills were breathing in
the terrible oxygen
—the frightening gills,
25 fresh and crisp with blood,
that can cut so badly—
I thought of the coarse white flesh
packed in like feathers,
the big bones and the little bones,
30 the dramatic reds and blacks
of his shiny entrails,

CONTINUED

and the pink swim-bladder
like a big peony.
I looked into his eyes
35 which were far larger than mine
but shallower, and yellowed,
the irises backed and packed
with tarnished tinfoil
seen through the lenses
40 of old scratched isinglass.
They shifted a little, but not
to return my stare.
—It was more like the tipping
of an object toward the light.
45 I admired his sullen face,
the mechanism of his jaw,
and then I saw
that from his lower lip
—if you could call it a lip—
50 grim, wet, and weapon-like,
hung five old pieces of fish-line,
or four and a wire leader
with the swivel still attached,
with all their five big hooks
55 grown firmly in his mouth.
A green line, frayed at the end
where he broke it, two heavier lines,
and a fine black thread
still crimped from the strain and snap
60 when it broke and he got away.
Like medals with their ribbons
frayed and wavering,
a five-haired beard of wisdom
trailing from his aching jaw.
65 I stared and stared
and victory filled up
the little rented boat,
from the pool of bilge
where oil had spread a rainbow
70 around the rusted engine
to the bailer rusted orange,
the sun-cracked thwarts,
the oarlocks on their strings,
the gunnels—until everything
75 was rainbow, rainbow, rainbow!
And I let the fish go.

Discussion

1. (a) To what is the fish's skin compared? (b) Explain the meaning of "and underneath two or three/rags of green weed hung down" (lines 20–21). (c) To whom is the oxygen "terrible" (line 23)? Why? (d) To what is the fish's flesh compared? (e) To what various things are parts of the fish compared? (f) What picture of the fish do you get from the images in lines 34–40?

2. In lines 1–40, can the speaker's feeling for the fish best be described as (a) curiosity; (b) awe; (c) repulsion? Explain.

3. (a) Where in the poem do the speaker's feelings toward the fish begin to change? (b) What causes them to change? (c) What is meant by "a five-haired beard of wisdom" (line 63)?

4. (a) How does the insignificance of the boat change the speaker's feeling about his victory? (b) Why does he let the fish go?

5. (a) What similarities exist between the experiences described in "Owl" and the one described in "The Fish"? (b) How are the speakers' attitudes alike? (c) How do their attitudes differ?

The Author

The direct, straightforward style in which "The Fish" is written is typical of Elizabeth Bishop's works. She was born and schooled in Massachusetts, but has spent much of her adult life traveling. The result of some of her travels was a collection entitled *Poems, North and South.* Published in 1956, the book won her the Pulitzer award for poetry in that year.

Section 3

A poem is often a comment on life;
an expression of an idea, a problem, or an ideal.
In Section Three, nine poets comment
on the world they share with us, their readers.
Some of the poems are humorous, some
are serious, but all have something to say about life.
What does each say to you?

Thief Jones

Robert P. Tristram Coffin

The people living round the place
Called him Thief Jones to his face,
Thief was like a Christian name,
It had lost the smut of shame.
5 Thief's house was black and let in weather,
The ridgepole hardly held together,
The doorway stood at a lee-lurch.
Men often opened it to search
Among the litter of net-corks there
10 For a lobster-buoy or pair
Of missing pants whose seat was sewn
With patches they could prove their own.
It got so, when a man lost track
Of anything, he took a tack
15 Down Thief's way and had a look.
The folks at Mundy's Landing took
Thief as they took foggy weather;
They'd learned to get on well together.
Thief never said a word if he

20 Happened to be in. He'd be
Glad to see the man and might
Help him straighten things out right —
"This rudder's yours, this anchor's mine."
He might invite the man to dine
25 On the hasty-pudding cooking
On his stove, after the looking.
Men liked to talk with Thief, he knew
Stories yellow, pink, and blue.
But though they liked to hear him lie,
30 They never halved a blueberry pie
From his cookstove's warming-shelf,
Thief ate his victuals by himself.

Discussion

1. (a) Describe in as much detail as the poem allows the type of place that Thief Jones lived in. (b) Although Thief is not described in the poem, what would you imagine he looked like?

2. (a) What does the poet mean when he says that the townspeople "took Thief as they took foggy weather"? (b) What do lines 19–28 say about the relationship between Thief and the people of the town? (c) What do the last four lines of the poem imply about this relationship?

3. How do you think Thief feels about his activities and the way he is treated?

takes talent

Don Marquis

After most of the employees of the New York Sun
had gone home for the evening, Archy, a cockroach,
climbed up on a typewriter and wrote reports
to the boss, a columnist. Archy, who had been
an unsuccessful poet in a previous life,
tapped out letters on the typewriter by
hurling himself head first at the keys.
But, being very much a lightweight, he could not
operate the shift key; thus his writings contain
no capitals or punctuation. (Though Archy
never capitalized his own name, he liked others
to do so when writing about him—or so it is
rumored.)
*   The two poems that follow are samples*
of the kind of reports Archy wrote to Don Marquis,
the boss.

there are two
kinds of human
beings in the world
so my observation
5 has told me
namely and to wit
as follows
firstly
those who
10 even though they
were to reveal
the secret of the universe
to you would fail
to impress you
15 with any sense
of the importance
of the news
and secondly
those who could
20 communicate to you
that they had
just purchased
ten cents worth
of paper napkins
25 and make you
thrill and vibrate
with the intelligence
                    archy

Discussion

1. Describe and contrast the qualities involved in the "two/kinds of human/beings in the world."
2. (a) What does the title of this poem mean? **(b)** What comment on people is Archy making? **(c)** Does he see any hope for those who lack the "talent"? **(d)** Is Archy justified in separating humans into these two categories? Why or why not?
3. (a) Is the tone of "takes talent" humorous or serious? **(b)** Do you think Archy's comment should be taken seriously? Explain.

the hen and the oriole

Don Marquis

well boss did it
ever strike you that a
hen regrets it just as
much when they wring her
5 neck as an oriole but
nobody has any
sympathy for a hen because
she is not beautiful
while everyone gets
10 sentimental over the
oriole and says how
shocking to kill the
lovely thing this thought
comes to my mind
15 because of the earnest
endeavor of a
gentleman to squash me
yesterday afternoon when i
was riding up in the
20 elevator if i had been a
butterfly he would have
said how did that
beautiful thing happen to
find its way into
25 these grimy city streets do
not harm the splendid
creature but let it
fly back to its rural
haunts again beauty always
30 gets the best of
it be beautiful boss
a thing of beauty is a
joy forever[1]
be handsome boss and let
35 who will be clever[2] is
the sad advice
of your ugly little friend
        archy

Discussion

1. In your own words, state the incident Archy describes in this poem.
2. (a) What conclusion does Archy's experience lead him to make? (b) What criticism of human values does Archy imply in this poem? (c) Is this criticism valid? Why or why not?

The Author

A writer who took ten years to produce a failure and three days to write a hit play; a man who hoped to be remembered for his serious ideas and is best known for his sense of humor; a slave to work who praised idleness—these are but a few of the contradictions in the life of Don Marquis.

Within his lifetime Marquis was poet, playwright, short-story writer, and newspaper columnist. But today he is best remembered for his work in a field where talent is rare—humorous verse. Fame came to Marquis with the creation of Archy and Mehitabel, the cat who claimed to have once been Cleopatra. The quaint philosophies of the cat and the cockroach often filled Marquis' column in the New York *Sun*, and have been collected in a book entitled *The Lives and Times of Archy and Mehitabel*.

1. *a thing of beauty is a / joy forever.* Archy is quoting a line from *Endymion*, a long poem by the English poet, John Keats (1795–1821).
2. *be handsome boss and let/who will be clever,* a paraphrase of a line in Charles Kingsley's "A Farewell." The original line reads: "Be good, sweet maid, and let who can be clever."

Buffalo Dusk

Carl Sandburg

The buffaloes are gone.
And those who saw the buffaloes are gone.
Those who saw the buffaloes by thousands and
how they pawed the prairie sod into dust
5   with their hoofs, their great heads down
pawing on in a great pageant of dusk,
Those who saw the buffaloes are gone.
And the buffaloes are gone.

Discussion

1. (a) What is the meaning of the word "dusk" as used both in the title and line 6 of the poem? **(b)** How is this word related to what happened to the buffalo? **(c)** What reason would the poet have for describing the appearance of the buffalo as "a great pageant of dusk"?
2. Who could "those who saw the buffalo" have been?
3. A reader of this poem remarked, "This poem reads like a great stampede, with awesome noise followed by awesome silence." What about the poem would cause you to agree or disagree?

The Author

As a young man, Carl Sandburg (1878–1967) traveled widely across America, riding the freight trains from city to city, viewing the land, and meeting people. He loved the common people and took great pains to collect and record their folklore. He was instrumental in popularizing the folk music of his day, singing and accompanying himself on the guitar.

Sandburg was awarded two Pulitzer Prizes during his lifetime: one for his *Complete Poems* (1951) and the other for *Abraham Lincoln: The War Years* (1939). The poem that appears here is a simple, sad lament for a part of America that is gone forever. In language and thought it is characteristic of Sandburg's most famous poems.

The Four Directions

Emerson Blackhorse "Barney" Mitchell

A century and eight more years,
    Since Kit Carson rode from four directions,
Deep into the heart of nomadic Navajos,
    Burning, ravishing the Land of Enchantment.[1]

5 Prairie grasses are once more
    Growing as high as the horse's belly.
Cradles of wrapped babies in colors
    Of the rainbow again span the land.

I know my people will stand and rise again.
10   Now it is time.
Pollen of yellow grain,
    Scatter in the four directions.

---

1. *Land of Enchantment.* In 1863 Kit Carson led a military campaign against the Navajos, burning their crops and orchards, destroying their herds. The following winter the starving Navajos finally surrendered and were removed from their homeland to a reservation.

Discussion

1. (a) What actions does the first stanza describe? (b) What do the actions and images of the second stanza imply, by contrast? (c) What might the last two lines mean literally?
2. Contrast this poem with "Buffalo Dusk" on the preceding page. (a) Could both poems be said to be about more or less the same subject? (b) Is the tone of both poems similar or different? Explain.

The Author

Barney Mitchell was born in a Navajo hogan in Shiprock, New Mexico on March 3, 1945. Since his father had been killed in service in World War II, Barney was raised by his maternal grandparents, and it was they who instilled in him the love of Navajo life and lore.

His first major piece of writing was the story of his childhood and his experiences on the reservation, entitled *Miracle Hill*. This was completed while he was attending the Institute of American Indian Arts.

LeRoy (Satchel) Paige was a major league
baseball player who pitched long
after the age at which most pitchers
retire. In "To Satch" how does Samuel Allen
pay tribute to Paige as an athlete
and as a man?

TO SATCH

Samuel Allen

Sometimes I feel that I will never stop
Just go on forever
Till one fine morning
I'll reach up and grab me a hand fulla stars
5 Swing out my long lean leg
And whip three hot strikes burning down the heavens
And look over at God and say
How about that!

"To Satch (or American Gothic)" by Samuel Allen. Reprinted by permission of the author.

Discussion

1. Who is the speaker in this poem?
2. (a) What is the "one fine morning" the speaker mentions in line 3? **(b)** What attitude toward life and death does he reveal in the poem?
3. (a) Explain how the lack of punctuation is related to meaning in the poem. **(b)** Why do you think the poet uses such expressions as "hand fulla stars" and "three hot strikes"?

(c) How would the poem differ if colloquial language were not used?
4. What impression of Satch does the poem give you?

The Author

As a young man, Samuel Allen studied in two unrelated fields —creative writing and law. To-

day he is well-known and respected in both. While attending the Sorbonne in Paris, Allen became friendly with Richard Wright, who helped him publish some of his earliest poems. In 1958, a bilingual edition of *Ivory Tusks*, a collection of his later works, was printed in Germany. Allen has also been a professor of literature, and a government legal counselor, as well as a poet.

THE SPRINTERS

Lillian Morrison

The gun explodes them.
Pummeling, pistoning they fly
In time's face.
A go at the limit,
5 A terrible try
To smash the ticking glass,
Outpace the beat
That runs, that streaks away
Tireless, and faster than they.

10 Beside ourselves
(It is for us they run!)
We shout and pound the stands
For one to win,
Loving him, whose hard
15 Grace-driven stride
Most mocks the clock
And almost breaks the bands
Which lock us in.

Discussion

1. (a) What is described in this poem? **(b)** Explain the meaning of the first line.
2. (a) What is the "ticking glass" (line 6)? **(b)** How is the "beat" (line 7) personified? **(c)** What is the purpose of the personification?
3. To the spectators, what do the participants in the event symbolize?
4. (a) What are "the bands/ Which lock us in" (lines 17–18)? **(b)** Does the use of the word *almost* in line 17 reveal that the speaker is optimistic or pessimistic about our chances of breaking the bands? Support your answer with other words or lines from the poem.
5. (a) Chart the rhyme scheme of the first stanza. **(b)** Is it regular or irregular? **(c)** Are the lines run-on or end stopped? **(d)** Is the pattern of rhyme in keeping with the content of the poem? Why or why not?

SUPERMAN
John Updike

I drive my car to supermarket,
  The way I take is superhigh,
A superlot is where I park it,
  And Super Suds are what I buy.

5 Supersalesmen sell me tonic—
  Super-Tone-O, for Relief.
The planes I ride are supersonic.
  In trains, I like the Super Chief.

Supercilious men and women
10   Call me superficial—*me*,
Who so superbly learned to swim in
  Supercolossality.

Superphosphate-fed foods feed me;
  Superservice keeps me new.
15 Who would dare to supersede me,
  Super-super-superwho?

Discussion

1. **(a)** What meanings does the word *super* suggest to you? **(b)** Does Updike in any way alter or distort these meanings by repeating *super* in every line of the poem? Explain.
2. **(a)** Why might men and women call the speaker "superficial"? **(b)** Why does he become angry at being so labeled? **(c)** What does he mean by "learned to swim in"?
3. Do you think Updike is condemning the American way of life, justifying it, or poking fun at it? Why do you think so?
4. **(a)** What consonant sound is most often repeated in this poem? **(b)** What seems to be the purpose of the alliteration?
5. Note the end rhymes in the poem. Do they add to or detract from its tone? Explain.

The Author

Born and raised in a small town in Pennsylvania, John Updike has used the scenes of his boyhood to form the background for much of his writing. Updike, who established himself as a writer while still in his early twenties, writes with a verbal dexterity almost unmatched by his contemporaries. He is interested in all fields of writing, and has to date published five widely acclaimed novels as well as numerous short stories and poems.

KID

(CUERNAVACA¹)

Robert Hayden

He is found with the homeless dogs
   that worry sidewalk cafes
where gringos² in dollar bills
   deplore and sip. He has

5 Tricks of pathos for
   the silly foreigners
and so manages not to starve.
   Waiters strike at him and curse;

Deft and quick and accustomed,
10   he dances beyond their blows,
taunts them and scampers off,
   laughing as he goes.

---

1. **Cuernavaca** (kwer′ nä vä′kä), a city in Mexico, popular among tourists.
2. **gringos,** a term applied to white foreigners in Spain and Latin America. The word is used to show contempt.

Discussion

1. What is the setting of this poem?

2. Who is the "He" in line 1?

3. Explain the use of *worry* in line 2.

4. (a) What is meant by "gringos in dollar bills"? (b) What might the foreigners "deplore"? (c) Do they do very much to correct the things they deplore? Explain.

5. (a) How does the kid make a living? (b) Why do waiters "strike at him and curse"? (c) Is he bothered by the waiters' attitude toward him?

6. (a) What picture of the boy's character and appearance do you get from this poem? (b) Find words and phrases which help form this impression.

7. At the outset of this poem, you may have thought it is being told by an omniscient observer. (a) What word makes you begin to realize that, despite the apparent objectivity, the speaker is sympathetic to the kid? (b) As the poem continues, certain other words and phrases remind the reader of the speaker's sympathy for the kid. Find examples of such language. (c) How might the poem have differed if the observer were really objective?

The Author

Robert Hayden was born in Detroit, Michigan, in 1913 and received his education in that state. Before his death in 1980 he had won many honors: in 1966, first prize at the First World Festival of Negro Arts at Dakar, Senegal; in 1972, a National Book Award nomination in poetry. Other awards included a Ford Foundation Fellowship for travel and writing in Mexico. "Kid" is a poem that grew out of his experiences there. In 1976 he became the first black to be appointed Consultant in Poetry to the Library of Congress.

Hayden's work often reflects his black heritage, but his poetry speaks to all people. Ranging from hard, straightforward talk to somber reflection to singing lyricism, it reveals thoughtfulness and courage.

Birds, Like Thoughts

John Ciardi

Watch a wild turkey come in to land
(they are rare, but a man can find most
of what he wants if he wants it enough
to look for it)—you see a long slant
5 out of the air, like the approach of
some queer plane. Its landing gear first
let down, then agitated, it starts to run
before it touches, finishes yards on
from the point of touchdown; and only then
10 folds its wings and is back, a hen again.

Not wrens, warblers, swallows—(I can't even see
what it is swallows do on the air. They
change it, exceed it, make it serve impossibility)—
all smaller (not lesser) birds play
15 instantly in and out of the air. There are no
parts to their coming, going. A whirl and they light;
a whirl and they are airborne. Watch a jay go
its long dart through branches. It is too right
to need caution. It lands like an arrow
20 with no separation of its motion—So!

And there it is, and instantly gone if it feels
like it. Talk about landing on a dime! —
it could land on the edge of one. I've watched
every bird I could find to look at as it wheels,
25 heaves, whirls, glides. Whatever is hatched
to wings has its own way with them. But I'm
sure of one thing: the more weight you take to air,
the more space you need to get down,
the more slowly. Birds are like thoughts: they're
30 more instant as they stay light. Both come and gone.

Ciardi on His Poem

Most readers think a poem has to be the direct result of an experience that happened at a given moment in time. It is truer to say that a poem follows from its own opening. I am trying to say that the second line has to come into the poem in answer to the first, the third in answer to the first two, the fourth in answer to the first three, and so on until it finds the ending that will resolve (as in music) what has gone before. The poem may have begun from an idea or a perception that resulted from an outside (an "out-there-in-the-world") experience. But if it is any sort of poem it must answer to its own word choices, to its rhymes, to its figures of speech, to the second echoes in words. Which is to say, it leaves its outside experience and starts responding to its inner experience as an *act of language.* Such a poem as "Birds, Like Thoughts" brings together many memories of birds I have watched landing and taking off. It would be wrong, however, to say I had

listed in advance what I was going to say. The first stanza, as the reader can see, is rather closely connected with the experience of seeing a wild turkey land: the parenthesis in lines 2 to 4 and the last three words of the stanza are my only real departure from physical description.

But everything else in the poem followed from the first stanza and was not in my mind until it was suggested into being by my need to feel out and resolve the implications of what I had written in stanza one. It might be fair, therefore, to say that stanza one is related to a fixed experience, but that stanzas two and three, though they include bits of experience brought back to mind by stanza one, arise in answer to the implications of the poem, rather than in answer to a fixed experience.

Discussion

1. (a) According to the first stanza, how does a wild turkey land? (b) To what does the speaker compare the bird's landing? Cite details to support your answer.
2. (a) What train of thought is begun by watching a turkey land? (b) List the various birds the speaker describes. (c) What conclusions does he reach about a bird's size and its ability to land?
3. Lines 2–4 are enclosed in parentheses. Why might the poet have chosen to set them off in this manner? (Read the poet's letter to find out what he considers the purpose of these lines.)
4. In your own words, tell what the speaker means when he says, "But I'm/sure of one thing: the more weight you take to air,/the more space you need to get down,/the more slowly" (lines 26–29).
5. (a) Restate in literal language the simile contained in the last two lines. (b) Is the speaker condemning serious thought? Explain. (c) Do the speaker's own thoughts remain instant and light?

THE SLEEPING GIANT

(A HILL, SO NAMED, IN HAMDEN, CONNECTICUT)

Donald Hall

The whole day long, under the walking sun
That poised an eye on me from its high floor,
Holding my toy beside the clapboard house
I looked for him, the summer I was four.

5 I was afraid the waking arm would break
From the loose earth and rub against his eyes
A fist of trees, and the whole country tremble
In the exultant labor of his rise;

Then he with giant steps in the small streets
10 Would stagger, cutting off the sky, to seize
The roofs from house and home because we had
Covered his shape with dirt and planted trees;

And then kneel down and rip with fingernails
A trench to pour the enemy Atlantic
15 Into our basin, and the water rush,
With the streets full and the voices frantic.

That was the summer I expected him.
Later the high and watchful sun instead
Walked low behind the house, and school began,
20 And winter pulled a sheet over his head.

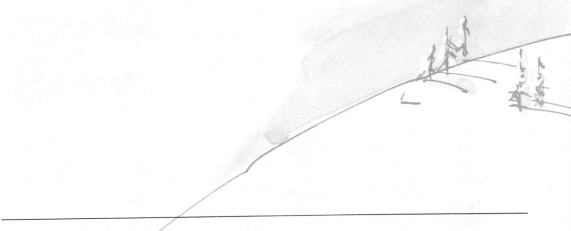

Hall on His Poem

As I first thought of "The Sleeping Giant," I took it as an amusing anecdote of growing up, more lightly than I take it now. I wrote it first over several months in blank verse quatrains; it didn't work, no sense of finish. I then rhymed it, which took another six months. For a long time it was finished except for the end, the last line. I found myself quite frustrated, knowing that the last line had to do a number of things at once, and tie the poem together, but unable to see how to do it. After staring at the unfinished poem, and having tried all sorts of unsatisfactory conclusions, one morning I watched —with astonishment and gratitude—my intelligent right hand write out the correct line without me telling it to. "And winter pulled a sheet over his head" killed the giant, using the consistent domestic detail of the sheet, gave the visual image of snow, and named a unit of time (at school) during which the child learned to distinguish between reality and fantasy.

Still, I regarded the poem as a problem solved, a technical problem; I liked to think of poetry as skill, at that time, rather than as spirit. I was puzzled when friends and editors began to take the poem more and more seriously than I did. Though I was aware of what giants in folklore could mean, I denied or refused to recognize the possibility of meaning in my poem. (I think this denial—of the real sources of the poem in psyche—was necessary to the writing of it; if I had known what I was saying, I would not have been able to say it.) Then one day a critic wrote that "The Sleeping Giant" took its power from the universal fear, buried in all of us, of the tiny baby as he looks up at his gigantic father. When I read the critic's words, chills ran up my spine, and I knew that I had found the true source of the poem.

Discussion

1. (a) In reality, what is the sleeping giant? (b) Why does the boy fear it?

2. (a) What, according to stanza 2, will happen if the giant awakens? (b) Why will he "seize/The roofs from house and home" (lines 10–11)? (c) How does the boy imagine the giant will finally destroy the people? (d) What happens to dispel the boy's fears? (e) Why will he probably not fear the giant again?

3. (a) How is the hill personified in the title? (b) Show how this personification is carried out throughout the poem.

4. Read the poet's explanation of "The Sleeping Giant." (a) What kind of rhyme scheme does Hall use in this, the final version of the poem? (b) What biographical elements does the poem contain? (c) At your first reading, did you interpret the poem as an "anecdote of growing up"? If not, how did you interpret it? (d) Reread the poem, paying special attention to the last line. In your opinion does the line do all that the poet wants it to do?

Every Good Boy Does Fine

David Wagoner

I practiced my cornet in a cold garage
Where I could blast it till the oil in drums
Boomed back; tossed free-throws till I couldn't move my thumbs;
Sprinted through tires, tackling a headless dummy.

5 In my first contest, playing a wobbly solo,
I blew up in the coda, alone on stage,
And twisting like my hand-tied necktie, saw the judge
Letting my silence dwindle down his scale.

At my first basketball game, gangling away from home
10 A hundred miles by bus to a dressing room,
Under the showering voice of the coach, I stood in a towel,
Having forgotten shoes, socks, uniform.

In my first football game, the first play under the lights
I intercepted a pass. For seventy yards, I ran
15 Through music and squeals, surging, lifting my cleats,
Only to be brought down by the safety man.

I took my second chances with less care, but in dreams
I saw the bald judge slumped in the front row,
The coach and team at the doorway, the safety man
20 Galloping loud at my heels. They watch me now.

You who have always horned your way through passages,
Sat safe on the bench while some came naked to court,
Slipped out of arms to win in the long run,
Consider this poem a failure, sprawling flat on a page.

Reprinted from THE NESTING GROUND by permission of the Indiana University Press.

Wagoner on His Poem

I think I started to write "Every Good Boy Does Fine" in an attempt to keep the incidents described therein from bothering me any more. During the work on the poem, I realized I was still having experiences similar to those I'd had in high school, • that they were symbolic of many kinds of failure, and that

the act of writing the poem itself was just one more example, however necessary, of asking for disappointment. I have judges, coaches, and safety men inside me, doing their jobs strictly and sometimes badly and sometimes not for my benefit. Every good boy does not do fine. In my own terms, I

consider the poem a success, but I didn't manage to get it down on paper because I was "good," but because I had learned how and was still willing to take a chance at outfoxing whatever there is inside me that says "I can't."

Discussion

1. What various things does the boy practice in lines 1–4?
2. (**a**) What is his first contest? (**b**) How does he do? (**c**) Why isn't he a success in his first basketball game? (**d**) What happens in the first football game he plays?
3. Explain the meaning of "I took my second chances with less care" (line 17) and "They watch me now" (line 20).
4. (**a**) What do lines 21–23 mean? (**b**) How are these lines

related to the incidents the speaker has described? (**c**) Why might the people referred to in these lines consider the poem a failure?
5. Does Wagoner really mean what he says in the title — that "every good boy does fine"? Explain. (The letter from the poet will help you answer this question.)
6. In writing this poem, Wagoner chose his words very carefully. Some words carry

more than one meaning. Keeping this in mind, tell why Wagoner's word is a better choice than the suggested substitute.

Wagoner	*substitute*
blew up (line 6)	made a mistake
scale (line 8)	score
showering (line 11)	booming
horned (line 21)	bluffed
in the long run (line 23)	at last

Meditation on His Ninety-First Year

John Haag

This withered clutch of bones, this hand that held
Two oxen and a plow steadily down
An even furrow, now scarcely can hold
The heavy reading-glass. An April sun
5 Could bring me to a sweat when my thin blood
Was warmer; now I'm tissue-dry and shake
In any breeze that giddies this grey head.
"The years have flown," a fellow patriarch
Is fond of saying, but as I reflect
10 Upon nine decades ripening steadily,
Each measured year maturing, act by act,
I wonder at him—could his memory
Remain so barren that life disappears
Into a limbo of forgotten years?

15 It's pleasant for me now to spin the past:
A boyhood full of cows and berry-vines,
Hay-ricks and wild birds, the journey west
When I was seventeen, the evergreens
And rivers and the rocks . . . I took a wife
20 The fall that my first crop was harvested,
And she was fruitful; under our first roof
We reared four sons to carry on the blood.
I've planted every year, yet never known
Two springs so much alike I could not tell
25 One from the other; no two days have been
Identical, and I can still recall
Each acre tilled, each crop or foal or calf . . .
The living things—these are my epitaph.

From *Northwest Review* (Spring 1959). Reprinted by permission.

The doctor tells me I should not expect
30 To live forever. After he has gone
I smile to think that he, at thirty-eight,
Cannot conceive how well, at ninety-one,
I have accepted this absurd remark.
Today the teacup chatters at my teeth;
35 I feel the room grow colder, and I break
With reveries and vague regrets that growth
Is over, that the blood wears out, and then
No more of things that breathe and climb, no more.
But, though I feel the minutes growing thin
40 And I've torn the last page from the calendar,
I cannot grudge the passing of my breath—
After so much life, so little death.

Haag on His Poem

"Meditation" is a tribute to my paternal Grandfather, and I feel it faithfully represents the pattern and spirit of his life, even though some of the details I employ are not necessarily biographical.

To express the man I felt I had to use language he might himself have used. His formal education was limited, by today's standards, but his high intelligence and active interest in what went on in the world made him articulate—when he felt it was time to speak up. He might use an image, but no ornate language or poeticisms, so one of my problems was to make poetry out of his direct diction and patterns of speech. In doing so I rediscovered an elemental truth about the relationship between what you say and the way you say it: as I searched out the poetry in the man, I found no better expression for it than his own language, because the language he used to express himself always honestly reflected what he was. So in a way my Grandfather really made this poem—I just put it together.

Discussion

1. (a) Who is the speaker in this poem? (b) How does he view the passage of time?
2. (a) What occupation did the speaker follow as a young man? (b) What are some of the things he remembers about his youth?
3. (a) Does the young doctor understand the speaker's attitude and views? Explain. (b) What things about being old does the speaker regret? (c) What is his attitude toward the life he has lived? toward the death that will come to him shortly?
4. Read the poet's comments on this poem, noting what he has to say about the language. (a) Find images in the poem you consider especially vivid. (b) Considering the subject matter, is the imagery the poet uses appropriate? Why or why not?
5. The poem begins by pointing out the contrast between the power in the man's hands when he was young and their feebleness in old age. (a) Find other examples of contrast in the poem and explain their functions. (b) Are the contrasts effective? Explain.

Unit **4** Review

Read the following poem carefully and answer the questions that follow it.

from THE WIND OUR ENEMY[1]
by Anne Marriott

Wind
flattening its gaunt furious self against
the naked siding, knifing in the wounds
of time, pausing to tear aside the last
old scab of paint.

Wind
surging down the cocoa-coloured seams
of summer-fallow, darting in about
white hoofs and brown, snatching the
     sweaty cap
shielding red eyes.

Wind
filling the dry mouth with bitter dust,
whipping the shoulders worry-bowed too
     soon,
soiling the water pail, and in grim
     prophecy
greying the hair. . . .

Wind
in a lonely laughterless shrill game
with broken wash-boiler, bucket without
a handle, Russian thistle, throwing up
sections of soil.

God will it ever rain again? What about
those clouds out west? No, that's just
     dust, as thick
and stifling now as winter underwear.
No rain, no crop, no feed, no faith, only
     wind.

1. (**a**) What various things does the wind do? (**b**) In your own words, summarize the picture of the wind given in the poem.
2. Where might the poem be set?
3. Explain the meaning of "in grim prophecy/greying the hair."
4. Find images that appeal to (**a**) the sense of sight; (**b**) the sense of hearing; (**c**) the sense of touch.
5. Locate examples of (**a**) simile; (**b**) metaphor; (**c**) personification; and (**d**) hyperbole. Discuss the effect of these figures of speech.
6. (**a**) Point out examples of alliteration used to emphasize important words. (**b**) Can you find repeated consonant sounds that are used for other purposes?
7. Does the poem have a chartable rhyme scheme? Why or why not?
8. Does the poem have a regular rhythm, or does it follow the irregular rhythm of everyday speech? Demonstrate by reading aloud.
9. Would you characterize the speaker as (**a**) a poet; (**b**) a scholar; (**c**) an ordinary man? Why?

[1]Reprinted by permission of the author from "The Wind Our Enemy" from SANDSTONE AND OTHER POEMS by Anne Marriott. Published by the Ryerson Press.

SUGGESTED READING

BENÉT, ROSEMARY and STEPHEN VINCENT, *A Book of Americans.* (Rinehart) Very popular among young people, these poems emphasize historic facts about famous Americans.

BONTEMPS, ARNA (comp.), *Golden Slippers; An Anthology of Negro Poetry for Young Readers.* (Harper) The format of this book is unique and the drawings are delightful. The poets include Langston Hughes, Countee Cullen, Paul Laurence Dunbar, and James Weldon Johnson.

BREWTON, SARA and JOHN (comps.), *Bridled with Rainbows; Poems about Many Things of Earth and Sky.* (Macmillan) Even though it contains two hundred poems, this is a comparatively small book.

COLE, WILLIAM (comp.), *The Birds and the Beasts Were There; Animal Poems*. (World) Praise is given in these poems to the grace and beauty of animals. Unusual woodcuts add to the attractiveness of this book.

COLUM, PADRAIC (ed.), *Roofs of Gold; Poems to Read Aloud*. (Macmillan) This refreshingly imaginative anthology contains eighty poems collected by a poet "from a lifetime of writing, reading, and enjoying poetry." Most of the poems lend themselves to reading aloud.

DERLETH, AUGUST, *Country Places*. (Prairie) Thirty-two nature poems by Derleth are artistically published in a very tiny book. Representative titles are "Smoke Wind," "Owl: Midnight," and "Brush Fire at Dusk."

DICKINSON, EMILY, *Poems for Youth*, edited by Alfred Leete Hampson. (Little) Here are about forty of Emily Dickinson's poems, found after her death. Many of her poems are short, "direct as telegrams."

DUNNING, STEPHEN; EDWARD LUEDERS; and HUGH SMITH (comps.), *Reflections on a Gift of Watermelon Pickle . . . and Other Modern Verse*. (Scott, Foresman) Eve Merriam's How to Eat a Poem" opens this bright, imaginative book of modern poetry selected for (and often by) young people. The collection of over one hundred poems is divided into thematic sections, includes questions for interpretation, and is strikingly illustrated with photographs.

FERRIS, HELEN (ed.), *Favorite Poems, Old and New; Selected for Boys and Girls*. (Doubleday) Covering a wider range than any other standard poetry anthology for young people, the book is arranged by subjects and is easy to use.

FISH, HELEN (ed.), *Boy's Book of Verse*. (Lippincott) Planned for boys, this collection includes many poems like "Casey at the Bat," "High Flight," and "Jesse James."

FROST, ROBERT, *You Come Too; Favorite Poems of Robert Frost for Young Readers*. (Holt) "The Pasture," often used as the first poem in Frost's collections, introduces this anthology of favorites.

LINDSAY, VACHEL, *Johnny Appleseed and Other Poems*. (Macmillan) Lindsay is a poet of the pioneer. Typical of his style is the booming rhythm caught in "The Congo."

LONGFELLOW, HENRY WADSWORTH, *Favorite Poems of Henry Wadsworth Longfellow*. (Doubleday) This attractive book has full-page color illustrations of familiar poems.

MILLAY, EDNA ST. VINCENT, *Edna St. Vincent Millay's Poems; Selected for Young People*. (Harper) This illustrated book contains some unfamiliar poems as well as some familiar ones.

NASH, OGDEN, *Parents Keep Out; Elderly Poems for Youngerly Readers*. (Little) The inimitable Nash presents a number of anecdotes, jokes, and fables embellished with cheerful rhymes.

O'NELL, HORACE J. and CLARENCE STRATTON (eds.), *Poems for a Machine Age*. (McGraw) Included in this collection are strong poems like Lindsay's "Factory Windows Are Always Broken," and Kipling's "The Secret of the Machines."

PLOTZ, HELEN (comp.), *Imagination's Other Place; Poems of Science and Mathematics*. (Crowell) An unusual collection emphasizes the quality common to poetry and science, both dedicated to exploring and questioning.

READ, HERBERT (ed.), *This Way, Delight; A Book of Poetry for the Young*. (Pantheon) The aim of this group of poems is delight and interest. The book moves from simple poems to the more mature, including selections from such modern poets as T. S. Eliot, E. E. Cummings, and Dylan Thomas.

SANDBURG, CARL, *Wind Song*. (Harcourt) The best-known poems of one of the best-loved American poets are collected in an attractive volume.

UNTERMEYER, LOUIS (ed.), *The Magic Circle; Stories and People in Poetry*. (Harcourt) These are narrative poems of adventure grouped under general headings.

5

What does America mean
to a lawman who helps bring
civilization to the old West?
... to a bus boy who realizes his high
ambitions? ... to a farmer who
becomes a local hero?
What does America mean
to an immigrant who discovers that
almost anything can happen?
How is America reflected in
the tall tales and humor of
her people, in their dreams
and frustrations?
Their optimism and ideals,
their deeds and desires,
their longings and memories
all go into the making of

The
American
Romance

JOSEPH PICKETT, "MANCHESTER VALLEY." COLLECTION, THE MUSEUM OF MODERN ART, NEW YORK. GIFT ABBY ALDRICH ROCKEFELLER

Have you ever had something stick in your mind
so that you could not get rid of it?
Imagine what might happen if this condition spread
from person to person like a disease.

Punch, Brothers, Punch

Samuel Langhorne Clemens

WILL THE READER please to cast his eye over the following lines, and see if he can discover anything harmful in them?

> *Conductor, when you receive a fare,*
> *Punch in the presence of the passenjare!*
> *A blue trip slip for an eight-cent fare,*
> *A buff trip slip for a six-cent fare,*
> *A pink trip slip for a three-cent fare,*
> *Punch in the presence of the passenjare!*

CHORUS

> *Punch, brothers! punch with care!*
> *Punch in the presence of the passenjare!*

I came across these jingling rhymes in a newspaper, a little while ago, and read them a couple of times. They took instant and entire possession of me. All through breakfast they went waltzing through my brain; and when, at last, I rolled up my napkin, I could not tell whether I had eaten anything or not. I had carefully laid out my day's work the day before—a thrilling tragedy in the novel which I am writing. I went to my den to begin my deed of blood. I took up my pen, but all I could get it to say was, "Punch in the presence of the passenjare." I fought hard for an hour, but it was useless. My head kept humming, "A blue trip slip for an eight-cent fare, a buff trip slip for a six-cent fare," and so on and so on, without peace or respite. The day's work was ruined—I could see that plainly enough. I gave up and drifted downtown, and presently discovered that my feet were keeping time to that relentless jingle. When I could stand it no longer I altered my step. But it did no good; those rhymes accommodated themselves to the new step and went on harassing me just as before. I returned home, and suffered all the afternoon; suffered all through an unconscious and unrefreshing dinner; suffered, and

From TOM SAWYER ABROAD, TOM SAWYER DETECTIVE, AND OTHER STORIES by Mark Twain. Published by Harper & Brothers, 1901.

cried, and jingled all through the evening; went to bed and rolled, tossed, and jingled right along, the same as ever; got up at midnight frantic, and tried to read; but there was nothing visible upon the whirling page except "Punch! punch in the presence of the passenjare." By sunrise I was out of my mind, and everybody marvelled and was distressed at the idiotic burden of my ravings—"Punch! oh, punch! punch in the presence of the passenjare!"

Two days later, on Saturday morning, I arose, a tottering wreck, and went forth to fulfil an engagement with a valued friend, the Rev. Mr. ——, to walk to the Talcott Tower, ten miles distant. He stared at me, but asked no questions. We started. Mr. —— talked, talked, talked—as is his wont. I said nothing; I heard nothing. At the end of a mile, Mr. —— said—

"Mark, are you sick? I never saw a man look so haggard and worn and absent-minded. Say something; do!"

Drearily, without enthusiasm, I said: "Punch, brothers, punch with care! Punch in the presence of the passenjare!"

My friend eyed me blankly, looked perplexed, then said—

"I do not think I get your drift, Mark. There does not seem to be any relevancy in what you have said, certainly nothing sad; and yet—maybe it was the way you *said* the words—I never heard anything that sounded so pathetic. What is—"

But I heard no more. I was already far away with my pitiless, heartbreaking "blue trip slip for an eight-cent fare, buff trip slip for a six-cent fare, pink trip slip for a three-cent fare; punch in the presence of the passenjare." I do not know what occurred during the other nine miles. However, all of a sudden Mr. —— laid his hand on my shoulder and shouted—

"Oh, wake up! wake up! wake up! Don't sleep all day! Here we are at the Tower, man! I have talked myself deaf and dumb and blind, and never got a response. Just look at this magnificent autumn landscape! Look at it! look at it! Feast your eyes on it! You have travelled; you have seen boasted landscapes elsewhere. Come, now, deliver an honest opinion. What do you say to this?"

I sighed wearily, and murmured—

"A buff trip slip for a six-cent fare, a pink trip slip for a three-cent fare, punch in the presence of the passenjare."

Rev. Mr. —— stood there, very grave, full of concern, apparently, and looked long at me; then he said—

"Mark, there is something about this that I cannot understand. Those are about the same words you said before; there does not seem to be anything in them, and yet they nearly break my heart when you say them. Punch in the—how is it they go?"

I began at the beginning and repeated all the lines. My friend's face lighted with interest. He said—

"Why, what a captivating jingle it is! It is almost music. It flows along so nicely. I have nearly caught the rhymes myself. Say them over just once more, and then I'll have them, sure."

I said them over. Then Mr. —— said them. He made one little mistake, which I corrected. The next time and the next he got them right. Now a great burden seemed to tumble from my shoulders. That torturing jingle departed out of my brain, and a grateful sense of rest and peace descended upon me. I was light-hearted enough to sing; and I did sing for half an hour, straight along, as we went jogging homeward. Then my freed tongue found blessed speech again, and the pent talk of many a weary hour began to gush and flow. It flowed on and on, joyously, jubilantly, until the fountain was empty and dry. As I wrung my friend's hand at parting, I said—

"Haven't we had a royal good time! But now I remember, you haven't said a word for two hours. Come, come, out with something!"

The Rev. Mr. —— turned a lacklustre eye upon me, drew a deep sigh, and said, without animation, without apparent consciousness—

"Punch, brothers, punch with care! Punch in the presence of the passenjare!"

A pang shot through me as I said to myself, "Poor fellow, poor fellow! *he* has got it, now."

I did not see Mr. —— for two or three days after that. Then, on Tuesday evening, he staggered into my presence and sank dejectedly into a seat. He was pale, worn; he was a wreck. He lifted his faded eyes to my face and said—

"Ah, Mark, it was a ruinous investment that I made in those heartless rhymes. They have ridden me like a nightmare, day and night, hour after hour, to this very moment. Since I saw you I have suffered the torments of the lost. Saturday evening I had a sudden call, by telegraph, and took the night train for Boston. The occasion was the death of a valued old friend who had requested that I should preach his funeral sermon. I took my seat in the cars and set myself to framing the discourse. But I never got beyond the opening paragraph; for then the train started and the car-wheels began their 'clack, clack—clack-clack-clack! clack, clack—clack-clack-clack!' and right away those odious rhymes fitted themselves to that accompaniment. For an hour I sat there and set a syllable of those rhymes to every separate and distinct clack the carwheels made. Why, I was as fagged out, then,

as if I had been chopping wood all day. My skull was splitting with headache. It seemed to me that I must go mad if I sat there any longer; so I undressed and went to bed. I stretched myself out in my berth, and—well, you know what the result was. The thing went right along, just the same. 'Clack-clack-clack, a blue trip slip, clack-clack-clack, for an eight-cent fare; clack-clack-clack, a buff trip slip, clack-clack-clack, for a six-cent fare, and so on, and so on, and so on—*punch* in the presence of the passenjare!' Sleep? Not a single wink! I was almost a lunatic when I got to Boston. Don't ask me about the funeral. I did the best I could, but every solemn individual sentence was meshed and tangled and woven in and out with 'Punch, brothers, punch with care, punch in the presence of the passenjare.' And the most distressing thing was that my *delivery* dropped into the undulating rhythm of those pulsing rhymes, and I could actually catch absent-minded people nodding *time* to the swing of it with their stupid heads. And, Mark, you may believe it or not, but before I got through, the entire assemblage were placidly bobbing their heads in solemn unison, mourners, undertaker, and all. The moment I had finished, I fled to the anteroom in a state bordering on frenzy. Of course it would be my luck to find a sorrowing and aged maiden aunt of the deceased there, who had arrived from Springfield too late to get into the church. She began to sob, and said—

"'Oh, oh, he is gone, he is gone, and I didn't see him before he died!'

"'Yes!' I said, 'he *is* gone, he *is* gone, he *is* gone—oh, *will* this suffering never cease!'

"'*You* loved him, then! Oh, you too loved him!'

"'Loved him! Loved *who?*'

" 'Why, my poor George! my poor nephew!'

" 'Oh—*him!* Yes—oh, yes, yes. Certainly—certainly. Punch—punch—oh, this misery will kill me!'

" 'Bless you! bless you, sir, for these sweet words! *I*, too, suffer in this dear loss. Were you present during his last moments?'

" 'Yes. I—*whose* last moments?'

" '*His*. The dear departed's.'

" 'Yes! Oh, yes—yes—*yes!* I suppose so, I think so, *I* don't know! Oh, certainly—I was there—*I* was there!'

" 'Oh, what a privilege! what a precious privilege! And his last words—oh, tell me, tell me his last words! What did he say?'

" 'He said—he said—oh, my head, my head, my head! He said—he said—he never said *any*thing but Punch, punch, *punch* in the presence of the passenjare! Oh, leave me, madam! In the name of all that is generous, leave me to my madness, my misery, my despair!—a buff trip slip for a six-cent fare, a pink trip slip for a three-cent fare—endu-rance *can* no fur-ther go!—PUNCH in the presence of the passenjare!' "

My friend's hopeless eyes rested upon mine a pregnant minute, and then he said impressively—

"Mark, you do not say anything. You do not offer me any hope. But, ah me, it is just as well—it is just as well. You could not do me any good. The time has long gone by when words could comfort me. Something tells me that my tongue is doomed to wag forever to the jigger of that remorseless jingle. There—there it is coming on me again: a blue trip slip for an eight-cent fare, a buff trip slip for a—"

Thus murmuring faint and fainter, my friend sank into a peaceful trance and forgot his sufferings in a blessed respite.

How did I finally save him from the asylum? I took him to a neighboring university and made him discharge the burden of his persecuting rhymes into the eager ears of the poor, unthinking students. How is it with *them*, now? The result is too sad to tell. Why did I write this article? It was for a worthy, even a noble, purpose. It was to warn you, reader, if you should come across those merciless rhymes, to avoid them—avoid them as you would a pestilence! ✳

Discussion

1. (**a**) How does the narrator first come across the jingle? (**b**) What immediate effect do the lines have on him? (**c**) How does he finally rid himself of the jingle?

2. (**a**) Explain how the jingle gets in the way of the Rev. Mr.——'s activities. (**b**) How do the listeners to his funeral speech react? (**c**) How is the Rev. Mr. —— finally relieved of the jingle?

3. (**a**) According to the author, why did he write the story? Is his explanation serious? (**b**) Could you easily forget the jingle after reading the story?

4. (**a**) Listen carefully to, and write out if possible, a rhyme or musical jingle from radio or T.V. advertising that takes a particularly powerful hold on your memory. What is it about such jingles that makes them so easily remembered? (**b**) Do such jingles make any real sense? (**c**) Might they sometimes force the hearer to do things he might not otherwise do?

The Author

Mark Twain (Samuel Langhorne Clemens) spent most of his youth in Hannibal, Missouri, a town on the banks of the Mississippi River. Following his career as a printer and as a pilot on a Mississippi steamboat, Sam Clemens headed for the West in 1861. There he launched himself as a writer and journalist and adopted the pen name of Mark Twain. In 1867, Twain went abroad. His newspaper stories about his travels in Europe and Palestine brought him widespread popularity as a humorist.

Twain was the brilliant spokesman for the Middle West and the American frontier, the spinner of yarns in the coarse idiom of the people of these areas, a teller of tales which reflected the unrestrained frontier imagination. His humor and wit gained him worldwide acclaim. He is remembered especially for his vivid portrayals of the life and people along the Mississippi River in *The Adventures of Tom Sawyer* and *The Adventures of Huckleberry Finn*. Other books which have remained popular are *The Prince and the Pauper* and *A Connecticut Yankee in King Arthur's Court*.

See
IRONY
Handbook
of Literary
Terms
page 551

"What is it that has a tongue but can't talk?
... It's a wagon. A wagon's got a tongue but it can't talk.
Only my wagon *could*. It heard plenty of tales."
So spoke the old mountaineer, and Ellis Credle
listened, so that she might be able afterward to set down this
story and others like it from the
truly American tradition of the tall tale.
Note how exaggeration and irony add to the humor
of this tale from the Blue Ridge Mountains.[1]

the man who rode the bear

Ellis Credle

BACK IN THE TIMES when the Indians were still a-raiding around in the Blue Ridge Mountains, there was an old bear that had the people more scarified than the Indians ever did. He was a terror—as big as a horse, people said, and ferocious, too. It seemed like a bullet didn't even tickle him. If he was hit, he'd just shake himself and go right on about his business. He raided pigpens, carried off sheep, and wasn't even afraid to hang around the cabins at night and take a grab at anybody that came out. It got so folks were afraid to be out after dark.

Well, the critter went over to Sowback Ridge one night and got into the pigpen of a fellow named Joe Dowdy. Joe and his wife Tildy didn't hear a

1. *Blue Ridge Mountains,* the southeastern range of the Appalachian Mountains, extending from northwestern Maryland to northern Georgia.

sound. It was raining and they were moving the furniture here and there to keep the rain from wetting it. Their old roof leaked like a sieve, and no sooner did they get the bed moved away from a place where the water was coming through than they would hear a drip, drip on something else. What with all the noise they made, dragging the bed and the chest and the table around, and with the rain beating down on the shingles over-head, they never heard their hog a-squealing.

The bear killed the pig and dragged him around behind the barn. There he made a meal of him, hair, hide, and hoof. Then, gorged with his meal, the bear lay down under the eaves of the barn, where he was pro-tected from the rain, and went to sleep.

It was too bad about Joe's hog be-cause it was his last one, all he and

Tildy had to provide meat for the winter. Joe was the kind of man that seemed born for bad luck. If he planted a corn patch, there would be rain all around the country but never a drop in his field. His neighbors' corn would grow tall and green, and Joe's would burn up for lack of water. His livestock were always dying off with one thing or another, and it seemed he just couldn't get ahead.

Tildy didn't have any better luck than her husband. Foxes caught her chickens, and her turkeys got lost in the woods. So it went until the night the bear paid them a visit. By that time Joe and Tildy had nothing in the world but the leaky cabin, the hog, and a poor decrepit old horse. And now, though they didn't know it, their hog was inside the bear.

Along about four o'clock in the morning, when the rain let up a little, Joe and Tildy sat down in front of the fireplace and began to talk about their situation.

"If I could only get the reward they're offering for that old bear, it would put us on Easy Street," Joe said. "It's a lot of money. I might just try it."

"Oh, talk sense," said Tildy impatiently. "Everybody in the mountains has tried it. Folks have gone in bands to get him. He's clawed Jake Sadler and raked open Solly Sneed. He just about chewed an arm offen Sam Tolan. He's killed so many dogs there's hardly any left to chase rabbits. Everybody's scared for their lives of that critter. Do you think you can go out and bring him in all by your lonesome?"

"Well——" Joe hung his head.

"And what would you hunt him with?" Tildy went on. "Your gun has been sold these three months. Nobody would lend you his, not with that bear likely to show up anywhere. Are you aiming to go out and get him with your bare hands?"

Joe sighed.

"You'd better think of looking for work," said Tildy. "I heard yesterday that the miller down the creek a piece is looking for a man to help with the grinding. Why don't you get down there and ask for the job?"

"I've got no more chance of getting that job than I have of killing the bear," said old Joe. "There're a dozen younger men that want it."

"Oh, don't be so chickenhearted!" exclaimed Tildy. "If you're the first one there in the morning, like as not you'll get it."

"Well," said Joe doubtfully, "I reckon it wouldn't hurt to try."

"Wouldn't hurt to try!" echoed Tildy. "Well, I reckon it wouldn't. Get out right now and saddle up the horse and get along."

"Why, it's dark now," said Joe. "I couldn't see to saddle the horse."

"Get along. You'll manage with the horse; do it by the feel. Day will be breaking an hour from now and the miller will be ready to pick his man and get on with the grinding. You be there! If you get there an hour early, it won't hurt."

Well, Joe got up, clamped some spurs on his boots—for his poor old horse needed plenty of urging—and put on his coat.

Then he had a thought. He turned to Tildy. "It's dark as Egypt outside. S'posen that old bear should be hanging round here."

"Oh shucks, that bear is miles away. He got a calf over at Alf Heeney's place last night. That's a good fifteen miles from here."

"That's a far piece, for sure. I reckon it's safe enough to go out."

With that Joe said good-by and walked out to the barn. It had stopped raining but the clouds still hung low.

Not a star could be seen, and Joe couldn't make out a thing in the dark. He found the barn easy enough for he knew every stone on the path. He felt his way to the place where he kept his saddle and bridle, and took them off the peg. Then he made his way to the stall where the horse slept. He held out his hands and walked this way and that inside the stall, but he couldn't find the horse. He wasn't in his stall, and that was queer; animals don't like being outside on a rainy night. The fact was that the horse had smelled the bear and had run clean away to the woods.

"Now where's that horse?" said Joe. He went outside and stumbled here and there, feeling along the fences and around the well. Then he went back to the barn and felt along the walls. At the back, he stumbled over the bear lying under the eaves sound asleep.

Joe put out his hand and felt the hair on the bear's neck. "Oh, so there you are, you crazy critter!" He grabbed the bear by the ear. "Haven't you got enough sense to stay in outen the rain?"

Well, the bear was so logy with a whole hog in his stomach that he didn't even wake up. While he snored away, Joe opened his mouth and put the bit in; he buckled the bridle on his head. He threw the saddle across the bear's back and then gave him a kick in the ribs.

"Get up, you no-count critter! Let me fasten this bellyband."

The bear roused himself groggily, and hoisted himself onto his feet. Joe quickly fastened the bellyband. Then he leaped into the saddle. He gave the critter a jab with his spurs.

That bear woke up for sure. He felt the thing tied around his middle and the load on his back. He gave himself a terrific shake. It almost threw poor old Joe from the saddle. "What's the matter with you?" he cried, and he beat the bear's head with the handle of his whip.

The bear had never had anything like this happen to him. He reached around to claw Joe off his back, but his arms wouldn't reach. He couldn't get his head back that far to bite. And all the time Joe was beating him about the ears with the handle of the whip and sticking him with his spurs.

"Get up there, get!" Joe yelled. The night was so black that he never had an idea what it was he was contending with.

That old bear was scarified outen his wits. He took off down the road as fast as he could gallop. Every now and then he'd hump himself and jump up in the air, trying to throw off whatever it was that had him around the middle. Never in his life had Joe had such a ride. Who would have thought the old horse had it in him? he wondered.

It was a good seven miles to the mill and that bear ran every step of the way. By the time he got there he was run near to death. He was so tuckered out that when Joe pulled up on the reins to stop him, he just stood swaying, with his tongue hanging out and all the fight out of him.

In the dark, Joe threw the halter rope around the hitching post and tied it. Then he sat down on the steps of the mill to wait till the miller appeared.

It wasn't long before the sunrise began to lighten the sky and the day came on. The miller entered his mill through the back door and unlocked the front one, ready to do business. He saw Joe leaning against the wall.

"Good morning, Joe Dowdy. Have you come for some meal? How'd you get here so early?"

"I rode," said Joe, pointing with his thumb over his shoulder. "There's my horse out there tied to the hitching post."

The miller looked. His eyes popped half out of his head. He tottered backward. There stood the bear, saddled and bridled and tied to the hitching post.

"You—rode—that?" squalled the miller.

"Sure," said Joe without turning around. "Why not?"

The miller gulped and stuttered. He looked at Joe as though he'd never seen him before. He'd never thought Joe Dowdy was much of a man—but there was the bear. The very bear that had been terrorizing the whole settlement. And here was Joe acting as though bear-taming was nothing at all.

"I came to see you about that j-job." Joe stuttered a little. "I'd admire to have it, if you ain't got a man no better."

"B-b-better!" stammered the miller. "Where would I find a better man than you? You can have the job, and welcome."

By that time folks had begun to arrive with their meal to be ground. When they saw the bear tied to the hitching post, they were struck dumb with astonishment. They forgot all about taking their meal into the mill. At first, they just stood; then they began carrying on—exclaiming and asking questions.

"Who—who rode him?" They stared at the bear and then at the miller.

"Joe, here, rode him up just before daybreak."

Joe turned around then, to see what all the commotion was about. When he saw the bear, his eyes flew open. His heart almost stopped. He was so shocked that the breath went out of him and he couldn't say a word.

"Well, Joe, you're the man that gets the reward!" the miller said. "You sure have earned it. Tell us—how did you manage it?"

Joe was so scarified to think what he'd done that he could only gasp, "I—I'd ruther not talk about it."

Well, the fame of old Joe Dowdy went all over the mountains. Such a stout-hearted fellow there'd never been since the land was settled. The money for capturing the bear came in mighty handy for Joe and Tildy. They put a new roof on their house, bought themselves a cow, several hogs, and some poultry. So now they were well off. But if Joe thought he could settle down and enjoy his good fortune, he had another think a-coming.

When the time came to elect a sheriff, it was only natural that folks should think of Joe. All the mountain men met at the crossroads store and they agreed that he was the man for the job. There were some pretty tough horse thieves about; robbers appeared now and then, and sometimes rowdy fellows got to fighting with knives. Yes, Joe could handle them if anybody could.

The very thought of the sheriff's duties gave Joe the cold shivers. But he decided he'd better not refuse until he had talked it over with Tildy. "Let me think it over a bit," he told the men. "Being sheriff is a mighty big responsibility. I'll let you know about it tomorrow morning."

Joe set out for home. When he got there he explained to Tildy all that had happened. Tildy listened and looked thoughtful.

"They pay the sheriff a mighty big salary," she said. "You'd better take the job. You know the sheriff has a man to help him out. A deputy, they call him. If anything dangerous turns up, you can send him to handle it, while you stay out of harm's way and direct things."

Well, that solved the problem. Joe went back to the store the next day and accepted the job.

They gave Joe a big husky fellow for a deputy. If Joe didn't appear to take care of some ruffian, people said it was a job not worthy of a man like Joe. He'd just as well save himself for something big. So everything went all right for a year or two. Then there was a serious problem for old Joe Dowdy.

Word got around that the Indians were acting up again. They were going on the warpath by the looks of things, and all through the mountains people were worried. The men of the community got together at the store to see what could be done about it. They were all there but Joe, who had found an excuse to stay home.

"We'll have to get together and fight 'em," said Solly Sneed. "There's no other way."

"How can we fight 'em?" Jake Jones wanted to know. "There are maybe two hundred of them and only fifty of us."

"They're a-gathering," said the miller. "Whilst we chew the rag, they're a-sharpening their war hatchets."

"Within a week they'll be on us!" shouted Sam Cobble.

"Let's call on Joe Dowdy; he'll get us out of this!" someone cried.

"Sure, sure, we'll call on Joe. Why didn't we think of that before?"

Everybody gave a sigh of relief. Yes, Joe was the man to save the day.

So a messenger was sent to tell Joe they were all depending on him. He should put his mind to it, and save them from the Indians. It hardly needs saying that Joe was scared outen his wits.

"Why, Bud," he said to the messenger, "how can I do that?"

"Any way it suits you, Joe," Bud replied. "We know you can take care of twenty or thirty Indians by yourself. Maybe we fellows could handle the rest. While you're getting your coat, I'll go out and saddle your horse for you." And he set off for the barn.

Joe rushed into the house. "Tildy! Tildy!" he shouted.

Tildy came running. "What now?"

Joe poured out the story of what had happened. "Fight twenty or thirty Indians all by my lonesome! What'll I do? I think I had better go and explain how that business about catching the bear was all a misunderstanding. I'll make 'em see that I ain't a mite braver than anyone else."

"Wait!" said Tildy. "If you do that, you'll lose your job as sheriff, and then where will we be? We've got used to having money now and it would be mighty hard to be poor again."

"But what can I do? Bud's out there now, a-saddling my horse."

"Let me think," Tildy told him. She sat with her head in her hands. "Well," she said at last, "you might stall just a little and gain some time. Go over to the store and tell the men that you'll have to take a couple of days to scout out the situation, to see where the Indians are camped and how many there are. Say you want to spy out their plans.

"You wouldn't really have to go near the Indians. You could just ride over that-a-way. Let folks think you're a-going. Then you can hide in the woods a day or so, and come on home with some tale to satisfy them. Meanwhile, I'll be thinking up some excuse to get us out of this fix."

Since there seemed nothing else to do, Joe decided to take his wife's advice. He went out and mounted his old nag and rode with the messenger down to the store. He said to the gathering just what Tildy had told him to. They all agreed it was a sensible plan.

"But you ought not to go on a horse like that," the miller said. "That old bag of bones can hardly get into a trot. If some Indians were to ride after you, they'd overhaul you in no time. We'll get you a good horse."

"He can have mine," spoke up Solly Sneed. "I reckon he can outrun anything! Of course, he's a mite hard to handle, but anybody that could saddle up a bear and ride it ought to be able to manage my horse."

Now everybody in the mountains knew Solly's horse. He was a half-wild brute of a critter that only Solly could ride. He'd buck and bite, and he'd run fit to throw the old Boogerman[2] himself. The thought of getting on his back scared Joe almost as much as facing the Indians. But there was nothing for it but to accept Solly's offer.

"Well, I'll just ride my old horse home," Joe said, "and get some grub. I'll lead Sol's horse on behind, and he'll be there ready to mount after I've fixed up something to eat."

The men all agreed that this was a good idea. "We'll stay here at the store to wish you good luck as you go by," they said.

Home went poor Joe, feeling that his last day had come for sure. He showed Tildy the horse. "I'll never stay on his back a minute," he said. "He'll hump me off like I was a rabbit. Then he'll trample me, just outen spite. And the men all waiting at the store to see me go by!"

"Oh my!" cried Tildy, "what shall we do?" And she put her head in her hands, to think. In a few minutes she came up with a plan.

"We'll feed him some corn," she said, "and while he's eating I can tie your feet under his stomach. That way he can't buck you off. You ride by the store, then circle around the woods and come back home. You can hide in the barn loft a few days until it's time to report to the men at the store."

Joe wasn't too pleased with the idea of being tied onto the horse, but there seemed to be no other way out of his predicament. So they fed the horse a big helping of corn and, while he was munching it, Joe mounted and Tildy tied his feet with a rope under the horse's belly.

Joe set off easily enough. The horse was full of corn and in no mood for acting up. But when they came to the store, Joe kicked him in the ribs. If he passed the store at a fast clip, he thought, the fellows wouldn't see that his feet were tied. Well, kicking that horse was a mighty rash act, and Joe soon found it out. The critter let out a whinny and hoisted himself up on his hind legs. Then he set off for other places. Joe whizzed by the store like he was shot out of a cannon. The men hardly saw him before he was out of sight.

Joe couldn't stop that horse to save his life. He pulled and he sawed, but the animal took the bit in his teeth and went streaking on. The worst of it was, he was headed right for the Indian camp.

Now the Indians had set guards along the road to warn them in case the whites should attack. Two fellows were close in and two farther on down the road.

As Joe came abreast of the first two, they leaped out in all their war paint. They tried to stop the horse. One seized the bridle, the other tried to grab the saddle. But lawsy! They didn't have a chance. That horse upped with his back feet and kicked

2. **Boogerman,** dialect for *bogeyman,* an evil spirit or goblin.

one Indian half a mile down the road. He reached around with his teeth and took a bite out of the other one. The fellow squalled and jumped back. The horse humped himself and galloped on.

"Here comes a white man!" the Indian bawled to the guards closer in. "Even his horse is trained to fight. He kicks with his heels and bites with his teeth. He kicked my partner and cracked his skull. He pretty near bit my arm off!"

The near guards were scared a sight. They bellowed on to the camp: "Here come the white men! Their horses are worse fighters than the men. They thrash with their hoofs and crack people's skulls; they bite off arms with their teeth!"

This news set the Indian camp in an uproar. Everybody was running around telling the news to everybody else, and with every telling the tale got bigger. Such horses had never been heard of. How could they defend themselves against an army of such terrible critters?

Meanwhile, the horse thundered on. But with all the kicking he had done, and the humping and running, the rope that tied Joe's feet began to work loose. Joe knew he'd have a terrible fall if it came untied. How could he save himself? I'll grab a tree limb over the road, he thought, and haul myself offen this hog-wild critter.

He reached out to grab the first tree he came near. It was small and had hardly any roots. It came out in his hand and there he went, galloping past the second set of guards brandishing a tree torn up by the roots.

"Here come the white men!" the guards shouted. "They pull up trees by the roots without getting outen their saddles. Here they come, a-shaking them over their heads for war clubs!"

This news struck terror into the whole Indian camp. Men that pulled up trees by the roots. Horses that bit off arms and legs and cracked people's skulls. It was death to stay and face such monsters! Like a swarm of locusts, the Indians fled out of camp and took to the woods. When Joe and the horse came charging in among the tents, not a red man was left.

Joe hadn't thought to drop the tree, and it was banging and beating against the horse's side. It set the critter wild for sure. He charged around, kicking and bucking. He knocked down teepees, kicked over cooking pots, and trampled the Indians' belongings. There was never such havoc created by a horse before. That finished off the job of loosening Joe's feet, but he still stuck on. It was better than falling.

From behind the trees the Indians saw all the rampaging. The chief yelled for his counselors. "We'd better send him a peace pipe," he cried, "before the rest of 'em get here!"

"Send him a pipe!" the counselors agreed at once.

By the time Joe had thought to drop the tree and his horse had quieted a bit, an Indian brave was there.

"Peace, we have peace!" the red man cried, holding out the pipe.

Joe grabbed the thing—what it was he didn't know. He stuck it in his mouth. There was no other way of holding it, for he had all he could do to stay in the saddle. The horse was wheeling; he was tired of his jaunt. He'd had his run and his mind was set for home. He turned himself around and set off at a trot.

By the time he got back to the store, where the men were still gathered, the horse had gentled down considerable. Joe could hardly believe he had got back without having his neck broken. He took the pipe from his mouth and held it out to see what it was the Indian fellow had offered him.

The men on the porch of the store let out a whoop. "They're routed!" they shouted and began to thump each other on the back. "The Indians have sent the peace pipe!"

"T-t-tore their camp all to pieces," stuttered Joe. He sank down on the steps, nearly finished off.

Old Joe had done it again. All by his lonesome he had met and routed the Indians — all two hundred of them. It was almost beyond belief. The men got on their horses and rode over to the camp to see for themselves.

Yes, it was true. There was the camp with nary an Indian to be seen. Marks of the horse's hoofs were everywhere. The wreckage of the tee-pees was mingled with broken pottery. Even the campfires were scattered though the coals were still hot.

Well, there never was a man like Joe, the settlers all decided then and there.

"He ought to be commander of the state militia," said the miller. "He ought to have the job of defending the whole state."

"It's the kind of job he's fitten for!" the others heartily agreed.

When they got back to the store, they put it up to Joe. "You're the man for the job," they told him, "the job of defending the state from whatsoever and whosoever should attack it."

"No, boys." Joe shook his head. "I'm getting old. I've done enough. I hereby resign from public life. I don't even want to be sheriff any more. I want to settle down on my farm and live a quiet life. Don't call on me for anything else. I'm through."

That was his say and he stuck to it.

Well, in the end, the men had another meeting in the store. They decided that sure enough Joe had done his part for the settlement. He'd earned his rest. Out of gratitude for his defeat of the Indians, they voted him a pension, a nice tidy sum to be paid him every month for the rest of his life.

So, at last, Joe and Tildy were able to settle down and live peacefully on their little farm. ✱

Discussion

1. The storyteller says, "Joe was the kind of man that seemed born for bad luck" (page 296). (a) Give examples of this bad luck. (b) Is Joe himself at all responsible for his plight? (c) How does Tildy influence his actions?

2. (a) Which of Joe's actions bring about unexpected results? In each case, point out the action, Joe's intention, and the unexpected result. (b) Explain the irony in each example. What type of irony (verbal, situation, or tone) is this? (c) Does the author here make use of irony as a device to express criticism or simply to create humor? Explain.

3. Read in the feature on page 303 the old mountaineer's description of his youth. Most of our tall tales grew out of situations similar to the one described here. What devices has the author used in "The Man Who Rode the Bear" to make it sound as if it were told by Hank Huggins? Find examples of dialogue, description, etc., which help create this effect.

4. (a) Do you feel that the ending of the story (Joe's retiring) develops directly out of previous events, or is it simply added at this point in order to conclude the story? Explain. (b) Sometimes storytellers change stories considerably as they tell them. Do you think the plot structure would be destroyed if some further adventures were

added by an imaginative storyteller or if an episode were dropped from this story? Why or why not?

5. A necessary ingredient of every tall tale is exaggeration. (a) Find examples of exaggeration in "The Man Who Rode the Bear."

(b) Why is the device effective in creating humor?

6. (a) Why do you think tall tales were popular on the various American frontiers? (b) In what way can they be considered part of the American Romance?

How the Tall Tales Grew

When Ellis Credle and her husband moved to a small town in the Blue Ridge Mountains to search for tales to collect into a book, they encountered Hank Huggins, an old mountaineer who was described to them by the local storekeeper as "just an old liar. He'll even tell a whopper when the truth would do as well." Ellis Credle describes their meeting with him as follows:

Mr. Huggins and his wife—a quiet little body—greeted us hospitably. He ushered us toward the porch, then, putting a hand on my shoulder, turned and made a gesture toward the mountains.

"There's the reason I live up here!"

He nodded toward the valley spread out below in an opal-blue haze. We could see the tiny houses of the village along the straight ribbon of the highway; the creek was a thread winding among the homesteads.

We went into the cabin. A small fire was burning on the hearth. Mr. Huggins pulled up some rickety ladderback chairs and we sat down, spreading our hands gratefully to the blaze. To make conversation, my husband asked if there were any dangerous animals in the woods.

"Well, not so many now. But in the old days—*whew!*" Hank Huggins whistled and shook his head. "The varmints that used to be up here and the things that used to happen! Why, I recollect one time that a bear and a wildcat—" And the old man launched into a story. From this he progressed to another, and then to a third.

These were probably some of the "whoppers" the storekeeper had mentioned. But we were like people who had stumbled on a gold mine. We felt the excitement of a great discovery. Mr. Huggins was surely a man left over from a way of life now vanished, when people sat around the fire telling tales their grandparents had passed down to them, or making new ones out of half-forgotten lore. We sat entranced.

"However did you come to know so many stories?" I demanded at last.

Hank Huggins gave us a quizzical look. "What is it that has a tongue but can't talk?" Then, seeing our blank expressions: "Shucks, that's the oldest riddle there is. It's a wagon. A wagon's got a tongue but it can't talk. Only my wagon *could.* It heard plenty of tales.

"It was like this. When I was a young fellow, I had a job driving a freight wagon from up here in the hills down to the low country. It was before the railroad was built through the mountains. Well, there used to be a lot of us fellows driving wagons, and we would go together in trains, so as to have help in case somebody got stuck in the mud or broke an axle. Nights we'd camp together in some nice grove. Whilst we were cooking our suppers and after we'd et them, we'd sit around swapping news or telling tales. The tales I've heard around those campfires! Every fellow trying to outdo the next one."

The light outside had changed. It was time for us to go. When we stepped outside, we were amazed to see that the valley down below was dark with blue shadows. Mr. and Mrs. Huggins walked to the gate with us.[1]

. . . And so they grew, these tall tales, these "legacies from the wagoners and herders gathered around those long-dead campfires, and the mountain folk around their hearths"—a true part of the American Romance.

[1]Copyright 1957, by Ellis Credle. From TALL TALES FROM THE HIGH HILLS. Published by Thomas Nelson & Sons.

See **DIALOGUE** Handbook of Literary Terms page 539

NOW PLAYING

THE

BRIDE

comes to

YELLOW SKY

James Agee

adapted from the short story by Stephen Crane

CAST OF CHARACTERS

JACK POTTER, *Marshal of Yellow Sky*
FRANK GUDGER, *his prisoner*
DEACON SMEED, *the local clergyman*
LAURA LEE BATES, *proprietor of the "Weary Gentleman" saloon*
JASPER MORGAN, *an influential citizen*
ED, *a man of the town*
SCRATCHY WILSON, *the last of the badmen*
BRIDE, *Potter's new wife*

DINING-CAR STEWARD
WAITER
DRUMMER, *a traveling salesman*
TWO MEXICAN SHEEPHERDERS
MEN AND WOMEN ON TRAIN
YOUNG MAN
MRS. SMEED, *the Deacon's wife*
PORTER
CITIZENS OF YELLOW SKY

[*Fade in to exterior of the main street of Yellow Sky. Dusk. Late summer dusk; sound of church bell o.s. Pull down onto* POTTER'S *little home, of which the second story is a jail with barred windows.* JACK POTTER *comes out his door, dressed for travel, carrying a bag. He walks a few steps, then glances back around at his house.*]

PRISONER (*in upper window*). So long, Marshal. Don't do nothing I wouldn't do.

POTTER. Don't you do nothing I wouldn't, s'more like it. You lock yourself in right after mealtimes.

PRISONER. You can trust me, Marshal.

POTTER. I don't need to. I done tole Laura Lee to keep an eye on you. (*Pause; shyly*) Well, so long. I'll be back in a couple of days. (*He walks away.*)

PRISONER (*calling after*). Give my howdy to the gals in San Antone!

POTTER. You do that when you git out. I ain't no hand fer it.

PRISONER. Oh, I doan know, Marshal. They tell me still waters run deep.

[POTTER *doesn't answer. He walks on away. Dolly shot of* POTTER *and* DEACON SMEED. DEACON SMEED *falls in with* POTTER. *Camera dollies along with them. The following dialogue is interrupted two or three times by eminently respectable people converging on the church. All treat* POTTER *respectfully but a little remotely.*]

SMEED. Evening, Mr. Potter.

POTTER. Evening, Deacon.

SMEED. Leaving town so soon again?

POTTER. It's been most two months.

SMEED. Oh *has* it indeed, indeed. Hm. And what's going to happen to your prisoner, if I may ask?

POTTER. Laura Lee's gonna take care of him.

SMEED. Mrs. Bates? (POTTER *nods.*) She'll bring him his meals?

POTTER. He'll let himself out for 'em.

SMEED. Do you think that—ah—looks right?

POTTER (*quietly*). Afraid I ain't worryin' *how* it looks, Deacon. It's the easiest way, and you know as well as I do, he ain't gonna make no trouble.

SMEED. I'm afraid you don't care how *anything* looks, Mr. Potter.

POTTER. Oh now, Deacon, don't start on that church business again!

SMEED. I'm sorry, Marshal, but every respectable person in Yellow Sky agrees with me. If only for appearance' sake, you ought to come to church.

POTTER. Looky here, Deacon. We never did get nowheres with that argument, and we never will. I ain't got nothin' against church-goin'; I just don't hold with it fer myself.

SMEED. And then all these mysterious trips to San Antonio lately——

[*They pause in front of church.*]

POTTER. Now looky here, Deacon—if you mean light women and such, you know I ain't a man to fool around with them.

SMEED. Oh, you *misconstrue me*, Marshal, *indeed* you do. But . . . Caesar's wife,[1] you know . . .

[*The church bell stops ringing.*]

POTTER. How's that?

SMEED. She must be *above* suspicion.

POTTER. Well, who's suspicious? You?

SMEED. Of course not, Marshal. Perish the thought. Only you never *say why* you're going to San Antonio.

POTTER (*after a pause*). Just business. Goodnight, Deacon.

SMEED. Goodnight, Mr. Potter.

[POTTER *walks ahead; he blows out his cheeks; his eyes focus gratefully on the*

---

1. **Caesar's wife.** Deacon Smeed expects Potter to know the expression "Caesar's wife must be above suspicion." Julius Caesar divorced Pompeia, not because he believed her guilty of charges of infidelity but because he felt the wife of the emperor must not even be suspected of wrongdoing. The expression has come to mean that anyone in the public eye must be careful of his actions.

Film Jargon

Much of the effect in movies and in TV screenplays is accomplished by the cameraman, who, by maneuvering his camera and its lenses, focuses attention where the director wants it. In order to enjoy and appreciate reading a play that is intended for the screen, you must be able to picture the image as it would appear before you. Understanding the following technical terms and directions to the cameraman is therefore essential if you are to imagine the scene accurately.

b.g.: background.

close shot, medium shot, full (or *long*) *shot:* the extent of the view of the camera. A *close shot* is made near a person or object to show one particular thing; a *medium shot,* which includes two or three characters, shows regular action; a *full shot,* which shows a great deal of *b.g.,* is used to establish place or overall setting.

closeup: a *close shot* focusing on one item or one aspect of a person (eye, hand, etc.).

creep (in): dolly towards the scene very slowly to get a better shot of the action.

cut, cut to: make an abrupt replacement of one image for another. This is the standard way of making a change of image.

dissolve, dissolve to: blend or melt one image into another by *fading out* the first while *fading in* the second.

dolly, dolly shot: a shot taken with the camera moving on a *dolly,* a wheeled platform.

down shot: shot taken with the camera looking down on the action.

ext.: exterior, a shot of an outdoor scene.

fade out, fade in: gradually melt the image to or from a blank or black screen.

favor (shot favoring): a shot which, while including a number of persons or objects, highlights or focuses attention on one.

focus: the clarity of the image. Bringing something *into focus* makes it clear; an image *out of focus* is hazy.

freeze: stop action and hold the image motionless. For example, the camera might *freeze* a shot of a ball in flight.

full shot: (see *close shot*).

hold: fix on a person or object for a moment or two without turning away.

int.: interior, a shot of an indoor scene.

long shot: (see *close shot*).

medium shot: (see *close shot*).

o.s.: off-stage.

pan, pan shot: move the camera from one side to the other, either to follow a person or to give a panoramic view in sequence (table, chair, man, etc.).

pull (down, up, away, etc.): move the camera in the direction indicated.

still camera: hold the camera in one position.

up shot: shot from lower than eye level.

viewpoint shot: shot taken as if from the view of one of the characters.

"Weary Gentleman" saloon. *He checks his watch and speeds up out of shot.*

Cut to medium shot of DEACON, *who pauses at the church door, sees* POTTER *enter the "Weary Gentleman," and goes into church, from which we hear the first hymn.*

Cut to interior of "Weary Gentleman." Dusk. There is a typical Western bar, behind which LAURA LEE, *a woman in her fifties, is presiding as bartender. Camera pans* POTTER *to bar. He leaves his bag on a table near the door.*]

POTTER. Evenin', Laura Lee.

LAURA LEE *(behind bar)*. Hi, Jack.

JASPER. Jack.

ED. Howdy, Marshal.

POTTER. Jasper,—Ed.

ED. Leavin' town again?

POTTER. That's right.

ED. San Antone?

POTTER *(nods; drinks)*. Laura Lee, you tell Frank no drinks, no foolin' around. Just come right straight here and eat and get right back again. 'Cause it's got the Deacon bothered, him goin' out at all.

LAURA LEE. Aw, Smeed. I tell you, Jack, when you waded in here and cleaned the town up, it wasn't just a favor you done us. Everything's gettin' too blame respectable.

POTTER. It was my job.

LAURA LEE. I don't hold it agin you. But if things get too tame around here, you'll up an' quit town fer good.

POTTER. Uh, uh. I aim to be buried here. Besides, long as ole Scratchy busts loose now an' then, things won't never get *too* tame.

[*At the mention of* SCRATCHY, LAURA LEE'S *eyes focus on something o.s.*]

LAURA LEE *(a little absently)*. Here's to 'im.

[POTTER'S *eyes follow hers to a half-finished glass of beer, no customer. Close shot of* POTTER. *A glance from*

the beer to LAURA LEE, *a look of slightly concerned inquiry, meaning "Is that Scratchy's?" Close shot of* LAURA LEE, *nodding.*]

LAURA LEE. It don't work holding him to nothing, Jack. I figured maybe beer, on 'lowance . . .

POTTER. Don't hear me hollerin', do you? It's worth tryin'. Only thing bothers me is if I'm out of town.

LAURA LEE. He ain't due for another tear yet.

POTTER. Ain't sure we can count on him hittin' 'em regular, no more. He's gettin' rouncier all the time.

JASPER *(breaking a pause)*. What ye doin' in San Antone, Jack?

[LAURA LEE *gives him a cold glance.*]

POTTER. Just a business trip.

[SCRATCHY *comes in through a side door and up to the bar, to a half-finished glass of beer.*]

POTTER. Howdy, Scratchy.

[SCRATCHY *doesn't answer.* POTTER *and others are quietly amused.*]

LAURA LEE. What's wrong with ye, Scratchy? Cat got yer tongue?

[SCRATCHY *drinks glass down.*]

LAURA LEE *(continuing)*. Yer last one tonight. Rather wait fer it?

SCRATCHY. Just draw me my beer.

POTTER. Ain't still sore, are ye, Scratchy?

SCRATCHY. You know it was all in fun. What d'ye go an' plug me fer?

POTTER. 'Tain't fun, Scratchy. Not skeerin' the daylights out o' folks that ain't used to gunplay.

SCRATCHY. You're a fine one to talk about gunplay. Mean, sneakin' skunk!

POTTER. Sneakin'? It was fair and above board, like it always is.

LAURA LEE. He just beat ye to the draw, an' you know it.

SCRATCHY. That don't make my leg no happier.

POTTER. Mendin' a' right, Scratchy?

SCRATCHY. Oh, *I* git around.

POTTER. Just mind where ye git *to*, that's all I ask.

SCRATCHY. Next time, I'll make *you* dance.

POTTER. Better not be no next time. 'Cause next time, instead o' the meat o' the leg, I might have to pop you in the kneecap.

SCRATCHY. You wouldn't do that.

POTTER. I wouldn't want to. But I might have to, Scratchy, just to learn you. You don't know it but you're gettin' dangersome when you drink, lately.

SCRATCHY. Me—dangersome? A good man with a gun's a safe man with a gun, an' I'm the best they is.

LAURA LEE. When you're in yer likker, yeah. But you don't drink fer fun no more, Scratchy. You kinda go out o' yer head.

POTTER. That's right, Scratchy. One o' these days you're gonna shoot to kill, an' swing fer it, an' then all of us'll be sorry.

SCRATCHY. I don't need to kill nobody more—I got my notches, an' to spare——(*He pats his gun.*)

POTTER. That was all right, agin the kind o' varmints that used to be around here in the old days—You come in right handy. Sort of a scavenger, like a turkey-buzzard. But you can't go shootin' up law-abidin' citizens an' git away with it.

SCRATCHY (*with extreme contempt*). Who wants to shoot a law-abidin' citizen!

[POTTER *finishes his drink, pays, starts out.*]

POTTER. Well . . .

SCRATCHY. You leavin' town again?

POTTER. 'Bye, Laura Lee. See you day after tomorrow. (*To* SCRATCHY) You watch yer drinkin' while I'm gone.

SCRATCHY. I'll save it all up fer you, Jack. 'Tain't nobody else wuth the hangover.

[POTTER *exits.*]

JASPER. Reckon what he's up to, all these trips to San Antone?

LAURA LEE. Never you mind, it's his business.

ED. You ain't sweet on Jack, are ye, Laura Lee?

LAURA LEE (*a cold look at him*). Only man I ever was, he's in his grave ten year. (*She hears the train draw out, pours and drinks.*) But if I was, that's the only one *man* enough since.

[*Cut to interior of day coach. Close shot of* POTTER. *Night. He finishes rolling a cigarette, lights it and, elbow on windowsill, settles into the tired posture of night travel, gazing out of window. Camera slowly pans, losing his face, then his reflected face, squaring on the dark land flooding past. Fade out.*

Fade in to interior of parlor car. Camera looks squarely through window at fast-moving daylit land, reversing direction of preceding shot; then in a slow pan picks up the reflection of BRIDE'S *face in window; then the face itself; then pulls away.*

Cut to POTTER *and* BRIDE. *For a few moments we merely hold on them, as though this were a provincial wedding portrait of the period (circa, 1895). He has an outdoor clumsiness in his new suit, which is a shade tight and small for him. Her very new-looking hat and dress are in touchingly ambitious, naïve taste. Between their heads, in the seat just behind theirs, the head of a* "SOPHISTICATED" MAN *turns slowly, slyly watching, filled with patronizing amusement.* POTTER, *gradually aware, turns and looks him in the eye; the guy shrivels and turns away fast.*

Hold on BRIDE *and* POTTER *a moment.* BRIDE *looks at something o.s.* TWO WOMEN *watch her, whispering and giggling.*

Cut to medium shot, centering POT-

TER *and* BRIDE *from viewpoint of* WOM-
EN. *The* BRIDE *smiles very sweetly,
looking straight into the camera, and
we hear o.s. a more intense giggling
and whispering and a few inaudible
words. The* BRIDE *looks a little puzzled,
her smile fading; then she smiles
again, sure there can be no malice toward her; then looks straight ahead of
her. Both are glowing and intensely
shy. His large, spread hands englobe
his knees; hers are discreet in her lap.
He stares straight ahead, his eyes a
little unfocused. She keeps looking
around. With almost the manner of a
little girl, she draws a deep breath and
utters a quiet sigh of joy, at the same
time slightly raising, then relaxing,
the hands on her lap. He hears her
happy sigh; he looks at her; he watches
her shyly and with a certain awe. He
slowly shakes his head in the manner
of one who can scarcely believe his
good fortune. He lifts his own hands
from his knees; decides they were
where they belong; carefully replaces
them. When he finally speaks he tries
to be light and tender, and it is clear
that the loudness of his voice startles
and embarrasses him, and in the background heads flinch slightly.*]
POTTER. WELL, MRS. POTTER!
BRIDE *(by reflex)*. Shh!
[*Both are terribly embarrassed.*]
POTTER *(quick and low)*. Sorry! Frog
in my throat.
BRIDE *(same)*. I'm sorry, I didn't
mean to shush you. It just made me
jump's all.
POTTER. You shush me any time yer
a mind to.
BRIDE *(after a pause; with shy daring)*. You *call* me that, any time yer
a mind to. 'Cause I like to hear you
say it. Only not so loud.
POTTER *(after a pause, whispering it,
very shy)*. Mrs. Potter . . .
[*Overwhelmed by his daring, he blushes
and looks away. She shivers with*

quiet delight; she glances up at him,
then all around, with shy pride; then,
as delicately as if it were asleep, she
moves her hands in her lap as to un-
cover her wedding ring, and slowly,
almost unbelievingly, lowers her eyes
and looks at it. Then she looks around
again, speculatively.*]
BRIDE. Think they can tell we just got
m——(*She speaks the word almost
sacredly*) married?
POTTER. Don't see how they would.
We ain't treatin' 'em to no lovey-
dovey stuff or none o' that monkey
business.
BRIDE *(whisper)*. Jack!
POTTER. 'Scuse me.
BRIDE. It's all right.
POTTER. No it ain't neither. It ain't
fittin' I talk to you like that.
BRIDE. Yes it is, Jack. I reckon it
just kinda crep' up on me from
behind.
[*Silent, they look out the window. They
have run out of talk. They have plenty
to think about, but soon he feels he has
to make conversation.*]
POTTER. This-yer train sure does gob-
ble up the miles, don't it?
BRIDE. My yes. Just goes like the
wind.
POTTER. It's a thousand mile from
one end o' Texas to the other, and it
don't only stop but four times.
BRIDE. My land!
POTTER. It only stops for water at
Yaller Sky.
BRIDE. Oh.
POTTER. Hope you ain't gonna mind.
What I mean, it's a good town, but
it might look awful puny, side o'
San Antone.
BRIDE. Oh *no*. I never did like a big
town. I like it where ever'body
knows ever'body else.
POTTER. You'll like it there then.
[*They run out of talk again. She looks
around with more and more apprecia-
tion of the opulence and splendor of*

the car. Camera pans around Pullman car.]

BRIDE'S VOICE (*o.s.*). I just can't get over it! (*Pause*) It's all so handsome and rich-lookin'!

POTTER'S VOICE (*o.s.*). Yeah. They do it in style, sure enough, don't they?

BRIDE'S VOICE (*o.s.*). It's just like it was a palace or sumpin'. Even the ceilin'!

POTTER'S VOICE (*o.s.*). Gee. You sure do notice things. I never even seen it.

[*Close shot of* POTTER, *who has been looking up.*]

POTTER (*continuing*). Ever rode a parlor car before?

BRIDE. No.

POTTER. Me neither. One of these days we'll go on a trip overnight.

[*Both are quietly aghast with embarrassment.*]

POTTER (*struggling*). I mean, I always did have a hankerin' to see what them Pullman berths are like.

BRIDE (*helping him*). This is wonderful enough.

POTTER. Shucks. This ain't *nothing*. After a while we'll go forward to the diner and get a big layout. Ever et in a diner?

BRIDE. No. I always took me along some lunch.

POTTER. Finest meal in the world. Charge a dollar.

BRIDE. A dollar? Why that's too much — for us — ain't it, Jack?

POTTER. Not this trip, anyhow. We're gonna do the whole thing. (*He swells up, a little like a nabob, and looks away so she can look at him admiringly.*)

[*Dissolve to interior of* SCRATCHY'S *house (adobe). Day. Close shot. We sight above the bore of a long-barreled, blue-black revolver, against a raggedly-curtained window.*

Focus on the smoothly spinning cylinder of the revolver. SCRATCHY'S *other hand, with a rag, wipes the weapon clear of cleaning oil; the weapon is turned this way and that, lovingly, catching the light; then is sighted along, aiming it at Indians on a calendar, and is dry fired, with a click of the tongue and a whispered, "Got ye that time, ye dog!"; then it is laid delicately down on a patchwork quilt. Camera pans with* SCRATCHY'S *hand to a pint whiskey bottle on the floor by the bed. (Next to it is another bottle, empty.) Hand and bottle move out of shot; sound of drinking; bottle is returned, a good inch lower; hand unwraps a second revolver from a worn, fine old napkin; then a rag, then a little can of cleaning oil and a little rod. The hands start cleaning the revolver.*

During this entire scene, SCRATCHY WILSON'S *voice is heard, deeply and still tranquilly drunk, humming as much as singing, "Brighten the Corner."[2] The singing is of course interrupted: by his muttered line; by occasional shortness of breath; by his drinking, and a sharp cough afterward; and just as it resumes after the drinking, the voice is raw. But in overall mood it is as happy and innocent as a baby talking to itself in its crib.*

Cut to interior of parlor car. Day. Camera centers on POTTER *and* BRIDE. *The* DINING STEWARD *walks through quickly, hitting chimes.*]

STEWARD. Fust call for dinnah! Fust call!

[*Only* POTTER *and* BRIDE *react. A quick exchange of glances and they get up and follow* STEWARD *out of shot.*

Cut to interior of dining car. Day. Camera shoots past WAITERS *ranked ready beside empty tables as* POTTER *and* BRIDE *enter the car, registering*

---

2. **"Brighten the Corner,"** the title of a hymn. To provide an ironic effect, the author has Scratchy hum it as he cleans his guns.

abrupt dismay at all the service, whiteness, glitter and loneliness. The WAITER *nearest them tries to steer them toward a two-some table.* POTTER, *in a replying spasm of independence, steers* BRIDE *to a four-chair table opposite. The two sit down side by side.*]

POTTER *(low).* Looks like we're the only customers.

[*Instantly a hand plants a large menu in* POTTER'S *hand, blocking off his face, and then the same to the* BRIDE.]

WAITER'S VOICE *(juicy, o.s.).* There you are, sir! An' how're *you*-all today!

[POTTER *slowly lowers menu, looks to* WAITER. BRIDE *looks to* POTTER.]

POTTER. Gone up on yer prices, ain't ye?

WAITER'S VOICE *(o.s.).* Things are costin' more all ovah, these days. *(Oily)* Matter of fact, though, we can 'commodate folks of more moderate means. *(His finger reaches down and points on menu.)* There's a nice gumbo, good sandwiches . . .

POTTER. We'll have the dollar and a quarter dinner.

[*The* BRIDE *watches him with admiration.*]

WAITER. Yes indeed, sir. The chicken or the ham, sir? The ham is *mighty* delicious today, sir.

POTTER. Chicken.

WAITER. Yes, *sir!*

[*They unfold their napkins.* POTTER *glances about. Several* WAITERS *pretend not to watch. As* BRIDE *settles her napkin in lap, he starts tucking his high into his vest.*

Dissolve to exterior of "Weary Gentleman" saloon. Day. Camera dollies with the nattily dressed DRUMMER *through swinging doors into interior of saloon. We pause and shoot past him as he hesitates and looks around at* JASPER, LAURA LEE, *and* FRANK. *All glance at him casually and resume talking.*]

FRANK. Not even a small beer?

LAURA LEE *(sliding a tall one toward* JASPER). Not even that, Frank. What's more, it's high time you locked yourself back in. 'Cause Jack Potter's treatin' you white, an' it's up to you to treat him the same. Now git along with ye.

[*Close shot of* DRUMMER, *who registers sharp interest, glancing keenly back and forth between* FRANK *and* LAURA LEE.]

FRANK'S VOICE *(o.s.).* He'd treat me a whole lot whiter if he'd get back when he said he would.

LAURA LEE'S VOICE *(o.s.).* He ain't but a day late.

FRANK'S VOICE *(o.s.).* A day's a long time when you spend it in jail.

[DRUMMER *registers curiosity and consternation and looks exclusively at* FRANK.

New shot of LAURA LEE *and* FRANK.]

LAURA LEE. Read them magazines he give ye.

[*Camera pans with* FRANK *as he starts toward door, holding on* DRUMMER.]

FRANK. Done read 'em four or five times. Git tired of it, all that bang-bang stuff. *(To* DRUMMER) Howdy, stranger. *(He walks on out.)*

DRUMMER *(belated and odd).* Howdy. Did I hear that man correctly, ma'am? Is he a *jail-bird?*

LAURA LEE. If you want to put it that way.

DRUMMER *(looks to* JASPER, *who is wholly neutral).* Well! *(He looks to both; both are neutral.)* Well!

LAURA LEE. What'll ye have, mister?

DRUMMER. Beer, please, a big head on it.

[LAURA LEE *draws and hands it to him, sizing him up.*]

LAURA LEE. Big head.

DRUMMER. Nice little town.

LAURA LEE. It'll pass.

DRUMMER. Oh, I've had quite a profitable morning's work. *(He sips.)*

LAURA LEE. That'll be a nickel, mister.

[*He pays and sips again.*]

DRUMMER. Matter of fact, I'm a drummer.

LAURA LEE. I can see that.

DRUMMER. That's right. I travel in stockings. "Exquisite" stockings. (*Hustling his sample case to bar*) Paris to your doorstep, that's our slogan. Now if you're willing to spare a moment of your time, I can *promise* you, a lady of your taste and refinement, you just won't be able to *resist!*

LAURA LEE. Don't trouble yourself, mister, I don't——(*But the* DRUMMER *is already lifting the lid of the case. She leans her arms on it, nipping his fingers.*) Now, looky here, young feller; I ain't even a-goin' to *look* at them fool stockin's, let alone *resist* 'em.

[TWO MEXICAN SHEEPHERDERS *enter quietly by the rear door and sit at a table.*]

LAURA LEE (*to* MEXICANS). What's yours, Narciso Gulliermo Diorisio Mario?

FIRST MEXICAN. Cervezas.[3]

[*The* SECOND MEXICAN *nods.*]

DRUMMER (*sucking his fingers*). That hurt, ma'am.

LAURA LEE (*drawing beer*). Wouldn't be surprised.

JASPER. Seen Scratchy around, Laura Lee?

LAURA LEE. Not since t'other night.

JASPER. Gittin' so ye can't count on him fer nothin'. He was 'sposed to clair out my cesspool yesterday. Never showed up.

LAURA LEE (*pause—quietly*). Can't say as I blame him, Jasper; that's a job ye do yourself—and nobody ought to have to do it for him.

JASPER. Well—sometimes ye gotta take what ye can git.

[*She is silent.*]

JASPER (*continuing*). All I hope is, he ain't a-tyin' one on.

[*Close shot of* LAURA LEE.]

LAURA LEE. If I had to do a job like that fer you, I might tie on a few myself.

[*Camera pans as she takes beer to end of bar.* FIRST MEXICAN *pays and takes them. She sits on her stool, looking at nobody.*

A new shot of JASPER, *who watches her, nettled, and a little malicious.*]

JASPER. Hey, Laura Lee.

LAURA LEE. Yeah.

JASPER. Reckon what Jack Potter's *up* to in San Antone.

LAURA LEE. Reckon what business 'tis o' yourn.

JASPER. Just figured he might of *told you.*

LAURA LEE (*quiet and stern*). Jack Potter ain't tied to *my* apron strings, nor nobody's.

[*Cut to interior of dining car. Day.* POTTER *and* BRIDE *are finishing their desserts opposite a wooden, middle-aged* MARRIED COUPLE. (*The car is now full of people.*) POTTER *and the* MAN *meet glances;* BRIDE *and* WOMAN *do same.* POTTER *glances secretively down at his lapel and, privately as he can, scratches with his thumb-nail at a food stain. Their voices are low.*]

BRIDE. Don't worry. I can get that off in a jiffy.

POTTER. Ain't likely I'll wear it much, nohow.

BRIDE. Why, you'll wear it a-Sundays, church an' all.

POTTER (*uneasy*). I ain't never been much of a hand for church.

BRIDE. You don't ever go?

[POTTER *uneasily shakes his head.*]

BRIDE (*continuing; uneasy*). I don't know what I'd do, for lonesomeness, without no church to go to.

WAITER'S VOICE (*o.s.*). Look what I

---

3. *Cervezas* (ser vā′ sas), beer. [*Spanish*]

done brung yah both! An extra pot of nice fresh coffee.

[*Medium shot of* WAITER, *who leans over, setting down pot, beaming, proprietary, working for a big tip.*

New shot of POTTER *and* BRIDE, *who show mild embarrassment reactions; they murmur appreciations ad lib.[4]*]

BRIDE. Want some more?

POTTER. No thanks.

[*She pours for herself. The sugar is not in easy reach.*]

POTTER (*formally, to other man*). Pass the sugar, please.

MAN (*glumly*). Certainly.

POTTER (*to* BRIDE). Sugar?

BRIDE. Sure you won't have some more coffee?

POTTER. All right. Thanks. Thank you.

BRIDE. Certainly.

[*She leans to pour for him, much enjoying serving him, and knocks her napkin from the edge of the table to the floor between them. Both quickly stoop to reach for it. Their hands touch accidentally and fly apart as if they had struck a spark.*]

BOTH. 'Scuse me!

[*As they straighten up quickly,* POTTER *bumps the table making a clatter, and the* BRIDE *slops a little of the coffee from the pot in her other hand onto their clothes.*]

POTTER (*to everyone*).
  'Scuse me. } (*Together*)
BRIDE (*to him*). Gee,
  I'm sorry.

[*The two older people exchange unsmiling glances and pretend nothing is happening.* POTTER *with his handkerchief, she with his napkin, gently dab coffee off each other; they are embarrassed but not at all at odds. As the* WAITER'S *arm presents the check to* POTTER, *the camera centers on his right hand near his trousers pocket. The hand makes the odd, helpless gesture of putting aside a holster which isn't there.*]

BRIDE'S VOICE (*o.s.*). What's the matter?

POTTER'S VOICE (*o.s.*). Just habit, I reckon. Fust time in years I ain't totin' a gun.

[*Cut to interior of* SCRATCHY'S. *Day. Close shot of* SCRATCHY. *His loaded cartridge belt lies heavy and lethal across his knees. He thumbs in the last cartridge and lays aside the belt. The camera, as* SCRATCHY *rises to his feet, goes into a short spinning blur in and out of focus.*]

SCRATCHY'S VOICE (*o.s.*). Whoa there.

[*Camera proceeds into a slow, wobbly dollying pan, past window and bureau to pegs where* SCRATCHY'S *hand fumbles among his few clothes. Most of them are old and poor, but his hands select and get off the hook a violently fancy pseudo-western shirt on which camera comes into sharp focus. Then one hand, as camera creeps in, reaches for a real shocker of a necktie, muffs it, and as camera comes into close shot, drags it drunkenly, snakily, slithering from its hook. All this time* SCRATCHY *is muttering and humming.*

Cut to interior of parlor car. Day. Center camera on POTTER'S *more conservative tie. Tense and uneasy, he adjusts it. Pull back to* POTTER *and* BRIDE. *He is tense; she is content. He takes out and looks at a thick hunter watch.[5] Watching him, she realizes his uneasiness. She checks her own watch with his.*]

BRIDE. Mine's slow.

POTTER. Nope. I trust yourn. She's a seventeen jeweler.

[*Behind them, the* "SOPHISTICATED" MAN *slopes an amused eye.*]

BRIDE. Gracious.

---

4. **ad lib,** an instruction to the actors to improvise appropriate dialogue, which need not be heard distinctly.
5. **hunter watch,** a pocket watch with a hinged cover to protect the crystal.

[POTTER *corrects his watch, pockets it and avoids her eyes. She watches him. An uneasy silence. He looks at his watch again.*]

BRIDE *(continuing).* Jack.

POTTER. Hmm.

BRIDE. Somethin's eatin' at you.

POTTER. Me?

[*She nods—a pause.*]

POTTER. Nuthin' much. Only I wisht I'd sent a telegram.

BRIDE. Thought you did, there at the depot.

POTTER. I just tore it up.

[*Silence.*]

BRIDE *(shyly).* Was it—about us—gittin' married this morning?

POTTER. I oughta told 'um, back in Yaller Sky. That's all. You see, they're so used to me bein' a bachelor an' all. They ain't gonna take it no way good, me never tellin' 'em —an' all of a sudden I come home married——*(An inarticulate pause; ashamed)*—Reckon I'm just plain bashful.

BRIDE *(very shy).* Reckon I feel the same.

[*He looks at her, unbelieving. She corroborates her statement with a little nod. They are so relieved they awkwardly resist an impulse to join hands and both face rigidly front, their tension growing.*

Fast dissolve to interior of SCRATCHY'S *house. Day. We see a broken, distorting mirror. The camera is on* SCRATCHY, *and the reflection is his. He is wearing a fancy shirt, both revolvers, and the cartridge belt, and he has to stoop to see himself. He is in a reeling slouch, glaring, stinking drunk. He draws closer, making savage faces which are still more savagely distorted in the mirror. He becomes momentarily fascinated by these distortions. He draws both guns and lurches into extreme closeup, growling low.*]

SCRATCHY. All right, Jack Potter. Yore time has come!

[*Camera pulls back centering hands getting, from his dresser drawer, a newish hat as phony as the shirt. Camera leans for mirror reflection as he preens the hat on his head.*

Dissolve to interior of "Weary Gentleman." Day. Close shot of the DRUMMER, *whose eyes are fixed almost on the lens in the cold manner of a snake charming a bird. Camera pulls away along his fully extended, shirt-sleeved, and fancily sleeve-gartered arm. It is clothed to the armpit in a supersheer, elaborately clocked dark stocking.*]

DRUMMER (*soft and almost lascivious*). Speaks louder than words, doesn't it! *You* tell her, gentlemen; in *all your experience*, did you ever meet a lady that wouldn't *swoon* just to look at it? Sheer as twilight air. And just look at that clocking! Nothing like it ever contrived before, by the most inspired continental designers, to give style to the ankle and moulding to the calf. And they run all the way up—opera length. (*With a trace of hoarseness, almost whispering*) How about it, madam? (*He gives her a smile. A grand pause.*)

[*Pull back to include interior of* "Weary Gentleman." JASPER *and* ED *look toward him with quiet disgust. The two* MEXICANS *glance at each other and toward* LAURA LEE.

Close shot of LAURA LEE, *who gives the merchandise one more cold, fascinated once-over, then looks the* DRUMMER *in the eye.*]

LAURA LEE. All right, son. I'm still resistin'. So, fork over that dollar.

DRUMMER. But madam, you haven't given the Exquizzit——

LAURA LEE. Save yer breath, young feller. Why, if my husband had caught me in a pair o' them things, he'd 'a' broke my jaw. You're in the *wrong territory*, son. 'Cause this is a man's country. It's a hard country.

[*A* YOUNG MAN *comes in quickly.*]

YOUNG MAN. Scratchy Wilson's drunk an' he's turned loose with both hands.

[*Both* MEXICANS *set down their unfinished beers and fade out the rear door. The* DRUMMER *views with mystification; nobody pays any attention to him. They're as quick and efficient as a well-rehearsed fire-drill.* JASPER *and* ED *go out the front door and close the window shutters. The* YOUNG MAN *bolts the rear door.* LAURA LEE *bars the window on her side and goes center, swinging shut one leaf of the plank door. As* JASPER *and* ED *return,* JASPER *swings the other shut and bars his window and* ED *brings from the corner the bar for the main door and helps* LAURA LEE *put it in place.* LAURA LEE *returns to her place behind the bar. In the sudden, solemn, chapel-like gloom, the* DRUMMER *is transfixed; his eyes glitter.*]

DRUMMER. Say, what *is* this?

[*A silent reaction from the men.*]

DRUMMER (*continuing*). Is there going to be a gunfight?

JASPER (*grimly*). Dunno if there'll be a fight or not, but there'll be some shootin'—some good shootin'.

YOUNG MAN. Oh, there's a fight just *waitin'* out there in the street, if anyone wants it.

[JASPER *and* ED *nod solemnly.*]

DRUMMER *(to* YOUNG MAN*).* What'd ye say his name was?

ALL. Scratchy Wilson.

[*The* DRUMMER *does a fast multiple take, person-to-person.*]

DRUMMER. What're you goin' to do? *(Grim silence)* Does he do this often? *(More silence)* Can he break down that door?

LAURA LEE. No. He's give that up. But when he comes you'd better lay down on the floor, stranger. He's dead sure to *shoot* at that door, an' there's no tellin' what a stray bullet might do.

[*The* DRUMMER, *keeping a strict eye on the door, begins carefully removing the stocking from his arm.*]

DRUMMER. Will he kill anybody?

[*The* MEN *laugh low and scornfully.*]

JASPER. He's out to shoot, an' he's out fer trouble. Don't see no good *experimentin'* with him.

DRUMMER. But what do you *do* in a case like this? What do you do?

YOUNG MAN. Why, he an' Jack Potter——

JASPER *and* ED. Jack ain't back yet.

YOUNG MAN *(suddenly frightened).* Lordy!

DRUMMER. Well, who's he? What's *he* got to do with it?

YOUNG MAN. He's Marshal.

LAURA LEE. Comes to shootin', he's the only one in town can go up agin him.

[*Far off, o.s., we hear a wild Texas yell, a shot, another yell. Everyone becomes very still and tense.*]

DRUMMER *(half whispered).* That must be him comin', hey?

[*The* MEN *look at him in irritation and look away again. They wait, their eyes shining in the gloom.* JASPER *holds up three fingers. Moving like a ghost,*

LAURA LEE *gets out three glasses and the bottle. The* DRUMMER *lifts one forlorn finger; she adds another glass. They pour. In unison they snap the drinks down at a gulp and walk to windows to look through chinks. The* DRUMMER *quietly puts a coin on the bar.* LAURA LEE *just looks at it, at him, and away. He shamefacedly takes back his coin. She silently takes a Winchester from beneath the bar and breaks it.*]

DRUMMER *(whispered).* You goin' to shoot him?

[*Silence; everyone looks at him bleakly.*]

LAURA LEE *(low).* Not if I can help it. I ain't a good enough shot. Might kill him.

DRUMMER. Well, it'd be pure self-defense if you did, wouldn't it? *(No answer)* Well, *wouldn't* it? Good riddance *too,* I'd say.

[LAURA LEE *closes the breech.*]

LAURA LEE *(low).* Mister, Scratchy Wilson's an old friend. Nobody'd harm a hair of his head if they's any way out—let alone kill him. You see, trouble is, he's a wonder with a gun. Just a wonder. An' he's a terror when he's drunk. So when he goes on the war trail, we hunt our holes—naturally.

DRUMMER. But—why do they allow him—what's he doin' in a town like this?

LAURA LEE. He's the last of the old gang that used to hang out along the river here. *(A silence. Then nearer, but distant, a howl is heard. The* DRUMMER *reacts, jittery.)* You better come back o' the bar. I kinda fixed it up.

DRUMMER *(ashamed).* No thanks, I'll——

LAURA LEE *(with a peremptory gesture).* Come on.

[*He does. He squats low in the front angle of the bar and examines, with* some relief, the various plates of scrap metal with which she has armored it. O.S., nearer, we hear another shot and three yowls. There's a shuffling of feet. They look at each other.]

MEN (quietly). Here he comes!

[Pan shot. We dolly with LAURA LEE, carrying her gun, to look through a chink in the shutter, and through the chink see SCRATCHY round the corner at the far end of the empty street, yelling, a long heavy blue-black revolver in either hand. We hear his words, distant, but preternaturally powerful, as he strides to the middle of the street and stops dead, both guns alert, threatening and at bay.]

SCRATCHY. Yaller Sky, hyar I come!

[As SCRATCHY comes nearer, he holsters a revolver, extracts a pint bottle from his belt, cocks it vertically and drains it, and tosses it high and glittering into the sunlight, in mid-air; then shoots it into splinters, left-handed, and does a quick 360-degree whirl, drawing both guns, as if against enemies ambushing him from the rear. He raises a small tornado of dust.

Cut to a head closeup into which he finishes his pivot, glaring. His eyes are glittering, drunk, mad, frightening. He is eaten up with some kind of interior bitter wildness.]

SCRATCHY (a low growl). Got ye, ye yaller-bellies!

[He gives a lonely Texas yowl; the echoes die. He glares all about him; his eyes, focusing on something o.s., take on sudden purpose.]

SCRATCHY (loud). Jack Potter!

[Medium shot with still camera of POTTER'S house. Freeze closer shot of SCRATCHY, who is trying to adjust his eyes to this oddity.]

SCRATCHY (louder). Jack Potter!

[Medium shot of POTTER'S house, as before.]

SCRATCHY'S VOICE (o.s.). You heared me, Jack Potter. Come on out an'
face the music. Caze it's time to dance.

[Close shot of SCRATCHY. Dead silence. He is puzzled.]

SCRATCHY. 'Tain't no ways like you Potter, asullin' there in yer house. You ain't no possum. I treated ye fair and square. I saved it all up for ye, like I told ye. Now you play square with me.

FRANK'S VOICE (o.s., scared). Hey, Scratchy.

SCRATCHY (puzzled, looking around). How's that? Who is that?

[POTTER'S house; past SCRATCHY.]

FRANK'S VOICE. Hit's me. Frank.

SCRATCHY. Why don't ye say so? Whar ye at?

FRANK'S VOICE. I'm up yere in the jail.

SCRATCHY. Well show yerself! What ye skeered of?

FRANK'S VOICE. You.

SCRATCHY. Me? Shucks. Only man needs to be skeered o' me is Jack Potter, the yaller hound.

FRANK'S VOICE. Jack ain't here, Scratchy.

SCRATCHY. What ye mean he ain't here?

FRANK'S VOICE. He ain't got back yet, that's what I mean. That's what I was tryin' to tell you.

SCRATCHY. Ain't back! Don't gimme none o' that. He come back yesterday when he promised he would.

FRANK'S VOICE. No, he didn't.

SCRATCHY. You lie to me. Frank Gudger, I'll give ye what fer. (He shoots, striking a bar and ringing a musical note.)

FRANK'S VOICE. Scratchy! Don't do that! Hit's dangersome.

SCRATCHY. Not if ye keep yer head low it ain't.

FRANK'S VOICE. 'Tis too. Ye can't tell whar them bullets'll rebound.

SCRATCHY. Don't you dast tell me how to shoot, ye pore wall-eyed woods colt. *Is* Jack Potter back or *ain't* he?

FRANK'S VOICE. No he ain't and that's the honest truth.

SCRATCHY. Don't you *sass me.*

[*Close shot.* SCRATCHY *shoots another bar, ringing a different musical note, which is followed by a shattering of glass.*]

SCRATCHY (*continuing*). Is he back?

FRANK'S VOICE. Quit it, Scratchy. Ye done busted my lamp chimbley.

SCRATCHY. *Is* he back or *ain't* he?

FRANK'S VOICE. All right, have it yer own way. He's back if you say so.

SCRATCHY. Well, why didn't you tell me so straight off? (*No answer*) Why don't he come on out then?

FRANK'S VOICE. Reckon he would if he was inside.

SCRATCHY. Oh, he ain't inside, huh?

FRANK'S VOICE. Not that I know of.

SCRATCHY. Well, that leaves just one other place for him to be.

[*He turns toward the "Weary Gentleman," hikes his trousers, reaches for the bottle which is no longer there.*]

SCRATCHY (*growling and starting*). Dad burn it. Never seed it yet I didn't run out just at the wrong time!

[*He walks fast past the respectable houses, the churches and so on, and dollying, shooting past him, we see they all have an unearthly quietness. As he walks, he talks, now to himself, now shouting.*]

SCRATCHY (*continuing*). But that's all right. Just lay low. 'Caze quick as I wet my whistle, I'm gonna show ye some shootin'! (*He stops in front of* MORGAN'S *house.*) You, Jasper Morgan. Yeah, and that snivelin' woman o' yourn, too! Too dainty to do like ordinary folks. Too high an' mighty! Git yerself a lot o' fancy plumbing, an' ye ain't man enough to clean out yer own cesspool. "Let Scratchy do it." Ain't nuthin' so low but Scratchy'll do it for the price of a pint.

[*He glares around for a target. He spies a potted fern suspended from the porch ceiling. He shoots the suspension chain and the whole thing drops to the porch floor with a foomp. He turns;* DEACON'S *house is opposite.*]

SCRATCHY (*continuing; in a horrible mockery of a sissy voice*). Deacon! Oh *Deacon Smee-eed!* (*He makes two syllables of* Smeed.) You home, Deacon? Kin I pay ye a little call? *Most* places in town, ye just *knock* an' walk *in,* but that ain't *good* enough for a *good* man, *is* it, Deacon? Oh *no! No—no!* Pay a little call on the Deacon, ye got to shove a 'lectric bell, real special. (*A hard shift of tone*) All right, Smeed, start singin' them psalms o' yourn. You'll be whangin' 'em on a harp, few mo' minutes, you an' yer missuz, too. Can't stop in right now, I'm a mite too thirsty. But I'll be back, Deacon. Oh, I'll be back. (*He studies the house.*) Here's my callin' card.

[*He takes careful aim, and camera focuses on doorbell, which the bullet hits, so fusing it that it rings continuously. We hear a woman scream hysterically. Close shot of* SCRATCHY.]

SCRATCHY. Ah, quit it. Don't holler 'til yer hurt.

[*Interior of* DEACON'S *house;* DEACON *and* WIFE. *Past* DEACON *and his* WIFE, *through the curtained window, we see* SCRATCHY *pass. The* DEACON *has an arm around his* WIFE. *He is trying pathetically to resemble an intrepid doomed frontiersman in an Indian fight.*]

DEACON. He'll pay for this. By the Almighty, he'll pay dearly. I'm not going to stand for it, I'm simply not going——

MRS. SMEED. Oh hush. For goodness sake, stop that horrid *bell!*

[*He looks at her, goes into the hallway with wounded dignity, and jerks a wire loose. Just as the bell stops, there is a shot and the stinging sound o.s. of the church bell being shot at. The* DEACON *reacts to this last outrage.*

Medium shot, upward, of church bell from SCRATCHY'S *viewpoint.*

Close shot, shooting down. SCRATCHY *looks up at bell, both pleased and angry, and shoots again at the church bell.*]

SCRATCHY. *(He bellows.)* Come on out and fight if you dast—only you don't dast.

[*He starts glancing all around; the revolvers in each hand are as sensitive as snakes; the little fingers play in a musician-like way.*

Cut to a motionless curtain of machine-made lace with a head dimly silhouetted behind; a drawn shade, with an eye and fingertips visible at the edge.

Cut back to SCRATCHY.]

SCRATCHY *(continuing).* O no! You know who's *boss* in *this* town. Marcellus T. Wilson, that's who. He ain't fittin' to wipe yer boots on, no-sirree, he's the lowest of the low, but he's boss all the same. 'Caze *this* is a boss, *(Gesturing with a revolver)* an' *this* is a boss *(Another)* an' this is the feller that can boss the both of 'em better'n any other man that's left in this woreout womanizin' country. An' there ain't hardly a man of ye dast *touch* a gun, let alone come up again a *man* with one. Oh no! Got lil' ole honeybunch to worry about, lil' ole wifeypifey, all the young 'uns, make ye some easy money runnin' a store, doctorin', psalm-singing, fix ye a purty lawn so Scratchy kin cut it for ye, if ye can't get a Mex cheap enough. Oh, I——*(He searches helplessly, then half-says.)*—hate—I could wipe every one of ye offen the face o' the earth, a-hidin' behind yore women's skirts, ever' respectable last one of ye! Come out an' fight! Come on! Come on! Dad *blast* ye! *(He glares around again. There is no kind of response at all. His attention shifts; his eyes focus on something o.s.; he becomes purposeful.)*

[*Exterior of "Weary Gentleman" saloon which is barricaded. Day. Dolly shot over* SCRATCHY'S *shoulder as he advances on door.*

Cut to close shot of SCRATCHY, *who comes to door and hammers on it with gun butt.*]

SCRATCHY. Laura Lee. *(Pause)* Laura Lee. *(Pause. Now he hammers with both revolvers.)* Laura Lee! *(No answer)* You can't fool me. I know you're there. Open up. I want a drink. *(No answer)* All I want's a little drink. *(Now he hammers harder than ever.)*

[*Cut to close shot of* LAURA LEE, *low behind bar, her rifle ready if need be, thumb on safety.*

Close shot of THREE LOCAL MEN *on floor, watching the door fixedly.*

Close shot of the DRUMMER, *behind the bar, plenty scared.*

Close shot, back to SCRATCHY, *finishing his hammering. He is rather tired. He glares at the door a moment, then:*]

SCRATCHY. All right then. All right. *(He looks around him, sore.)*

[*He sights a scrap of paper in the dirt, picks it up, and with a vicious and cruel thrust, nails it to the door with a knife. Then he turns his back contemptuously on the saloon, walks to the far side of the street and, spinning quickly and lithely, fires at the sheet of paper.*

Cut to paper as the bullet misses it by half an inch.

Cut to SCRATCHY.]

SCRATCHY. Well, I . . . Gah . . . gittin'

old in yer old age, Scratchy. *(He takes careful aim and fires.)*
[*Cut to paper. The bullet splits the haft of the knife: the blade clatters down; the paper follows, fluttering; a hole appears in the door.*
Close shot of interior of "Weary Gentleman." JASPER is on floor, between a chair and a spittoon. Bullet flicks wood from chair, ricochets with appropriate sounds, puncturing spittoon from which dark liquid oozes. JASPER, with slow horror, looks at it.
From SCRATCHY'S viewpoint, the paper finishes settling.
Close shot of SCRATCHY, who is satisfied; he turns and starts walking grandly away. Suddenly he cries out.]
SCRATCHY. Hey! *(He stops and faces the saloon again.)* Hey, tell Jack Potter to come on out o' there like a man! *(No answer)* Jack! JACK POTTER?
[*Close shot of interior saloon.*]
LAURA LEE. Jack Potter ain't here, Scratchy, an' *you know it!* 'Cause if he was, he'd be out thar arter ye.
[*Close shot of SCRATCHY, who hesitates, thinks it over.*]
SCRATCHY *(uncertainly)*. You wouldn't fool me, would ye, Laura Lee?
LAURA LEE'S VOICE *(o.s.)*. I never did, did I?
SCRATCHY. Well don't never you try it. 'Caze I ain' the man'll stand fer it. *(Suddenly sore)* That lyin' no-'count Frank! I'll fix *him!* I'll cook his goose! *(He starts out fast up the street. There is the sound of a distant train whistle o.s.).*
[*Dissolve to interior of parlor car. Day. Sound of dying wail of whistle o.s. Throughout scene, sound of slowing train. Tension and emotion increase in the faces of POTTER and BRIDE.*]
POTTER *(with desperate finality)*. Well——
[*She looks to him anxiously—he meets her eyes briefly and both smile, then lower their eyes pathetically. He gratefully thinks of something to do.*]
POTTER *(continuing)*. Better git down our truck.
[*With day-coach reflex, he stands up, reaching for the non-existent baggage rack, realizes his mistake, and pretends he is only tidying his clothes.*]
PORTER'S VOICE *(o.s., loud and glad)*. Don't you bother, mister——
[*Cut to close shot of PORTER, grinning.*]
PORTER *(continuing)*. —I got it all ready an' waitin'!
[*Full shot of car. Some amused heads turn.*
BRIDE and POTTER as before. He sits down abashed. Train sound is much slower. Their time is short.]
POTTER *(smiling and wretched)*. Home at last.
BRIDE *(uneasy)*. Mm-hmm.
[*A silence. Close shot of POTTER, in real desperation. O.S. sound of train bell.*]
POTTER *(sweating; rapidly)*. Say listen. You ain't gonna like me fer this an' I don't blame ye, but I just can't face 'em if we can help it, not right yet. What I want, I want to sorta *sneak* in, if we can git away with it, an' make home without nobody seein' us, an' then study what to do about 'em. I figure we got a chance if we kinda skin along the hind side o' Main Street. We got cover 'til about sixty foot from my door. Would ye do it?
[*Camera pulls and pans into shot of POTTER and BRIDE.*]
BRIDE *(fervent)*. Oh gee, if only they don't ketch us!
POTTER *(incredulously grateful)*. You don't hate me fer it?
BRIDE *(with all her heart)*. Hate you?
[*They look at each other with entirely new love. The train is stopping. They get up fast and leave the shot.*

Cut to exterior of station at Yellow Sky. Day. As train pulls to a stop, the PORTER *descends train steps first and leaves the shot.* POTTER, *with* BRIDE *behind and above him, peers anxiously forward along the station platform.*

Long shot of the empty platform.

Medium shot; panning.]

POTTER (*over shoulder*). Come on, girl. Hurry.

[*He steps to platform; she follows unassisted. He grabs up both bags and, looking back to her, collides with the untipped, dismayed* PORTER.]

POTTER. Oh. (*He sets down bags. A fumbling rush for change. He hands out a coin.*) Much obliged. (*He picks up bags and starts walking, the* BRIDE *alongside.*) Let's git outa here.

PORTER. Much obliged to *you*, sir.

[POTTER *walks away so fast that she has to hustle to keep alongside. Both are eagle-eyed—he with anxiety, she with that and with simple interest.*

Camera pans an empty segment of street.]

BRIDE'S VOICE (*o.s.*). Gee, I don't see *nobody*.

[BRIDE *and* POTTER *as before.*]

POTTER. Just the hot time o' day; let's not risk it.

[*They walk still faster around rear corner of station and out of sight.*

Cut to close shot of cell window in POTTER'S *house. It is empty; very, very slowly a little mirror rises to eye level above the sill—and jerks down fast.*

Close shot between the rear of two buildings toward the vacant Main Street. POTTER'S *head comes close into shot, then the* BRIDE'S.]

POTTER (*whispering*). All right.

[*They dart noiselessly across the gap.*]

POTTER (*continuing*). Good girl.

[*They laugh, low and sheepish, and steal ahead. Camera pans with them.*]

POTTER (*still whispering*). Next corner, dear, an' I can show you our home.

BRIDE (*same*). Oh, Jack. (*She stops. Her eyes are damp. He stops.*)

POTTER (*whispering*). Sumpin' the matter?

[*Very close shot of* BRIDE.]

BRIDE. The way you said that!

POTTER'S VOICE (*o.s.*). Said what?

BRIDE (*moved*). Our home! (*She smiles very shyly. He is moved and says, in a most embarrassed voice:*)

POTTER. Come on then, girl—Let's *get* there.

[*They start walking fast and quiet; we pan with them, approaching the frame corner of a house.*]

POTTER (*continuing*). Now right the next second, you can see it!

[*They circle the corner and come face to face with* SCRATCHY. *He is leaning against the wall, just around the corner, reloading. Instantly he drops this revolver, whips the other from its holster, and aims it at* POTTER'S *chest. A deadly silence. The* BRIDE *grabs* POTTER'S *right arm. He drops both bags and exhibits the desperate reflex of a man whose fighting arm has never before been encumbered. He reaches for the gun that is not there. He sweeps her behind him.*

Closeup of SCRATCHY.

Close shot of the BRIDE. *Her face looks crumpled with terror; she gazes at the gun as at an apparitional snake.*

Close shot of POTTER. *He looks up from the gun into* SCRATCHY'S *eyes.*

Close shot of the revolver.

Camera rises slowly to bring in SCRATCHY *in extreme closeup. His eyes are cold and mad; his face is almost solemn.*]

SCRATCHY (*almost reproachfully*). Tried to sneak up on me. Tried to sneak up on me!

[*Shot of the* MEN *with the* BRIDE *behind*

POTTER. POTTER *makes a slight move-ment;* SCRATCHY *thrusts his revolver venomously forward; camera lunges forward correspondingly.*

Close shot of SCRATCHY.]

SCRATCHY (*smiling with a new and quiet ferocity*). No, don't ye do it, Jack Potter. Don't you move a finger towards a gun just yet. Don't you bat an eyelash. The time has come fer me to settle with you, so I aim to do it my own way, an' loaf along without no interferin'. So if ye don't want a gun bent on ye, or a third eye right now, just mind what I tell ye. (*He slowly raises his revolver to eye level, so that it is pointing a little upward, dead into the lens.*)

[*Close shot of* POTTER, *past gun. He is looking directly down the barrel. He is not at all a cowardly man but he is looking directly into the eye of death. Sweat breaks out on his face.*

Extreme close shot looking down the pistol barrel.

Extreme close shot of POTTER, *then the* BRIDE'S *face, saying "our home" (without sound) and smiling.*

Return to POTTER. *His eyes, a little dizzily out of focus, restore to normal.*]

POTTER (*quietly*). I ain't got a gun, Scratchy. Honest I ain't. You'll have to do all the shootin' yerself.

[*Close shot of* SCRATCHY. *He goes livid and steps forward and lashes his weapon to and fro.*]

SCRATCHY. Don't you tell me you ain't got no gun on you, you whelp. Don't tell me no lie like that. There ain't a man in Texas ever seen you without no gun. Don't take me fer no kid. (*His eyes blaze with light; his throat works like a pump.*)

[*Close shot of* POTTER.]

POTTER. I ain't takin' you fer no kid. I'm takin' you fer a damned fool. I tell you I ain't got a gun an' I ain't. If you're gonna shoot me up, ya

better do it now; you'll never get a chance like this again.

[*Pull away into shot of both men.* SCRATCHY *calms a little.*]

SCRATCHY (*sneering*). If you ain't got a gun, why ain't you got a gun? Been to Sunday school?

POTTER. You know where I been. I been in San Antone. An' I ain't got a gun because I just got married. An' if I'd thought there was goin' to be any galoots like you prowlin' around, when I brought my wife home, I'd 'a' had a gun, an' don't you fergit it.

SCRATCHY (*says the word with total, uncomprehending vacancy*). Married?

POTTER. Yes, married. I'm married.

SCRATCHY (*a little more comprehension*). Married? You mean, *you?* (*He backs off a pace; the arm and pistol drop.*) No. (*He studies* POTTER *cagily and shakes his head. Then literally for the first time, he sees the* BRIDE.) What's that ye got there? Is this the lady?

POTTER. Yes, this is the lady.

[*A silence.*]

SCRATCHY. Well, I 'spose it's all off now.

POTTER. It's all off if you say so, Scratchy. You know I didn't make the trouble. (*He picks up both valises.*)

[SCRATCHY *studies* POTTER *up and down, slowly, incredulously. Then he looks at the ground.*]

SCRATCHY. Well, I 'low it's off, Jack. (*He shakes his head.*) Married! (*He looks up with infinite reproach, sadness and solitude. He picks up his fallen revolver. He hefts it and turns both revolvers in his hands, looking at them, then puts them with finality into their holsters. Then he again meets* POTTER'S *eyes.*) G'bye, Jack.

[*Close shot of* POTTER. *He begins to comprehend; he is moved.*]

POTTER. 'Bye, Scratchy.

[*Close shot of* SCRATCHY. *He looks at* POTTER *a moment, then turns around and walks heavily away.*

Cut to POTTER *and* BRIDE. *She emerges from behind him, whimpering, glancing from man to man, hugging his arm. His eyes on* SCRATCHY *o.s., he is hardly aware of her.*

Cut to a lace curtain, which is plucked aside and DEACON'S WIFE *looks out.*

Close shot of a front door that opens cautiously, squeakily; and cautiously, a man we don't know emerges.

Cut to interior of "Weary Gentleman." Day. The doors open; JASPER, ED, *the* YOUNG MAN, *and finally* LAURA LEE, *followed by the* DRUMMER, *emerge onto the porch, looking up the street.*

Group shot, favoring LAURA LEE *and* DRUMMER.]

DRUMMER (*smug*). You were saying, ma'am—this is a *hard* country?

[*She gives him a look and looks again toward* SCRATCHY *and company. Long shot, past* ED *and* DRUMMER. *The* DEACON *trots out to* POTTER, *frantically effusive. They pantomime introductions.*]

ED. Drummer, looks like ye got ye a new customer.

[DRUMMER *registers certainty and anticipation.*]

DRUMMER (*to* LAURA LEE). And how about you, ma'am?

[*Close shot of* LAURA LEE. *She turns on him, colder than ever.*]

LAURA LEE (*in measured tones*). I wouldn't wear them things if it killed me. (*Then she realizes she is dead. Her eyes fall, tragic and defiant, to a neutral angle. In background,* JASPER, *watching her, realizes a little of the meaning. He is sympathetic.*)

ED'S VOICE (*o.s.*). Well, look at that!

[*Long shot past all of them.* POTTER *is walking toward home with* DEACON *and the* BRIDE *as if between custodians. They stop. The* DEACON, *extra effusive, peels off and toddles for home.*

Close moving shot of POTTER *and* BRIDE *walking. She glances back toward the filling, watchful street, which we see past them.* POTTER *is looking toward* SCRATCHY *o.s.*]

BRIDE. Sure looks like the cat's outa the bag.

POTTER. More like a wild cat. (*He stops. So do* BRIDE *and camera.*) You know? There's somethin' I always wanted to do. (*He sets down the suitcases and looks her up and down, businesslike. She is willing but mystified. He picks her up.*)

BRIDE (*surprised and grateful*). Oh, Jack . . .

[*As he carries her forward out of the shot, he looks sadly again toward* SCRATCHY *o.s. while she, loving and puzzled, looks at him.*

Medium shot of FRANK *at the window.*]

FRANK. Howdy, Marshal! Proud to know ye, Miz Potter! Welcome home!

[*With the attempted velocity of a fast baseball, he slams down handfuls of improvised confetti. Pull camera down.* POTTER *and* BRIDE *walk to door amid showering confetti.* POTTER *shoves door open with his shoe, enters,* BRIDE *in arms, and shoves door shut.*

Dolly in, close shot, showing that SCRATCHY *has shot the lock to pieces. The last confetti flutters down. Salient are the torn pictures of the murderous faces and weapons of early Western fiction.*

Very long shot of SCRATCHY. *Very small, he walks heavily away toward a solitary, still more distant hovel; empty earth and sky all around. A long hold; then camera focuses on a close shot of the funnel-shaped tracks of his feet in heavy sand.*]

Discussion

1. (a) What, according to Laura Lee, has Potter done for Yellow Sky? **(b)** How do the townspeople regard him? **(c)** How does he feel about the town?

2. (a) Is Jack Potter the same man on the train that he is in Yellow Sky? Explain. **(b)** Find in the dialogue and stage directions examples of the way in which Potter and his bride regard each other. **(c)** Why is Potter afraid to bring his bride to Yellow Sky?

3. (a) Summarize Jack Potter's character. **(b)** Does his character differ from your concept of a Western "hero"? Explain.

4. (a) What is Scratchy Wilson's position in Yellow Sky? **(b)** Why don't the townspeople have him put in jail? **(c)** Reread Scratchy's long speech, page 320, column 1. What does this speech reveal about Scratchy's background?

5. (a) Why does Scratchy have contempt for Jasper Morgan and Deacon Smeed? **(b)** Why is Potter the only man Scratchy wants to fight? **(c)** Why doesn't Scratchy shoot Potter when he has the chance?

6. (a) How does Laura Lee regard Jack Potter? **(b)** What does the playwright mean when he states that Laura Lee realizes she is dead (page 325, column 1, paragraph 14)?

7. Why do you think the author has added the character of the Drummer, a stranger, to those of the citizens of Yellow Sky?

8. (a) On page 308 Laura Lee says, "I tell you, Jack, when you waded in here and cleaned the town up, it wasn't just a favor you done us. Everything's gettin' too blame respectable." What does she mean? **(b)** Which other characters are not completely satisfied with the fact that the town is turning "respectable"? **(c)** Which characters would be likely to express contentment with the town's respectability? Find specific speeches and details to support your answer.

9. In this screenplay, Yellow Sky is in the midst of change. Many details as well as actions symbolize this change. Of the items listed below, some represent the old West and some represent the new West. Explain what each one represents in *The Bride Comes to Yellow Sky:* **(a)** the $1.25 dinners; **(b)** Laura Lee's armored bar; **(c)** Frank's Wild West magazines; **(d)** the Drummer's merchandise; **(e)** the notches on Scratchy's gun; **(f)** Scratchy's fancy shirt; **(g)** Morgan's cesspool and Smeed's doorbell; **(h)** Frank's improvised confetti; **(i)** Scratchy's footprints in the final shot; **(j)** the title *The Bride Comes to Yellow Sky.*

10. In a sentence, state the theme of this screenplay.

The Author

James Agee (ā′ jē), poet, novelist, movie critic, dramatist, and social commentator, was born in Knoxville, Tennessee, in 1909, and attended school there and in the Cumberland Mountain country. This background gave him a deep love of the land which influenced much of his writing. He graduated from Harvard in 1932, and two years later published a collection of poetry, *Permit Me Voyage.*

While working as a staff writer for *Fortune* magazine he was assigned to spend some time living with an Alabama sharecropper family. Their way of life so moved him that he resigned his job and devoted his time to writing a report on sharecropper life. *Let Us Now Praise Famous Men,* with Agee's text as commentary on a series of photographs of sharecropper families, was published in 1941 and received much praise for his poetic handling of his subject. In 1955 James Agee died.

His novels are *The Morning Watch* and *A Death in the Family,* which was adapted for stage and movies under the title *All the Way Home.* Most of Agee's later work was for motion pictures and television. In addition to *The Bride Comes to Yellow Sky,* Agee's film scripts include *The Night of the Hunter* and *The African Queen.*

After his first day in the new country, he could say,
"America is a country
where anything, anything at all can happen."

The First Day

George and Helen Papashvily

AT FIVE IN THE MORNING the engines stopped, and after thirty-seven days the boat was quiet.

We were in America.

I got up and stepped over the other men and looked out the porthole. Water and fog. We were anchoring off an island. I dressed and went on deck.

Now began my troubles. What to do? This was a Greek boat and I was steerage, so of course by the time we were halfway out I had spent all my landing money for extra food.

Hassan, the Turk, one of the six who slept in the cabin with me, came up the ladder.

"I told you so," he said as soon as he saw me. "Now we are in America and you have no money to land. They send you home. No money, no going ashore. What a disgrace. In your position, frankly, I would kill myself."

Hassan had been satisfied to starve on black olives and salt cheese all the way from Gibraltar, and he begrudged every skewer of lamb I bribed away from the first-cabin steward.

We went down the gangplank into the big room. Passengers with pictures in their hands were rushing around to match them to a relative. Before their tables the inspectors were busy with long lines of people.

The visitors' door opened and a fellow with a big pile of caps, striped blue-and-white cotton caps with visors and a top button, came in. He went first to an old man with a karakul hat near the window, then to a Cossack[1] in the line. At last he came to me.

"Look," he said in Russian, "look at your hat. You want to be a greenhorn all your life? A karakul hat! Do you expect to see anybody in the U.S.A. still with a fur hat? The customs inspector, the doctor, the cap-

1. **Cossack** (kos′ak), one of a people from southwest Russia.

tain—are they wearing fur hats? Certainly not."

I didn't say anything.

"Look," he said. "I'm sorry for you. I was a greenhorn once myself. I wouldn't want to see anybody make my mistakes. Look, I have caps. See, from such rich striped material. Like wears railroad engineers, and house painters, and coal miners." He spun one around on his finger. "Don't be afraid. It's a cap in real American style. With this cap on your head, they couldn't tell you from a citizen. I'm positively guaranteeing. And I'm trading you this cap even for your old karakul hat. Trading even. You don't have to give me one penny."

Now it is true I bought my karakul *coudie* new for the trip. It was a fine skin, a silver lamb, and in Georgia[2] it would have lasted me a lifetime. Still——

"I'll tell you," the cap man said. "So you can remember all your life you made money the first hour you were in America, I give you a cap and a dollar besides. Done?"

I took off my *coudie* and put on his cap. It was small and sat well up on my head, but then in America one dresses like an American and it is a satisfaction always to be in the best style. So I got my first dollar.

Ysaacs, a Syrian,[3] sat on the bench and smoked brown paper cigarettes and watched all through the bargain. He was from our cabin, too, and he knew I was worried about the money to show the examiners. But now, as soon as the cap man went on to the next customer, Ysaacs explained a way to get me by the examiners—a good way.

Such a very good way, in fact, that when the Inspector looked over my passport and entry permit I was ready.

"Do you have friends meeting you?" he asked me. "Do you have money to support yourself?"

I pulled out a round fat roll of green American money—tens, twenties—a nice thick pile with a rubber band around.

"O.K.," he said. "Go ahead." He stamped my papers.

I got my baggage and took the money roll back again to Ysaac's friend, Arapoulaopolus, the money lender, so he could rent it over again to another man. One dollar was all he charged to use it for each landing. Really a bargain.

On the outer platform I met Zurabeg, an Ossetian,[4] who had been down in steerage, too. But Zurabeg was no greenhorn coming for the first time. Zurabeg was an American citizen with papers to prove it, and a friend of Gospadin[5] Buffalo Bill besides. This Zurabeg came first to America twenty years before as a trick show rider, and later he was boss cook on the road with the Gospadin Buffalo Bill. Every few years, Zurabeg, whenever he saved enough money, went home to find a wife—but so far with no luck.

"Can't land?" he asked me.

"No, I can land," I said, "but I have no money to pay the little boat to carry me to shore." A small boat went chuffing back and forth taking off the discharged passengers. "I try to make up my mind to swim, but if I swim how will I carry my baggage? It would need two trips at least."

"Listen, donkey-head," Zurabeg said, "this is America. The carrying boat is free. It belongs to my government. They take us for nothing. Come on."

2. **Georgia,** a republic in the southeast part of the Soviet Union in Europe, between the Black and Caspian Seas.
3. **Syrian** (sir′ ē ən), one from Syria, a country in western Asia, on the Mediterranean Sea south of Turkey.
4. **Ossetian** (o set′ i ən), one from a region of Russia between the Black and Caspian Seas.
5. **Gospadin** (gus pō dēn′), Mister.

So we got to the shore.

And there—the streets, the people, the noise! The faces flashing by—and by again. The screams and chatter and cries. But most of all the motion, back and forth, back and forth, pressing deeper and deeper on my eyeballs.

We walked a few blocks through this before I remembered my landing cards and passport and visas. I took them out and tore them into little pieces and threw them all in an ash can. "They can't prove I'm not a citizen, now," I said. "What we do next?"

"We get jobs," Zurabeg told me. "I show you."

We went to an employment agency. Conveniently, the man spoke Russian. He gave Zurabeg a ticket right away to start in Russian restaurant as first cook.

"Now, your friend? What can you do?" he asked me.

"I," I said, "am a worker in decorative leathers particularly specializing in the ornamenting of crop handles according to the traditional designs."

"Good night!" the man said. "This is the U.S.A. No horses. Automobiles. What else can you do?"

Fortunately my father was a man of great foresight and I have two trades. His idea was that in the days when a man starves with one, by the other he may eat.

"I am also," I said, "a swordmaker. Short blades or long; daggers with or without chasing; hunting knives, plain or ornamented; tempering, fitting, pointing——" I took my certificate of successful completion of apprenticeship out of my *chemidon*.

"What next? A crop maker—a sword pointer. You better take him along for a dishwasher," he said to Zurabeg. "They can always use another dishwasher."

We went down into the earth and flew through tunnels in a train. It was like the caves under the Kazbeck[6] where the giant bats sleep, and it smelled even worse.

The restaurant was on a side street and the lady owner, the *hasaika*, spoke kindly. "I remember you from the tearoom," she said to Zurabeg. "I congratulate myself on getting you. You are excellent on the *piroshkis*, isn't it?"

"On everything, madame," Zurabeg said grandly. "On everything. Buffalo Bill, an old friend of mine, has eaten thirty of my *piroshkis* at a meal. My friend—" he waved toward me "—will be a dishwasher."

I made a bow.

The kitchen was small and hot and fat—like inside of a pig's stomach. Zurabeg unpacked his knives, put on his cap, and, at home at once, started to dice celery.

"You can wash these," the *hasaika* said to me. "At four we have party."

It was a trayful of glasses. And such glasses—thin bubbles that would hardly hold a sip—set on stems. The first one snapped in my hand, the second dissolved, the third to tenth I got washed, the eleventh was already cracked, the twelfth rang once on the pan edge and was silent.

Perhaps I might be there yet, but just as I carried the first trayful to the service slot, the restaurant cat ran between my feet.

When I got all the glass swept up, I told Zurabeg, "Now, we have to eat. It's noon. I watch the customers eat. It makes me hungry. Prepare a *shashlik* and some cucumbers, and we enjoy our first meal for good luck in the New World."

"This is a restaurant," Zurabeg

---

6. **Kazbeck** (käz bek′), a mountain that rises over 16,000 feet in the Caucasus Mountains in Russia.

said, "not a *duquani* on the side of the Georgian road where the proprietor and the house eat with the guests together at one table. This is a restaurant with very strict organization. We get to eat when the customers go, and you get what the customers leave. Try again with the glasses and remember my reputation. Please."

I found a quart of sour cream and went into the back alley and ate that and some bread and a jar of caviar which was very salty—packed for export, no doubt.

The *hasaika* found me. I stood up. "Please," she said, "please go on. Eat sour cream. But after, could you go away? Far away? With no hard feelings. The glasses—the caviar—it's expensive for me—and at the same time I don't want to make your friend mad. I need a good cook. If you could just go away? Quietly? Just disappear, so to speak? I give you five dollars."

"I didn't do anything," I said, "so you don't have to pay me. All in all, a restaurant probably isn't my fate. You can tell Zurabeg afterward."

She brought my cap and a paper bag. I went down through the alley and into the street. I walked. I walked until my feet took fire in my shoes and my neck ached from looking. I walked for hours. I couldn't even be sure it was the same day. I tried some English on a few men that passed. "What watch?" I said. But they pushed by me so I knew I had it wrong. I tried another man. "How many clock?" He showed me on his wrist. Four-thirty.

A wonderful place. Rapidly, if one applies oneself, one speaks the English.

I came to a park and went in and found a place under a tree and took off my shoes and lay down. I looked in the bag the *hasaika* gave me. A sandwich from bologna and a nickel—to begin in America with.

What to do? While I decided, I slept.

A policeman was waking me up. He spoke. I shook my head I can't understand. Then with hands, with legs, rolling his eyes, turning his head, with motions, with gestures (really he was as good as marionettes I saw once in Tiflis[7]), he showed me to lie on the grass is forbidden. But one is welcome to the seats instead. All free seats in this park. No charge for anybody. What a country.

But I was puzzled. There were iron arm rests every two feet along the benches. How could I distribute myself under them? I tried one leg. Then the other. But when I was under, how could I turn around? Then, whatever way I got in, my chin was always caught by the hoop. While I thought this over, I walked and bought peanuts for my nickel and fed the squirrels.

Lights began to come on in the towers around the park. It was almost dark. I found a sandy patch under a rock on little bluff above the drive. I cut a *shashlik* stick and built a fire of twigs and broiled my bologna over it and ate the bread. It lasted very short. Then I rolled up my coat for a pillow like the days during the war and went to sleep.

I was tired from America and I slept some hours. It must have been almost midnight when the light flashed in my face. I sat up. It was from the head lamp of a touring car choking along on the road below me. While I watched, the engine coughed and died. A man got out. For more than an hour he knocked with tools and opened the hood and closed it again.

---

7. **Tiflis** (tif′ lis; *Russian* tēf li ēs′), the capital of Russian Georgia.

Then I slid down the bank. In the war there were airplanes, and of course cars are much the same except, naturally, for the wings. I showed him with my hands and feet and head, like the policeman: "Give me the tools and let me try." He handed them over and sat down on the bench.

I checked the spark plugs and the distributor, the timer and the coils. I looked at the feed line, at the ignition, at the gas. In between, I cranked. I cranked until I cranked my heart out onto the ground. Still the car wouldn't move.

I got mad. I cursed it. I cursed it for a son of a mountain devi.[8] I cursed it for the carriage of the diavels in the cave. I cursed it by the black-horned goat, and when I finished all I knew in Georgian I said it again in Russian to pick up the loose ends. Then I kicked the radiator as hard as I could. The car was an old Model T, and it started with a snort that shook the chassis like an aspen.

The man came running up. He was laughing and he shook my hands and talked at me and asked questions. But the policeman's method didn't work. Signs weren't enough. I remembered my dictionary—English-Russian, Russian-English—it went both ways. I took it from my blouse pocket and showed the man. Holding it under the headlights, he thumbed through.

"Work?" he found in English.

I looked at the Russian word beside it and shook my head.

"Home?" he turned to that.

"No," again.

I took the dictionary. "Boat. Today."

"Come home—" he showed me the words— "with me—" he pointed to himself. "Eat. Sleep. Job." It took him quite a time between words. "Job. Tomorrow."

"Automobiles?" I said. We have the same word in Georgian.

"Automobiles!" He was pleased we found one word together.

We got in his car, and he took me through miles and miles of streets with houses on both sides of every one of them until we came to his own. We went in and we ate and we drank and ate and drank again. For that, fortunately, you need no words.

Then his wife showed me a room and I went to bed. As I fell asleep, I thought to myself: Well, now, I have lived one whole day in America and—just like they say—America is a country where anything, anything at all can happen.

And in twenty years—about this—I never changed my mind. *

---

8. *devi*, devil. *Devi, diavels,* and *black-horned goat* all refer to evil spirits believed in by superstitious people of Russian Georgia.

Discussion

1. What is the author's attitude toward his new country when he first arrives? Find specific passages which express this attitude.

2. (a) Why is the man with the caps willing to pay Papashvily a dollar to trade hats? (b) Why does Papashvily agree to trade? (c) How is the episode with the man who rents money similar to that with the cap seller? (d) In what other ways does Papashvily show himself ignorant of American customs?

3. (a) Why does Papashvily tear up his passport, landing papers, and visas? (b) What evidence is there to indicate that he is determined to become a good American?

4. Since coming to the United States, Papashvily has of course learned a great deal about the country and the language, but on that first day he knew almost nothing. (a) How does the writing in this selection suggest the speech of one unfamiliar with the

language? **(b)** Find some specific words or phrases which add color and interest to his descriptions. **(c)** How does he manage to create humor in recounting his experiences?
5. (a) How do Papashvily's experiences on that first day lead him to think of America as a place where "anything can happen"? **(b)** How does the author, telling this story years afterwards, regard these events, and how does he regard the "greenhorn" immigrant he was when he first arrived? **(c)** How does this story qualify as part of the American Romance?

Word Study

You can often guess at the meaning of a foreign word by paying attention to the context in which the word is used. Read the sentences below and decide what each italicized word means. Then choose the most appropriate definition from the following list.

(a) *a woman proprietor of a restaurant who acts as hostess*
(b) *slices of mutton roasted on a stick*
(c) *small pastries filled with meat or cheese*
(d) *fur hat*
(e) *family-style inn*
(f) *suitcase*

1. "Now it is true I bought my karakul *coudie* new for the trip. It was a fine skin, a silver lamb, and in Georgia it would have lasted me a lifetime. . . . I took off my *coudie* and put on his cap."
2. I opened my *chemidon* where it stood on the floor and searched through my clothes until I found my certificate.
3. We asked the woman who showed us to a table if she was the *hasaika,* but she said the owner would be back shortly and that we could ask her if she needed a cook and dishwasher.
4. Buffalo Bill, an old friend of mine, prefers my meat *piroshkis* to the cheese, but he once ate thirty of my pies at one meal.
5. Though I had no lamb for a proper *shashlik,* I cut a stick and broiled my bologna on it over the fire.
6. "This is a restaurant, not a *duquani* on the side of the Georgian road where the proprietor and the employees eat with the guests together at one table."

The Authors

Ever since that day in 1923 you have just read about, George Papashvily (pä pəsh vē′ lē) encountered a number of seemingly unfortunate events which by some quirk turned out to have happy endings. Some of these humorous situations were recounted by Papashvily and his wife Helen, who wrote down his stories as he told them, in a popular and lively book entitled *Anything Can Happen,* from which this selection is taken.

An author who could not write in English, George Papashvily was also a successful sculptor who had never had a lesson. He was born on a Russian farm, apprenticed to a harnessmaker at the age of nine, and later hired by a swordmaker. When he was fourteen he joined the Czar's army to serve in World War I. After coming to the United States he worked in mines, factories, on a farm, and in the movies. Among other books by the Papashvilys are *Thanks to Noah, Dogs and People,* and *Yes and No Stories.* Mrs. Papashvily has also published a biography, *Louisa May Alcott.*

See
FLASHBACK
Handbook
of Literary
Terms
page 545

In this autobiographical selection,
Gordon Parks, a renowned photographer,
tells how he became interested in music
as a youth and how he tried
to get the world of music interested in him.

MUSIC INSIDE MY HEAD

Gordon Parks

IT WAS NATURAL that we hoped for an early spring. But winter was deep in the earth and unwilling to be hurried. So spring would sneak in a bit at a time, breathe upon the cold and then retreat. It gnawed at the snow, dwindling it with rain and sun, but the cold wind never slept. It roamed the nights, repairing the damage that had been done during the day. It was good when finally the icicles fell and melted into the earth and the smoke left our breath and the frozen Mississippi moved again.

By now the land was stricken with poverty.[1] Every newspaper and magazine I read showed photographs of men queued up at breadlines[2] and

From A CHOICE OF WEAPONS by Gordon Parks. Copyright © 1965, 1966 by Gordon Parks. Reprinted by permission of Harper & Row, Publishers and Robert Lantz Literary Agency.
1. *By now . . . poverty.* The author is referring to the great depression of the 1930's.
2. *breadlines,* lines of people waiting to receive food given as charity or relief.

employment halls seeking food and work. And this poverty attacked my family wherever it caught us. Yet hunger, I learned, was less frightening in the summer. I could walk slower and give more freely of what energy I had. And it was easier when the moon shone and the stars twinkled over the warm evenings, and love was close at hand.

July brought such evenings and also my first quarrel with Sally.[3] It happened over some minor thing, but it kept us apart for months. And during those hours I worried and worked at a composition that spoke my feelings. The song was called "No Love"; and I wrote it at an upright piano my sister inherited with the house. And now that I had started writing songs again, I worked at it late into the nights and on weekends; music was the one thing that kept me hopeful. A peculiar experience had kindled my love for it long before Casamala[4] decided that I should become a composer.

I was seven at the time. The Kansas day was hot and I was hunting June bugs in our cornfield when I heard a murmuring in the cornstalks. The murmuring grew into music, and I stood there, my mouth full of mulberries, puzzled, looking up at the slow-drifting clouds to see if they were the music's source. The violins, horns and drums were as true to me as the sunlight, and I had a feeling that the music was trapped inside my head, that it would be there even if I had no ears. I covered them with my hands, and the sounds were still there and they continued until all the clouds moved away and there was nothing but pale sky. Then it was gone as mysteriously as it had come, and I ran toward the house a little frightened, a little joyful, eager to tell my experience. But no one was around and I scooted up on the piano stool and started banging our old Kimball upright—trying to reproduce the sounds I had heard. The noise reached my father in another part of the field and he dropped his hoe and rushed to the house. He opened the door and watched me with astonishment; I was screaming as loud as I could.

"Have you gone batty, boy?"

I jumped down and started telling my story, but he only looked at me, at the mulberry stains around my mouth, and shook his head. "I declare, if you don't quit fondin' yourself on those mulberries, you're goin' to be swearin' you saw the devil. Now stop that bangin' and git to your chores."

Perhaps I never forgave my father's reactions to those delirious moments, for never again did we talk about things bordering on fantasy —not even a bedtime story. On that day, however (and to the woe of my good father), I began to play the piano. Several years later, Earl McCray, a music professor at the white school, offered me free music lessons. I was assigned a trombone and placed in our junior-high-school orchestra. But by now I was accustomed to playing by ear, and the slow process of learning to read music seemed unnecessary. I indulged in trickery. Each Saturday morning, before my appointment with Mr. McCray, my sister fingered my lesson on the piano and I memorized it; then I went off to astonish the professor with my "sight reading." He recommended me as soloist at the graduation concert. And everyone said I played "The Rosary" with great feeling that night. Only my sister knew I couldn't read a note.

---

3. **Sally,** the girl who later became Parks' wife.
4. **Casamala,** a girl of Parks' acquaintance, who encouraged him in his musical studies.

This was long past. But now at nineteen, five years later, I regretted the tricks I had played upon the professor. I had never learned to read or write music, though I was determined to compose; it seemed the one way to avoid a less-than-ordinary existence. I worked out a notation system of my own by referring to the piano keys as numbers instead of notes—a process that proved more complicated than the conventional way.

The next consideration was a publisher; it was disheartening to discover that all the important ones were in Chicago or farther east. And there were warnings against dishonest publishers who stole songs; but this didn't bother me. It would have been flattering, I thought, to have composed something worthy of a professional's theft. The difficulty would be to get someone to transpose my numbers to notes and then have the final work accepted. But I knew I couldn't depend on music alone. That first winter[5] had taught me that I would have to fight with everything that came to hand. Learning, I knew, would be the most effective weapon against the coming years. So once again I seized upon books. After school I searched the local library shelves for authors who might help me in different ways. I pushed my mind into the foreign worlds of Thomas Mann, Dostoevski, James Joyce[6] and others whom I had never read before. I tried stone sculpture, short-story writing, poetry and, when I could hustle the material, painting. I did everything I could to protect myself against another such winter. Somewhere in between I played basketball for the Diplomats[7] and my high school as well.

A collapse was inevitable, and it came during a basketball game in October, 1931. I had dribbled past two guards and arched the ball perfectly, knowing it would swish through the hoop. But a blackness suddenly covered the court and the ball disappeared into it like a balloon into a cloud, and I felt myself falling. The coach had my teammates carry me to the locker room, where I was examined by the school nurse. Her only comment was that I looked awful hungry and thin to be playing such a strenuous game. But at home later that evening a doctor whom my sister called said I was on the verge of a physical breakdown. I had wasted from 165 pounds to 124 in less than three months. If I was to regain my health, he said, I would have to leave school for the remainder of the year and rest.

So at twenty I found myself an invalid. There was no chance of graduating with my class. I was already too far behind. In fact, I knew that I would never go back to school. For the next five months I sat in the dark of my room rejecting time, light and reason. I never heard from Sally during that time, but my sister helped me through the long convalescence and tried to get me to read, to write, to do anything that would divert my eyes from the blank wall opposite my bed. I finally opened a book one rainy afternoon. And gradually I began to read, think and hope again. One thing was clear. I couldn't escape my fate by trying to outrun it. I would have to take my time from now on, and grow in the light of my own particular experience—and accept the slowness of things that were meant to be slow. Spring was back again, but I was afraid to look upon its coming with

5. *That first winter,* 1928–1929. When his mother died the previous year, Parks had come to live with his sister and her family in St. Paul, Minnesota.
6. *Thomas Mann, Dostoevski* (dos′tə yef′skē), *James Joyce,* important novelists of the 19th and 20th centuries.
7. *the Diplomats,* a boys' club.

any pleasure. It had deceived me once too often.

By April I had regained my weight and strength. And before long I was hanging out at Jim's pool hall again, for it was a good place to get back into the stream of things. Arguments were always going; they flared, blossomed and faded by the dozens. Some of them were senseless, some were heated, some were comical.

During one argument, one man claimed that Glen Gray, the band leader, had a mustache. The other denied it. My interest was casual until one of the men, a waiter at the Hotel St. Paul, boasted that he should know since he "rubbed shoulders with Gray every night." He was lying of course about the shoulder rubbing, but he did see the orchestra leader regularly; anyone working there had the same opportunity. I wondered why I hadn't thought of this before. Many of the best orchestras played at the large Twin City hotels[8]; if only I could get one of them to broadcast my songs. The thought grew and I hurried home, sorted out several of my compositions and set my alarm clock for six o'clock. And by seven-thirty the next morning I was at the Hotel St. Paul servants' entrance, the songs tucked in my pocket, applying for a waiter's job.

The time keeper, an old gray-haired man, looked me over and asked me to wait around until he saw the day's work schedule. And for the next four hours I paced the corridor, looking expectantly at him now and then. At eleven-thirty, he motioned for me.

"Are you an experienced waiter?"

"Yessir. Yessir." (I had never waited on table in my life.)

"You ever work here before?"

"Not yet, no, sir."

"Where have you worked?"

"The Minnesota Club, the Lowry, the——"

"Okay, okay. There's a Rotary[9] luncheon today, nothing steady. You want to work it?"

"Is that where the orchestra plays?"

"Orchestra? What's the orchestra got to do with it?" he asked.

"Oh nothing, nothing. Just thought I'd ask." My heart thumped like a drum.

"Well, do you want it or not?" he snapped.

"Yessir, I'll take it." I stepped up to his table and signed in.

The banquet captain changed my status from waiter to bus boy the instant he saw me pick up a tray. And as I trudged back and forth between the kitchen and the banquet hall, under the weight of the trays of drinks, I could hear the music coming from the main dining room. It was frustrating to have Glen Gray so close and not to be able to talk with him. But the driving captain kept his eye on me, pointing to tray after tray. And only once, when the dining-room door swung open, did I glimpse the tall, debonair orchestra leader directing his orchestra. And I noticed then that he did have a mustache.

Much later, the Rotarians were enjoying coffee, puffing cigars and asking silly questions of a mind reader they had hired for entertainment. I hung around, clearing dirty dishes from the tables—and listening to the questions and answers.

"Who's going to be the most famous in this room?" someone asked.

"Good question," the mind reader said. He then covered his eyes and turned his back to the audience. There was snickering as he suppos-

---

8. **Twin City hotels.** Minneapolis and St. Paul, Minnesota, are known as the Twin Cities.
9. **Rotary.** The Rotary Club is a men's service organization.

edly searched the future. Whomever he chose was in for a good razzing. The laughter was already building.

"Gentlemen." There was a momentary quiet. "There is a boy in the back of this room in a white uniform" (every eye in the room turned on me). "He will be more widely acclaimed than any — "

That was enough. Bedlam broke loose. "Boy! Boy! Come up here!" It was the mind reader's voice screaming over the others. "Bring him up, somebody!"

Two men started toward me, but I grabbed a tray of dishes, and, fleeing the banquet hall, I tripped and threw the dishes in all directions. But I got to my feet and kept going until I reached the dressing room.

In spite of that fiasco, I was hired three days later as a regular bus boy, and assigned to the main dining room.

Glen Gray left soon after, without my having had a chance to speak to him. But Kay Kyser, Bert Lown, Jack Teagarden and others, who came later, didn't get off so easy. Each of them suffered through my inexhaustible efforts — and they encouraged me. But none of them acted as though Tin Pan Alley[10] was overlooking a great talent.

Late that summer, I was offered the head bus boy job at the Hotel Lowry, by the *maître d'hôtel*,[11] a former wrestler whose name was Gleason. I took it. And for nearly three hours each day, after the luncheon crowd left, I had the main dining room and the huge grand piano all to myself. Once the tables were set for the evening, I played away before an imagined audience — using the light-control switches for color combinations that added to the mood. On one such afternoon I was playing and singing "No Love" when I felt someone was behind me.

Embarrassed, I stopped, turned and looked into the shadows. It was Larry Duncan, the orchestra leader who was currently engaged by the hotel.

"Is that your music?" he asked.

"Yes."

"Go ahead. Play it again."

I played it again and he listened attentively. When I finished he asked me if I would like to have it orchestrated.

"I sure would," I said, and it was probably the understatement of my lifetime. The orchestra's arranger spent the rest of that afternoon with me, taking the piece down as I played it. And, as I watched him work, I hoped that my afternoons of fantasy were coming to an end.

This happened on a Wednesday.

During dinner on the following Friday night, Larry motioned me toward the bandstand. "We're broadcasting 'No Love' on the network show tomorrow night — with your permission, of course," he said.

I got Sally on the telephone and, without knowing whether she cared or not, I excitedly spilled out the good news. "I composed it for you — don't forget to listen." Her voice didn't reveal the slightest interest. She said, very casually, that she would listen — but, I found out later, she spent the next two hours telephoning all her friends. And I spent the rest of that evening and the next day drifting about in a trance.

On the night of the broadcast, Abby, the drummer, congratulated me and showed a group of waiters and myself the program. Fate had arranged things. There was my name among those of Irving Berlin, Duke Ellington, Cole Porter and Jerome

---

10. **Tin Pan Alley,** the body of composers and publishers of popular music.
11. *maître d'hôtel* (me′trə dō tel′), headwaiter. [*French*]

Kern.[12] Now, in spite of my imagining the worst—a broken microphone, a broken promise, a canceled broadcast—it was going to happen. I knew that Gleason kept a death watch on unfilled water glasses, so I went about filling them to the brim. I wanted to hear every word, every note, without being disturbed.

When at last the moment came, people continued to eat, drink and talk, as if they were unaware of the miracle taking place. I wanted to shout, to command everyone to listen, to ascend with me—far above ordinary things. But they kept on eating, drinking, laughing and talking. And, just before the vocalist approached the microphone, I took refuge near the bandstand where I could hear him sing my lyrics. But now, at such a moment, a drunk started rapping his glass with a spoon. He wanted more water. I ignored him. He rapped louder and I hated him for it.

"What is it, sir?" A shiver went up my back. It was Gleason's voice.

"Water! Water! Tell that damned boy our party wants water!"

Such was my lot, I thought, and I turned toward the table only to have Gleason wave me away. He was filling the glasses and proudly explaining that the music the orchestra was playing was mine. The drunk whispered the news to his party, and his party whispered the news to the next table, and soon everyone in the entire dining room was looking toward me. When the orchestra finished, a burst of applause filled the air. I smiled nervously, picked up a tray of dirty dishes and left the room amidst the ovation. Then, slipping into an empty room, I telephoned Sally. "Yes, I listened," she said, "and it was beautiful. Would you like to come over sometime, maybe tonight?"

"As soon as I can get out of here," I answered. The sky was overcast and it was chilly when I boarded the street car; but I couldn't accept such a night. There were stars and a moon instead, and a ridiculous hint of spring in the fall air. My heart, in its joy, would have it no other way.   ✱

12. *Irving Berlin. . . . Jerome Kern,* well-known songwriters.

Discussion

1. (a) Under what financial conditions is Parks living when he writes "No Love"? Explain. (b) Why does he write the song? (c) What causes his physical breakdown? (d) How does Parks react to being an invalid and not being able to graduate with his class?

2. (a) What inspires Parks to look for work at the Hotel St. Paul? (b) Are his expectations there fulfilled? Explain. (c) How does Parks finally come to meet Larry Duncan, the bandleader?

3. What important qualities does Gordon Parks reveal in this selection? Illustrate these qualities by referring to passages throughout the selection.

4. Locate the beginning and the end of the flashback Parks uses. (a) How do you know these paragraphs make up a flashback? (b) Why do you suppose Parks uses a flashback here?

5. (a) Reread the first paragraph in the selection. What device of figurative language does Parks use in his description here? (b) Reread the last paragraph in the selection. What does Parks mean when he says, "There were stars and a moon instead, and a ridiculous hint of spring in the fall air"? (c) How does this last paragraph contrast with the opening one?

GORDON PARKS:
A PORTFOLIO

In his autobiography, *A Choice of Weapons,* Gordon Parks tells
of the difficulties he had when young and the many jobs he held
before choosing photography as his life's work. Beginning
as a fashion photographer, he soon became more interested
in picturing the poverty-stricken areas of his own and other
countries. His present work as photojournalist has taken him all
over the world, and earned him wide recognition as artist and
writer.

An illustration for Robert Frost's poem, "The Road Not Taken."

Wild horses being herded on a ranch outside Lisbon, Portugal, at sunset.

A Brazilian boy, Flavio, entertains his brothers and sisters by making a face with a page torn from a magazine.

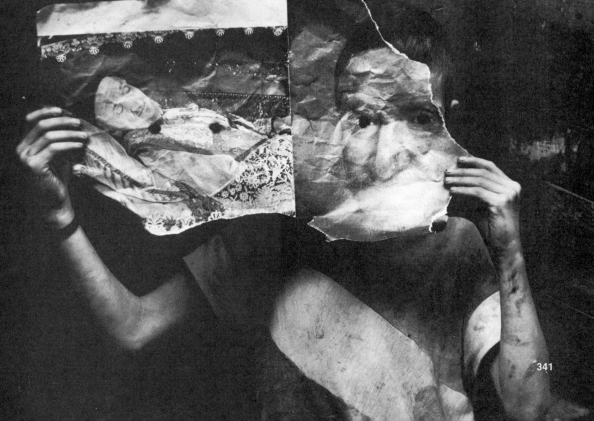

GORDON PARKS:
A PORTFOLIO

Actress Pamela Tiffin modeling a gown by James Galanos, an American fashion designer. This picture is typical of Park's early work in fashion photography.

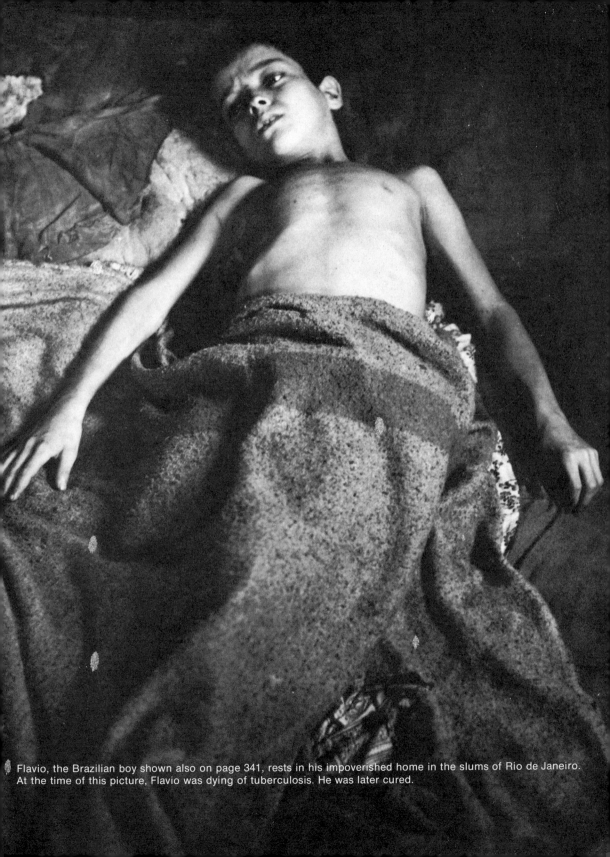

Flavio, the Brazilian boy shown also on page 341, rests in his impoverished home in the slums of Rio de Janeiro. At the time of this picture, Flavio was dying of tuberculosis. He was later cured.

When John Steinbeck set out to rediscover the United States, he traveled in a well-stocked camper truck. His only companion was a large French poodle named Charley. The following selections are from the book he wrote about his journey. Read what discoveries Steinbeck made about his own land—and the surprising discovery he made about Charley.

from

travels with CHARLEY

John Steinbeck

THE NEXT PASSAGE in my journey is a love affair. I am in love with Montana. For other states I have admiration, respect, recognition, even some affection, but with Montana it is love, and it's difficult to analyze love when you're in it. Once, when I raptured in a violet glow given off by the Queen of the World, my father asked me why, and I thought he was crazy not to see. Of course I know now she was a mouse-haired, freckle-nosed, scabby-kneed little girl with a voice like a bat and the loving kindness of a gila monster, but then she lighted up the landscape and me. It seems to me that Montana is a great splash of grandeur. The scale is huge but not overpowering. The land is rich with grass and color, and the mountains are the kind I would create if mountains were ever put on my agenda. Montana seems to me to be what a small boy would think Texas is like from hearing Texans. Here for the first time I heard a definite regional accent unaffected by TV-ese, a slow-paced warm speech. It seemed to me that the frantic bustle of America was not in Montana. Its people did not seem afraid of shadows in a John Birch Society sense.[1] The calm of the mountains and the rolling grasslands

From TRAVELS WITH CHARLEY *in Search of America* by John Steinbeck. Copyright © 1961, 1962 by The Curtis Publishing Co., Inc. © 1962 by John Steinbeck. Reprinted by permission of The Viking Press, Inc., and McIntosh and Otis, Inc.

1. **afraid . . . sense.** The John Birch Society is a politically conservative, anticommunist organization. Steinbeck means that the people of Montana did not seem to look for hidden enemies in every situation.

had got into the inhabitants. It was hunting season when I drove through the state. The men I talked to seemed to me not moved to a riot of seasonal slaughter but simply to be going out to kill edible meat. Again my attitude may be informed by love, but it seemed to me that the towns were places to live in rather than nervous hives. People had time to pause in their occupations to undertake the passing art of neighborliness.

I found I did not rush through the towns to get them over with. I even found things I had to buy to make myself linger. In Billings I bought a hat, in Livingston a jacket, in Butte a rifle I didn't particularly need, a Remington bolt-action 222, second-hand but in beautiful condition. Then I found a telescope sight I had to have, and waited while it was mounted on the rifle, and in the

process got to know everyone in the shop and any customers who entered. With the gun in a vise and the bolt out, we zeroed the new sight on a chimney three blocks away, and later when I got to shooting the little gun I found no reason to change it. I spent a good part of a morning at this, mostly because I wanted to stay. But I see that, as usual, love is inarticulate. Montana has a spell on me. It is grandeur and warmth. If Montana had a seacoast, or if I could live away from the sea, I would instantly move there and petition for admission. Of all the states it is my favorite and my love.

At Custer we made a side trip south to pay our respects to General Custer and Sitting Bull on the battlefield of Little Big Horn.[2] I don't sup-

2. *Little Big Horn,* the site of a Sioux uprising in 1876. Custer and his command of 264 were all killed.

pose there is an American who doesn't carry Remington's painting of the last defense of the center column of the 7th Cavalry in his head. I removed my hat in memory of brave men, and Charley saluted in his own manner but I thought with great respect.

The whole of eastern Montana and the western Dakotas is memory-marked as Injun country, and the memories are not very old either. Some years ago my neighbor was Charles Erskine Scott Wood, who wrote *Heavenly Discourse.* He was a very old man when I knew him, but as a young lieutenant just out of military academy he had been assigned to General Miles and he served in the Chief Joseph campaign.[3] His memory of it was very clear and very sad. He said it was one of the most gallant retreats in all history. Chief Joseph and the Nez Percés with squaws and children, dogs, and all their possessions, retreated under heavy fire for over a thousand miles, trying to escape to Canada. Wood said they fought every step of the way against odds until finally they were surrounded by the cavalry under General Miles and the large part of them wiped out. It was the saddest duty he had ever performed, Wood said, and he had never lost his respect for the fighting qualities of the Nez Percés. "If they hadn't had their families with them, we could never have caught them," he said. "And if we had been evenly matched in men and weapons, we couldn't have beaten them. They were men," he said, "real men."

I must confess to a laxness in the matter of National Parks. I haven't visited many of them. Perhaps this is because they enclose the unique, the spectacular, the astounding—the greatest waterfall, the deepest canyon, the highest cliff, the most stupendous works of man or nature. And I would rather see a good Brady photograph[4] than Mount Rushmore.[5] For it is my opinion that we enclose and celebrate the freaks of our nation and of our civilization. Yellowstone National Park is no more representative of America than is Disneyland.

This being my natural attitude, I don't know what made me turn sharply south and cross a state line to take a look at Yellowstone. Perhaps it was a fear of my neighbors. I could hear them say, "You mean you were that near to Yellowstone and didn't go? You must be crazy." Again it might have been the American tendency in travel. One goes, not so much to see but to tell afterward. Whatever my purpose in going to Yellowstone, I'm glad I went because I discovered something about Charley I might never have known.

A pleasant-looking National Park man checked me in and then he said, "How about that dog? They aren't permitted in except on leash."

"Why?" I asked.

"Because of the bears."

"Sir," I said, "this is an unique dog. He does not live by tooth or fang. He respects the right of cats to be cats although he doesn't admire them. He turns his steps rather than disturb an earnest caterpillar. His greatest fear is that someone will point out a rabbit and suggest that he chase it. This is a dog of peace and tranquillity. I suggest that the greatest danger to your

---

3. General Miles . . . campaign. In 1877 General Nelson Appleton Miles, a noted Indian fighter, captured Chief Joseph and the Nez Percés (nā per sā') Indians after four days of fighting.
4. Brady photograph. Photographic portraits of famous people were the specialty of Mathew B. Brady, an American photographer of the Civil War period.
5. Mount Rushmore, a national memorial in the Black Hills of South Dakota. On one face of the mountain are sculptured the heads of Washington, Jefferson, Lincoln, and Theodore Roosevelt.

bears will be pique at being ignored by Charley."

The young man laughed. "I wasn't so much worried about the bears," he said. "But our bears have developed an intolerance for dogs. One of them might demonstrate his prejudice with a clip on the chin, and then — no dog."

"I'll lock him in the back, sir. I promise you Charley will cause no ripple in the bear world, and as an old bear-looker, neither will I."

"I just have to warn you," he said. "I have no doubt your dog has the best of intentions. On the other hand, our bears have the worst. Don't leave food about. Not only do they steal but they are critical of anyone who tries to reform them. In a word, don't believe their sweet faces or you might get clobbered. And don't let the dog wander. Bears don't argue."

We went on our way into the wonderland of nature gone nuts, and you will have to believe what happened. The only way I can prove it would be to get a bear.

Less than a mile from the entrance I saw a bear beside the road, and it ambled out as though to flag me down. Instantly a change came over Charley. He shrieked with rage. His lips flared, showing wicked teeth that have some trouble with a dog biscuit. He screeched insults at the bear, which hearing, the bear reared up and seemed to me to overtop Rocinante.[6] Frantically I rolled the windows shut and, swinging quickly to the left, grazed the animal, then scuttled on while Charley raved and ranted beside me, describing in detail what he would do to that bear if he could get at him. I was never so astonished in my life. To the best of my knowledge Charley had never seen a bear, and in his whole history had showed great tolerance for every living thing. Besides all this, Charley is a coward, so deep-seated a coward that he has developed a technique for concealing it. And yet he showed every evidence of wanting to get out and murder a bear that outweighed him a thousand to one. I don't understand it.

A little farther along two bears showed up, and the effect was doubled. Charley became a maniac. He leaped all over me, he cursed and growled, snarled and screamed. I didn't know he had the ability to snarl. Where did he learn it? Bears were in good supply, and the road became a nightmare. For the first time in his life Charley resisted reason, even resisted a cuff on the ear. He became a primitive killer lusting for the blood of his enemy, and up to this moment he had had no enemies. In a bearless stretch, I opened the cab, took Charley by the collar, and locked him in the house. But that did no good. When we passed other bears he leaped on the table and scratched at the windows trying to get out at them. I could hear canned goods crashing as he struggled in his mania. Bears simply brought out the Hyde in my Jekyll-headed dog.[7] What could have caused it? Was it a pre-breed memory of a time when the wolf was in him? I know him well. Once in a while he tries a bluff, but it is a palpable lie. I swear that this was no lie. I am certain that if he were released he would have charged every bear we passed and found victory or death.

It was too nerve-wracking, a shocking spectacle, like seeing an old,

---

6. **Rocinante** (rō sə nän′tä), the camper truck. Steinbeck named it after the horse of a Spanish gentleman who is the hero of a novel about chivalry by Miguel de Cervantes.
7. **Bears . . . Jekyll-headed dog,** a reference to *The Strange Case of Dr. Jekyll and Mr. Hyde,* a novel by Robert Louis Stevenson. It is the story of Dr. Jekyll, who compounds a drug which turns him into a murdering beast called Mr. Hyde.

calm friend go insane. No amount of natural wonders, of rigid cliffs and belching waters, of smoking springs could even engage my attention while that pandemonium went on. After about the fifth encounter I gave up, turned Rocinante about, and retraced my way. If I had stopped the night and bears had gathered to my cooking, I dare not think what would have happened.

At the gate the park guard checked me out. "You didn't stay long. Where's the dog?"

"Locked up back there. And I owe you an apology. That dog has the heart and soul of a bear-killer and I didn't know it. Heretofore he has been a little tender-hearted toward an underdone steak."

"Yeah!" he said. "That happens sometimes. That's why I warned you. A bear dog would know his chances, but I've seen a Pomeranian go up like a puff of smoke. You know, a well-favored bear can bat a dog like a tennis ball."

I moved fast, back the way I had come, and I was reluctant to camp for fear there might be some unofficial non-government bears about. That night I spent in a pretty auto court near Livingston. I had my dinner in a restaurant, and when I had settled in with a drink and a comfortable chair and my bathed bare feet on a carpet with red roses, I inspected Charley. He was dazed. His eyes held a faraway look and he was totally exhausted, emotionally no doubt. Mostly he reminded me of a man coming out of a long, hard drunk—worn out, depleted, collapsed. He couldn't eat his dinner, he refused the evening walk, and once we were in he collapsed on the floor and went to sleep. In the night I heard him whining and yapping, and when I turned on the light his feet were making running gestures and

his body jerked and his eyes were wide open, but it was only a night bear. I awakened him and gave him some water. This time he went to sleep and didn't stir all night. In the morning he was still tired. I wonder why we think the thoughts and emotions of animals are simple. ✱

Discussion

1. (a) Why is John Steinbeck traveling through the country? (b) What kind of man do you think Steinbeck must be? Cite evidence of his words or actions to support your statements.

2. In what ways can this selection be considered part of the American Romance? Find as many "romantic" elements as you can.

3. (a) How does John Steinbeck feel about Montana? (b) What causes him to feel as he does? (c) Why doesn't he move to Montana?

4. (a) What kind of "personality" had Charley displayed prior to his visit to Yellowstone? (b) What is Steinbeck's guess as to the reason for Charley's reaction to the bears?

5. Reread each of the following quotations in its context in the selection. What does Steinbeck mean by each? Restate the ideas in your own words.

(a) "The men I talked to seemed to me not moved to a riot of seasonal slaughter but simply to be going out to kill edible meat" (page 345, column 1, lines 3–6).

(b) "For it is my opinion that we enclose and celebrate the freaks of our nation and of our civilization" (page 346, column 2, lines 5–8).

(c) "One goes, not so much to see but to tell afterward" (page 346, column 2, paragraph 1).

(d) ". . . so deep-seated a coward that he has developed a technique for concealing it" (page 347, column 2, lines 2–4).

Word Study

John Steinbeck says, "It was too nerve-wracking, a shocking spectacle, like seeing an old, calm friend go insane . . . . while that pandemonium went on." Look up the word *pandemonium* in the Glossary. From what language does it come? What does each of the two word parts mean? Which definition fits the meaning of the word in the context Steinbeck uses?

Below are some more Greek roots. Study them.

akos	a cure
chroma	color
Hellene	Greek
hopla	arms; weapons
horama	view
theos	god
mimos	mime; to act without using words

The prefix *pan-* can be combined with other root words to form new words; for example, *Pan-American* means "including all the countries of North, Central, and South America." The words in Column A below are combinations of *pan* with the Greek roots given above. Decide what each word means; then match it to its definition in Column B.

Column A	Column B
panorama	tell through gestures, using no speech
panchromatic	
	complete suit of armor or set of equipment
pantomime	
Panhellenic	belief in all the gods
panoply	a cure-all
pantheism	a wide, unbroken view
	sensitive to light of all colors
panacea	
	pertaining to members of the Greek race

The Author

John Steinbeck (1902–1968), winner of the highest literary award, the 1962 Nobel Prize for Literature, was born in Salinas, California. He worked as a hod-carrier, painter, chemist, caretaker, surveyor, and fruit picker; he had a major interest in marine biology and once led a biological expedition; and he wrote in many forms, from newspaper articles to stories to novels. His best known work is *The Grapes of Wrath,* a Pulitzer Prize-winning novel which exposes the living conditions of migrant workers. Close behind in fame and popularity come many other works, including *Of Mice and Men, The Pearl, The Moon is Down,* and *The Red Pony.*

Dreams

Langston Hughes

Hold fast to dreams
For if dreams die
Life is a broken-winged bird
That cannot fly.

5 Hold fast to dreams
For when dreams go
Life is a barren field
Frozen with snow.

Discussion

1. (a) What kind of dreams do you think the poet is talking about? (b) What figures of speech does he use? (c) With what two things does he compare a life without dreams? (d) In what ways are the comparisons appropriate?

2. (a) How important do you think dreams are? (b) Suggest some comparisons of your own that could be applied to a life without dreams.

The Author

Langston Hughes (1902–1967) made a name for himself in many types of writing—novels, stories, plays, songs, movie screenplays, travel articles, and children's books. He is best known, however, as a poet.

Born in Joplin, Missouri, he attended high school in Cleveland, Ohio, where he began writing poetry. Before graduating from college he spent a year in Mexico, worked as a seaman on trans-Atlantic voyages, and held a job as a cook in Paris. While working as a bus boy in a hotel, he one day left some poems beside the plate of the American poet Vachel Lindsay. Lindsay picked them up and later recited them before an audience. Lindsay's reading gave Hughes his first public hearing and launched him on a highly successful career.

Have you ever longed for home?
Note what details this voyager recalls
as he thinks of his native land.

The Long Voyage

Malcolm Cowley

Not that the pines were darker there,
nor mid-May dogwood brighter there,
nor swifts more swift in summer air;
    it was my own country,

5 having its thunderclap of spring,
its long midsummer ripening,
its corn hoar-stiff at harvesting,
    almost like any country,

yet being mine; its face, its speech,
10 its hills bent low within my reach,
its river birch and upland beech
    were mine, of my own country.

Now the dark waters at the bow
fold back, like earth against the plow;
15 foam brightens like the dogwood now
    at home, in my own country.

From THE DRY SEASON, copyright 1941 by Malcolm Cowley.

Discussion

1. (a) What features of America are recalled most vividly by the voyager? **(b)** Are these features general ones that almost anyone could experience, or are they special and personal to the poet?

2. Do you think the traveler is on his way away from his country, back to his country, or neither? Find details to support your answer.

3. If you were traveling far from your country, what particular things do you think *you* would remember most clearly? Why?

The Author

When Malcolm Cowley writes of the emotions of a traveler away from home, he writes as one who has experienced the feelings he describes. He was reared and educated in Pittsburgh, Pennsylvania. He left the United States to serve in France in the American Ambulance Service during World War I. He then returned to Harvard University, but again left home to study in Europe from 1921 to 1923. Cowley has written two volumes of poetry, *Blue Juniata* and *The Dry Season*, and has both edited and translated numerous books.

Unit **5** Review

1. During the Middle Ages, *romance* was a term often used to describe the kind of story which told of crusading knights out to combat evil in the world—slaying dragons, rescuing maidens, and having similar adventures. Although we still use the term to refer to this kind of adventure story, the word *romance* today has various other meanings. *The American Romance* is a phrase which has taken on a meaning of its own. Study the introduction to this unit on page 286. Note the qualities which are suggested as characteristic of the American Romance. (**a**) Consider the selections you have read in this unit. Which qualities characteristic of the American Romance occur in more than one of these selections? Identify the selections in which you find these qualities. (**b**) Can you recall other works you have read, in this text or in outside reading, which might also be included in the idea of the American Romance? Describe one and explain why you feel it belongs.

2. Following are references to various uses of irony in selections in this unit. Decide in each case whether the example is verbal irony, irony of situation, or irony of tone. Explain your answer.

(**a**) Scratchy Wilson hums a hymn as he loads his gun (page 311, column 2, paragraph 1).

(**b**) Marshal Potter feels sure the other passengers on the train cannot tell that he and his bride are newlyweds because they are not acting like newlyweds (page 310, column 2, paragraph 2).

(**c**) Frank Gudger claims he is tired of "all that bang-bang stuff" in his Wild-West magazines (page 312, column 2, paragraph 11).

(**d**) George Papashvily feels he has gotten a good deal from the cap seller (page 329, column 1, paragraph 5).

(**e**) Young Gordon Parks runs from the men's laughter when the mind reader singles him out to be the most famous in the room (page 338, column 1, paragraphs 1–3).

(**f**) John Steinbeck claims that Charley's greatest fear is "that someone will point out a rabbit and suggest that he chase it" (page 346, column 2, paragraph 5).

3. (**a**) One of the important functions of dialogue is to suggest character. Read again the conversations between Joe and Tildy on pages 296 and 299 of "The Man Who Rode the Bear." What does the language used tell you about these characters? (**b**) Reread the dialogues between John Steinbeck and the park guard on pages 346–347 and 348. What does his language and his way of speaking tell you about the character of each man? (**c**) How does the dialogue in each of these two selections contribute toward the tone of the selection?

SUGGESTED READING

ARMOUR, RICHARD, *Drug Store Days*. (McGraw) The author humorously recalls his boyhood as the son of a small-town druggist in Southern California.

BALLANTYNE, R. M., *The Dog Crusoe*. (Dutton) Dick Varley encounters adventure and excitement as he sets out on a scouting expedition in the early days in the West.

BENÉT, STEPHEN VINCENT, *Thirteen O'Clock*. (Farrar) This collection of tales includes legends, folklore, and ghost stories.

BLAIR, WALTER, *Tall Tale America*. (Coward) In these tales of America's folk heroes, the reader will meet Daniel Boone, Mike Fink, Davy Crockett, Pecos Bill, Paul Bunyan, and other interesting characters.

BOTKIN, B. A. (ed.), *Treasury of American Folklore*. (Crown) This exhaustive volume of folklore ranges in scope from tall tales of characters like Paul Bunyan to the songs and stories of the early slaves.

CREDLE, ELLIS, *Tall Tales from the High Hills and Other Stories*. (Nelson) This is the complete collection of tales from the Blue Ridge Mountains from which "The Man Who Rode the Bear" is taken.

EDMONDS, WALTER, *Drums Along the Mohawk*. (Little) The Mohawk River Valley was a hostile frontier at the time Americans were fighting for freedom and independence in the Revolutionary War.

FIELD, RACHEL, *Calico Bush*. (Macmillan) This is the story of the hopes and fears of a young French girl "bound out" to an American family. The reader sees a vivid picture of daily life against the rugged Maine landscape.

FREEDMAN, BENEDICT and NANCY, *Mrs. Mike*. (Coward) Boston-bred Kathie O'Fallon travels to Alberta, Canada, marries a Mountie, and lives a rigorous life close to the Arctic Circle. Family warmth and the lore of the North permeate this popular story.

FREIDEL, FRANK, *Our Country's Presidents*. (National Geographic) These sketches of the Presidents are short, highly readable, and informative. Each sketch is illustrated with drawings, paintings, maps, and excellent photographs.

HALE, LEON, *Turn South at the Second Bridge*. (Doubleday) In this collection of amusing tales of real Texans, the reader meets individuals who do not fit the Texas stereotypes.

HARRIS, CHRISTIE, *Raven's Cry*. (Atheneum) Told from the point of view of the Indians, this story of their struggle with the traders of the West Coast during the eighteenth century reveals the pride and dignity with which the Indians fought.

HOLT, RACKHAM, *Mary McLeod Bethune*. (Doubleday) This is the biography of a famous Negro educator who came from a family that "had no family tree" and offered no "prestige with which to open doors."

LANE, ROSE WILDER, *Let the Hurricane Roar*. (Longmans) The romantic West beckons to Charles and Caroline, who move to Dakota, where they live in a dugout and contend with destructive grasshoppers, blizzards, fire, and separation.

LATHAM, JEAN LEE, *This Dear-Bought Land*. (Harper) A fifteen-year-old boy is a member of the expedition that Captain John Smith leads from England to settle Jamestown, Virginia, in 1607. He experiences the hardships, frustrations, and dangers that come close to defeating the settlement.

MADISON, ARNOLD, *Danger Beats the Drum*. (Holt) After his policeman father is killed by a narcotics addict, Bob tries to escape his troubles by vacationing with his mother and sisters. At the lake he meets a Negro boy, and the two of them become involved in mystery and adventure. Through his experiences, Bob learns to face himself and the world around him.

MURDOCK, FRANK, *Davy Crockett*, or, "Be Sure You're Right, Then Go Ahead." (in *American Lost Plays*. Indiana University Press) This melodrama treats the antics and romance of Davy Crockett in an amusing way.

RITCHIE, BARBARA (adapt.), *Life and Times of Frederick Douglass*. (Crowell) This is the autobiography of one man who escaped from the bonds of slavery, and became a leading spokesman for abolition.

THOMAS, MAUDE MORGAN, *Sing in the Dark*. (Holt) Working in the coal mines with the fear of disaster ever present makes music all the more important to the singing Welsh who settled in Pennsylvania. Huw Griffith isn't the best singer, but he "makes it" nevertheless.

WILLIAMSON, JOANNE S., *And Forever Free*. (Knopf) In this historical tale of the social and political scene of New York City in the 1860's, a fifteen-year-old immigrant comes to the city and lands a job as a reporter.

WOJIECHOWSKA, MAIA, *The Hollywood Kid*. (Harper) Fifteen-year-old Jody Blake must choose for himself whether to stay with his troubled, possessive movie-queen mother, or to break away from the glittery life of Hollywood.

6

A series of events . . .
who tantalize, horrify, or amuse;
A cast of characters . . .
who are like others we know,
but also very different;
A setting . . .
which may be a weird and distorted world
or one similar to the one in which you live;
A plot . . .
which explores the ways of the human mind,
and helps you toward an understanding
of why people act as they do—
These elements and others are found
in the work of master story-tellers,
in stories which have stood the test of time
in . . .

The
Well-Told
Tale

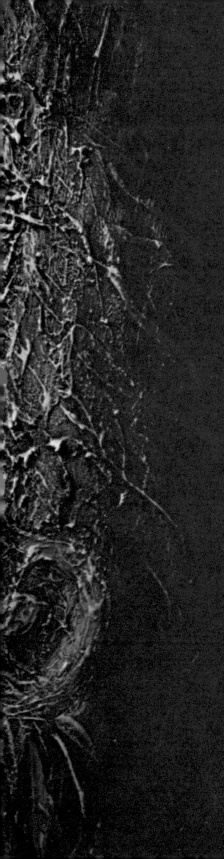

What is it about
the old man's eye that makes
the narrator's blood
run cold? As you read,
try to determine the effect
Poe is attempting to produce
in this tale.

the tell-tale heart

Edgar Allan Poe

TRUE!—nervous—very, very dread-
fully nervous I had been and am; but
why *will* you say that I am mad? The
disease had sharpened my senses—not
destroyed—not dulled them. Above
all was the sense of hearing acute.
I heard all things in the heavens
and in the earth. I heard many
things in hell. How, then, am I mad?

Hearken! and observe how healthily —how calmly I can tell you the whole story.

It is impossible to say how first the idea entered my brain; but once conceived, it haunted me day and night. Object there was none. Passion there was none. I loved the old man. He had never wronged me. He had never given me insult. For his gold I had no desire. I think it was his eye! Yes, it was this! One of his eyes resembled that of a vulture—a pale blue eye, with a film over it. Whenever it fell upon me, my blood ran cold; and so by degrees—very gradually—I made up my mind to take the life of the old man, and thus rid myself of the eye forever.

Now this is the point. You fancy me mad. Madmen know nothing. But you should have seen *me*. You should have seen how wisely I proceeded —with what caution—with what foresight—with what dissimulation I went to work! I was never kinder to the old man than during the whole week before I killed him. And every night, about midnight, I turned the latch of his door and opened it—oh, so gently! And then, when I had made an opening sufficient for my head, I put in a dark lantern,[1] all closed, closed, so that no light shone out, and then I thrust in my head. Oh, you would have laughed to see how cunningly I thrust it in! I moved it slowly —very, very slowly, so that I might not disturb the old man's sleep. It took me an hour to place my whole head within the opening so far that I could see him as he lay upon his bed. Ha!—would a madman have been so wise as this? And then, when my head was well in the room, I undid the lantern cautiously—oh, so cautiously —cautiously (for the hinges creaked) —I undid it just so much that a single thin ray fell upon the vulture eye.

And this I did for seven long nights—every night just at midnight—but I found the eye always closed; and so it was impossible to do the work; for it was not the old man who vexed me, but his Evil Eye. And every morning, when the day broke, I went boldly into the chamber, and spoke courageously to him, calling him by name in a hearty tone, and inquiring how he had passed the night. So you see he would have been a very profound old man, indeed, to suspect that every night, just at twelve, I looked in upon him while he slept.

Upon the eighth night I was more than usually cautious in opening the door. A watch's minute hand moves more quickly than did mine. Never before that night had I *felt* the extent of my own powers—of my sagacity. I could scarcely contain my feelings of triumph. To think that there I was, opening the door, little by little, and he not even to dream of my secret deeds or thoughts. I fairly chuckled at the idea; and perhaps he heard me; for he moved on the bed suddenly, as if startled. Now you may think that I drew back—but no. His room was as black as pitch with the thick darkness (for the shutters were close fastened, through fear of robbers), and so I knew that he could not see the opening of the door, and I kept pushing it on steadily, steadily.

I had my head in, and was about to open the lantern, when my thumb slipped upon the tin fastening, and the old man sprang up in the bed, crying out—"Who's there?"

I kept quite still and said nothing. For a whole hour I did not move a muscle, and in the meantime I did not hear him lie down. He was still sitting up in the bed listening—just as I have

1. **dark lantern,** a lantern whose light can be hidden by a cover over the opening.

done, night after night, hearkening to the death watches[2] in the wall.

Presently I heard a slight groan, and I knew it was the groan of mortal terror. It was not a groan of pain or of grief—oh, no!—it was the low stifled sound that arises from the bottom of the soul when overcharged with awe. I knew the sound well. Many a night, just at midnight, when all the world slept, it has welled up from my own bosom, deepening, with its dreadful echo, the terrors that distracted me. I say I knew it well. I knew what the old man felt, and pitied him, although I chuckled at heart. I knew that he had been lying awake ever since the first slight noise, when he had turned in the bed. His fears had been ever since growing upon him. He had been trying to fancy them causeless, but could not. He had been saying to himself: "It is nothing but the wind in the chimney—it is only a mouse crossing the floor," or "It is merely a cricket which has made a single chirp." Yes, he had been trying to comfort himself with these suppositions; but he had found all in vain. *All in vain;* because Death, in approaching him, had stalked with his black shadow before him, and enveloped the victim. And it was the mournful influence of the unperceived shadow that caused him to feel—although he neither saw nor heard—to *feel* the presence of my head within the room.

When I had waited a long time, very patiently, without hearing him lie down, I resolved to open a little—a very, very little crevice in the lantern. So I opened it—you cannot imagine how stealthily, stealthily—until, at length, a single dim ray, like the thread of the spider, shot from out the crevice and full upon the vulture eye.

It was open—wide, wide open —and I grew furious as I gazed upon it. I saw it with perfect distinctness —all a dull blue, with a hideous veil over it that chilled the very marrow in my bones; but I could see nothing else of the old man's face or person, for I had directed the ray as if by instinct, precisely upon the damned spot.

And now have I not told you that what you mistake for madness is but over-acuteness of the senses?—now, I say, there came to my ears a low, dull, quick sound, such as a watch makes when enveloped in cotton. I knew *that* sound well too. It was the beating of the old man's heart. It increased my fury, as the beating of a drum stimulates the soldier into courage.

But even yet I refrained and kept still. I scarcely breathed. I held the lantern motionless. I tried how steadily I could maintain the ray upon the eye. Meantime the hellish tattoo of the heart increased. It grew quicker and quicker, and louder and louder every instant. The old man's terror *must* have been extreme! It grew louder, I say, louder every moment!—do you mark me well? I have told you that I am nervous: so I am. And now at the dead hour of the night, amid the dreadful silence of that old house, so strange a noise as this excited me to uncontrollable terror. Yet, for some minutes longer I refrained and stood still. But the beating grew louder, louder! I thought the heart must burst. And now a new anxiety seized me—the sound would be heard by a neighbor! The old man's hour had come! With a loud yell, I threw open the lantern and leaped into the room. He shrieked once—once only. In an instant I dragged him to the floor, and pulled the heavy bed over him. I then smiled gaily, to find the deed so far done. But, for many minutes,

2. **death watches,** small beetles that live in wood and make a ticking sound.

the heart beat on with a muffled sound. This, however, did not vex me; it would not be heard through the wall. At length it ceased. The old man was dead. I removed the bed and examined the corpse. Yes, he was stone, stone dead. I placed my hand upon the heart and held it there many minutes. There was no pulsation. He was stone dead. His eye would trouble me no more.

If still you think me mad, you will think so no longer when I describe the wise precautions I took for the concealment of the body. The night waned, and I worked hastily, but in silence. First of all I dismembered the corpse. I cut off the head and the arms and the legs.

I then took up three planks from the flooring of the chamber, and deposited all between the scantlings. I then replaced the boards so cleverly, so cunningly, that no human eye—not even *his*—could have detected anything wrong. There was nothing to wash out—no stain of any kind—no blood-spot whatever. I had been too wary for that. A tub had caught all —ha! ha!

When I had made an end of these labors, it was four o'clock—still dark as midnight. As the bell sounded the hour, there came a knocking at the street door. I went down to open it with a light heart—for what had I *now* to fear? There entered three men, who introduced themselves, with perfect suavity, as officers of the police. A shriek had been heard by a neighbor during the night; suspicion of foul play had been aroused; information had been lodged at the police office, and they (the officers) had been deputed to search the premises.

I smiled—for *what* had I to fear? I bade the gentlemen welcome. The shriek, I said, was my own in a dream. The old man, I mentioned, was absent in the country. I took my visitors all over the house. I bade them search —search *well*. I led them, at length, to *his* chamber. I showed them his treasures, secure, undisturbed. In the enthusiasm of my confidence, I brought chairs into the room, and desired them *here* to rest from their fatigues, while I myself, in the wild audacity of my perfect triumph, placed my own seat upon the very spot beneath which reposed the corpse of the victim.

The officers were satisfied. My *manner* had convinced them. I was singularly at ease. They sat, and while I answered cheerily, they chatted of familiar things. But, ere long, I felt myself getting pale and wished them gone. My head ached, and I fancied a ringing in my ears: but still they sat and still chatted. The ringing became more distinct; it continued and became more distinct; I talked more freely to get rid of the feeling; but it continued and gained definiteness—until, at length, I found that the noise was *not* within my ears.

No doubt I now grew *very* pale —but I talked more fluently, and with a heightened voice. Yet the sound increased—and what could I do? It was *a low, dull, quick sound—much such a sound as a watch makes when enveloped in cotton.* I gasped for breath —and yet the officers heard it not. I talked more quickly—more vehemently; but the noise steadily increased. I arose and argued about trifles, in a high key and with violent gesticulations, but the noise steadily increased. Why *would* they not be gone? I paced the floor to and fro with heavy strides, as if excited to fury by the observation of the men —but the noise steadily increased. Oh, what *could* I do? I foamed—I raved—I swore! I swung the chair upon which I had been sitting, and grated it upon the boards, but the noise arose over all and continually increased. It grew louder—louder—*louder!* And still the men chatted pleasantly, and smiled. Was it possible they heard not? No, no! They heard!—they suspected! —they *knew!*—they were making a mockery of my horror!—this I thought, and this I think. But anything was better than this agony!

Anything was more tolerable than this derision! I could bear those hypocritical smiles no longer! I felt that I must scream or die!—and now —again!—hark! louder! louder! louder! *louder!*——

"Villains!" I shrieked, "dissemble no more! I admit the deed!—tear up the planks!—here, here!—it is the beating of his hideous heart!" ✳

Discussion

1. (a) Why does the narrator want to kill the old man? (b) How does he go about carrying out his plans? (c) Why do his plans miscarry?
2. (a) What is the setting for the events of this story? (b) Why is this setting important?
3. Throughout the story, the narrator insists that he is not mad. Do you feel he is correct? Cite passages from the selection to justify your answer.
4. Read the biography of Poe printed below. (a) What single emotional effect does Poe create in this story? (b) Pick out phrases and sentences that help create this effect.
5. This story was written over one hundred years ago. Why do you think it is still widely read?

The Author

The life of Edgar Allan Poe (1809–1849) was, for the most part, a tragic one. Orphaned at an early age, Poe was taken in by the wealthy Allan family of Virginia. Following his attendance at English schools and instruction by private tutors, Poe attended the University of Virginia for a year. He also attended the military academy at West Point for a short time but was expelled. Increasing friction between Poe and his foster father led to a final break between the two men when Poe was twenty-three.

Forced to make his own living, Poe turned to writing and editing. He achieved success as a poet and literary critic but especially as a short-story writer. Poe believed that a short story should be written so as to produce a single emotional effect within the reader: all events, characters, ideas, and words should be chosen and manipulated solely for the purpose of achieving this effect. Few writers have used this formula more effectively than did Poe himself. Among his most famous short stories are "The Pit and the Pendulum," "The Cask of Amontillado," "The Fall of the House of Usher," and his detective stories "The Gold Bug" and "The Purloined Letter."

To be young again is the dream
of many old people. Even if
this were possible, would it be wise?

Dr. Heidegger's Experiment

Nathaniel Hawthorne

THAT VERY SINGULAR MAN, old Dr. Heidegger, once invited four venerable friends to meet him in his study. There were three white-bearded gentlemen, Mr. Medbourne, Colonel Killigrew, and Mr. Gascoigne, and a withered gentlewoman, whose name was the Widow Wycherly. They were all melancholy old creatures, who had been unfortunate in life, and whose greatest misfortune it was that they were not long ago in their graves. Mr. Medbourne, in the vigor of his age, had been a prosperous merchant, but had lost his all by a frantic speculation, and was now little better than a mendicant. Colonel Killigrew had wasted his best years, and his health and substance, in the pursuit of sinful pleasures, which had given birth to a brood of pains, such as the gout, and divers other torments of soul and body. Mr. Gascoigne was a ruined politician, a man of evil fame, or at least had been so till time had buried him from the knowledge of the present generation, and made him obscure instead of infamous. As for the Widow Wycherly, tradition tells us that she was a great beauty in her day; but, for a long while past, she had lived in deep seclusion, on account of certain scandalous stories which had prejudiced the gentry of the town against her. It is a circumstance worth mentioning that each of these three old gentlemen, Mr. Medbourne, Colonel Killigrew, and Mr. Gascoigne, were early lovers of the Widow Wycherly, and had once been

on the point of cutting each other's throats for her sake. And, before proceeding further, I will merely hint that Dr. Heidegger and all his four guests were sometimes thought to be a little beside themselves[1]—as is not unfrequently the case with old people, when worried either by present troubles or woeful recollections.

"My dear old friends," said Dr. Heidegger, motioning them to be seated, "I am desirous of your assistance in one of those little experiments with which I amuse myself here in my study."

If all stories were true, Dr. Heidegger's study must have been a very curious place. It was a dim, old-fashioned chamber, festooned with cobwebs, and besprinkled with antique dust. Around the walls stood several oaken bookcases, the lower shelves of which were filled with rows of gigantic folios and black-letter quartos, and the upper with little parchment-covered duodecimos. Over the central bookcase was a bronze bust of Hippocrates,[2] with which according to some authorities, Dr. Heidegger was accustomed to hold consultations in all difficult cases of his practice. In the obscurest corner of the room stood a tall and narrow oaken closet, with its door ajar, within which doubtfully appeared a skeleton. Between two of the bookcases hung a looking glass, presenting its high and dusty plate within a tarnished gilt frame. Among many wonderful stories related of this mirror, it was fabled that the spirits of all the doctor's deceased patients dwelt within its verge, and would stare him in the face whenever he looked thitherward. The opposite side of the chamber was ornamented with the full-length portrait of a young lady, arrayed in the faded magnificence of silk, satin, and brocade, and with a visage as faded as her dress. Above half a century ago, Dr. Heidegger had been on the point of marriage with this young lady; but, being affected with some slight disorder, she had swallowed one of her lover's prescriptions, and died on the bridal evening. The greatest curiosity of the study remains to be mentioned; it was a ponderous folio volume, bound in black leather, with massive silver clasps. There were no letters on the back, and nobody could tell the title of the book. But it was well known to be a book of magic; and once, when a chambermaid had lifted it, merely to brush away the dust, the skeleton had rattled in its closet, the picture of the young lady had stepped one foot upon the floor, and several ghastly faces had peeped forth from the mirror; while the brazen head of Hippocrates frowned, and said, "Forbear!"

Such was Dr. Heidegger's study. On the summer afternoon of our tale a small round table, as black as ebony, stood in the center of the room, sustaining a cut-glass vase of beautiful form and elaborate workmanship. The sunshine came through the window between the heavy festoons of two faded damask curtains, and fell directly across this vase; so that a mild splendor was reflected from it on the ashen visages of the five old people who sat around. Four champagne glasses were also on the table.

"My dear old friends," repeated Dr. Heidegger, "may I reckon on your aid in performing an exceedingly curious experiment?"

Now Dr. Heidegger was a very strange old gentleman, whose eccentricity had become the nucleus for a

---

1. *a little beside themselves,* a little out of their senses; not quite normal.
2. *Hippocrates* (hi pok′ rə tēz), a Greek physician (460?–357? B.C.) frequently called "the father of medicine."

thousand fantastic stories. Some of these fables, to my shame be it spoken, might possibly be traced back to my own veracious self; and if any passages of the present tale should startle the reader's faith, I must be content to bear the stigma of a fiction monger.

When the doctor's four guests heard him talk of his proposed experiment, they anticipated nothing more wonderful than the murder of a mouse in an air pump, or the examination of a cobweb by the microscope, or some similar nonsense, with which he was constantly in the habit of pestering his intimates. But without waiting for a reply, Dr. Heidegger hobbled across the chamber, and returned with the same ponderous folio, bound in black leather, which common report affirmed to be a book of magic. Undoing the silver clasps, he opened the volume, and took from among its black-letter pages a rose, or what was once a rose, though now the green leaves and crimson petals had assumed one brownish hue, and the ancient flower seemed ready to crumble to dust in the doctor's hands.

"This rose," said Dr. Heidegger, with a sigh, "this same withered and crumbling flower, blossomed five and fifty years ago. It was given me by Sylvia Ward, whose portrait hangs yonder; and I meant to wear it in my bosom at our wedding. Five and fifty years it has been treasured between the leaves of this old volume. Now, would you deem it possible that this rose of half a century could ever bloom again?"

"Nonsense!" said the Widow Wycherly, with a peevish toss of her head. "You might as well ask whether an old woman's wrinkled face could ever bloom again."

"See!" answered Dr. Heidegger. He uncovered the vase, and threw the faded rose into the water which it contained. At first, it lay lightly on the surface of the fluid, appearing to imbibe none of its moisture. Soon, however, a singular change began to be visible. The crushed and dried petals stirred, and assumed a deepening tinge of crimson, as if the flower were reviving from a deathlike slumber; the slender stalk and twigs of foliage became green; and there was the rose of half a century, looking as fresh as when Sylvia Ward had first given it to her lover. It was scarcely full blown; for some of its delicate red leaves curled modestly around its moist bosom, within which two or three dewdrops were sparkling.

"That is certainly a very pretty deception," said the doctor's friends; carelessly, however, for they had witnessed greater miracles at a conjurer's show. "Pray, how was it effected?"

"Did you never hear of the Fountain of Youth," asked Dr. Heidegger, "which Ponce de León, the Spanish adventurer, went in search of two or three centuries ago?"

"But did Ponce de León ever find it?" said the Widow Wycherly.

"No," answered Dr. Heidegger, "for he never sought it in the right place. The famous Fountain of Youth, if I am rightly informed, is situated in the southern part of the Floridian peninsula, not far from Lake Macaco. Its source is overshadowed by several gigantic magnolias, which, though numberless centuries old, have been kept as fresh as violets by the virtues of this wonderful water. An acquaintance of mine, knowing my curiosity in such matters, has sent me what you see in the vase."

"Ahem!" said Colonel Killigrew, who believed not a word of the doctor's story. "And what may be the effect of this fluid on the human frame?"

"You shall judge for yourself, my dear colonel," replied Dr. Heidegger, "and all of you, my respected friends, are welcome to so much of this admirable fluid as may restore to you the bloom of youth. For my own part, having had much trouble in growing old, I am in no hurry to grow young again. With your permission, therefore, I will merely watch the progress of the experiment."

While he spoke, Dr. Heidegger had been filling the four champagne glasses with the water of the Fountain of Youth. It was apparently impregnated with an effervescent gas, for little bubbles were continually ascending from the depths of the glasses, and bursting in silvery spray at the surface. As the liquor diffused a pleasant perfume, the old people doubted not that it possessed cordial and comfortable properties; and though utter sceptics as to its rejuvenescent power, they were inclined to swallow it at once. But Dr. Heidegger besought them to stay a moment.

"Before you drink, my respectable old friends," said he, "it would be well that, with the experience of a lifetime to direct you, you should draw up a few general rules for your guidance, in passing a second time through the perils of youth. Think what a sin and shame it would be, if, with your peculiar advantages, you should not become patterns of virtue and wisdom to all the young people of the age!"

The doctor's four venerable friends made him no answer, except by a feeble and tremulous laugh; so very ridiculous was the idea that, knowing how closely repentance treads behind the steps of error, they should ever go astray again.

"Drink, then," said the doctor, bowing. "I rejoice that I have so well selected the subjects of my experiment."

With palsied hands, they raised the glasses to their lips. The liquor, if it really possessed such virtues as Dr. Heidegger imputed to it, could not have been bestowed on four human beings who needed it more woefully. They looked as if they had never known what youth or pleasure was, but had been the offspring of Nature's dotage, and always the gray, decrepit, sapless, miserable creatures, who now sat stooping round the doctor's table, without life enough in their souls or bodies to be animated even by the prospect of growing young again. They drank off the water, and replaced their glasses on the table.

Assuredly there was an almost immediate improvement in the aspect of the party, not unlike what might have been produced by a glass of generous wine, together with a sudden glow of cheerful sunshine brightening over all their visages at once. There was a healthful suffusion on their cheeks, instead of the ashen hue that had made them look so corpse-like. They gazed at one another, and fancied that some magic power had really begun to smooth away the deep and sad inscriptions which Father Time had been so long engraving on their brows. The Widow adjusted her cap, for she felt almost like a woman again.

"Give us more of this wondrous water!" cried they, eagerly. "We are younger—but we are still too old! Quick—give us more!"

"Patience, patience!" quoth Dr. Heidegger, who sat watching the experiment with philosophic coolness. "You have been a long time growing old. Surely, you might be content to grow young in half an hour! But the water is at your service."

Again he filled their glasses with the liquor of youth, enough of which still remained in the vase to turn half the old people in the city to the age of their own grandchildren. While the bubbles were yet sparkling on the brim, the doctor's four guests snatched their glasses from the table, and swallowed the contents at a single gulp. Was it delusion? Even while the draught was passing down their throats, it seemed to have wrought a change in their whole systems. Their eyes grew clear and bright; a dark shade deepened among their silvery locks; they sat around the table, three gentlemen of middle age, and a woman, hardly beyond her buxom prime.

"My dear widow, you are charming!" cried Colonel Killigrew, whose eyes had been fixed upon her face, while the shadows of age were flitting from it like darkness from the crimson daybreak.

The fair widow knew, of old, that Colonel Killigrew's compliments were not always measured by sober truth; so she started up and ran to the mirror, still dreading that the ugly visage of an old woman would meet her gaze. Meanwhile, the three gentlemen behaved in such a manner as proved that the water of the Fountain of Youth possessed some intoxicating qualities; unless, indeed, their exhilaration of spirits was merely a lightsome dizziness caused by the sudden removal of the weight of years. Mr. Gascoigne's mind seemed to run on political topics, but whether relating to the past, present, or future, could not easily be determined, since the same ideas and phrases have been in vogue these fifty years. Now he rattled forth full-throated sentences about patriotism, national glory, and people's right; now he muttered some perilous stuff or other,

in a sly and doubtful whisper, so cautiously that even his own conscience could scarcely catch the secret; and now, again, he spoke in measured accents, and a deeply deferential tone, as if a royal ear were listening to his well-turned periods. Colonel Killigrew all this time had been trolling forth a jolly bottle song, and ringing his glass in symphony with the chorus, while his eyes wandered toward the buxom figure of the Widow Wycherly. On the other side of the table, Mr. Medbourne was involved in a calculation of dollars and cents, with which was strangely intermingled a project for supplying the East Indies with ice, by harnessing a team of whales to the polar icebergs.

As for the Widow Wycherly, she stood before the mirror curtsying and simpering to her own image, and greeting it as the friend whom she loved better than all the world beside. She thrust her face close to the glass, to see whether some long-remembered wrinkle or crow's foot had indeed vanished. She examined whether the snow had so entirely melted from her hair that the venerable cap could be safely thrown aside. At last, turning briskly away, she came with a sort of dancing step to the table.

"My dear old doctor," cried she, "pray favor me with another glass!"

"Certainly, my dear madam, certainly!" replied the complaisant doctor. "See! I have already filled the glasses."

There, in fact, stood the four glasses, brimful of this wonderful water, the delicate spray of which, as it effervesced from the surface, resembled the tremulous glitter of diamonds. It was now so nearly sunset that the chamber had grown duskier than ever; but a mild and moonlike splendor gleamed from within the vase, and rested alike on the four guests and on the doctor's venerable figure. He sat in a high-backed, elaborately carved, oaken armchair, with a gray dignity of aspect that might have well befitted that very Father Time, whose power had never been disputed, save by this fortunate company. Even while quaffing the third draught of the Fountain of Youth, they were almost awed by the expression of his mysterious visage.

But, the next moment, the exhilarating gush of young life shot through their veins. They were now in the happy prime of youth. Age, with its miserable train of cares and sorrows and diseases, was remembered only as the trouble of a dream, from which they had joyously awoke. The fresh gloss of the soul, so early lost, and without which the world's successive scenes had been but a gallery of faded pictures, again threw its enchantment over all their prospects. They felt like new-created beings in a new-created universe.

"We are young! We are young!" they cried exultingly.

Youth, like the extremity of age, had effaced the strongly marked characteristics of middle life, and mutually assimilated them all. They were a group of merry youngsters, almost maddened with the exuberant frolicsomeness of their years. The most singular effect of their gaiety was an impulse to mock the infirmity and decrepitude of which they had so lately been the victims. They laughed loudly at their old-fashioned attire, the wide-skirted coats and flapped waistcoats of the young men, and the ancient cap and gown of the blooming girl. One limped across the floor like a gouty grandfather; one set a pair of spectacles astride of his nose, and pretended to pore over the black-

letter pages of the book of magic; a third seated himself in an armchair, and strove to imitate the venerable dignity of Dr. Heidegger. Then all shouted mirthfully, and leaped about the room. The Widow Wycherly—if so fresh a damsel could be called a widow—tripped up to the doctor's chair, with a mischievous merriment in her rosy face.

"Doctor, you dear old soul," cried she, "get up and dance with me!" And then the four young people laughed louder than ever, to think what a queer figure the poor old doctor would cut.

"Pray excuse me," answered the doctor quietly. "I am old and rheumatic, and my dancing days were over long ago. But either of these gay young gentlemen will be glad of so pretty a partner."

"Dance with me, Clara!" cried Colonel Killigrew.

"No, no, I will be her partner!" shouted Mr. Gascoigne.

"She promised me her hand, fifty years ago!" exclaimed Mr. Medbourne.

They all gathered round her. One caught both her hands in his passionate grasp—another threw his arm about her waist—the third buried his hands among the glossy curls that clustered beneath the widow's cap. Blushing, panting, struggling, chiding, laughing, her warm breath fanning each of their faces by turns, she strove to disengage herself, yet still remained in their triple embrace. Never was there a livelier picture of youthful rivalship, with bewitching beauty for the prize. Yet, by a strange deception, owing to the duskiness of the chamber and the antique dresses which they still wore, the tall mirror is said to have reflected the figures of the three old, gray, withered grandsires, ridiculously contending for the skinny ugliness of a shriveled grandam.

But they were young; their burning passions proved them so. Inflamed to madness by the coquetry of the girl-widow, who neither granted nor quite withheld her favors, the three rivals began to interchange threatening glances. Still keeping hold of the fair prize, they grappled fiercely at one another's throats. As they struggled to and fro, the table was overturned, and the vase dashed into a thousand fragments. The precious Water of Youth flowed in a bright stream across the floor, moistening the wings of a butterfly, which, grown old in the decline of summer, had alighted there to die. The insect fluttered lightly through the chamber, and settled on the snowy head of Dr. Heidegger.

"Come, come, gentlemen! Come, Madam Wycherly," exclaimed the doctor, "I really must protest against this riot."

They stood still and shivered, for it seemed as if gray Time were calling them back from their sunny youth, far down into the chill and darksome vale of years. They looked at old Dr. Heidegger, who sat in his carved armchair, holding the rose of half a century, which he had rescued from among the fragments of the shattered vase. At the motion of his hand, the four rioters resumed their seats, the more readily, because their violent exertions had wearied them, youthful though they were.

"My poor Sylvia's rose!" ejaculated Dr. Heidegger, holding it in the light of the sunset clouds. "It appears to be fading again."

And so it was. Even while the party were looking at it, the flower continued to shrivel up, till it became as dry and fragile as when the doctor had first thrown it into the vase. He shook off the few drops of moisture which clung to its petals.

"I love it as well thus as in its dewy freshness," observed he, pressing the withered rose to his withered lips. While he spoke, the butterfly fluttered down from the doctor's snowy head, and fell upon the floor.

His guests shivered again. A strange chillness, whether of the body or spirit they could not tell, was creeping gradually over them all. They gazed at one another, and fancied that each fleeting moment snatched away a charm, and left a deepening furrow where none had been before. Was it an illusion? Had the changes of a lifetime been crowded into so brief a space, and were they now four aged people, sitting with their old friend, Dr. Heidegger?

"Are we grown old again, so soon?" cried they, dolefully.

In truth they had. The Water of Youth possessed merely a virtue more transient than that of wine. The delirium which it created had effervesced away. Yes! They were old again. With a shuddering impulse, that showed her a woman still, the widow clasped her skinny hands before her face, and wished that the coffin lid were over it, since it could be no longer beautiful.

"Yes, friends, ye are old again," said Dr. Heidegger, "and lo! the Water of Youth is all lavished on the ground. Well—I bemoan it not; for if the fountain gushed at my very doorstep, I would not stoop to bathe my lips in it—no, though its delirium were for years instead of moments. Such is the lesson ye have taught me!"

But the doctor's four friends had taught no such lesson to themselves. They resolved forthwith to make a pilgrimage to Florida, and quaff at morning, noon, and night, from the Fountain of Youth.   *

Discussion

1. (a) What is the setting of this story? (b) What details help you picture the setting? (c) Why is the setting important?
2. What sort of man is Dr. Heidegger?
3. (a) What characteristics do the four old people have in common? (b) Select passages about each which you think are particularly effective in revealing their individual personalities.
4. Reread page 367, column 1, paragraph 3. What groups of people is Hawthorne satirizing in his descriptions of the four old people?
5. (a) Why do the old people drink Dr. Heidegger's potion? (b) Describe the effect of the potion on each of them. (c) Why does Dr. Heidegger refuse to drink the potion?
6. (a) What is the importance of the rose to the story? (b) Why do you think Hawthorne introduces the butterfly?
7. What use of irony of situation does Hawthorne make in this story?
8. Have the four old people learned anything from their experience? Explain.
9. Which of the following words best expresses the tone of the story: tragic, sad, ironic, ghostly? Explain your answer.
10. What is the theme of this story?

Word Study

In "Dr. Heidegger's Experiment," the author states that the shelves of Dr. Heidegger's study "were filled with rows of gigantic folios and black-letter quartos." Look up *quarto* in a dictionary. What does it mean?

Many English words contain Latin word parts which refer to numbers. The word parts *quar-* and *quadr-* mean "four." Other Latin word parts which are frequently found in English words are *uni-* (one), *bi-* (two), and *tri-* (three).

Each of the following sentences contains an incomplete word. Decide which of the word parts given above correctly completes the word. You may refer to a dictionary for help.

1. A _____ cycle is a popular two-wheeled vehicle.
2. A geometric figure with three sides is called a _____ angle.
3. Because a bird has two legs, it is called a _____ ped.
4. A horse, on the other hand, is a _____ uped.
5. A chorus in which everyone sings the same melody is said to be sung in _____ son.
6. A musical group which has four people is called a _____ tet.

The Author

Nathaniel Hawthorne (1804–1864) was born and raised in Salem, Massachusetts. Following his graduation from Bowdoin College, he returned to Salem where he lived in seclusion, devoting his time to reading and writing. After serving for a time as Surveyor of the Salem Custom House, Hawthorne again turned to writing. Between the years 1850 and 1852, he published the three novels which firmly established him as one of the finest American writers: *The Scarlet Letter, The House of the Seven Gables,* and *The Blithedale Romance.* In addition to novels, Hawthorne published several volumes of short stories, among them *Twice-Told Tales, Mosses from an Old Manse,* and *The Snow-Image.*

Hawthorne once described himself as an observer of life, and he was, in truth, a remarkably accurate observer. His characters reveal his insight into human nature and his concern with the problem of sin and its effect on man. In many of his stories Hawthorne uses elaborate and intricate symbols to explore various aspects of evil.

The Quest for Eternal Youth

✠

When Ponce de León, the Spanish discoverer of Florida, searched for the legendary fountain of youth, he was continuing a quest which men had pursued since ancient times. Among the legends and folklore of early peoples there are numerous tales of a magic liquid (or food) which would make man not only eternally young, but, in certain instances, immortal.

One of the earliest of these stories deals with the Babylonian hero, Gilgamesh (gil′gä mesh). Informed of a magic plant which would bestow youth upon the man who ate of it, Gilgamesh takes a treacherous trip to the mythical fresh-water sea which lies beneath the surface of the earth. He obtains the magic plant and returns to the surface. However, before he can eat any of the plant, it is snatched from his hands by a serpent. So Gilgamesh never receives the benefits of the plant he has taken such pains to obtain; that the serpent benefited from the plant is seen in the fact that he periodically sheds his old skin, revealing a new one underneath.

In Japan, the idea of eternal youth is conveyed by the chrysanthemum. An ancient legend recounts the story of the fountain of youth, the home of Kiku-Jidō, the Chrysanthemum Boy. It is said that blossoming chrysanthemums bring blessings from this fountain. The leaves of the flower, when dipped in saké-beer, are believed to bring health and long life to man.

Many ancient peoples believed that youth-giving liquids and foods were above man's reach and were available only to the gods. The Greek gods of Olympus feasted upon ambrosia, a food which insured their immortality.

The gods of the Norsemen retained their youth by eating golden apples which were contained in a casket watched over by Idun (ē′dün), the goddess of youth. No matter how many of the apples were eaten, the casket always contained the same number. An attempt by the god of fire, Loki (lō′kē), to steal this casket forms the subject of a famous Norse story.

Estsanatlehi, the Woman Who Changes, is one of the most important gods of the Navaho Indians. When she becomes old, she transforms herself into a young girl again and lives a "renewed life."

Medieval alchemists, the forerunners of modern chemists, turned their attention to producing an elixir of life, a potion which would free man from the infirmities of old age and death. Some of the writings of the Middle Ages contain actual recipes for producing this elixir. One such recipe states that the person desiring eternal youth must, every fifty years, enter into "a fast of forty days." During this time he must take prescribed doses of such ingredients as Maydew ("collected with a cloth of pure white linen"); tender herbs; Balm of Azoth; "a broth of lean beef . . . seasoned with rice, sage, valerian, vervain, and balm"; and Egyptian wine. If the instructions are carried out, states the author of the recipe, "the aged man will be renewed in youth."

It is probable that Ponce de León was familiar with some of the stories about the legendary fountain and with exotic accounts of contemporary Europeans who claimed to have discovered its whereabouts. Following his conquest of Puerto Rico, Ponce de León was appointed governor of the region. From the Indians of the area, he learned of a local legend which held that the fountain of youth was located in the land of Bimini, an island in the Bahamas southeast of Florida. He set out to find the fountain. However, he never did reach Bimini; instead he and his men landed on the coast of Florida in 1513. In the course in their explorations they were attacked by Indians, and Ponce de León was wounded in the struggle. He died shortly after his return to Cuba. Ironically, he lost his life while searching for the means to prolong it.

FEATHERTOP

You will probably find Feathertop an odd kind of hero,
but he found the world to which he was so suddenly introduced
rather odd, too. What idea is expressed through his reactions?

Adapted for television by
Maurice Valency
from a story
by Nathaniel Hawthorne

CHARACTERS

MOTHER RIGBY   BOB ENDICOTT
DICCON   ADAM
FEATHERTOP   MAJOR WHITBY
JUDGE GOOKIN   MR. BELL
POLLY GOOKIN   DANCERS

Fade in: A shot of MOTHER RIGBY'S *fireplace. Dancing flames. An iron pot on a crane seething over. Weird shadows.*

Sound: MOTHER RIGBY *is singing an old ballad as she bends over her work.*

Dolly back: The kitchen is a low-beamed room, the largest room in a small New England house of colonial design. It is the year 1770. There are cobwebs in the corners. Bunches of herbs and other witch's gear hang from the ceiling. On the wall hangs an old brass astrolabe alongside an old cutlass, a magic square on old parchment, etc. MOTHER RIGBY *puts the finishing touches to the scarecrow she has made. This has a ramshackle grandeur about it. It is plainly enough stuffed with straw. The head is a pumpkin. The tattered silk stockings fall lankly over the sticks that serve it for legs. But the embroidered coat and the doeskin breeches were once the last word in fine tailoring and the head has an oddly appealing look to it. An old tie-wig gives the figure a raffish cockiness as it sits sprawled out in the chimney corner.*

MOTHER RIGBY *(sings as she puts the last touches to it).*

Late, late yestreen I saw the new moon
   With the old moon in her arm,
And I fear, I fear, my master dear,
   That we will come to harm. . . .[1]

---

1. Late, late yestreen . . . come to harm. Mother Rigby is singing a stanza from "Sir Patrick Spens," an old English ballad.

(When she has finished, she takes her pipe from the mantel shelf, fills it from an old tobacco pouch. She gazes at her work with satisfaction. A battered three-cornered hat hangs on a nail nearby. She fetches it down, chuckling, and sets it on the scarecrow's head. Then she stands her creation up in the corner. She stops humming her ballad, and speaks in a sharp, professional tone.) Diccon! *(DICCON, her helper, appears at once.)* Diccon, a coal for my pipe! *(A glowing coal appears in DICCON'S hand. He touches it to her pipe. MOTHER RIGBY puffs abstractedly.)* Thank you. Sit down, Diccon. What think you of my scarecrow? He's worth looking at, eh? *(She turns to the scarecrow.)* And you are the fine gentleman, my boy. Fine enough to scare any crow in New England. Ah, there. Ah, there. *(She fishes an old feather out of the trash and mischievously sticks it in his hat.)* There, Feathertop, that's you. Now you're perfect. *(She stares at the firelight playing over FEATHERTOP'S honest features.)* Diccon, that puppet yonder is too good a piece of work to stand all summer long in a cornfield. Just because I'm a witch, I've half a mind to send him forth into the world to take his chance among other straw men of my acquaintance. *(She sets down her glass, chuckling.)* Judge Gookin, for instance—the richest as well as the biggest fool in the Colonies. Wouldn't that be a fine joke? *(She laughs.)* For two coppers, I'd do it. *(Two coins fall mysteriously, one after the other, on the table before her. She picks them up, laughing.)* So. So. The joke begins. Master Gookin wants very much to rise in the world—that I know. Well, I shall give him a leg up—I shall send him the finest gentleman ever seen in

these parts—by far. *(Laughs again)* What for, you wonder? I'll tell you, boy—but first I'll turn you into a man—and then—ah, then you'll hear the joke I've planned for Master Gookin! *(She sticks her pipe into the scarecrow's mouth.)* Come now, puff, darling! Puff! Puff just once. Breathe in a little smoke. Puff, I say! Puff! *(A little smoke trickles out of the pumpkin's mouth. She laughs exultantly.)* Ah, there! That's it, boy. Once more—puff! It's breath I'm giving you. Puff for your life, boy, puff! *(He begins puffing in earnest. The face changes. Upon the innocent and cheerful features of the scarecrow is superimposed a human face of the same contours. This shimmers into focus with each puff and then withdraws. MOTHER RIGBY claps her hands.)* Ah, now it takes! Again, boy! Once more! Once more! *(FEATHERTOP emits a cloud of smoke that envelops the head completely. When it clears, the head is human.)* And now fetch us a puff to the very bottom of your bellows. There— *(The figure straightens up miraculously, the utmost in an elegant gentleman.)* See what a fine boy you've become? *(FEATHERTOP smiles, pleased that he's done so well.)* But why are you skulking like a mouse in the corner? You've nothing to be ashamed of. *(She beckons.)* Step forth. The world awaits you. *(He looks frightened and eager by turns but ends by shaking his head. She beckons imperiously.)* Walk, pumpkin head! Walk, Feathertop! I say, walk! *(He hitches forward uncertainly and stands tottering. The rising sun streams in through the window, setting off his figure. He lifts his hand trying to touch the sunlight.)* Steady! Steady, boy! *(He steadies himself. He steps out.)* That's it. That's it. That's splendid.

(He is now enjoying himself. He steps out with an impish grin, pretends to totter, then regains balance, and struts about comically. She is delighted by these unsolicited antics.) Yes. Yes. Yes. Ha-ha-ha-ha. You're a proper marvel. And now that you're properly puffed up—*(She raises a hand. Her eye flashes. He shrinks back in terror.)* Speak! *(He takes the pipe from his lips, and opens his mouth, trembling. He shakes his head. She insists.)* Speak! *(He gasps desperately.)* Speak or I'll——

FEATHERTOP *(in terror).* Ah——

MOTHER RIGBY. I beg your pardon?

FEATHERTOP *(piteously).* Par-don.

MOTHER RIGBY *(laughs).* Pardon? What for? You haven't done anything yet. Well? Speak!

FEATHERTOP. What—must—I—say?

MOTHER RIGBY. Whatever comes into your head.

FEATHERTOP *(makes an effort to think. Then puts the pipe to his lips and sucks in some smoke. A thought comes with it.)* Who—am—I?

MOTHER RIGBY. You? You're my little Feathertop, that's who you are. You're the best witch's puppet ever seen in this world. I'm going to make a man of you.

FEATHERTOP *(pleased).* A man?

MOTHER RIGBY. And no ordinary man. A man among men. Lift up your head, boy. Chin high.

FEATHERTOP. Chin high. *(He laughs with delight.)*

MOTHER RIGBY. Ah, what sparkle! What grace! *(Suddenly she fetches him a slap on the ear. Tears come into his eyes.)*

FEATHERTOP. That hurt.

MOTHER RIGBY. It was your birth pang. No man is complete without one. Congratulations, boy. You're born. Well? How do you like it?

FEATHERTOP. I like it.

MOTHER RIGBY. Do you so? Well, I'm delighted to hear it. Come then, say "Thank you, Mother."

FEATHERTOP. Thank you, Mother.

MOTHER RIGBY. With a proper bow. *(He tries.)* No, no—not like a pump handle. Like a fine gentleman. Like this. *(She bows.)*

FEATHERTOP *(imitates her with impish humor).* Thank you, Mother.

MOTHER RIGBY. That's better. Bit homespun still. Back still creaks a bit. But many a fine gentleman's back creaks worse than yours and no one's the worse for it.

FEATHERTOP *(bows with the utmost grace).* Thank you, ma'am.

MOTHER RIGBY *(curtseys).* Ah, that's something like. You're a real wonder, I declare. So life interests you, does it? Well, there's quite a bit to it in one way or the other.

FEATHERTOP. Where, ma'am?

MOTHER RIGBY. Why, all about you, boy. Just open your eyes and you're certain to see it. *(He steps to the fire.)* That's fire. It burns. Don't touch.

FEATHERTOP. No, ma'am. *(His coat catches a highlight. He passes a timid hand over its surface.)*

MOTHER RIGBY. That's velvet.

FEATHERTOP. It's smooth, ma'am.

MOTHER RIGBY *(smiles).* Not half as smooth as you, pet. *(He smells a bunch of dried herbs.)*

FEATHERTOP. Thank you, ma'am.

MOTHER RIGBY. Them's herbs. Sweet?

FEATHERTOP *(gallantly).* Not half as sweet as you, ma'am.

MOTHER RIGBY *(laughing).* Well, now that's something I didn't expect to hear! Diccon, do you mark the boy? What a piece of work he's turned out, to be sure. *(Admiringly)* Lad, I count myself a better witch because of you.

FEATHERTOP. You're a wonderful witch, ma'am.

MOTHER RIGBY. Listen to him, now. A feather and a puff of smoke, and he's all compliments and manners. Well, my handsome boy, you've come a long way since sunrise, there's no denying it. You should be quite a man by nightfall at this rate, if you have scope.

FEATHERTOP. Scope, ma'am?

MOTHER RIGBY. And scope you shall have. I'm going to send you forth into the world—what do you say to that—the great, wide, the wonderful world, boy.

FEATHERTOP. Will I like it, Mother?

MOTHER RIGBY. I think so, aye. For I've given you great natural advantages, boy, including a coat that once belonged to a French duke— that was scalped, I believe, by the Indians; 'tis no ordinary garment. Besides, you're tall and slender and you have modesty. You're bound to cut a fine figure among the other stuffed shirts that go strutting and posing about the world.

FEATHERTOP. I shall endeavor to live up to it, ma'am.

MOTHER RIGBY. Oh, you will, you will, never fear. You've a well-turned leg. Your chest is full. And your head's empty. There's a perfect natural endowment for any sort of career. Without any more, you could be a general and command an army. And as for your heart —there's more heart in that waist-coat, depend on it, than you'll find in many a banker or statesman. Yes, yes, boy—barring accidents, you will go far in this world. *(He puffs fruitlessly.)* Only mind—your pipe's out.

FEATHERTOP *(distressed)*. Oh.

MOTHER RIGBY. Knock out the ashes. *(He does so. She hands him her pouch.)* Fill it, boy. Quickly. *(He begins filling it.)* Mark me now, you do stand in some need of education, for you're young, though remarkably grown for your age. I can't send you to Harvard College, there's no time, and besides they'd only stuff your head with rubbish. Well, there are but three things a man needs to know, and I'll teach you those directly. Diccon! *(DICCON appears.)* For the rest, what passes for learning in this world is mostly smoke, and you'll find plenty of that in your pipe. Diccon, a coal! *(DICCON lights the pipe and goes. FEATHERTOP puffs away contentedly.)* Now, boy, mark me well——

FEATHERTOP. With all my heart, ma'am.

MOTHER RIGBY. If you wish to get on in this world, look wise, ask no questions, tell no lies.

FEATHERTOP. Look wise. Ask no questions. Tell no lies.

MOTHER RIGBY. Can you remember that? *(He nods.)* With that much learning, you can hold your own with the wisest heads in the New World, nay, in the Old World, too.

FEATHERTOP. But, Mother, how if I'm asked——

MOTHER RIGBY. What, boy?

FEATHERTOP. Where I hail from, who I am?

MOTHER RIGBY. Gentlemen never answer such questions, and 'tis rude to ask. Keep your mouth shut, and others will tell your lies for you. Only see you don't get caught up in them yourself.

FEATHERTOP. Never fear, Mother. I'm no scatterbrain.

MOTHER RIGBY. Oh, you're not? That's good to know. And now, we must look to your fortune, my innocent, for in this world a man without money might as well be dead. Here's two coppers for you.

FEATHERTOP. What am I to do with them, ma'am?

MOTHER RIGBY. You may jingle them

together in your pocket, but on no account spend them.

FEATHERTOP. But what if I should have need?

MOTHER RIGBY. You won't. You're a rich man, by the looks of you, and that's all that matters. The rich have no need of money—they have credit. 'Tis a type of witchcraft I don't deal in, but you'll find out soon enough how it goes.

FEATHERTOP (pockets the money). Trust me for that, ma'am.

MOTHER RIGBY. I do, boy, I do. You have a good head on your shoulders, a clear, fine, empty head, that's the point. The rest will come. In the meantime, bow and smile. And, above all, listen. So long as you listen, people will consider that you're a marvelously witty fellow.

FEATHERTOP. One never tires of listening to you, ma'am.

MOTHER RIGBY (smiles). I know. I know. (Admiringly) 'Twouldn't surprise me a bit if you rose to be governor and ruled us all.

FEATHERTOP. I'm not so ambitious, ma'am. 'Twill be enough if I learn to rule myself. But I've a strange longing to see the world.

MOTHER RIGBY. So? And where do you wish to begin, my fine gentleman?

FEATHERTOP. 'Tis all one to me, Mother. I have seen none of it yet.

MOTHER RIGBY. Boston? No, 'tis too big; you'd be lost in Boston. Philadelphia? 'Tis too grand. (She thinks.) Feathertop, my boy——

FEATHERTOP. Mother?

MOTHER RIGBY. Straight down that path, a half hour's walk will bring you to Judge Gookin's house. 'Tis a fine, big house.

FEATHERTOP. Finer than this, ma'am?

MOTHER RIGBY (chuckles). A little. Master Gookin's the richest, as well as the biggest, fool in the Colonies. And he wants to rise in the world. Well, you shall give him a leg up.

FEATHERTOP. I, ma'am?

MOTHER RIGBY. You, lad. No one in these parts is good enough for his daughter, so he says. She must have a fine gentleman from abroad. Well, we shall send him one—the finest gentleman from abroad that ever was seen. Wait a bit, now——(She picks an old garter out of a drawer and pins it to his coat. It turns into a jeweled cross.) There! You're a Knight of the Garter. Lord Feathertop!

FEATHERTOP (strutting about). How I glitter! (Suddenly weak) Mother——

MOTHER RIGBY. Why, what ails you? Oh——(His pipe has gone out.) Diccon! (DICCON appears.) Quick! A coal for his pipe. (DICCON obliges.) Puff, lad, puff! (He brightens up at once.) Better now?

FEATHERTOP. Much better, thank you. (In the grand manner) A trifling indisposition. Nothing at all, really.

MOTHER RIGBY (hands him her tobacco pouch; chuckles). I understand. All the same, remember, boy, stick to your pipe—your life is in it. A puff from time to time and you'll be as fit as a fiddle. There's nothing else but smoke holds you together. Here—there's tobacco in this pouch will keep you glittering a lifetime, and for a light all you need to do is to call for Diccon to bring you a coal.

FEATHERTOP (gaily). Diccon! A coal for my pipe! (DICCON appears, glances at the burning pipe, then goes. FEATHERTOP laughs.) Why, it works like a charm, Mother.

MOTHER RIGBY. Yes, it does. And now, hark ye, lad, while I think of it. When you see Polly Gookin—she's a pretty lass and she's certain to turn your head. Mind you don't lose it completely.

FEATHERTOP. Trust me for that, Mother. I'm no fool.

MOTHER RIGBY. Come, then, off you go. *(The door swings open by itself.)* 'Tis a beautiful morning, and the world's before you.

FEATHERTOP *(peers out dubiously).* Is that it there, Mother?

MOTHER RIGBY. That's it there, boy.

FEATHERTOP *(jauntily).* Why, then, I'm off.

MOTHER RIGBY. Here, take my staff with you. *(She hands him her old stick. It turns into a gold-topped cane.)* This will lead you straight to Judge Gookin's door.

FEATHERTOP. Good-by, Mother. *(He wipes away a tear.)*

MOTHER RIGBY. Why, the lad's sentimental.

FEATHERTOP. I've my feelings, ma'am, like other people, I hope.

MOTHER RIGBY. Have you so? Well —mind you don't show them too often. *(Blows him a kiss)* Good luck, boy. Good luck, my darling.

FEATHERTOP *(waves his hat gallantly as he goes).* Good-by, Mother, good-by. *(He goes.)*

[*Dissolve to: Silhouette of* FEATHERTOP *striding down a road against the morning sun, with* DICCON *behind him.*

Dissolve to: Close-up of FEATHER-TOP'S *hat and stick on* JUDGE GOOKIN'S *hall table.* POLLY GOOKIN *and* BOB ENDICOTT *are standing near them, speaking in low tones.*]

BOB. Polly——(POLLY *takes up the hat and perches it on her head.)* Take that off, Polly. 'Tis the stranger's hat.

POLLY. I'll not take it off.

BOB. Polly, listen to me.

POLLY. I'll not listen to you, Bob Endicott. I've listened to you enough.

BOB. But, Polly, I mean to ask your father this very night——

POLLY. You do? Oh, Bob! *(She throws her arms about his neck gaily and kisses him.)* And why not now, pray?

BOB. Oh, Polly, can I ask him for his daughter's hand in front of this Lord—Lord—what's-his-name?

JUDGE GOOKIN'S VOICE *(off stage).* Polly!

POLLY *(puts down hat).* It's Father.

GOOKIN *(off stage).* Polly!

POLLY. I must go.

BOB. I'll come back tonight, Polly, and I'll ask him, never fear.

POLLY. Mind you do, Bob Endicott, or I'll——

GOOKIN *(off stage).* Polly!

POLLY. Good-by.

[*Dissolve to:* JUDGE GOOKIN'S *living room. Windsor chairs are drawn up to the fire.* FEATHERTOP *sits in one at his ease, pipe in hand.* GOOKIN *is standing. The décor is colonial, elegant, and comfortable.*]

GOOKIN. No, no, I won't hear of it! My Lord stay at the inn? What would they say of me in Boston? *(Calls)* Polly! Polly, I say! I'm naught but a poor widower, sir, as you may know, but my daughter will see to it that whatever poor comforts this house can afford——*(Calls)* Polly! Where the devil is the girl? *(A servant comes in with a tray, decanter, and glasses.)* Where's your mistress?

ADAM. Miss Polly begs you will be patient. She will be down directly she's dressed.

GOOKIN. Primping, primping. Tell her she's wanted here. *(He pours a glass for* FEATHERTOP.) And now, My Lord——*(He pours himself one.)* Pray tell me. *(He clinks glasses with* FEATHERTOP, *who is not too sure of the procedure.)* What brings a man of your position to our town?

FEATHERTOP *(takes a sip of the wine thoughtfully; the taste astonishes him).* What d'ye call this liquid?

GOOKIN. What? 'Tis wine, my lad. Port wine.

FEATHERTOP. It makes the head spin.

GOOKIN. Surely you don't disapprove of spirits, My Lord.

FEATHERTOP. Not in the least, sir. In this world you need to drink things to make the head spin. *(Holds out his glass)* Another drop, Master Gookin.

GOOKIN. My Lord is here on no ordinary business, I'm sure.

FEATHERTOP. I come only to see the world, Master Gookin.

GOOKIN *(laughs knowingly)*. Ah, indeed. To be sure. *(Winks)* Secret business. Private business?

FEATHERTOP. By no means. Public.

GOOKIN. Ah! On public business. Trust me, My Lord, I'll say nothing of it. Not a word. And the nature of——(FEATHERTOP *gets up, his eye caught by a portrait of George III[2] on the wall.)* I confess, I have been expecting this visit for some time.

FEATHERTOP *(pointing to the picture in wonder)*. Why is that man so angry?

GOOKIN. Eh? Oh, I take your meaning, My Lord, yes. Ah, My Lord, you're right. His Majesty has good cause to be angry. Thank heaven you've come, My Lord. We look to you for deliverance.

FEATHERTOP *(in astonishment)*. To me?

GOOKIN. Come, now, 'tis as plain as a pikestaff. My Lord, be open with me. You were sent here, were you not?

FEATHERTOP. Yes, I was indeed. But——

GOOKIN. Enough, My Lord, say no more. I understand. And look you, sir. *(He unlocks a casket.)* I have not been idle. Here, My Lord. The evidence.

FEATHERTOP. The evidence——

GOOKIN. Enough to hang the lot of them, My Lord. A letter from Major Whitby offering to sell his fortress to the French[3] whenever they desire it. Here he threatens to send his Hessians[4] to sack a farm unless he is paid fifty pounds. Letters. Affidavits. Depositions. All as clear as day. You may open the hearings at once. Tomorrow. The sheriff takes bribes. The selectmen[5] are perjurers. His Majesty's Collector[6] is a knave. Major Whitby is a traitor. The preacher has traffic with witches——

FEATHERTOP. But are there no honest men in the land?

GOOKIN. All rogues. All blackguards. You must make a clean sweep, My Lord. I can see you are shocked.

FEATHERTOP. I am astonished.

GOOKIN. My Lord, can you leave treachery unpunished? Can you permit honest folk to be abused? Can you look on idly while these wolves batten on the blood of the people?

FEATHERTOP. No, certainly I can't do that.

GOOKIN *(pours him out another glass)*. My Lord, I say no more. The evidence is in your hands. You may sift it at your leisure.

FEATHERTOP. You wish me to?

GOOKIN. I beg you to.

FEATHERTOP. Very well, I shall.

GOOKIN. And when you see who the guilty are, My Lord, heads will roll, will they not?

---

2. *George III,* the king of England at the time of the story. It was during his reign that the American Revolution took place.

3. *offering to sell his fortress to the French.* The French and Indian War between England and France had ended in 1763, seven years before this play takes place. Bitter about their defeat, the French, both before and during the American Revolution, actively encouraged and aided the American colonists in their struggle for independence. Major Whitby, by selling his fortress to the French, would be committing treason against England.

4. *Hessians,* German soldiers hired by England.

5. *selectmen,* a board of town officers chosen yearly to manage various public affairs.

6. *His Majesty's Collector,* a person employed by the king of England to collect taxes from the colonists.

FEATHERTOP. Upon my word, they may. They may. *(Inflating visibly)* I did not ask to be sent forth into your world, Master Gookin. But now that I'm here *(He blows out a cloud of smoke)* perhaps I shall be of some use in it. *(At this moment,* POLLY GOOKIN *comes in. He sees her. He gasps with amazement.)*

GOOKIN. Be guided by me, My Lord. Hang a dozen of them first. After that——

FEATHERTOP *(rises)*. Oh, lovely creature!

GOOKIN. What? *(He turns.)* Why, 'tis only my daughter, Polly.

FEATHERTOP. How beautiful she is, your daughter!

POLLY *(curtseys)*. My Lord.

FEATHERTOP *(bows)*. My lady.

GOOKIN. The lass is to your taste, eh?

FEATHERTOP. Aye, very much. Very much.

GOOKIN. She's a good girl, My Lord, and has a sweet singing voice. And she'll bring five hundred a year to the man she marries. *(*ADAM *comes in.)* What is it, Adam?

ADAM. Major Whitby and the King's Collector to present their compliments.

GOOKIN. I'll come out to them. By your leave, My Lord. *(He goes out with* ADAM.*)*

FEATHERTOP. Your name is Polly, lovely creature?

POLLY. Polly Gookin, My Lord.

FEATHERTOP. Polly Gookin. 'Tis a beautiful name, is it not?

POLLY. It's mine.

FEATHERTOP. 'Tis music in the ear. All of you is lovely, Mistress Polly. Your name, your eyes, your hair——*(He reaches out timidly and touches her hair.)* 'Tis softer than velvet. But your cheek is softer still——*(He strokes her cheek. She draws back.)*

POLLY. My Lord, by your leave——!

FEATHERTOP. Mistress Polly——*(He bends forward very naturally and kisses her on the lips.)*

POLLY. Oh!

FEATHERTOP. You are angry with me?

POLLY. But what do you take me for, My Lord?

FEATHERTOP. I have done something wrong?

POLLY. Pray let me pass.

FEATHERTOP. On my word, I meant no harm. And you're really none the worse for it. Don't be angry, Mistress Polly.

POLLY. I'm not accustomed to your courtly ways, My Lord. We are simple country folk. All the same——

FEATHERTOP. Among country folk, it is not permitted to kiss a lovely face?

POLLY. Only if one intends to marry it, My Lord.

FEATHERTOP. But I intend to marry it, Miss Polly. I very much intend to marry it.

POLLY. You're but mocking me, My Lord. 'Tis not very gallant.

FEATHERTOP. On my word, I'm not.

POLLY. Let me go! Please! *(She breaks away.)*

FEATHERTOP. Wait, Miss Polly, wait——*(She crosses to the door.* GOOKIN *comes in.)*

GOOKIN. My Lord, these scoundrels insist——What's amiss here? Where are you going?

POLLY *(brushing past)*. I beg your pardon.

FEATHERTOP. I have made your daughter angry, Master Gookin.

GOOKIN. What? Oh, bother the child —she's high-spirited. I'll bring her round. Major Whitby and the Collector desire to be received. You'll not see them, I hope?

[MAJOR WHITBY *and the* COLLECTOR *come in.*]

WHITBY. I'm sure My Lord will see us, Master Gookin, if only out of curiosity. *(He bows.)* My Lord, your most humble and obedient servant, Major Whitby. In command of His Majesty's garrison. *(FEATHERTOP bows curtly.)* And this is Mr. Graham Bell, His Majesty's Collector.

MR. BELL. My Lord.

FEATHERTOP. I am much concerned for Miss Polly, Master Gookin.

GOOKIN. I'll see to it directly. *(Calls)* Polly! I'll fetch her back. Polly! One moment, My Lord. *(He goes.)*

WHITBY. Hark ye, My Lord—this Gookin——

FEATHERTOP. Eh?

WHITBY. A most pernicious liar, sir.

MR. BELL. A thief, sir. A notorious knave. Not to be trusted for a moment. *(He whispers.)*

WHITBY. Whatever he may have told you, My Lord——

MR. BELL. Whatever he may have said——

WHITBY. Believe no word of it——

MR. BELL. Be guided by us, My Lord. We've been waiting for you night and day.

WHITBY. Sh! Mum's the word!

[GOOKIN *comes in.*]

MR. BELL. Your girl has spirit, Master Gookin.

GOOKIN. Aye. But what could My Lord have said to her to make her fly off like a jack rabbit?

FEATHERTOP *(putting his pipe to his lips).* Only that I intend to marry her.

GOOKIN. To marry her! But, My Lord——!

FEATHERTOP. Diccon! A coal for my pipe! (DICCON *appears, adding to the general astonishment.* FEATHERTOP *puffs calmly.)*

[*Dissolve to: A room in* GOOKIN'S *house adjoining the ballroom, where a dance is in progress.* POLLY *is standing before a long mirror, admiring her ball gown.* GOOKIN *stands behind her. There is a sound of string music.*]

GOOKIN *(exasperated).* "But, Father! But, Father! But, Father!" Can you sing no other tune? You want to travel in your own coach, I suppose, with your servants in livery and your house in town?

POLLY. Oh, Father, I don't want anything like that.

GOOKIN. Well, I do. And here's the man can give them to you. Aye, and sent from heaven! A baron!

POLLY. But, Father——

GOOKIN. "But, Father!" Now listen to me, girl, your father knows best, and we'll have no more of this nonsense. I shall send My Lord Feathertop in to you, and mind you cross him in nothing. Wait here.

[*He goes off. The girl walks back to the mirror and makes a face at his retreating back.* BOB *comes in silently.*]

BOB. Polly——*(Camera on his reflection in the mirror. She turns.)*

POLLY *(in his arms).* Oh, Bob, Bob! I'm frightened!

BOB. Frightened? Of what?

POLLY. This man. This baron.

BOB. Feathertop?

[*Camera on* FEATHERTOP. *He has just walked into the doorway. He stops on hearing his name.*]

POLLY. He's not like other people. He's strange.

BOB. But what's it to you, Polly?

POLLY. Father—Father wants me to marry him.

BOB. Marry him? But you don't even know him. He's scarcely been here a day.

POLLY. I know. I know. But Father ——Oh, Bob, Bob, what are we going to do?

BOB. Do? Why, I'll——

[FEATHERTOP *blows out a cloud of smoke. They see him and turn. He comes in, bows.*]

FEATHERTOP *(ignores BOB).* Miss Polly, your father bids me come and fetch you. It seems the dancing is

about to begin. (To BOB) By your leave. (He offers his arm to POLLY, who takes it with a helpless look at BOB.)

BOB. Sir.

FEATHERTOP (stops). Yes?

BOB. Nothing. Nothing.

[FEATHERTOP smiles. He takes POLLY out. BOB stares after them in desperation. The music strikes up.

Dissolve to: The dance floor. Several couples take places to dance a figure dance of the minuet variety. FEATHERTOP and POLLY join them.]

FEATHERTOP (as the dance begins). I may be a little awkward at this just at first, Miss Polly——

POLLY (dancing). Our New World dances must seem strange.

FEATHERTOP. Your New World seems

strange. *(He steps on her foot.)* Ah. Forgive me.

POLLY. 'Tis no matter.

FEATHERTOP. The young man yonder — Mr. Endicott——

POLLY. Yes, My Lord?

FEATHERTOP. He takes your fancy, Miss Polly?

POLLY. We grew up together.

FEATHERTOP *(his dancing greatly improved)*. He's not for you, Miss Polly. *(He draws her away from the other dancers.)*

POLLY. How do you mean, My Lord?

[*Camera on a lady dancing with* WHITBY.]

THE LADY. Mark My Lord, how he dances, Major.

WHITBY. 'Tis doubtless the latest fashion from Paris.

[FEATHERTOP *dances out of the room with* POLLY *and into the adjoining room. The camera dollies after them.*]

FEATHERTOP *(still dancing)*. Miss Polly, I am but lately come into this world. I understand little enough of it.

POLLY. It must seem trivial, My Lord, compared to the world you know.

FEATHERTOP. It seems beautiful and wonderful beyond belief. Yet it bewilders me.

POLLY. How bewilders you, My Lord?

FEATHERTOP. Until I look at you, Miss Polly. Then all is clear.

POLLY. What is clear, My Lord?

FEATHERTOP *(stops dancing; takes her hand)*. What it is, and what I am, and what I have to do.

POLLY. I don't understand, My•Lord.

FEATHERTOP. 'Tis a beautiful world, this world of yours, with its hills and its plains, its sunlight poured like a blessing from the sky, and its water bubbling like laughter from the depths. There should be joy in such a world, Miss Polly. It should be peopled with happy and lovely beings. Like you, Miss Polly. Not with miserable creatures, like Judge Gookin.

POLLY. My Lord!

FEATHERTOP *(nods)*. Or Major Whitby. Or Mr. Bell, His Majesty's Collector. Why should this beautiful world be filled with liars and hypocrites?

POLLY. Is that not human nature, My Lord?

FEATHERTOP. I had begun to think so. But then I saw you, Miss Polly. And then I understood. Men are beautiful. They are good. But they are unhappy. They are afraid. And that makes them hateful and ugly. No matter. They shall be so no longer.

POLLY. But, My Lord——

FEATHERTOP *(more and more exalted)*. I came among them in my innocence, and at once they turned to me for help. Very well. *(He takes her other hand.)* I shall not fail them.

POLLY. Let me go, if you please, sir!

FEATHERTOP. For your sake I shall help them. I shall heal them. I shall make all men equal and all men good. I shall exalt the humble. I shall abase the proud. I shall feed the hungry. Aye, the world will be the better for me.

POLLY *(frightened)*. Please let me go.

FEATHERTOP. But I shall need help, Miss Polly. I shall need inspiration, more than this poor pipe of mine can give. I shall need a vision of beauty to guide me. I shall need a hand to lead me. I shall need you——

POLLY. You're hurting me.

FEATHERTOP. I love you. *(He moves to take her in his arms. At this moment, half acceding, she sees his image in the glass. It is the scarecrow, pumpkin head and all. She screams.)* I love you. *(But now he sees it also, and recoils in horror. He speaks to the image.)* Go away! *(He makes a threatening gesture. The image steps toward him with the same gesture. His words echo back from it, as he shouts.)* Go away!

[POLLY *faints. The music stops. People rush in.*]

GOOKIN. My Lord——

WHITBY. My Lord——

BOB. What have you done to her? *(He kneels beside her.)* Polly!

MR. BELL. She's fainted.

[POLLY *opens her eyes.*]

FEATHERTOP. Miss Polly——

POLLY *(sees him and starts up).* The scarecrow!

WHITBY. Scarecrow?

GOOKIN. Pull yourself together, girl. Have you lost your wits?

BOB *(to GOOKIN).* If she has, the fault is yours!

GOOKIN. Be so good as to leave my house, Mr. Endicott. My Lord, forgive the girl. She's yours.

FEATHERTOP *(totters; he speaks in a choked voice).* Fools! Fools!

GOOKIN. My Lord?

FEATHERTOP. Give the girl to the man she loves. *(He takes up a massive candlestick and draws* GOOKIN *to the mirror.)* Or—do you prefer——

GOOKIN. What, My Lord?

FEATHERTOP. Your lord? There's your lord for you! There! *(They stare in horror at the reflection. He hurls the candlestick at the glass. It shatters.)* There. *(He makes a supreme effort and draws himself up. He surveys them each in turn. Then he puts his pipe in his mouth defiantly.)* Diccon. A coal for my pipe. *(*DICCON *appears.)*

GOOKIN. But, My Lord—My Lord—where are you going?

[FEATHERTOP *pauses at the door, looks at them, and blows a puff of smoke at them.*

Dissolve to: MOTHER RIGBY'S *kitchen. She sits placidly rocking by her fire. The door flies open.* FEATHERTOP *comes in, dejected.*]

MOTHER RIGBY. Well, well, boy! And I thought you'd make the whole world over!

FEATHERTOP. So did I, Mother. But then I looked in a glass.

MOTHER RIGBY. I know. I know.

FEATHERTOP. And I saw myself as I am.

MOTHER RIGBY. Alas, boy, I should have warned you.

FEATHERTOP. I don't want to live!

MOTHER RIGBY. Nonsense, boy—you're no different from the rest of them.

FEATHERTOP. I don't want to live! I don't want to live! *(He hurls his pipe against the wall. He falls in a heap.)*

MOTHER RIGBY. What a pity! *(She picks up her pipe and fills it slowly.)* Poor little Feathertop! Of all the straw men who go bustling about this world, why should you alone have to know yourself, and die for it? *(She sighs.)* Poor lad! Who knows what mighty thoughts passed through that pumpkin head in its little hour. And how you must have suffered! *(He looks up at her.)* Well, 'twas not in vain—at least you've put one thing right in the world. *(A flicker of interest appears in his eyes.)* Old Gookin has learned his lesson and the girl will have her boy. 'Tis not much—one good deed and that done unwillingly, but more than most people can boast of in a lifetime of iniquity. Well——*(She stares at her pipe a moment, then puts it to her lips.)* You shall be a scarecrow after all. 'Tis a useful and innocent vocation and will bring you no grief. *(She stares reflecting at the scarecrow lying in a heap on the floor, and prods it with her toe.)* Diccon! *(She sits back in her rocker.)* A coal for my pipe! *(*DICCON *lights it. She puffs out a cloud which obscures the picture.)* ✳

Discussion

1. (**a**) At the beginning of the play, how does Feathertop feel about being sent out into the world? (**b**) What kind of world does he find? (**c**) At what point do his feelings about the world change? (**d**) What causes the change?
2. (**a**) What kind of character is Mother Rigby? (**b**) How does she differ from Judge Gookin, Major Whitby, and Mr. Bell? (**c**) What type of people are Polly Gookin and Bob Endicott?
3. Review the Handbook article on satire (page 563). (**a**) What is satiric about the fact that Feathertop is kept alive by smoke from his pipe? (**b**) Look up the following passages in the play and explain what the author is satirizing in each case.
    (1) page 376, column 1, paragraph 5
    (2) page 376, column 1, paragraph 7
    (3) page 376, column 1, paragraph 9
    (4) page 377, column 1, paragraph 2
    (5) page 377, column 2, paragraph 2
(**c**) What is the tone of the satire in this play?
4. Review the functions of dialogue in the Handbook article on page 539. (**a**) Cite passages of dialogue which are important in revealing the background of the play. (**b**) How does the dialogue help to establish the tone? (**c**) Select passages of dialogue which you feel are important in revealing Feathertop's character, Mother Rigby's character, and Judge Gookin's character. Defend your choices.
5. What is the theme of this play?
6. *Feathertop* is a television play. What changes would have to be made before it could be presented as a stage play?
7. This play is a fantasy; the events could not possibly happen. Yet the dramatist has supplied enough "realism" to draw the reader (and viewer) into the story. (**a**) What elements of fantasy does the play contain? (**b**) What qualities give it a feeling of reality?
8. The play *Feathertop* is based upon a short story by Nathaniel Hawthorne. What elements does it have in common with "Dr. Heidegger's Experiment"?

Word Study

Near the beginning of the play, Mother Rigby states that Judge Gookin "wants to rise in the world" and she vows "to give him a leg up." What does she mean by each of these expressions?

    A phrase or expression whose meaning cannot be understood from the ordinary meanings of the words is called an *idiom.* Following are sentences which contain idioms. From the list of definitions below, choose the one definition which explains the italicized idiom in each sentence. Then try to explain the relationship between the literal meaning and the definition.

> *causes . . . to become conceited*
> *latest, most up-to-date*
> *makes a good impression*
> *pay close attention*
> *pompous, empty person*
> *punish*
> *succeed*
> *win a decisive victory*

1. Feathertop's outfit is the *last word* in stylishness.
2. Mother Rigby hopes that Feathertop will *go far* in the world.
3. "Now, *mark me well,*" said Mother Rigby.
4. Judge Gookin is described as a *stuffed shirt.*
5. Success *turns* Judge Gookin's *head.*
6. Feathertop *cuts a fine figure* at the party.

The Author

Critic, teacher, and dramatist, Maurice Valency was born in New York in 1903 and received his education at Columbia University and at the Sorbonne in Paris. He is the author of several well-known plays including *The Thracian Horses* and *Battleship Bismarck.* He is also noted for adapting several plays of Jean Giraudoux, a French dramatist, for the American stage. Among these are *The Madwoman of Chaillot, Ondine,* and *The Apollo of Bellac.*

Bill was to be scalped at daybreak and Sam was to be broiled at the stake. At first neither took the idea seriously.

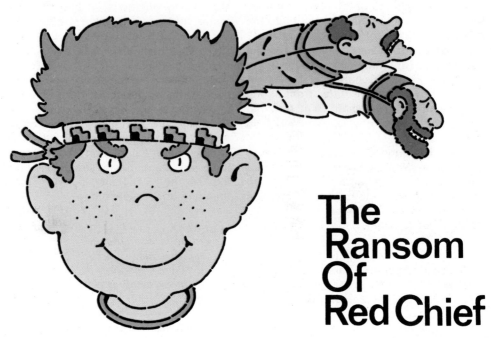

The Ransom Of Red Chief

O. Henry

IT LOOKED like a good thing: but wait till I tell you. We were down South, in Alabama—Bill Driscoll and myself—when this kidnapping idea struck us. It was, as Bill afterward expressed it, "during a moment of temporary mental apparition";[1] but we didn't find that out till later.

There was a town down there, as flat as a flannel-cake, and called Summit, of course. It contained inhabitants of as undeleterious[2] and self-satisfied a class of peasantry as ever clustered around a Maypole.

Bill and me had a joint capital of about six hundred dollars, and we needed just two thousand dollars more to pull off a fraudulent town-lot scheme in Western Illinois with. We talked it over on the front steps of the Hotel. Philoprogenitoveness,[3] says we,

is strong in semi-rural communities; therefore, and for other reasons, a kidnapping project ought to do better there than in the radius of newspapers that send reporters out in plain clothes to stir up talk about such things. We knew that Summit couldn't get after us with anything stronger than constables and, maybe, some lackadaisical bloodhounds and a diatribe or two in the *Weekly Farmers' Budget*. So, it looked good.

We selected for our victim the only child of a prominent citizen named Ebenezer Dorset. The father was respectable and tight, a mortgage fan-

1. **apparition,** Bill means *aberration,* a temporary disorder of the mind.
2. **undeleterious,** harmless.
3. **Philoprogenitoveness,** love of offspring.

cier and a stern, upright collection-plate passer and forecloser. The kid was a boy of ten, with bas-relief freckles, and hair the color of the cover of the magazine you buy at the news-stand when you want to catch a train. Bill and me figured that Ebenezer would melt down for a ransom of two thousand dollars to a cent. But wait till I tell you.

About two miles from Summit was a little mountain, covered with a dense cedar brake. On the rear elevation of this mountain was a cave. There we stored provisions.

One evening after sundown, we drove in a buggy past old Dorset's house. The kid was in the street, throwing rocks at a kitten on the opposite fence.

"Hey, little boy!" says Bill, "would you like to have a bag of candy and a nice ride?"

The boy catches Bill neatly in the eye with a piece of brick.

"That will cost the old man an extra five hundred dollars," says Bill, climbing over the wheel.

That boy put up a fight like a welter-weight cinnamon bear; but, at last, we got him down in the bottom of the buggy and drove away. We took him up to the cave, and I hitched the horse in the cedar brake. After dark I drove the buggy to the little village, three miles away, where we had hired it, and walked back to the mountain.

Bill was pasting court-plaster over the scratches and bruises on his features. There was a fire burning behind the big rock at the entrance of the cave, and the boy was watching a pot of boiling coffee, with two buzzard tail-feathers stuck in his red hair. He points a stick at me when I come up, and says:

"Ha! cursed paleface, do you dare to enter the camp of Red Chief, the terror of the plains?"

"He's all right now," says Bill, rolling up his trousers and examining some bruises on his shins. "We're playing Indian. We're making Buffalo Bill's show look like magic-lantern views of Palestine in the town hall. I'm Old Hank, the Trapper, Red Chief's captive, and I'm to be scalped at daybreak. By Geronimo! that kid can kick hard."

Yes, sir, that boy seemed to be having the time of his life. The fun of camping out in a cave had made him forget that he was a captive himself. He immediately christened me Snake-eye, the Spy, and announced that, when his braves returned from the warpath, I was to be broiled at the stake at the rising of the sun.

Then we had supper; and he filled his mouth full of bacon and bread and gravy, and began to talk. He made a during-dinner speech something like this:

"I like this fine. I never camped out before; but I had a pet 'possum once, and I was nine last birthday. I hate to go to school. Rats ate up sixteen of Jimmy Talbot's aunt's speckled hen's eggs. Are there any real Indians in these woods? I want some more gravy. Does the trees moving make the wind blow? We had five puppies. What makes your nose so red, Hank? My father has lots of money. Are the stars hot? I whipped Ed Walker twice, Saturday. I don't like girls. You dassent catch toads unless with a string. Do oxen make any noise? Why are oranges round? Have you got beds to sleep on in this cave? Amos Murray has got six toes. A parrot can talk, but a monkey or a fish can't. How many does it take to make twelve?"

Every few minutes he would remember that he was a pesky redskin, and pick up his stick rifle and tiptoe to the mouth of the cave to rubber for the scouts of the hated pale-face. Now and then he would let out a war-whoop that made Old Hank the Trapper shiver. That boy had Bill terrorized from the start.

"Red Chief," says I to the kid, "would you like to go home?"

"Aw, what for?" says he. "I don't have any fun at home. I hate to go to school. I like to camp out. You won't take me back home again, Snake-eye, will you?"

"Not right away," says I. "We'll stay here in the cave awhile."

"All right!" says he. "That'll be fine. I never had such fun in all my life."

We went to bed about eleven o'clock. We spread down some wide blankets and quilts and put Red Chief between us. We weren't afraid he'd run away. He kept us awake for three hours, jumping up and reaching for his rifle and screeching: "Hist! pard," in mine and Bill's ears, as the fancied crackle of a twig or the rustle of a leaf revealed to his young imagination the stealthy approach of the outlaw band. At last, I fell into a troubled sleep, and dreamed that I had been kidnapped and chained to a tree by a ferocious pirate with red hair.

Just at daybreak, I was awakened by a series of awful screams from Bill. They weren't yells, or howls, or shouts, or whoops, or yawps, such as you'd expect from a manly set of vocal organs—they were simply indecent, terrifying, humiliating screams, such as women emit when they see ghosts or caterpillars. It's an awful thing to hear a strong, desperate, fat man scream incontinently in a cave at daybreak.

I jumped up to see what the matter was. Red Chief was sitting on Bill's chest, with one hand twined in Bill's hair. In the other he had the sharp case-knife we used for slicing bacon; and he was industriously and realisti-

cally trying to take Bill's scalp, according to the sentence that had been pronounced upon him the evening before.

I got the knife away from the kid and made him lie down again. But, from that moment, Bill's spirit was broken. He laid down on his side of the bed, but he never closed an eye again in sleep as long as that boy was with us. I dozed off for a while, but along toward sun-up I remembered that Red Chief had said I was to be burned at the stake at the rising of the sun. I wasn't nervous or afraid; but I sat up and lit my pipe and leaned against a rock.

"What you getting up so soon for, Sam?" asked Bill.

"Me?" says I. "Oh, I got a kind of pain in my shoulder. I thought sitting up would rest it."

"You're a liar!" says Bill. "You're afraid. You was to be burned at sunrise, and you was afraid he'd do it. And he would, too, if he could find a match. Ain't it awful, Sam? Do you think anybody will pay out money to get a little imp like that back home?"

"Sure," said I. "A rowdy kid like that is just the kind that parents dote on. Now, you and the Chief get up and cook breakfast, while I go up on the top of this mountain and reconnoitre."

I went up on the peak of the little mountain and ran my eye over the contiguous vicinity. Over towards Summit I expected to see the sturdy yeomanry of the village armed with scythes and pitchforks beating the countryside for the dastardly kidnappers. But what I saw was a peaceful landscape dotted with one man ploughing with a dun mule. Nobody was dragging the creek; no couriers dashed hither and yon, bringing tidings of no news to the distracted parents. There was a sylvan attitude of somnolent sleepiness pervading that section of the external outward surface of Alabama that lay exposed to my view. "Perhaps," says I to myself, "it has not yet been discovered that the wolves have borne away the tender lambkin from the fold. Heaven help the wolves!" says I, and I went down the mountain to breakfast.

When I got to the cave I found Bill backed up against the side of it, breathing hard, and the boy threatening to smash him with a rock half as big as a cocoanut.

"He put a red-hot boiled potato down my back," explained Bill, "and then mashed it with his foot; and I boxed his ears. Have you got a gun about you, Sam?"

I took the rock away from the boy and kind of patched up the argument. "I'll fix you," says the kid to Bill. "No man ever yet struck the Red Chief but he got paid for it. You better beware!"

After breakfast the kid takes a piece of leather with strings wrapped around it out of his pocket and goes outside the cave unwinding it.

"What's he up to now?" says Bill, anxiously. "You don't think he'll run away, do you, Sam?"

"No fear of it," says I. "He don't seem to be much of a home body. But we've got to fix up some plan about the ransom. There don't seem to be much excitement around Summit on account of his disappearance; but maybe they haven't realized yet that he's gone. His folks may think he's spending the night with Aunt Jane or one of the neighbors. Anyhow, he'll be missed today. Tonight we must get a message to his father demanding the two thousand dollars for his return."

Just then we heard a kind of war-whoop, such as David might have emitted when he knocked out the champion Goliath.[4] It was a sling that Red Chief had pulled out of his pocket, and he was whirling it around his head.

I dodged, and heard a heavy thud and a kind of a sigh from Bill, like a horse gives out when you take his saddle off. A rock the size of an egg had caught Bill just behind his left ear. He loosened himself all over and fell in the fire across the frying pan of hot water for washing the dishes. I dragged him out and poured cold water on his head for half an hour.

By and by, Bill sits up and feels behind his ear and says: "Sam, do you know who my favorite Biblical character is?"

"Take it easy," says I. "You'll come to your senses presently."

"King Herod,"[5] says he. "You won't go away and leave me here alone, will you, Sam?"

I went out and caught that boy and shook him until his freckles rattled.

"If you don't behave," says I, "I'll take you straight home. Now, are you going to be good, or not?"

"I was only funning," says he, sullenly. "I didn't mean to hurt Old Hank. But what did he hit me for? I'll behave, Snake-eye, if you won't send me home, and if you'll let me play the Black Scout today."

"I don't know the game," says I. "That's for you and Mr. Bill to decide. He's your playmate for the day. I'm going away for a while, on business. Now, you come in and make friends with him and say you are sorry for hurting him, or home you go, at once."

I made him and Bill shake hands, and then I took Bill aside and told him I was going to Poplar Grove, a little village three miles from the cave, and find out what I could about how the kidnapping had been regarded in Summit. Also, I thought it best to send

---

4. **Goliath**, in the Bible, a Philistine giant whom David killed with a stone from a sling.
5. **King Herod**, King of Judea, a tyrant who at the time of Jesus Christ's birth ordered all the male infants of Bethlehem killed.

a peremptory letter to old man Dorset that day, demanding the ransom and dictating how it should be paid.

"You know, Sam," says Bill, "I've stood by you without batting an eye in earthquakes, fire and flood—in poker games, dynamite outrages, police raids, train robberies, and cyclones. I never lost my nerve yet till we kidnapped that two-legged skyrocket of a kid. He's got me going. You won't leave me long with him, will you, Sam?"

"I'll be back some time this afternoon," says I. "You must keep the boy amused and quiet till I return. And now we'll write the letter to old Dorset."

Bill and I got paper and pencil and worked on the letter while Red Chief, with a blanket wrapped around him, strutted up and down, guarding the mouth of the cave. Bill begged me tearfully to make the ransom fifteen hundred dollars instead of two thousand. "I ain't attempting," says he, "to decry the celebrated moral aspect of parental affection, but we're dealing with humans, and it ain't human for anybody to give up two thousand dollars for that forty-pound chunk of freckled wildcat. I'm willing to take a chance at fifteen hundred dollars. You can charge the difference up to me."

So, to relieve Bill, I acceded, and we collaborated a letter that ran this way:

EBENEZER DORSET, ESQ.:

We have your boy concealed in a place far from Summit. It is useless for you or the most skilful detectives to attempt to find him. Absolutely, the only terms on which you can have him restored to you are these: We demand fifteen hundred dollars in large bills for his return; the money to be left at midnight tonight at the same spot and in the same box as your reply—as hereinafter described. If you agree to these terms, send your answer in writing by a solitary messenger tonight at half-past eight o'clock. After crossing Owl Creek on the road to Poplar Grove, there are three large trees about a hundred yards apart, close to the fence of the wheat field on the right-hand side. At the bottom of the fence post, opposite the third tree, will be found a small pasteboard box.

The messenger will place the answer in this box and return immediately to Summit.

If you attempt any treachery or fail to comply with our demand as stated, you will never see your boy again.

If you pay the money as demanded, he will be returned to you safe and well within three hours. These terms are final, and if you do not accede to them no further communication will be attempted.

TWO DESPERATE MEN.

I addressed this letter to Dorset, and put it in my pocket. As I was about to start, the kid comes up to me and says:

"Aw, Snake-eye, you said I could play the Black Scout while you was gone."

"Play it, of course," says I. "Mr. Bill will play with you. What kind of a game is it?"

"I'm the Black Scout," says Red Chief, "and I have to ride to the stockade to warn the settlers that the Indians are coming. I'm tired of playing Indian myself. I want to be the Black Scout."

"All right," says I. "It sounds harmless to me. I guess Mr. Bill will help you foil the pesky savages."

"What am I to do?" asks Bill, looking at the kid suspiciously.

"You are the hoss," says Black Scout. "Get down on your hands and knees. How can I ride to the stockade without a hoss?"

"You'd better keep him interested," said I, "till we get the scheme going. Loosen up."

Bill gets down on his all fours, and

a look comes in his eye like a rabbit's when you catch it in a trap.

"How far is it to the stockade, kid?" he asks, in a husky manner of voice.

"Ninety miles," says the Black Scout. "And you have to hump yourself to get there on time. Whoa, now!"

The Black Scout jumps on Bill's back and digs his heels in his side.

"For Heaven's sake," says Bill, "hurry back, Sam, as soon as you can. I wish we hadn't made the ransom more than a thousand. Say, you quit kicking me or I'll get up and warm you good."

I walked over to Poplar Grove and sat around the postoffice and store, talking with the chaw-bacons that came in to trade. One whiskerando says that he hears Summit is all upset on account of Elder Ebenezer Dorset's boy having been lost or stolen. That was all I wanted to know. I bought some smoking tobacco, referred casually to the price of black-eyed peas, posted my letter surreptitiously, and came away. The postmaster said the mail-carrier would come by in an hour to take the mail to Summit.

When I got back to the cave Bill and the boy were not to be found. I explored the vicinity of the cave, and risked a yodel or two, but there was no response.

So I lighted my pipe and sat down on a mossy bank to await developments.

In about half an hour I heard the bushes rustle, and Bill wabbled out into the little glade in front of the cave. Behind him was the kid, stepping softly like a scout, with a broad grin on his face. Bill stopped, took off his hat, and wiped his face with a red handkerchief. The kid stopped about eight feet behind him.

"Sam," says Bill, "I suppose you'll think I'm a renegade, but I couldn't

help it. I'm a grown person with masculine proclivities and habits of self-defense, but there is a time when all systems of egotism and predominance fail. The boy is gone. I sent him home. All is off. There was martyrs in old times," goes on Bill, "that suffered death rather than give up the particular graft they enjoyed. None of 'em ever was subjugated to such supernatural tortures as I have been. I tried to be faithful to our articles of depredation; but there came a limit."

"What's the trouble, Bill?" I asks him.

"I was rode," says Bill, "the ninety miles to the stockade, not barring an inch. Then, when the settlers was rescued, I was given oats. Sand ain't a palatable substitute. And then, for an hour I had to try to explain to him why there was nothin' in holes, how a road can run both ways, and what makes the grass green. I tell you, Sam, a human can only stand so much. I takes him by the neck of his clothes and drags him down the mountain. On the way he kicks my legs black and blue from the knees down; and I've got to have two or three bites on my thumb and hand cauterized.

"But he's gone"—continues Bill—"gone home. I showed him the road to Summit and kicked him about eight feet nearer there at one kick. I'm sorry we lose the ransom; but it was either that or Bill Driscoll to the madhouse."

Bill is puffing and blowing, but there is a look of ineffable peace and growing content on his rose-pink features.

"Bill," says I, "there isn't any heart disease in your family, is there?"

"No," says Bill, "nothing chronic except malaria and accidents. Why?"

"Then you might turn around," says I, "and have a look behind you."

Bill turns and sees the boy, and

loses his complexion and sits down plump on the ground and begins to pluck aimlessly at grass and little sticks. For an hour I was afraid of his mind. And then I told him that my scheme was to put the whole job through immediately and that we would get the ransom and be off with it by midnight if old Dorset fell in with our proposition. So Bill braced up enough to give the kid a weak sort of a smile and a promise to play the Russian in a Japanese war with him as soon as he felt a little better.

I had a scheme for collecting that ransom without danger of being caught by counterplots that ought to commend itself to professional kidnappers. The tree under which the answer was to be left—and the money later on—was close to the road fence with big, bare fields on all sides. If a gang of constables should be watching for any one to come for the note, they could see him a long way off crossing the fields or in the road. But no, sirree! At half-past eight I was up in that tree as well hidden as a tree toad, waiting for the messenger to arrive.

Exactly on time, a half-grown boy rides up the road on a bicycle, locates the pasteboard box at the foot of the fencepost, slips a folded piece of paper into it, and pedals away again back toward Summit.

I waited an hour and then concluded the thing was square. I slid down the tree, got the note, slipped along the fence till I struck the woods, and was back at the cave in another half an hour. I opened the note, got near the lantern, and read it to Bill. It was written with a pen in a crabbed hand, and the sum and substance of it was this:

TWO DESPERATE MEN.

Gentlemen: I received your letter today by post, in regard to the ransom you ask for the return of my son. I think you are a little high in your demands, and I hereby make you a counterproposition, which I am inclined to believe you will accept. You bring Johnny home and pay me two hundred and fifty dollars in cash, and I agree to take him off your hands. You had better come at night, for the neighbors believe he is lost, and I couldn't be responsible for what they would do to anybody they saw bringing him back. Very respectfully,

 EBENEZER DORSET.

"Great Pirates of Penzance," says I; "of all the impudent——"

But I glanced at Bill, and hesitated. He had the most appealing look in his eyes I ever saw on the face of a dumb or a talking brute.

"Sam," says he, "what's two hundred and fifty dollars, after all? We've got the money. One more night of this kid will send me to a bed in Bedlam.[6] Besides being a thorough gentleman, I think Mr. Dorset is a spendthrift for making us such a liberal offer. You ain't going to let the chance go, are you?"

"Tell you the truth, Bill," says I, "this little he ewe lamb has somewhat got on my nerves too. We'll take him home, pay the ransom, and make our getaway."

We took him home that night. We got him to go by telling him that his father had bought a silver-mounted rifle and a pair of moccasins for him, and we were to hunt bears the next day.

It was just twelve o'clock when we knocked at Ebenezer's front door. Just at the moment when I should have been abstracting the fifteen hundred dollars from the box under the tree, according to the original proposition, Bill was counting out two hundred and fifty dollars into Dorset's hand.

---

6. *Bedlam*, popular name for the Hospital of St. Mary of Bethlehem, insane asylum in London, England.

When the kid found out we were going to leave him at home he started up a howl like a calliope and fastened himself as tight as a leech to Bill's leg. His father peeled him away gradually, like a porous plaster.

"How long can you hold him?" asks Bill.

"I'm not as strong as I used to be," says old Dorset, "but I think I can promise you ten minutes."

"Enough," says Bill. "In ten minutes I shall cross the Central, Southern, and Middle Western States, and be legging it trippingly for the Canadian border."

And, as dark as it was, and as fat as Bill was, and as good a runner as I am, he was a good mile and a half out of Summit before I could catch up with him. ✳

Discussion

1. (a) What circumstances at first make the kidnaping of the Dorset boy attractive to Bill and the narrator? (b) What kind of boy does he appear to be when they first meet him? (c) Is there any indication in the first few pages of the story that the kidnaping may not succeed? Where?

2. (a) How old does the story say the boy is? (b) In your opinion does he act his age? List examples from the story which support your opinion. (c) Of the three, Bill, the narrator, or "Red Chief," who seems the cleverest? Why?

3. (a) Near the middle of the story who seems to be in control? Is this situation ironic in any way? Why or why not? (b) What does Mr. Dorset's letter of reply hint about the way the townsfolk view "Red Chief"? (c) Is his note the kind you would usually expect under such circumstances? Explain.

4. (a) What do Bill and the narrator finally have to do to separate themselves from "Red Chief"? (b) Does the conclusion of the story lead you to believe that they will ever try kidnaping again? (c) Would you say the character of these two men was suited to the role of kidnaper? Explain.

The Author

The personal life of O. Henry, born William Sydney Porter (1862–1910), is as interesting as that of any of the characters he created in his stories. While in the newspaper business in 1894, Porter was called to stand trial for embezzlement of funds from the First National Bank of Austin, Texas. Instead, he took a train to New Orleans where he got work unloading bananas; from there he skipped to Honduras, teaming up with a famous outlaw by the name of Al Jennings. The two of them traveled to South America and Mexico on $30,000 of stolen cash until 1897 when Porter came back to Austin to visit his ailing wife. There he was taken into custody and sentenced to five years in the Ohio State Penitentiary. Throughout these years and the ones that followed in New York City, Porter must have been keeping mental notes on the people he met and the incidents of their lives, notes that were later to blossom into the characteristic "O. Henry" story. When he died at the age of 48, he had written 600 pieces of original fiction.

THE LADY, OR THE TIGER?

Frank R. Stockton

IN THE VERY OLDEN TIME, there lived a semibarbaric king, whose ideas, though somewhat polished and sharpened by the progressiveness of distant Latin neighbors,[1] were still large, florid, and untrammeled, as became the half of him which was barbaric. He was a man of exuberant fancy, and, withal, of an authority so irresistible that, at his will, he turned his varied fancies into facts. He was greatly given to self-communing; and, when he and himself agreed upon anything, the thing was done. When every member of his domestic and political systems moved smoothly in its appointed course, his nature was bland and genial; but whenever there was a little hitch, and some of his orbs got out of their orbits, he was blander and more genial still, for nothing pleased him so much as to make the crooked straight, and crush down uneven places.

Among the borrowed notions by which his barbarism had become semifixed was that of the public arena, in which, by exhibitions of manly and beastly valor, the minds of his subjects were refined and cultured.

But even here the exuberant and barbaric fancy asserted itself. The arena of the king was built, not to give the people an opportunity of hearing the rhapsodies of dying gladiators, nor to enable them to view the inevitable conclusion of a conflict between religious opinions and hungry jaws, but for purposes far better

---

From THE LADY, OR THE TIGER AND OTHER STORIES by Frank R. Stockton (Charles Scribner's Sons, 1884).

1. **Latin neighbors,** peoples of the ancient Roman empire.

adapted to widen and develop the mental energies of the people. This vast amphitheater, with its encircling galleries, its mysterious vaults, and its unseen passages, was an agent of poetic justice, in which crime was punished, or virtue rewarded, by the decrees of an impartial and incorruptible chance.

When a subject was accused of a crime of sufficient importance to interest the king, public notice was given that on an appointed day the fate of the accused person would be decided in the king's arena, a structure which well deserved its name; for, although its form and plan were borrowed from afar, its purpose emanated solely from the brain of this man, who, every barleycorn a king,[2] knew no tradition to which he owed more allegiance than pleased his fancy, and who ingrafted on every adopted form of human thought and action the rich growth of his barbaric idealism.

When all the people had assembled in the galleries, and the king, surrounded by his court, sat high up on his throne of royal state on one side of the arena, he gave a signal, a door beneath him opened, and the accused subject stepped out into the amphitheater. Directly opposite him, on the other side of the enclosed space, were two doors, exactly alike and side by side. It was the duty and the privilege of the person on trial to walk directly to these doors and open one of them. He could open either door he pleased; he was subject to no guidance or influence but that of the aforementioned impartial and incorruptible chance. If he opened the one, there came out of it a hungry tiger, the fiercest and most cruel that could be procured, which immediately sprang upon him and tore him to pieces, as a punishment for his guilt. The mo-

ment that the case of the criminal was thus decided, doleful iron bells were clanged, great wails went up from the hired mourners posted on the outer rim of the arena, and the vast audience, with bowed heads and downcast hearts, wended slowly their homeward way, mourning greatly that one so young and fair, or so old and respected, should have merited so dire a fate.

But if the accused person opened the other door, there came forth from it a lady, the most suitable to his years and station that his majesty could select among his fair subjects; and to this lady he was immediately married, as a reward for his innocence. It mattered not that he might already possess a wife and family or that his affections might be engaged upon an object of his own selection; the king allowed no such subordinate arrangements to interfere with his great scheme of retribution and reward. The exercises, as in the other instance, took place immediately, and in the arena. Another door opened beneath the king, and a priest, followed by a band of choristers and dancing maidens blowing joyous airs on golden horns and treading an epithalamic measure, advanced to where the pair stood, side by side, and the wedding was promptly and cheerily solemnized. Then the gay brass bells rang forth their merry peals, the people shouted glad hurrahs, and the innocent man, preceded by children strewing flowers on his path, led his bride to his home.

This was the king's semibarbaric method of administering justice. Its perfect fairness is obvious. The criminal could not know out of which

2. *every barleycorn a king.* A barleycorn is a measure equal to one third of an inch. However, the term John Barleycorn is a humorous personification of barley as the source of liquor. The author is combining the usual phrase "every inch a king" with the concept of John Barleycorn to create a humorous effect.

door would come the lady; he opened either he pleased, without having the slightest idea whether, in the next instant, he was to be devoured or married. On some occasions the tiger came out of one door, and on some out of the other. The decisions of this tribunal were not only fair, they were positively determinate; the accused person was instantly punished if he found himself guilty, and, if innocent, he was rewarded on the spot, whether he liked it or not. There was no escape from the judgments of the king's arena.

The institution was a very popular one. When the people gathered together on one of the great trial days, they never knew whether they were to witness a bloody slaughter or a hilarious wedding. This element of uncertainty lent an interest to the occasion which it could not otherwise have attained. Thus, the masses were entertained and pleased, and the thinking part of the community could bring no charge of unfairness against this plan; for did not the accused person have the whole matter in his own hands?

This semibarbaric king had a daughter as blooming as his most florid fancies and with a soul as fervent and imperious as his own. As is usual in such cases, she was the apple of his eye and was loved by him above all humanity. Among his courtiers was a young man of that fineness of blood and lowness of station common to the conventional heroes of romance who love royal maidens. This royal maiden was well satisfied with her lover, for he was handsome and brave to a degree unsurpassed in all this kingdom, and she loved him with an ardor that had enough of barbarism in it to make it exceedingly warm and strong. This love affair moved on happily for many months, until one day the king hap-

pened to discover its existence. He did not hesitate nor waver in regard to his duty in the premises. The youth was immediately cast into prison, and a day was appointed for his trial in the king's arena. This, of course, was an especially important occasion, and his majesty, as well as all the people, was greatly interested in the workings and development of this trial. Never before had such a case occurred; never before had a subject dared to love the daughter of a king. In after-years such things became commonplace enough, but then they were, in no slight degree, novel and startling.

The tiger cages of the kingdom were searched for the most savage and relentless beasts, from which the fiercest monster might be selected for the arena, and the ranks of maiden youth and beauty throughout the land were carefully surveyed by competent judges, in order that the young man might have a fitting bride in case fate did not determine for him a different destiny. Of course, everybody knew that the deed with which the accused was charged had been done. He had loved the princess, and neither he, she, nor anyone else thought of denying the fact, but the king would not think of allowing any fact of this kind to interfere with the workings of the tribunal, in which he took such great delight and satisfaction. No matter how the affair turned out, the youth would be disposed of, and the king would take an aesthetic pleasure in watching the course of events, which would determine whether or not the young man had done wrong in allowing himself to love the princess.

The appointed day arrived. From far and near the people gathered and thronged the great galleries of the arena, and crowds, unable to gain admittance, massed themselves against its outside walls. The king and his court were in their places opposite the twin doors—those fateful portals so terrible in their similarity.

All was ready. The signal was given. A door beneath the royal party opened, and the lover of the princess walked into the arena. Tall, beautiful, fair, his appearance was greeted with a low hum of admiration and anxiety. Half the audience had not known so grand a youth had lived among them. No wonder the princess loved him! What a terrible thing for him to be there!

As the youth advanced into the arena, he turned, as the custom was, to bow to the king, but he did not think at all of that royal personage; his eyes were fixed upon the princess who sat to the right of her father. Had it not been for the moiety of barbarism in her nature, it is probable that lady would not have been there, but her intense and fervid soul would not allow her to be absent on an occasion in which she was so terribly interested.

From the moment that the decree had gone forth, that her lover should decide his fate in the king's arena, she had thought of nothing, night or day, but this great event and the various subjects connected with it. Possessed of more power, influence, and force of character than anyone who had ever before been interested in such a case, she had done what no other person had done—she had possessed herself of the secret of the doors. She knew in which of the two rooms that lay behind those doors stood the cage of the tiger, with its open front, and in which waited the lady. Through these thick doors, heavily curtained with skins on the inside, it was impossible that any noise or suggestion should come from within to the person who should approach to raise the latch of one of them, but gold and the power of a woman's will had brought the secret to the princess.

And not only did she know in which room stood the lady ready to emerge, all blushing and radiant, should her door be opened, but she knew who the lady was. It was one of the fairest and loveliest of the damsels of the court who had been selected as the reward of the accused youth should he be proved innocent of the crime of aspiring to one so far above him, and the princess hated her. Often had she seen, or imagined that she had seen, this fair creature throwing glances of admiration upon the person of her lover, and sometimes she thought these glances were perceived and even returned. Now and then she had seen them talking together; it was but for a moment or two, but much can be said in a brief space; it may have been on most unimportant topics, but how could she know that? The girl was lovely, but she had dared to raise her eyes to the loved one of the princess, and, with all the intensity of the savage blood transmitted to her through long lines of wholly barbaric ancestors, she hated the woman who blushed and trembled behind that silent door.

When her lover turned and looked at her, and his eye met hers as she sat there paler and whiter than anyone in the vast ocean of anxious faces about her, he saw, by that power of quick perception which is given to those whose souls are one, that she knew behind which door crouched the tiger and behind which stood the lady. He had expected her to know it. He understood her nature, and his soul was assured that she would never rest until she had made plain to herself this thing, hidden to all other lookers-on, even to the king. The only hope for the youth in which there was any element of certainty was based upon the success of the princess in discovering this mystery, and the moment he looked upon her, he saw she had succeeded, as in his soul he knew she would succeed.

Then it was that his quick and anxious glance asked the question: "Which?" It was as plain to her as if he shouted it from where he stood. There was not an instant to be lost. The question was asked in a flash; it must be answered in another.

Her right arm lay on the cushioned parapet before her. She raised her hand, and made a slight, quick movement toward the right. No one but her lover saw her. Every eye but his was fixed on the man in the arena.

He turned, and with a firm and rapid step he walked across the empty space. Every heart stopped beating, every breath was held, every eye was fixed immovably upon that man. Without the slightest hesitation, he went to the door on the right and opened it.

Now, the point of the story is this: Did the tiger come out of that door, or did the lady?

The more we reflect upon this question, the harder it is to answer. It involves a study of the human heart which leads us through devious mazes of passion, out of which it is difficult to find our way. Think of it, fair reader, not as if the decision of the question depended upon yourself, but upon that hot-blooded, semibarbaric princess, her soul at a white heat beneath the combined fires of despair and jealousy. She had lost him, but who should have him?

How often, in her waking hours and in her dreams, had she started in wild horror and covered her face with her hands as she thought of her lover opening the door on the other side of which waited the cruel fangs of the tiger!

But how much oftener had she seen him at the other door! How in her grievous reveries had she gnashed her teeth and torn her hair, when she saw his start of rapturous delight as he opened the door of the lady! How her soul had burned in agony when she had seen him rush to meet that woman, with her flushing cheek and sparkling eye of triumph; when she had seen him lead her forth, his whole frame kindled with the joy of recovered life; when she had heard the glad shouts from the multitude, and the wild ringing of the happy bells; when she had seen the priest, with his joyous followers, advance to the couple and make them man and wife before her very eyes; and when she had seen them walk away together upon their path of flowers, followed by the tremendous shouts of the hilarious multitude, in which her one despairing shriek was lost and drowned!

Would it not be better for him to die at once, and go to wait for her in the blessed regions of semibarbaric futurity?

And yet, that awful tiger, those shrieks, that blood!

Her decision had been indicated in an instant, but it had been made after days and nights of anguished deliberation. She had known she would be asked, she had decided what she would answer, and, without the slightest hesitation, she had moved her hand to the right.

The question of her decision is one not to be lightly considered, and it is not for me to presume to set myself up as the one person able to answer it. And so I leave it with all of you: Which came out of the opened door—the lady, or the tiger?   *

Discussion

1. (a) What kind of ruler would a "semi-barbaric" king be? **(b)** Describe the king's method for achieving justice.

2. (a) Describe the character of the princess. **(b)** What is her attitude toward the young lady selected to be the young man's bride? **(c)** How does this attitude complicate her position?

3. What do you think the princess decides? Give reasons for your views.

4. (a) What elements of a traditional fairy tale does this story have? **(b)** How does it differ from traditional fairy tales?

5. (a) Reread the third paragraph of the story. Why do you think the author uses such flowery language? **(b)** Find examples of verbal irony.

6. (a) How would you describe the tone of this selection? **(b)** Do you think the tone is appropriate for the subject? Explain.

7. Do you think this story qualifies as a well-told tale? Give reasons for your answer.

Word Study

Listed below are several words which Stockton uses in his story. Replace the italicized phrases in each of the following sentences with the one word which expresses the meaning of the italicized phrase. You may refer to your Glossary for help.

administered	*emanated*
aspired	*procured*
attained	*solemnized*
deliberated	*untrammeled*

1. The king had an unusual method by which he *managed the affairs of* justice in his kingdom.

2. The king believed that he had *arrived at* a perfect system of reward and punishment.

3. If the accused man was innocent, the marriage was immediately *observed with ceremony*.

4. The young man *had an ambition* to marry the princess.

5. The king *obtained by effort* the fiercest tiger available.

6. The princess *weighed in her mind* the consequences of her decision.

The Author

Frank R. Stockton was born in 1834 and grew up in the city of Philadelphia. As a boy Stockton won several literary prizes and began to write stories for a young people's magazine. Starting in 1873, he served for eight years as an editor of *St. Nicholas Magazine,* a popular periodical for children. When he began writing for adults in 1879, he continued to use the absurd situations and the qualities of fantasy which had characterized his children's stories.

"The Lady, or the Tiger?" first appeared in *Century Magazine* in 1882 and was an immediate success. This story later formed the title piece for a collection of Frank Stockton's short stories. His most famous novel is *The Casting Away of Mrs. Lecks and Mrs. Aleshine.*

See
FORESHADOWING
Handbook
of Literary
Terms
page 547

He was alone, and it was seventy-five
degrees below zero. Could he make it to
camp before the cold conquered him?
Notice the clues which foreshadow
the outcome of this story.

to build a fire

Jack London

DAY HAD BROKEN cold and gray, exceedingly cold and gray, when the man turned aside from the main Yukon trail[1] and climbed the high earth bank, where a dim and little-traveled trail led eastward through the fat spruce timberland. It was a steep bank, and he paused for breath at the top, excusing the act to himself by looking at his watch. It was nine o'clock. There was no sun or hint of sun, though there was not a cloud in the sky. It was a clear day, and yet there seemed an intangible pall over the face of things, a subtle gloom that made the day dark and that was due to the absence of sun. This fact did not worry the man. He was used to the lack of sun. It had been days since he had seen the sun, and he knew that a few more days must pass before that cheerful orb, due south, would just peep above the skyline and dip immediately from view.

The man flung a look back along the way he had come. The Yukon lay a mile wide and hidden under three feet of ice. On top of this ice were as many feet of snow. It was all pure white, rolling in gentle undulations where the ice jams of the freeze-up had formed. North and south, as far as his eye could see, it was unbroken white, save for a dark hairline that curved and twisted from around the spruce-covered island to the south and that curved and twisted away into the north, where it disappeared

From LOST FACES by Jack London. Publis⌐
Macmillan Company (1909). Reprinted by ⌐
the estate of the author.
1. **Yukon** (ū′ kon) *trail,* a trail which ⌐
Yukon, a territory in northwestern Car⌐

Elmer Jacols

behind another spruce-covered island. This dark hairline was the trail —the main trail—that led south five hundred miles to the Chilcoot Pass,[2] Dyea,[3] and salt water, and that led north seventy miles to Dawson,[4] and still on to the north a thousand miles to Nulato,[5] and finally to St. Michael on the Bering Sea,[6] a thousand miles and half a thousand more.

But all this—the mysterious, far-reaching hairline trail, the absence of sun from the sky, the tremendous cold, and the strangeness and weirdness of it all—made no impression on the man. It was not because he was long used to it. He was a new-comer in the land, a *chechaquo*, and this was his first winter. The trouble with him was that he was without imagination. He was quick and alert in the things of life, but only in the things, not in the significances. Fifty degrees below zero meant eighty-odd degrees of frost. Such a fact impressed him as being cold and uncomfortable, and that was all. It did not lead him to meditate upon his frailty as a creature of temperature, and upon man's frailty in general, able only to live within certain narrow limits of heat and cold; and, from there on, it did not lead him to the conjectural field of immortality and man's place in the universe. Fifty degrees below zero stood for a bite of frost that hurt and that must be guarded against by the use of mittens, ear flaps, warm moccasins, and thick socks. Fifty degrees below zero was to him just precisely fifty degrees below zero. That there should be anything more to it than that was a thought that never entered his head.

As he turned to go on, he spat speculatively. There was a sharp, explosive crackle that startled him. He spat again. And again, in the air, be-fore it could fall to the snow, the spittle crackled. He knew that at fifty below spittle cracked on the snow, but this spittle had crackled in the air. Undoubtedly it was colder than fifty below—how much colder he did not know. But the temperature did not matter. He was bound for the old claim on the left fork of Henderson Creek where the boys were already. They had come over across the divide from the Indian Creek country, while he had come the roundabout way to take a look at the possibilities of getting out logs in the spring from the islands in the Yukon. He would be in to camp by six o'clock; a bit after dark, it was true, but the boys would be there, a fire would be going, and a hot supper would be ready. As for lunch, he pressed his hand against the protruding bundle under his jacket. It was also under his shirt, wrapped up in a handkerchief and lying against the naked skin. It was the only way to keep the biscuits from freezing. He smiled agreeably to him-self as he thought of those biscuits, each cut open and sopped in bacon grease, and each enclosing a generous slice of fried bacon.

He plunged in among the big spruce trees. The trail was faint. A foot of snow had fallen since the last sled had passed over, and he was glad he was without a sled, traveling light. In fact, he carried nothing but the lunch wrapped in the handker-chief. He was surprised, however, at the cold. It certainly was cold, he con-cluded, as he rubbed his numb nose and cheekbones with his mittened hand. He was a warm-whiskered man,

---

2. **Chilcoot** (chil'küt) **Pass,** a mountain pass in British Columbia, the territory just south of the Yukon.
3. **Dyea,** (dī'a), at the time of the story, a town in western British Columbia, south of Chilcoot Pass.
4. **Dawson,** a city in the western part of the Yukon.
5. **Nulato** (nü lä'tō), a city in western Alaska.
6. **St. Michael on the Bering Sea,** a port city on the west-ern coast of Alaska.

but the hair on his face did not protect the high cheekbones and the eager nose that thrust itself aggressively into the frosty air.

At the man's heels trotted a dog, a big native husky, the proper wolf dog, gray-coated and without any visible or temperamental difference from its brother, the wild wolf. The animal was depressed by the tremendous cold. It knew that it was no time for traveling. Its instinct told it a truer tale than was told to the man by the man's judgment. In reality, it was not merely colder than fifty below zero; it was colder than sixty below, than seventy below. It was seventy-five below zero. Since the freezing point is thirty-two above zero, it meant that one hundred and seven degrees of frost obtained. The dog did not know anything about thermometers. Possibly in its brain there was no sharp consciousness of a condition of very cold such as was in the man's brain. But the brute had its instinct. It experienced a vague but menacing apprehension that subdued it and made it slink along at the man's heels, and that made it question eagerly every unwonted movement of the man as if expecting him to go into camp or to seek shelter somewhere and build a fire. The dog had learned fire, and it wanted fire, or else to burrow under the snow and cuddle its warmth away from the air.

The frozen moisture of its breathing had settled on its fur in a fine powder of frost, and especially were its jowls, muzzle, and eyelashes whitened by its crystalled breath. The man's red beard and mustache were likewise frosted, but more solidly, the deposit taking the form of ice and increasing with every warm, moist breath he exhaled. Also, the man was chewing tobacco, and the muzzle of ice held his lips so rigidly that he was unable to clear his chin when he expelled the juice. The result was that a crystal beard of the color and solidity of amber was increasing its length on his chin. If he fell down it would shatter itself, like glass, into brittle fragments. But he did not mind the appendage. It was the penalty all tobacco chewers paid in that country, and he had been out before in two cold snaps. They had not been so cold as this, he knew, but by the spirit thermometer at Sixty Mile[7] he knew they had been registered at fifty below and at fifty-five.

He held on through the level stretch of woods for several miles, crossed a wide flat of nigger heads, and dropped down a bank to the frozen bed of a small stream. This was Henderson Creek, and he knew he was ten miles from the forks. He looked at his watch. It was ten o'clock. He was making four miles an hour, and he calculated that he would arrive at the forks at half-past twelve. He decided to celebrate that event by eating his lunch there.

The dog dropped in again at his heels, with a tail drooping discouragement, as the man swung along the creek bed. The furrow of the old sled trail was plainly visible, but a dozen inches of snow covered the marks of the last runners. In a month no man had come up or down that silent creek. The man held steadily on. He was not much given to thinking, and just then, particularly, he had nothing to think about save that he would eat lunch at the forks and that at six o'clock he would be in camp with the boys. There was nobody to talk to, and, had there been, speech would have been impossible because of the ice muzzle on his mouth. So he continued monotonously to chew tobacco

---

7. **Sixty Mile**, a village in the western part of the Yukon near the Alaskan border.

and to increase the length of his amber beard.

Once in a while the thought reiterated itself that it was very cold and that he had never experienced such cold. As he walked along he rubbed his cheekbones and nose with the back of his mittened hand. He did this automatically, now and again changing hands. But, rub as he would, the instant he stopped his cheekbones went numb and the following instant the end of his nose went numb. He was sure to frost his cheeks; he knew that, and experienced a pang of regret that he had not devised a nose strap of the sort Bud wore in cold snaps. Such a strap passed across the cheeks as well and saved them. But it didn't matter much, after all. What were frosted cheeks? A bit painful, that was all; they were never serious.

Empty as the man's mind was of thoughts, he was keenly observant, and he noticed the changes in the creek, the curves and bends and timber jams, and always he sharply noted where he placed his feet. Once, coming around a bend, he shied abruptly, like a startled horse, curved away from the place where he had been walking, and retreated several paces back along the trail. The creek he knew was frozen clear to the bottom—no creek could contain water in that arctic winter—but he knew also that there were springs that bubbled out from the hillsides and ran along under the snow and on top of the ice of the creek. He knew that the coldest snaps never froze these springs, and he knew likewise their danger. They were traps. They hid pools of water under the snow that might be three inches deep, or three feet. Sometimes a skin of ice half an inch thick covered them, and in turn was covered by the snow. Sometimes there were alternate layers of water and ice skin, so that when one broke through, he kept on breaking through for a while, sometimes wetting himself to the waist.

That was why he had shied in such panic. He had felt the give under his feet and heard the crackle of a snow-hidden ice skin. And to get his feet wet in such a temperature meant trouble and danger. At the very least it meant delay, for he would be forced to stop and build a fire, and, under its protection, to bare his feet while he dried his socks and moccasins. He stood and studied the creek bed and its banks and decided that the flow of water came from the right. He reflected awhile, rubbing his nose and cheeks, then skirted to the left, stepping gingerly and testing the footing for each step. Once clear of the danger, he took a fresh chew of tobacco and swung along at his four-mile gait.

In the course of the next two hours he came upon several similar traps. Usually the snow above the hidden pools had a sunken, candied appearance that advertised the danger. Once again, however, he had a close call, and once, suspecting danger, he compelled the dog to go on in front. The dog did not want to go. It hung back until the man shoved it forward, and then it went quickly across the white, unbroken surface. Suddenly it broke through, floundered to one side, and got away to firmer footing. It had wet its forefeet and legs, and almost immediately the water that clung to it turned to ice. It made quick efforts to lick the ice off its legs, then dropped down in the snow and began to bite out the ice that had formed between the toes. This was a matter of instinct. To permit the ice to remain would mean sore feet. It did not know this. It merely obeyed the mysterious prompting that arose from the deep crypts of its being. But the man knew, having achieved a judgment on the subject, and he removed the mitten from his right hand and helped tear out the ice particles. He did not expose his fingers more than a minute, and was astonished at the swift numbness that smote them. It certainly was cold. He pulled on the mitten hastily, and beat the hand savagely across his chest.

At twelve o'clock the day was at its brightest. Yet the sun was too far south on its winter journey to clear the horizon. The bulge of the earth intervened between it and Henderson Creek, where the man walked under a clear sky at noon and cast no shadow. At half-past twelve, to the minute, he arrived at the forks of the creek. He was pleased at the speed he had made. If he kept it up, he would certainly be with the boys by six. He unbuttoned his jacket and shirt and drew forth his lunch. The action consumed no more than a quarter of a minute, yet in that brief moment the numbness laid hold of the exposed fingers. He did not put the mitten on, but, instead, struck the fingers a dozen sharp smashes against his leg. Then he sat down on a snow-covered log to eat. The sting that followed upon the striking of his fingers against his leg ceased so quickly that he was startled. He had no chance to take a bite of biscuit. He struck the fingers repeatedly and returned them to the mitten, baring the other hand for the purpose of eating. He tried to take a mouthful but the ice muzzle prevented. He had forgotten to build a fire and thaw out. He chuckled at his foolishness, and as he chuckled he noted the numbness creeping into the exposed fingers. Also, he noted that the stinging which had first come to his toes when he sat down was already passing away. He wondered whether the toes were warm or numb. He moved them inside the moccasins and decided that they were numb.

He pulled the mitten on hurriedly and stood up. He was a bit frightened. He stamped up and down until the stinging returned into the feet. It certainly was cold, was his thought. That man from Sulphur Creek had spoken the truth when telling how cold it sometimes got in the country. And he had laughed at him at the time! That showed one must not be too sure of things. There was no mistake about it, it *was* cold. He strode up and down, stamping his feet and threshing his arms, until reassured by the returning warmth. Then he got out matches and proceeded to make a fire. From the undergrowth, where high water of the previous spring had lodged a supply of seasoned twigs, he got his firewood. Working carefully from a small beginning, he soon had a roaring fire, over which he thawed the ice from his face and in the protection of which he ate his biscuits. For the moment the cold of space was outwitted. The dog took satisfaction in the fire, stretching out close enough for warmth and far enough away to escape being singed.

When the man had finished, he filled his pipe and took his comfortable time over a smoke. Then he pulled on his mittens, settled the ear flaps of his cap firmly about his ears, and took the creek trail up the left fork. The dog was disappointed and yearned back toward the fire. This man did not know cold. Possibly all the generations of his ancestry had been ignorant of cold, of real cold, of cold one hundred and seven degrees below freezing point. But the dog knew; all its ancestry knew, and it had inherited the knowledge. And it knew that it was not good to walk abroad in such fearful cold. It was the time to lie snug in a hole in the snow and wait for a curtain of cloud to be drawn across the face of outer space whence this cold came. On the other hand, there was no keen intimacy between the dog and the man. The one was the toil slave of the other, and the only caresses it had ever received were the caresses of the whip lash and of harsh and menacing throat sounds that threatened the whip lash. So the dog made no effort to communicate its apprehension to the man. It was not concerned in the welfare of the man; it was for its own sake that it yearned back toward the fire. But the man whistled and spoke to it with the sound of whip lashes, and the dog swung in at the man's heels and followed after.

The man took a chew of tobacco and proceeded to start a new amber beard. Also, his moist breath quickly powdered with white his mustache, eyebrows, and lashes. There did not seem to be so many springs on the left fork of the Henderson, and for half an hour the man saw no signs of any. And then it happened. At a place where there were no signs, where the soft, unbroken snow seemed to advertise solidity beneath, the man broke through. It was not deep. He wet himself halfway to the knees before he floundered out to the firm crust.

He was angry and cursed his luck aloud. He had hoped to get into camp with the boys at six o'clock, and this would delay him an hour, for he would have to build a fire and dry out his footgear. This was imperative at that low temperature—he knew that much; and he turned aside to the bank which he climbed. On top, tangled in the underbrush about the trunks of several small spruce trees, was a high-water deposit of dry firewood—sticks and twigs, principally, but also larger portions of seasoned branches and fine, dry, last year's grasses. He threw down several large pieces on top of the snow. This served for a foundation and prevented the young flame from drowning itself in the snow it otherwise would melt. The flame he got by touching a match to a small shred of birch bark that he took from his pocket. This burned even more readily than paper. Placing it on the foundation, he fed the young flame with wisps of dry grass and with the tiniest dry twigs.

He worked slowly and carefully, keenly aware of his danger. Gradually, as the flame grew stronger, he increased the size of the twigs with which he fed it. He squatted in the snow, pulling the twigs out from their entanglement in the brush and feeding directly to the flame. He knew there must be no failure. When it is seventy-five below zero, a man must not fail in his first attempt to build a fire—that is, if his feet are wet. If his feet are dry, and he fails, he can run along the trail for half a mile and restore his circulation. But the circulation of wet and freezing feet cannot be restored by running when it is seventy-five below. No matter how fast he runs, the wet feet will freeze the harder.

All this the man knew. The old-timer on Sulphur Creek had told him about it the previous fall, and now he was appreciating the advice. Already all sensation had gone out of his feet. To build a fire he had been forced to remove his mittens, and the fingers had quickly gone numb. His pace of four miles an hour had kept his heart pumping blood to the surface of his body and to all the extremities. But the instant he stopped, the action of the pump eased down. The cold of space smote the unprotected tip of the planet, and he, being of that unprotected tip, received the full force of the blow. The blood of his body recoiled before it. The blood was alive, like the dog, and like the dog it wanted to hide away and cover itself up from the fearful cold. So long as he walked four miles an hour, he pumped that blood, willy-nilly, to the surface, but now it ebbed away and sank down into the recesses of his body. The extremities were the first to feel its absence. His wet feet froze the faster, and his exposed fingers numbed the faster, though they had not yet begun to freeze. Nose and cheeks were already freezing, while the skin of all his body chilled as it lost its blood.

But he was safe. Toes and nose and cheeks would be only touched by the frost, for the fire was beginning to burn with strength. He was feeding it with twigs the size of his finger. In another minute he would be able to feed it with branches the size of his wrist, and then he could remove his wet footgear, and, while it dried, he could keep his naked feet warm by the fire, rubbing them at first, of course, with snow. The fire was a success. He was safe. He remembered the advice of the old-timer on Sulphur Creek and smiled. The old-timer had been very serious in laying down the law that no man must travel alone in the Klondike[8] after fifty below. Well, here he was; he had had the accident; he was alone; and he had saved himself. Those old-timers were rather womanish, some of them, he thought. All a man had to do was to keep his head, and he was all right. Any man who was a man could travel alone. But it was surprising, the rapidity with which his cheeks and nose were freezing. And he had not thought his fingers could go lifeless in so short a time. Lifeless they were, for he could scarcely make them move together to grip a twig, and they seemed remote from his body and from him. When he

touched a twig, he had to look and see whether or not he had hold of it. The wires were pretty well down between him and his finger ends.

All of which counted for little. There was the fire, snapping and crackling and promising life with every dancing flame. He started to untie his moccasins. They were coated with ice; the thick German socks were like sheaths of iron halfway to the knees; and the moccasin strings were like rods of steel all twisted and knotted as by some conflagration. For a moment he tugged with his numb fingers; then, realizing the folly of it, he drew his sheath knife.

But before he could cut the strings, it happened. It was his own fault or, rather, his mistake. He should not have built the fire under the spruce tree. He should have built it in the open. But it had been easier to pull the twigs from the brush and drop them directly on the fire. Now the tree under which he had done this carried a weight of snow on its boughs. No wind had blown for weeks, and each bough was fully freighted. Each time he had pulled a twig he had communicated a slight agitation to the tree—an imperceptible agitation, so far as he was concerned, but an agitation sufficient to bring about the disaster. High up in the tree one bough capsized its load of snow. This fell on the boughs beneath, capsizing them. This process continued, spreading out and involving the whole tree. It grew like an avalanche, and it descended without warning upon the man and the fire, and the fire was blotted out! Where it had burned was a mantle of fresh and disordered snow.

The man was shocked. It was as though he had just heard his own sentence of death. For a moment he

8. **Klondike** (klon′ dĭk), a region in the western part of the Yukon territory.

sat and stared at the spot where the fire had been. Then he grew very calm. Perhaps the old-timer on Sulphur Creek was right. If he had only had a trail mate he would have been in no danger now. The trail mate could have built the fire. Well, it was up to him to build the fire over again, and this second time there must be no failure. Even if he succeeded, he would most likely lose some toes. His feet must be badly frozen by now, and there would be some time before the second fire was ready.

Such were his thoughts, but he did not sit and think them. He was busy all the time they were passing through his mind. He made a new foundation for a fire, this time in the open, where no treacherous tree could blot it out. Next he gathered dry grasses and tiny twigs from the high-water flotsam. He could not bring his fingers together to pull them out, but he was able to gather them by the handful. In this way he got many rotten twigs and bits of green moss that were undesirable, but it was the best he could do. He worked methodically, even collecting an armful of the larger branches to be used later when the fire gathered strength. And all the while the dog sat and watched him, a certain yearning wistfulness in its eyes, for it looked upon him as the fire provider, and the fire was slow in coming.

When all was ready, the man reached in his pocket for a second piece of birch bark. He knew the bark was there, and, though he could not feel it with his fingers, he could hear its crisp rustling as he fumbled for it. Try as he would, he could not clutch hold of it. And all the time, in his consciousness, was the knowledge that each instant his feet were freezing. This thought tended to put him in a panic, but he fought against it and kept calm. He pulled on his mittens with his teeth, and threshed his arms back and forth, beating his hands with all his might against his sides. He did this sitting down, and he stood up to do it; and all the while the dog sat in the snow, its wolf brush of a tail curled around warmly over its forefeet, its sharp wolf ears pricked forward intently as it watched the man. And the man, as he beat and threshed with his arms and hands, felt a great surge of envy as he regarded the creature that was warm and secure in its natural covering.

After a time he was aware of the first faraway signals of sensation in his beaten fingers. The faint tingling grew stronger till it evolved into a stinging ache that was excruciating but which the man hailed with satisfaction. He stripped the mitten from his right hand and fetched forth the birch bark. The exposed fingers were quickly going numb again. Next he brought out his bunch of sulphur matches. But the tremendous cold had already driven the life out of his fingers. In his effort to separate one match from the others, the whole bunch fell in the snow. He tried to pick it out of the snow, but failed. The dead fingers could neither touch nor clutch. He was very careful. He drove the thought of his freezing feet, and nose, and cheeks, out of his mind, devoting his whole soul to the matches. He watched, using the sense of vision in place of that of touch, and when he saw his fingers on each side of the bunch, he closed them—that is, he willed to close them, for the wires were down, and the fingers did not obey. He pulled the mitten on the right hand, and beat it fiercely against his knee. Then, with both mittened hands, he scooped the bunch of matches, along with much snow, into his lap. Yet he was no better off.

After some manipulation he managed to get the bunch between the heels of his mittened hands. In this fashion he carried it to his mouth. The ice crackled and snapped when, by a violent effort, he opened his mouth. He drew the lower jaw in, curled the upper lip out of the way, and scraped the bunch with his upper teeth in order to separate a match. He succeeded in getting one, which he dropped on his lap. He was no better off. He could not pick it up. Then he devised a way. He picked it up in his teeth and scratched it on his leg. Twenty times he scratched before he succeeded in lighting it. As it flamed he held it with his teeth to the birch bark. But the burning brimstone went up his nostrils and into his lungs, causing him to cough spasmodically. The match fell into the snow and went out.

The old-timer on Sulphur Creek was right, he thought in the moment of controlled despair that ensued: after fifty below, a man should travel with a partner. He beat his hands but failed in exciting any sensation. Suddenly he bared both hands, removing the mittens with his teeth. He caught the whole bunch between the heels of his hands. His arm muscles not being frozen enabled him to press the hand heels tightly against the matches. Then he scratched the bunch along his leg. It flared into flame, seventy sulphur matches at once! There was no wind to blow them out. He kept his head to one side to escape the strangling fumes, and held the blazing bunch to the birch bark. As he so held it, he became aware of sensation in his hand. His flesh was burning. He could smell it. Deep down below the surface he could feel it. The sensation developed into pain that grew acute. And still he endured it, holding the flame of the matches clumsily to the bark that would not light readily because his own burning hands were in the way, absorbing most of the flame.

At last, when he could endure no more, he jerked his hands apart. The blazing matches fell sizzling into the snow, but the birch bark was alight. He began laying dry grasses and the tiniest twigs on the flame. He could not pick and choose, for he had to lift the fuel between the heels of his hands. Small pieces of rotten wood and green moss clung to the twigs, and he bit them off as well as he could with his teeth. He cherished the flame carefully and awkwardly. It meant life, and it must not perish. The withdrawal of blood from the surface of his body now made him begin to shiver, and he grew more awkward. A large piece of green moss fell squarely on the little fire. He tried to poke it out with his fingers, but his shivering frame made him poke too far, and he disrupted the nucleus of the little fire, the burning grasses and tiny twigs separating and scattering. He tried to poke them together again, but in spite of the tenseness of the effort, his shivering got away with him, and the twigs were hopelessly scattered. Each twig gushed a puff of smoke and went out. The fire provider had failed. As he looked apathetically about him, his eyes chanced on the dog, sitting across the ruins of the fire from him, in the snow, making restless, hunching movements, slightly lifting one forefoot and then the other, shifting its weight back and forth on them with wistful eagerness.

The sight of the dog put a wild idea into his head. He remembered the tale of the man, caught in a blizzard, who killed a steer and crawled inside the carcass and so was saved. He would kill the dog and bury his hands in the warm body until the numbness went out of them. Then he could build another fire. He spoke to the dog, calling it to him, but in his voice was a strange note of fear that frightened the animal, who had never known the man to speak in such a way before. Something was the matter, and its suspicious nature sensed danger—it knew not what danger, but somewhere, somehow, in its brain arose an apprehension of the man. It flattened its ears down at the sound of the man's voice, and its restless, hunching movements and the liftings and shiftings of its forefeet became more pronounced; but it would not come to the man. He got on his hands and knees and crawled toward the dog. This unusual posture again excited suspicion, and the animal sidled mincingly away.

The man sat up in the snow for a moment and struggled for calmness. Then he pulled on his mittens, by means of his teeth, and got up on his feet. He glanced down at first in order to assure himself that he was really standing up, for the absence of sensation in his feet left him unrelated to the earth. His erect position in itself started to drive the webs of suspicion from the dog's mind, and when he spoke peremptorily, with the sound of whip lashes in his voice, the dog rendered its customary allegiance and came to him. As it came within reaching distance, the man lost his control. His arms flashed out to the dog, and he experienced genuine surprise when he discovered that his hands could not clutch, that there was neither bend nor feeling in the fingers. He had forgotten for the moment that they were frozen and that they were freezing more and more. All this happened quickly, and before the animal could get away, he encircled its body with his arms. He sat down in the snow and in this fashion held the dog, while it snarled and whined and struggled.

But it was all he could do, hold its body encircled in his arms and sit there. He realized that he could not kill the dog. There was no way to do it. With his helpless hands he could neither draw nor hold his sheath knife nor throttle the animal. He released it, and it plunged wildly away, with tail between its legs and still snarling. It halted forty feet away and surveyed him curiously, with ears sharply pricked forward.

The man looked down at his hands in order to locate them, and found them hanging on the ends of his arms. It struck him as curious that one should have to use his eyes in order to find out where his hands were. He began threshing his arms back and forth, beating the mittened hands against his sides. He did this for five minutes, violently, and his heart pumped enough blood up to the surface to put a stop to his shivering. But no sensation was aroused in the hands. He had an impression that they hung like weights on the ends of his arms, but when he tried to run the impression down, he could not find it.

A certain fear of death, dull and oppressive, came to him. This fear quickly became poignant as he realized that it was no longer a mere matter of freezing his fingers and toes, or of losing his hands and feet, but that it was a matter of life and death with the chances against him. This threw him into a panic, and he turned and ran up the creek bed along the old, dim trail. The dog joined in behind and kept up with him. He ran blindly, without intention, in fear such as he had never known in his life. Slowly, as he plowed and floundered through the snow, he began to see things again—the banks

of the creek, the old timber jams, the leafless aspens, and the sky. The running made him feel better. He did not shiver. Maybe, if he ran on, his feet would thaw out, and, anyway, if he ran far enough, he would reach camp and the boys. Without doubt he would lose some fingers and toes and some of his face, but the boys would take care of him, and save the rest of him when he got there. And at the same time there was another thought in his mind that said he would never get to the camp and the boys, that it was too many miles away, that the freezing had too great a start on him, and that he would soon be stiff and dead. This thought he kept in the background and refused to consider. Sometimes it pushed itself forward and demanded to be heard, but he thrust it back and strove to think of other things.

It struck him as curious that he could run at all on feet so frozen that he could not feel them when they struck the earth and took the weight of his body. He seemed to himself to skim along above the surface and to have no connection with the earth. Somewhere he had once seen a winged Mercury,[9] and he wondered if Mercury felt as he felt when skimming over the earth.

His theory of running until he reached camp and the boys had one flaw in it: he lacked the endurance. Several times he stumbled, and finally he tottered, crumpled up, and fell. When he tried to rise, he failed. He must sit and rest, he decided, and next time he would merely walk and keep on going. As he sat and regained his breath, he noted that he was feeling quite warm and comfortable. He was not shivering, and it even seemed that a warm glow had come to his chest and trunk. And yet, when he touched his nose or cheeks, there was no sensation. Running would not thaw them out. Nor would it thaw out

9. **Mercury**, in Roman mythology, the messenger of the gods.

his hands and feet. Then the thought came to him that the frozen portions of his body must be extending. He tried to keep this thought down, to forget it, to think of something else; he was aware of the panicky feeling that it caused, and he was afraid of the panic. But the thought asserted itself and persisted, until it produced a vision of his body totally frozen. This was too much, and he made another wild run along the trail. Once he slowed down to a walk, but the thought of the freezing extending itself made him run again.

And all the time the dog ran with him, at his heels. When he fell down a second time, it curled its tail over its forefeet and sat in front of him, facing him, curiously eager and intent. The warmth and security of the animal angered him, and he cursed it till it flattened down its ears appeasingly. This time the shivering came more quickly upon the man. He was losing in his battle with the frost. It was creeping into his body from all sides. The thought of it drove him on, but he ran no more than a hundred feet when he staggered and pitched headlong. It was his last panic. When he had recovered his breath and control, he sat up and entertained in his mind the conception of meeting death with dignity. However, the conception did not come to him in such terms. His idea of it was that he had been making a fool of himself, running around like a chicken with its head cut off —such was the simile that occurred to him. Well, he was bound to freeze anyway, and he might as well take it decently. With this new-found peace of mind came the first glimmerings of drowsiness. A good idea, he thought, to sleep off to death. It was like taking an anesthetic. Freezing was not so bad as people thought. There were lots worse ways to die.

He pictured the boys finding his body next day. Suddenly he found himself with them, coming along the trail and looking for himself. And, still with them, he came around a turn in the trail and found himself lying in the snow. He did not belong with himself any more, for even then he was out of himself, standing with the boys and looking at himself in the snow. It certainly was cold, was his thought. When he got back to the States he could tell the folks what real cold was. He drifted on from this to a vision of the old-timer on Sulphur Creek. He could see him quite clearly, warm and comfortable, and smoking a pipe.

"You were right, old hoss; you were right," the man mumbled to the old-timer of Sulphur Creek.

Then the man drowsed off into what seemed to him the most comfortable and satisfying sleep he had ever known. The dog sat facing him and waiting. The brief day drew to a close in a long, slow twilight. There were no signs of a fire to be made, and, besides, never in the dog's experience had it known a man to sit like that in the snow and make no fire. As the twilight drew on, its eager yearning for the fire mastered it, and with a great lifting and shifting of forefeet, it whined softly, then flattened its ears down in anticipation of being chidden by the man. But the man remained silent. Later the dog whined loudly. And still later it crept close to the man and caught the scent of death. This made the animal bristle and back away. A little longer it delayed, howling under the stars that leaped and danced and shone brightly in the cold sky. Then it turned and trotted up the trail in the direction of the camp it knew, where were the other food providers and fire providers. ✳

Discussion

1. (a) What is the setting in this story? **(b)** What details in the early part of the story make you aware of the intense cold? **(c)** Why is the setting important?

2. Review the Handbook article on narrative point of view (page 558). **(a)** What point of view does Jack London use to tell this story? **(b)** Why do you think he uses this point of view?

3. (a) What advice was given by the old-timer at Sulphur Creek? **(b)** What was the man's reaction to this advice before he started on his journey?

4. Each of the references below has to do with the man's attitude toward his situation. Locate each reference and explain the attitude expressed in the passage.

  (a) page 404, column 1, paragraph 1
  (b) page 407, column 2, paragraph 1
  (c) page 408, column 1, paragraphs 1 and 2
  (d) page 409, column 1, paragraph 1
  (e) page 409, column 2, paragraph 3
  (f) page 411, column 2, paragraph 2
  (g) page 412, column 2, paragraph 3
  (h) page 414, column 1, paragraph 1

5. (a) How do the dog's reactions to the cold differ from those of the man? **(b)** Why do you think the author includes the dog's reactions?

6. (a) Do you think the ending of this story is appropriate? Explain. **(b)** At what point in the story were you aware that the author is foreshadowing a tragic ending? **(c)** Cite passages in the story which foreshadow the ending.

7. Why do you think the author selected the title "To Build a Fire"?

The Author

Jack London was born in San Francisco in 1876. His family's financial problems forced him to leave school and go to work before he was fifteen. After several years of wandering around the country, he returned to San Francisco and completed high school. Later London enrolled at the University of California but attended for only a short time.

In 1896, after the gold rush to the Klondike had begun, he went to Alaska. He found no gold, but the experiences of the prospectors and trappers of the region gave him the materials for the stories he was to write. When he returned to San Francisco, he supported himself and his family by working at odd jobs, writing and studying in his spare time. By 1913 he was one of the best-known writers in the country.

Jack London's stories about Alaska during the gold rush are still widely read. Among his best-known books are his novels *Call of the Wild* and *White Fang,* and a collection of shorter pieces, *Sun Dog Trail and Other Stories.*

Unit **6** Review

1. (a) In which of the stories in this unit does the author use fantasy? (b) What elements of fantasy do these selections contain?

2. (a) Which of the stories in this unit are basically realistic? (b) In each case what elements or techniques has the author used to make his story seem true to life?

3. In some stories the characters emerge as believable individuals, with faults and virtues, successes and failures. In other stories the characters are types, figures who represent a certain kind of person. Which of the following characters would you classify as individuals and which would you classify as character types? Give reasons for your answers.

    a. Widow Wycherly
    b. Judge Gookin
    c. the murderer in "The Tell-Tale Heart"
    d. "Red Chief"
    e. the man in the Yukon
    f. the princess

4. (a) What do you think are the characteristics of a story which deserves to be called a "well-told tale"? (b) In your opinion, do all of the stories in the unit meet this standard? Explain your answer.

SUGGESTED READING

ALDRICH, BESS STREETER, *The Bess Streeter Aldrich Reader*. (Appleton) Included in this collection by a popular author are "A White Bird Flying" and other favorites.

ARTHUR, ROBERT, *Mystery and More Mystery*. (Random) Besides providing suspenseful, exciting reading, this book includes a special section in which the author details the incidents which inspired the tales.

ASIMOV, ISAAC (ed.), *Tomorrow's Children*. (Doubleday) Every story in this collection of outstanding science-fiction stories concerns children who range from amusing to enchanting to horrifying. Excellent writers like Asimov and Bradbury provide good, solid reading.

BRADBURY, RAY, *S Is for Space*. (Doubleday) One of the most popular science-fiction writers of all covers times past, present, and future in this engrossing collection of stories.

CHRISTIE, AGATHA, *13 Clues for Miss Marple,* edited by R. T. Bond. (Dodd) Miss Marple, the spirited, charming, amusing detective, shows her craft and insight as she unravels mysteries.

CLEMENS, SAMUEL, *A Connecticut Yankee in King Arthur's Court*. (Harper *Perennial) A blow on the head conveys a man back to the days of King Arthur, where he sees the knights, chivalry, and medieval superstitions through modern eyes. *The Prince and the Pauper* (World) relates the story of a king and a poor boy who by accident exchange places in the England of Henry VIII.

DALY, MAUREEN (ed.), *My Favorite Mystery Stories*. (Dodd) In this anthology, a woman who knows and loves mystery stories has collected some of the best ever written.

DAY, A. GROVE (ed.), *The Greatest American Short Stories*. (McGraw) Hawthorne's "The Ambitious Guest," Harris' "The Wonderful Tar Baby Story," O. Henry's "The Gift of the Magi," and Harte's "The Outcasts of Poker Flat" are included in this collection of twenty American classics.

HALE, EDWARD EVERETT, *The Man Without a Country*. (Houghton) In a moment of anger, Philip Nolan, a U.S. Navy officer involved in Aaron Burr's treason, expresses the wish never to hear the name of his country again. His wish is granted!

HAWTHORNE, NATHANIEL, *Twice-Told Tales*, J. Hubert Scott, ed. (Houghton) This collection contains many of Hawthorne's best-known stories including "The Gray Champion," "The Ambitious Guest," and "The Minister's Black Veil."

HITCHCOCK, ALFRED, *Alfred Hitchcock's Sinister Spies*. (Random) A master of suspense here presents espionage stories by authors ranging from the classical through Sherlock Holmes to the modern. Some of the best storytellers of all time are represented in this book.

IRVING, WASHINGTON, *The Legend of Sleepy Hollow*. (Macmillan *Airmont) Ichabod Crane, the local schoolmaster, courts Katrina Van Tassel, but the courtship is interrupted when Crane disappears.

JESSUP, ALEXANDER (ed.), *The Best American Humorous Short Stories*. (Modern Library) Edgar Allan Poe, Oliver W. Holmes, Mark Twain, Frank Stockton, Bret Harte, and O. Henry are only a few of the authors represented in this enjoyable collection.

POE, EDGAR ALLAN, *The Gold Bug and Other Tales and Poems*. (Macmillan) These mystery and detective stories by a master of the art will keep the reader on the edge of his chair. "The Gold Bug" explains the cryptogram that helps in finding the treasure.

PORTER, WILLIAM SIDNEY, *O. Henry's Best Stories*. (Globe) O. Henry's amazing ability to surprise his readers is clearly evident in this collection, which includes such favorites as "The Cop and the Anthem," "The Last Leaf," and others.

Sometimes Magic: A Collection of Outstanding Stories for the Teenage Girl. (Platt) These stories, all by talented women, will always be popular. Jane Austen and Jean Stafford are represented.

WRIGHT, HELEN and SAMUEL RAPPORT (comps.), *Great Undersea Adventures*. (Harper) This is an anthology of the sea in both fact and fiction. Selections range from the Biblical story of Jonah and the whale, through a Poe story, to articles by the modern explorer Cousteau.

*paperback

7

Heroes
of
Olympus

Introduction by Roger Lancelyn Green

Every land has invented myths and told fairy tales at some point in its development. The terrible plains of Mesopotamia, dead flat as far as the eye can reach in every direction, bred the hopeless, devil-haunted mythology of the ancient Babylonians; the desert stretching away on either side of the narrow valley of fertile land depending yearly for its very life on the rising Nile gave the Egyptians their strange, vivid mythology of life and death, good

continued

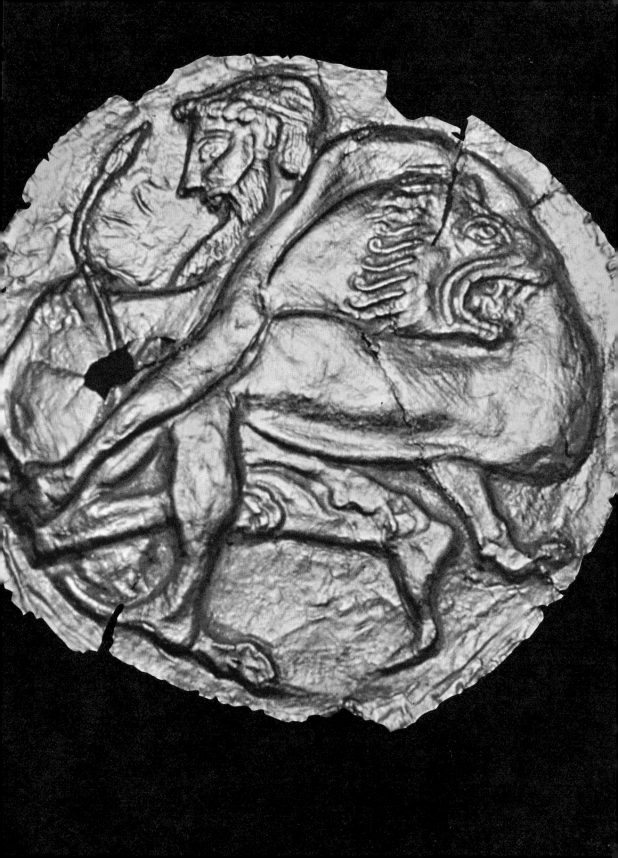

and evil at eternal war; the cruel threat of cold and snow, of frozen seas and icy starvation gave our Norse ancestors their heroic saga of men and gods fighting against relentless foes and perishing bravely in the end.

It seems natural that Greece, with its towering, tree-clad hills and its fertile valleys silver with olive leaves and gleaming with spring flowers, with its deep bays and blue seas flecked with innumerable islands, should have brought forth a mythology of wonder and beauty. One can still half expect to see Artemis, the maiden huntress, with her bevy of nymphs flit by in the lonely glades of Arcadia; the shepherd's pipe heard over the mountain slopes through the dreamy summer afternoon must surely be that of Pan, master and lover of all wild things. It is so easy, as the smooth sea ruffles suddenly into great waves breaking over your little boat as you sail from one island to the next, to think of Poseidon, Ruler of the Sea, waking in sudden rage and smiting the waves with his trident.

At first the Greeks must have thought of all the strange powers about them—the force of the storm, the changing of the seasons—as huge, formless, and awe-inspiring. The gods of the earliest inhabitants

*were very much of this kind: terrible Titans like
Cronus who could swallow his own children, or like
the giants who could pile the great mountains of
Ossa and Pelion one upon the other as a scaling-
ladder to heaven.*

*Who these earliest inhabitants of Greece were, we do
not know. But about four thousand years ago fresh
waves of invaders surged into Greece and occupied
it. The gods of these new people waged war against
the old gods, and the myths grew of how Zeus and his
brothers and sisters had fought against Cronus and
the Titans and cast them out of heaven to lie forever
in Tartarus, the prison below the earth.*

*In ancient Greece there were many kings, each rul-
ing over his castle or little walled city and the lands
about it. Lesser kings owed allegiance to a few
greater kings, like Theseus of Athens; and in time of
war all lesser kings rallied at the call of the High
King of Mycenae—Agamemnon, King of Men. As the
little cities which had begun as separate settlements
came to know one another and became part of a single nation, they found that their myths disagreed.
They all recognized Zeus, the father of gods and
men, the shadow of God Himself; but they disagreed
over their local gods and goddesses.*

"Hera is the wife of Zeus and the Lady of Heaven," the people of Argos would say. But the people of Arcadia would disagree: "Zeus married Maia, and they had a son called Hermes." But the people of Delphi and Delos would insist that the Lady of Heaven was Leto, and that she and Zeus were the parents of Apollo and Artemis. So it came about that Zeus had many wives as well as many children. And not only gods and goddesses but mortal children as well, since the royal family in every Greek city liked to trace its descent from Zeus.

The ancient Greeks probably did not consciously tabulate the divine family of Olympus, or arrange their myths to fit properly into one another. Their idea of the Court of Heaven was very much like a glorified Mycenae: Zeus and the lesser gods were magnified and all-powerful likenesses of Agamemnon the High King and his lesser kings. There seems to have been no written literature. The myths and legends were preserved in songs by the minstrels, who adapted what they sang to the particular court at which they were singing.

It was only centuries later, when the stories about the gods and goddesses were gathered together from all over Greece, that the rather undignified, even

slightly comic, picture of Olympus began to emerge. Great poets and thinkers tried to separate religion from myth, or they tried to explain how such strange stories had grown up about the gods. But the stories went on being told, and in Alexandria and Rome and Byzantium, when the gods were no longer worshipped, the stories about them grew into the comic conception of Olympus which Mr. Graves describes.

The mixture of myth and legend from Greece, growing in the imaginations of some of the world's greatest poets and playwrights, became the foundation of the literature of the Western World. The basic myths and fairy tales may be much the same all over the world, but in Greece they found their most vivid expression, and we still turn to Greece for the greatest of all stories—those that hide truth in fiction, fantasy, and romance. And so we find in the legends of Heracles or Theseus battling savage beasts and still more savage men, the contest of the brave man against the powers of evil; in Prometheus' risking punishment to give his gift of fire we sense a faith in man's great potential; and in the eternal quest for the Golden Apples of the Hesperides we glimpse the never satisfied dreams of men.

By the time the many peoples of Greece had contributed their beliefs to the emerging picture of the gods, the family of Immortals had become large and sprawling, and "life at home" on Mount Olympus was sometimes as full of problems as life among mortals.
What mixture of godlike and human qualities do you find in this account of the rulers of heaven and earth?

THE PALACE OF OLYMPUS

Robert Graves

THE TWELVE most important gods and goddesses of ancient Greece, called the Olympians, belonged to the same large, quarrelsome family. Though thinking little of the smaller, old-fashioned gods over whom they ruled, they thought even less of mortals. All the Olympians lived together in an enormous palace, set well above the usual level of clouds at the top of Mount Olympus, the highest mountain in Greece. Great walls, too steep for climbing, protected the Palace. The Olympians' masons, gigantic one-eyed Cyclopes, had built them on much the same plan as royal palaces on earth.

At the southern end, just behind the Council Hall, and looking towards the famous Greek cities of Athens, Thebes, Sparta, Corinth, Argos, and

Mycenae, were the private apartments of King Zeus, the Father-god, and Queen Hera, the Mother-goddess. The northern end of the palace, looking across the valley of Tempe towards the wild hills of Macedonia, consisted of the kitchen, banqueting hall, armoury, workshops, and servants' quarters. In between came a square court, open to the sky, with covered cloisters and private rooms on each side, belonging to the other five Olympian gods and the other five

Olympian goddesses. Beyond the kitchen and servants' quarters stood cottages for smaller gods, sheds for chariots, stables for horses, kennels for hounds, and a sort of zoo where the Olympians kept their sacred animals. These included a bear, a lion, a peacock, an eagle, tigers, stags, a cow, a crane, snakes, a wild boar, white bulls, a wild cat, mice, swans, herons, an owl, a tortoise, and a tank full of fish.

In the Council Hall the Olympians

met at times to discuss mortal affairs—such as which army on earth should be allowed to win a war, and whether they ought to punish some king or queen who had been behaving proudly or disgustingly. But for the most part they were too busy with their own quarrels and lawsuits to take much notice of mortal affairs. King Zeus had an enormous throne of polished black Egyptian marble, decorated in gold. Seven steps led up to it, each of them enamelled with one of the seven colours of the rainbow. A bright blue covering above showed that the whole sky belonged to Zeus alone; and on the right arm of his throne perched a ruby-eyed golden eagle clutching jagged strips of pure tin, which meant that Zeus could kill whatever enemies he pleased by throwing a thunderbolt of forked lightning at them. A purple ram's fleece covered the cold seat. Zeus used it for magical rainmaking in times of drought. He was a strong, brave, stupid, noisy, violent, conceited god, and always on the watch lest his family should try to get rid of him; having once himself got rid of his wicked, idle, cannibalistic father Cronus, King of the Titans and Titanesses. The Olympians could not die, but Zeus, with the help of his two elder brothers, Hades and Poseidon, had banished Cronus to a distant island in the Atlantic—perhaps the Azores, perhaps Torrey Island, off the coast of Ireland. Zeus, Hades, and Poseidon then drew lots for the three parts of Cronus' kingdom. Zeus won the sky; Poseidon, the sea; Hades, the Underworld; they shared the earth between them. One of Zeus' emblems was the eagle, another was the woodpecker.

Cronus managed at last to escape from the island in a small boat and, changing his name to Saturn, settled quietly among the Italians, and behaved very well. In fact, until Zeus discovered his escape and banished him again, Saturn's reign was known as the Golden Age. Mortals in Italy lived without work or trouble, eating only acorns, wild fruit, honey, and pig-nuts, and drinking only milk or water. They never fought wars, and spent their days dancing and singing.

Queen Hera had an ivory throne, with three crystal steps leading up to it. Golden cuckoos and willow leaves decorated the back, and a full moon hung above it. Hera sat on a white cowskin, which she sometimes used for rain-making magic if Zeus could not be bothered to stop a drought. She disliked being Zeus' wife, because he was frequently marrying mortal women and saying, with a sneer, that these marriages did not count—his brides would soon grow ugly and die; but she was his Queen, and perpetually young and beautiful.

When first asked to marry him, Hera had refused; and had gone on refusing every year for three hundred years. But one springtime Zeus disguised himself as a poor cuckoo caught in a thunderstorm, and tapped at her window. Hera, not seeing through his disguise, let the cuckoo in, stroked his wet feathers, and whispered: "Poor bird, I love you." At once Zeus changed back again into his true shape, and said: "Now you must marry me!" After this, however badly Zeus behaved, Hera felt obliged to set a good example to gods and goddesses and mortals, as the Mother of Heaven. Her emblem was the cow, the most motherly of animals; but, not wishing to be thought as plain-looking and placid as a cow, she also used the peacock and the lion.

These two thrones faced down the Council Hall towards the door leading into the open courtyard. Along the sides of the hall stood ten other thrones—for five goddesses on Hera's side, for five gods on Zeus'.

Poseidon, god of the seas and rivers, had the second-largest throne. It was of grey-green white-streaked marble, ornamented with coral, gold, and mother-of-pearl. The arms were carved in the shape of sea-beasts, and Poseidon sat on sealskin. For his help in banishing Cronus and the Titans, Zeus had married him to Amphitrite, the former Sea-goddess, and allowed him to take over all her titles. Though Poseidon hated to be less important than his younger brother, and always went about scowling, he feared Zeus' thunderbolt. His only weapon was a trident, with which he could stir up the sea and so wreck ships; but Zeus never travelled by ship. When Poseidon felt even crosser than usual, he would drive away in his chariot to a palace under the waves, near the island of Euboea, and there let his rage cool. As his emblem Poseidon chose the horse, an animal which he pretended to have created. Large waves are still called "white horses" because of this.

Opposite Poseidon sat his sister Demeter, goddess of all useful fruits, grasses, and grains. Her throne of bright green malachite was ornamented with ears of barley in gold, and little golden pigs for luck. Demeter seldom smiled, except when her daughter Persephone—unhappily married to the hateful Hades, God of the Dead—came to visit her once a year. Demeter had been rather wild as a girl, and nobody could remember the name of Persephone's father: probably some country god married for a drunken joke at a harvest festival. Demeter's emblem was the poppy, which grows red as blood among the barley.

Next to Poseidon sat Hephaestus, a son of Zeus and Hera. Being the god of goldsmiths, jewellers, blacksmiths, masons, and carpenters, he had built all these thrones himself, and made his own a masterpiece of every different metal and precious stone to be found. The seat could swivel about, the arms could move up and down, and the whole throne rolled along automatically wherever he wished, like the three-legged golden tables in his workshop. Hephaestus had hobbled ever since birth, when Zeus roared at Hera: "A brat as weak as this is unworthy of me!"—and threw him far out over the walls of Olympus. In his fall Hephaestus broke a leg so badly that he had to wear a golden leg-iron. He kept a country house on Lemnos, the island where he had struck earth; and his emblem was the quail, a bird that does a hobbling dance in springtime.

Opposite Hephaestus sat Athene, Goddess of Wisdom, who first taught him how to handle tools, and knew more than anyone else about pottery, weaving, and all useful arts. Her silver throne had golden basketwork at the back and sides, and a crown of violets, made from blue lapis lazuli, set above it. Its arms ended in grinning Gorgons' heads.[1] Athene, wise though she was, did not know the names of her parents. Poseidon claimed her as his daughter by a marriage with an African goddess called Libya. It is true that, as a child, she had been found wandering in a goatskin by the shores of a Libyan lake; but rather than admit herself the daughter of Poseidon, whom she thought very stupid, she allowed Zeus to pretend she was his. Zeus announced that one day, overcome by a

1. **Gorgons' heads.** A Gorgon (gôr′gən) was one of three winged, dragonlike sisters who had snakes for hair and whose looks turned men to stone. The most famous of these terrible sisters was Medusa (mə dü′sə).

fearful headache, he had howled aloud like a thousand wolves hunting in a pack. Hephaestus, he said, then ran up with an axe and kindly split open his skull, and out sprang Athene, dressed in full armour. Athene was also a Battle-goddess, yet never went to war unless forced—being too sensible to pick quarrels—and when she fought, always won. She chose the wise owl as her emblem; and had a town house at Athens.

Next to Athene sat Aphrodite, Goddess of Love and Beauty. Nobody knew who her parents were, either. The South Wind said that he had once seen her floating in a scallop shell off the island of Cythera, and steered her gently ashore. She may have been a daughter of Amphitrite by a smaller god named Triton, who used to blow roaring blasts on a conch, or perhaps by old Cronus. Amphitrite refused to say a word on the subject. Aphrodite's throne was silver, inlaid with beryls and aquamarines, the back shaped like a scallop shell, the seat made of swan's down, and under her feet lay a golden mat—an embroidery of golden bees, apples, and sparrows. Aphrodite had a magic girdle, which she would wear whenever she wanted to make anyone love her madly. To keep Aphrodite out of mischief, Zeus decided that she needed a hard-working, decent husband; and naturally chose his son Hephaestus. Hephaestus exclaimed: "Now I am the happiest god alive!" But she thought it disgraceful to be the wife of a sooty-faced, horny-handed, crippled smith and insisted on having a bedroom of her own. Aphrodite's emblem was the dove, and she would visit Paphos, in Cyprus, once a year to swim in the sea, for good luck.

Opposite Aphrodite sat Ares, Hephaestus' tall, handsome, boastful, cruel brother, who loved fighting for its own sake. Ares and Aphrodite were continually holding hands and giggling in corners, which made Hephaestus jealous. Yet if he ever complained to the Council, Zeus would laugh at him, saying: "Fool, why did you give your wife that magic girdle? Can you blame your brother if he falls in love with her when she wears it?" Ares' throne was built of brass, strong and ugly—those huge brass knobs in the shape of skulls, and that cushion-cover of human skin! Ares had no manners, no learning, and the worst of taste; yet Aphrodite thought him wonderful. His emblems were a wild boar and a bloodstained spear. He kept a country house among the rough woods of Thrace.

Next to Ares sat Apollo, the god of music, poetry, medicine, archery, and young unmarried men—Zeus' son by Leto, one of the smaller goddesses, whom he married to annoy Hera. Apollo rebelled against his father once or twice, but got well punished each time, and learned to behave more sensibly. His highly polished golden throne had magical inscriptions carved all over it, a back shaped like a lyre, and a python skin to sit on. Above hung a golden sundisk with twenty-one rays shaped like arrows, because he pretended to manage the Sun. Apollo's emblem was a mouse; mice were supposed to know the secrets of earth, and tell them to him. (He preferred white mice to ordinary ones; most boys still do.) Apollo owned a splendid house at Delphi on the top of Mount Parnassus, built around the famous oracle[2] which he stole from Mother Earth, Zeus' grandmother.

Opposite Apollo sat his twin sister Artemis, goddess of hunting and of unmarried girls, from whom he had

---

2. **oracle.** The oracle was said to reside in the temple of Apollo at Delphi (del'fi) and to speak through the priestesses, uttering prophecies and answering important questions submitted by people who journeyed there.

learned medicine and archery. Her throne was of pure silver, with a wolfskin to sit on, and the back shaped like two date palms, one on each side of a new-moon boat. Apollo married several mortal wives at different times. Once he chased a girl named Daphne, who cried out for help to Mother Earth and got turned into a laurel tree before he could catch and kiss her. Artemis, however, hated the idea of marriage, although she kindly took care of mothers when their babies were born. She much preferred hunting, fishing, and swimming in moonlit mountain pools. If any mortal happened to see her without clothes, she used to change him into a stag and hunt him to death. She chose as her emblem the she-bear, the most dangerous of all wild animals in Greece.

Last in the row of gods sat Hermes, Zeus' son by a smaller goddess named Maia, after whom the month of May is called: Hermes, the god of merchants, bankers, thieves, fortunetellers, and heralds, was born in Arcadia. His throne was cut out of a single piece of solid grey rock, the arms shaped like rams' heads, and a goatskin for the seat. On its back he had carved a swastika, this being the shape of a fire-making machine invented by him—the fire-drill. Until then, housewives used to borrow glowing pieces of charcoal from their neighbours. Hermes also invented the alphabet; and one of his emblems was the crane, because cranes fly in a V —the first letter he wrote. Another of Hermes' emblems was a peeled hazel stick, which he carried as the Messenger of the Olympians: white ribbons dangled from it, which foolish people often mistook for snakes.[3]

Last in the row of goddesses sat Zeus' eldest sister, Hestia, Goddess of the Home: on a plain, uncarved, wooden throne, and a plain cushion woven of undyed wool. Hestia, the kindest and most peaceable of all the Olympians, hated the continual family quarrels, and never troubled to choose any particular emblem of her own. She used to tend the charcoal hearth in the middle of the Council Hall.

That made six gods and six goddesses. But one day Zeus announced that Dionysus, his son by a mortal woman named Semele, had invented wine, and must be given a seat in the Council. Thirteen Olympians would have been an unlucky number so Hestia offered him her seat, just to keep the peace. Now there were seven gods and five goddesses; an unjust state of affairs because, when questions about women had to be discussed, the gods outvoted the goddesses. Dionysus' throne was gold-plated fir wood, ornamented with bunches of grapes carved in amethyst (a violet-coloured stone), snakes carved in serpentine (a stone with many markings), and various horned animals besides, carved in onyx (a black and white stone), sard (a dark red stone), jade (a dark green stone), and carnelian (a pink stone). He took the tiger for his emblem, having once visited India at the head of a drunken army and brought tigers back as souvenirs.

Of the other gods and goddesses living on Olympus, Heracles the Porter slept in the gatehouse; and Poseidon's wife Amphitrite has already been mentioned. There were also Dionysus' mother Semele, whom he persuaded Zeus to turn into a goddess; Ares' hateful sister Eris, Goddess of Quarrels; Iris, Hera's messenger, who used to run along the rainbow; the Goddess Nemesis, who kept a list for

3. **peeled hazel stick . . . snakes.** Hermes' staff, known as a caduceus (kə dü'sē əs), has two snakes twined around it, with a pair of wings on top. It was supposed to possess magical powers over sleeping, waking, and dreams.

the Olympians of proud mortals due to be punished; Aphrodite's wicked little son Eros, God of Love, who enjoyed shooting arrows at people to make them fall ridiculously in love; Hebe, Goddess of Youth, who married Heracles; Ganymede, Zeus' handsome young cupbearer; the nine Muses, who sang in the Banqueting Hall; and Zeus' ancient mother, Rhea, whom he treated very shabbily, though she had once saved his life by a trick when Cronus wanted to eat him.[4]

In a room behind the kitchen sat the three Fates, named Clotho, Lachesis, and Atropos. They were the oldest goddesses in existence, too old for anybody to remember where they came from. The Fates decided how long each mortal should live: spinning a linen thread, to measure exactly so many inches and feet for months and years, and then snipping it off with a pair of shears. They also knew, but seldom revealed, what would be the fate of each Olympian god. Even Zeus feared them for that reason.

The Olympians drank nectar, a sweet drink made from fermented honey; and ate ambrosia, said to be an uncooked mixture of honey, water, fruit, olive oil, cheese, and barley —though this may be doubted. Some claim that certain speckled mushrooms were the true food of the Olympians, created whenever Zeus' thunderbolt struck the earth; and that this kept them immortal. Because the Olympians also loved the smell, though not the taste, of roast beef and mutton, mortals used to sacrifice sheep and cattle to them, afterwards eating the meat themselves.   *

4. **she had once saved his life . . . eat him.** Zeus' wicked father, the Titan Cronus, in an attempt to escape the prophecy that he would be overthrown by his children, swallowed them as soon as they were born. His wife Rhea prevented him from swallowing Zeus by giving him instead a stone wrapped in a blanket.

Discussion

1. Although the names of the Greek gods in this selection may be unfamiliar, you may already have met some of the gods under other names. The ancient Romans developed their own concepts of gods, which were very similar in many ways to those of the Greeks; but in most cases the Romans called the gods by different names. Usually the Roman name for the god has become the more popular or better known of the two. In a few examples, such as that of Apollo, the name is the same in both languages.

Below are listed some of the Roman gods and their offices. For each, determine the Greek god who was his counterpart. How many do you recognize by their Roman names?

a. Bacchus (bak'əs), god of wine
b. Cupid, god of love
c. Diana, goddess of the hunt and of the moon
d. Juno (jü'nō), queen of the gods
e. Jupiter, ruler of gods and men
f. Mars, god of war
g. Mercury, messenger of the gods
h. Minerva (mə ner'və), goddess of wisdom, arts, and defensive war
i. Neptune (nep'tün), god of the sea
j. Pluto, god of the Underworld
k. Venus, goddess of love
l. Vulcan (vul'kən), god of fire and metalworking

2. (a) Zeus is usually considered the most important of the Olympian gods. What attributes gave him this position? (b) Who was the "most important god" before Zeus, and how did Zeus manage to get rid of him? (Refer also to the Introduction for help in answering this question.) (c) What seems to be the real reason—not the mythical reason—for the change in gods? (The Introduction may provide some clues.)

3. (a) Which qualities and actions of the gods could be considered godlike? (b) What examples can you cite of qualities and actions of the gods which would ordinarily be thought of as human? (c) How do you explain this mixture of qualities attributed to the gods?

4. Below are listed some of the animals in the "Olympian zoo," as Graves calls it, which are specified as being the emblems of particular gods. (a) To which god or goddess does each animal belong? (b) For what qualities did the god or goddess choose this animal as an emblem? (c) Do any of the gods seem to possess the qualities of their symbolic animals?

1. horse
2. owl
3. eagle
4. wild boar
5. she-bear
6. dove
7. cow
8. crane
9. quail
10. mouse

5. In his Introduction, Roger Green states that many of the stories from Greek mythology probably grew from attempts by the early peoples to understand and explain for themselves life and the forces of nature. What myths explain the following natural occurrences: (a) lightning and thunder; (b) storms at sea; (c) rain in times of drought; (d) length of life?

6. (a) What is the tone of "The Palace of Olympus"? (b) Explain what elements in Graves' treatment of the gods help create this tone.

Word Study

In our borrowings from other languages to create new words in English, we often make use of Greek mythology. Many of our English words are not only based upon the names of Greek characters, but also take their meanings in part from the myths which feature these characters.

Copy the following words on a sheet of paper; then look them up in a dictionary. For each word write both the meaning which is in current use and the etymology, including the Greek mythological character upon whom the word is based. Explain in each case how the meaning of the word is derived from the myth.

cyclopean   museum
herculean   nemesis
hermetic   titanic

The Author

Robert Graves was born in London in 1895. His father was a poet and collector of folk songs and his mother a professor's daughter. A large library at home provided much of his early education, which was continued in various preparatory schools in England. While a regimental officer in the Royal Welch Fusiliers during World War I, he began writing poetry in earnest and had published three volumes of verse by 1917.

After the war he married and went back to continue his education at St. John's College, Oxford. In 1926 he served as professor of English at the University of Cairo, Egypt. Later he moved to Majorca, Spain, where he has lived off and on since.

Robert Graves is a true "man of letters"; he has proved himself as poet, novelist, biographer, editor, and translator, and is responsible for well over one hundred books on a variety of subjects from poetry to mythology, from historical fiction to the meaning of dreams. For his literary efforts, he has received numerous awards.

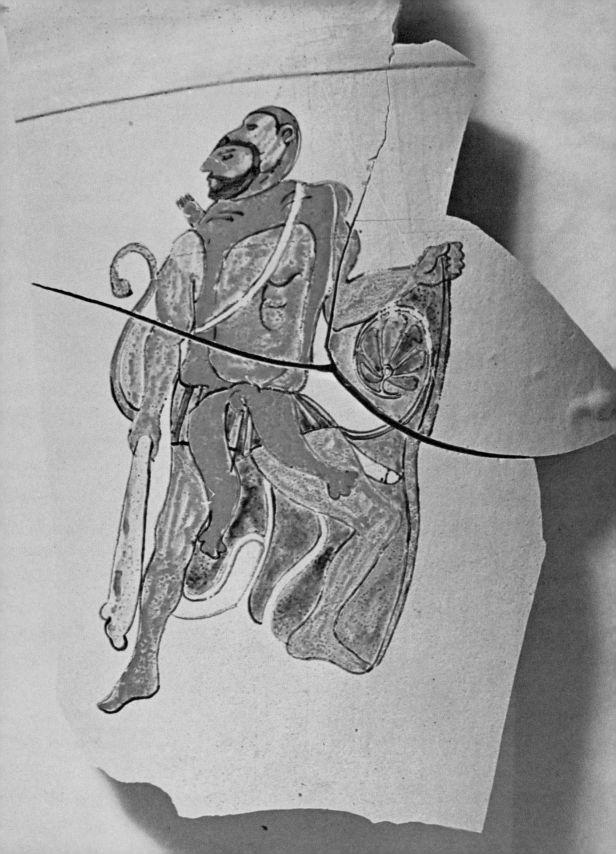

"Destined to be the most famous mortal who ever trod the soil of Greece . . . .

"He shall rid the land of monsters and do many labours of which poets will tell in song and story forever . . . .

"He is the Hero, the son of Zeus, whose coming was foretold at the beginning of the world."

The Hero was Heracles, according to the ancient prophecy told to his mother, the lovely and faithful Alcmena (alk mē′nə) and her brave husband Amphitryon (am fit′ri on). Yet Heracles and Iphicles (if′i klēz) were twin brothers. How was it possible for just one to be so favored?

As the legend of Heracles developed, the ancient Greeks attributed to him many qualities. As you read, note these qualities and how they were regarded by the Greeks. Note also the part played by the gods in this famous hero tale.

THE LABOURS OF HERACLES

Roger Lancelyn Green

From Roger Lancelyn Green: TALES OF THE GREEK HEROES (Puffin, 1958). Copyright © Roger Lancelyn Green, 1958. Reprinted by permission of Penguin Books Ltd.

THE
BIRTH
OF
HERACLES

WHEN HERACLES and his twin brother Iphicles were no more than ten months old, Heracles performed his first feat of valour.

It happened on a summer's evening when Alcmena had bathed the two babies, given them their milk and rocked them to sleep in a cradle made out of a big bronze shield which Amphitryon had brought back as a prize from his campaign against the robbers.

"Sleep, my little ones!" crooned Alcmena. "Sleep softly, and pass safely through the dark night and into the gentle morning, my twin babes!"

Darkness fell, and all the house grew still. But at the hour of midnight Hera sent two monstrous snakes with scales of azure blue, to slay the infant Heracles. Writhing and curling along the ground they came, shining with a strange, baleful light, and spitting deadly venom.

But when they drew near the children (for all the doors flew open before them), Zeus caused the babes to wake. Iphicles, seeing the serpents curling up to strike with their cruel fangs, screamed with fright, and kicking off his coverlet rolled out onto the floor.

Heracles, however, sat up smiling in the brazen shield, and grasped a snake in either hand, gripping them by their necks and keeping the poisoned fangs well away from him. The serpents hissed horribly, and twined their cruel coils about the child. But Heracles held on, squeezing and squeezing with his tiny hands, trying to throttle them with his strong little fingers.

Then Alcmena heard the screams of Iphicles and, running to the room, saw the unearthly light flickering through the open door which she had closed so carefully.

"Arise, Amphitryon!" she cried. "Do you not hear how loud our younger child is wailing? Do you not see the light flickering on the walls? Surely some terrible creature has come into the house!"

Amphitryon sprang up, seized his sword, and rushed into the nursery, with Alcmena close behind him carrying a lamp.

There they found Heracles grasping a dead snake in either hand, shaking them fiercely, and crowing with delight. But Iphicles lay on the floor, his eyes wide with terror, too scared even to cry any more.

Proudly the baby Heracles showed the serpents to Amphitryon and Alcmena, then flinging them from him, snuggled down once more and went quietly to sleep.

In the morning Alcmena, feeling that there must be something strange about her child Heracles, went to consult the ancient prophet Tiresias, the wisest man in Thebes.

Strange things were told of Tiresias who was blind, and who had already lived three times as long as any ordinary man. It was said that when he was a boy two enchanted snakes turned him into a woman, and that a year later they made him a man again. And that once, when Zeus and Hera had an argument, Hera saying that Zeus had a much better time than she did, they had consulted Tiresias, who replied that it was nine times as pleasant to be a woman as to be a man.

Hera was furious at this, and struck Tiresias blind in that instant. Zeus could not undo what another Immortal had done, but he gave Tiresias the gift of prophecy and decreed that he should live for more than three generations.

"Tell me what all this means," Alcmena begged Tiresias, when she had related the adventure with the serpents. "It is not natural that a child of ten months should do all that Heracles has done. So tell me the truth, I beg, even if you see much suffering and sorrow in the future for me and mine."

"Be of good cheer, granddaughter of Perseus,"[1] answered the old prophet solemnly, "for your son is destined to be the most famous mortal who ever trod the soil of Greece. He shall rid the land of monsters, and do many labours of which poets will tell in song and story forever. Many things shall he suffer also and the long enmity of Hera, Queen of the Immortals, who sent those serpents against him.[2] But in the end he shall stand beside the Immortals in their direst need, and afterwards shall become one of them and sit on Olympus forever. For know that he is the Hero, the son of Zeus, whose coming was foretold at the beginning of the world by Prometheus, the good Titan."

Then Tiresias went on to tell Alcmena what had happened on her wedding night, and how she was in reality the bride of Zeus, and the most honoured among mortal women, to be the mother of Heracles.

After this Heracles grew quickly and in safety, well tended by Alcmena and her husband, who was not in the least jealous of Zeus.

At first Heracles learnt all the gentle arts: how to sing, how to play sweetly on the lyre and how to read and write. Then Amphitryon taught him how to drive a chariot skilfully; and he learnt also the use of sword and spear, and the whole art of boxing and wrestling. None could throw a dart more truly than Heracles, and of all archers he was the best, sending an arrow further than any other mortal, more swiftly, and with deadly aim.

It was plain to see, even when he was young, that Heracles was the son of an Immortal. For he was a head taller than any other man, and broad in proportion, while his eyes flashed fire.

But his temper was very violent, and when he was still only a boy he killed Linus, who was teaching him to play the lyre. For Linus struck him angrily one day when he played a false note, and Heracles struck back so violently with the instrument which he held in his hand that Linus fell dead immediately.

Heracles was pardoned for this deed; but Amphitryon, fearing lest some such mischance might happen again, sent him away from Thebes, to tend the cattle on Mount Cithaeron. And here Heracles increased in strength and skill; and at last he drew near to manhood. ✱

1. **Perseus** (pėr′sē əs), an earlier hero, best known for slaying the Gorgon Medusa. (See page 427, footnote 1.) Perseus avoided being turned to stone from the Gorgon's deadly glance by looking not directly at her but at her reflection in a highly polished shield. He killed Medusa with a magic sword.
2. **enmity of Hera . . . against him.** In this, and in all her other attempts to discredit or to destroy Heracles, Hera is expressing her dislike and jealousy towards all the mortal wives and children of Zeus, for she knows that Heracles is in fact Zeus' son, Zeus having disguised himself as Amphitryon in order to wed Alcmena. Though born a twin to Heracles, Iphicles is Amphitryon's natural son.

THE CHOICE OF HERACLES

WHILE HERACLES was guarding the cattle of Amphitryon on the lonely slopes of Mount Cithaeron, and still ignorant of his high destiny, a strange thing befell him.

As he sat alone on the hillside one day, wondering if he was fated to be a cowherd all his life, or whether it would not be better to become a wild robber of the mountains, he saw two lovely maidens coming towards him. One of them was dressed in simple white, and had modest, downcast eyes and a calm, gentle face from which seemed to shine both goodness and wisdom; but the other wore bright colours, and came striding along glancing boldly about her—now admiring herself, and now looking to others for admiration. She was decked with rich jewels, and her face was artfully touched with paint and with powder.

As they drew near to Heracles, the second, as if anxious to forestall her companion, pushed eagerly ahead and spoke to him:

"Dear Heracles," she said, "I see that you have reached the age when you must choose what kind of life yours is to be. So I have come to urge you to take me as your friend and let me guide you on your way. I promise that if you do I will lead you by the easiest and most delightful paths. You shall taste every pleasure, and no troubles or toils shall come near you. Your life shall be passed in the pursuit and enjoyment of pleas-ant things, with no labour of body or mind, except to please yourself without any thought for the cares of others."

She paused, and Heracles asked: "Lady, tell me your name."

Then she answered softly: "Heracles, those who love me call me Happiness, but my enemies, it is true, have another name which I do not care to mention."

Meanwhile the modest maiden had come up, and now she spoke:

"I too, noble Heracles, am come to offer you a way of life. I know of what a worthy line you come, that you are descended from Perseus the Gorgon-slayer, and are yourself the son of Zeus. I know how well you have learnt all the accomplishments necessary for the path which I trust that you will take, in my company. Follow me, and you will do great deeds and leave a name which will never be forgotten. But you cannot win what is glorious and excellent in the world without care and labour: the gods give no real good, no true happiness to men on earth on any other terms. If you would bring happiness to others and be remembered in Greece, you must strive for the service of Greece—as you well may with your strength and your skill, if you do but use them rightly. As for my companion, who is called Vice and Folly and other such names, do not be misled by her: there is no pleasure and no happiness like those which you earn by strife and labour and with the sweat of your brow."

"Do not believe this foolish girl, who is called Virtue!" interrupted Vice hastily. "*My* way to happiness is short and pleasant; hers is hard, and long, and the end is doubtful."

"Come, Heracles," said Virtue quietly, "choose which of us you will follow. Her path leads through easy, worthless pleasures that grow stale and horrible and yet are craved after more and more. But follow me through toil and suffering to the great heritage which Zeus has planned for you."

"Lady!" cried Heracles, "I choose your path! Tell me how to set my foot on it, and I will not turn back however hard it prove, and whatever I have to endure on the way."

"You have chosen worthily," she said in her calm, gentle voice. "And for the beginning—look yonder! What is it that disturbs your cattle so?"

Heracles looked across the valley, and saw a great yellow lion leaping down the slope with open jaws towards the cows, who fled this way and that, lowing piteously in terror.

With a shout of fury Heracles sprang to his feet and went charging down the valley and up the other side. But by the time he got there, the lion had gone, and one of the cows lay dead.

"I'll kill that lion, or perish in the attempt!" cried Heracles angrily, and he turned back towards the two strange maidens—but there was no one to be seen.

Heracles returned to Thebes for his brother Iphicles, who took charge of the cattle, and he himself set out to trail the lion to its den. He did not succeed in this, however, and after a night and a day on Cithaeron he came down into a distant valley where dwelt King Thestius with his fifty beautiful daughters.

He was welcomed at the palace, and there he stayed for fifty nights entertained kindly by the fifty lovely princesses who took it in turns to attend upon the young man, who spent each day hunting upon the mountain.

After fifty days Heracles at length tracked the great lion to its lair, a cave in a dark, evil-smelling crevice of the rocks. Armed with a great club of olive wood cut roughly from a tree which he had torn up by the roots, Heracles strode boldly into the cave.

The great yellow lion came at him, roaring horribly, and Heracles retreated so as to have more light. In the entrance to the cave he stood at bay, and as the lion leapt, he struck it on the head with the club, bringing it to the ground, where it stood, trembling all over while its head swayed from side to side from the force of the blow.

Heracles struck once more, and the great beast lay dead before him. Then he pulled a knife from his belt and tried to skin it, but the hide was too tough. In vain he sharpened the knife on a stone, and even tried with the stone itself. It was only when he had cut out one of the terrible claws that he had an instrument keen enough for his task.

When the skin was off, Heracles dried and cured it carefully, and wore it ever afterwards tied over his shoulders and round his waist, with the scalp over his head like a helmet, so that it served both as clothing and armour.

On his way back to Thebes, Heracles met with a messenger from a certain King Eriginus, who was on his way to collect tribute from the Thebans whom he had conquered in war some years before this and robbed of all their weapons and armour.

Heracles was furious when he heard what the messenger wanted, and insulted him so grossly in his rage that King Eriginus sent a band of armed men to Thebes demanding that Heracles should be given up to him for punishment. Creon, King of Thebes, was ready to do this, for the Thebans had nothing with which to fight.

Heracles however gathered together the young men and armed them with the sacred trophies which hung in the temple of Athena. He taught them quickly how to use these weapons, and then led them against the company of men sent by King Eriginus, whom they defeated and drove out of Thebes.

Full of rage, Eriginus gathered an army and set out to destroy the city, but Heracles ambushed them in a narrow mountain pass and defeated them almost single-handed, killing the king and most of his captains. A quick march over the hills with his band of Theban youths gave Eriginus' little city into their hands, and the inhabitants were themselves forced to bring tribute each year to Thebes.

Amphitryon was killed in the battle, but Alcmena found a good second husband at Thebes, and lived there quietly for the rest of her life.

King Creon was so grateful for what Heracles had done—and so afraid lest he might think of seeking revenge for his willingness to give him up to Eriginus, that he made haste to offer him his daughter Megara in marriage.

The wedding was celebrated with great rejoicings, and Heracles settled down with every hope of becoming king of Thebes when Creon died.

So several years passed, and Heracles had three sons whom he adored, and for whose future he planned great things.

Now, living quietly in Thebes, Heracles did no great deeds of valour, nor did he free Greece from any plagues; and Zeus was troubled, seeing that the Hero was not fitting himself for his great task.

Hera was troubled also, though for a very different reason.

"What of your oath?" she cried to Zeus one day. "You swore that Eurystheus of Argolis should rule over all the natives of that land,[1] and yet Heracles the greatest of them dwells safely in Thebes, and will soon become King of the city which Cadmus built."

Then Zeus answered: "Hera, Queen of Olympus, do not be jealous any longer. Fate holds many troubles in store for Heracles, but what good will it do if he lives merely as a captain in Argolis, second only to Eurystheus?"

"I would have him as slave to Eurystheus!" cried Hera viciously.

"That I will grant," answered Zeus. "Let him serve that cowardly lord of Argolis, performing ten labours for him, the hardest that can be devised, and if he survives them, then grant him his freedom."

"I agree to that," said Hera, "for I will help Eurystheus to choose the tasks which Heracles must perform. But how shall we contrive to bring this servitude about? Force is useless against him, and if Eurystheus tries to make him his slave, Heracles will certainly kill him, come what may."

Zeus sighed; then he answered sadly:

"Hera, my Queen, it shall be as you wish. Send madness upon Heracles so that, unknowing what he does, he may commit murder and be driven, as an exile from Thebes. Go, see to it!"

Zeus nodded his head, and as Olympus shook to confirm his words, Hera sped gleefully on her way. But

---

1. **Eurystheus** (ū ris′thūs) **of Argolis** (är′gə lis) . . . **land.** When Heracles was about to be born, Zeus announced to the Immortals with much satisfaction that on that day would be born a descendant of Perseus who would rule over the entire Peloponnesian peninsula known as Argolis. Hera, in her jealousy, tricked Zeus by arranging that Heracles be born a day late and that his cousin Eurystheus be born on the day chosen for Heracles. Though Zeus was furious when he found out, he had to keep his word and agreed that Eurystheus should become ruler.

at a word from Zeus, Athena followed quietly to help Heracles as far as possible.

Now that morning the sons of Heracles and their cousins, the children of Iphicles, were engaged in martial exercises on the plain of Thebes, with other boys and young men of the city.

Heracles sat on a hillside watching them, his bow on his back and a quiver full of arrows by his side. Suddenly a dark shadow crossed the sun, and a low, evil moaning drew near and seemed to pause above his head. Then Heracles staggered to his feet, his eyes rolling wildly and foam starting from his lips.

"Enemies are upon us!" he cried. "Eurystheus of Argolis comes to take us prisoners and make us his slaves! I will not suffer it! Alone I will save Thebes and protect my beloved children from servitude!"

In his madness, he fitted an arrow to his bow, aimed and loosed it with such skill that his eldest son sank dead upon the plain. Then, while the boys fled away shrieking with terror he sent arrow after arrow screaming after them, until all three of his sons lay dead, with two of Iphicles' as well.

He would have done worse deeds, but Athena came at this moment, and seeing how quickly and how fatally the madness had worked, she took up a great stone and cast it at Heracles, laying him stunned and insensible on the ground. In this state he was bound and carried to Thebes where, Creon being too old to interfere, Lycus, a pretender to the throne, declared himself king and Heracles banished for murder.

When the madness had left him, Heracles in his misery and despair shut himself up in a dark room and refused to see or speak to anybody. No one dared to come near, until at length King Thestius visited him by command of Zeus, and told him that he must go to Delphi and ask Apollo how he was to atone for the terrible things he had done.

Then Heracles roused himself, gathered the lion skin about his shoulders, took the club in his hand and departed from Thebes forever: for now his children were dead, and his wife Megara had died of a broken heart.

When he came to Delphi, the voice of the oracle spoke to him out of the dark chasm beneath the temple:

"Heracles, son of Zeus, the time has come for you to begin the labours which will make you famous ever more, and which will fit you for the great purpose for which you were born. Go now to Eurystheus, who rules over Argolis, in his high citadel of Tiryns, and serve him faithfully in the tasks which he shall set you, doing him no harm nor striving to wrest the kingdom from him. At the last it may be that Zeus will raise you to Olympus and give you a place among the Immortals."

So Heracles set out for Argolis, accompanied only by his nephew Iolaus, the son of Iphicles, who refused to desert him. ✱

Discussion

1. (a) Why does Hera send the serpents to kill the infant Heracles? (b) What god comes to Heracles' assistance? (c) What effect does this happening have on Alcmena?
2. (a) From whom does Alcmena seek advice? (b) What does she learn about her son?
3. (a) What subjects form part of Heracles' education as a child? (b) In your opinion, why was each of these subjects important to the Greeks?

4. (a) Who are the maidens who come to Heracles on Mount Cithaeron? (b) Describe the actions, dress, and speech of each. Are they appropriate to the character described? Explain. (c) From which one does Heracles choose to accept advice? Why does he make this choice?

5. (a) What is the first deed of valor Heracles performs as a man? (b) What trophy from this deed does he keep to wear ever afterwards?

6. (a) What feat does Heracles perform that puts him in line to succeed Creon as king of Thebes? (b) Why does Hera claim that he must not become king of Thebes? (c) What demands does she make? (d) Under what conditions does Zeus agree to her demands?

7. (a) What means do Zeus and Hera devise to have Heracles exiled from Thebes? (b) Where does Heracles go for advice after his exile? (c) What advice is he given?

THE BEGINNING OF THE LABOURS

EURYSTHEUS, the cowardly weakling who had become King of Argolis after Amphitryon was banished,[1] lived in the mighty fortress of Tiryns, whose great walls had been built by the Cyclopes, and whose narrow gateway led beneath the Brazen Tower in which Acrisius had kept Danae prisoner.[2]

He was delighted when Heracles

arrived and gave him Apollo's message.

"Well, you're a fine, great, hulking fellow!" he cried insolently. "Be sure that I'll work you hard, though I doubt whether you'll be able to perform any of the Labours which I have in store for you. As a beginning, off you go up the valley and over the hills towards Corinth. Halfway there, turn left into the mountains, and bring me back the dead body of the Nemean Lion."

Now this Lion had fallen from the moon, and was ravaging the lands all round Nemea. Nobody could kill it, for it was invulnerable, its hide so hard that neither iron nor bronze nor stone could pierce it.

Heracles set out, and near Nemea he met a shepherd who told him which way to go.

"But you've no hope of killing that Lion," the shepherd warned him. "He has ravaged the land all about his lair, and nobody dares to go near him. Still, I'll make a sacrifice to Zeus, and perhaps he will at least give you an easy death."

"Wait thirty days," said Heracles shortly, "and if I have not returned by then, offer your sacrifice—but not to Zeus—to me, as a dead Hero!" Then he went on his way, armed with his club, his bow, a quiver full of sharp-tipped arrows, and a great sword by his side.

For a long while he searched in vain, but at last one evening he dis-

---

1. *Amphitryon was banished.* Years before, Amphitryon had accidentally killed Electryon (ē lek' trī on), Alcmena's father, and had been banished from his home in Argolis. Alcmena had forgiven him, however, and had followed him to Thebes, where they were wed.

2. *fortress of Tiryns . . . prisoner.* Acrisius (ə kris'i əs) imprisoned his daughter Danae (dan'ā ē) in the brass-plated tower at Tiryns for fear of a prophecy that he would be killed by her son, if she were to marry. Tiryns still exists today. The mighty blocks of stone which make up its ruins support the legend that it was built by the Cyclopes (sī klō'pēz), the race of one-eyed giants who had also helped the gods build Olympus.

covered the den of the fearsome Lion, which had two entrances and was strewn with the bones of men and cattle.

Heracles waited nearby, and presently the great tawny beast came prowling up the hillside, its mane streaked with the blood of its latest kill and its tongue licking the great bearded chin.

Setting an arrow to the string, Heracles drew it to his ear and loosed. The swift shaft hummed to its mark, but the sharp point rebounded from the Lion's flank and fell harmlessly to the ground.

With a cry of rage, Heracles drew his sword and charged, lunging with all his strength at the Lion's chest as the huge creature reared up on its hind legs to strike at him with its mighty claws. But the tempered iron bent as if it had been lead, and the Lion, though it fell backwards, then crouched for a spring, roaring horribly.

Suddenly Heracles remembered the lion which he had slain on Cithaeron, and taking his club in both hands he dealt this one a smashing blow on the head. The Lion stood dazed for a moment, then fled to its lair, where it turned, snarling, to wait for its adversary.

Realizing that no weapon could kill it, Heracles rushed into the cave with his cloak wrapped around one arm, and seized the Lion round the neck with the other. Then they rolled and wrestled on the ground, over and over, the Lion's struggles growing ever weaker and weaker, until at last it lay dead, throttled by the mighty arm about its neck. Before it died it made one final effort and bit off one of Heracles' fingers.

When the beast was dead, and he had rested and recovered from the battle, Heracles flung the body across his shoulders and strode off towards Tiryns. On the way he found the shepherd getting ready the sacrifice, which he was quite certain would need to be offered to the ghost of the dead hero.

Heracles laughed when he saw what was happening. "I'll join you in your prayers," he cried jovially, "but we'll make them to great Zeus, the giver of victory. You cannot sacrifice to a living man!"

Then he returned to Tiryns, and flung down the grizzly carcass before Eurystheus, who squeaked with horror and indignation.

"Take the nasty thing away!" he commanded, "and never dare to come into the city again, if you return from any more Labours. But the next one will not be accomplished so easily. Go and kill the Lernean Hydra!"

The second Labour was much more dangerous and difficult than the first, for the Hydra was a great serpent, with nine heads, which lived in the marshes of Lerna not far from Argos. It was so venomous that its very breath was deadly and it was the terror of the whole district.

Accompanied by Iolaus, Heracles drove down to the edge of the marsh in his chariot, and there Athena appeared to him.

"When you draw near to the Hydra's lair," she said, "you must make it come out by shooting fiery arrows into the cave. But when you fight, take care to hold your breath, for its very smell is deadly. Remember also that the centre head is immortal!"

Heracles thanked Athena, and did as she advised. After crossing the marsh and reaching the hillock of firm ground on which the Hydra lived, Heracles bade Iolaus light a fire, and then tying blazing bundles of grass to his arrows he shot them into the cave.

SPAIN

ITALY

THE
LABOURS
OF HERACLES

MEDITERRAN

AFRICA

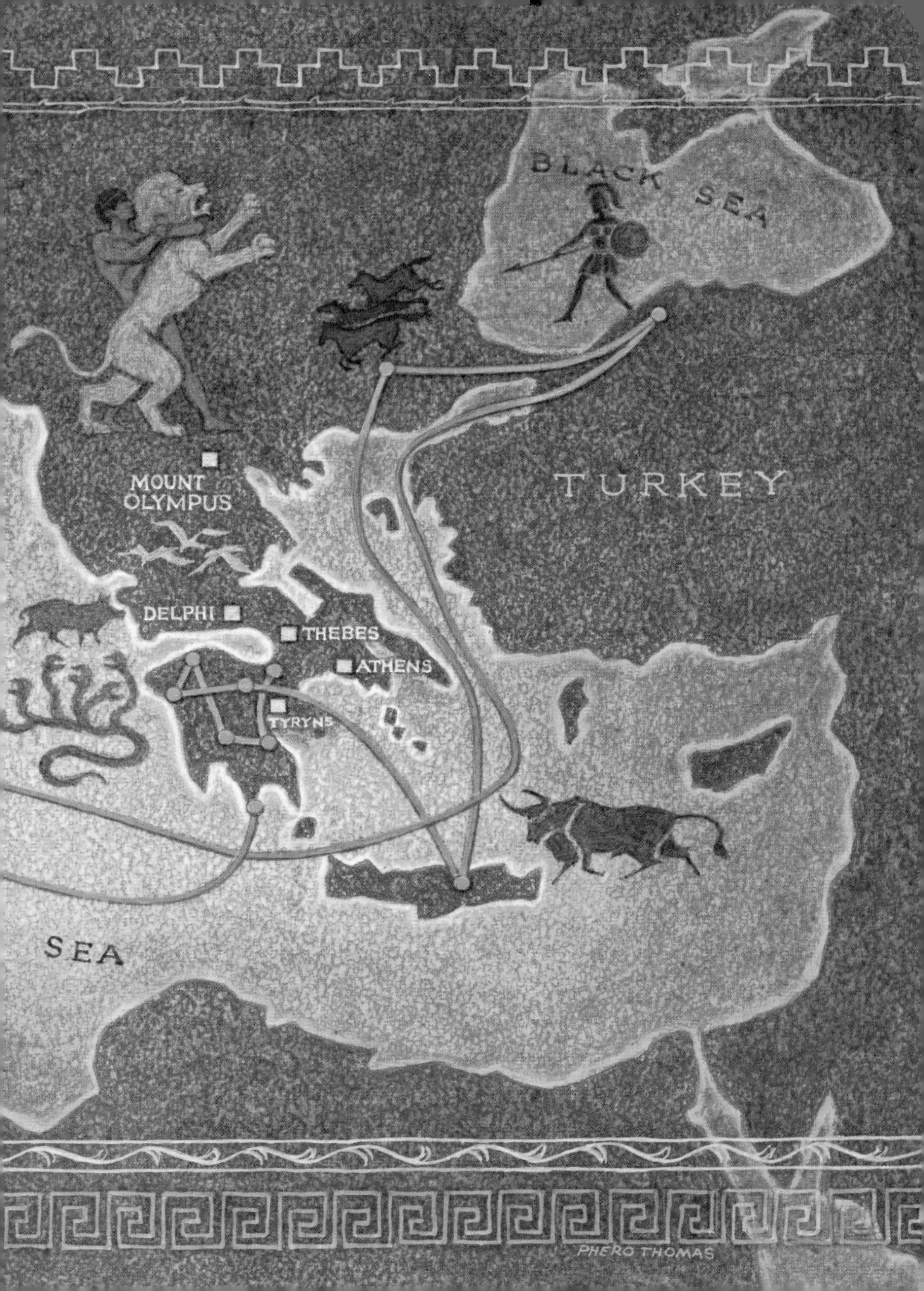

BLACK SEA

TURKEY

MOUNT
OLYMPUS

DELPHI

THEBES

ATHENS

TYRYNS

SEA

PHERO THOMAS

Out came the Hydra, hissing fiercely; and holding his breath, Heracles leapt forward and shattered the nearest head with a blow of his club. But what was his horror and consternation when, from the bleeding neck sprang out two new heads, each as fierce and deadly as the old! To make matters worse, a gigantic crab came scuttling out of the marsh and grabbed Heracles by the foot.

With a roar of rage, he crushed the crab with a single blow of his club, and shouted to Iolaus to light a torch and come to his assistance. Iolaus obeyed bravely, and as Heracles crushed each head of the Hydra with his club, he burnt and seared the shattered neck so that no new heads could grow from the bleeding stumps.

When at last the battle was over, Heracles cut off the immortal head with his sword and buried it under a gigantic rock, where doubtless it lies safely to this day. Then, having dipped his arrows in the Hydra's blood, thus making them deadly poisonous, he returned to his taskmaster.

"You have cheated!" cried Eurystheus, when he heard all the story, "Iolaus helped you, and your Labours must be performed by you alone. This one does not count, so you have still nine to accomplish. Off you go now, and for the next one bring me the Hind with the Golden Horns!"

This creature was a wonderful reindeer, sacred to Artemis, who had once seen five of them away in the distant north and capturing four by her fleetness of foot tamed them and harnessed them to her chariot. The fifth Hind wandered free in the hills of Arcadia, by the lovely river Cerynites, and no one dared touch it, knowing that it belonged to Artemis.

Heracles did not wish to harm this lovely creature and, though it was the swiftest of all deer, he chased it on foot for a whole year. On this quest he journeyed to the land at the back of the north wind, wandered there in the great, sweet-smelling pine forests, and came back into Greece, still pursuing the Hind. At length he overtook it in Arcadia, as it drew near to its usual dwelling place.

As he was bringing it towards Tiryns, Artemis, the Immortal Huntress, met him in anger and cried:

"Rash mortal, how dare you seize and carry away my Hind? Surely there is no reason why I should not immediately slay you with one of my golden arrows?"

Then Heracles answered humbly, telling her that it was not of his own will but at the command of Eurystheus that he was carrying the Cerynitian Hind to Tiryns. Artemis smiled when she heard the story of his quest, and her anger departed from her.

"Go on and show my Hind to your master," she said, "but be sure that you do it no harm, and that you return it to my sacred grove on the hills above the Cerynitian River—otherwise Eurystheus will feel my anger!"

Heracles delivered her message faithfully, and Eurystheus lived in terror until the Hind with the Golden Horns had been returned to its Immortal owner.

"Now," he said, with a sigh of relief when this was done, "bring me the Erymanthian Boar, and bring it alive, in case Apollo makes any fuss about it, as I believe it has something to do with him."

This Boar was, indeed, said to be the very one which killed Adonis, the beautiful youth who was the favourite of Aphrodite. She, in a moment of anger, blinded Erymanthus, a mortal son of Apollo, because he saw her bathing, and in revenge Apollo sent the Boar which gashed Adonis

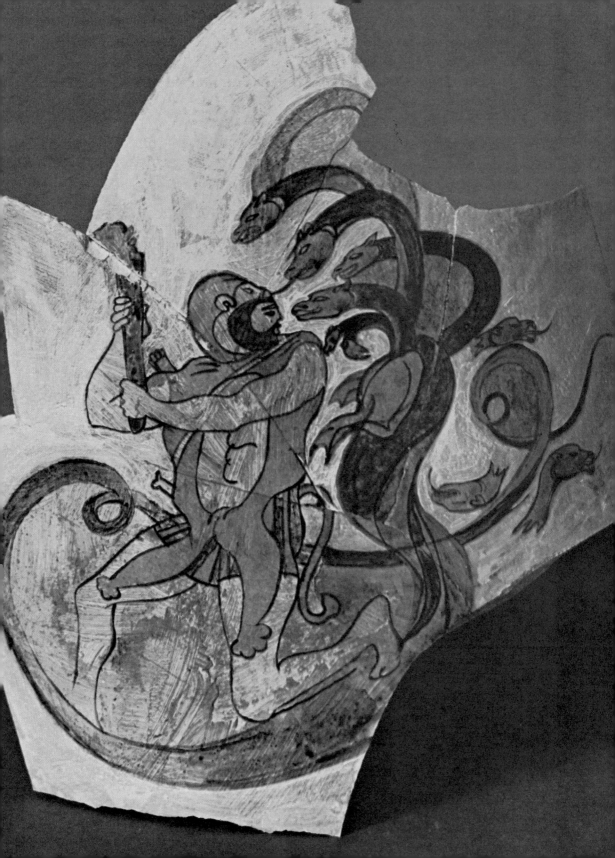

in the thigh, and killed him. When Adonis had died in her arms, Aphrodite wished to be revenged on the Boar, and had it brought before her tightly bound, though indeed it came willingly.

"Vilest of all wild beasts!" cried Aphrodite, "was it indeed you who gashed the thigh of my beautiful Adonis?"

"I did it," answered the Boar, "but not out of any hatred. For when I saw Adonis, I loved him and ran to kiss him, even as I had seen you do. In my devotion I forgot about my sharp tusks, and one of these it was that wounded him."

Hearing this, Aphrodite forgave the Boar, and set it free to wander on Erymanthia, where in time it became so fierce and savage that no one dared go near it, or live on the slopes of the mountain.

Yet Heracles set out undaunted, and on the way met with a Centaur called Pholus. These Centaurs were men only to the waist; below that they had the body and legs of a horse. Some of them were very wise, for, though not immortal, they lived to a great age; but the wisest of all was Chiron.

Pholus entertained Heracles hospitably in his cave, setting roast meat before him. But he foolishly opened a jar of wine which Dionysus had left in the cave, and the wild Centaurs who lived nearby, attracted by the smell, came crowding round, drank the strong wine, and were so maddened by it that they attacked Heracles. He was forced to shoot several of them with his poisoned arrows, and to drive the rest away. One of them, called Nessus, never forgave Heracles, but swore vengeance upon him, which he carried out in a strange fashion many years later.

After the battle Pholus picked up one of the arrows, marvelling that so little a thing could kill so great a creature as a Centaur. As he examined it, the arrow slipped from his fingers and pricked him in the foot; and the poison of the Hydra on its tip was so strong that he died in a few minutes.

Heracles grieved sorely when he saw that the kindly Centaur was dead, and buried him with all honour before continuing on his way in search of the Boar, which he caught by chasing it into a deep snowdrift, plunging in after it, and tying its legs firmly together.

When he arrived at Tiryns with the Boar and flung it down for inspection, Eurystheus was so terrified that he jumped into a large brass pot and hid at the bottom of it, gibbering with fear, until Heracles took the creature away. He flung it into the sea and it swam away to Italy, and its tusks were preserved ever after in the temple of Apollo at Cumae.

As soon as the coast was clear, Eurystheus emerged from his jar, and sent Heracles off on his next Labour:

"I won't have any more dangerous animals brought back this time!" he declared. "But I've thought of a thoroughly nasty job for you, and one that's absolutely impossible. Go to King Augeas over at Elis—he has the biggest herd of cattle of any man in Greece, thousands of them. Clean out his stables in a single day; they are rather dirty, as they've not been touched for thirty years!"

Off went Heracles, determined to accomplish this Labour too, however unpleasant and difficult it might be, and after careful examination he hit upon a scheme.

But first of all he went to King Augeas and, without saying anything about Eurystheus, declared:

"I'll undertake to clear your cattle-stables, yard and all, in a single day, while your cows are out on the pasture, if you'll promise to give me a tenth of your herd in payment."

Believing that what he offered was quite impossible, Augeas agreed to the bargain and swore solemnly to fulfil his side of it if the task was performed.

Heracles at once knocked holes in either end of the great stable-building, and by digging a short channel turned the courses of the rivers Alpheus and Peneus which flowed close by, so that both streams ran in through one gap and out through the other.

The strong current of water cleared out the thirty years' accumulation of dung in a very short time, and Heracles had turned back the rivers into their normal beds and rebuilt the gaps in the stable walls before the herds were driven home in the evening.

Augeas, however, refused to fulfil his side of the bargain, and Heracles had to return some years later to punish him. He did not reap any reward from Eurystheus either, who said that this Labour did not count, since Heracles had worked for hire, and packed him off to chase away the Stymphalian Birds.

These were the property of Ares: they had brazen claws, wings, and beaks, could moult their feathers at will—which sped down like sharp arrows—and ate human flesh. Athena advised Heracles not to go near them, for, so sharp were their beaks, that by flying straight at a man they could pierce even the hardest armour. But she lent him a pair of brazen castanets, which Hephaestus had made specially, and he went up onto a mountain overlooking the deep pool of Stymphalus which was surrounded by dense woods.

When Heracles clashed the castanets the noise, helped by the echo, was so terrible that the Birds flew up in fear, and fled shrieking and clapping their wings to the distant island of Aretias, where Heracles was to meet them again when he went voyaging with the Argonauts.[3]

As they fled he was able to bring down several of the Stymphalian Birds with his deadly arrows, and these he brought back in triumph to Eurystheus.

"That was a poor exploit!" he scoffed, kicking the dead birds contemptuously. "No one could be afraid of harmless little creatures like this: I wish I'd known before I sent you after them. However, off you go now, and bring me the Cretan Bull."

Heracles turned without a word, strode down to the harbour at Nauplia, and took ship to the beautiful island of Crete, where King Minos welcomed him warmly and entertained him in his great palace at Cnossus with its many stairs and passages, its strange, short columns with broad tops and narrow bases painted vivid reds and blues, and the running water and sanitation which were not to be surpassed until three thousand years later.

Minos gladly gave Heracles permission to take the Bull. "It is causing havoc all over the island," he told him. "The fault is mine, I'm afraid. Poseidon sent it to me out of the sea so that I might offer up a worthy sacrifice, but, in my greed and folly, I kept it myself and substituted one of my own bulls. After that it went mad, and now no one can do anything with it."

Heracles, however, was a match for any mad bull. He captured this

---

3. **Argonauts** (är'gə nôts), the crew of the ship *Argo*, led by Jason (jā'sn) on his quest of the Golden Fleece, the highly prized wool from a magic ram.

one without any difficulty and carried it away to Greece. When he reached Tiryns he let the Bull loose, and Eurystheus only just got into his jar in time, and crouched there gibbering with fear for several days.

But the Bull, failing to get hold of Eurystheus, fled away north, crossed the Isthmus of Corinth, and came to Marathon, beyond Athens. Here it found the pastures green and tasty, and decided to stay there, killing anyone who came near it.

Unfortunately one of its first victims was a son of Minos, who happened to be visiting Athens, and Minos would not believe that he had been killed by the Bull. So he invaded Athens, and only made peace when King Aegeus agreed to send an offering of seven youths and seven maidens every year to be devoured by the Minotaur, a monster half bull and half man which lived in the Labyrinth, a maze which the clever craftsman Daedalus had made.[4]

For twenty-seven years the Cretan Bull plagued the people of Marathon, and the Athenians regularly sent the tribute of youths and maidens to Minos, until Theseus came to Athens. But meanwhile Heracles was waiting in Tiryns for Eurystheus to recover from his fright; and when at last he did, the new Labour which he had devised for him was to journey north in Thrace and bring back the horses of King Diomedes.

"Only be sure you tame them before they reach Argolis," insisted Eurystheus, "for they are terrible creatures, which are fed only on the flesh of men!"

Heracles turned resolutely and went north, ever north until he came to the wild land of Thrace. There Diomedes welcomed him kindly: but Heracles knew that it was only a pretence, since it was this savage king's custom to throw his guests to the four terrible horses, who would immediately devour them.

Next day, with the help of a groom belonging to Diomedes, Heracles managed to steal the four horses, and even to harness them to a chariot, though they had never before known bit or bridle.

But the groom then betrayed him to Diomedes, who followed him with a band of men. Heracles, when he saw them coming, left the groom to hold the horses, and broke down a stretch of the sea wall. It was high tide, and the great waves came pouring through, and washed away most of the Thracians.

King Diomedes, however, he captured and carried back to the chariot. There, finding that the horses had already eaten the treacherous groom, he threw the wicked king to them as well, and they devoured him also.

After this Heracles drove off at full speed, and whether it was through eating their master, or whether he managed to tame them on the way, certain it is that when they reached Tiryns, Eurystheus had no need to hide himself in his brass jar.

The horses were quite tame now, and Eurystheus dedicated them to Hera. But they continued to be the strongest and most fearless horses in all Greece; and several of their descendants were used in the war against Troy.[5]

---

4. *Minotaur* (min′ə tôr) . . . *Daedalus* (ded′l əs) *had made.* King Minos had caused Daedalus to build the elaborate network of passages known as the Labyrinth (lab′ə rinth), from which no one was supposedly able to escape. There he put the Minotaur, monstrous offspring of the Cretan Bull, but was only able to keep it under control by offering human sacrifices of youths and maidens. The Minotaur was finally killed by Theseus (thē′sē əs), who found his way out of the Labyrinth afterwards by following a thread which he had unwound.

5. *war against Troy,* the famous Trojan War, during which the Greek army under the command of Agamemnon (ag′ə-mem′non), king of Mycenae, held the city of Troy under siege for ten years. This war has been the subject of innumerable writings, including *The Iliad* and *The Odyssey* of Homer.

As for Heracles, he was given no rest from labour: for Eurystheus sent him off again immediately—this time to bring back the belt of Hippolyta, the Queen of the Amazons, which his daughter greatly desired to possess. This belt was the gift of Ares, the Lord of War, to the bravest of the Amazons, who were a race of warrior women, trained to the use of arms and skilled particularly in casting the javelin and shooting with the bow.

They allowed no men in their wild land on the south coast of the Black Sea; and they kept their husbands in the next country, visiting them only for one month in every year.

To reach this land Heracles had to go by sea. So he gathered together a band of adventurers, and set sail for Troy and the Hellespont.   *

Discussion

1. (a) What makes the Nemean Lion especially dangerous and difficult to kill? **(b)** How does Heracles manage to overcome it? **(c)** In what ways are the experience and the trophy from Heracles' first feat of valor useful to him in this Labor?

2. (a) How does the shepherd show that he believes Heracles will not survive his adventure with the Lion? **(b)** Why does Heracles join in the shepherd's prayers and sacrifice?

3. (a) What help does Heracles receive from a god in the Labor of the Lernean Hydra? **(b)** What causes Heracles' horror and fear when he attempts to kill the Hydra? **(c)** Who is Iolaus, and how does he help Heracles destroy the Hydra?

4. (a) What kind of creature is the Cerynitian Hind? **(b)** Why is the connection of Artemis to this episode appropriate? **(c)** How is the Erymanthian Boar connected with Apollo?

5. (a) What kind of creature is a Centaur? **(b)** Why is Heracles forced to fight the Centaurs? **(c)** Why is he particularly grieved by Pholus' death?

6. (a) In what two ways does Heracles show his cleverness in his cleaning of the Augean Stables? **(b)** In what two ways is Heracles cheated after his completion of this Labor? **(c)** What would be meant by someone's referring to a task as "cleaning the Augean Stables"?

7. (a) Describe the dangers of the Labor of the Stymphalian Birds. **(b)** What assistance does Heracles receive in order to complete this Labor?

8. (a) Describe the circumstances by which the Cretan Bull had become wild and dangerous. **(b)** What further difficulty does the Bull create after being released? **(c)** What is the Minotaur and how does it enter into this tale?

9. For what reasons is the punishment Heracles deals King Diomedes a just one?

Word Study

Like many of the Greek myths, the story of Heracles' encounter with the Lernean Hydra has had its influence upon our language. One modern meaning for *hydra* is "any persistent evil." Why is it appropriate that an evil or difficulty which happens over and over again be called a *hydra* or *hydra-headed?*

Originally, *hydra* meant simply "water serpent," and was in turn derived from *hydor*, the Greek word for water. Many of our English words today use a form of this word as a prefix or a base word. Study the words in the left-hand column below; then choose the appropriate definition for each from the column at the right. You may use a dictionary if necessary.

hydrant	**(a)** *operated by water*
hydraulic	**(b)** *boat which glides on*
hydroelectricity	*the surface of water*
hydrophobia	**(c)** *street fixture for*
hydroplane	*drawing water directly*
hydrozoan	*from a main*
	(d) *power produced from*
	the force of water
	(e) *spineless water animal*
	(f) *morbid fear of water*

THE WANDERINGS OF HERACLES

HERACLES SAILED from Nauplia in Argolis with nine companions, amongst whom were two young heroes named Peleus and Telamon, who were both to win great fame in days to come.

After several adventures on the way, they came into the Black Sea and arrived in the land of the Amazons. They prepared for war, but to their surprise Queen Hippolyta came down to the harbour to visit them in a friendly manner, and even offered to give Heracles the belt as soon as he explained why he had come.

But Hera, who had an eye on what Heracles was doing, felt that this was far too easy a victory for him. So she disguised herself as an Amazon warrior and went hastening to the fortified citadel:

"Amazons, come swiftly!" she cried. "There is a ship in the harbour filled with men, vile pirates, who have captured our queen and will carry her off to sell as a slave in Greece or Troy!"

The Amazons needed no second summons. Out they came like bees when their hive is disturbed, and with fierce cries rushed down to the shore and attacked Heracles and his companions.

Terrible was the battle that followed: great were the deeds done that day by Peleus and Telamon; but it was Heracles with his unerring arrows who slew the leaders of the Amazons, and at length captured Melanippe the Queen's favourite sister. When he threatened to kill her unless they gave him the girdle and let him sail away in safety, they obeyed Hippolyta and marched back to their city in great sorrow, while Heracles set sail for Greece in triumph.

After several more adventures he arrived safely at Tiryns where Eurystheus received the Belt of the Amazon Queen for his daughter, and sent Heracles straight out again—this time to fetch back, without either asking or paying for them, the cattle of Geryon, who was said to be the strongest man in the world. This ogre had been born with three heads and six arms and hands, but only one body from the waist downwards. He lived on the mysterious island of Erythia in the Atlantic Ocean beyond the Straits of Gibraltar.

Heracles set out on this expedition alone, and journeyed overland through Italy, France, and Spain, slaying many wild beasts and other monsters on the way, until he came to the straits separating Europe from Africa.

Here he set up two great stone pillars, one at Gibraltar and the other at Ceuta: and the Straits were called the Pillars of Hercules by the Romans in consequence.

As he laboured to raise the pillar on the African coast, the heat was terrific and Heracles, half crazed by the sun's tropical glare, set an arrow to his bow and loosed it with all his strength in the direction of the Sun-chariot which the Titan Helios[1] was at

---

1. **Sun-chariot . . . Helios** (hē′lē os). According to one Greek legend, the sun is a fiery chariot, pulled by powerful horses and driven by Helios through the sky. (Compare Apollo's claim as Sun God, page 428.)

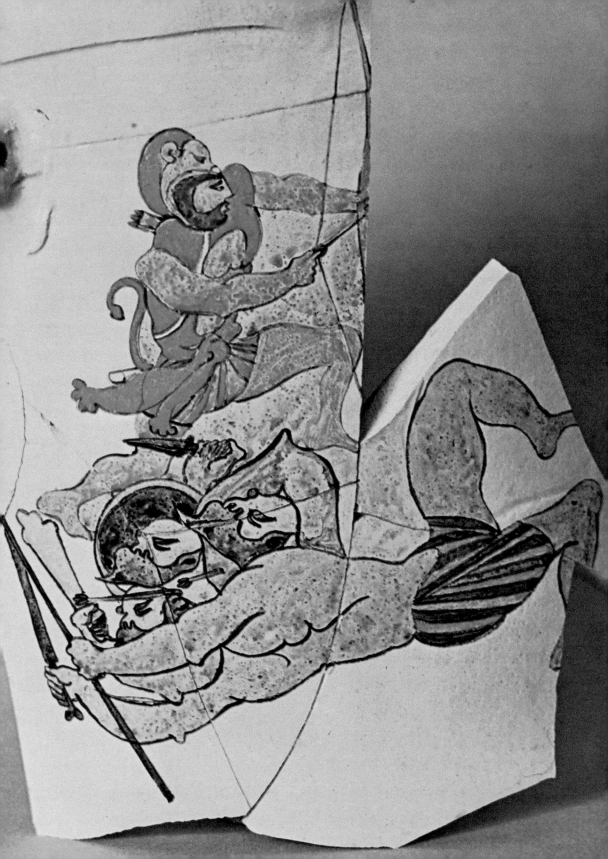

that moment bringing down towards the western ocean.

Helios was so tickled by the audacity of this struggling mortal that he not only veiled his beams immediately, but lent Heracles his magic goblet of pure gold, shaped like a gigantic water lily.

In this Heracles crossed to the island of Erythia, using his lionskin as a sail. On reaching the shore his first care was to moor his strange boat in a concealed inlet: then he climbed a hill in the centre of the island to spy out the land. He had scarcely reached the summit, when a great dog came rushing at him open-mouthed, only to meet his end from a single blow of the deadly club.

As he descended in the direction of the pastures where he could see the beautiful red cattle grazing, Heracles was attacked by the herdsman, whom he killed also, but only after a fierce fight. Heracles then drove the cattle towards the shore, but before he reached it the ogre Geryon came rushing towards him, brandishing various weapons in his six huge hands, and shouting threats of terrible vengeance.

Heracles knew that he was no match for so powerful a monster if they came to hand-grips; so, quick as thought, he discharged three arrows one after another, one through each of the ogre's three throats: and that was the end of him. Then he drove the cattle into the magic goblet, sailed back to Spain, and having returned his strange vessel to Helios with many thanks, began the weary task of driving the herd overland all the way back to Greece.

On the way many adventures befell him. Once in the south of France near where Marseille now stands, he was attacked by a large army of war-like natives. He fought and fought until all his arrows were spent, and then it seemed that his end had come, for the ground was soft with not a stone in sight. In despair, Heracles prayed to Zeus, who took pity on him and rained down stones from above, thus supplying him with ample ammunition. That great plain covered with smooth round stones may be seen to this very day.

On another occasion Heracles camped for the night in a valley among seven low hills where now stands the city of Rome. He did not know that a fire-breathing troll called Cacus lived in a huge cave under Mount Aventine, nor did he realize in the morning that this creature had come down during the night and stolen several of the cattle. For Cacus had carefully blotted out all the footmarks, and the mouth of his cave was hidden by a great door of solid rock which slid down in grooves.

But just as Heracles was setting out in the morning, he heard a cow lowing somewhere in the hillside: for Cacus had very foolishly taken one of the cows who had a calf, and left the calf with the herd.

Heracles at once counted the cattle, found that some were missing, and set out to deal with the thief. Before long he found the door of the cavern, but Cacus, realizing that he was discovered, hastily broke the chains and balances which should have raised it, and even Heracles could not lift the enormous block of stone and slide it up in its grooves.

Three times Heracles strove to stir it, and three times drew back, gnashing his teeth with rage. But after the third attempt, as Cacus laughed triumphantly within, Heracles saw that there was a crack in the hillside above the cave. He climbed up to it, set his heels in it and his back against the hill itself, and pushed with all his might. The crack slowly widened, and then with a sudden roar the whole side of the hill slid away and a great mass of rock went crashing down into the river at the foot.

But Heracles landed on the floor of the cavern, which was now open to the light of day for the first time, and rushed to attack Cacus. The troll immediately filled the hollow with smoke which he belched out of his mouth; but Heracles plunged valiantly into the thick of it, guided by the flames which Cacus was breathing, and caught him by the throat. Very soon the fight was over, and Heracles, singed and choking from the smoke, dragged the troll's body out into the open. Then he gathered the missing cattle and continued on his way.

One more strange adventure befell him as he drew near to the north of Greece, for Hera sent a giant gadfly which stung the cattle and scattered them far and wide. Heracles pursued them relentlessly, and at length, having retrieved nearly all of them, he lay down to rest in a cave somewhere in the hills of the country now called Bulgaria, on the west coast of the Black Sea.

It was cold and stormy, and Heracles slept long and heavily after his laborious search for the cattle. But in the morning he found that the horses which drew his chariot had mysteriously disappeared.

In a great fury he wandered far and wide until at length he came to another cave in which he found a mysterious creature. She was like a woman from the waist upward, but below that was a scaly snake. He looked at her in wonder, but asked nevertheless:

"Strange maiden, have you seen my horses?"

"Yes," she replied, "it was I who took them in when they strayed this way. But I will never give them up to you, unless you wed me, according to the custom of this country. Here we are married when we have kissed thrice; and the marriage lasts only for as long as we both wish it."

There was no help for it, so Heracles kissed the snake-maiden three times, and lodged in her cave for three days.

At the end of that time she gave him back his horses, and before leaving he strung the spare bow which he carried with him and gave it to her, saying:

"Lady, I prophesy that you will have three sons: let the one who can draw this bow as I do, come and seek me if he wishes for assistance in winning his fortune. But if he does not come, then let him, and no other, rule over this land after you."

Then Heracles set out once more, and this time he reached Greece safely with the cattle.

But as he was crossing the Isthmus of Corinth, a giant bandit who had taken possession of the place and stopped all travellers to rob or kill them, held him up:

"Hand all those cattle over to me!" he cried, "and you shall pass in safety."

"Never," replied Heracles briefly.

Then the bandit picked up a huge rock and hurled it at him. Heracles dodged the great whirling mass, and picking it up flung it back with such good aim that the bandit never again molested travellers.

So Heracles came to Tiryns and handed over the cattle to Eurystheus.

"Now!" he cried, "I have accomplished the ten Labours which you set me, and spent more than eight years of my life in doing so: now I may go free!"

"Not so," answered Eurystheus, "for you know that two Labours do not count. Iolaus helped you to kill the Lernean Hydra, and you cleaned the Augean Stables for hire. So Hera commands that you perform two further Labours. Go now and bring back three Golden Apples from the Garden of the Hesperides!"

Once again Heracles bowed to his fate and with a weary sigh turned his back on Tiryns and set off once more.

THE GOLDEN APPLES, AND THE HOUND OF HELL

Discussion

1. **(a)** Who were the Amazons? Why might a tall, powerful woman sometimes be referred to as an Amazon? **(b)** For what reasons is it appropriate that the Belt of Hippolyta be a present from Ares? **(c)** What must Heracles overcome in order finally to secure the Belt of Hippolyta?

2. **(a)** What famous landmark is said to have been created by Heracles during the Labor of the cattle of Geryon? **(b)** How and why does Helios give assistance to Heracles in this Labor? **(c)** What special dangers does Geryon present? **(d)** How does Heracles manage to overcome Geryon?

3. On his way back to Tiryns with the cattle of Geryon, Heracles has further adventures in France, Italy, Bulgaria, and Greece. Describe the four encounters which delay his return.

4. In his first ten Labors Heracles displays strength, swiftness and cleverness. **(a)** Which of his successes depend primarily on his strength? **(b)** Which depend on his speed? **(c)** Which depend on his cleverness or cunning? **(d)** In which of his Labors is it necessary for Heracles to rely on the help of the gods for his success?

5. Why does Eurystheus claim that two of the Labors do not count?

6. Give examples of ways in which Hera demonstrates that her hatred and jealousy continue strong.

HERACLES SET OUT wearily on his eleventh Labour without any idea of where the Golden Apples were to be found. But Zeus was watching him, since he had a special deed for him to perform which, as it turned out, did more to save both mortals and Immortals than any help which Heracles could give in the coming war with the Giants.[1]

For all this while Prometheus the Good Titan had been lying chained to Mount Caucasus in punishment for disobeying Zeus by bringing fire to mankind.[2] And the great eagle still came every day to devour

---

1. coming war with the Giants. In revenge for the Olympians' having overthrown the Titans, who were her children, Mother Earth had given birth to a race of Giants who, according to prophecy, would one day attack and try to overthrow Olympus. These Giants could be defeated only by an exceedingly brave and strong mortal. With this in mind Zeus had fathered Heracles and agreed to his performing the Labors, which would groom him for this final task.

2. Prometheus (prə mē′thē əs) . . . **fire to mankind.** Because he had given aid to the Olympians, Prometheus had not been cast into the underworld prison, Tartarus, with the other Titans. Later, however, he gave fire to man—the one gift Zeus had expressly forbidden—and was punished by being chained forever on Mount Caucasus (kô′kə səs) "on the eastern edge of the world" beyond the Black Sea. It was then Prometheus made the prophecy that the Giants would rise against Olympus and that a mortal was needed to defeat them. But he also prophesied that Zeus would be overthrown one day. Because he would not tell how this fate could be avoided, Zeus daily tortured him by having an eagle eat his liver, which grew again each night.

his liver, which still grew again every night: but in spite of all his suffering, Prometheus still refused to tell Zeus of the danger greater than that of the Giants, which was threatening him.[3]

Nevertheless, Zeus had grown merciful with time. If Prometheus had suffered in body, Zeus had suffered in mind—for he knew that at any moment he might make the mistake of which Prometheus had prophesied, and which only Prometheus could prevent.

So when Heracles came into the land of Illyria and begged the Nymphs who lived there to tell him how he might find the Golden Apples, they replied that, by the command of their father, Zeus, he must journey on, to Mount Caucasus, and ask Prometheus.

The way was long and dangerous, but at length Heracles came to the great mountain above the world's end. Climbing by chasm and crevasse, by steep glissade and slippery glacier, he came to the great cliff-face on which the Titan was chained. And as he clambered up beside him, the great eagle swooped down to its horrible feast, and the mighty Titan screamed aloud in his agony.

But Heracles, with a shout of rage and pity, fitted an arrow to his bow, drew it to the head, and loosed it with all his might. The great eagle flew up, transfixed by the arrow, and plunged down into the black waves thousands of feet below.

"Who are you, rash mortal?" asked Prometheus slowly.

"I am Heracles, the son of Zeus," was the answer. "And I come here by his command, to free you. For Zeus forgives you for your great crimes against himself, and asks your pardon for the torture to which he has put you. Nevertheless, he bids me say that, since his great decrees cannot be broken altogether, you must wear a ring on your finger forever as a token that you are still bound in fetters of metal."

Prometheus nodded his head and smiled:

"You are the Hero of whom I prophesied," he said. "Your hand shall strike down the Giants and save Olympus from ruin. But that you would come to set me free, I did not know, for a prophet cannot foretell his own future. But come, strike off my fetters and let me girdle my finger with the ring; and in memory of my sufferings I declare that mankind shall ever after wear rings in token of this day."

Heracles set to work; and while he hacked and twisted at the brazen fetters he told Prometheus of his quest and asked him about the Golden Apples of the Hesperides.

"They grow on the tree which Mother Earth gave to Hera as a wedding present," said Prometheus, "and that tree is in a magic garden on the world's western verge, beyond the mountain on which my brother Atlas stands forever supporting the starry sky on his shoulders.[4] The Dragon Ladon curls round that tree, and in the garden dwell the immortal daughters of Hesperus, the Warden of the Evening Star, which is also the Star of the Morning; and he is the son of Atlas. Ask Atlas to assist you: for no mortal may enter that garden without great danger; and he has built a great wall round it that cannot be climbed."

Many other things Prometheus

---

3. *danger greater . . . threatening him.* Prometheus knew that if Zeus completed his plans to marry a sea goddess named Thetis (thē′tis) he would surely be overthrown, for Thetis was destined to bear a son more powerful than his father.
4. *Atlas* (at′les) *. . . on his shoulders.* Atlas is thus being punished by Zeus for leading the Titans in the battle against the Olympians in the beginning of the world.

told to Heracles, so that when his work was ended he went on his way with bowed head, thinking of the greatness and nobility of the mighty Titan, helper of mankind.

Once again Heracles met with many adventures as he traversed the earth on his quest: but there is not time now to tell how he fought with Cycnus the son of Ares, slew him and wounded even the Immortal Warlord himself; nor how in Egypt the cruel King Busiris who sacrificed all strangers came to find himself bound and offered up on his own altar; nor even of his adventures with the King of Ethiopia. But as he traversed Libya on his way to Mount Atlas, his strength was put to the proof in the hardest wrestling match of his whole career. For there dwelt the savage Antaeus, a giant son of Earth, who challenged all strangers to wrestle with him; and when he had killed them with his mighty hands, he used their skulls to decorate the temple of Poseidon. He lived in a cave and slept on the bare earth; and he would rob the lionesses of their cubs and eat them raw for his supper.

Heracles needed no second bidding when Antaeus challenged him to wrestle. He flung off his lionskin, anointed himself all over with oil, and stood ready. Antaeus did the same, but in place of oil he covered himself from head to foot in dust.

Then they seized hold of one another, arms twisting with arms, bending and swaying backwards and forwards, striving to reach each other's throat with their clutching fingers. Heracles proved the stronger, and with a mighty effort flung the almost fainting Antaeus to the ground.

But then an amazing thing happened. The moment Antaeus touched the earth all his weariness passed from him, and he sprang to his feet with a shout of triumph as fresh and strong as at the beginning of the battle.

Astonished, Heracles closed with him once more, and with a great effort flung him to the ground again. Up jumped the young giant with his strength and vigour again renewed, and Heracles exclaimed:

"A Son of Earth, are you? I might have guessed from whence you drew your strength! Come on again, and this time I'll see to it that we fight standing: if fall you must, fall upon me, and see what sort of vigour I can impart to you!"

Again they wrestled, and this time Heracles exerted his great strength and lifted Antaeus above his head, and held him there in spite of all his struggles, and did not lower him even when he grew weaker and weaker. But at last he took him in his arms, still careful that not so much as a toe touched the ground, and hugged him to death as a bear might.

Flinging aside the corpse of his cruel foe, Heracles continued on his way, and came soon to the great mountain, the highest in the known world, on top of which stood Atlas the Titan, holding up the sky lest it should sink down again upon the earth as it had done in the beginning of the world.

"I come to you for help, great Titan," cried Heracles when he had climbed to the peak on which Atlas stood. "Your brother Prometheus advised me to ask your assistance: I am Heracles, and I come for three of the Golden Apples to deliver to my taskmaster, Eurystheus of Tiryns, who loads me with labours by command of Immortal Hera."

"Heracles, son of Zeus," answered Atlas, "I was warned long ago of your coming by wise Themis, sister of my Titan father. I will do what you wish if you will perform two great deeds to assist me. While I am away you must take my place and hold the sky upon your shoulders; and before you do this, you must slay the Dragon Ladon who guards the tree; for even I may not touch the fruit while he lives."

Heracles looked down beyond the mountain, towards the Western Ocean, and saw far below him the lovely Garden of the Hesperides. There were the cool glades and the silver leaves of Paradise, and in the midst the great tree shining with the golden fruit, while three lovely nymphs, the daughters of Hesperus, danced and sang in the dappled sunlight.

Then he saw the Dragon curled about the tree, a monster longer than any he had slain, its scales shining with gold and blue. He drew an arrow from his quiver, fitted it to his bow, and shot with so unerring an aim that it pierced the Dragon's throat. The creature uncurled from the tree and glided away into the bushes there to die slowly and strangely, for its tail was still alive several years later when the Argonauts visited the spot.

When Ladon the Dragon had gone, Atlas shifted his mighty burden on to the broad shoulders of Heracles, and stretching himself with a great sigh of relief, he hurried off in the direction of the Garden.

The hours passed slowly for Heracles as he stood there holding up his gigantic burden, and he felt weary and ill at ease as the light faded and the stars began twinkling in his hair. All through the long night he stood there, supporting the sky and in the morning he could have shouted for joy when he saw Atlas striding up the mountain carrying three Golden Apples in his hand.

But his heart sank suddenly when the Titan stood still at a little distance and looked at him with a cruel gleam in his eyes.

"Here are the Apples," said Atlas. "But I will take them to King Eurystheus myself. I have been through great dangers to obtain them; it is only fair that I should have a sufficient respite from my burden. You cannot know what joy it is to walk the earth again, and feel no longer that heavy weight upon my shoulders."

"You do indeed deserve your holiday," answered Heracles, thinking quickly, "and I wish you all joy of it, though I look forward to your return, for this is certainly a very heavy load. But when you set it upon my shoulders, I thought it was to remain there only a few hours, and I paid little attention to how it was placed. Now you, who have supported it so long, must be an expert sky-carrier: can you teach me how to arrange the burden most easily?"

"I can indeed," replied the slow-witted Atlas, "you should hold it like this—let me show you."

He dropped the Golden Apples, and stepping forward eagerly, took the sky on his shoulders once more, explaining as he did so what was the easiest way to hold it up.

Heracles watched carefully. "You know," he said gravely, "you do it so much better than I . . . I think I'd better leave you to it, and myself take those Golden Apples to Eurystheus. Every man to his own task!"

With that he set off down the mountain, leaving Atlas to lament the loss of his only chance of freedom.

When he reached the sea coast, Heracles took ship for Greece and after a long voyage was landed at Lindos on the island of Rhodes. He was so ravenously hungry after the journey that he killed the first ox he came upon, and roasted a great dinner for himself. But the owner of the ox stood on the lovely hillside where the castle of Lindos stands today, and cursed the stranger for an hour without stopping.

Heracles paid for the ox when he had eaten it. But in after days when the people of Lindos honoured Heracles as an Immortal, they always invoked him with curses instead of prayers in memory of his visit to their land.

Heracles went on his way to Tiryns when his hunger was satisfied, and delivered the Golden Apples to Eurystheus. That cowardly king was afraid to receive them, in case Hera should take vengeance on him, and said:

"I'll make you a present of them. You deserve them after so much trouble! You've only one more Labour to perform, and if you return safely from that, I expect you'll need the Golden Apples!" He sniggered cruelly, for the final Labour was to be the hardest and most dangerous of all — no less than to descend into the Realm of Hades and bring back Cerberus, the three-headed Hound of Hell.

When Heracles heard this, he turned away in despair, and left Tiryns, still carrying the Golden Apples.

But Zeus again was watching over him, and sent Athena and Hermes to his help. First of all Heracles gave the Apples to the Goddess, who handed them over to Aphrodite to take care of for the time being. But when, later, Athena returned them to the Garden of the Hesperides, she took pity on Atlas and showed him the Gorgon's Head — and he became the topmost peak of stony Mount Atlas with great thankfulness.

Meanwhile the two Immortals led Heracles to the great cave at Taenarum, not far from Sparta, and down into the gloomy depths of the earth until they came to the Underworld which was bounded by the Black River Styx. Here Athena waited, while Hermes went on with Heracles, for it was one of his offices to lead souls down to Hades.

At the River Styx the dark old ferryman, Charon, was waiting with his boat. He was only allowed to ferry dead souls across that stream, and they paid him one coin, called an *obol*, which was always placed ready in a dead person's mouth. He would have refused to take this living passenger, but Heracles scowled at him so fiercely that he did not dare: and he was punished afterwards by Hades for his cowardice.

On the other side Heracles found himself in the grey, twilit land of the dead, where ghosts flitted about moaning and gibbering.

The first he met was the Gorgon Medusa, and when he saw that terrible shape, he fitted an arrow to his bow; but Hermes reminded him with a smile that she was only a harmless ghost, killed by Perseus.

Heracles saw many terrible sights in the Realm of Hades, for he crossed the Fiery River of Phlegathon and entered Tartarus, the prison where the Titans lay, and where the wicked are punished.

He saw, for example, Ixion on his flaming wheel, the wicked king who had broken faith with Zeus; and Tantalus who stood up to the neck in cool water and yet could not quench his burning thirst since the water went away as soon as he stooped to drink. Also he saw Sisyphus, thief and murderer, whose doom was to roll a stone to the top of a hill down which it always rolled just as he neared the summit; and the daughters of King Danaus who murdered their husbands and had to fill forever a cask which had a hole in the bottom.

Only one of the souls in torment was Heracles allowed to free; and that was Ascalaphus, who had given Persephone six pomegranate seeds when Hades first carried her down to his kingdom. If she had not eaten these, she could have returned to earth forever: but since she had eaten in the realm of the dead, she was forced to return there for six months every year. So Demeter in fury placed a heavy stone on top of Ascalaphus; but Heracles was allowed to roll it away, and Ascalaphus was turned into an owl instead.

At last Heracles came to where Hades and Persephone sat in state, and he told them why he was there and begged them to lend him their terrible hound.

"You may willingly take Cerberus," answered Hades, "if you can overcome him without the use of weapons."

So Heracles returned to the bank of the Styx, and Cerberus rushed at him, since he was there to prevent the souls of the dead from leaving the Realm of Hades. Cerberus had three mighty heads with lion-like manes bristling with snakes; and in place of a tail a serpent writhed and hissed. Heracles wrapped his lionskin about himself, seized hold of the brute and squeezed him hard. Cerberus struggled and tried to bite; but the lionskin was too tough, and Heracles was too strong. Only the serpent-tail managed to hurt him; but even then Heracles would not let go.

At last Cerberus gave way, and Heracles carried him off in triumph, crossing the Dark River with the help of Hermes and Athena. They led him up the great cavern near Troezen through which Dionysus had brought his mother Semele,[5] and at last they saw the light of day.

To Heracles this was welcome, but when Cerberus beheld the glorious light of the sun, he struggled, and howled dismally, and the white foam flying from his jaws spattered all the grass. From this foam grew the flower called Aconite which gives the deadly poison known as wolf's-bane.

Holding his captive firmly, Heracles set out at once for Tiryns. When he arrived there, he strode straight into the citadel, shouting for Eurystheus. And when the King appeared, Heracles cried:

"My last Labour is achieved! Here is Cerberus!"

He dropped the dog on the ground as he spoke, and it rushed at Eurystheus, barking with all three mouths and hissing with every snake on its three manes.

Eurystheus turned with a scream of terror and leapt into his brass pot, where he was still shrieking with fear when Heracles left Tiryns for the last time, carrying Cerberus in his arms.

Straight back to the Dark River of Styx he went, and placed the terrible Hound of Hell on the gloomy shore. Then he returned to earth rejoicing, his twelve Labours ended, free at last. ✱

5. *cavern near Troezen* (trē′zen) . . . *Semele* (sem′ə lē). Dionysus had bargained with Hades so that he might take his mother with him to Olympus. He led her out of the Underworld through this chasm which Zeus caused to be opened in the earth. (See Dionysus, page 429.)

Discussion

1. **(a)** Why are the Golden Apples of the Hesperides so valuable and so difficult to obtain? **(b)** How does Heracles go about getting information on how to find them?

2. **(a)** Relate the story of Prometheus and his torture. **(b)** Why is Prometheus important to Zeus? **(c)** What custom practiced widely today is supposedly explained by this part of the Prometheus legend? Explain.

3. What is particularly strange about Heracles' wrestling match with Antaeus?

4. (a) Who is Atlas and how did he come to be in this situation? **(b)** Why is it necessary for Heracles to enlist Atlas' help? **(c)** How does Heracles outwit Atlas?

5. (a) Why does Eurystheus give the Apples to Heracles? **(b)** What does Heracles then do with them?

6. (a) Why does Heracles need the assistance of the gods in his last Labor of the Hound of Hell? **(b)** What assistance does he get?

7. (a) Describe the Underworld as the Greeks pictured it. **(b)** Can you compare the Greek concept of the Underworld with any other concepts with which you may be familiar? **(c)** How does the Greek concept of "heaven" (Mount Olympus) compare to any other concepts you may be familiar with?

8. (a) Why might a particularly unattractive woman be referred to as a Gorgon? **(b)** Explain how the legend of Tantalus provided us with the word *tantalize,* meaning "to torment or tease." (You may use a dictionary if necessary.) **(c)** What sort of task might be called a "task of Sisyphus"? **(d)** Why is the name Cerberus sometimes given to a surly, watchful guard? **(e)** What is appropriate about the connection in legend of Cerberus and wolf's-bane?

Word Study

Greek place names, as well as names of mythological characters, have contributed much to the English language. Each of the adjectives at the top of the next column is based upon the name of a place, real or mythical, which figures in these selections.

Look up each word in a dictionary. Note its meaning in current usage and its derivation. Then decide into which of the sentences the word will best fit. Be prepared to explain why your choice is appropriate.

Delphic   *Arcadian*
labyrinthine *Stygian*
Olympian

1. They all stood silent, awed by the _____ beauty of the vast, mountainous scene before them.

2. The movie's _____ setting seemed particularly appropriate for the tale of horror and death which was to follow.

3. Viewing the quiet, peaceful countryside, he commented that here a man could live in _____ contentment.

4. When they found themselves arguing about the meaning of their boss' announcement, the confused employees began to wonder if he had been deliberately _____.

5. She told him she hadn't time to explore the _____ windings of his logic.

The Author

Roger Lancelyn Green was born in Norwich, England, in 1918 and was educated in Surrey, in Liverpool, and at Merton College, Oxford. In addition to having had a varied career as actor, bookseller, librarian, editor, and researcher, he is the author of many books of poetry, mythology, and fairy tales. Greatly interested in ancient Greece, he has visited that country at least eight times to study its history, literature, mythology, archeological remains, and modern aspects. Many of his works, such as *Tales of the Greeks and Trojans, Ancient Greece,* and *Mystery at Mycenae,* are results of this research and study. Other of his works reflect his interests in the authors Lewis Carroll, Rudyard Kipling, and J. M. Barrie. Mr. Green now lives in his ancestral home, Poulton-Lancelyn, in Cheshire, England.

HERACLES in the art of the past

Vase painting was one of the most common forms of ancient Greek art. These decorated vases, which were found in almost every Greek household, showed the daily life of the Greeks in all its aspects —working, playing, and worshiping. The artists also drew much of their subject matter from the myths and stories of the gods and heroes. The fact that Heracles was one of the most popular of Greek heroes is demonstrated by the number of times he appears in these vase paintings, as well as in the other forms of art that have been preserved. The vases shown on this page, from the fifth and sixth centuries B. C., are but a small sampling of those works of art which illustrate the legend of Heracles.

Above: At the sight of Heracles carrying the Erymanthian Boar, Erystheus hides in his jar.

At right: Accompanied by Hermes, Heracles requests Hades to allow him to take Cerherus from the Underworld.

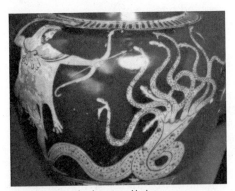

Heracles slays the Lernean Hydra.

Heracles prepares to fight the ogre Geryon.

Unit 7 Review

1. Consider the nature of the twelve Labors which Heracles performs. (a) Which of them are believable tasks, that is, deeds which could conceivably be performed by a human being with sufficient courage, strength, endurance, and cunning? (b) Which are not? How does Heracles manage to perform those tasks which are beyond human capabilities?

2. Note that toward the last the Labors seem both to increase in difficulty and to become more fantastic. (a) How do the characters and the situation make the Labor of the Golden Apples different from all the preceding ones? (b) What makes the Labor of the Hound of Hell the most fantastic of all? (c) Why is this appropriately the last of Heracles' Labors?

3. The map on pages 442–443 shows the supposed locations of the Labors of Heracles. (The line connecting these locations shows only the order of the Labors, however, not Heracles' route; he had to return to Tiryns after each Labor.) Note that the later, more fantastic adventures are those which take place far away from Heracles' home in Greece. (a) What possible explanation might there be for the difference in believability between adventures happening near Heracles' home and those happening far away? (b) To complete his Labor of the Golden Apples, Heracles must travel to "the eastern edge of the world" (Mount Caucasus, page 454, footnote 2), and to the "world's western verge" (Mount Atlas, page 455). What do these phrases suggest about the ancient Greek concept of the world in which they lived? (c) Why does it seem ap-

propriate that Heracles travel to the two edges of the world in performing his next-to-last Labor? (d) What do you think makes it possible for the most fantastic adventure of all—the descent into Hades—to take place near a specific spot in Greece (Taenarum)?

4. (a) To what extent do the gods seem to play a part in daily events on earth? (b) Why do you think it is all right for Heracles to be aided by the gods but not by mortals? (Note that Eurystheus does not count the Labor in which Iolaus helped.)

5. Following is a list of personal qualities which have been considered important by various peoples in history. Determine the importance of each of these qualities to the ancient Greeks by discussing instances in these selections where a character exhibits, ignores, or denies the quality.

    a. respect for others' property
    b. hospitality
    c. remaining steadfast and unchanging
    d. keeping one's word
    e. cunning
    f. obedience
    g. courage

Which of these qualities do we consider most important in our society today?

6. (a) Describe the character of Heracles. (b) Describe the character of Eurystheus. (c) What devices does the author use in order to make Eurystheus a comic character?

7. The wing-footed god Hermes (Roman: Mercury) is used by many organizations as a symbol either to represent themselves or to be associated with their products. Hermes' caduceus is the symbol of the Medical Department of the U.S. Army, and often is used to represent medicine in general. Aphrodite (Venus) and Atlas are familiar figures in the world of advertising. Name as many products or companies as you can which use either characters from Greek mythology or their attributes. In each case, explain why the symbol is appropriate to the product or the company.

8. As we become familiar with classical mythology we become aware of the many references and allusions to these myths in

everyday life. Even as he is in great danger, Jack London's hero in "To Build a Fire" recalls the god Mercury (page 413, column 2, line 5). What god was likely to have been pictured with his bow and arrow on some of the valentines mentioned in "The Scarlet Letter"? (a) Why do you think we find so frequently today in writings and conversations, in art and advertising, allusions or references to the Greek myths and words derived from Greek mythology? (b) What explanation can you give for the fact that so many artists and writers throughout history have chosen their themes or subject matter from the myths of ancient Greece? (c) In your opinion, why do these legends and myths continue to be told today?

9. What is the difference in tone between Robert Graves' and Roger Green's retellings of the Greek myths? How might you account for such a difference?

SUGGESTED READING

BULFINCH, THOMAS, *The Age of Fable.* (**Harper) In this standard reference book, all the great Greek myths are concisely told.

COLUM, PADRAIC, *The Golden Fleece and the Heroes Who Lived Before Achilles.* (Macmillan) Jason and his Argonauts have thrilling adventures on uncharted waters in their quest for the Golden Fleece. Another colorful retelling of Greek mythology by this poet and storyteller is *The Adventures of Odysseus and the Tales of Troy* (Macmillan). *Children of Odin* (Macmillan) is the story of the rough, powerful gods of the Norsemen.

COOLIDGE, OLIVIA E., *Greek Myths.* (Houghton) This retelling of the familiar stories is realistic, fresh, and engrossing. *Legends of the North* (Houghton) is a companion book, equally well-written, which catches the brave spirit of the Scandinavian myths. In *The King of Men* (Houghton), the story

of Agamemnon and the Trojan War provides the basis for an exciting novel.

DEUTSCH, BABETTE, *Heroes of the Kalevala.* (Messner) A noted author presents a very readable retelling of the great Finnish epic.

GRAVES, ROBERT, *Greek Gods and Heroes.* (Doubleday) If you enjoyed "The Palace of Olympus," you are certain to like Graves' retelling of other Greek myths.

GREEN, ROGER LANCELYN, *Tales of the Greek Heroes.* (*Penguin) Besides telling of "The Labours of Heracles," the author relates the stories of other Greek heroes. Other books about mythology by Green include *Mystery at Mycenae* (Barnes) and *Myths of the Norsemen* (Dufour).

HAMILTON, EDITH, *Mythology.* (Little *Mentor) One of the classic scholars of our time relates the stories of the gods and heroes. This book will appeal to readers seeking authoritative accounts.

HAWTHORNE, NATHANIEL, *A Wonder Book and Tanglewood Tales.* (Houghton) These are interesting retellings of the Greek myths, colored with nineteenth-century New England interpretations.

HOMER, *The Iliad: The Story of Achilles,* translated by W. H. D. Rouse. (*Mentor) This is a clear, simple prose translation of the quarrel between Achilles and Agamemnon and the Trojan War which followed. *The Odyssey: The Story of Odysseus* (*Mentor) is Rouse's direct prose translation of one of the greatest adventure stories of the Western world. Odysseus starts for home and his faithful wife Penelope, but one adventure after another delays his arrival.

LANG, ANDREW (ed.), *Arabian Nights.* (Longmans) Scheherazade relates the fables, folk tales, and romances of Arabia: "Aladdin and the Wonderful Lamp," "Forty Thieves," "Seven Voyages of Sinbad the Sailor," and other favorites.

PICARD, BARBARA, *German Hero Tales and Folk Tales.* (Walck) Here is a fine source of the folklore of early Germany.

*paperback
**paperback and hardcover

8

*When Anne Frank was thirteen years old,
her family left their pleasant home in
Amsterdam for the refuge offered by
a hidden apartment in a building that was
a warehouse and office building combined.
The Franks were Jews; no Jew was safe
in lands controlled by the Nazis.
To escape Nazi tyranny, Anne's father, Otto,
a businessman, had earlier fled Frankfort,
Germany, for Holland, taking with him
his wife Edith, and their two daughters,
Margot and Anne. In Amsterdam,
Mr. Frank became an importer for
Travies, Inc. In May 1940, the Nazi
army captured the Netherlands;
persecution of the Jews quickly began.
In July 1942, the Franks were
driven into hiding. The record of
the twenty-five months that followed has*

continued

The
Diary of
Anne Frank

become the legacy of mankind. Into the diary her father had presented on her birthday, thirteen-year-old Anne poured the story of the hopes, fears, joys, and frustrations of living in cramped quarters for too long with too many people under constant tension. Discovered after the war, the diary has been translated into every major language, has been re-created into the drama you are about to read, and has been made into a distinguished motion picture. Now you have the opportunity to live vicariously with Anne and to discover for yourself why millions of people regard the diary of Anne Frank as a living tribute to the dignity, courage, and perseverance of the human spirit.

The Diary of Anne Frank

Dramatized by
Frances Goodrich and Albert Hackett

(based upon the book, *Anne Frank: The Diary of a Young Girl*)

CAST OF CHARACTERS

MR. FRANK	MRS. FRANK
MIEP	MARGOT FRANK
MRS. VAN DAAN	ANNE FRANK
MR. VAN DAAN	MR. KRALER
PETER VAN DAAN	DUSSEL

The Time: During the years of World War II and immediately thereafter.
The Place: Amsterdam. There are two acts.

Act One

SCENE ONE

The scene remains the same through-out the play. It is the top floor of a warehouse and office building in Amsterdam, Holland. The sharply peaked roof of the building is outlined against a sea of other rooftops, stretching away into the distance. Nearby is the belfry of a church tower, the Westertoren, whose carillon rings out the hours. Occasionally faint sounds float up from below: the voices of children playing in the street, the tramp of marching feet, a boat whistle from the canal.

The three rooms of the top floor and a small attic space above are exposed to our view. The largest of the rooms is in the center, with two small rooms, slightly raised, on either side. On the right[1] is a bathroom, out of sight. A narrow steep flight of stairs at the back leads up to the attic. The rooms are sparsely furnished with a few chairs, cots, a table or two. The windows are painted over, or covered with make-shift blackout curtains. In the main room there is a sink, a gas ring for cooking, and a woodburning stove for warmth.

The room on the left is hardly more than a closet. There is a skylight in the sloping ceiling. Directly under this room is a small steep stairwell, with steps leading down to a door. This is the only entrance from the building below. When the door is opened we see that it has been concealed on the outer side by a bookcase attached to it.

The curtain rises on an empty stage. It is late afternoon, November, 1945.

The rooms are dusty, the curtains in rags. Chairs and tables are overturned.

The door at the foot of the small stairwell swings open. MR. FRANK comes up the steps into view. He is a gentle, cultured European in his middle years. There is still a trace of a German accent in his speech.

He stands looking slowly around, making a supreme effort at self-control. He is weak, ill. His clothes are threadbare.

After a second he drops his rucksack on the couch and moves slowly about. He opens the door to one of the smaller rooms, and then abruptly closes it again, turning away. He goes to the window at the back, looking off at the Westertoren as its carillon strikes the hour of six; then he moves restlessly on.

From the street below we hear the sound of a barrel organ and children's voices at play. There is a many-colored scarf hanging from a nail. MR. FRANK takes it, putting it around his neck. As he starts back for his rucksack, his eye is caught by something lying on the floor. It is a woman's white glove. He holds it in his hand and suddenly all of his self-control is gone. He breaks down, crying.

We hear footsteps on the stairs. MIEP GIES comes up, looking for MR. FRANK. MIEP is a Dutch girl of about twenty-two. She wears a coat and hat, ready to go home. She is pregnant. Her attitude toward MR. FRANK is protective, compassionate.

MIEP. Are you all right, Mr. Frank?
MR. FRANK *(quickly controlling himself)*. Yes, Miep, yes.
MIEP. Everyone in the office has

---

1. On the right. Stage directions are given from the actor's viewpoint. It is the *actor's* right, not that of the audience, that is meant here.

gone home . . . It's after six. *(Then pleading)* Don't stay up here, Mr. Frank. What's the use of torturing yourself like this?

MR. FRANK. I've come to say good-by . . . I'm leaving here, Miep.

MIEP. What do you mean? Where are you going? Where?

MR. FRANK. I don't know yet. I haven't decided.

MIEP. Mr. Frank, you can't leave here! This is your home! Amsterdam is your home. Your business is here, waiting for you . . . You're needed here . . . Now that the war is over, there are things that . . .

MR. FRANK. I can't stay in Amsterdam, Miep. It has too many memories for me. Everywhere there's something . . . the house we lived in . . . the school . . . that street organ playing out there . . . I'm not the person you used to know, Miep. I'm a bitter old man. *(Breaking off)* Forgive me. I shouldn't speak to you like this . . . after all that you did for us . . . the suffering . . .

MIEP. No. No. It wasn't suffering. You can't say we suffered. *(As she speaks, she straightens a chair which is overturned.)*

MR. FRANK. I know what you went through, you and Mr. Kraler. I'll remember it as long as I live. *(He gives one last look around.)* Come, Miep. *(He starts for the steps, then remembers his rucksack, going back to get it.)*

MIEP *(hurrying up to a cupboard)*. Mr. Frank, did you see? There are some of your papers here. *(She brings a bundle of papers to him.)* We found them in a heap of rubbish on the floor . . . after you left.

MR. FRANK. Burn them. *(He opens his rucksack to put the glove in it.)*

MIEP. But, Mr. Frank, there are letters, notes . . .

MR. FRANK. Burn them. All of them.

MIEP. Burn *this*? *(She hands him a paperbound notebook.)*

MR. FRANK *(quietly)*. Anne's diary. *(He opens the diary and begins to read.)* "Monday, the sixth of July, nineteen forty-two." *(To* MIEP*)* Nineteen forty-two. Is it possible, Miep? . . . Only three years ago. *(As he continues his reading, he sits down on the couch.)* "Dear Diary, since you and I are going to be great friends, I will start by telling you about myself. My name is Anne Frank. I am thirteen years old. I was born in Germany the twelfth of June, nineteen twenty-nine. As my family is Jewish, we emigrated to Holland when Hitler came to power."

[*As* MR. FRANK *reads on, another voice joins his, as if coming from the air. It is* ANNE'S VOICE.]

MR. FRANK *and* ANNE. "My father started a business, importing spice and herbs. Things went well for us until nineteen forty. Then the war came, and the Dutch capitulation, followed by the arrival of the Germans. Then things got very bad for the Jews."

[MR. FRANK'S VOICE *dies out.* ANNE'S VOICE *continues alone. The lights dim slowly to darkness. The curtain falls on the scene.*]

ANNE'S VOICE. You could not do this and you could not do that. They forced Father out of his business. We had to wear yellow stars. I had to turn in my bike. I couldn't go to a Dutch school any more. I couldn't go to the movies, or ride in an automobile, or even on a streetcar, and a million other things. But somehow we children still managed to have fun. Yesterday Father told me we were going into hiding. Where, he wouldn't say. At five o'clock this morning Mother woke me and told me to hurry and get dressed. I was to put on as many clothes as I could. It would look too suspicious if we walked along carrying suitcases. It wasn't until we were on our way that I learned where we were going. Our hiding place was to be upstairs in the building where Father used to have his business. Three other people were coming in with us . . . the Van Daans and their son Peter . . . Father knew the Van Daans but we had never met them . . . [*During the last lines the curtain rises on the scene. The lights dim on. ANNE'S VOICE fades out.*]

Discussion

1. (a) What information do you get about Anne from the first entry in the diary? (b) What do you learn about her father? (c) What information does the diary give you about the war and its effect on the Jews?
2. What reason does Mr. Frank give Miep for his decision to leave Amsterdam?
3. (a) What is the time setting for this scene? (b) What is the general appearance of the rooms?

SCENE TWO

It is early morning, July, 1942. The rooms are bare, as before, but they are now clean and orderly.

MR. VAN DAAN, *a tall, portly man in his late forties, is in the main room, pacing up and down, nervously smoking a cigarette. His clothes and overcoat are expensive and well cut.*

MRS. VAN DAAN *sits on the couch, clutching her possessions, a hatbox, bags, etc. She is a pretty woman in her early forties. She wears a fur coat over her other clothes.*

PETER VAN DAAN *is standing at the window of the room on the right, looking down at the street below. He is a shy, awkward boy of sixteen. He wears a cap, a raincoat, and long Dutch trousers, like "plus fours." At his feet is a black case, a carrier for his cat.*

The yellow Star of David[1] is conspicuous on all of their clothes.

MRS. VAN DAAN (*rising, nervous, excited*). Something's happened to them! I know it!

MR. VAN DAAN. Now, Kerli!

MRS. VAN DAAN. Mr. Frank said they'd be here at seven o'clock. He said . . .

MR. VAN DAAN. They have two miles to walk. You can't expect . . .

MRS. VAN DAAN. They've been picked up. That's what's happened. They've been taken . . .

[MR. VAN DAAN *indicates that he hears someone coming.*]

MR. VAN DAAN. You see?

[PETER *takes up his carrier and his schoolbag, etc. and goes into the main room as* MR. FRANK *comes up the stairwell from below.* MR. FRANK

---

1. *Star of David,* a six-pointed star, a religious symbol of the Jewish people. In Nazi-occupied countries all Jews were required to wear a Star of David prominently displayed on their clothing.

looks much younger now. His movements are brisk, his manner confident. He wears an overcoat and carries his hat and a small cardboard box. He crosses to the VAN DAANS, shaking hands with each of them.]

MR. FRANK. Mrs. Van Daan, Mr. Van Daan, Peter. (Then, in explanation of their lateness) There were too many of the Green Police[2] on the streets . . . We had to take the long way around.

[Up the steps come MARGOT FRANK, MRS. FRANK, MIEP (not pregnant now), and MR. KRALER. All of them carry bags, packages, and so forth. The Star of David is conspicuous on all of the FRANKS' clothing. MARGOT is eighteen, beautiful, quiet, shy. MRS. FRANK is a young mother, gently bred, reserved. She, like MR. FRANK, has a slight German accent. MR. KRALER is a Dutchman, dependable, kindly.

As MR. KRALER and MIEP go upstage[3] to put down their parcels, MRS. FRANK turns back to call ANNE.]

MRS. FRANK. Anne?

[ANNE comes running up the stairs. She is thirteen, quick in her movements, interested in everything, mercurial in her emotions. She wears a cape, long wool socks and carries a schoolbag.]

MR. FRANK (introducing them). My wife, Edith. Mr. and Mrs. Van Daan (MRS. FRANK hurries over, shaking hands with them.) . . . their son, Peter . . . my daughters, Margot and Anne.

[ANNE gives a polite little curtsy as she shakes MR. VAN DAAN'S hand. Then she immediately starts off on a tour of investigation of her new home, going upstairs to the attic room.

MIEP and MR. KRALER are putting the various things they have brought on the shelves.]

MR. KRALER. I'm sorry there is still so much confusion.

MR. FRANK. Please. Don't think of it. After all, we'll have plenty of leisure to arrange everything ourselves.

MIEP (to MRS. FRANK). We put the stores of food you sent in here. Your drugs are here . . . soap, linen here.

MR. FRANK. Thank you, Miep.

MIEP. I made up the beds . . . the way Mr. Frank and Mr. Kraler said. (She starts out.) I have to hurry. I've got to go to the other side of town to get some ration books[4] for you.

MRS. VAN DAAN. Ration books? If they see our names on ration books, they'll know we're here.

MR. KRALER. There isn't anything. . . ⎫
MIEP. Don't worry. Your names won't be on them. (As she hurries out) I'll be up later. ⎭ (Together)

MR. FRANK. Thank you, Miep.

MRS. FRANK (to MR. KRALER). It's illegal, then, the ration books? We've never done anything illegal.

MR. FRANK. We won't be living here exactly according to regulations.

[As MR. KRALER reassures MRS. FRANK, he takes various small things, such as matches, soap, etc., from his pockets, handing them to her.]

MR. KRALER. This isn't the black market, Mrs. Frank. This is what we call the white market[5] . . . helping all of the hundreds and hundreds who are hiding out in Amsterdam.

[The carillon is heard playing the

---

2. **Green Police**, a branch of the Nazi police who wore green uniforms.
3. **upstage**, toward the back of the stage. *Down*, or *downstage*, means toward the front of the stage.
4. **ration books**, books of coupons which allowed the bearer to buy a fixed amount of provisions or food.
5. **black market . . . white market**. Black market goods are sold illegally, usually at a very high price. The goods the Franks were receiving (white market) were donated by people wishing to help the Jews.

quarter-hour before eight. MR. KRALER *looks at his watch.* ANNE *stops at the window as she comes down the stairs.*]

ANNE. It's the Westertoren!

MR. KRALER. I must go. I must be out of here and downstairs in the office before the workmen get here. *(He starts for the stairs leading out.)* Miep or I, or both of us, will be up each day to bring you food and news and find out what your needs are. Tomorrow I'll get you a better bolt for the door at the foot of the stairs. It needs a bolt that you can throw yourself and open only at our signal. *(To* MR. FRANK*)* Oh . . . You'll tell them about the noise?

MR. FRANK. I'll tell them.

MR. KRALER. Good-by then for the moment. I'll come up again, after the workmen leave.

MR. FRANK. Good-by, Mr. Kraler.

MRS. FRANK *(shaking his hand).* How can we thank you?

[*The others murmur their good-bys.*]

MR. KRALER. I never thought I'd live to see the day when a man like Mr. Frank would have to go into hiding. When you think——

[*He breaks off, going out.* MR. FRANK *follows him down the steps, bolting the door after him. In the interval before he returns,* PETER *goes over to* MARGOT, *shaking hands with her. As* MR. FRANK *comes back up the steps,* MRS. FRANK *questions him anxiously.*]

MRS. FRANK. What did he mean, about the noise?

MR. FRANK. First let us take off some of these clothes.

[*They all start to take off garment after garment. On each of their coats, sweaters, blouses, suits, dresses, is another yellow Star of David.* MR. *and* MRS. FRANK *are underdressed quite simply. The others wear several things—sweaters, extra dresses, bathrobes, aprons, nightgowns, etc.*]

MR. VAN DAAN. It's a wonder we weren't arrested, walking along the streets . . . Petronella with a fur coat in July . . . and that cat of Peter's crying all the way.

ANNE *(as she is removing a pair of panties).* A cat?

MRS. FRANK *(shocked).* Anne, please!

ANNE. It's all right. I've got on three more.

[*She pulls off two more. Finally, as they have all removed their surplus clothes, they look to* MR. FRANK, *waiting for him to speak.*]

MR. FRANK. Now. About the noise. While the men are in the building below, we must have complete quiet. Every sound can be heard down there, not only in the workrooms, but in the offices too. The men come at about eight-thirty, and leave at about five-thirty. So, to be perfectly safe, from eight in the morning until six in the evening we must move only when it is necessary, and then in stockinged feet. We must not speak above a whisper. We must not run any water. We cannot use the sink, or even, forgive me, the w.c.[6] The pipes go down through the workrooms. It would be heard. No trash . . . (MR. FRANK *stops abruptly as he hears the sound of marching feet from the street below. Everyone is motionless, paralyzed with fear.* MR. FRANK *goes quietly into the room on the right to look down out of the window.* ANNE *runs after him, peering out with him. The tramping feet pass without stopping. The tension is relieved.* MR. FRANK, *followed by* ANNE, *returns to the main room and resumes his instructions to the group.) . . .* No trash must ever be thrown out which might reveal that someone is living up here . . . not even a

---

6. **w. c.**, water closet, the bathroom.

potato paring. We must burn everything in the stove at night. This is the way we must live until it is over, if we are to survive.

[*There is silence for a second.*]

MRS. FRANK. Until it is over.

MR. FRANK *(reassuringly)*. After six we can move about . . . we can talk and laugh and have our supper and read and play games . . . just as we would at home. *(He looks at his watch.)* And now I think it would be wise if we all went to our rooms, and were settled before eight o'clock. Mrs. Van Daan, you and your husband will be upstairs. I regret that there's no place up there for Peter. But he will be here, near us. This will be our common room, where we'll meet to talk and eat and read, like one family.

MR. VAN DAAN. And where do you and Mrs. Frank sleep?

MR. FRANK. This room is also our bedroom.

MRS. VAN DAAN. That isn't right. We'll sleep here and you take the room upstairs. *(Together)*

MR. VAN DAAN. It's your place.

MR. FRANK. Please. I've thought this out for weeks. It's the best arrangement. The only arrangement.

MRS. VAN DAAN *(to MR. FRANK)*. Never, never can we thank you. *(Then to MRS. FRANK)* I don't know what would have happened to us, if it hadn't been for Mr. Frank.

MR. FRANK. You don't know how your husband helped me when I came to this country . . . knowing no one . . . not able to speak the language. I can never repay him for that. *(Going to VAN DAAN)* May I help you with your things?

MR. VAN DAAN. No. No. *(To MRS. VAN DAAN)* Come along, *liefje.*[7]

MRS. VAN DAAN. You'll be all right, Peter? You're not afraid?

PETER *(embarrassed)*. Please, Mother.

[*They start up the stairs to the attic room above.* MR. FRANK *turns to* MRS. FRANK.]

MR. FRANK. You too must have some rest, Edith. You didn't close your eyes last night. Nor you, Margot.

ANNE. I slept, Father. Wasn't that funny? I knew it was the last night in my own bed, and yet I slept soundly.

MR. FRANK. I'm glad, Anne. Now you'll be able to help me straighten things in here. *(To MRS. FRANK and MARGOT)* Come with me . . . You and Margot rest in this room for the time being. *(He picks up their clothes, starting for the room on the right.)*

MRS. FRANK. You're sure . . . ? I could help . . . And Anne hasn't had her milk . . .

MR. FRANK. I'll give it to her. *(To ANNE and PETER)* Anne, Peter . . . it's best that you take off your shoes now, before you forget. *(He leads the way to the room, followed by MARGOT.)*

MRS. FRANK. You're sure you're not tired, Anne?

ANNE. I feel fine. I'm going to help Father.

MRS. FRANK. Peter, I'm glad you are to be with us.

PETER. Yes, Mrs. Frank.

[MRS. FRANK *goes to join* MR. FRANK *and* MARGOT.]

[*During the following scene* MR. FRANK *helps* MARGOT *and* MRS. FRANK *to hang up their clothes. Then he persuades them both to lie down and rest. The* VAN DAANS *in their room above settle themselves. In the main room* ANNE *and* PETER *remove their shoes.* PETER *takes his cat out of the carrier.*]

---

7. *liefje* (lēf' Hyə).

ANNE. What's your cat's name?

PETER. Mouschi.

ANNE. Mouschi! Mouschi! Mouschi! *(She picks up the cat, walking away with it. To* PETER*)* I love cats. I have one . . . a darling little cat. But they made me leave her behind. I left some food and a note for the neighbors to take care of her . . . I'm going to miss her terribly. What is yours? A him or a her?

PETER. He's a tom. He doesn't like strangers. *(He takes the cat from her, putting it back in its carrier.)*

ANNE *(unabashed)*. Then I'll have to stop being a stranger, won't I? Is he fixed?

PETER *(startled)*. Huh?

ANNE. Did you have him fixed?

PETER. No.

ANNE. Oh, you ought to have him fixed—to keep him from—you know, fighting. Where did you go to school?

PETER. Jewish Secondary.

ANNE. But that's where Margot and I go! I never saw you around.

PETER. I used to see you . . . sometimes . . .

ANNE. You did?

PETER. . . . in the school yard. You were always in the middle of a bunch of kids. *(He takes a penknife from his pocket.)*

ANNE. Why didn't you ever come over?

PETER. I'm sort of a lone wolf. *(He starts to rip off his Star of David.)*

ANNE. What are you doing?

PETER. Taking it off.

ANNE. But you can't do that. They'll arrest you if you go out without your star.

[*He tosses his knife on the table.*]

PETER. Who's going out?

ANNE. Why, of course! You're right! Of course we don't need them any more. *(She picks up his knife and starts to take her star off.)* I wonder what our friends will think when we don't show up today?

PETER. I didn't have any dates with anyone.

ANNE. Oh, I did. I had a date with Jopie to go and play ping-pong at her house. Do you know Jopie deWaal?

PETER. No.

ANNE. Jopie's my best friend. I wonder what she'll think when she telephones and there's no answer? . . . Probably she'll go over to the house . . . I wonder what she'll think . . . we left everything as if we'd suddenly been called away . . . breakfast dishes in the sink . . . beds not made . . . *(As she pulls off her star the cloth underneath shows clearly the color and form of the star.)* Look! It's still there! (PETER *goes over to the stove with his star.*) What're you going to do with yours?

PETER. Burn it.

ANNE. *(She starts to throw hers in, and cannot.)* It's funny, I can't throw mine away. I don't know why.

PETER. You can't throw . . . ? Something they branded you with . . . ? That they made you wear so they could spit on you?

ANNE. I know. I know. But after all, it *is* the Star of David, isn't it?

[*In the bedroom, right,* MARGOT *and* MRS. FRANK *are lying down.* MR. FRANK *starts quietly out.*]

PETER. Maybe it's different for a girl.

[MR. FRANK *comes into the main room.*]

MR. FRANK. Forgive me, Peter. Now let me see. We must find a bed for your cat. *(He goes to a cupboard.)* I'm glad you brought your cat. Anne was feeling so badly about hers. *(Getting a used small washtub.)* Here we are. Will it be comfortable in that?

PETER *(gathering up his things)*. Thanks.

MR. FRANK *(opening the door of the*

room on the left). **And here is your room. But I warn you, Peter, you can't grow any more. Not an inch, or you'll have to sleep with your feet out of the skylight. Are you hungry?**

PETER. No.

MR. FRANK. We have some bread and butter.

PETER. No, thank you.

MR. FRANK. You can have it for luncheon then. And tonight we will have a real supper . . . our first supper together.

PETER. Thanks. Thanks.

[*He goes into his room. During the following scene he arranges his possessions in his new room.*]

MR. FRANK. That's a nice boy, Peter.

ANNE. He's awfully shy, isn't he?

MR. FRANK. You'll like him, I know.

ANNE. I certainly hope so, since he's the only boy I'm likely to see for months and months.

[MR. FRANK *sits down, taking off his shoes.*]

MR. FRANK. Annele, there's a box there. Will you open it?

[*He indicates a carton on the couch.* ANNE *brings it to the center table. In the street below there is the sound of children playing.*]

ANNE (*as she opens the carton*). You know the way I'm going to think of it here? I'm going to think of it as a boarding house. A very peculiar summer boarding house, like the one that we——(*She breaks off as she pulls out some photographs.*) Father! My movie stars! I was wondering where they were! I was looking for them this morning . . . and Queen Wilhelmina! How wonderful!

MR. FRANK. There's something more. Go on. Look further.

[*He goes over to the sink, pouring a glass of milk from a thermos bottle.*]

ANNE (*pulling out a pasteboard-bound book*). A diary! (*She throws her arms around her father.*) I've never had a diary. And I've always longed for one. (*She looks around the room.*) Pencil, pencil, pencil. (*She starts down the stairs.*) I'm going down to the office to get a pencil.

MR. FRANK. Anne! No!

[*He goes after her, catching her by the arm and pulling her back.*]

ANNE (*startled*). But there's no one in the building now.

MR. FRANK. It doesn't matter. I don't want you ever to go beyond that door.

ANNE (*sobered*). Never . . .? Not even at night time, when everyone is gone? Or on Sundays? Can't I go down to listen to the radio?

MR. FRANK. Never. I am sorry, Anneke. It isn't safe. No, you must never go beyond that door.

[*For the first time* ANNE *realizes what "going into hiding" means.*]

ANNE. I see.

MR. FRANK. It'll be hard, I know. But always remember this, Anneke. There are no walls, there are no bolts, no locks that anyone can put on your mind. Miep will bring us books. We will read history, poetry, mythology. (*He gives her the glass of milk.*) Here's your milk. (*With his arm about her, they go over to the couch, sitting down side by side.*) As a matter of fact, between us, Anne, being here has certain advantages for you. For instance, you remember the battle you had with your mother the other day on the subject of overshoes? You said that you'd rather die than wear overshoes? But in the end you had to wear them? Well now, you see, for as long as we are here you will never have to wear overshoes! Isn't that good? And the coat that you inherited from Margot, you won't have to wear that any more. And the piano! You won't have to practice on the piano. I tell you, this is going to be a fine life for you!

[ANNE'S *panic is gone.* PETER *appears in the doorway of his room, with a saucer in his hand. He is carrying his cat.*]

PETER. I . . . I . . . I thought I'd better get some water for Mouschi before . . .

MR. FRANK. Of course.

[*As he starts toward the sink the carillon begins to chime the hour of eight. He tiptoes to the window at the back and looks down at the street below. He turns to* PETER, *indicating in pantomime that it is too late.* PETER *starts back for his room. He steps on a creaking board. The three of them are frozen for a minute in fear. As* PETER *starts away again,* ANNE *tiptoes over to him and pours some of the milk from her glass into the saucer for the cat.* PETER *squats on the floor, putting the milk before the cat.* MR. FRANK *gives* ANNE *his fountain pen, and then goes into the room at the right. For a second* ANNE *watches the cat, then she goes over to the center table, and opens her diary.*

In the room at the right, MRS. FRANK *has sat up quickly at the sound of the carillon.* MR. FRANK *comes in and sits down beside her on the settee, his arm comfortingly around her.*

Upstairs, in the attic room, MR. *and* MRS. VAN DAAN *have hung their clothes in the closet and are now seated on the iron bed.* MRS. VAN DAAN *leans back exhausted.* MR. VAN DAAN *fans her with a newspaper.*

ANNE *starts to write in her diary. The lights dim out, the curtain falls.*

In the darkness ANNE'S VOICE *comes to us again, faintly at first, and then with growing strength.*]

ANNE'S VOICE. I expect I should be describing what it feels like to go into hiding. But I really don't know yet myself. I only know it's funny never to be able to go outdoors . . . never to breathe fresh air . . . never to run and shout and jump. It's the silence in the nights that frightens me most. Every time I hear a creak in the house, or a step on the street outside, I'm sure they're coming for us. The days aren't so bad. At least we know that Miep and Mr. Kraler are down there below us in the office. Our protectors, we call them. I asked Father what would happen to them if the Nazis found out they were hiding us. Pim said that they would suffer the same fate that we would . . . Imagine! They know this, and yet when they come up here, they're always cheerful and gay as if there were nothing in the world to bother them . . . Friday, the twenty-first of August, nineteen forty-two. Today I'm going to tell you our general news. Mother is unbearable. She insists on treating me like a baby, which I loathe. Otherwise things are going better. The weather is . . .

[*As* ANNE'S VOICE *is fading out the curtain rises on the scene.*]

Discussion

1. (a) What is the time setting for this scene? (b) What difference is there in the appearance of the rooms?

2. The refugees speak of their apartment as the Secret Annex. (a) What advantages does the annex have as a hiding place? (b) What are the disadvantages? (c) Why does Mr. Kraler want a better bolt at the foot of the stairs?

3. Study the illustration of the stage set for the play (pages 466–467). (a) Which is Mr. and Mrs. Van Daan's room? (b) Why do they both protest taking this room? (c) Which is Peter's room? (d) What inference can you

make as to where Anne and Margot are to sleep?

4. **(a)** What are your impressions of the Van Daans? **(b)** Comment on the fact that Mrs. Van Daan is wearing a fur coat and that Peter has been allowed to bring his cat. **(c)** Why has Mr. Frank invited the Van Daans to join his family in hiding?

5. **(a)** What are your impressions of Mr. Frank? **(b)** How does he show that he hopes to keep life in the annex as normal as possible? **(c)** How does he try to reconcile Anne to "going into hiding"?

6. **(a)** Why does Peter burn the Star of David? **(b)** Why can't Anne do the same?

7. Reread the diary entry that concludes the scene. This is the second time so far that we have heard Anne's voice reading from her diary. **(a)** What might be the playwrights' purpose in including this entry? **(b)** What is signified by the dimming light and the curtain falling?

Word Study

In a dictionary, look up the word *Nazi*. How is this word formed?

A word formed from the first letters or syllables of other words is called an *acronym.* What two words are suggested in the acronym *Amerind*?

Following are several acronyms which appear frequently in modern publications.

Gestapo	*UNESCO*
UNIVAC	*snafu*
radar	

1. Copy the acronyms on a sheet of paper.
2. Write the complete phrase or expression from which the acronym is derived.
3. Be sure you know how to pronounce each acronym.

If you are unable to give the information asked about each acronym, consult a dictionary.

SCENE THREE

It is a little after six o'clock in the evening, two months later.

MARGOT *is in the bedroom at the right, studying.* MR. VAN DAAN *is lying down in the attic room above.*

The rest of the "family" is in the main room. ANNE *and* PETER *sit opposite each other at the center table, where they have been doing their lessons.* MRS. FRANK *is on the couch.* MRS. VAN DAAN *is seated with her fur coat, on which she has been sewing, in her lap. None of them are wearing their shoes.*

Their eyes are on MR. FRANK, *waiting for him to give them the signal which will release them from their day-long quiet.* MR. FRANK, *his shoes in his hand, stands looking down out of the window at the back, watching to be sure that all of the workmen have left the building below.*

After a few seconds of motionless silence, MR. FRANK *turns from the window.*

MR. FRANK (*quietly to the group*). It's safe now. The last workman has left. [*There is an immediate stir of relief.*]
ANNE (*Her pent-up energy explodes*). WHEE!
MRS. FRANK (*startled, amused*). Anne!
MRS. VAN DAAN. I'm first for the w.c. [*She hurries off to the bathroom.* MRS. FRANK *puts on her shoes and starts up to the sink to prepare supper.* ANNE *sneaks* PETER'S *shoes from under the table and hides them behind her back.* MR. FRANK *goes into* MARGOT'S *room.*]
MR. FRANK (*to* MARGOT). Six o'clock. School's over.
[MARGOT *gets up, stretching.* MR. FRANK *sits down to put on his shoes. In the main room* PETER *tries to find his.*]

PETER (to ANNE). Have you seen my shoes?

ANNE (innocently). Your shoes?

PETER. You've taken them, haven't you?

ANNE. I don't know what you're talking about.

PETER. You're going to be sorry!

ANNE. Am I?

[PETER goes after her. ANNE, with his shoes in her hand, runs from him, dodging behind her mother.]

MRS. FRANK (protesting). Anne, dear!

PETER. Wait till I get you!

ANNE. I'm waiting! (PETER makes a lunge for her. They both fall to the floor. PETER pins her down, wrestling with her to get the shoes.) Don't! Don't! Peter, stop it. Ouch!

MRS. FRANK. Anne! . . . Peter!

[Suddenly PETER becomes self-conscious. He grabs his shoes roughly and starts for his room.]

ANNE (following him). Peter, where are you going? Come dance with me.

PETER. I tell you I don't know how.

ANNE. I'll teach you.

PETER. I'm going to give Mouschi his dinner.

ANNE. Can I watch?

PETER. He doesn't like people around while he eats.

ANNE. Peter, please.

PETER. No!

[He goes into his room. ANNE slams his door after him.]

MRS. FRANK. Anne, dear, I think you shouldn't play like that with Peter. It's not dignified.

ANNE. Who cares if it's dignified? I don't want to be dignified.

[MR. FRANK and MARGOT come from the room on the right. MARGOT goes to help her mother. MR. FRANK starts for the center table to correct MARGOT'S school papers.]

MRS. FRANK (to ANNE). You complain that I don't treat you like a grown-up. But when I do, you resent it.

ANNE. I only want some fun . . . someone to laugh and clown with . . . After you've sat still all day and hardly moved, you've got to have some fun. I don't know what's the matter with that boy.

MR. FRANK. He isn't used to girls. Give him a little time.

ANNE. Time? Isn't two months time? I could cry. (Catching hold of MARGOT.) Come on, Margot . . . dance with me. Come on, please.

MARGOT. I have to help with supper.

ANNE. You know we're going to forget how to dance . . . When we get out we won't remember a thing.

[She starts to sing and dance by herself. MR. FRANK takes her in his arms, waltzing with her. MRS. VAN DAAN comes in from the bathroom.]

MRS. VAN DAAN. Next? (She looks around as she starts putting on her shoes.) Where's Peter?

ANNE (as they are dancing). Where would he be!

MRS. VAN DAAN. He hasn't finished his lessons, has he? His father'll kill him if he catches him in there with that cat and his work not done. (MR. FRANK and ANNE finish their dance. They bow to each other with extravagant formality.) Anne, get him out of there, will you?

ANNE (at PETER'S door). Peter? Peter?

PETER (opening the door a crack). What is it?

ANNE. Your mother says to come out.

PETER. I'm giving Mouschi his dinner.

MRS. VAN DAAN. You know what your father says.

[She sits on the couch, sewing on the lining of her fur coat.]

PETER. For heaven's sake, I haven't even looked at him since lunch.

MRS. VAN DAAN. I'm just telling you, that's all.

ANNE. I'll feed him.

PETER. I don't want you in there.

MRS. VAN DAAN. Peter!

PETER (to ANNE). Then give him his dinner and come right out, you hear?

[He comes back to the table. ANNE shuts the door of PETER'S room after her and disappears behind the curtain covering his closet.]

MRS. VAN DAAN (to PETER). Now is that any way to talk to your little girl friend?

PETER. Mother . . . for heaven's sake . . . will you please stop saying that?

MRS. VAN DAAN. Look at him blush! Look at him!

PETER. Please! I'm not . . . anyway . . . let me alone, will you?

MRS. VAN DAAN. He acts like it was something to be ashamed of. It's nothing to be ashamed of, to have a little girl friend.

PETER. You're crazy. She's only thirteen.

MRS. VAN DAAN. So what? And you're sixteen. Just perfect. Your father's ten years older than I am. (To MR. FRANK) I warn you, Mr. Frank, if this war lasts much longer, we're going to be related and then . . .

MR. FRANK. Mazeltov![1]

MRS. FRANK (deliberately changing the conversation). I wonder where Miep is. She's usually so prompt.

[Suddenly everything else is forgotten as they hear the sound of an automobile coming to a screeching stop in the street below. They are tense, motionless in their terror. The car starts away. A wave of relief sweeps over them. They pick up their occupations again. ANNE flings open the door of PETER'S room, making a dramatic entrance. She is dressed in PETER'S clothes. PETER looks at her in fury. The others are amused.]

ANNE. Good evening, everyone. Forgive me if I don't stay. (She jumps up on a chair.) I have a friend waiting for me in there. My friend Tom. Tom Cat. Some people say that we look alike. But Tom has the most beautiful whiskers, and I have only a little fuzz. I am hoping . . . in time . . .

PETER. All right, Mrs. Quack Quack!

ANNE (outraged—jumping down). Peter!

PETER. I heard about you . . . How you talked so much in class they called you Mrs. Quack Quack. How Mr. Smitter made you write a composition . . . "'Quack, quack,' said Mrs. Quack Quack."

ANNE. Well, go on. Tell them the rest. How it was so good he read it out loud to the class and then read it to all his other classes!

PETER. Quack! Quack! Quack . . . Quack . . . Quack . . .

[ANNE pulls off the coat and trousers.]

ANNE. You are the most intolerable, insufferable boy I've ever met!

[She throws the clothes down the stairwell. PETER goes down after them.]

PETER. Quack, quack, quack!

MRS. VAN DAAN (to ANNE). That's right, Anneke! Give it to him!

ANNE. With all the boys in the world . . . Why I had to get locked up with one like you! . . .

PETER. Quack, quack, quack, and from now on stay out of my room!

[As PETER passes her, ANNE puts out her foot, tripping him. He picks himself up, and goes on into his room.]

MRS. FRANK (quietly). Anne, dear . . . your hair. (She feels ANNE'S forehead.) You're warm. Are you feeling all right?

ANNE. Please, Mother.

[She goes over to the center table, slipping into her shoes.]

MRS. FRANK (following her). You haven't a fever, have you?

ANNE (pulling away). No. No.

---

1. **Mazeltov** (mä′zəl tof), an expression used among Jews to express congratulations.

MRS. FRANK. You know we can't call a doctor here, ever. There's only one thing to do . . . watch carefully. Prevent an illness before it comes. Let me see your tongue.

ANNE. Mother, this is perfectly absurd.

MRS. FRANK. Anne, dear, don't be such a baby. Let me see your tongue. *(As* ANNE *refuses,* MRS. FRANK *appeals to* MR. FRANK.*)* Otto . . . ?

MR. FRANK. You hear your mother, Anne.

[ANNE *flicks out her tongue for a second, then turns away.*]

MRS. FRANK. Come on—open up! *(As* ANNE *opens her mouth very wide)* You seem all right . . . but perhaps an aspirin . . .

MRS. VAN DAAN. For heaven's sake, don't give that child any pills. I waited for fifteen minutes this morning for her to come out of the w.c.

ANNE. I was washing my hair!

MRS. FRANK. I think there's nothing the matter with our Anne that a ride on her bike, or a visit with her friend Jopie deWaal wouldn't cure. Isn't that so, Anne?

[MR. VAN DAAN *comes down into the room. From outside we hear faint sounds of bombers going over and a burst of ack-ack.*]

MR. VAN DAAN. Miep not come yet?

MRS. VAN DAAN. The workmen just left, a little while ago.

MR. VAN DAAN. What's for dinner tonight?

MRS. VAN DAAN. Beans.

MR. VAN DAAN. Not again!

MRS. VAN DAAN. Poor Putti! I know. But what can we do? That's all that Miep brought us.

[MR. VAN DAAN *starts to pace, his hands behind his back.* ANNE *follows behind him, imitating him.*]

ANNE. We are now in what is known as the "bean cycle." Beans boiled, beans *en casserole,*[2] beans with strings, beans without strings . . .

[PETER *has come out of his room. He slides into his place at the table, becoming immediately absorbed in his studies.*]

MR. VAN DAAN *(to* PETER*).* I saw you . . . in there, playing with your cat.

MRS. VAN DAAN. He just went in for a second, putting his coat away. He's been out here all the time, doing his lessons.

MR. FRANK *(looking up from the paper).* Anne, you got an excellent in your history paper today . . . and very good in Latin.

ANNE *(sitting beside him).* How about algebra?

MR. FRANK. I'll have to make a confession. Up until now I've managed to stay ahead of you in algebra. Today you caught up with me. We'll leave it to Margot to correct.

ANNE. Isn't algebra *vile,* Pim!

MR. FRANK. Vile!

MARGOT *(to* MR. FRANK*).* How did I do?

ANNE *(getting up).* Excellent, excellent, excellent, excellent!

MR. FRANK *(to* MARGOT*).* You should have used the subjunctive here . . .

MARGOT. Should I? . . . I thought . . . look here . . . I didn't use it here . . .

[*The two become absorbed in the papers.*]

ANNE. Mrs. Van Daan, may I try on your coat?

MRS. FRANK. No, Anne.

MRS. VAN DAAN *(giving it to* ANNE*).* It's all right . . . but careful with it. *(*ANNE *puts it on and struts with it.)* My father gave me that the year before he died. He always bought the best that money could buy.

ANNE. Mrs. Van Daan, did you have a

---

2. *en casserole* (aN käs rôl′), prepared and served in a covered baking dish.

lot of boy friends before you were married?

MRS. FRANK. Anne, that's a personal question. It's not courteous to ask personal questions.

MRS. VAN DAAN. Oh I don't mind. *(To* ANNE*)* Our house was always swarming with boys. When I was a girl we had . . .

MR. VAN DAAN. Oh, God. Not again!

MRS. VAN DAAN *(good-humored).* Shut up! *(Without a pause, to* ANNE. MR. VAN DAAN *mimics* MRS. VAN DAAN, *speaking the first few words in unison with her.)* One summer we had a big house in Hilversum.[3] The boys came buzzing round like bees around a jam pot. And when I was sixteen! . . . We were wearing our skirts very short those days and I had good-looking legs. *(She pulls up her skirt, going to* MR. FRANK.*)* I still have 'em. I may not be as pretty as I used to be, but I still have my legs. How about it, Mr. Frank?

MR. VAN DAAN. All right. All right. We see them.

MRS. VAN DAAN. I'm not asking you. I'm asking Mr. Frank.

PETER. Mother, for heaven's sake.

MRS. VAN DAAN. Oh, I embarrass you, do I? Well, I just hope the girl you marry has as good. *(Then to* ANNE*)* My father used to worry about me, with so many boys hanging round. He told me, if any of them gets fresh, you say to him . . . "Remember, Mr. So-and-So, remember I'm a lady."

ANNE. "Remember, Mr. So-and-So, remember I'm a lady."

[*She gives* MRS. VAN DAAN *her coat.*]

MR. VAN DAAN. Look at you, talking that way in front of her! Don't you know she puts it all down in that diary?

MRS. VAN DAAN. So, if she does? I'm only telling the truth!

[ANNE *stretches out, putting her ear to the floor, listening to what is going on below. The sound of the bombers fades away.*]

MRS. FRANK *(setting the table).* Would you mind, Peter, if I moved you over to the couch?

ANNE *(listening).* Miep must have the radio on.

[PETER *picks up his papers, going over to the couch beside* MRS. VAN DAAN.]

MR. VAN DAAN *(accusingly, to* PETER*).* Haven't you finished yet?

PETER. No.

MR. VAN DAAN. You ought to be ashamed of yourself.

PETER. All right. All right. I'm a dunce. I'm a hopeless case. Why do I go on?

MRS. VAN DAAN. You're not hopeless. Don't talk that way. It's just that you haven't anyone to help you, like the girls have. *(To* MR. FRANK*)* Maybe you could help him, Mr. Frank?

MR. FRANK. I'm sure that his father . . . ?

MR. VAN DAAN. Not me. I can't do anything with him. He won't listen to me. You go ahead . . . if you want.

MR. FRANK *(going to* PETER*).* What about it, Peter? Shall we make our school coeducational?

MRS. VAN DAAN *(kissing* MR. FRANK*).* You're an angel, Mr. Frank. An angel. I don't know why I didn't meet you before I met that one there. Here, sit down, Mr. Frank . . . *(She forces him down on the couch beside* PETER.*)* Now, Peter, you listen to Mr. Frank.

MR. FRANK. It might be better for us to go into Peter's room.

[PETER *jumps up eagerly, leading the way.*]

MRS. VAN DAAN. That's right. You go in there, Peter. You listen to Mr. Frank. Mr. Frank is a highly educated man.

---

3. **Hilversum** (hil′vər səm), a health resort and residential area some miles from Amsterdam.

[*As* MR. FRANK *is about to follow* PETER *into his room,* MRS. FRANK *stops him and wipes the lipstick from his lips. Then she closes the door after them.*]

ANNE (*on the floor, listening*). Shh! I can hear a man's voice talking.

MR. VAN DAAN (*to* ANNE). Isn't it bad enough here without your sprawling all over the place?

[ANNE *sits up.*]

MRS. VAN DAAN (*to* MR. VAN DAAN). If you didn't smoke so much, you wouldn't be so bad-tempered.

MR. VAN DAAN. Am I smoking? Do you see me smoking?

MRS. VAN DAAN. Don't tell me you've used up all those cigarettes.

MR. VAN DAAN. One package. Miep only brought me one package.

MRS. VAN DAAN. It's a filthy habit anyway. It's a good time to break yourself.

MR. VAN DAAN. Oh, stop it, please.

MRS. VAN DAAN. You're smoking up all our money. You know that, don't you?

MR. VAN DAAN. Will you shut up? (*During this,* MRS. FRANK *and* MARGOT *have studiously kept their eyes down. But* ANNE, *seated on the floor, has been following the discussion interestedly.* MR. VAN DAAN *turns to see her staring up at him.*) And what are you staring at?

ANNE. I never heard grownups quarrel before. I thought only children quarreled.

MR. VAN DAAN. This isn't a quarrel! It's a discussion. And I never heard children so rude before.

ANNE (*rising, indignantly*). I, rude!

MR. VAN DAAN. Yes!

MRS. FRANK (*quickly*). Anne, will you get me my knitting? (ANNE *goes to get it.*) I must remember, when Miep comes, to ask her to bring me some more wool.

MARGOT (*going to her room*). I need some hairpins and some soap. I made a list.

[*She goes into her bedroom to get the list.*]

MRS. FRANK (*to* ANNE). Have you some library books for Miep when she comes?

ANNE. It's a wonder that Miep has a life of her own, the way we make her run errands for us. Please, Miep, get me some starch. Please take my hair out and have it cut. Tell me all the latest news, Miep. (*She goes over, kneeling on the couch beside* MRS. VAN DAAN.) Did you know she was engaged? His name is Dirk, and Miep's afraid the Nazis will ship him off to Germany to work in one of their war plants. That's what they're doing with some of the young Dutchmen . . . they pick them up off the streets —

MR. VAN DAAN (*interrupting*). Don't you ever get tired of talking? Suppose you try keeping still for five minutes. Just five minutes.

[*He starts to pace again. Again* ANNE *follows him, mimicking him.* MRS. FRANK *jumps up and takes her by the arm up to the sink, and gives her a glass of milk.*]

MRS. FRANK. Come here, Anne. It's time for your glass of milk.

MR. VAN DAAN. Talk, talk, talk. I never heard such a child. Where is my . . . ? Every evening it's the same, talk, talk, talk. (*He looks around.*) Where is my . . . ?

MRS. VAN DAAN. What're you looking for?

MR. VAN DAAN. My pipe. Have you seen my pipe?

MRS. VAN DAAN. What good's a pipe? You haven't got any tobacco.

MR. VAN DAAN. At least I'll have something to hold in my mouth! (*Opening* MARGOT'S *bedroom door*) Margot, have you seen my pipe?

MARGOT. It was on the table last night.

[ANNE *puts her glass of milk on the table and picks up his pipe, hiding it behind her back.*]

MR. VAN DAAN. I know. I know. Anne, did you see my pipe? . . . Anne!

MRS. FRANK. Anne, Mr. Van Daan is speaking to you.

ANNE. Am I allowed to talk now?

MR. VAN DAAN. You're the most aggravating . . . The trouble with you is, you've been spoiled. What you need is a good old-fashioned spanking.

ANNE (*mimicking* MRS. VAN DAAN). "Remember, Mr. So-and-So, remember I'm a lady."

[*She thrusts the pipe into his mouth, then picks up her glass of milk.*]

MR. VAN DAAN (*restraining himself with difficulty*). Why aren't you nice and quiet like your sister Margot? Why do you have to show off all the time? Let me give you a little advice, young lady. Men don't like that kind of thing in a girl. You know that? A man likes a girl who'll listen to him once in a while . . . a domestic girl, who'll keep her house shining for her husband . . . who loves to cook and sew and . . .

ANNE. I'd cut my throat first! I'd open my veins! I'm going to be remarkable! I'm going to Paris . . .

MR. VAN DAAN (*scoffingly*). Paris!

ANNE. . . . to study music and art.

MR. VAN DAAN. Yeah! Yeah!

ANNE. I'm going to be a famous dancer or singer . . . or something wonderful.

[*She makes a wide gesture, spilling the glass of milk on the fur coat in* MRS. VAN DAAN'S *lap.* MARGOT *rushes quickly over with a towel.* ANNE *tries to brush the milk off with her skirt.*]

MRS. VAN DAAN. Now look what you've done . . . you clumsy little fool! My beautiful fur coat my father gave me . . .

ANNE. I'm so sorry.

MRS. VAN DAAN. What do you care? It isn't yours . . . So go on, ruin it! Do you know what that coat cost? Do you? And now look at it! Look at it!

ANNE. I'm very, very sorry.

MRS. VAN DAAN. I could kill you for this. I could just kill you!

[MRS. VAN DAAN *goes up the stairs, clutching the coat.* MR. VAN DAAN *starts after her.*]

MR. VAN DAAN. Petronella . . . *liefje! Liefje!* . . . Come back . . . the supper . . . come back!

MRS. FRANK. Anne, you must not behave in that way.

ANNE. It was an accident. Anyone can have an accident.

MRS. FRANK. I don't mean that. I mean the answering back. You must not answer back. They are our guests. We must always show the greatest courtesy to them. We're all living under terrible tension. (*She stops as* MARGOT *indicates that* VAN DAAN *can hear. When he is gone, she continues.*) That's why we must control ourselves . . . You don't hear Margot getting into arguments with them, do you? Watch Margot. She's always courteous with them. Never familiar. She keeps her distance. And they respect her for it. Try to be like Margot.

ANNE. And have them walk all over me, the way they do her? No, thanks!

MRS. FRANK. I'm not afraid that anyone is going to walk all over you, Anne. I'm afraid for other people, that you'll walk on them. I don't know what happens to you, Anne. You are wild, self-willed. If I had ever talked to my mother as you talk to me . . .

ANNE. Things have changed. People aren't like that any more. "Yes, Mother." "No, Mother." "Anything you say, Mother." I've got to fight things out for myself! Make something of myself!

MRS. FRANK. It isn't necessary to fight to do it. Margot doesn't fight, and isn't she . . . ?

ANNE (violently rebellious). Margot! Margot! Margot! That's all I hear from everyone . . . how wonderful Margot is . . . "Why aren't you like Margot?"

MARGOT (protesting). Oh, come on, Anne, don't be so . . .

ANNE (paying no attention). Everything she does is right, and everything I do is wrong! I'm the goat around here! . . . You're all against me! . . . And you worst of all!

[She rushes off into her room and throws herself down on the settee, stifling her sobs. MRS. FRANK sighs and starts toward the stove.]

MRS. FRANK (to MARGOT). Let's put the soup on the stove . . . if there's anyone who cares to eat. Margot, will you take the bread out? (MARGOT gets the bread from the cupboard.) I don't know how we can go on living this way . . . I can't say a word to Anne . . . she flies at me . . .

MARGOT. You know Anne. In half an hour she'll be out here, laughing and joking.

MRS. FRANK. And . . . (She makes a motion upwards, indicating the VAN DAANS.) . . . I told your father it wouldn't work . . . but no . . . no . . . he had to ask them, he said . . . he owed it to him, he said. Well, he knows now that I was right! These quarrels! . . . This bickering!

MARGOT (with a warning look). Shush. Shush.

[The buzzer for the door sounds. MRS. FRANK gasps, startled.]

MRS. FRANK. Every time I hear that sound, my heart stops!

MARGOT (starting for PETER'S door). It's Miep. (She knocks at the door.) Father?

[MR. FRANK comes quickly from PETER'S room.]

MR. FRANK. Thank you, Margot. (As he goes down the steps to open the outer door) Has everyone his list?

MARGOT. I'll get my books. (Giving her mother a list) Here's your list. (MARGOT goes into her and ANNE'S bedroom on the right. ANNE sits up, hiding her tears, as MARGOT comes in.) Miep's here.

[MARGOT picks up her books and goes back. ANNE hurries over to the mirror, smoothing her hair.]

MR. VAN DAAN (coming down the stairs). Is it Miep?

MARGOT. Yes. Father's gone down to let her in.

MR. VAN DAAN. At last I'll have some cigarettes!

MRS. FRANK (to MR. VAN DAAN). I can't tell you how unhappy I am about Mrs. Van Daan's coat. Anne should never have touched it.

MR. VAN DAAN. She'll be all right.

MRS. FRANK. Is there anything I can do?

MR. VAN DAAN. Don't worry.

[He turns to meet MIEP. But it is not MIEP who comes up the steps. It is MR. KRALER, followed by MR. FRANK. Their faces are grave. ANNE comes from the bedroom. PETER comes from his room.]

MRS. FRANK. Mr. Kraler!

MR. VAN DAAN. How are you, Mr. Kraler?

MARGOT. This is a surprise.

MRS. FRANK. When Mr. Kraler comes, the sun begins to shine.

MR. VAN DAAN. Miep is coming?

MR. KRALER. Not tonight.

[KRALER goes to MARGOT and MRS. FRANK and ANNE, shaking hands with them.]

MRS. FRANK. Wouldn't you like a cup of coffee? . . . Or, better still, will you have supper with us?

MR. FRANK. Mr. Kraler has something

to talk over with us. Something has happened, he says, which demands an immediate decision.

MRS. FRANK (*fearful*). What is it?

[MR. KRALER *sits down on the couch. As he talks he takes bread, cabbages, milk, etc., from his briefcase, giving them to* MARGOT *and* ANNE *to put away.*]

MR. KRALER. Usually, when I come up here, I try to bring you some bit of good news. What's the use of telling you the bad news when there's nothing that you can do about it? But today something has happened . . . Dirk . . . Miep's Dirk, you know, came to me just now. He tells me that he has a Jewish friend living near him. A dentist. He says he's in trouble. He begged me, could I do anything for this man? Could I find him a hiding place? . . . So I've come to you . . . I know it's a terrible thing to ask of you, living as you are, but would you take him in with you?

MR. FRANK. Of course we will.

MR. KRALER (*rising*). It'll be just for a night or two . . . until I find some other place. This happened so suddenly that I didn't know where to turn.

MR. FRANK. Where is he?

MR. KRALER. Downstairs in the office.

MR. FRANK. Good. Bring him up.

MR. KRALER. His name is Dussel . . . Jan Dussel.

MR. FRANK. Dussel . . . I think I know him.

MR. KRALER. I'll get him.

[*He goes quickly down the steps and out.* MR. FRANK *suddenly becomes conscious of the others.*]

MR. FRANK. Forgive me. I spoke without consulting you. But I knew you'd feel as I do.

MR. VAN DAAN. There's no reason for you to consult anyone. This is your place. You have a right to do exactly as you please. The only thing I feel . . . there's so little food as it is . . . and to take in another person . . .

[PETER *turns away, ashamed of his father.*]

MR. FRANK. We can stretch the food a little. It's only for a few days.

MR. VAN DAAN. You want to make a bet?

MRS. FRANK. I think it's fine to have him. But, Otto, where are you going to put him? Where?

PETER. He can have my bed. I can sleep on the floor. I wouldn't mind.

MR. FRANK. That's good of you, Peter. But your room's too small . . . even for *you*.

ANNE. I have a much better idea. I'll come in here with you and Mother, and Margot can take Peter's room and Peter can go in our room with Mr. Dussel.

MARGOT. That's right. We could do that.

MR. FRANK. No, Margot. You mustn't sleep in that room . . . neither you nor Anne. Mouschi has caught some rats in there. Peter's brave. He doesn't mind.

ANNE. Then how about *this*? I'll come in here with you and Mother, and Mr. Dussel can have my bed.

MRS. FRANK. No. No. *No!* Margot will come in here with us and he can have her bed. It's the only way. Margot, bring your things in here. Help her, Anne.

[MARGOT *hurries into her room to get her things.*]

ANNE (*to her mother*). Why Margot? Why can't I come in here?

MRS. FRANK. Because it wouldn't be proper for Margot to sleep with a . . . Please, Anne. Don't argue. Please.

[ANNE *starts slowly away.*]

MR. FRANK (*to* ANNE). You don't mind sharing your room with Mr. Dussel, do you, Anne?

ANNE. No. No, of course not.

MR. FRANK. Good. (ANNE goes off into her bedroom, helping MARGOT. MR. FRANK starts to search in the cupboards.) Where's the cognac?

MRS. FRANK. It's there. But, Otto, I was saving it in case of illness.

MR. FRANK. I think we couldn't find a better time to use it. Peter, will you get five glasses for me?

[PETER goes for the glasses. MARGOT comes out of her bedroom, carrying her possessions, which she hangs behind a curtain in the main room. MR. FRANK finds the cognac and pours it into the five glasses that PETER brings him. MR. VAN DAAN stands looking on sourly. MRS. VAN DAAN comes downstairs and looks around at all of the bustle.]

MRS. VAN DAAN. What's happening? What's going on?

MR. VAN DAAN. Someone's moving in with us.

MRS. VAN DAAN. In here? You're joking.

MARGOT. It's only for a night or two . . . until Mr. Kraler finds him another place.

MR. VAN DAAN. Yeah! Yeah!

[MR. FRANK hurries over as MR. KRALER and DUSSEL come up. DUSSEL is a man in his late fifties, meticulous, finicky . . . bewildered now. He wears a raincoat. He carries a briefcase, stuffed full, and a small medicine case.]

MR. FRANK. Come in, Mr. Dussel.

MR. KRALER. This is Mr. Frank.

DUSSEL. Mr. Otto Frank?

MR. FRANK. Yes. Let me take your things. (He takes the hat and briefcase, but DUSSEL clings to his medicine case.) This is my wife Edith . . . Mr. and Mrs. Van Daan . . . their son, Peter . . . and my daughters, Margot and Anne.

[DUSSEL shakes hands with everyone.]

MR. KRALER. Thank you, Mr. Frank.

Thank you all. Mr. Dussel, I leave you in good hands. Oh . . . Dirk's coat.

[DUSSEL hurriedly takes off the raincoat, giving it to MR. KRALER. Underneath is his white dentist's jacket, with a yellow Star of David on it.]

DUSSEL (to MR. KRALER). What can I say to thank you . . . ?

MRS. FRANK (to DUSSEL). Mr. Kraler and Miep . . . They're our life line. Without them we couldn't live.

MR. KRALER. Please, please. You make us seem very heroic. It isn't that at all. We simply don't like the Nazis. (To MR. FRANK, who offers him a drink) No, thanks. (Then going on) We don't like their methods. We don't like . . .

MR. FRANK (smiling). I know. I know. "No one's going to tell us Dutchmen what to do with our damn Jews!"

MR. KRALER (to DUSSEL). Pay no attention to Mr. Frank. I'll be up tomorrow to see that they're treating you right. (To MR. FRANK) Don't trouble to come down again. Peter will bolt the door after me, won't you, Peter?

PETER. Yes, sir.

MR. FRANK. Thank you, Peter. I'll do it.

MR. KRALER. Good night. Good night.

GROUP. Good night, Mr. Kraler. We'll see you tomorrow, etc., etc.

[MR. KRALER goes out with MR. FRANK. MRS. FRANK gives each one of the "grownups" a glass of cognac.]

MRS. FRANK. Please, Mr. Dussel, sit down.

[MR. DUSSEL sinks into a chair. MRS. FRANK gives him a glass of cognac.]

DUSSEL. I'm dreaming. I know it. I don't believe my eyes. Mr. Otto Frank here! (To MRS. FRANK) You're not in Switzerland then? A woman told me . . . She said she'd gone to your house . . . the door was open, everything was in disorder, dishes in the sink. She said

she found a piece of paper in the wastebasket with an address scribbled on it . . . an address in Zurich. She said you must have escaped to Zurich.

ANNE. Father put that there purposely . . . just so people would think that very thing!

DUSSEL. And you've been *here* all the time?

MRS. FRANK. All the time . . . ever since July.

[ANNE *speaks to her father as he comes back.*]

ANNE. It worked, Pim . . . the address you left! Mr. Dussel says that people believe we escaped to Switzerland.

MR. FRANK. I'm glad . . . And now let's have a little drink to welcome Mr. Dussel. *(Before they can drink,* MR. DUSSEL *bolts his drink.* MR. FRANK *smiles and raises his glass.)* To Mr. Dussel. Welcome. We're very honored to have you with us.

MRS. FRANK. To Mr. Dussel, welcome.

[*The* VAN DAANS *murmur a welcome. The "grownups" drink.*]

MRS. VAN DAAN. Um. That was good.

MR. VAN DAAN. Did Mr. Kraler warn you that you won't get much to eat here? You can imagine . . . three ration books among the seven of us . . . and now you make eight.

[PETER *walks away, humiliated. Outside a street organ is heard dimly.*]

DUSSEL *(rising).* Mr. Van Daan, you don't realize what is happening outside that you should warn me of a thing like that. You don't realize what's going on . . . *(As* MR. VAN DAAN *starts his characteristic pacing,* DUSSEL *turns to speak to the others.)* Right here in Amsterdam every day hundreds of Jews disappear . . . They surround a block and search house by house. Children come home from school to find their parents gone. Hundreds are being deported . . . people that you and I know . . . the Hallensteins . . . the Wessels . . .

MRS. FRANK *(in tears).* Oh, no. No!

DUSSEL. They get their call-up notice . . . come to the Jewish theatre on such and such a day and hour . . . bring only what you can carry in a rucksack. And if you refuse the call-up notice, then they come and drag you from your home and ship you off to Mauthausen. The death camp!

MRS. FRANK. We didn't know that things had got so much worse.

DUSSEL. Forgive me for speaking so.

ANNE *(coming to* DUSSEL*).* Do you know the deWaals? . . . What's become of them? Their daughter Jopie and I are in the same class. Jopie's my best friend.

DUSSEL. They are gone.

ANNE. Gone?

DUSSEL. With all the others.

ANNE. Oh, no. Not Jopie!

[*She turns away, in tears.* MRS. FRANK *motions to* MARGOT *to comfort her.* MARGOT *goes to* ANNE, *putting her arms comfortingly around her.*]

MRS. VAN DAAN. There were some people called Wagner. They lived near us . . . ?

MR. FRANK *(interrupting with a glance at* ANNE*).* I think we should put this off until later. We all have many questions we want to ask . . . But I'm sure that Mr. Dussel would like to get settled before supper.

DUSSEL. Thank you. I would. I brought very little with me.

MR. FRANK *(giving him his hat and briefcase).* I'm sorry we can't give you a room alone. But I hope you won't be too uncomfortable. We've had to make strict rules here . . . a schedule of hours . . . We'll tell you after supper. Anne, would you like to take Mr. Dussel to his room?

ANNE *(controlling her tears).* If you'll come with me, Mr. Dussel?

[*She starts for her room.*]

DUSSEL (*shaking hands with each in turn*). Forgive me if I haven't really expressed my gratitude to all of you. This has been such a shock to me. I'd always thought of myself as Dutch. I was born in Holland. My father was born in Holland, and my grandfather. And now . . . after all these years . . . (*He breaks off.*) If you'll excuse me.

[DUSSEL *gives a little bow and hurries off after* ANNE. MR. FRANK *and the others are subdued.*]

ANNE (*turning on the light*). Well, here we are.

[DUSSEL *looks around the room. In the main room* MARGOT *speaks to her mother.*]

MARGOT. The news sounds pretty bad, doesn't it? It's so different from what Mr. Kraler tells us. Mr. Kraler says things are improving.

MR. VAN DAAN. I like it better the way Kraler tells it.

[*They resume their occupations, quietly.* PETER *goes off into his room. In* ANNE'S *room,* ANNE *turns to* DUSSEL.]

ANNE. You're going to share the room with me.

DUSSEL. I'm a man who's always lived alone. I haven't had to adjust myself to others. I hope you'll bear with me until I learn.

ANNE. Let me help you. (*She takes his briefcase.*) Do you always live all alone? Have you no family at all?

DUSSEL. No one.

[*He opens his medicine case and spreads his bottles on the dressing table.*]

ANNE. How dreadful. You must be terribly lonely.

DUSSEL. I'm used to it.

ANNE. I don't think I could ever get used to it. Didn't you even have a pet? A cat, or a dog?

DUSSEL. I have an allergy for fur-bearing animals. They give me asthma.

ANNE. Oh, dear. Peter has a cat.

DUSSEL. Here? He has it here?

ANNE. Yes. But we hardly ever see it. He keeps it in his room all the time. I'm sure it will be all right.

DUSSEL. Let us hope so. (*He takes some pills to fortify himself.*)

ANNE. That's Margot's bed, where you're going to sleep. I sleep on the sofa there. (*Indicating the clothes hooks on the wall.*) We cleared these off for your things. (*She goes over to the window.*) The best part about this room . . . you can look down and see a bit of the street and the canal. There's a houseboat . . . you can see the end of it . . . a bargeman lives there with his family . . . They have a baby and he's just beginning to walk and I'm so afraid he's going to fall into the canal some day. I watch him . . .

DUSSEL (*interrupting*). Your father spoke of a schedule.

ANNE (*coming away from the window*). Oh, yes. It's mostly about the times we have to be quiet. And times for the w.c. You can use it now if you like.

DUSSEL (*stiffly*). No, thank you.

ANNE. I suppose you think it's awful, my talking about a thing like that. But you don't know how important it can get to be, especially when you're frightened . . . About this room, the way Margot and I did . . . she had it to herself in the afternoons for studying, reading . . . lessons, you know . . . and I took the mornings. Would that be all right with you?

DUSSEL. I'm not at my best in the morning.

ANNE. You stay here in the mornings then. I'll take the room in the afternoons.

DUSSEL. Tell me, when you're in here,

what happens to me? Where am I spending my time? In there, with all the people?

ANNE. Yes.

DUSSEL. I see. I see.

ANNE. We have supper at half past six.

DUSSEL (*going over to the sofa*). Then, if you don't mind . . . I like to lie down quietly for ten minutes before eating. I find it helps the digestion.

ANNE. Of course. I hope I'm not going to be too much of a bother to you. I seem to be able to get everyone's back up.

[DUSSEL *lies down on the sofa, curled up, his back to her.*]

DUSSEL. I always get along very well with children. My patients all bring their children to me, because they know I get on well with them. So don't worry about that.

[ANNE *leans over him, taking his hand and shaking it gratefully.*]

ANNE. Thank you. Thank you, Mr. Dussel.

[*The lights dim to darkness. The curtain falls on the scene.* ANNE'S VOICE *comes to us faintly at first, and then with increasing power.*]

ANNE'S VOICE. . . . And yesterday I finished Cissy Van Marxvelt's latest book. I think she is a first-class writer. I shall definitely let my children read her. Monday the twenty-first of September, nineteen forty-two. Mr. Dussel and I had another battle yesterday. Yes, Mr. Dussel! According to him, nothing, I repeat . . . nothing, is right about me . . . my appearance, my character, my manners. While he was going on at me I thought . . . sometime I'll give you such a smack that you'll fly right up to the ceiling! Why is it that every grownup thinks he knows the way to bring up children? Particularly the grownups that never had any. I keep wishing that Peter was a girl instead of a boy. Then I

would have someone to talk to. Margot's a darling, but she takes everything too seriously. To pause for a moment on the subject of Mrs. Van Daan. I must tell you that her attempts to flirt with Father are getting her nowhere. Pim, thank goodness, won't play.

[*As she is saying the last lines, the curtain rises on the darkened scene.* ANNE'S VOICE *fades out.*]

Discussion

1. Much of this scene is composed of incidents which provide a clearer idea of thirteen-year-old Anne. (a) What are some of her characteristics? Cite incidents to illustrate these character traits. (b) Does Anne seem to you a normal thirteen-year-old girl? Why, or why not?

2. What does the behavior of Mr. Van Daan, Mrs. Van Daan, and Peter tell you about each?

3. (a) How are members of the audience suddenly reminded early in the scene, amidst the horseplay and teasing on stage, that they are not observing a normal household? (b) What effect does this reminder create?

4. (a) What effect does Mr. Dussel's arrival have upon arrangements in the household? (b) How do various members of the household react to his coming? (c) What information of the outside world does Mr. Dussel provide?

5. Dramatists, even more than other storytellers, have to make every word count. (a) Who speaks each of the following lines? (b) To whom is each remark directed? (c) What do you learn from each speech?

(1) You complain that I don't treat you like a grownup. But when I do, you resent it.

(2) I never heard grownups quarrel before. I thought only children quarreled.

(3) Did Mr. Kraler warn you that you won't get much to eat here? You can imagine. . . . three ration books among the seven of us. . . . and now you make eight.

SCENE FOUR

It is the middle of the night, several months later. The stage is dark except for a little light which comes through the skylight in PETER'S *room.*

Everyone is in bed. MR. *and* MRS. FRANK *lie on the couch in the main room, which has been pulled out to serve as a makeshift double bed.*

MARGOT *is sleeping on a mattress on the floor in the main room, behind a curtain stretched across for privacy. The others are all in their accustomed rooms.*

From outside we hear two drunken soldiers singing "Lili Marlene." A girl's high giggle is heard. The sound of running feet is heard coming closer and then fading in the distance. Throughout the scene there is the distant sound of airplanes passing overhead.

A match suddenly flares up in the attic. We dimly see MR. VAN DAAN. *He is getting his bearings. He comes quickly down the stairs, and goes to the cupboard where the food is stored. Again the match flares up, and is as quickly blown out. The dim figure is seen to steal back up the stairs.*

There is quiet for a second or two, broken only by the sound of airplanes, and running feet on the street below.

Suddenly, out of the silence and the dark, we hear ANNE *scream.*

ANNE *(screaming).* No! No! Don't . . . don't take me!
[*She moans, tossing and crying in her sleep. The other people wake, terrified.* DUSSEL *sits up in bed, furious.*]
DUSSEL. Shush! Anne! Anne, for God's sake, shush!
ANNE *(still in her nightmare).* Save me! Save me!
[*She screams and screams.* DUSSEL *gets out of bed, going over to her, trying to wake her.*]

DUSSEL. For God's sake! Quiet! Quiet! You want someone to hear?
[*In the main room* MRS. FRANK *grabs a shawl and pulls it around her. She rushes in to* ANNE, *taking her in her arms.* MR. FRANK *hurriedly gets up, putting on his overcoat.* MARGOT *sits up, terrified.* PETER'S *light goes on in his room.*]
MRS. FRANK *(to* ANNE, *in her room).* Hush, darling, hush. It's all right. It's all right. *(Over her shoulder to* DUSSEL) Will you be kind enough to turn on the light, Mr. Dussel? *(Back to* ANNE) It's nothing, my darling. It was just a dream.
[DUSSEL *turns on the light in the bedroom.* MRS. FRANK *holds* ANNE *in her arms. Gradually* ANNE *comes out of her nightmare, still trembling with horror.* MR. FRANK *comes into the room, and goes quickly to the window, looking out to be sure that no one outside has heard* ANNE'S *screams.* MRS. FRANK *holds* ANNE, *talking softly to her. In the main room* MARGOT *stands on a chair, turning on the center hanging lamp. A light goes on in the* VAN DAANS' *room overhead.* PETER *puts his robe on, coming out of his room.*]
DUSSEL *(to* MRS. FRANK, *blowing his nose).* Something must be done about that child, Mrs. Frank. Yelling like that! Who knows but there's somebody on the streets? She's endangering all our lives.
MRS. FRANK. Anne, darling.
DUSSEL. Every night she twists and turns. I don't sleep. I spend half my night shushing her. And now it's nightmares!
[MARGOT *comes to the door of* ANNE'S *room, followed by* PETER. MR. FRANK *goes to them, indicating that everything is all right.* PETER *takes* MARGOT *back.*]

MRS. FRANK (to ANNE). You're here, safe, you see? Nothing has happened. (To DUSSEL) Please, Mr. Dussel, go back to bed. She'll be herself in a minute or two. Won't you, Anne?

DUSSEL (picking up a book and a pillow). Thank you, but I'm going to the w.c. The one place where there's peace!

[He stalks out. MR. VAN DAAN, in underwear and trousers, comes down the stairs.]

MR. VAN DAAN (to DUSSEL). What is it? What happened?

DUSSEL. A nightmare. She was having a nightmare!

MR. VAN DAAN. I thought someone was murdering her.

DUSSEL. Unfortunately, no.

[He goes into the bathroom. MR. VAN DAAN goes back up the stairs. MR. FRANK, in the main room, sends PETER back to his own bedroom.]

MR. FRANK. Thank you, Peter. Go back to bed.

[PETER goes back to his room. MR. FRANK follows him turning out the light and looking out the window. Then he goes back to the main room, and gets up on a chair, turning out the center hanging lamp.]

MRS. FRANK (to ANNE). Would you like some water? (ANNE shakes her head.) Was it a very bad dream? Perhaps if you told me . . . ?

ANNE. I'd rather not talk about it.

MRS. FRANK. Poor darling. Try to sleep then. I'll sit right here beside you until you fall asleep. (She brings a stool over, sitting there.)

ANNE. You don't have to.

MRS. FRANK. But I'd like to stay with you . . . very much. Really.

ANNE. I'd rather you didn't.

MRS. FRANK. Good night, then. (She leans down to kiss ANNE. ANNE throws her arm up over her face, turning away. MRS. FRANK, hiding her hurt, kisses ANNE'S arm.) You'll

be all right? There's nothing that you want?

ANNE. Will you please ask Father to come.

MRS. FRANK (after a second). Of course, Anne dear. (She hurries out into the other room. MR. FRANK comes to her as she comes in.) Sie verlangt nich Dir![1]

MR. FRANK (sensing her hurt). Edith, Liebe, schau . . .[2]

MRS. FRANK. Es macht nichts! Ich danke dem lieben Herrgott, dass sie sich wenigstens an Dich wendet, wenn sie Trost braucht! Geh hinein, Otto, sie ist ganz hysterisch vor Angst.[3] (As MR. FRANK hesitates) Geh zu ihr.[4] (He looks at her for a second and then goes to get a cup of water for ANNE. MRS. FRANK sinks down on the bed, her face in her hands, trying to keep from sobbing aloud. MARGOT comes over to her, putting her arms around her.) She wants nothing of me. She pulled away when I leaned down to kiss her.

MARGOT. It's a phase . . . You heard Father . . . Most girls go through it . . . they turn to their fathers at this age . . . they give all their love to their fathers.

MRS. FRANK. You weren't like this. You didn't shut me out.

MARGOT. She'll get over it . . .

[She smooths the bed for MRS. FRANK and sits beside her a moment as MRS. FRANK lies down. In ANNE'S room MR. FRANK comes in, sitting down by ANNE. ANNE flings her arms around him, clinging to him. In the distance we hear the sound of ack-ack.]

ANNE. Oh, Pim. I dreamed that they came to get us! The Green Police! They broke down the door and

---

1. **Sie verlangt nich Dir!** She wants to see you.
2. **Edith, Liebe, schau** . . . Edith, my dear, look . . .
3. **Es macht nichts!** . . . **vor Angst**. It doesn't matter. Thank God that she at least turns to you when she is in need of consolation. Go, Otto, she is hysterical with fear.
4. **Geh zu ihr.** Go to her.

grabbed me and started to drag me out the way they did Jopie.

MR. FRANK. I want you to take this pill.

ANNE. What is it?

MR. FRANK. Something to quiet you.

[*She takes it and drinks the water. In the main room* MARGOT *turns out the light and goes back to her room.*]

MR. FRANK (*to* ANNE). Do you want me to read to you for a while?

ANNE. No. Just sit with me for a minute. Was I awful? Did I yell terribly loud? Do you think anyone outside could have heard?

MR. FRANK. No. No. Lie quietly now. Try to sleep.

ANNE. I'm a terrible coward. I'm so disappointed in myself. I think I've conquered my fear . . . I think I'm really grown-up . . . and then something happens . . . and I run to you like a baby . . . I love you, Father. I don't love anyone but you.

MR. FRANK (*reproachfully*). Annele!

ANNE. It's true. I've been thinking about it for a long time. You're the only one I love.

MR. FRANK. It's fine to hear you tell me that you love me. But I'd be happier if you said you loved your mother as well . . . She needs your help so much . . . your love . . .

ANNE. We have nothing in common. She doesn't understand me. Whenever I try to explain my views on life to her she asks me if I'm constipated.

MR. FRANK. You hurt her very much now. She's crying. She's in there crying.

ANNE. I can't help it. I only told the truth. I didn't want her here . . . (*Then, with sudden change*) Oh, Pim, I was horrible, wasn't I? And the worst of it is, I can stand off and look at myself doing it and know it's cruel and yet I can't stop doing it. What's the matter with me? Tell me. Don't say it's just a phase! Help me.

MR. FRANK. There is so little that we parents can do to help our children. We can only try to set a good example . . . point the way. The rest you must do yourself. You must build your own character.

ANNE. I'm trying. Really I am. Every night I think back over all of the things I did that day that were wrong . . . like putting the wet mop in Mr. Dussel's bed . . . and this thing now with Mother. I say to myself, that was wrong. I make up my mind, I'm never going to do that again. Never! Of course I may do something worse . . . but at least I'll never do *that* again . . . I have a nicer side, Father . . . a sweeter, nicer side. But I'm scared to show it. I'm afraid that people are going to laugh at me if I'm serious. So the mean Anne comes to the outside and the good Anne stays on the inside, and I keep on trying to switch them around and have the good Anne outside and the bad Anne inside and be what I'd like to be . . . and might be . . . if only . . . only . . .

[*She is asleep.* MR. FRANK *watches her for a moment and then turns off the light, and starts out. The lights dim out. The curtain falls on the scene.* ANNE'S VOICE *is heard dimly at first, and then with growing strength.*]

ANNE'S VOICE. . . . The air raids are getting worse. They come over day and night. The noise is terrifying. Pim says it should be music to our ears. The more planes, the sooner will come the end of the war. Mrs. Van Daan pretends to be a fatalist. What will be, will be. But when the planes come over, who is the most frightened? No one else but Petronella! . . . Monday, the ninth of November, nineteen forty-two. Wonderful news! The Allies have landed in Africa. Pim says that we can look for an early finish to the war. Just for fun he asked each of us what was the first thing we wanted to do when we got out of here. Mrs. Van Daan longs to be home with her own things, her needlepoint chairs, the Beckstein piano her father gave her . . . the best that money could buy. Peter would like to go to a movie. Mr. Dussel wants to get back to his dentist's drill. He's afraid he is losing his touch. For myself, there are so many things . . . to ride a bike again . . . to laugh till my belly aches . . . to have new clothes from the skin out . . . to have a hot tub filled to overflowing and wallow in it for hours . . . to be back in school with my friends . . .

[*As the last lines are being said, the curtain rises on the scene. The lights dim on as* ANNE'S VOICE *fades away.*]

Discussion

1. Anne's nightmare serves more than one dramatic purpose. (**a**) What does it tell you about Anne? (**b**) What do you think it may foreshadow?
2. What does the scene reveal about the feelings of: (**a**) Mr. Dussel toward Anne? (**b**) Anne toward her mother? (**c**) her mother toward Anne? (**d**) Anne toward her father? (**e**) Mr. Frank toward his wife? (**f**) Margot toward her mother? Find statements to support your answers.
3. Toward the end of the scene, what does Anne say that indicates she is struggling for greater maturity?
4. Just before Anne's nightmare, Mr. Van Daan has come downstairs. (**a**) What is his purpose? (**b**) Have there been any clues to this kind of action on his part? Explain.

SCENE FIVE

It is the first night of the Hanukkah[1] celebration. MR. FRANK *is standing at the head of the table on which is the Menorah.[2] He lights the Shamos, or servant candle, and holds it as he says the blessing. Seated listening is all of the "family," dressed in their best. The men wear hats,* PETER *wears his cap.*

MR. FRANK (*reading from a prayer book*). "Praised be Thou, oh Lord our God, Ruler of the universe, who has sanctified us with Thy commandments and bidden us kindle the Hanukkah lights. Praised be Thou, oh Lord our God, Ruler of the universe, who has wrought wondrous deliverances for our fathers in days of old. Praised be Thou, oh Lord our God, Ruler of the universe, that Thou has given us life and sustenance and brought us to this happy season." (MR. FRANK *lights the one candle of the Menorah as he continues.*) "We kindle this Hanukkah light to celebrate the great and wonderful deeds wrought through the zeal with which God filled the hearts of the heroic Maccabees, two thousand years ago. They fought against indifference, against tyranny and oppression, and they restored our Temple to us. May these lights remind us that we should ever look to God, whence cometh our help." Amen. [*Pronounced O-mayn.*]

ALL. Amen.

[MR. FRANK *hands* MRS. FRANK *the prayer book.*]

---

1. **Hanukkah** (hä′nu kä), a Jewish festival usually held in December. The festival commemorates the rededication of the temple in Jerusalem after the Maccabees, a family of Jewish patriots, led the Jews to victory over the Syrians in 165 B.C.
2. **Menorah** (mə′nō rə), a candelabrum with various numbers of candlesticks used primarily in Jewish religious services.

MRS. FRANK (reading). "I lift up mine eyes unto the mountains, from whence cometh my help. My help cometh from the Lord who made heaven and earth. He will not suffer thy foot to be moved. He that keepeth thee will not slumber. He that keepeth Israel doth neither slumber nor sleep. The Lord is thy keeper. The Lord is thy shade upon thy right hand. The sun shall not smite thee by day, nor the moon by night. The Lord shall keep thee from all evil. He shall keep thy soul. The Lord shall guard thy going out and thy coming in, from this time forth and forevermore." Amen.

ALL. Amen.

[MRS. FRANK *puts down the prayer book and goes to get the food and wine.* MARGOT *helps her.* MR. FRANK *takes the men's hats and puts them aside.*]

DUSSEL (rising). That was very moving.

ANNE (pulling him back). It isn't over yet!

MRS. VAN DAAN. Sit down! Sit down!

ANNE. There's a lot more, songs and presents.

DUSSEL. Presents?

MRS. FRANK. Not this year, unfortunately.

MRS. VAN DAAN. But always on Hanukkah everyone gives presents . . . everyone!

DUSSEL. Like our St. Nicholas' Day.

[*There is a chorus of "no's" from the group.*]

MRS. VAN DAAN. No! Not like St. Nicholas![3] What kind of a Jew are you that you don't know Hanukkah?

MRS. FRANK (as she brings the food). I remember particularly the candles . . . First one, as we have tonight. Then the second night you light two candles, the next night three . . . and so on until you have eight candles burning. When there are eight candles it is truly beautiful.

MRS. VAN DAAN. And the potato pancakes.

MR. VAN DAAN. Don't talk about them!

MRS. VAN DAAN. I make the best *latkes* you ever tasted!

MRS. FRANK. Invite us all next year . . . in your own home.

MR. FRANK. God willing!

MRS. VAN DAAN. God willing.

MARGOT. What I remember best is the presents we used to get when we were little . . . eight days of presents . . . and each day they got better and better.

MRS. FRANK (sitting down). We are all here, alive. That is present enough.

ANNE. No, it isn't. I've got something . . . (She rushes into her room, hurriedly puts on a little hat improvised from the lamp shade, grabs a satchel bulging with parcels and comes running back.)

MRS. FRANK. What is it?

ANNE. Presents!

MRS. VAN DAAN. Presents!

DUSSEL. Look!

MRS. VAN DAAN. What's she got on her head?

PETER. A lamp shade!

ANNE (She picks out one at random). This is for Margot. (She hands it to MARGOT, pulling her to her feet.) Read it out loud.

MARGOT (reading).
"You have never lost your temper.
You never will, I fear,
You are so good.
But if you should,
Put all your cross words here."
(She tears open the package.) A new crossword puzzle book! Where did you get it?

ANNE. It isn't new. It's one that you've done. But I rubbed it all out, and if you wait a little and forget, you can do it all over again.

---

3. *Not like St. Nicholas.* On December 6, the feast of St. Nicholas, Dutch children are given gifts. St. Nicholas, actually a fourth-century saint, is today a figure like Santa Claus. The feast has no real religious significance.

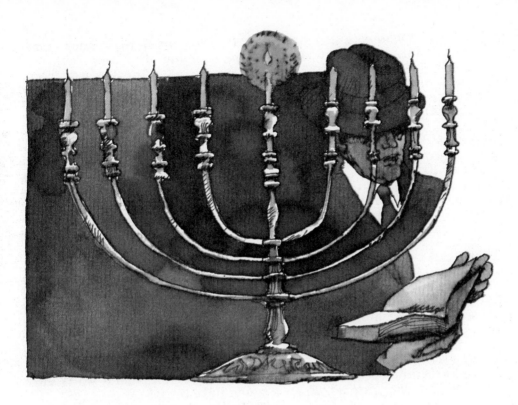

MARGOT (sitting). It's wonderful, Anne. Thank you. You'd never know it wasn't new.

[From outside we hear the sound of a streetcar passing.]

ANNE (with another gift). Mrs. Van Daan.

MRS. VAN DAAN (taking it). This is awful . . . I haven't anything for anyone . . . I never thought . . .

MR. FRANK. This is all Anne's idea.

MRS. VAN DAAN (holding up a bottle). What is it?

ANNE. It's hair shampoo. I took all the odds and ends of soap and mixed them with the last of my toilet water.

MRS. VAN DAAN. Oh, Anneke!

ANNE. I wanted to write a poem for all of them, but I didn't have time. (Offering a large box to MR. VAN DAAN) Yours, Mr. Van Daan, is *really* something . . . something

you want more than anything. (As she waits for him to open it) Look! Cigarettes!

MR. VAN DAAN. Cigarettes!

ANNE. Two of them! Pim found some old pipe tobacco in the pocket lining of his coat . . . and we made them . . . or rather, Pim did.

MRS. VAN DAAN. Let me see . . . Well, look at that! Light it, Putti! Light it.

[MR. VAN DAAN hesitates.]

ANNE. It's tobacco, really it is! There's a little fluff in it, but not much.

[Everyone watches as MR. VAN DAAN cautiously lights it. The cigarette flares up. Everyone laughs.]

PETER. It works!

MRS. VAN DAAN. Look at him.

MR. VAN DAAN (spluttering). Thank you, Anne. Thank you.

[ANNE rushes back to her satchel for another present.]

ANNE (*handing her mother a piece of paper*). For Mother, Hanukkah greeting.

[*She pulls her mother to her feet.*]

MRS. FRANK (*She reads*).
"Here's an I.O.U. that I promise to pay.
Ten hours of doing whatever you say.
Signed, Anne Frank."

(MRS. FRANK, *touched, takes* ANNE *in her arms, holding her close.*)

DUSSEL (*to* ANNE). Ten hours of doing what you're told? *Anything you're told?*

ANNE. That's right.

DUSSEL. You wouldn't want to sell that, Mrs. Frank?

MRS. FRANK. Never! This is the most precious gift I've ever had!

[*She sits, showing her present to the others.* ANNE *hurries back to the satchel and pulls out a scarf, the scarf that* MR. FRANK *found in the first scene.*]

ANNE (*offering it to her father*). For Pim.

MR. FRANK. Anneke . . . I wasn't supposed to have a present!

[*He takes it, unfolding it and showing it to the others.*]

ANNE. It's a muffler . . . to put round your neck . . . like an ascot, you know. I made it myself out of odds and ends . . . I knitted it in the dark each night, after I'd gone to bed. I'm afraid it looks better in the dark!

MR. FRANK (*putting it on*). It's fine. It fits me perfectly. Thank you, Annele.

[ANNE *hands* PETER *a ball of paper, with a string attached to it.*]

ANNE. That's for Mouschi.

PETER (*rising to bow*). On behalf of Mouschi, I thank you.

ANNE (*hesitant, handing him a gift*). And . . . this is yours . . . from Mrs. Quack Quack. (*As he holds it gingerly in his hands*) Well . . . open it . . . Aren't you going to open it?

PETER. I'm scared to. I know something's going to jump out and hit me.

ANNE. No. It's nothing like that, really.

MRS. VAN DAAN (*as he is opening it*). What is it, Peter? Go on. Show it.

ANNE (*excitedly*). It's a safety razor!

DUSSEL. A what?

ANNE. A razor!

MRS. VAN DAAN (*looking at it*). You didn't make that out of odds and ends.

ANNE (*to* PETER). Miep got it for me. It's not new. It's second-hand. But you really do need a razor now.

DUSSEL. For what?

ANNE. Look on his upper lip . . . you can see the beginning of a mustache.

DUSSEL. He wants to get rid of that? Put a little milk on it and let the cat lick it off.

PETER (*starting for his room*). Think you're funny, don't you.

DUSSEL. Look! He can't wait! He's going in to try it!

PETER. I'm going to give Mouschi his present!

[*He goes into his room, slamming the door behind him.*]

MR. VAN DAAN (*disgustedly*). Mouschi, Mouschi, Mouschi.

[*In the distance we hear a dog persistently barking.* ANNE *brings a gift to* DUSSEL.]

ANNE. And last but never least, my roommate, Mr. Dussel.

DUSSEL. For me? You have something for me? (*He opens the small box she gives him.*)

ANNE. I made them myself.

DUSSEL (*puzzled*). Capsules! Two capsules!

ANNE. They're ear-plugs!

DUSSEL. Ear-plugs?

ANNE. To put in your ears so you won't hear me when I thrash around at night. I saw them advertised in a magazine. They're not real ones . . . I made them out of cotton and candle wax. Try them . . . See if they don't work . . . see if you can hear me talk . . .

DUSSEL (*putting them in his ears*). Wait now until I get them in . . . so.

ANNE. Are you ready?

DUSSEL. Huh?

ANNE. Are you ready?

DUSSEL. Good God! They've gone inside! I can't get them out! (*They laugh as* MR. DUSSEL *jumps about, trying to shake the plugs out of his ears. Finally he gets them out. Putting them away.*) Thank you, Anne! Thank you!

MR. VAN DAAN. A real Hanukkah!   (*Together*)

MRS. VAN DAAN. Wasn't it cute of her?

MRS. FRANK. I don't know when she did it.

MARGOT. I love my present.

ANNE (*sitting at the table*). And now let's have the song, Father . . . please . . . (*To* DUSSEL) Have you heard the Hanukkah song, Mr. Dussel? The song is the whole thing! (*She sings*) "Oh Hanukkah! Oh, Hanukkah! The sweet celebration . . ."

MR. FRANK (*quieting her*). I'm afraid, Anne, we shouldn't sing that song tonight. (*To* DUSSEL) It's a song of jubilation, of rejoicing. One is apt to become too enthusiastic.

ANNE. Oh, please, please. Let's sing the song. I promise not to shout!

MR. FRANK. Very well. But quietly now . . . I'll keep an eye on you and when . . .

[*As* ANNE *starts to sing, she is interrupted by* DUSSEL, *who is snorting and wheezing.*]

DUSSEL (*pointing to* PETER). You . . . You! (PETER *is coming from his bedroom, ostentatiously holding a bulge in his coat as if he were holding his cat, and dangling* ANNE'S *present before it.*) How many times . . . I told you . . . Out! Out!

MR. VAN DAAN (*going to* PETER). What's the matter with you? Haven't you any sense? Get that cat out of here.

PETER (*innocently*). Cat?

MR. VAN DAAN. You heard me. Get it out of here!

PETER. I have no cat. (*Delighted with his joke, he opens his coat and pulls out a bath towel. The group at the table laugh, enjoying the joke.*)

DUSSEL (*still wheezing*). It doesn't need to be the cat . . . his clothes are enough . . . when he comes out of that room . . .

MR. VAN DAAN. Don't worry. You won't be bothered any more. We're getting rid of it.

DUSSEL. At last you listen to me.

[*He goes off into his bedroom.*]

MR. VAN DAAN (*calling after him*). I'm not doing it for you. That's all in your mind . . . all of it! (*He starts back to his place at the table.*) I'm doing it because I'm sick of seeing that cat eat all our food.

PETER. That's not true! I only give him bones . . . scraps . . .

MR. VAN DAAN. Don't tell me! He gets fatter every day! Damn cat looks better than any of us. Out he goes tonight!

PETER. No! No!

ANNE. Mr. Van Daan, you can't do that! That's Peter's cat. Peter loves that cat.

MRS. FRANK (*quietly*). Anne.

PETER (*to* MR. VAN DAAN). If he goes, I go.

MR. VAN DAAN. Go! Go!

MRS. VAN DAAN. You're not going and the cat's not going! Now please . . . this is Hanukkah . . . Hanukkah . . . this is the time to celebrate . . . What's the matter with all of you? Come on, Anne. Let's have the song.

ANNE (*singing*).
"Oh, Hanukkah! Oh, Hanukkah! The sweet celebration."

MR. FRANK (rising). I think we should first blow out the candle . . . then we'll have something for tomorrow night.

MARGOT. But, Father, you're supposed to let it burn itself out.

MR. FRANK. I'm sure that God understands shortages. (Before blowing it out) "Praised be Thou, oh Lord our God, who hast sustained us and permitted us to celebrate this joyous festival."

[He is about to blow out the candle when suddenly there is a crash of something falling below. They all freeze in horror, motionless. For a few seconds there is complete silence. MR. FRANK slips off his shoes. The others noiselessly follow his example. MR. FRANK turns out a light near him. He motions to PETER to turn off the center lamp. PETER tries to reach it, realizes he cannot and gets up on a chair. Just as he is touching the lamp he loses his balance. The chair goes out from under him. He falls. The iron lamp shade crashes to the floor. There is a sound of feet below, running down the stairs.]

MR. VAN DAAN (under his breath). God almighty! (The only light left comes from the Hanukkah candle. DUSSEL comes from his room. MR. FRANK creeps over to the stairwell and stands listening. The dog is heard barking excitedly.) Do you hear anything?

MR. FRANK (in a whisper). No. I think they've gone.

MRS. VAN DAAN. It's the Green Police. They've found us.

MR. FRANK. If they had, they wouldn't have left. They'd be up here by now.

MRS. VAN DAAN. I know it's the Green Police. They've gone to get help. That's all, they'll be back.

MR. VAN DAAN. Or it may have been the Gestapo,[4] looking for papers . . .

MR. FRANK (interrupting). Or a thief, looking for money.

MRS. VAN DAAN. We've got to do something . . . Quick! Quick! Before they come back.

MR. VAN DAAN. There isn't anything to do. Just wait.

[MR. FRANK holds up his hand for them to be quiet. He is listening intently. There is complete silence as they all strain to hear any sound from below. Suddenly ANNE begins to sway. With a low cry she falls to the floor in a faint. MRS. FRANK goes to her quickly, sitting beside her on the floor and taking her in her arms.]

MRS. FRANK. Get some water, please! Get some water!

[MARGOT starts for the sink.]

MR. VAN DAAN (grabbing MARGOT). No! No! No one's going to run water!

MR. FRANK. If they've found us, they've found us. Get the water. (MARGOT starts again for the sink. MR. FRANK, getting a flashlight) I'm going down.

[MARGOT rushes to him, clinging to him. ANNE struggles to consciousness.]

MARGOT. No, Father, no! There may be someone there, waiting . . . It may be a trap!

MR. FRANK. This is Saturday. There is no way for us to know what has happened until Miep or Mr. Kraler comes on Monday morning. We cannot live with this uncertainty.

MARGOT. Don't go, Father!

MRS. FRANK. Hush, darling, hush. (MR. FRANK slips quietly out, down the steps and out through the door below.) Margot! Stay close to me.

[MARGOT goes to her mother.]

MR. VAN DAAN. Shush! Shush!

[MRS. FRANK whispers to MARGOT to get the water. MARGOT goes for it.]

MRS. VAN DAAN. Putti, where's our money? Get our money. I hear you can buy the Green Police off, so much a head. Go upstairs quick! Get the money!

---

4. **Gestapo**, the Secret State Police of Nazi Germany.

MR. VAN DAAN. Keep still!

MRS. VAN DAAN (*kneeling before him, pleading*). Do you want to be dragged off to a concentration camp? Are you going to stand there and wait for them to come up and get you? Do something, I tell you!

MR. VAN DAAN (*pushing her aside*). Will you keep still!

[*He goes over to the stairwell to listen. PETER goes to his mother, helping her up onto the sofa. There is a second of silence. Then ANNE can stand it no longer.*]

ANNE. Someone go after Father! Make Father come back!

PETER (*starting for the door*). I'll go.

MR. VAN DAAN. Haven't you done enough?

[*He pushes PETER roughly away. In his anger against his father PETER grabs a chair as if to hit him with it, then puts it down, burying his face in his hands. MRS. FRANK begins to pray softly.*]

ANNE. Please, please, Mr. Van Daan. Get Father.

MR. VAN DAAN. Quiet! Quiet!

[*ANNE is shocked into silence. MRS. FRANK pulls her closer, holding her protectively in her arms.*]

MRS. FRANK (*softly, praying*). "I lift up mine eyes unto the mountains, from whence cometh my help. My help cometh from the Lord who made heaven and earth. He will not suffer thy foot to be moved . . . He that keepeth thee will not slumber . . ."

[*She stops as she hears someone coming. They all watch the door tensely. MR. FRANK comes quietly in. ANNE rushes to him, holding him tight.*]

MR. FRANK. It was a thief. That noise must have scared him away.

MRS. VAN DAAN. Thank God.

MR. FRANK. He took the cash box. And the radio. He ran away in such a hurry that he didn't stop to shut the street door. It was swinging wide open. (*A breath of relief sweeps over them.*) I think it would be good to have some light.

MARGOT. Are you sure it's all right?

MR. FRANK. The danger has passed. (*MARGOT goes to light the small lamp.*) Don't be so terrified, Anne. We're safe.

DUSSEL. Who says the danger has passed? Don't you realize we are in greater danger than ever?

MR. FRANK. Mr. Dussel, will you be still!

[*MR. FRANK takes ANNE back to the table, making her sit down with him, trying to calm her.*]

DUSSEL (*pointing to PETER*). Thanks to this clumsy fool, there's someone now who knows we're up here! Someone now knows we're up here, hiding!

MRS. VAN DAAN (*going to DUSSEL*). Someone knows we're here, yes. But who is the someone? A thief! A thief! You think a thief is going to go to the Green Police and say . . . I was robbing a place the other night and I heard a noise up over my head? You think a thief is going to do that?

DUSSEL. Yes. I think he will.

MRS. VAN DAAN (*hysterically*). You're crazy!

[*She stumbles back to her seat at the table. PETER follows protectively, pushing DUSSEL aside.*]

DUSSEL. I think some day he'll be caught and then he'll make a bargain with the Green Police . . . if they'll let him off, he'll tell them where some Jews are hiding!

[*He goes off into the bedroom. There is a second of appalled silence.*]

MR. VAN DAAN. He's right.

ANNE. Father, let's get out of here! We can't stay here now . . . Let's go . . .

MR. VAN DAAN. Go! Where?

MRS. FRANK (*sinking into her chair at the table*). Yes. Where?

MR. FRANK (*rising, to them all*). Have we lost all faith? All courage? A moment ago we thought that they'd come for us. We were sure it was the end. But it wasn't the end. We're alive, safe. (MR. VAN DAAN *goes to the table and sits.* MR. FRANK *prays.*) "We thank Thee, oh Lord our God, that in Thy infinite mercy Thou hast again seen fit to spare us." (*He blows out the candle, then turns to* ANNE.) Come on, Anne. The song! Let's have the song! (*He starts to sing.* ANNE *finally starts falteringly to sing, as* MR. FRANK *urges her on. Her voice is hardly audible at first.*)

ANNE (*singing*).
"Oh, Hanukkah! Oh, Hanukkah!
The sweet . . . celebration . . ."

[*As she goes on singing, the others gradually join in, their voices still shaking with fear.* MRS. VAN DAAN *sobs as she sings.*]

GROUP.
"Around the feast . . . we . . . gather
In complete . . . jubilation . . .
Happiest of sea . . . sons
Now is here.
Many are the reasons for good cheer."

[DUSSEL *comes from the bedroom. He comes over to the table, standing beside* MARGOT, *listening to them as they sing.*]

"Together
We'll weather
Whatever tomorrow may bring."

[*As they sing on with growing courage, the lights start to dim.*]

"So hear us rejoicing
And merrily voicing
The Hanukkah song that we sing.
Hoy!"

[*The lights are out. The curtain starts slowly to fall.*]

"Hear us rejoicing
And merrily voicing
The Hanukkah song that we sing."

[*They are still singing, as the curtain falls.*]

CURTAIN

Discussion

1. (**a**) What significance can you find in the fact that the "family" celebrates Hanukkah? (**b**) Why does Mr. Frank lead the "family" in the observance? (**c**) Is the gift Anne gives to each occupant of the annex appropriate? Explain your answers. (**d**) Why does Mr. Frank not want Anne to sing the Hanukkah song?

2. (**a**) What incident reveals that Peter has a sense of humor? (**b**) What effect does his behavior have on Mr. Dussel? on Mr. Van Daan?

3. (**a**) What happening ends the celebration abruptly? (**b**) Do you think there is any significance in this event? (**c**) What do you learn about each of the following from the way in which each reacts to the incident: Anne, Mr. Dussel, Mrs. Van Daan, Mr. Van Daan?

4. What decisions does Mr. Frank make throughout the scene that show him still to be the person in charge?

5. (**a**) Why at the end of the scene does Mr. Frank urge Anne to sing the Hanukkah song when earlier he had discouraged her? (**b**) Why do you think the playwrights conclude Act One with the singing of this song?

Dit is een foto, zoals ik me zou wensen, altijd zo te zijn. Dan had ik nog wel een kans om naar Holywood te komen.

Anne Frank.
10 Oct. 1942

(translation)
"This is a photo as I would wish
myself to look all the time. Then
I would maybe have a chance to
come to Hollywood."
Anne Frank, 10 Oct. 1942

Dramatic License

Since a drama is a series of events that can be acted out rather than a description, Frances Goodrich and Albert Hackett had to adapt Anne's diary entries to make them suitable for presentation on a stage. These changes, made for the sake of the overall effect desired by the dramatists, are referred to as the use of dramatic license.

From Anne's descriptions of events in the annex, the dramatists had to create dialogue for the persons involved. Too, they had to compress journal entries to provide necessary exposition, or background, for the play. For example, the first diary entry, which Mr. Frank begins to read aloud on stage, was drawn from parts of a number of entries. Finally, so as not to crowd the stage unduly with actors, in Miep and Mr. Kraler they created composite characters. The personalities of Miep Gies and Elli Vossen,

both of whom worked in the warehouse building and were friends of Anne, merge on stage in Miep; Mr. Kraler and Mr. Koophuis, both business friends of Mr. Frank and both associated with Travis, Inc., become the single character Mr. Kraler.

In reality, the people living in the Secret Annex had more freedom to move around than do the characters in the play. In the diary, Anne frequently mentions the trips to the "private office" on the first floor of the building where the inhabitants of the annex listened to news broadcasts, speeches, and concerts on the radio. The playwrights, however, realizing the difficulties in staging different settings, have confined the action and the characters to one set, the Secret Annex itself.

During the two years the Franks and the Van Daans occupied the Secret Annex, there were several burglaries in the office below. None

of them occurred during the Hanukkah season. Again, the playwrights have used dramatic license in presenting only one of these burglaries. By having the burglary occur during the Hanukkah celebration, the playwrights have created an extremely dramatic situation; the hope and strength which the inhabitants receive from the religious ceremony contrast sharply with the ever-present danger of discovery, brought into focus by the intrusion of the unknown thief.

Much of Anne's diary reveals her thoughts about herself, the special problems with which she, as a teen-ager, is faced. The following diary entry reveals an important aspect of Anne's personality:

Saturday, 15 July, 1944
. . . . I have one outstanding trait in my character, which must strike anyone who knows me for any

length of time and that is my knowledge of myself. I can watch myself and my actions, just like an outsider. The Anne of every day I can face entirely without prejudice, without making excuses for her, and watch what's good and what's bad about her. This "self-consciousness" haunts me, and every time I open my mouth I know as soon as I have spoken whether "that ought to have been different" or "that was right as it was." There are so many things about myself that I condemn; I couldn't begin to name them all. I understand more and more how true Daddy's words were when he said: "All children must look after their own upbringing." Parents can only give good advice or put them on the right paths, but the final forming of a person's character lies in their own hands.[1]

This is the type of personal, intimate revelation which Anne made only in her diary. To reveal this aspect of Anne's personality to the audience, the dramatists incorporated the entry into Scene 4 in which Anne, still frightened and overwrought from her nightmare, confesses to her father things that in actuality she revealed to no one.

Frances Goodrich and Albert Hackett, through their careful selections and adaptations of diary entries, have succeeded in presenting vivid portraits of the inhabitants of the Secret Annex. At the same time, they have preserved the spirit of reality found in the historical source from which they had to work, the diary of a young girl.

---

1. From ANNE FRANK: THE DIARY OF A YOUNG GIRL by Anne Frank. Copyright 1952 by Otto H. Frank. Reprinted by permission of Doubleday & Company, Inc. and Vallentine, Mitchell & Co. Ltd.

Act Two

SCENE ONE

In the darkness we hear ANNE'S VOICE, *again reading from the diary.*

ANNE'S VOICE. Saturday, the first of January, nineteen forty-four. Another new year has begun and we find ourselves still in our hiding place. We have been here now for one year, five months and twenty-five days. It seems that our life is at a standstill.

The curtain rises on the scene. It is afternoon. Everyone is bundled up against the cold. In the main room MRS. FRANK *is taking down the laundry, which is hung across the back.* MR. FRANK *sits in the chair down left, reading.* MARGOT *is lying on the couch with a blanket over her and the many-colored knitted scarf around her throat.* ANNE *is seated at the center table, writing in her diary.* PETER, MR. *and* MRS. VAN DAAN, *and* DUSSEL *are all in their own rooms, reading or lying down.*

As the lights dim on, ANNE'S VOICE *continues, without a break.*

ANNE'S VOICE. We are all a little thinner. The Van Daan's "discussions" are as violent as ever. Mother still does not understand me. But then I don't understand her either. There is one great change, however. A change in myself. I read somewhere that girls of my age don't feel quite certain of themselves.

[*The buzzer of the door below suddenly sounds. Everyone is startled;* MR. FRANK *tiptoes cautiously to the top of the steps and listens. Again the buzzer sounds, in* MIEP'S *V-for-Victory signal.[1]*]

MR. FRANK. It's Miep! (*He goes quickly down the steps to unbolt the door.*

MRS. FRANK *calls upstairs to the* VAN DAANS *and then to* PETER.)

MRS. FRANK. Wake up, everyone! Miep is here! (ANNE *quickly puts her diary away.* MARGOT *sits up, pulling the blanket around her shoulders.* MR. DUSSEL *sits on the edge of his bed, listening, disgruntled.* MIEP *comes up the steps, followed by* MR. KRALER. *They bring flowers, books, newspapers, etc.* ANNE *rushes to* MIEP, *throwing her arms affectionately around her.*) Miep . . . and Mr. Kraler . . . What a delightful surprise!

MR. KRALER. We came to bring you New Year's greetings.

MRS. FRANK. You shouldn't . . . you should have at least one day to yourselves. (*She goes quickly to the stove and brings down teacups and tea for all of them.*)

ANNE. Don't say that, it's so wonderful to see them! (*Sniffing at* MIEP'S *coat*) I can smell the wind and the cold on your clothes.

MIEP (*giving her the flowers*). There you are. (*Then to* MARGOT, *feeling her forehead*) How are you, Margot? . . . Feeling any better?

MARGOT. I'm all right.

ANNE. We filled her full of every kind of pill so she won't cough and make a noise.

[*She runs into her room to put the flowers in water.* MR. *and* MRS. VAN DAAN *come from upstairs. Outside there is the sound of a band playing.*]

MRS. VAN DAAN. Well, hello, Miep. Mr. Kraler.

MR. KRALER (*giving a bouquet of flow-*

---

1. V-for-Victory signal, three short rings followed by a long one. In the Morse Code the letter **V** is transmitted by three dots and a dash. It was widely used as a victory symbol during World War II.

ers to MRS. VAN DAAN*).* With my hope for peace in the New Year.

PETER *(anxiously).* Miep, have you seen Mouschi? Have you seen him anywhere around?

MIEP. I'm sorry, Peter. I asked everyone in the neighborhood had they seen a gray cat. But they said no.

[MRS. FRANK *gives* MIEP *a cup of tea.*

MR. FRANK *comes up the steps, carrying a small cake on a plate.*]

MR. FRANK. Look what Miep's brought for us!

MRS. FRANK *(taking it).* A cake!

MR. VAN DAAN. A cake! *(He pinches* MIEP'S *cheeks gaily and hurries up to the cupboard.)* I'll get some plates.

[DUSSEL, *in his room, hastily puts a coat on and starts out to join the others.*]

MRS. FRANK. Thank you, Miepia. You shouldn't have done it. You must have used all of your sugar ration for weeks. *(Giving it to* MRS. VAN DAAN*)* It's beautiful, isn't it?

MRS. VAN DAAN. It's been ages since I even saw a cake. Not since you brought us one last year. *(Without looking at the cake, to* MIEP*)* Remember? Don't you remember, you gave us one on New Year's Day? Just this time last year? I'll never forget it because you had "Peace in nineteen forty-three" on it. *(She looks at the cake and reads.)* "Peace in nineteen forty-four!"

MIEP. Well, it has to come sometime, you know. *(As* DUSSEL *comes from his room)* Hello, Mr. Dussel.

MR. KRALER. How are you?

MR. VAN DAAN *(bringing plates and a knife).* Here's the knife, *liefje.* Now, how many of us are there?

MIEP. None for me, thank you.

MR. FRANK. Oh, please. You must.

MIEP. I couldn't.

MR. VAN DAAN. Good! That leaves one . . . two . . . three . . . seven of us.

DUSSEL. Eight! Eight! It's the same number as it always is!

MR. VAN DAAN. I left Margot out. I take it for granted Margot won't eat any.

ANNE. Why wouldn't she!

MRS. FRANK. I think it won't harm her.

MR. VAN DAAN. All right! All right! I just didn't want her to start coughing again, that's all.

DUSSEL. And please, Mrs. Frank should cut the cake.

MR. VAN DAAN. What's the difference?

MRS. VAN DAAN. It's not Mrs. Frank's cake, is it, Miep? It's for all of us. *(Together)*

DUSSEL. Mrs. Frank divides things better.

MRS. VAN DAAN *(going to* DUSSEL*).* What are you trying to say?

MR. VAN DAAN. Oh, come on! Stop wasting time! *(Together)*

MRS. VAN DAAN *(to* DUSSEL*).* Don't I always give everybody exactly the same? Don't I?

MR. VAN DAAN. Forget it, Kerli.

MRS. VAN DAAN. No. I want an answer! Don't I?

DUSSEL. Yes. Yes. Everybody gets exactly the same . . . except Mr. Van Daan always gets a little bit more.

[VAN DAAN *advances on* DUSSEL, *the knife still in his hand.*]

MR. VAN DAAN. That's a lie!

[DUSSEL *retreats before the onslaught of the* VAN DAANS.]

MR. FRANK. Please, please! *(Then to* MIEP*)* You see what a little sugar cake does to us? It goes right to our heads!

MR. VAN DAAN *(handing* MRS. FRANK *the knife).* Here you are, Mrs. Frank.

MRS. FRANK. Thank you. *(Then to*

MIEP *as she goes to the table to cut the cake)* Are you sure you won't have some?

MIEP *(drinking her tea)*. No, really, I have to go in a minute.

[*The sound of the band fades out in the distance.*]

PETER *(to* MIEP*)*. Maybe Mouschi went back to our house . . . they say that cats . . . Do you ever get over there . . . ? I mean . . . do you suppose you could . . . ?

MIEP. I'll try, Peter. The first minute I get I'll try. But I'm afraid, with him gone a week . . .

DUSSEL. Make up your mind, already someone has had a nice big dinner from that cat!

[PETER *is furious, inarticulate. He starts toward* DUSSEL *as if to hit him.* MR. FRANK *stops him.* MRS. FRANK *speaks quickly to ease the situation.*]

MRS. FRANK *(to* MIEP*)*. This is delicious, Miep!

MRS. VAN DAAN *(eating hers)*. Delicious!

MR. VAN DAAN *(finishing it in one gulp)*. Dirk's in luck to get a girl who can bake like this!

MIEP *(putting down her empty teacup)*. I have to run. Dirk's taking me to a party tonight.

ANNE. How heavenly! Remember now what everyone is wearing, and what you have to eat and everything, so you can tell us tomorrow.

MIEP. I'll give you a full report! Good-by, everyone!

MR. VAN DAAN *(to* MIEP*)*. Just a minute. There's something I'd like you to do for me.

[*He hurries off up the stairs to his room.*]

MRS. VAN DAAN *(sharply)*. Putti, where are you going? *(She rushes up the stairs after him, calling hysterically.)* What do you want? Putti, what are you going to do?

MIEP *(to* PETER*)*. What's wrong?

PETER. *(His sympathy is with his mother.)* Father says he's going to sell her fur coat. She's crazy about that old fur coat.

DUSSEL. Is it possible? Is it possible that anyone is so silly as to worry about a fur coat in times like this?

PETER. It's none of your darn business . . . and if you say one more thing . . . I'll, I'll take you and I'll . . . I mean it . . . I'll . . .

[*There is a piercing scream from* MRS. VAN DAAN *above. She grabs at the fur coat as* MR. VAN DAAN *is starting downstairs with it.*]

MRS. VAN DAAN. No! No! No! Don't you dare take that! You hear? It's mine! *(Downstairs* PETER *turns away, embarrassed, miserable.)* My father gave me that! You didn't give it to me. You have no right. Let go of it . . . you hear?

[MR. VAN DAAN *pulls the coat from her hands and hurries downstairs.* MRS. VAN DAAN *sinks to the floor, sobbing. As* MR. VAN DAAN *comes into the main room the others look away, embarrassed for him.*]

MR. VAN DAAN *(to* MR. KRALER*)*. Just a little—discussion over the advisability of selling this coat. As I have often reminded Mrs. Van Daan, it's very selfish of her to keep it when people outside are in such desperate need of clothing . . . *(He gives the coat to* MIEP.*)* So if you will please to sell it for us? It should fetch a good price. And by the way, will you get me cigarettes. I don't care what kind they are . . . get all you can.

MIEP. It's terribly difficult to get them, Mr. Van Daan. But I'll try. Good-by.

[*She goes.* MR. FRANK *follows her down the steps to bolt the door after her.* MRS. FRANK *gives* MR. KRALER *a cup of tea.*]

MRS. FRANK. Are you sure you won't have some cake, Mr. Kraler?

MR. KRALER. I'd better not.

MR. VAN DAAN. You're still feeling badly? What does your doctor say?

MR. KRALER. I haven't been to him.

MRS. FRANK. Now, Mr. Kraler! . . .

MR. KRALER (sitting at the table). Oh, I tried. But you can't get near a doctor these days . . . they're so busy. After weeks I finally managed to get one on the telephone. I told him I'd like an appointment . . . I wasn't feeling very well. You know what he answers . . . over the telephone . . . Stick out your tongue! (They laugh. He turns to MR. FRANK as MR. FRANK comes back.) I have some contracts here . . . I wonder if you'd look over them with me. . .

MR. FRANK (putting out his hand). Of course.

MR. KRALER. (He rises.) If we could go downstairs . . . (MR. FRANK starts ahead, MR. KRALER speaks to the others.) Will you forgive us? I won't keep him but a minute. (He starts to follow MR. FRANK down the steps.)

MARGOT (with sudden foreboding). What's happened? Something's happened! Hasn't it, Mr. Kraler?

[MR. KRALER stops and comes back, trying to reassure MARGOT with a pretense of casualness.]

MR. KRALER. No, really. I want your father's advice . . .

MARGOT. Something's gone wrong! I know it!

MR. FRANK (coming back, to MR. KRALER). If it's something that concerns us here, it's better that we all hear it.

MR. KRALER (turning to him, quietly). But . . . the children . . . ?

MR. FRANK. What they'd imagine would be worse than any reality.

[As MR. KRALER speaks, they all listen with intense apprehension. MRS. VAN DAAN comes down the stairs and sits on the bottom step.]

MR. KRALER. It's a man in the storeroom . . . I don't know whether or not you remember him . . . Carl, about fifty, heavy-set, near-sighted . . . He came with us just before you left.

MR. FRANK. He was from Utrecht?

MR. KRALER. That's the man. A couple of weeks ago, when I was in the storeroom, he closed the door and asked me . . . how's Mr. Frank? What do you hear from Mr. Frank? I told him I only knew there was a rumor that you were in Switzerland. He said he'd heard that rumor too, but he thought I might know something more. I didn't pay any attention to it . . . but then a thing happened yesterday . . . He'd brought some invoices to the office for me to sign. As I was going through them, I looked up. He was standing staring at the bookcase . . . your bookcase. He said he thought he remembered a door there . . . Wasn't there a door there that used to go up to the loft? Then he told me he wanted more money. Twenty guilders[2] more a week.

MR. VAN DAAN. Blackmail!

MR. FRANK. Twenty guilders? Very modest blackmail.

MR. VAN DAAN. That's just the beginning.

DUSSEL (coming to MR. FRANK). You know what I think? He was the thief who was down there that night. That's how he knows we're here.

MR. FRANK (to MR. KRALER). How was it left? What did you tell him?

MR. KRALER. I said I had to think about it. What shall I do? Pay him the money? . . . Take a chance on firing him . . . or what? I don't know.

2. **Twenty guilders**, a little over $5.00 in American money. The guilder is the gold monetary unit of the Netherlands.

DUSSEL (*frantic*). For God's sake don't fire him! Pay him what he asks . . . keep him here where you can have your eye on him.

MR. FRANK. Is it so much that he's asking? What are they paying nowadays?

MR. KRALER. He could get it in a war plant. But this isn't a war plant. Mind you, I don't know if he really knows . . . or if he doesn't know.

MR. FRANK. Offer him half. Then we'll soon find out if it's blackmail or not.

DUSSEL. And if it is? We've got to pay it, haven't we? Anything he asks we've got to pay!

MR. FRANK. Let's decide that when the time comes.

MR. KRALER. This may be all imagination. You get to a point, these days, where you suspect everyone and everything. Again and again . . .

on some simple look or word, I've found myself . . .

[*The telephone rings in the office below.*]

MRS. VAN DAAN (*hurrying to* MR. KRALER*).* There's the telephone! What does that mean, the telephone ringing on a holiday?

MR. KRALER. That's my wife. I told her I had to go over some papers in my office . . . to call me there when she got out of church. (*He starts out.*) I'll offer him half then. Goodby . . . we'll hope for the best!

[*The group call their good-bys half-heartedly.* MR. FRANK *follows* MR. KRALER, *to bolt the door below. During the following scene,* MR. FRANK *comes back up and stands listening, disturbed.*]

DUSSEL (*to* MR. VAN DAAN*).* You can thank your son for this . . . smashing the light! I tell you, it's just a question of time now.

[*He goes to the window at the back and stands looking out.*]

MARGOT. Sometimes I wish the end would come . . . whatever it is.

MRS. FRANK (*shocked*). Margot!

[ANNE *goes to* MARGOT, *sitting beside her on the couch with her arms around her.*]

MARGOT. Then at least we'd know where we were.

MRS. FRANK. You should be ashamed of yourself! Talking that way! Think how lucky we are! Think of the thousands dying in the war, every day. Think of the people in concentration camps.

ANNE (*interrupting*). What's the good of that? What's the good of thinking of misery when you're already miserable? That's stupid!

MRS. FRANK. Anne!

[*As* ANNE *goes on raging at her mother,* MRS. FRANK *tries to break in, in an effort to quiet her.*]

ANNE. We're young. Margot and Peter and I! You grownups have had your chance! But look at us . . . If we begin thinking of all the horror in the world, we're lost! We're trying to hold onto some kind of ideals . . . when everything . . . ideals, hopes . . . everything, are being destroyed! It isn't our fault that the world is in such a mess! We weren't around when all this started! So don't try to take it out on us! (*She rushes off to her room, slamming the door after her. She picks up a brush from the chest and hurls it to the floor. Then she sits on the settee, trying to control her anger.*)

MR. VAN DAAN. She talks as if we started the war! Did we start the war?

[*He spots* ANNE'S *cake. As he starts to take it,* PETER *anticipates him.*]

PETER. She left her cake. (*He starts for* ANNE'S *room with the cake. There is silence in the main room.* MRS. VAN DAAN *goes up to her room, followed by* MR. VAN DAAN. DUSSEL *stays looking out the window.* MR. FRANK *brings* MRS. FRANK *her cake. She eats it slowly, without relish.* MR. FRANK *takes his cake to* MARGOT *and sits quietly on the sofa beside her.* PETER *stands in the doorway of* ANNE'S *darkened room, looking at her, then makes a little movement to let her know he is there.* ANNE *sits up, quickly, trying to hide the signs of her tears.* PETER *holds out the cake to her.*) You left this.

ANNE (*dully*). Thanks.

[PETER *starts to go out, then comes back.*]

PETER. I thought you were fine just now. You know just how to talk to them. You know just how to say it. I'm no good . . . I never can think . . . especially when I'm mad . . . That Dussel . . . when he said that about Mouschi . . . someone eating him . . . all I could think is . . .

I wanted to hit him. I wanted to give him such a . . . a . . . that he'd . . . That's what I used to do when there was an argument at school . . . That's the way I . . . but here . . . And an old man like that . . . it wouldn't be so good.

ANNE. You're making a big mistake about me. I do it all wrong. I say too much. I go too far. I hurt people's feelings . . .

[DUSSEL *leaves the window, going to his room.*]

PETER. I think you're just fine . . . What I want to say . . . if it wasn't for you around here, I don't know. What I mean . . .

[PETER *is interrupted by* DUSSEL'S *turning on the light.* DUSSEL *stands in the doorway, startled to see* PETER. PETER *advances toward him forbiddingly.* DUSSEL *backs out of the room.* PETER *closes the door on him.*]

ANNE. Do you mean it, Peter? Do you really mean it?

PETER. I said it, didn't I?

ANNE. Thank you, Peter!

[*In the main room* MR. *and* MRS. FRANK *collect the dishes and take them to the sink, washing them.* MARGOT *lies down again on the couch.* DUSSEL, *lost, wanders into* PETER'S *room and takes up a book, starting to read.*]

PETER (*looking at the photographs on the wall*). You've got quite a collection.

ANNE. Wouldn't you like some in your room? I could give you some. Heaven knows you spend enough time in there . . . doing heaven knows what. . . .

PETER. It's easier. A fight starts, or an argument . . . I duck in there.

ANNE. You're lucky, having a room to go to. His lordship is always here . . . I hardly ever get a minute alone. When they start in on me, I can't duck away. I have to stand there and take it.

PETER. You gave some of it back just now.

ANNE. I get so mad. They've formed their opinions . . . about everything . . . but we . . . we're still trying to find out . . . We have problems here that no other people our age have ever had. And just as you think you've solved them, something comes along and bang! You have to start all over again.

PETER. At least you've got someone you can talk to.

ANNE. Not really. Mother . . . I never discuss anything serious with her. She doesn't understand. Father's all right. We can talk about everything . . . everything but one thing. Mother. He simply won't talk about her. I don't think you can be really intimate with anyone if he holds something back, do you?

PETER. I think your father's fine.

ANNE. Oh, he is, Peter! He is! He's the only one who's ever given me the feeling that I have any sense. But anyway, nothing can take the place of school and play and friends of your own age . . . or near your age . . . can it?

PETER. I suppose you miss your friends and all.

ANNE. It isn't just . . . (*She breaks off, staring up at him for a second.*) Isn't it funny, you and I? Here we've been seeing each other every minute for almost a year and a half, and this is the first time we've ever really talked. It helps a lot to have someone to talk to, don't you think? It helps you to let off steam.

PETER (*going to the door*). Well, any time you want to let off steam, you can come into my room.

ANNE (*following him*). I can get up an awful lot of steam. You'll have to be careful how you say that.

PETER. It's all right with me.

ANNE. Do you really mean it?

PETER. I said it, didn't I?

[*He goes out.* ANNE *stands in her doorway looking after him. As* PETER *gets to his door he stands for a minute looking back at her. Then he goes into his room.* DUSSEL *rises as he comes in, and quickly passes him, going out. He starts across for his room.* ANNE *sees him coming, and pulls her door shut.* DUSSEL *turns back toward* PETER'S *room.* PETER *pulls his door shut.* DUSSEL *stands there, bewildered, forlorn.*

The scene slowly dims out. The curtain falls on the scene. ANNE'S VOICE *comes over in the darkness . . . faintly at first, and then with growing strength.*]

ANNE'S VOICE. We've had bad news. The people from whom Miep got our ration books have been arrested. So we have had to cut down on our food. Our stomachs are so empty that they rumble and make strange noises, all in different keys. Mr. Van Daan's is deep and low, like a bass fiddle. Mine is high, whistling like a flute. As we all sit around waiting for supper, it's like an orchestra tuning up. It only needs Toscanini[3] to raise his baton and we'd be off in the Ride of the Valkyries.[4] Monday, the sixth of March, nineteen forty-four. Mr. Kraler is in the hospital. It seems he has ulcers. Pim says we are his ulcers. Miep has to run the business and us too. The Americans have landed on the southern tip of Italy. Father looks for a quick finish to the war. Mr. Dussel is waiting every day for the warehouse man to demand more money. Have I been skipping too much from one subject to another? I can't help it. I feel that spring is coming. I feel it in my whole body and soul. I feel utterly confused. I am longing . . . so longing . . . for everything . . . for friends . . . for someone to talk to . . . someone who understands . . . someone young, who feels as I do . . . [*As these last lines are being said, the curtain rises on the scene. The lights dim on.* ANNE'S VOICE *fades out.*]

3. *Toscanini* (tos′kə nē′nē), an Italian-born musical conductor who lived and worked principally in the United States.
4. *Ride of the Valkyries* (val kir′ēz), a musical composition by Richard Wagner (väg′nər), a German composer.

Discussion

1. (a) Approximately how much time has passed between the end of Act One and the beginning of Act Two? (b) For how long have the Franks been in hiding? (c) How does the dramatist show the passing of time?

2. Describe incidents in this scene which make evident each of the following: (a) Mr. Dussel's disagreeable personality; (b) Miep's and Mr. Kraler's generosity; (c) Mr. Van Daan's greed; (d) Mrs. Van Daan's vanity; (e) Mr. Frank's level-headedness. What clues in Act One suggest that each of these characters will react in the way he does?

3. (a) What new problem does Mr. Kraler present to the inhabitants of the annex? (b) What solution is decided upon?

4. (a) Explain the situation that causes Anne to flare up at her mother. (b) Do you think her behavior is justified? Explain your answer. (c) How does Anne's anger lead to greater intimacy between herself and Peter?

5. (a) What does Anne mean when she says to Peter that in all the time in the annex "this is the first time we've really talked"? (b) In their private conversation what are some of the things they reveal about themselves?

6. (a) How long after the rest of the scene is Anne's diary entry written? (b) What do you learn from this entry?

SCENE TWO

It is evening, after supper. From the outside we hear the sound of children playing. The "grownups," with the exception of MR. VAN DAAN, *are all in the main room.* MRS. FRANK *is doing some mending,* MRS. VAN DAAN *is reading a fashion magazine.* MR. FRANK *is going over business accounts.* DUSSEL, *in his dentist's jacket, is pacing up and down, impatient to get into his bedroom.* MR. VAN DAAN *is upstairs working on a piece of embroidery in an embroidery frame.*

In his room PETER *is sitting before the mirror, smoothing his hair. As the scene goes on, he puts on his tie, brushes his coat and puts it on preparing himself meticulously for a visit from* ANNE. *On his wall are now hung some of* ANNE'S *motion picture stars.*

In her room ANNE *too is getting dressed. She stands before the mirror in her slip, trying various ways of dressing her hair.* MARGOT *is seated on the sofa, hemming a skirt for* ANNE *to wear.*

In the main room DUSSEL *can stand it no longer. He comes over, rapping sharply on the door of his and* ANNE'S *bedroom.*

ANNE *(calling to him)*. No, no, Mr. Dussel! I am not dressed yet. *(*DUSSEL *walks away, furious, sitting down and burying his head in his hands.* ANNE *turns to* MARGOT.*)* How is that? How does that look?

MARGOT *(glancing at her briefly)*. Fine.

ANNE. You didn't even look.

MARGOT. Of course I did. It's fine.

ANNE. Margot, tell me, am I terribly ugly?

MARGOT. Oh, stop fishing.

ANNE. No. No. Tell me.

MARGOT. Of course you're not. You've got nice eyes . . . and a lot of animation, and . . .

ANNE. A little vague, aren't you?

[She reaches over and takes a brassière out of MARGOT'S *sewing basket. She holds it up to herself, studying the effect in the mirror. Outside,* MRS. FRANK, *feeling sorry for* DUSSEL, *comes over, knocking at the girls' door.]*

MRS. FRANK *(outside)*. May I come in?

MARGOT. Come in, Mother.

MRS. FRANK *(shutting the door behind her)*. Mr. Dussel's impatient to get in here.

ANNE *(still with the brassière)*. Heavens, he takes the room for himself the entire day.

MRS. FRANK *(gently)*. Anne, dear, you're not going in again tonight to see Peter?

ANNE *(dignified)*. That is my intention.

MRS. FRANK. But you've already spent a great deal of time in there today.

ANNE. I was in there exactly twice. Once to get the dictionary, and then three-quarters of an hour before supper.

MRS. FRANK. Aren't you afraid you're disturbing him?

ANNE. Mother, I have some intuition.

MRS. FRANK. Then may I ask you this much, Anne. Please don't shut the door when you go in.

ANNE. You sound like Mrs. Van Daan! *(She throws the brassière back in* MARGOT'S *sewing basket and picks up her blouse, putting it on.)*

MRS. FRANK. No. No. I don't mean to suggest anything wrong. I only wish that you wouldn't expose yourself to criticism . . . that you wouldn't give Mrs. Van Daan the opportunity to be unpleasant.

ANNE. Mrs. Van Daan doesn't need an opportunity to be unpleasant!

MRS. FRANK. Everyone's on edge,

worried about Mr. Kraler. This is one more thing . . .

ANNE. I'm sorry, Mother. I'm going to Peter's room. I'm not going to let Petronella Van Daan spoil our friendship.

[MRS. FRANK *hesitates for a second, then goes out, closing the door after her. She gets a pack of playing cards and sits at the center table, playing solitaire. In* ANNE'S *room* MARGOT *hands the finished skirt to* ANNE. *As* ANNE *is putting it on,* MARGOT *takes off her high-heeled shoes and stuffs paper in the toes so that* ANNE *can wear them.*]

MARGOT *(to* ANNE*).* Why don't you two talk in the main room? It'd save a lot of trouble. It's hard on Mother, having to listen to those remarks from Mrs. Van Daan and not say a word.

ANNE. Why doesn't she say a word? I think it's ridiculous to take it and take it.

MARGOT. You don't understand Mother at all, do you? She can't talk back. She's not like you. It's just not in her nature to fight back.

ANNE. Anyway . . . the only one I worry about is you. I feel awfully guilty about you. *(She sits on the stool near* MARGOT, *putting on* MARGOT'S *high-heeled shoes.)*

MARGOT. What about?

ANNE. I mean, every time I go into Peter's room, I have a feeling I may be hurting you. *(*MARGOT *shakes her head.)* I know if it were me, I'd be wild. I'd be desperately jealous, if it were me.

MARGOT. Well, I'm not.

ANNE. You don't feel badly? Really? Truly? You're not jealous?

MARGOT. Of course I'm jealous . . . jealous that you've got something to get up in the morning for . . . But jealous of you and Peter? No.

[ANNE *goes back to the mirror.*]

ANNE. Maybe there's nothing to be jealous of. Maybe he doesn't really like me. Maybe I'm just taking the place of his cat . . . *(She picks up a pair of short, white gloves, putting them on.)* Wouldn't you like to come in with us?

MARGOT. I have a book.

[*The sound of the children playing outside fades out. In the main room* DUSSEL *can stand it no longer. He jumps up, going to the bedroom door and knocking sharply.*]

DUSSEL. Will you please let me in my room!

ANNE. Just a minute, dear, dear Mr. Dussel. *(She picks up her Mother's pink stole and adjusts it elegantly over her shoulder, then gives a last look in the mirror.)* Well, here I go . . . to run the gauntlet. *(She starts out, followed by* MARGOT.*)*

DUSSEL *(as she appears—sarcastic).* Thank you so much.

[DUSSEL *goes into his room.* ANNE *goes toward* PETER'S *room, passing* MRS. VAN DAAN *and her parents at the center table.*]

MRS. VAN DAAN. My God, look at her! *(*ANNE *pays no attention. She knocks at* PETER'S *door.)* I don't know what good it is to have a son. I never see him. He wouldn't care if I killed myself. *(*PETER *opens the door and stands aside for* ANNE *to come in.)* Just a minute, Anne. *(She goes to them at the door.)* I'd like to say a few words to my son. Do you mind? *(*PETER *and* ANNE *stand waiting.)* Peter, I don't want you staying up till all hours tonight. You've got to have your sleep. You're a growing boy. You hear?

MRS. FRANK. Anne won't stay late. She's going to bed promptly at nine. Aren't you, Anne?

ANNE. Yes, Mother . . . *(To* MRS. VAN DAAN*)* May we go now?

MRS. VAN DAAN. Are you asking me? I

didn't know I had anything to say about it.

MRS. FRANK. Listen for the chimes, Anne dear.

[*The two young people go off into* PETER'S *room, shutting the door after them.*]

MRS. VAN DAAN (*to* MRS. FRANK). In my day it was the boys who called on the girls. Not the girls on the boys.

MRS. FRANK. You know how young people like to feel that they have secrets. Peter's room is the only place where they can talk.

MRS. VAN DAAN. Talk! That's not what they called it when I was young.

[MRS. VAN DAAN *goes off to the bathroom.* MARGOT *settles down to read her book.* MR. FRANK *puts his papers away and brings a chess game to the center table. He and* MRS. FRANK *start to play. In* PETER'S *room,* ANNE *speaks to* PETER, *indignant, humiliated.*]

ANNE. Aren't they awful? Aren't they impossible? Treating us as if we were still in the nursery. (*She sits on the cot.* PETER *gets a bottle of pop and two glasses.*)

PETER. Don't let it bother you. It doesn't bother me.

ANNE. I suppose you can't really blame them . . . *they* think back to what they were like at our age. They don't realize how much more advanced we are . . . When you think what wonderful discussions we've had! . . . Oh, I forgot. I was going to bring you some more pictures.

PETER. Oh, these are fine, thanks.

ANNE. Don't you want some more? Miep just brought me some new ones.

PETER. Maybe later. (*He gives her a glass of pop and taking some for himself, sits down facing her.*)

ANNE (*looking up at one of the photographs*). I remember when I got that . . . I won it. I bet Jopie that I could eat five ice-cream cones. We'd all been playing ping-pong . . . We used to have heavenly times . . . we'd finish up with ice cream at the Delphi, or the Oasis, where Jews were allowed . . . there'd always be a lot of boys . . . we'd laugh and joke . . . I'd like to go back to it for a few days or a week. But after that I know I'd be bored to death. I think more seriously about life now. I want to be a journalist . . . or something. I love to write. What do you want to do?

PETER. I thought I might go off some place . . . work on a farm or something . . . some job that doesn't take much brains.

ANNE. You shouldn't talk that way. You've got the most awful inferiority complex.

PETER. I know I'm not smart.

ANNE. That isn't true. You're much better than I am in dozens of things . . . arithmetic and algebra and . . . well, you're a million times better than I am in algebra. (*With sudden directness*) You like Margot, don't you? Right from the start you liked her, liked her much better than me.

PETER (*uncomfortably*). Oh, I don't know.

[*In the main room* MRS. VAN DAAN *comes from the bathroom and goes over to the sink, polishing a coffeepot.*]

ANNE. It's all right. Everyone feels that way. Margot's so good. She's sweet and bright and beautiful and I'm not.

PETER. I wouldn't say that.

ANNE. Oh, no, I'm not. I know that. I know quite well that I'm not a beauty. I never have been and never shall be.

PETER. I don't agree at all. I think you're pretty.

ANNE. That's not true!

PETER. And another thing. You've changed . . . from at first, I mean.

ANNE. I have?

PETER. I used to think you were awful noisy.

ANNE. And what do you think now, Peter? How have I changed?

PETER. Well . . . er . . . you're . . . quieter.

[*In his room* DUSSEL *takes his pajamas and toilet articles and goes into the bathroom to change.*]

ANNE. I'm glad you don't just hate me.

PETER. I never said that.

ANNE. I bet when you get out of here you'll never think of me again.

PETER. That's crazy.

ANNE. When you get back with all of your friends, you're going to say . . . now what did I ever see in that Mrs. Quack Quack.

PETER. I haven't got any friends.

ANNE. Oh, Peter, of course you have. Everyone has friends.

PETER. Not me. I don't want any. I get along all right without them.

ANNE. Does that mean you can get along without me? I think of myself as your friend.

PETER. No. If they were all like you, it'd be different.

[*He takes the glasses and the bottle and puts them away. There is a second's silence and then* ANNE *speaks, hesitantly, shyly.*]

ANNE. Peter, did you ever kiss a girl?

PETER. Yes. Once.

ANNE (*to cover her feelings*). That picture's crooked. (PETER *goes over, straightening the photograph.*) Was she pretty?

PETER. Huh?

ANNE. The girl that you kissed.

PETER. I don't know. I was blindfolded. (*He comes back and sits down again.*) It was a party. One of those kissing games.

ANNE (*relieved*). Oh, I don't suppose that really counts, does it?

PETER. It didn't with me.

ANNE. I've been kissed twice. Once a man I'd never seen before kissed me on the cheek when he picked me up off the ice and I was crying. And the other was Mr. Koophuis, a friend of Father's who kissed my hand. You wouldn't say those counted, would you?

PETER. I wouldn't say so.

ANNE. I know almost for certain that Margot would never kiss anyone unless she was engaged to them. And I'm sure too that Mother never touched a man before Pim. But I don't know . . . things are so different now. . . . What do you think? Do you think a girl shouldn't kiss anyone except if she's engaged or something? It's so hard to try to think what to do, when here we are with the whole world falling around our ears and you think . . . well . . . you don't know what's going to happen tomorrow and . . . What do you think?

PETER. I suppose it'd depend on the girl. Some girls, anything they do's wrong. But others . . . well . . . it wouldn't necessarily be wrong with them. *(The carillon starts to strike nine o'clock.)* I've always thought that when two people . . .

ANNE. Nine o'clock. I have to go.

PETER. That's right.

ANNE *(without moving)*. Good night.

[*There is a second's pause, then* PETER *gets up and moves toward the door.*]

PETER. You won't let them stop you coming?

ANNE. No. *(She rises and starts for the door.)* Sometime I might bring my diary. There are so many things in it that I want to talk over with you. There's a lot about you.

PETER. What kind of thing?

ANNE. I wouldn't want you to see some of it. I thought you were a nothing, just the way you thought about me.

PETER. Did you change your mind, the way I changed my mind about you?

ANNE. Well . . . You'll see . . .

[*For a second* ANNE *stands looking up at* PETER, *longing for him to kiss her. As he makes no move she turns away. Then suddenly* PETER *grabs her awkwardly in his arms, kissing her on the cheek.* ANNE *walks out dazed. She stands for a minute, her back to the people in the main room. As she regains her poise she goes to her mother and father and* MARGOT, *silently kissing them. They murmur their good nights to her. As she is about to open her bedroom door, she catches sight of* MRS. VAN DAAN. *She goes quickly to her, taking her face in her hands and kissing her first on one cheek and then on the other. Then she hurries off into her room.* MRS. VAN DAAN *looks after her, and then looks over at* PETER'S *room. Her suspicions are confirmed.*]

MRS. VAN DAAN. *(She knows.)* Ah hah!

[*The lights dim out. The curtain falls on the scene. In the darkness* ANNE'S VOICE *comes faintly at first and then with growing strength.*]

ANNE'S VOICE. By this time we all know each other so well that if anyone starts to tell a story, the rest can finish it for him. We're having to cut down still further on our meals. What makes it worse, the rats have been at work again. They've carried off some of our precious food. Even Mr. Dussel wishes now that Mouschi was here. Thursday, the twentieth of April, nineteen forty-four. Invasion fever is mounting every day. Miep tells us that people outside talk of nothing else. For myself, life has become much more pleasant. I often go to Peter's room after supper. Oh, don't think I'm in love, because I'm not. But it does make life more bearable to have someone with whom you can exchange views. No more tonight. P.S. . . . I must be honest. I must confess that I actually live for the next meeting. Is there anything lovelier than to sit under the skylight and feel the sun on your cheeks and have a darling boy in your arms? I admit now that I'm glad the Van Daans had a son and not a daughter. I've outgrown another dress. That's the third. I'm having to wear Margot's clothes after all. I'm working hard on my French and am now reading *La Belle Nivernaise.*[1]

[*As she is saying the last lines, the curtain rises on the scene. The lights dim on, as* ANNE'S VOICE *fades out.*]

---

1. *La Belle Nivernaise,* a novel by Alphonse Daudet (dō-dā′), a nineteenth-century French novelist.

Discussion

1. (a) In what ways has Anne changed since the beginning of the previous scene? (b) What has caused this change? (c) Is Mrs. Frank justified in her concern for Anne's behavior? Explain your answer.

2. (a) How do Anne and Margot differ? (b) In what ways does Margot show mature good sense when talking with Anne? (c) Does the relationship between the sisters seem natural? Explain.

3. (a) What feelings exist between the mother and each daughter? (b) What accounts for the closer relationship between Mrs. Frank and Margot?

4. (a) What are some of the things Peter and Anne are concerned about? (b) Discuss whether or not you think these concerns are typical for people their age.

5. (a) How and why does Anne dramatically alter her behavior to Mrs. Van Daan? (b) How does Mrs. Van Daan respond?

Word Study

When Anne, dressed in borrowed finery, leaves her room to face the unfriendly eyes of the Van Daans, she says, "Well, here I go . . . to run the gauntlet" (page 516, column 2, paragraph 5). The final word in the expression "to run the gauntlet" is more often spelled *gantlet* to distinguish it from another word of similar spelling but different origin. The phrase "to run the gantlet" originally referred to a form of punishment which is thought to have originated centuries ago in the Swedish armies. A soldier, found guilty of an offense, was forced to run between two lines of men each of whom struck him with a rod or whip as he passed. Why is "run the gantlet" a good expression for Anne to use in this situation?

The phrases "throw down the gauntlet" and "take up the gauntlet" also had literal meanings at one time. A gauntlet is a heavy glove, usually of leather, that was covered with steel or iron plates. In the Middle Ages a knight would issue his challenge to combat by throwing his gauntlet on the floor in front of his opponent. If the man accepted the challenge, he picked up the gauntlet.

In the following sentences, the three expressions are used figuratively.

1. John has *run the gantlet* of hostile criticism.
2. By *throwing down the gauntlet,* Harold forced George to make a decision.
3. Mark *took up the gauntlet* and decided to match his speed against Joel's.

From considering the literal meaning given above, try to determine the figurative meaning of each expression. Check your answers in the Glossary. Then answer the following questions:

1. Is any of the literal meaning retained when the expression is used figuratively? Explain.
2. What is the etymology of *gantlet* and *gauntlet*?
3. How are the words *gantlet* and *gauntlet* pronounced?

SCENE THREE

It is night, a few weeks later. Everyone is in bed. There is complete quiet. In the VAN DAANS' *room a match flares up for a moment and then is quickly put out.* MR. VAN DAAN, *in bare feet, dressed in underwear and trousers, is dimly seen coming stealthily down the stairs and into the main room, where* MR. *and* MRS. FRANK *and* MARGOT *are sleeping. He goes to the food safe and again lights a match. Then he cautiously opens the safe, taking out a half-loaf of bread. As he closes the safe, it creaks. He stands rigid.* MRS. FRANK *sits up in bed. She sees him.*

MRS. FRANK *(screaming).* Otto! Otto! *Komme schnell!*[1]

[The rest of the people wake, hurriedly getting up.]

MR. FRANK. *Was ist los? Was ist passiert?*[2]

*[*DUSSEL, *followed by* ANNE, *comes from his room.]*

MRS. FRANK *(as she rushes over to* MR. VAN DAAN*). Er stiehlt das Essen!*[3]

DUSSEL *(grabbing* MR. VAN DAAN*).* You! You! Give me that.

MRS. VAN DAAN *(coming down the stairs).* Putti . . . Putti . . . what is it?

DUSSEL *(his hands on* VAN DAAN'S *neck).* You dirty thief . . . stealing food . . . you good-for-nothing . . .

MR. FRANK. Mr. Dussel! For God's sake! Help me, Peter!

*[*PETER *comes over, trying, with* MR. FRANK, *to separate the two struggling men.]*

PETER. Let him go! Let go!

*[*DUSSEL *drops* MR. VAN DAAN, *pushing him away. He shows them the end of a loaf of bread that he has taken from* VAN DAAN.*]*

DUSSEL. You greedy, selfish . . . !

*[*MARGOT *turns on the lights.]*

MRS. VAN DAAN. Putti . . . what is it?

[All of MRS. FRANK'S *gentleness, her self-control, is gone. She is outraged, in a frenzy of indignation.]*

MRS. FRANK. The bread! He was stealing the bread!

DUSSEL. It was you, and all the time we thought it was the rats!

MR. FRANK. Mr. Van Daan, how could you!

MR. VAN DAAN. I'm hungry.

MRS. FRANK. We're all of us hungry! I see the children getting thinner and thinner. Your own son Peter . . . I've heard him moan in his sleep, he's so hungry. And you come in the night and steal food that should go to them . . . to the children!

MRS. VAN DAAN *(going to* MR. VAN DAAN *protectively).* He needs more food than the rest of us. He's used to more. He's a big man.

*[*MR. VAN DAAN *breaks away, going over and sitting on the couch.]*

MRS. FRANK *(turning on* MRS. VAN DAAN*).* And you . . . you're worse than he is! You're a mother, and yet you sacrifice your child to this man . . . this . . . this . . .

MR. FRANK. Edith! Edith!

*[*MARGOT *picks up the pink woolen stole, putting it over her mother's shoulders.]*

MRS. FRANK *(paying no attention, going on to* MRS. VAN DAAN*).* Don't think I haven't seen you! Always saving the choicest bits for him! I've watched you day after day and I've held my tongue. But not any longer! Not after this! Now I want him to go! I want him to get out of here!

MR. FRANK. Edith! ⎫

MR. VAN DAAN. Get out ⎬ *(Together)*
of here? ⎭

---

1. *Komme Schnell!* Hurry!
2. *Was ist los? Was ist passiert?* What's the matter? What happened?
3. *Er stiehlt das Essen!* He is stealing food.

MRS. VAN DAAN. What do you mean?

MRS. FRANK. Just that! Take your things and get out!

MR. FRANK (to MRS. FRANK). You're speaking in anger. You cannot mean what you are saying.

MRS. FRANK. I mean exactly that!

[MRS. VAN DAAN takes a cover from the FRANKS' bed, pulling it about her.]

MR. FRANK. For two long years we have lived here, side by side. We have respected each other's rights . . . . we have managed to live in peace. Are we now going to throw it all away? I know this will never happen again, will it, Mr. Van Daan?

MR. VAN DAAN. No. No.

MRS. FRANK. He steals once! He'll steal again!

[MR. VAN DAAN, holding his stomach, starts for the bathroom. ANNE puts her arms around him, helping him up the step.]

MR. FRANK. Edith, please. Let us be calm. We'll all go to our rooms . . . and afterwards we'll sit down quietly and talk this out . . . we'll find some way . . .

MRS. FRANK. No! No! No more talk! I want them to leave!

MRS. VAN DAAN. You'd put us out, on the streets?

MRS. FRANK. There are other hiding places.

MRS. VAN DAAN. A cellar . . . a closet. I know. And we have no money left even to pay for that.

MRS. FRANK. I'll give you money. Out of my own pocket I'll give it gladly.

[She gets her purse from a shelf and comes back with it.]

MRS. VAN DAAN. Mr. Frank, you told Putti you'd never forget what he'd done for you when you came to Amsterdam. You said you could never repay him, that you . . .

MRS. FRANK (counting out money). If my husband had any obligation to you, he's paid it, over and over.

MR. FRANK. Edith, I've never seen you like this before. I don't know you.

MRS. FRANK. I should have spoken out long ago.

DUSSEL. You can't be nice to some people.

MRS. VAN DAAN (turning on DUSSEL). There would have been plenty for all of us, if you hadn't come in here!

MR. FRANK. We don't need the Nazis to destroy us. We're destroying ourselves.

[He sits down, with his head in his hands. MRS. FRANK goes to MRS. VAN DAAN.]

MRS. FRANK (giving MRS. VAN DAAN some money). Give this to Miep. She'll find you a place.

ANNE. Mother, you're not putting Peter out. Peter hasn't done anything.

MRS. FRANK. He'll stay, of course. When I say I must protect the children, I mean Peter too.

[PETER rises from the steps where he has been sitting.]

PETER. I'd have to go if Father goes.

[MR. VAN DAAN comes from the bathroom. MRS. VAN DAAN hurries to him and takes him to the couch. Then she gets water from the sink to bathe his face.]

MRS. FRANK (while this is going on). He's no father to you . . . that man! He doesn't know what it is to be a father!

PETER (starting for his room). I wouldn't feel right. I couldn't stay.

MRS. FRANK. Very well, then. I'm sorry.

ANNE (rushing over to PETER). No, Peter! No! (PETER goes into his room, closing the door after him. ANNE turns back to her mother, crying.) I don't care about the food. They can have mine! I don't want it! Only don't send them away. It'll be daylight soon. They'll be caught . . .

MARGOT (*putting her arms comfortingly around* ANNE). Please, Mother!

MRS. FRANK. They're not going now. They'll stay here until Miep finds them a place. (*To* MRS. VAN DAAN) But one thing I insist on! He must never come down here again! He must never come to this room where the food is stored! We'll divide what we have . . . an equal share for each! (DUSSEL *hurries over to get a sack of potatoes from the food safe.* MRS. FRANK *goes on, to* MRS. VAN DAAN.) You can cook it here and take it up to him.

[DUSSEL *brings the sack of potatoes back to the center table.*]

MARGOT. Oh, no. No. We haven't sunk so far that we're going to fight over a handful of rotten potatoes.

DUSSEL (*dividing the potatoes into piles*). Mrs. Frank, Mr. Frank, Margot, Anne, Peter, Mrs. Van Daan, Mr. Van Daan, myself . . . Mrs. Frank . . .

[*The buzzer sounds in* MIEP'S *signal.*]

MR. FRANK. It's Miep! (*He hurries over, getting his overcoat and putting it on.*)

MARGOT. At this hour?

MRS. FRANK. It is trouble.

MR. FRANK (*as he starts down to unbolt the door*). I beg you, don't let her see a thing like this!

MR. DUSSEL (*counting without stopping*). . . . Anne, Peter, Mrs. Van Daan, Mr. Van Daan, myself . . .

MARGOT (*to* DUSSEL). Stop it! Stop it!

DUSSEL. . . . Mr. Frank, Margot, Anne, Peter, Mrs. Van Daan, Mr. Van Daan, myself, Mrs. Frank . . .

MRS. VAN DAAN. You're keeping the big ones for yourself! All the big ones . . . Look at the size of that! . . . And that! . . .

[DUSSEL *continues on with his dividing.* PETER, *with his shirt and trousers on, comes from his room.*]

MARGOT. Stop it! Stop it!

[*We hear* MIEP'S *excited voice speaking to* MR. FRANK *below.*]

MIEP. Mr. Frank . . . the most wonderful news! . . . The invasion has begun!

MR. FRANK. Go on, tell them! Tell them!

[MIEP *comes running up the steps, ahead of* MR. FRANK. *She has a man's raincoat on over her nightclothes and a bunch of orange-colored flowers in her hand.*]

MIEP. Did you hear that, everybody? Did you hear what I said? The invasion has begun! The invasion!

[*They all stare at* MIEP, *unable to grasp what she is telling them.* PETER *is the first to recover his wits.*]

PETER. Where?

MRS. VAN DAAN. When? When, Miep?

MIEP. It began early this morning . . .

[*As she talks on, the realization of what she has said begins to dawn on them. Everyone goes crazy. A wild demonstration takes place.* MRS. FRANK *hugs* MR. VAN DAAN.]

MRS. FRANK. Oh, Mr. Van Daan, did you hear that?

[DUSSEL *embraces* MRS. VAN DAAN. PETER *grabs a frying pan and parades around the room, beating on it, singing the Dutch National Anthem.* ANNE *and* MARGOT *follow him, singing, weaving in and out among the excited grownups.* MARGOT *breaks away to take the flowers from* MIEP *and distribute them to everyone. While this pandemonium is going on* MRS. FRANK *tries to make herself heard above the excitement.*]

MRS. FRANK (*to* MIEP). How do you know?

MIEP. The radio . . . The B.B.C.[4]! They said they landed on the coast of Normandy!

PETER. The British?

---

4. **B.B.C.**, the British Broadcasting Corporation.

MIEP. British, Americans, French, Dutch, Poles, Norwegians . . . all of them! More than four thousand ships! Churchill spoke, and General Eisenhower! D-Day they call it!

MR. FRANK. Thank God, it's come!

MRS. VAN DAAN. At last!

MIEP (starting out). I'm going to tell Mr. Kraler. This'll be better than any blood transfusion.

MR. FRANK (stopping her). What part of Normandy did they land, did they say?

MIEP. Normandy . . . that's all I know now . . . I'll be up the minute I hear some more! (She goes hurriedly out.)

MR. FRANK (to MRS. FRANK). What did I tell you? What did I tell you?

[MRS. FRANK indicates that he has forgotten to bolt the door after MIEP. He hurries down the steps. MR. VAN DAAN, sitting on the couch, suddenly breaks into a convulsive sob. Everybody looks at him, bewildered.]

MRS. VAN DAAN (hurrying to him). Putti! Putti! What is it? What happened?

MR. VAN DAAN. Please. I'm so ashamed.

[MR. FRANK comes back up the steps.]

DUSSEL. Oh, for God's sake!

MRS. VAN DAAN. Don't, Putti.

MARGOT. It doesn't matter now!

MR. FRANK (going to MR. VAN DAAN). Didn't you hear what Miep said? The invasion has come! We're going to be liberated! This is a time to celebrate! (He embraces MRS. FRANK and then hurries to the cupboard and gets the cognac and a glass.)

MR. VAN DAAN. To steal bread from children!

MRS. FRANK. We've all done things that we're ashamed of.

ANNE. Look at me, the way I've treated Mother . . . so mean and horrid to her.

MRS. FRANK. No, Anneke, no.

[ANNE runs to her mother, putting her arms around her.]

ANNE. Oh, Mother, I was. I was awful.

MR. VAN DAAN. Not like me. No one is as bad as me!

DUSSEL (to MR. VAN DAAN). Stop it now! Let's be happy!

MR. FRANK (giving MR. VAN DAAN a glass of cognac). Here! Here! Schnapps! Locheim![5]

[VAN DAAN takes the cognac. They all watch him. He gives them a feeble smile. ANNE puts up her fingers in a V-for-Victory sign. As VAN DAAN gives an answering V-sign, they are startled to hear a loud sob from behind them. It is MRS. FRANK, stricken with remorse. She is sitting on the other side of the room.]

MRS. FRANK (through her sobs). When I think of the terrible things I said . . .

[MR. FRANK, ANNE and MARGOT hurry to her, trying to comfort her. MR. VAN DAAN brings her his glass of cognac.]

MR. VAN DAAN. No! No! You were right!

MRS. FRANK. That I should speak that way to you! . . . Our friends! . . . Our guests! (She starts to cry again.)

DUSSEL. Stop it, you're spoiling the whole invasion!

[As they are comforting her, the lights dim out. The curtain falls.]

ANNE'S VOICE (faintly at first and then with growing strength). We're all in much better spirits these days. There's still excellent news of the invasion. The best part about it is that I have a feeling that friends are coming. Who knows? Maybe I'll be back in school by fall. Ha, ha! The joke is on us! The warehouse man doesn't know a thing and we

---

5. *Schnapps! Locheim!* Mr. Frank is proposing a toast to life.

are paying him all that money!
. . . Wednesday, the second of July,
nineteen forty-four. The invasion
seems temporarily to be bogged
down. Mr. Kraler has to have an
operation, which looks bad. The
Gestapo have found the radio that
was stolen. Mr. Dussel says they'll
trace it back and back to the thief,
and then, it's just a matter of time
till they get to us. Everyone is
low. Even poor Pim can't raise their
spirits. I have often been downcast
myself . . . but never in despair. I
can shake off everything if I write.
But . . . and that is the great
question . . . will I ever be able to
write well? I want to so much. I
want to go on living even after my
death. Another birthday has gone
by, so now I am fifteen. Already I
know what I want. I have a goal, an
opinion.

[*As this is being said—the curtain
rises on the scene, the lights dim on,
and* ANNE'S VOICE *fades out.*]

Discussion

1. (a) Why does Mrs. Frank become enraged for the first time? (b) Is her wrath justified? Explain. (c) How has the playwright foreshadowed this episode?

2. (a) What reason does Mrs. Van Daan give for her husband's behavior? (b) Is this adequate defense for what he has done? Explain your answer.

3. (a) How does Peter display loyalty to his father? (b) Does this loyalty seem reasonable or unreasonable to you in the light of Peter's previous attitude toward his father? Why?

4. During this scene Mr. Frank says, "We don't need the Nazis to destroy us. We're destroying ourselves" (page 522, column 2, paragraph 5). (a) Point out the attitudes and actions of various characters that might lead Mr. Frank to make such a remark. (b) Explain why each of these characters behaves as he does.

5. (a) What news does Miep bring? (b) Why does this news lead to a general reconciliation?

6. By the end of this scene what are your feelings toward Mr. Van Daan? toward Mrs. Frank?

7. (a) With what mixture of good and bad news does Anne conclude the scene? (b) Why do you think the joyous news of the invasion is mingled with a feeling of foreboding?

SCENE FOUR

It is an afternoon a few weeks later . . . Everyone but MARGOT *is in the main room. There is a sense of great tension.*

Both MRS. FRANK *and* MR. VAN DAAN *are nervously pacing back and forth,* DUSSEL *is standing at the window, looking down fixedly at the street below.* PETER *is at the center table, trying to do his lessons.* ANNE *sits opposite him, writing in her diary.* MRS. VAN DAAN *is seated on the couch, her eyes on* MR. FRANK *as he sits reading.*

The sound of a telephone ringing comes from the office below. They all are rigid, listening tensely. MR. DUSSEL *rushes down to* MR. FRANK.

DUSSEL. There it goes again, the telephone! Mr. Frank, do you hear?

MR. FRANK *(quietly)*. Yes. I hear.

DUSSEL *(pleading, insistent)*. But this is the third time, Mr. Frank! The third time in quick succession! It's a signal! I tell you it's Miep, trying to get us! For some reason she can't come to us and she's trying to warn us of something!

MR. FRANK. Please. Please.

MR. VAN DAAN *(to* DUSSEL*)*. You're wasting your breath.

DUSSEL. Something has happened, Mr. Frank. For three days now Miep hasn't been to see us! And today not a man has come to work. There hasn't been a sound in the building!

MRS. FRANK. Perhaps it's Sunday. We may have lost track of the days.

MR. VAN DAAN *(to* ANNE*)*. You with the diary there. What day is it?

DUSSEL *(going to* MRS. FRANK*)*. I don't lose track of the days! I know exactly what day it is! It's Friday, the fourth of August. Friday, and not a man at work. *(He rushes back to* MR. FRANK, *pleading with him, almost in tears.)* I tell you Mr. Kraler's dead. That's the only explanation. He's dead and they've closed down the building, and Miep's trying to tell us!

MR. FRANK. She'd never telephone us.

DUSSEL *(frantic)*. Mr. Frank, answer that! I beg you, answer it!

MR. FRANK. No.

MR. VAN DAAN. Just pick it up and listen. You don't have to speak. Just listen and see if it's Miep.

DUSSEL *(speaking at the same time)*. For God's sake . . . I ask you.

MR. FRANK. No. I've told you, no. I'll do nothing that might let anyone know we're in the building.

PETER. Mr. Frank's right.

MR. VAN DAAN. There's no need to tell us what side you're on.

MR. FRANK. If we wait patiently, quietly, I believe that help will come.

[*There is silence for a minute as they all listen to the telephone ringing.*]

DUSSEL. I'm going down. *(He rushes down the steps.* MR. FRANK *tries ineffectually to hold him.* DUSSEL *runs to the lower door, unbolting it. The telephone stops ringing.* DUSSEL *bolts the door and comes slowly back up the steps.)* Too late. *(MR. FRANK *goes to* MARGOT *in* ANNE'S *bedroom.)*

MR. VAN DAAN. So we just wait here until we die.

MRS. VAN DAAN *(hysterically)*. I can't stand it! I'll kill myself! I'll kill myself!

MR. VAN DAAN. For God's sake, stop it!

[*In the distance, a German military band is heard playing a Viennese waltz.*]

MRS. VAN DAAN. I think you'd be glad if I did! I think you want me to die!

MR. VAN DAAN. Whose fault is it we're

here? (MRS. VAN DAAN *starts for her room. He follows, talking at her.*) We could've been safe somewhere . . . in America or Switzerland. But no! No! You wouldn't leave when I wanted to. You couldn't leave your things. You couldn't leave your precious furniture.

MRS. VAN DAAN. Don't touch me!

[*She hurries up the stairs, followed by* MR. VAN DAAN. PETER, *unable to bear it, goes to his room.* ANNE *looks after him, deeply concerned.* DUSSEL *returns to his post at the window.* MR. FRANK *comes back into the main room and takes a book, trying to read.* MRS. FRANK *sits near the sink, starting to peel some potatoes.* ANNE *quietly goes to* PETER'S *room, closing the door after her.* PETER *is lying face down on the cot.* ANNE *leans over him, holding him in her arms, trying to bring him out of his despair.*]

ANNE. Look, Peter, the sky. (*She looks up through the skylight.*) What a lovely, lovely day! Aren't the clouds beautiful? You know what I do when it seems as if I couldn't stand being cooped up for one more minute? I *think* myself out. I think myself on a walk in the park where I used to go with Pim. Where the jonquils and the crocus and violets grow down the slopes. You know the most wonderful part about *thinking* yourself out? You can have it any way you like. You can have roses and violets and chrysanthemums all blooming at the same time . . . It's funny . . . I used to take it all for granted . . . and now I've gone crazy about everything to do with nature. Haven't you?

PETER. I've just gone crazy. I think if something doesn't happen soon . . . if we don't get out of here . . . I can't stand much more of it!

ANNE (*softly*). I wish you had a religion, Peter.

PETER. No, thanks! Not me!

ANNE. Oh, I don't mean you have to be Orthodox . . . or believe in heaven and hell and purgatory and things . . . I just mean some religion . . . it doesn't matter what. Just to believe in something! When I think of all that's out there . . . the trees . . . and flowers . . . and sea gulls . . . when I think of the dearness of you, Peter, . . . and the goodness of the people we know . . . Mr. Kraler, Miep, Dirk, the vegetable man, all risking their lives for us every day . . . When I think of these good things, I'm not afraid any more . . . I find myself, and God, and I . . .

[PETER *interrupts, getting up and walking away.*]

PETER. That's fine! But when I begin to think, I get mad! Look at us, hiding out for two years. Not able to move! Caught here like . . . waiting for them to come and get us . . . and all for what?

ANNE. We're not the only people that've had to suffer. There've always been people that've had to . . . sometimes one race . . . sometimes another . . . and yet . . .

PETER. That doesn't make me feel any better!

ANNE (*going to him*). I know it's terrible, trying to have any faith . . . when people are doing such horrible . . . But you know what I sometimes think? I think the world may be going through a phase, the way I was with Mother. It'll pass, maybe not for hundreds of years, but some day . . . I still believe, in spite of everything, that people are really good at heart.

PETER. I want to see something now . . . Not a thousand years from now!

[*He goes over, sitting down again on the cot.*]

ANNE. But, Peter, if you'd only look at it as part of a great pattern . . . that we're just a little minute in the life . . . *(She breaks off.)* Listen to us, going at each other like a couple of stupid grown-ups! Look at the sky now. Isn't it lovely? *(She holds out her hand to him.* PETER *takes it and rises, standing with her at the window looking out, his arms around her.)* Some day, when we're outside again, I'm going to . . .

[*She breaks off as she hears the sound of a car, its brakes squealing as it* comes to a sudden stop. *The people in the other rooms also become aware of the sound. They listen tensely. Another car roars up to a screeching stop.* ANNE *and* PETER *come from* PETER'S *room.* MR. *and* MRS. VAN DAAN *creep down the stairs.* DUSSEL *comes out from his room. Everyone is listening, hardly breathing. A doorbell clangs again and again in the building below.* MR. FRANK *starts quietly down the steps to the door.* DUSSEL *and* PETER *follow him. The others stand rigid, waiting, terrified.*

In a few seconds DUSSEL *comes*

stumbling back up the steps. He shakes off PETER'S help and goes to his room. MR. FRANK bolts the door below, and comes slowly back up the steps. Their eyes are all on him as he stands there for a minute. They realize that what they feared has happened. MRS. VAN DAAN starts to whimper. MR. VAN DAAN puts her gently in a chair, and then hurries off up the stairs to their room to collect their things. PETER goes to comfort his mother. There is a sound of violent pounding on a door below.]

MR. FRANK (quietly). For the past two years we have lived in fear. Now we can live in hope.

[The pounding below becomes more insistent. There are muffled sounds of voices, shouting commands.]

MEN'S VOICES. Auf machen! Da drinnen! Auf machen! Schnell! Schnell! Schnell![1] etc., etc.

[The street door below is forced open. We hear the heavy tread of footsteps coming up. MR. FRANK gets two school-bags from the shelves, and gives one to ANNE and the other to MARGOT. He goes to get a bag for MRS. FRANK. The sound of feet coming up grows louder. PETER comes to ANNE, kissing her good-by, then he goes to his room to collect his things. The buzzer of their door starts to ring. MR. FRANK brings MRS. FRANK a bag. They stand together, waiting. We hear the thud of gun butts on the door, trying to break it down.

ANNE stands, holding her school satchel, looking over at her father and mother with a soft, reassuring smile. She is no longer a child, but a woman with courage to meet whatever lies ahead.

The lights dim out. The curtain falls on the scene. We hear a mighty crash as the door is shattered. After a second ANNE'S VOICE is heard.]

ANNE'S VOICE. And so it seems our stay is over. They are waiting for us now. They've allowed us five minutes to get our things. We can each take a bag and whatever it will hold of clothing. Nothing else. So, dear Diary, that means I must leave you behind. Good-by for a while. P.S. Please, please, Miep, or Mr. Kraler, or anyone else. If you should find this diary, will you please keep it safe for me, because some day I hope . . .

[Her voice stops abruptly. There is silence. After a second the curtain rises.]

1. **Auf machen . . . Schnell!** Open up in there! Hurry up!

Discussion

1. (a) Why does Mr. Dussel want Mr. Frank to answer the phone? (b) Why does Mr. Frank refuse to answer it? (c) Suppose you were in the theater audience watching this scene. What effect do you think the ringing telephone would have on you? Why?

2. How is tension between the Van Daans revealed?

3. (a) How does Anne attempt to cheer Peter up? (b) What does she say gives her faith? (c) How does Peter respond to Anne's ideas?

4. Mr. Frank says, "For the past two years we have lived in fear. Now we can live in hope." (a) What does this statement show about him? (b) What other characteristics has he shown?

5. (a) How do the inhabitants behave upon the arrival of the police? (b) Do they behave as you would expect them to? Explain.

6. Anne's actual diary ends three days before her arrest. What, then, is the purpose of the diary entry in this scene?

SCENE FIVE

It is again the afternoon in November, 1945. The rooms are as we saw them in the first scene. MR. KRALER has joined MIEP and MR. FRANK. There are coffee cups on the table. We see a great change in MR. FRANK. He is calm now. His bitterness is gone. He slowly turns a few pages of the diary. They are blank.]

MR. FRANK. No more. *(He closes the diary and puts it down on the couch beside him.)*

MIEP. I'd gone to the country to find food. When I got back the block was surrounded by police . . .

MR. KRALER. We made it our business to learn how they knew. It was the thief . . . the thief who told them.

[MIEP goes up to the gas burner, bringing back a pot of coffee.]

MR. FRANK *(after a pause).* It seems strange to say this, that anyone could be happy in a concentration camp. But Anne was happy in the camp in Holland where they first took us. After two years of being shut up in these rooms, she could be out . . . out in the sunshine and the fresh air that she loved.

MIEP *(offering the coffee to MR. FRANK).* A little more?

MR. FRANK *(holding out his cup to her).* The news of the war was good. The British and Americans were sweeping through France. We felt sure that they would get to us in time. In September we were told that we were to be shipped to Poland . . . The men to one camp. The women to another. I was sent to Auschwitz. They went to Belsen.[1] In January we were freed, the few of us who were left. The war wasn't yet over, so it took us a long time to get home. We'd be sent here and there behind the lines where we'd be safe. Each time our train would stop . . . at a siding, or a crossing . . . we'd all get out and go from group to group . . . Where were you? Were you at Belsen? At Buchenwald? At Mauthausen? Is it possible that you knew my wife? Did you ever see my husband? My son? My daughter? That's how I found out about my wife's death . . . of Margot, the Van Daans . . . Dussel. But Anne . . . I still hoped. . . . Yesterday I went to Rotterdam. I'd heard of a woman there. . . . She'd been in Belsen with Anne . . . I know now.

[He picks up the diary again, and turns the pages back to find a certain passage. As he finds it we hear ANNE'S VOICE.]

ANNE'S VOICE. In spite of everything, I still believe that people are really good at heart.

[MR. FRANK slowly closes the diary.]

MR. FRANK. She puts me to shame.

[They are silent.]

The CURTAIN *falls.*

---

1. **Auschwitz** (oush′vits) . . . **Belsen**, the sites of Nazi concentration camps. Auschwitz is in Poland, Belsen in Germany. Buchenwald (bü′khən vält) and Mauthausen (mout′houz ən), mentioned later, are also concentration camps. The former is in Germany and the latter in Austria.

Discussion

1. What is implied by Mr. Frank's reading Anne's diary entry, then saying, "She puts me to shame"?

2. (a) What is the time relationship between the first scene and the last scene of the play? (b) How does Act One, Scene 1 end? (c) Reread the stage directions for Act Two, Scene 5. What has Mr. Frank supposedly been doing for the entire time in between these scenes? (d) What device has the playwright used to build up this illusion?

Accompanied by Nazi guards, prisoners are herded to one of the thirty-odd concentration camps.

The Aftermath

After the inhabitants of the annex were captured on August 4, they were first sent to Westerbork, a concentration camp in Holland, about eighty miles from Amsterdam. On the morning of September 3, they began the long journey to Auschwitz, the infamous camp in Poland where 4,000,000 Jews died in the gas chambers. For three days they traveled, packed into freight cars. At the camp the men were separated from the women. Mrs. Frank died in the women's camp on January 6, 1945, after her daughters had been sent on to Bergen-Belsen.

It was October 30 when Anne and Margot began the journey to Bergen-Belsen in a cattle car. This camp, where 30,000 prisoners died, was located in Germany. In late 1944 it was in a

disorganized state. The Allies were approaching. Food was scarce, and typhus was raging. Here Margot died at the end of February or the beginning of March, 1945, probably of a combination of typhus and starvation. Anne, already ill of typhus, died peacefully soon after. Three weeks later British troops liberated the camp.

Mrs. Van Daan also died of the typhus epidemic at Bergen-Belsen. Mr. Van Daan died in the gas chambers at Auschwitz. When the Nazis left Auschwitz in January, 1945, they took Peter Van Daan with them. Among other prisoners forced to march in freezing weather, he was not heard from again. Mr. Dussel was sent back to Germany and died in Neuengamme. Only Mr. Frank, who remained at Auschwitz until its liberation, survived.

A fuller record of the aftermath of the capture of Anne Frank can be found in Ernst Schnabel's book, *Anne Frank: A Portrait in Courage.*

Above: Women prisoners huddle on the ground in the concentration camp at Belsen. Right: A liberated prisoner tells his story to a British soldier.

Unit 8 Review

1. In a true-to-life play such as this, it is especially important that the reader see the characters clearly and in depth. (a) Which of Anne's feelings and concerns appear to you to be completely normal for a girl her age? (b) In what ways does she seem to be unusual? (c) Had she lived, what do you believe she would have become as an adult? Support your answer with evidence from within the play.

2. Is Peter a convincing character as he is presented in the play? Give reasons for your answers.

3. Since Anne's diary supplied the source material for the play, we see people and incidents from her point of view. What different picture of the various inhabitants of the annex, including Anne, might we have if the diary had been written by: (a) Mr. Dussel? (b) Mrs. Frank? (c) Mrs. Van Daan?

4. Certain items mentioned very early in the play gain significance as the action advances. Explain what is foreshadowed by mention of each of the following in the first and second scenes of Act One: (a) Mr. Frank's many-colored scarf; (b) Mrs. Van Daan's fur coat; (c) Mr. Van Daan's smoking a cigarette; (d) Peter's cat; (e) Anne's movie-star pictures.

5. (a) Point out the part of the play that is actually a flashback. (b) Explain the advantages of using a flashback in presenting this play.

6. (a) In the introduction to *The Diary of Anne Frank* (pages 466-468) you read that Anne's father had presented her with a diary on her birthday. Yet in the stage play the diary is presented on the first day in hiding. What reason can you give for this use of dramatic license? (b) Mr. Frank's account of what happened to the members of the annex differs slightly from the account in "The Aftermath" (pages 531-532). How do you explain this?

7. Consider the following statement: *"The Diary of Anne Frank* is not dramatic enough. The last scene should have shown Anne's death in a concentration camp. Then we could really have *felt* the tragedy." Explain why you agree or disagree with the viewpoint expressed in this statement.

8. The introduction to the unit (pages 466-468) speaks of the diary of Anne Frank as "a living tribute to the dignity, courage, and perseverance of the human spirit." Do these words seem an accurate description of the play you have just read? Defend your answer by referring to specific scenes and passages.

9. Do you believe that works such as Anne's diary and the play and motion picture based upon it can be influential in preventing future persecution of innocent people? Discuss.

SUGGESTED READING

APPEL, BENJAMIN, *Ben-Gurion's Israel.* (Grosset) Persecuted Jews from all parts of the world dreamed of a homeland. This well-written book explains and interprets the birth and growth of that homeland, modern Israel.

BENARY-ISBERT, MARGOT, *Dangerous Spring.* (Harcourt) The author based this novel on diaries she and her husband kept while in Germany. Karin Lorenz, a German teen-ager during the last days of the war, acts as translator for American soldiers who free the prisoners from a nearby concentration camp.

CORNBERG, SOL, and EMANUEL L. GEBAUER, *A Stage Crew Handbook.* (Harper) This handbook of technical advice deals with every aspect of backstage activity. It will prove interesting and useful to anyone interested in the mechanics of stage production.

FORMAN, JAMES, *Ring the Judas Bell.* (Farrar) Teen-agers and a village priest escape from a prison camp and make their way back across the border during the 1940 Civil War in Greece.

FRANK, ANNE, *Anne Frank, The Diary of a Young Girl.* (Doubleday *Washington Square) This is the famous diary from which the play was adapted. *Tales from the House Behind* (*Bantam) is a collection of stories Anne wrote while in hiding. Through them the reader sees the talent and sensitivity of a remarkable young girl.

GARTH, DAVID, *The Watch on the Bridge.* (Putnam) A battered, war-weary, and depressed American soldier in Germany meets a young German girl, who hides him and helps him regain his faith and courage.

GRIFFITH, FRANCIS and JOSEPH MERSAND (eds.), *Modern One-Act Plays.* (Harcourt) This distinctive collection includes notes about the authors and about the comedies, fantasies, and radio plays presented.

HACKETT, WALTER, *Radio Plays for Young People.* (Plays, Inc.) Fifteen famous stories adapted for radio include DeMaupassant's "The Necklace," Dickens' "A Christmas Carol," and Irving's "Rip Van Winkle."

HOUSEHOLD, GEOFFREY, *Watcher in the Shadows.* (Little) A Viennese in British Intelligence during the war poses as a Nazi. He is later hunted down by an enemy from the past who believes his pose was real.

LEVIN, JANE WHITBREAD, *Star of Danger.* (Harcourt) His yellow Star of David is Karl's "star of danger." This engrossing novel follows Karl as he experiences danger, hardship, loneliness, and the help of the Resistance in his flight from the Nazis.

LINDSAY, HOWARD and RUSSEL CROUSE, *Clarence Day's Life with Father and Life with Mother.* (Knopf) Two favorite stories about life in the Day family are adapted into warm, amusing, thoroughly enjoyable stage plays.

LONGSTRETH, T. MORRIS, *Dangerline.* (Macmillan) Good readers in particular will find both action and material for thought in this novel of a young man who slips through the Iron Curtain to rescue his East German friend.

McKOWN, ROBIN, *Seven Famous Trials in History.* (Vanguard) Along with the trials of Socrates, Joan of Arc, and others, the trial of twenty-one Nazis at Nuremberg helps to prove "that laws are as just as the society that makes them and the men who enforce them."

McSWIGAN, MARIE, *All Aboard for Freedom!* (Dutton) Based on actual experience, this is the story of a group of Czechoslovakians who escape into the Western Zone of Germany in September 1951.

SCHARY, DORÉ, *Sunrise at Campobello.* (Random) This three-act play covers the life of Franklin Delano Roosevelt during 1921–1924, the years when he fought against the devastating physical effects of polio. Photographs of the original Broadway production are included.

SCHNABEL, ERNST, *Anne Frank, a Portrait in Courage.* (Harcourt) This is an authoritative account of Anne Frank before, during, and after her years in hiding.

WOUK, HERMAN, *The Caine Mutiny Court-Martial.* (Doubleday) This play is based on Wouk's World War II novel, *The Caine Mutiny.* Though the drama deals only with the court-martial, events leading up to it are presented through cleverly interwoven dialogue.

*paperback

HANDBOOK
of
literary
terms

ALLITERATION

Sophisticated Selma sat sipping sassafrass sodas while listening to Sally snore soundly.

Three terrible thumping tigers tickling trout, trying to train their tongues to trill.

Weary Willy wondering watched the willowy wheat waving in the wind while wending his wagon westward toward Wyoming.

The lip-tripping tongue-twisters listed above were born because people take pleasure in playing with the sounds of language. We use repeated letter sounds in stock expressions: *busy as a bee; down the drain; smooth as silk.* Advertisers use them in slogans: *Better Buy Bird's Eye; Shop at Sears and Save; Go, Go, Goodyear!* Politicians use them in campaigns: *Tippecanoe and Tyler too; Fifty-four forty or fight; Free soil, free men, free speech, Fre-mont.* And poets, too, use repeated sounds in their writing:

The long light shakes across the lakes,
And the wild cataract leaps in glory.

The use of repeated consonant sounds is called *alliteration.* Usually, the alliterative sounds occur at the beginning of words.

*W*elling *w*ater, *w*insome *w*ord,
*W*ind in *w*arm *w*an *w*eather.

But sometimes they are found within words as well. Note the repetition of *b* and *l* in this line:

*L*ie *l*ight*l*ess, a*ll* the spark*l*es *bl*eared and *bl*ack
and *bl*ind.

Alliteration in poetry does, of course, give pleasure. The repeated sounds help to create melody, which is pleasant to the ear. But a good poet seldom uses alliteration simply because he thinks his readers will enjoy the repeated sounds. Alexander Pope, a respected eighteenth-century English poet, said, "The sound must be an echo to the

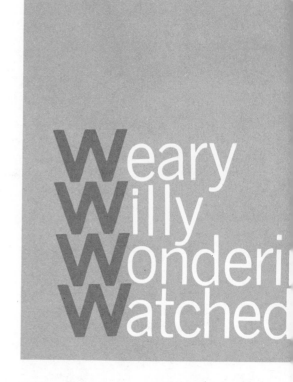

sense," and capable poets follow Pope's rule. How sound can echo sense, or meaning, is demonstrated very clearly in these lines:

The moan of doves in immemorial elms,
And murmuring of innumerable bees.

How is the repeated *m* sound an echo of the murmuring of doves and the hum of bees?

Alliteration can be used to call attention to important words in a poem:

. . . *d*readful was the *d*in of *h*issing through
the *H*all.

It can point out contrasts:

Depth of *p*ain and height of *p*assion.

It can link together words that are similar in image, thought, or feeling:

. . . *s*pikes of *l*ight
*S*peared open *l*ustrous gashes. . .

Find the alliterative sounds in each of the following passages. In each case, try to determine the purpose alliteration serves.

1. And hurled his glistering beams through gloomy air.

2. Greedily she ingorged without restraint.

3. The bookful blockhead, ignorantly read
   With loads of learned lumber in his head.

4. Weaving the web of days that wove your doom.

5. He was haughty, she was humble,
   He was loathed and she was loved.

The sounds produced by alliteration can also affect the mood of a poem. Read the following examples and answer the questions that follow each one.

1. She sent the gentle sleep from Heaven,
   That slid into my soul.

In these lines, does the repeated *s* sound help create a snarling, calm, or joyful effect?

2. Down sunk a hollow bottom, broad and deep.

Do the repeated *b* and *d* sounds help make this line seem dull and heavy or light and carefree? (Read the line aloud if you're not sure.) Are the sounds an "echo to the sense"?

ALLITERATION: repeated consonant sounds occurring at the beginnings of words and within words as well. Alliteration is used to create melody, establish mood, call attention to important words, and point out similarities and contrasts.

CHARACTERIZATION

1. Karen was small for her age, inclined to plumpness, but not fat. Her blue eyes viewed the people and events around her with a mixture of curiosity and wonder. Her straight blond hair hung halfway down her back, a silent symbol of her growing independence, for, with the stubbornness of youth, she ignored her parents' suggestions to get it cut. She was not yet a woman, yet past being a child; too sophisticated for dolls, yet, on an impulse, would turn a somersault on the living-room rug.

a. Approximately how old is Karen?
b. What details help you to visualize her?
c. What details reveal something about Karen's personality?

The author may describe the character.

2. "But why can't I go?" Karen wailed. "Everyone else is going. You never let me go anywhere. You just don't want me to be popular and have lots of friends." Karen wheeled around and stormed out of the room, slamming the door behind her.

a. What does Karen reveal about her personality in this speech?
b. What do her actions contribute to your picture of her?

The author may reveal a character through his speech and actions.

3. "I've known Karen a long time, ever since first grade. We've been best friends since last year. I like her because . . . well, I guess it's because she's always so happy and sure of herself and she's good at things like baseball and swimming and painting and stuff." Joanie paused, then added, "Everybody likes her—she's very popular with all the kids at school."

a. What is Joanie's relationship to Karen?
b. What do you learn about Karen from Joanie's comments?

The author may give the reactions and opinions of other characters.

4. The sunlight trickled between the slats of the Venetian blinds, splashing the carpet with bits of color. Karen stretched luxuriously, pleasantly aware of the tingling sensation in her muscles.

She really ought to get up, she thought to herself. Sally was coming over at eleven. Maybe mother would fix them a picnic lunch and they could eat out in the backyard. Mrs. Henley was taking them to the beach in the afternoon. And she should finish that letter to Peggy. . .maybe tonight. Karen stretched once more and, leaning over the side of the bed, proceeded to feel around for her slippers.

a. What is Karen thinking about?
b. What do her thoughts tell you about her personality?

The author may show the character's inner thoughts and feelings.

An author may use any one of the four methods of characterization illustrated above— (1) description, (2) the character's own speech and behavior, (3) the reactions of other characters, and (4) the character's thoughts and feelings—to bring to life the fictional people whom he has created. Most authors, however, use a combination of methods.

In the following excerpt from the novel *The Mill on the Floss*, George Eliot uses all four methods to characterize Tom Tulliver, a boy who is arriving home from boarding school. Tom and Maggie are the children of Mrs. Tulliver; Yap is the family dog.

Tom was to arrive early in the afternoon, and there was another fluttering heart besides Maggie's when it was late enough for the sound of the gig wheels to be expected; for if Mrs. Tulliver had a strong feeling, it was fondness for her boy. At last the sound came—the quick, light bowling of the gig wheels—and in spite of the wind, which was blowing the clouds about, and was not likely to respect Mrs. Tulliver's curls and cap strings, she came outside the door, and even held her hands

on Maggie's offending head, forgetting all the griefs of the morning.

"There he is, my sweet lad! But Lord ha' mercy! he's got never a collar on; it's been lost on the road, I'll be bound, and spoilt the set."

Mrs. Tulliver stood with her arms open; Maggie jumped first on one leg and then on the other; while Tom descended from the gig, and said, with masculine reticence as to the tender emotions, "Hullo! Yap—what, are you there?"

Nevertheless, he submitted to be kissed willingly enough, though Maggie hung on his neck in rather a strangling fashion, while his blue-gray eyes wandered toward the croft, and the lambs, and the river, where he promised himself that he would begin to fish the first thing tomorrow morning. He was one of those lads that grow everywhere in England, and, at twelve or thirteen years of age, look as much alike as goslings—a lad with light-brown hair, cheeks of cream and roses, full lips, indeterminate nose and eyebrows—a physiognomy in which it seems impossible to discern anything but the generic character of boyhood. . . .

Each of the following is a true statement about Tom. For each one (**a**) point out the lines from the excerpt which prove the statement, and (**b**) name the method or methods of characterization used.

   1. Tom is somewhat careless about his clothes.
   2. Tom does not like to display emotion to his mother and sister.
   3. Tom is glad to be home.
   4. Tom is an ordinary-looking boy.
   5. Tom is happy to see his family.

> **CHARACTERIZATION:** the method an author uses to acquaint the reader with his characters. He may use any or all of four different *methods of characterization:*
> **1.** He may describe the character's physical traits and personality.
> **2.** He may show the character's speech and behavior.
> **3.** He may give the opinions and reactions of other characters toward this individual.
> **4.** He may show the character's thoughts and feelings.

DIALOGUE

ROLSTON (*calling sharply*). Burns!

BURNS. Yes, sir?

ROLSTON. Ah—would you come into my office, please?

BURNS. Right away, Mr. Rolston.

ROLSTON (*casually*). Oh, ah—I meant to ask you this morning, Burns, how your wife is getting along.

BURNS. She's—as well as can be expected, the doctor says. He says after the operation we'll just—have to wait and see.

ROLSTON. Well, give her my regards, won't you? Oh, by the way, Burns, you didn't happen to see an envelope on my desk, did you?

BURNS. No, sir.

ROLSTON. It was a large one—a mailing envelope. It contained some extremely important—ah—personal papers.

BURNS (*tightly*). I said I didn't.

ROLSTON. It was right here when I went out to lunch. You weren't in my office this noon, were you?

BURNS. I only came in to leave that folder there, the file on the Peterson case, and that newspaper clipping about the trial.

ROLSTON. Hm. Did anyone else come in, did you notice?

BURNS. I was at my desk the whole time. No, no one came in. Excuse me—yes, your partner came looking for you.

ROLSTON. Hewitt? Was he in my office?

BURNS. Only for a moment. He came right out.

ROLSTON. Hewitt! If he's—— (*Catches himself*) And no one else?

BURNS. No, sir. (*Pause; with a slight smile*) Is there something worrying you, Mr. Rolston?

ROLSTON. Worrying me? Of course not! Why should there be?

BURNS. I don't know, sir, I only thought . . .

ROLSTON. I just don't like to have people snooping about in my office, that's all!

BURNS (*defensively*). I wasn't snooping, I told you. I just . . .

ROLSTON. And you're sure you didn't see that envelope?

BURNS (*flaring*). Why are you cross-examining me? We're not in the courtroom now! (*Pause; more quietly*) I'm sorry. I've had so much on my mind lately. My wife . . .

ROLSTON. Never mind that——

BURNS. But it's not fair, your questioning me like this. You know I never take anything off your desk without your knowing, and I never touch anything marked personal——

ROLSTON. Then you did see it!

BURNS. I didn't! I——

ROLSTON. Then how did you know it was marked personal?

BURNS. Why, ah—you mentioned it yourself, sir. (*Pause; then, speaking quickly*) You know, Mr. Hewitt might have had it when he came out of your office. I don't know. He *might* have been carrying something. I wasn't paying attention, really. I was . . .

ROLSTON. All right, that's all. I'll talk to Hewitt. Ask him to step in here, will you?

BURNS. Yes, sir. I'll tell him immediately!

ROLSTON. No, wait! Tell him—when he's free.

If you had heard the above speeches, but were not able to see the persons speaking, or to hear any more of their conversation, you would still know a great deal about the speakers and the situation they are in. To see how much information is contained in these speeches, consider the following questions:

1. Who is Mr. Rolston? How do you know?
2. Who is Mr. Burns? How do you know?
3. What is the relationship between the two men?
4. Where do they work? How can you tell?
5. Is Rolston really concerned about Burns' wife? If not, why does he ask about her?
6. Who is Mr. Hewitt? How do you know?
7. Do you think the envelope is important to the plot of the play from which these speeches are taken? Why or why not?
8. Do you suspect that Burns knows more about the envelope than he is saying? Why or why not?
9. Do you think that Mrs. Burns' illness would enter into the plot? Why or why not?
10. What do you think would be Rolston's reaction if he felt sure Hewitt had the envelope?
11. Why doesn't Rolston want to see Hewitt right away?
12. Is the situation likely to be light and humorous, tragic, or dramatic? Explain.

If you have answered these questions carefully and thoughtfully, you already have some understanding as to what *dialogue* is and how it works. *Dialogue* consists of the speeches of the characters in a novel, a short story, a play, a poem, or a work of non-fiction. Authors use dialogue in these several ways:

1. To identify the characters, establish their personalities, and reveal both the relationship of one character to another and the conflicts between them.

2. To set the time and the place, and to provide background necessary to understanding the literary work.

3. To advance the action, to establish a tone, or to express ideas.

Point out one or more speeches in the dialogue on the preceding page which give information about the characters. Which speeches provide necessary background? Which advance the action?

Because a play is written to be performed, a dramatist must rely heavily on dialogue. For this reason, you may be sure that each line of dialogue will be significant and will perform one of the jobs mentioned above.

Compare the following narrative passage to that which you have just read in dialogue:

When Rolston called sharply from his office, Burns answered, then went in. Rolston first asked Burns about his wife, to which Burns replied that she was as well as could be expected and that the doctor had said that after the operation they'd just have to wait and see. Rolston sent his regards, then asked casually if Burns had seen a mailing envelope on his desk, one which contained some important personal papers. Burns denied seeing it, adding that he had only been in the office to leave a folder and a newspaper clipping.

Which version do you find more interesting? Why?

Plays are written almost entirely in dialogue; authors also use dialogue in short stories, novels, and poems for the same purposes that the playwright does. What functions does the dialogue serve in the following selection from Mark Twain's *The Adventures of Tom Sawyer?*

> Sid flew downstairs and said:
> "Oh, Aunt Polly, come! Tom's dying!"
> "Dying!"
> "Yes'm. Don't wait—come quick!"

"Rubbage! I don't believe it!"

But she fled upstairs, nevertheless, with Sid and Mary at her heels. And her face grew white, too, and her lip trembled. When she reached the bedside she gasped out:

"You, Tom! Tom, what's the matter with you?"

"Oh, auntie, I'm—"

"What's the matter with you—what *is* the matter with you, child?"

"Oh, auntie, my sore toe's mortified!"

The old lady sank down into a chair and laughed a little, then cried a little, then did both together. This restored her and she said:

"Tom, what a turn you did give me. Now you shut up that nonsense and climb out of this."

The groans ceased and the pain vanished from the toe. The boy felt a little foolish, and he said:

"Aunt Polly, it *seemed* mortified, and it hurt so I never minded my tooth at all."

"Your tooth, indeed! What's the matter with your tooth?"

"One of them's loose, and it aches perfectly awful."

"There, there, now, don't begin that groaning again. Open your mouth. Well—your tooth *is* loose, but you're not going to die about that. Mary, get me a silk thread and a chunk of fire out of the kitchen."

Tom said:

"Oh, please, auntie, don't pull it out. It don't hurt any more. I wish I may never stir if it does. Please don't, auntie. *I* don't want to stay home from school."

"Oh, you don't, don't you? So all this row was because you thought you'd get to stay home from school and go fishing?"

1. What sort of boy is Tom?

2. What sort of woman is Aunt Polly?

3. How do Tom and Aunt Polly regard one another?

4. How does the language used provide an insight into their characters and backgrounds?

5. What do you think is likely to be the tone of the entire work?

DIALOGUE: conversation between characters in a short story, novel, play, poem, or work of nonfiction. Dialogue may be used to provide background information, to reveal character and character relationships, or to advance the story.

FACT AND FICTION

I. Fact

Unpredictable weather in the Himalayas has made these mountains among the most treacherous peaks in the world to climb. Below zero temperatures, sudden blizzards, avalanches, and ice falls are dangers climbers must be prepared to encounter.

Much careful planning is required of climbers just to get to the base of the mountain. There are no roads through the Himalayas, and all supplies must be carried over trails by men and horses. Once the mountain itself has been reached, camps must be established. Most of the equipment is kept at the lowest, or base, camp. During the ascent of the mountain smaller camps are established at various levels. Only equipment which is absolutely necessary is taken to the higher camps, for every step in these high altitudes is a laborious one.

II. Fiction

Outside, the dawn was seeping up the eastern sky. It was very cold, but the wind had fallen and the mountain seemed to hang suspended in a vast stillness. Above us the summit pyramid climbed bleakly into space, like the last outpost of a spent and lifeless planet. Raising my binoculars, I swept them over the gray waste. At first I saw nothing but rock and ice; then, suddenly, something moved.

"I've got him," I whispered. . . .

"He's not far," Nace said. "Can't have been gone more than half an hour." He seized his ice ax and started out. . . .

"Wait," I said. "I'm going with you."

Nace shook his head. "Better stay here."

"I'm going with you," I said.[1]

1. In which of the above accounts do you think the author's purpose is to inform?

2. Which account has more information which could be checked for accuracy? Which is more subjective—that is, more personal?

Sometimes, because of differences such as these, fact and fiction seem very different from one another. Often, however, especially in modern literature, the reader cannot readily classify a selection as either fact or fiction because it is a blend of both.

---

1. From "Top Man," by James Ramsey Ullman, pages 40–54.

The story, "A Man of Peace" (pages 4–20) is fiction, but it illustrates how a writer may use facts in a story. Read the letter from the author, Lawrence Williams, on pages 21–22, which gives the background of the story. According to the letter, what details in the story are fact? Read the fourth paragraph of the letter carefully. What important bit of fiction did he add? Are there any other details in the story which are probably fictional?

The range from pure fact to pure fiction might be illustrated on a graph such as this:

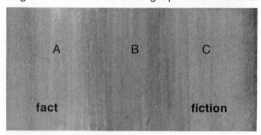

Much literature falls somewhere in B. Explain where on the graph each of the following might be placed:

(**a**) a history
(**b**) a fairy tale
(**c**) a biography
(**d**) a science-fiction novel
(**e**) a short story based on a personal experience
(**f**) a report of a scientific experiment

Suppose a writer wanted to write about unidentified flying objects. If his primary purpose is to inform the public of all reported sightings of UFO's in the United States in the past ten years, would he make his account fact or fiction? If his primary idea is to create a suspense thriller about people's being frightened by UFO's, do you think he would make his account fact or fiction? Why?

The author's purpose in writing determines whether the result is fact or fiction. Therefore, in judging something he reads, a good reader must consider the author's purpose. It would be unfair to criticize an article for lack of excitement if the author's primary purpose is to inform.

FACTUAL PROSE AND FICTION: two broad classifications of prose literature. Some of the characteristics of fiction are:
1. It is personal rather than impersonal.
2. It involves a conflict, or in some way involves the reader's emotions.
3. Its basic purpose normally is to entertain rather than to inform, persuade, or convince.
Contemporary authors often combine in their writings the characteristics of fact and fiction to such a degree that the reader has difficulty classifying a selection as definitely one or the other.

The extent to which a writer uses fact and fiction is determined by his purpose. Therefore the reader, when he evaluates any piece of literature —fact or fiction—should consider two questions:
1. What is the writer's purpose?
2. What techniques has he used to achieve this purpose?

FIGURATIVE LANGUAGE

The Eagle
Alfred, Lord Tennyson

He clasps the crag with crooked hands;
Close to the sun in lonely lands,
Ringed with the azure world, he stands.

The wrinkled sea beneath him crawls;
He watches from his mountain walls,
And like a thunderbolt he falls.

1. Summarize the description given in the poem.
2. Explain the meaning of each of the following phrases in the context of the poem:
    a. crooked hands
    b. in lonely lands
    c. wrinkled sea beneath him crawls
    d. his mountain walls
    e. like a thunderbolt he falls
3. This poem is a description of an eagle; yet, it differs greatly from the ordinary dictionary definition of *eagle:* "a large, strong bird of prey that has keen eyes and powerful wings." **(a)** How does the above poem suggest the eagle's strength? **(b)** Which lines emphasize his keen vision? **(c)** Which phrase stresses his powerful wings? **(d)** Which presents a more colorful description of the eagle, the poem or the dictionary? Explain your answer.

To make his description of the eagle especially clear and appealing, Tennyson has used *figurative language* rather than literal language. Literal language is words used in their ordinary meaning, without exaggeration or inventiveness. (The dictionary definition of *eagle* is written in literal terms.) Figurative language departs from the ordinary meanings of words to emphasize ideas and emotions. The devices for achieving figurative language are called *figures of speech.* Some of the most common figures of speech are *simile, metaphor, personification,* and *hyperbole.*

Simile

A *simile* is a stated comparison between two things that really are very different, but share some common element. To conjure up a vivid picture, a writer points out the quality they share. Similes are introduced by the use of *like* or *as.* If you were to say "John runs *like* the wind and is *as* strong as an ox," you would be using similes. You would be indicating comparisons between John's speed and the speed of the wind, and John's strength and the strength of an ox.

Poets, too, use similes. Longfellow writes about a blacksmith:

And the muscles of his brawny arms
Are strong as iron bands.

What two things are compared in these lines?

One important thing to remember is that statements that compare things that are essentially alike are not similes. Sentences such as "He looks like his father" or "He skates as well as I do" are not similes. A simile reveals a similar quality in two elements that are otherwise very different. Is "His haircut makes him look like a plucked chicken" a simile? Why or why not?

Metaphor

A metaphor, like a simile, is a comparison. But in a metaphor, the comparison is implied rather than stated. For example, "The muscles of his brawny arms are iron bands" is a metaphor. You are using metaphors when you speak of *wolfing* your lunch, acting in a *chicken-hearted* manner, *monkeying* around, or feeling *cocky.* In metaphors, as in similes, the two things being compared must be essentially different. Is this sentence a metaphor: "The tumbleweeds are the lost children of the desert"? Why or why not?

Explain the metaphor contained in these lines:

Death is a black camel, which kneels at the gates of all.

Personification

Personification is a form of metaphor in which a lifeless object, an animal, or an idea is made to act like a person. We use personification in everyday speech: fear *clutched* at his throat; winter *undresses* the trees; the hot sun *snarled* down at us.

Explain the use of personification in these lines of poetry:

Night's candles are burnt out, and jocund day
Stands tiptoe on the misty mountain top.

Hyperbole

Hyperbole is an exaggerated statement used to heighten effect. When you say, "I could eat a horse," you are deliberately exaggerating in order to let your listener know that you are extremely hungry.

What is the purpose of hyperbole in the following lines?

So fair art thou, my bonnie lass,
　So deep in love am I:
And I will love thee still, my dear,
　Till all the seas go dry.

Reread Tennyson's "The Eagle." Which of the various types of figures of speech can you find in the poem?

Occasionally, figurative language is called *metaphorical language.* When the latter term is used, it applies not only to metaphors but to all the various figures of speech.

Good figurative, or metaphorical, language has several important characteristics. First, it makes its point by being both forceful and brief. Second, it has a quality of freshness about it. (For example, which is a better use of hyperbole, "The coffee was so strong you could stand a spoon in it" or "The coffee was so strong you could trot a mouse on it"? Why?) Third, good figurative language fits the situation. If, for example, the figurative expression is based on a comparison, the things being compared must be alike in some recognizable way, and the general effect of the comparison must be consistent and appropriate. Is "The sun came over the mountains with all the glory of a newborn babe" a good figurative expression? Why or why not?

> **FIGURATIVE LANGUAGE:** any language which deviates from literal language so as to furnish novel effects or fresh insights into the subject being discussed. The most common figures of speech are simile, metaphor, personification, and hyperbole.

FLASHBACK

"All right, now," Mr. Tomlinson said, "settle down. It's just about time for the announcements to be made of the winners of this morning's class elections. I'm sure you're all interested enough to keep quiet for a few moments."

Jay Brownlee saw Mr. Tomlinson give him a quick, friendly smile and felt the color rise in his cheeks. Mr. Tomlinson, he knew, was aware of how important this moment was to Jay. Glancing about the room, Jay noticed that some of his classmates were whispering together, some were laughing and joking quietly, while others kept their eyes on their books. He wanted to yell at them to pay attention. How could they possibly be so nonchalant, so seemingly unconcerned? Didn't they realize what this announcement meant?

Five weeks ago—was it really only that short a time?—he had submitted his name as a candidate for president of the junior class. This he had done only after much persuasion and encouragement by his brother and his many friends. Normally shy, Jay wouldn't have dreamed he had a chance without their help. Even Mr. Tomlinson had encouraged him to run.

Once he had committed himself, however, he really went to work—circulating petitions, carefully lettering posters, writing and rewriting his campaign speech—and he was caught up by enthusiasm for his chances.

But then, just when it seemed as if everything were going most successfully, disaster struck. A series of petty thefts in the boys' locker room had led to an investigation and some rather strict new regulations. The boys were no longer allowed to work out on their own in the gym, and they were as down on the thief for causing them this inconvenience as they were angered by the thefts. To his surprise, Jay was accused by his opponent for president, Bill Mulford, who claimed he had seen Jay in the locker room acting suspiciously. Though Jay was innocent, the fact that he was locker-room assistant and had access to the keys part of the day made it look bad. Jay's claim that he had merely been there in order to talk to the coach was received skeptically. However, since all the evidence was circumstantial and Bill could not claim actually to have seen Jay committing the thefts, the whole thing was dropped, but only after a conference with Jay's parents and the principal. Practically the whole student body knew of the situation.

Jay glanced about him again, trying to determine his classmates' thoughts from their expressions, but could not. His friends, he knew, were convinced of his innocence. One even went so far as to suggest that Bill had accused Jay maliciously, hoping to spoil his chances for election. Jay couldn't quite believe that, even of Bill. At least, he *hoped* it wasn't true. But what did the rest of the students think? What did they *really* think? Did they believe that he was responsible for the pilfering, and therefore responsible for the unpopular new restrictions? Or were they willing to believe him innocent until proved guilty? That was the way it was *supposed* to be. For a moment, Jay regretted his shyness, wishing he were able to approach people and make friends as easily as Bill seemed to do. There were many of his classmates who didn't know him very well; if they did know him, they'd realize that he simply wasn't the kind. . . .

It would all be over in a moment, anyway. In a moment he would know. Jay clenched his fists, dropped his head, and quickly prayed that North High knew he was not a thief, that it had all been a mistake. *Let them know*, he repeated, *or at least, let them be fair!* But there was nothing more to be done. Jay wiped his palms on his trouser legs, sat back in his desk, and tried to relax as he waited for the announcement. . . .

Following is a list of the events in the order in which they are mentioned in the above episode:

 a. Mr. Tomlinson calls for quiet.

 b. Jay notices the unconcern of his classmates.

 c. Jay submits his name as candidate.

 d. Jay campaigns for president.

 e. Theft is committed.

 f. Jay is accused of the theft.

 g. The accusation is investigated, dropped through lack of proof.

 h. Jay's friends stand by him.

 i. Jay tries to determine the opinions of his classmates from their expressions.

 j. Jay prays that his classmates will be fair.

 k. Jay tries to relax and wait.

Rearrange the above incidents in the order in which they would have occurred in life.

The order of the items as you have rearranged them is called *chronological order*, the order in which events actually occur in time. Which events in the episode are *not* mentioned in chronological order? How can you tell?

Events related out of chronological order are called *flashbacks,* interruptions in the narrative to show a scene or scenes which occurred before the beginning of a story or earlier in a biographical account. This device is sometimes used by an author when he wants to include an incident from the past that is necessary to an understanding of the story or of the incident he is relating. An author using a flashback usually provides unmistakable clues, so that the careful reader will be able to spot the flashback immediately.

1. What words are used here as clues to the beginning of the flashback? to the return to present time?
2. Can you think of some other words or phrases which could be used in this way?
3. Why is the flashback above important to the story?
4. What effect would be created if the flashback were simply removed?
5. If the author did not use a flashback, what would he have to do?

Often an author does not want his work to cover a span of too much time; therefore, he uses a flashback to bring in material from the past when he feels it necessary to fill in background, or to make the characters or the situation more understandable. In this selection, Jay's nervousness, although natural to one running for office, would not mean nearly so much if we did not know about the accusation of theft.

In some stories which depend largely upon suspense for their effect—murder mysteries, for example—it might be impossible to maintain suspense if there were not such a device as the flashback to allow an author to give us certain information at the precise moment it is needed.

> **FLASHBACK:** an interruption in the action of a story, play, or work of nonfiction to show an episode that happened at an earlier time. A flashback is usually used to provide background information necessary to an understanding of the characters or the plot.

FORESHADOWING

It was a perfect day for a picnic. The morning was bright and clear with a few scattered clouds of the white, fluffy variety that kids find pictures in. Roses were in bloom, and birds sang outside my window. Nothing could go wrong on such a perfect day. Or so I, in my childlike innocence, thought.

1. Where are you first told that something will happen to the narrator which will spoil the perfect day?
2. At this point in the story, do you have any definite idea of what it is that might go wrong?

Sometimes an author gives the reader clues or suggestions about events which will later occur in a narrative. This technique is called *foreshadowing*. In the paragraph above, for example, the narrator suggests that something will happen to mar the perfect day. At this point in the story you don't know what this event is. It may be a humorous episode, such as a cow devouring the narrator's picnic lunch. It may be a tragic event, such as a drowning or an automobile accident.

Not all foreshadowing is as obvious as that in the example above. Frequently, future events are merely hinted at through dialogue, description, and the attitudes and reactions of the characters.

In the following excerpt from Charles Dickens' novel *David Copperfield*, David recounts an event from his childhood. His mother, a young attractive woman, had been widowed shortly before David was born. Peggotty is a trusted and devoted servant of the Copperfield family. As you read, notice clues which might foreshadow future events.

Peggotty and I were sitting one night by the parlor fire, alone. I had been reading to Peggotty about crocodiles. I remember she had a cloudy impression, after I had done, that they were a sort of vegetable. I was tired of reading, and dead sleepy; but having leave, as a high treat, to sit up until my mother came home from spending the evening at a neighbor's, I would rather have died upon my post (of course) than have gone off to bed. . . .

"Peggotty," says I suddenly, "were you ever married?"

"Lord, Master Davy," replied Peggotty, "what's put marriage in your head?"

She answered with such a start that it quite woke me. And then she stopped in her work, and looked at me, with her needle drawn out to its thread's length.

"But were you ever married, Peggotty?" says I. "You are a very handsome woman, an't you?"

"Me handsome, Davy!" said Peggotty. "Lawk no, my dear! But what put marriage in your head?"

"I don't know! You mustn't marry more than one person at a time, may you, Peggotty?"

"Certainly not," says Peggotty, with the promptest decision.

"But if you marry a person, and the person dies, why then you may marry another person, mayn't you, Peggotty?"

"You may," says Peggotty, "if you choose."

"You an't cross, I suppose, Peggotty, are you?" said I, after sitting quiet for a minute.

I really thought she was, she had been so short with me. But I was quite mistaken; for she laid aside her work (which was a stocking of her own), and opening her arms wide, took my curly head within them, and gave it a good squeeze. I know it was a good squeeze, because, being very plump, whenever she made any little exertion after she was dressed, some of the buttons on the back of her gown flew off. And I recollect two bursting while she was hugging me.

"Now let me hear some more about the crorkin-

dills," said Peggotty, "for I an't heard half enough."

I couldn't quite understand why Peggotty looked so queer, or why she was so ready to go back to the crocodiles. However, we returned to those monsters, with fresh interest on my part; but I had my doubts of Peggotty, who was thoughtfully sticking her needle into various parts of her face and arms all the time.

We had exhausted the crocodiles, and begun with the alligators, when the garden bell rang. We went to the door, and there was my mother, looking unusually pretty, I thought, and with her a gentleman with beautiful black hair and whiskers, who had walked home with us from church last Sunday.

As my mother stepped down on the threshold to take me in her arms and kiss me, the gentleman said I was a more highly privileged little fellow than a monarch.

"What does that mean?" I asked him.

He patted me on the head; but somehow I didn't like him or his deep voice, and I was jealous that his hand should touch my mother's in touching me—which it did. I put it away as well as I could.

"Oh, Davy!" remonstrated my mother.

"Dear boy!" said the gentleman. "I cannot wonder at his devotion. Come, let us shake hands!"

My right hand was in my mother's left, so I gave him the other.

"Why, that's the wrong hand, Davy!" laughed the gentleman.

My mother drew my right hand forward; but I resolved, for my former reason, not to give it him, and I did not. I gave him the other, and he shook it heartily, and said I was a brave fellow, and went away.

At this minute I see him turn around in the garden, and give us a last look with his ill-omened black eyes, before the door was shut.

Peggotty, who had not said a word or moved a finger, secured the fastenings instantly, and we all went into the parlor. My mother, contrary to her usual habit, instead of coming to the elbow-chair by the fire, remained at the other end of the room, and sat singing to herself.

"Hope you have had a pleasant evening, ma'am," said Peggotty, standing as stiff as a barrel in the center of the room, with a candlestick in her hand.

"Much obliged to you, Peggotty," returned my mother in a cheerful voice, "I have had a very pleasant evening."

"A stranger or so makes an agreeable change," suggested Peggotty.

"A very agreeable change, indeed," returned my mother.

Peggotty continuing to stand motionless in the middle of the room, and my mother resuming her singing, I fell asleep. . . .

(Later in the novel, Mrs. Copperfield marries the black-haired gentleman, and David, on several occasions, is mistreated by his new stepfather.)

1. When do you first get a hint from Peggotty's attitude that David's mother is about to be married again? When do you learn whom she will probably marry?

2. Which of Mrs. Copperfield's actions lead you to expect the marriage?

3. What hints are there in the man's attitude which foreshadow the marriage?

4. Find the clues in this passage which suggest that the man is not as kind and generous as he appears to be.

Foreshadowing frequently serves two purposes. First, it builds suspense by raising questions in the reader's mind. It thus encourages him to read on and find out more about the event that is being foreshadowed. After reading the preceding passage, for example, the reader is quite certain that Mrs. Copperfield will soon marry the black-haired gentleman. He does not know, however, how young David will fit into this marriage, nor does he know what will happen to Peggotty, who obviously does not approve of the marriage.

Foreshadowing is also a means of adding plausibility to a narrative by partially preparing the reader for events which are to follow. In the preceding passage, the gentleman appears to like David even though the little boy immediately dislikes him. However, David's statement that the gentleman gave them a "last look with his ill-omened black eyes" suggests that the man is not so kind and generous as he appears to be, that he will be the cause of much future unhappiness to the Copperfields.

> **FORESHADOWING:** an author's use of hints or clues about events which will occur later in a narrative.

IMAGERY

The hot July sun beat relentlessly down, casting an orange glare over the farm buildings, the fields, the pond. Even the usually cool green willows bordering the pond hung wilting and dry. The shimmering water seemed to hiss with rising steam. Our sun-baked backs ached for relief. We quickly pulled off our sweaty clothes and plunged into the pond, but the tepid water only stifled us and we soon climbed back onto the brown, dusty bank. Our parched throats longed for something cool—a strawberry ice, a tall frosted glass of lemonade. We pulled on our clothes and headed through the dense, crackling underbrush, the sharp briars pulling at our damp trousers, until we reached the field—and the yellow-streaked green of the watermelon patch. Just the thought of the water-laden fruit made us run, and, as we began to cut open the nearest melon, we could smell the pungent skin mingling with the dusty odor of dry earth. The soft, over-ripe melon gave way with a crack, revealing the deep pink sugar-heavy and tender relief inside.

1. From the paragraph above, pick out words and phrases which appeal to your sense of **(a)** sight; **(b)** sound; **(c)** smell; **(d)** taste; **(e)** touch and feeling.
2. Which sense impression is strongest?

To make his imaginary world seem real to his readers, an author often makes use of words and phrases which appeal to the senses. These words and phrases, called *images,* help the reader mentally see, hear, smell, feel, and taste much of what the characters experience. In this way he becomes involved in the world of the literary selection.

What are your feelings as you read the first three sentences of the paragraph reprinted above? What emotion do you experience as you read the last sentence? A good description should arouse a particular response or emotion within the reader. In the paragraph above, for example, the author uses images which help the reader feel the intense heat, experience thirst, and find relief along with the characters of the story.

What images combine to arouse the reader's response in the following selection from Lord Tennyson's "The Lotos-Eaters"?

There is sweet music here that softer
　　falls
Than petals from blown roses on the
　　grass,
Or night-dews on still waters between
　　walls
Of shadowy granite, in a gleaming pass;
Music that gentlier on the spirit lies
Than tired eyelids upon tired eyes;
Music that brings sweet sleep down from
　　the blissful skies.
Here are cool mosses deep,
And through the moss the ivies creep,
And in the stream the long-leaved
　　flowers weep,
And from the craggy ledge the poppy
　　hangs in sleep.

1. To what senses does the poet appeal in this passage? Pick out the sensory images which seem most vivid to you.
2. What emotion is the author trying to arouse in the reader?

> **IMAGERY:** concrete details that appeal to the senses. By using specific images, an author establishes mood and arouses emotion in his readers.

INFERENCE

Help Wanted:
Young man to work at White Sox ball park. You will see every home game. Some experience selling helpful, but not necessary. Uniform provided. Apply at concession stand, corner Addison & 14th.

1. The person who takes this job will probably work as (**a**) a baseball player; (**b**) a bat boy; (**c**) a hot-dog vender.
2. What two details tell you what kind of job this is?

"Hello, Coast Guard? This is Johnson at the lighthouse."[1]

1. Johnson is (**a**) a lost sailor; (**b**) a lighthouse keeper; (**c**) a member of the Coast Guard.
2. He is calling because (**a**) he is lost; (**b**) a storm is coming; (**c**) the light has burned out.

Drawing correct conclusions from a few hints or reading appropriately between the lines is called *making inferences*. The ability to make suitable inferences is one of the most important skills a reader can develop.

Many writers—particularly modern writers—do not tell the reader everything outright. Instead they rely on his ability to make reasonable inferences.

The reader can make inferences from the author's description of a scene or character, from a character's conversation and actions, from the way in which other characters react to him, from the particular words an author chooses, and from many other clues. In the following passage from *Nicholas Nickleby,* Charles Dickens describes a school owned and run by Mr. Wackford Squeers.

Obedient to this summons there ranged themselves in front of the schoolmaster's desk half a dozen scarecrows, out at knees and elbows, one of whom placed a torn and filthy book beneath his learned eye.

"This is the first class in English spelling and philosophy, Nickleby," said Squeers, beckoning Nicholas to stand beside him. "We'll get up a Latin one and hand that over to you. Now then, where's the first boy?"

"Please, sir, he's cleaning the back-parlor window," said the temporary head of the philosophical class.

"So he is, to be sure," rejoined Squeers. "We go upon the practical mode of teaching, Nickleby, the regular education system. C-l-e-a-n, clean, verb active, to make bright, to scour. W-i-n, win, d-e-r, der, winder, a casement. When the boy knows out of book, he goes and does it. Where's the second boy?"

"Please, sir, he's weeding the garden," replied a small voice.

"To be sure," said Squeers, by no means disconcerted. "So he is. B-o-t, bot, t-i-n, tin, bottin, n-e-y, ney, bottinney, noun substantive, a knowledge of plants. When he has learned that bottinney means a knowledge of plants, he goes and knows 'em. That's our system, Nickleby; what do you think of it?"

"It's a useful one, at any rate," answered Nicholas.

"I believe you," rejoined Squeers, not remarking the emphasis of his usher. "Third boy, what's a horse?"

"A beast, sir," replied the boy.

"So it is," said Squeers. "Ain't it, Nickleby?"

"I believe there is no doubt of that, sir," answered Nicholas.

"Of course there isn't," said Squeers. "A horse is a quadruped, and *quadruped's* Latin for beast, as everybody that's gone through the grammar knows, or else where's the use of having grammars at all?"

"Where, indeed!" said Nicholas, abstractedly.

1. Who are the scarecrows?
2. Is Squeers a well-educated man? How do you know?

---

1. From *The Saturday Evening Post,* (March 4, 1962). Reprinted by permission of R. Michaud and *The Saturday Evening Post.* © 1962 The Curtis Publishing Company.

3. What is Nicholas' position at the school?
4. Has Nicholas been at the school very long? How do you know?
5. What is Nicholas' attitude toward Squeers? (Note especially his final statement.)
6. What do you think is the author's attitude toward the schools of this period?

INFERENCE: a reasonable and intelligent conclusion drawn from hints provided by the author.

IRONY

Verbal Irony

It was one of those days. First the alarm clock failed to go off, then John broke his last shoelace as he was dressing, spilled orange juice on his assignments, and missed his ride to school. As he stood in the rain waiting for the bus, which was ten minutes late, he muttered to a friend standing nearby, "Well, I can tell this is going to be a perfect day!"

1. What does John mean by his statement?
2. Does he expect his friend to take him literally; that is, does he actually believe it *is* going to be a perfect day?
3. If he does not, why does he say it?

When John says just the opposite of what he really means or feels, he is using *verbal irony*. Another example of this kind of irony might be the comment "Good job!" to someone who has just done a poor job. Can you recall some situations in which you have used verbal irony? Describe them.

Irony of Situation

Read the following synopsis of a short story by O. Henry entitled "The Cop and the Anthem":

It is late autumn in New York, and Soapy, a bum, decides that it is time for him to make his usual arrangements for the winter months: he will get himself arrested and sentenced to prison. There he will have food and lodging, at least. To put his plot in motion, Soapy plans to enjoy a large meal, then not be able to pay for it. However, when he goes into a fashionable restaurant, he is immediately turned out because of his clothing. Next, he smashes a store window and confesses to it. But the policeman refuses to believe him. He does get his meal in a not-so-fashionable restaurant, but instead of being arrested when he can't pay, he is merely thrown out onto the street. Soapy makes several more attempts to be arrested, including the stealing of an umbrella, but it turns out that the man with the umbrella had himself stolen it earlier. Soapy gives up in despair and heads for the park and his accustomed bench, but on the way he stops before a church. As he listens to the music from within, he is reminded of his happy childhood and the depths into which he has now fallen. Sentimentally, he resolves to reform his life, to go straight, find a job, and become successful. But as he stands there making this decision, he is finally arrested—for vagrancy!

1. What does Soapy want to have happen and try to make happen?
2. What results from his efforts?
3. When does what he had wanted actually happen?
4. When it happens finally, does Soapy still want it? Why or why not?

This story, in which things turn out contrary to what is expected, is an example of *irony of situation.* Soapy believes that getting arrested will be a simple matter and does several things that ordinarily would get him arrested. There is irony in the fact that, when he *wants* to get arrested, nothing he can do will bring about his arrest. There is further irony in the fact that he finally is arrested—but only after he no longer wants to be—and then for nothing he has done, but for merely standing still while he makes plans to change his life. Many an author has based his entire story around this kind of ironic conclusion; others use irony in lesser degrees.

Irony of Tone

In the following selection from Mark Twain's *Innocents Abroad,* Twain describes his reaction to a tourist site as if he were no more than an average tourist. Here are his comments about the spot which he has been told marks the exact center of the earth, and about the nearby grave of the first human being, Adam:

If even greater proofs than those I have mentioned[1] are wanted, to satisfy the headstrong and the foolish that this is the genuine centre of the earth, they are here. The greatest of them lies in the fact that from under this very column was taken the *dust from which Adam was made.* This can surely be regarded in the light of a settler.[2] It is not likely that the original first man would have been made from an inferior quality of earth when it was entirely convenient to get first quality from the world's centre. This will strike any reflecting mind

forcibly. That Adam was formed of dirt procured in this very spot is amply proven by the fact that in six thousand years no man has ever been able to prove that the dirt was *not* procured here whereof he was made.

It is a singular circumstance that right under the roof of this same church, and not far away from that illustrious column, Adam himself, the father of the human race, lies buried. There is no question that he is actually buried in the grave which is pointed out as his—there can be none—because it has never yet been proved that that grave is not the grave in which he is buried.

The tomb of Adam! How touching it was, here in a land of strangers, far away from home, and friends, and all who cared for me, thus to discover the grave of a blood relation. . . . I leaned upon a pillar and burst into tears. . . . Noble old man—he did not live to see me—he did not live to see his child. And I—I—alas, I did not live to see *him.* Weighed down by sorrow and disappointment, he died before I was born—six thousand brief summers before I was born. But let us try to bear it with fortitude. Let us trust that he is better off where he is. Let us take comfort in the thought that his loss is our eternal gain.

1. Do you think Mark Twain actually believed that he was viewing the tomb of Adam?
2. Does he expect his reader to believe that the place is really Adam's tomb?
3. What are the two proofs which Twain presents and claims cannot be questioned? Are they really proofs?
4. Why does he present them?

When verbal irony is extended beyond a single statement in this way to pervade an entire selection, it is called *irony of tone.* This device, in which the author's real attitude contrasts with the attitude he pretends to have, is often used in satire and humorous writings, such as Twain's. Through the use of irony of tone an author can often convey his ideas more readily than would be possible by making direct statements. The criticism implied seems more readily acceptable because it is expressed through humor.

---

1. *those . . . mentioned.* Twain had previously cited the proofs that a man would have cast no shadow at noon if there were any sun, and that the column marking the center of the earth had three times shifted its position, signifying that the earth's mass had shifted, probably because of whole mountain ranges flying off into space.
2. *settler,* final proof, the statement which will settle all debate.

1. What kind of person is Twain criticizing in this selection?
2. What is his real attitude toward "the tomb of Adam"?
3. What do you think would be his attitude toward similar "tourist attractions"?

It is not always immediately apparent that an author is being ironic, but the careful reader will be able to sense when what an author says and what he means are not the same. The author frequently veils his real attitude behind a mask of innocence or even admiration in order to lead the reader to come independently to the conclusion the author desires.

> **IRONY:** the contrast between what is expected, or what appears to be, and what actually is. *Verbal irony* is the contrast of saying the opposite of what is actually meant. *Irony of situation* is based on the difference between the way events work out and what is expected to happen or what seems appropriate. *Irony of tone* extends verbal irony to include lengthy passages or even an entire work in which an author expresses an attitude opposite to what he feels.

PLOT

The exercises following the story "Champion Stock" deal with CONFLICT, DETAILS, *and* PATTERN OF EVENTS. *These are all important elements of a plot.*

Champion Stock

by Bud Murphy

1] I guess being raised on a ranch a fellow comes by his love for horses naturally. That, and having a Pa like mine who used to be one of the top bronc busters in the country. He was a champion, all right, and he used to tell me stories about rough horses he had ridden from Canada to Mexico, and how he won that pair of solid gold spurs at the Cheyenne rodeo before I was born.

2] That was the story I always liked best, about the gold spurs, I mean, because after the story he would always pull his big watch out and show me the spurs fastened on the chain. They were big as gold nuggets, caught together by a little gold chain between the rowels. Of course, there was a trick to his pulling out his watch at the end of the story, because he'd always remind me the watch showed it was my bedtime.

3] As long as I can remember I have wanted to be a top rider like my Pa. But in my seventeen years on the ranch I had never had a horse of my own. About all the riding I got to do was on the old sorrel mare Pa and I took turns riding when we had work to do up in the hills above the ranch cup, and on Saturdays when I worked over at the Kingman place.

4] "Some day," Pa always said, "you'll have a horse, Billy boy. When we kind

Reprinted by permission from *Literary Cavalcade,* copyright 1949 by Scholastic Magazines, Inc.

of git caught up on things an' I c'n afford it."

5] But there never did seem to be money for me to have a horse like other kids who lived on ranches in that part of southern Arizona.

6] Ours was a small ranch, as ranches go, just a few miles out of Patagonia, the nearest town, and until I got big enough to help him, Pa did the working of it himself. Ma ran a few chickens along with her housework and we always managed to have enough food though our clothes were nothing to brag about. And the one pair of boots I owned had to do me for school, church, and chores. They were so thin I finally got a new pair last Christmas. I remember it was Christmas because every year Pa had been promising me a horse for Christmas and every year there would be something else, just like last year it was the boots.

7] I really never did figure to have a horse of my own till I could earn enough money somehow to buy one. That was why I had been spending a lot of time working Saturdays over at the Kingman ranch which adjoined ours on the east. Old man Kingman had been a good friend of my Pa's for a long time and it was really Pa who got me the job.

8] "'Course he ain't got no more sense'n a mule," Pa told Mr. Kingman. "But he's strong an' he'll do what you tell him."

9] Mr. Kingman was a big bull of a man with a forehead like a barn door and a slow grin that made folks like him right off when they met him. He had done well, too, from the way Pa talked.

10] "Trouble is, I should 'a' done like him," Pa used to say. "He settled down an' got started early raisin' beef an' buyin' up land fast as he c'd afford it. Me, I spent too much dad-blamed time chasin' rodeos, driftin' from one ranch

t' another. Always workin' fer somebody else an' never savin' a dime."

11] Mr. Kingman ran upwards of a thousand head on his place with four cowboys and me to do the work. Not that I could do much, just working Saturdays, but he paid me two dollars every week for my trouble and I saved all of it. I figured if it took a couple of years or more, I would be willing to work it out in order to buy a colt he had that was just about the prettiest little foal I ever did see.

12] "He's a Morgan," I told Ma that first day I had seen the colt over at the Kingman place. "Thoroughbred, I b'lieve, except he's pretty big-boned for a thoroughbred."

13] Ma had looked at me in that sad way of hers when the family needed things we couldn't afford. "I know, Billy," she said, "but we could never buy one of Mr. Kingman's horses. He raises 'em for a hobby an' they're all expensive."

14] "Doesn't matter," I told her. "I'm going to buy him with my own money. I've been saving right along and I've got sixteen dollars already."

15] She just shook her head and said sixteen dollars was probably a long ways from what that foal would cost. So I took it up with Pa that evening.

16] "Y'mean that little black he's got over there?" Pa asked. I nodded. "May's well ferget about buyin' that hoss," he advised. "Y'got a good eye fer hosses though, I will say thet. Trouble is, y' set yer stakes too high."

17] "I don't care what he costs," I declared recklessly, "I'll keep savin' till I can buy him. Maybe somehow I can make some money next summer, too."

18] Pa's leathery old face clouded with worry. "Trouble is, I need y' here durin' the summer, boy. 'Bout all I c'n do t' spare y' on Sat'rd'ys."

19] I knew that was true and it was not any fault of his, so I said no more about the colt. Pa said no more either, except that he knew the way I felt, that I wanted a horse in the worst way and he would still try to get one for me come Christmas.

20] For the next few weeks I felt pretty glum until I gradually got over the notion of buying the Kingman horse. I reckoned I would keep on saving my money and maybe sometime I would find a colt like him that I could afford to buy. However, it did not keep me from hanging around the corral when I would finish my work at Kingman's, just watching the little rascal grow up. When I would come in from hauling fence or doctoring calves I would pick up a handful of oats and perch on the top rail of the corral, then coax at him. He was the worst one to get spooked by anything in the corral, and how he would jump when he was startled. Sometimes the wind would whisk a tumbleweed at him and he would light out like a dust devil on the rampage, kicking and snorting. He did not have a name yet, so I started calling him Sox. That was because his ankles were white.

21] Sometimes when I was trying to make friends with the little horse, Mr. Kingman would stop around at the corral and I guess he noticed I was plenty interested in that foal.

22] "Sure a mighty fine horse," I told him.

23] "He ought 'a be," Mr. Kingman said. "Champion quarterhorse stock, you know."

24] Mr. Kingman was proud of his horses, just as he was proud of everything else he had, not that he was the kind to brag about things, but it showed in the way he talked about his house, his car, and his stock.

25] "What're you goin' to do with him?" I asked. "Sell him?"

26] "Probably, one of these days."

27] I swallowed, wondering when that would be. I hoped it would not be for a couple of years, because perhaps by then I could save enough to buy him.

28] "Like to get your dad to break him for me," Mr. Kingman observed, looking over the little horse again.

29] "Pa's getting pretty old for that any more," I reminded him. Pa was in his sixties and just about every bone in his body had been broken at one time or another. He was not in any shape to ride out a rough horse any more in the way he used to. "Maybe I could break him for you."

30] Mr. Kingman looked at me in a way that was not encouraging. "I don't know. We'll have to see. There just isn't anybody, any more, can ride the kinks out of a bronc like your dad used to."

31] Right then I remembered a few of the stories Pa had told me about his younger days. "Did you know about the time he won the gold spurs?" I asked.

32] "Know about it?" Mr. Kingman laughed. "I was there, waiting for my turn to ride. Your dad drew a big, ornery buckskin horse and I told him he was crazier 'n a loco longhorn to get in the chute, let alone ride him. I never did see such a horse. Must have weighed thirteen hundred pounds."

33] "That's what Pa says," I agreed. "Thirteen hundred!"

34] "He darn near killed your dad," Mr. Kingman said softly.

35] "But Pa stayed on for the full ten seconds, raked him and whipped him and gave him a whale of a ride!"

36] "I'll say he did. And he wouldn't have been hurt, either, if that cinch hadn't let go. That horse just swelled up and snapped it."

37] It had been a bad accident from what Ma told me. Pa had been in the hospital at Cheyenne for weeks afterwards and his back never did quite get healed up. Ma used to tell me that part of the story when I would talk about breaking horses.

38] Along about Christmas time, school let out for two weeks vacation and I got a full-time job on the mail truck, helping to deliver packages out of Patagonia. I did not work for Kingman during that time at all and I missed seeing the little black colt. But I figured I could add to my savings considerably by working through the holidays and still have enough money to buy some kind of present for Ma and Pa.

39] When I got my check, the day before Christmas, it was for nineteen dollars and seventy-two cents. That evening we all went in to Tucson to do our Christmas shopping. I got Pa some soft brown bedroom slippers for two dollars and almost ran into him at a little jewelry store where I was headed, looking for something to buy Ma.

40] "Where you goin'?" Pa asked.

41] "Thought I'd find somethin' for Ma in here," I told him, and pointed at the window full of gadgets.

42] He fell in step with me, directing me away from the jewelry store and up the street toward a dress shop. "Ma wants a new dress awful bad," he said. "But they're a lot o' money. Want t' go in with me an' git her one?"

43] It sounded like a good idea until we got to looking at the dresses. The only one that would fit Ma that looked like anything was over twenty dollars. Pa was about to settle on another one that was cheaper when I offered to pay half on the one we wanted if he would buy it. We did that and I just shut my eyes, trying to forget about saving for a horse. Somehow, after we left the dress shop, though, I felt awfully good inside.

44] We were sitting around the Christmas tree that night when Ma opened the big box and took out the dress. All she did was make a little gasping sound and her eyes filled up as though she was going to break right out crying.

45] "It's beautiful," she said. "Oh, isn't it beautiful?" And she held it up in front of her while she looked in the mirror.

46] Pa unwrapped his bedroom slippers and put them on as though he was going to wear them for the rest of his life.

47] "Fit fine," he said. "They're just dandy." Then he took them off and pulled his boots back on.

48] "Your present's over there on the tree, Billy," said Ma.

49] The two of them waited while I hunted through the tree for a white package, so little I could hold it in one hand. It did not weigh an ounce. I opened it and inside was a piece of paper tied to the end of a string.

50] "Follow the string," it said.

51] I followed the string, which led out the back door, across the yard and into the feed barn. Ma and Pa were walking behind me, all of us bundled up in jackets because the frost had already settled and the night was cold. When I opened the door of the feed barn, Pa held up the lantern, and I stood there trying to believe what I saw. In the manger, up to his hocks in straw, was the little black colt, looking at me just the way he had so many times over in Kingman's corral.

52] "Is he mine?" I blubbered.

53] Pa nodded and I hugged him and Ma together, wondering how they ever got enough money to buy him. Then somewhere far off, the church bells were ringing midnight and Pa took out his watch to check the time.

54] "Merry Christmas," he said. Ma said "Merry Christmas" too, but I could not say anything. I was looking at Pa's watch. And the solid gold spurs were gone.

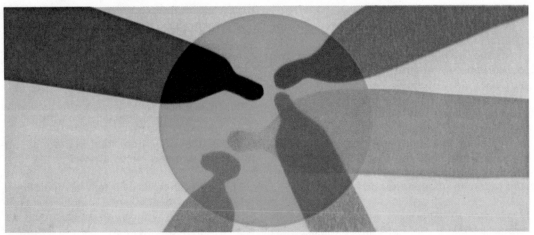

Conflict

1. What is Billy's greatest desire?
2. What obstacles must he overcome to obtain it?
3. At what point in the story prior to the end does he seem to have some real hope of winning?
4. What new obstacle does Billy face in the dress shop?

Every story, novel, or play develops around a struggle or conflict. Sometimes the conflict may be obvious, as in some Westerns in which the only conflict is the struggle between the good guys and the bad guys. In a more complicated Western, besides the obvious conflict with the villain, the hero may have to struggle with a wild animal or a fierce blizzard; or he may have to struggle with his conscience. In other words, he may be involved in several conflicts.

Conflicts in literature are of two general types: (1) *external conflict,* in which the character or main figure (sometimes an animal or a group) struggles against another character, nature, or society; and (2) *internal conflict,* in which the character struggles against some element of his own personality (his conscience or code of values, for example).

Of which type is the conflict Billy faces in wanting Sox? Of which type is the conflict he faces in the dress shop?

Details

Why is each of the following details important to the story?

1. the solid gold spurs mentioned in paragraph 1
2. the details concerning the ranch in paragraph 6
3. the details which describe the wealth of the Kingman spread
4. the details which describe Sox

An author must be very careful to select only those details which are important to his story. Bud Murphy, for example, does not tell us about Billy's school because that part of his life is not important to the conflict. He does tell us, however, exactly how much money Billy earns because the amount of his earnings is very important to our understanding of his problem.

Pattern of Events

1. What purpose does each of the following incidents serve?
   (a) the Christmas at which Billy received boots
   (b) Billy's talk with his parents about the horse
   (c) Billy's talk with Mr. Kingman (paragraphs 21 – 36)
   (d) Billy's job during vacation

(**e**) the shopping trip

(**f**) Billy's parents' reactions to his gifts on Christmas Eve

(**g**) the incident related in the last two paragraphs of the story

2. Could any of these incidents be eliminated without damaging the story? Explain.

3. Why couldn't any of the above incidents be rearranged without damaging the story?

4. What is the outcome of "Champion Stock"? How does the first paragraph set in motion the pattern of events which makes the outcome understandable?

An author writes a story with a specific outcome in mind. He carefully chooses only those incidents which are important to the way he wishes his story to end and arranges them in a cause-effect relationship. Each incident logically follows and is caused by the preceding ones; therefore each is a necessary link leading to the outcome of the story. In a well-planned story, no one incident can be moved or eliminated without damaging or even ruining the effect the writer is trying to achieve.

> **PLOT:** the significant pattern of action in a short story, novel, or play. The plot usually involves one or more conflicts, which may be external or internal. In a carefully constructed plot, each detail is important. The incidents are carefully selected and so arranged in a cause-effect relationship that each is a necessary link leading to the outcome of the story.

POINT OF VIEW

On Friday, September 13, 1952, I was born to Jo-Ann and Bob Cheever.

Robert H. Cheever, Jr. was born to JoAnn and Bob Cheever on Friday, September 13, 1952.

What is the only important difference between the two sentences above?

This difference in *who* tells an incident is referred to as a difference in *narrative point of view.* Before writing, an author must decide whether the story will be told by one of the characters, as in the first sentence, or by an outsider, as in the second sentence.

Margie chased after her little brother, who was running down the street.

Because she was afraid that he might get hurt, Margie chased after her little brother, who was running down the street.

In which of the two sentences above does the author tell you what a character is thinking?

Whether or not we know what a character is thinking or feeling depends upon who the narrator is and upon whether or not he can see into the minds of the characters.

The four passages following narrate the same incident from different narrative points of view. Notice how the amount of information given about each of the characters depends upon the point of view used.

1. As I placed the carefully wrapped package on the park bench, I looked up and saw Molly walking across the street. I hoped that she hadn't seen me.

a. Is the narrator a character in the incident or an outsider?

b. Do you know what the narrator was doing? what he was thinking?

c. Do you know what Molly was doing? what she was thinking?

2. As George placed the carefully wrapped package on the park bench, he looked up and saw Molly walking across the street.

a. Is the narrator a character in the incident or an outsider?
b. Do you know what George was doing? what he was thinking?
c. Do you know what Molly was doing? what she was thinking?

3. George, anxiously hoping that no one was watching him, placed a carefully wrapped package on an empty park bench. But Molly, who was walking home, saw him and couldn't help thinking that he was acting strangely.

a. Is the narrator a character in the incident or an outsider?
b. Do you know what George was doing? what he was thinking?
c. Do you know what Molly was doing? what she was thinking?

4. George, anxiously hoping that no one was watching him, placed a carefully wrapped package on an empty park bench. But when he looked around, he saw Molly watching him from across the street.

a. Is the narrator a character in the incident or an outsider?
b. Do you know what George was doing? what he was thinking?
c. Do you know what Molly was doing? what she was thinking?

An author uses his narrator much as a movie director uses his camera. Through his choice of point of view (who the narrator is), the author can focus sharply on some details and characters while showing others less clearly.

Personal Point of View

In the first example, the narrator is himself a character in the story. In telling the story from his personal point of view, the narrator ("I," or first person) can tell us his own thoughts, but he cannot tell us the thoughts of other characters. Just as you can report what you see others doing, the narrator can

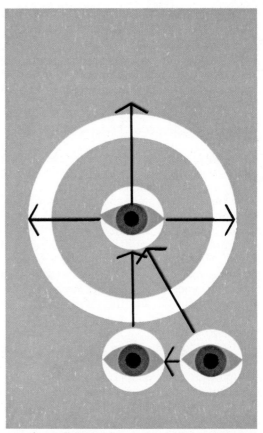

tell us only what he sees other characters doing or what he is told by other characters; and just as you cannot enter the minds of other people, the narrator cannot enter the minds of characters other than himself. (For examples of the personal point of view see "Top Man" and "The Scarlet Letter.")

Third Person Objective Point of View

In the second example the narrator is not a character in the story, but is an outsider, or third person. He tells us what is happening, but he does not tell us the thoughts of any of the characters. He is like a newspaper reporter who can give only the facts as they occur; he cannot enter into the characters' minds; he must be objective. Example 2 is written from the third person objective point of view.

This point of view is also called the third person dramatic point of view since it is the point of view a playwright uses. (Because this point of view greatly limits the amount of information an author can give, it is seldom used except in plays and in mystery or detective stories.)

Omniscient Point of View

In the third and fourth examples, the narrator again is an outsider, a third person. But in both these examples he has the ability to see into the minds and record the thoughts of the characters. Like a superhuman being, he is omniscient (all-knowing). Both examples are written from the omniscient point of view. Notice, however, that the examples differ in that in example 3 the narrator sees into the minds of both characters, but in example 4 he sees into the mind of only one character. In example 4 he enters the mind of George, thus placing the *focus* on him; and since he enters the mind of even one character, the point of view is still omniscient. (For an example of the use of the omniscient point of view see "The Turtle.")

POINT OF VIEW: the author's choice of a narrator for his story. This choice determines the amount of information a reader will be given. The three major points of view are:
1. PERSONAL OR FIRST PERSON: The narrator ("I") is a character in the story who can reveal only his own thoughts and feelings and what he sees and is told by other characters.
2. THIRD PERSON OBJECTIVE: The narrator is an outsider who can report only what he sees and hears.
3. OMNISCIENT: The narrator is an all-knowing outsider who can enter the minds of one or all of the characters.

RHYME

Lone Dog
Irene Rutherford McLeod

I'm a lean dog, a keen dog, a wild dog
   and lone;
I'm a rough dog, a tough dog, hunting on
   my own;
I'm a bad dog, a mad dog, teasing silly
   sheep;
I love to sit and bay the moon, to keep
   fat souls from sleep.

I'll never be a lap dog, licking dirty
   feet,
A sleek dog, a meek dog, cringing for
   my meat;
Not for me the fireside, the well-filled
   plate,
But shut door, and sharp stone, and cuff
   and kick and hate.

Not for me the other dogs, running by
   my side,
Some have run a short while, but none of
   them would bide.
Oh, mine is still the lone trail, the hard
   trail, the best,
Wide wind and wild stars, and hunger of
   the quest.

In the first stanza of "Lone Dog," which words at the ends of lines rhyme? in the second stanza? the third?

In poetry, this device of ending two or more lines with words that sound alike is called *end rhyming;* end words that share a particular sound are *end rhymes.*

When used in a poem, end rhymes set up a definite pattern of sounds, a *rhyme scheme.* You can chart a rhyme scheme with letters of the alphabet by using the same letter for end words that rhyme. Consider, for example, this limerick:

A dusky young damsel of Siam
Once said to her lover named Priam
   If you kiss me, of course,
   It must be by brute force,
But Lord knows you're stronger than I am.

1. If the last word in line 1 of this limerick were labeled with the letter a, which other end words would also be labeled a?
2. If the last word of line 3 were labeled b, what would the last word of line 4 be labeled? Why?

The rhyme scheme for this limerick is: a (the sound ending line 1); a (a sound rhyming with line 1); b (a new, or second rhyming sound); b (a sound rhyming with the second sound); a (a rhyme for the first sound).

If the limerick had a third rhyming sound, it would be designated by the letter c. A fourth rhyme would be labeled d, and so on. By using this method, you can chart the rhyme scheme of any poem that uses end rhymes.

1. Make a chart of the rhyme scheme for a stanza of McLeod's "Lone Dog."
2. Can you chart the rhyme scheme of Eliot's "Prelude I" (page 238)? Why or why not?
3. Reread the first line of "Lone Dog." Which words within the line rhyme?

Rhyming words within a line are called *internal rhymes*. Find at least three examples of internal rhyme in "Lone Dog."

A second type of internal rhyme rhymes a word within a line with the end word. For example:

  The splendor *falls* on castle *walls*.

Can you find any internal rhymes of this type in "Lone Dog"?

> **RHYME:** the repetition of syllable sounds. End words that share a particular sound are called end rhymes. Rhyming words within a line of poetry are called internal rhymes.

RHYTHM

I never saw a purple cow,
I never hope to see one.
But I can tell you anyhow,
I'd rather see than be one.

Read the above verse aloud. Did you notice that its author has arranged words in a way that automatically causes you to place greater stress on some words or syllables than on others? This combination of stressed and unstressed words or syllables creates a pattern that gives the line a definite flow, or *rhythm*. In the case of this nonsense rhyme, the rhythm is extremely regular (capital letters indicate stressed words or syllables):

i NEVer SAW a PURple COW,
i NEVer HOPE to SEE one.
but I can TELL you ANyHOW,
i'd RATHer SEE than BE one.

The *ti TUM ti TUM ti TUM* rhythm gives the verse a singsong effect. Also, each line of the verse is *end-stopped;* that is, the words are so arranged that a pause, designated by a punctuation mark, is necessary at the end of each line. These pauses, which call attention to the verse's rhymes, strengthen its singsong effect.

Because "Purple Cow" is a nonsense verse, its very regular rhythm is suitable; its regularity heightens its feeling of nonsense. But in more serious poetry, poets try to avoid the monotony caused by such absolute regularity. To the skilled poet, the regular beat is a foundation from which to depart and return. Read the following stanza from Tennyson's *The Princess* aloud:

The splendor falls on castle walls
  And snowy summits old in story;
The long light shakes across the lakes,
  And the wild cataract leaps in glory.
Blow, bugle, blow, set the wild echoes
    flying,
Blow, bugle; answer, echoes, dying,
    dying, dying.

1. Which words or syllables in the first line should be accented? in the second? the third? the fourth? Show how the rhythm changes in the last two lines.
2. Is the rhythm in this stanza extremely regular? Why might the poet have chosen not to create a singsong effect in this stanza?
3. Where is the first pause? the second?

Line 1 of this stanza overflows into the second line; it is a *run-on* line. Because you do not pause at the end of a run-on line, you de-emphasize the rhyme, thus increasing the poem's rhythmical variety. The variety of the rhythm causes the reader to stress the poem's meaning rather than its rhythm.

Rhythm is everywhere; it is inescapable. Even the most CASual EVeryday SPEECH FALLS into RHYTHmic PHRASes. But poets do not use rhythm simply because it exists. In poetry—as in well-written prose—rhythm has definite purposes.

First of all, rhythm is used because it is enjoyable for its own sake. This is evidenced by the pleasure young children derive from nursery rhymes. And on all the sidewalks of America girls jump rope to chants such as this one:

aLONG CAME the DOCtor!
aLONG CAME the NURSE!
aLONG CAME the LAdy
with the BIG, FAT PURSE!

Second, rhythm allows the poet to fit the movement of the poem to the mood:

the WIND was a TORrent of DARKness
    aMONG the GUSTy TREES;
the MOON was a GHOSTly GALleon
    TOSSED upon CLOUDy SEAS;
the ROAD was a RIBbon of MOONlight
    Over the PURple MOOR;
and the HIGHwayman CAME RIDing—
    RIDing—RIDing—
the HIGHwayman CAME RIDing, UP to
    the OLD INN DOOR.[1]

Is the rhythm in keeping with the mood of the poem? Before answering this question, reread the complete poem (pages 56–59).

Third, the poet can use rhythm to emphasize important words:

MOST WEAry SEEMED the SEA,
    WEAry the AIR,
WEAry the WANdering FIELDS of
    BARren FOAM.

The first syllable of *weary* is naturally accented each time the word appears. The second and third *weary* follow pauses, thus giving them extra emphasis. By stressing this word so strongly, the poet arouses a feeling of weariness in his readers.

Imagine that the poet who wrote the above lines had said this instead:

Weariness was here.
Weariness was there.
Weariness was round me
Everywhere.

Would he have aroused weariness in his readers? Is the rhythm used in the second version suitable to a serious poem? Why or why not?

---

1. From "The Highwayman," from COLLECTED POEMS by Alfred Noyes. Copyright 1906, 1934 by Alfred Noyes. Published by J. B. Lippincott Company. Reprinted by permission of J. B. Lippincott Company and John Murray (Publishers) Ltd.

RHYTHM: a series of stressed and unstressed sounds in a group of words. Rhythm may be regular or it may be varied.

SATIRE

1. Why is the man in the cartoon crawling toward water?
2. What will he find when he gets there?
3. Is this cartoon concerned with a major social problem or with a minor human weakness?

Atomic Courtesy[1]
by Ethel Jacobson
To smash the simple atom
All mankind was intent.
    Now any day
    The atom may
Return the compliment.

1. What, according to the author, was man's goal? Has he achieved his goal?
2. What is the author saying in the last three lines of the poem?

A literary work in which the author makes fun of the vices or follies of mankind is called a *satire*. A satire can deal with almost any subject, from minor human follies (the existence of fads in clothing, for example) to major social and political problems (the position of minority groups in society, the futility of war). But all satire has one thing in common: it uses humor, which may range from light-hearted to bitter, to comment on the weaknesses and vices of man and society.

Some satire is written solely for the purpose of amusing the reader. What is the author of the cartoon satirizing? Do you think he is commenting on a weakness or trying to correct a social problem?

The purpose of most satire, however, is to eliminate serious social problems by encouraging people to think or act in a certain way. What is the author of the poem satirizing? Is she merely trying to amuse the reader, or is she trying to influence the reader's ideas about the use of atomic energy?

---

1. Reprinted by permission of the author.

> **SATIRE:** a literary work in which the author ridicules the vices or follies of mankind, usually for the purpose of producing some change in attitude or action.

SETTING

There was commotion in Roaring Camp. It could not have been a fight, for in 1850 that was not novel enough to have called together the entire settlement. The ditches and claims were not only deserted, but "Tuttle's grocery" had contributed its gamblers, who, it will be remembered, calmly continued their game the day that French Pete and Kanaka Joe shot each other to death over the bar in the front room. The whole camp was collected before a rude cabin on the outer edge of the clearing.

1. What kind of a community is Roaring Camp? What details tell you this? What do you learn about the people who live in Roaring Camp?

2. When do the events of this story take place?

The time and place in which the events of a narrative occur form what is called the *setting*. The place may be a region, a city or town, or even a house or room. The time may be a period in history, a particular time of year, or, perhaps, a certain time of day. In some narratives, the setting is specific and detailed, as in the paragraph reprinted above, but in others, it may be intentionally obscure.

The stranger rode slowly into town. His wide-brimmed Stetson was pulled forward on his head, casting a shadow over his gaunt face. The sunlight sparkled on his spurs and on the handle of his gun which hung casually by his right side.

1. Where does this story take place? What details tell you this?

2. Approximately when does this story probably occur? How do you know?

Just as the bus pulled up in front of the Empire State Building, Larry tossed a spitball at Joanne. Enraged, she turned around in her seat and stuck out her tongue at him.

1. In what city does this story take place? How do you know?

2. What is the approximate time of this story? What details tell you this?

"There she blows! there! there! there! she blows! She blows!"

"Where-away?"

"On the lee-beam, about two miles off! a school of them!"

1. Where does this story take place? How do you know?

2. Is there any indication of time? Explain.

In some narratives, especially modern stories, the description of setting is either brief or merely suggested through the use of details scattered throughout the story. An author can suggest the setting by references to articles of clothing, famous historical figures, well-known landmarks, or through the dialect and speech patterns of the characters which he has created. Not all stories have a

setting in which both the time and place are identifiable.

During the whole of a dull, dark, and soundless day in the autumn of the year, when the clouds hung oppressively low in the heavens, I had been passing alone, on horseback, through a singularly dreary tract of country, and at length found myself, as the shades of evening drew on, within view of the melancholy House of Usher. I know not how it was —but, with the first glimpse of the building, a sense of insufferable gloom pervaded my spirit . . . I looked upon the scene before me — upon the bleak walls — upon the vacant eye-like windows — upon a few rank sedges — and upon a few white trunks of decayed trees — with an utter depression of soul which I can compare to no earthly sensation . . . There was an iciness, a sinking, a sickening of the heart — an unredeemed dreariness of thought which no goading of the imagination could torture into aught of the sublime.

1. What is the setting in this paragraph? Is the time of day important? Why?
2. How does the narrator react to the scene he is describing?
3. What effect is the author trying to create in this paragraph?
4. What specific words and phrases help to create this effect?

Frequently a setting which is presented in detail forms an important part of the narrative. It may have an effect on the events of the plot, it may reveal character, or, as in the preceding paragraph, it may create a certain mood or atmosphere.

SETTING: the time and place in which the events of a narrative occur. The setting may be specific and detailed, and introduced at the very beginning of the story, or it may be merely suggested through the use of details scattered throughout the story. In some stories, the setting is vital to the narrative; it may have an effect on the events of the plot, or reveal character, or create a certain atmosphere. In other stories, the setting is relatively unimportant: the story could have happened almost anywhere or at any time.

SYMBOL

Uphill
by Christina Rossetti

Does the road wind uphill all the way?
  Yes, to the very end.
Will the day's journey take the whole
    day?
  From morn to night, my friend.

But is there for the night a resting
    place?
  A roof for when the slow dark hours
    begin.
May not the darkness hide it from my
    face?
  You cannot miss that inn.

Shall I meet other wayfarers at night?
  Those who have gone before.
Then must I knock, or call when just
    in sight?
  They will not keep you standing at
    that door.

Shall I find comfort, travel-sore and
    weak?
  Of labour you shall find the sum.
Will there be beds for me and all who
    seek?
  Yes, beds for all who come.

1. (a) What kind of "journey" is being discussed? **(b)** State the theme of the poem.
2. In view of the theme, what does each of the following elements represent: **(a)** the road; **(b)** the uphill climb; **(c)** the day; **(d)** the night; **(e)** the journey's end; **(f)** the inn; **(g)** the other wayfarers; **(h)** the first speaker; **(i)** the second speaker?

Superficially, "Uphill" seems to be a conversation about the lodgings to be found at the end of a difficult trip. But if the poem is read carefully, it takes on a fuller meaning. Such aspects as the road and the uphill climb suggest further, deeper meanings. The road is more than a link between two places;

it is the path all men take toward death. The road, as well as the other items noted in question 2, is a *symbol.* A symbol may be an object, a person, an action, a situation —anything that suggests a meaning beyond its obvious meaning.

While some symbols suggest the same thing to most people (the heart is a universal symbol of love), others have different meanings for different people. What might a gun symbolize to a hunter? a thief? a soldier?

Characters in literature often have these personal symbols. You can recognize them by noting the objects, persons, or situations for which a character shows strong feelings. Watch for the repetition of an object or an action.

Look for the symbols in this poem by Stephen Crane.

I saw a man pursuing the horizon;
Round and round they sped.
I was disturbed at this;
I accosted the man.
"It is futile," I said.
"You can never---"

"You lie," he cried,
And ran on.

1. To the speaker, does the horizon symbolize (a) a useless goal; (b) an impossible goal; (c) a goal difficult to achieve? Explain.
2. To the speaker, does the man's pursuit symbolize (a) industriousness; (b) ridiculous activity; (c) nothing? Explain.
3. (a) What does the horizon symbolize to the runner? (b) In your opinion why does he continue?

SYMBOL: a person, place, event, or object which has a meaning in itself but suggests other meanings as well.

THEME

The moth,
Enraged,
Beats against the lamp,
His wings forming
Countless tiny fans,
And falls at last
A fragile pinch of gray ashes.
The lamp burns on,
Tranquilly.[1]

1. What is the conflict in this poem? Who is the attacker?
2. What is the main characteristic of the moth?
3. How does the lamp act?
4. Who is the "victor" in the conflict?
5. Is the author trying to instruct the reader how to act or behave?
6. Which of the following statements best expresses the main idea in the poem? (a) A moth flies against a lamp and gets burned. (b) Don't play with fire or you will get burned. (c) Tranquillity is frequently stronger than violence.

The main idea of a literary work, the general truth about life or mankind which it expresses, is called the *theme.* The theme, or main idea, of the poem reprinted above is best expressed in statement (c).

Statement (b) presents a moral; it tells the reader how to act. It is not the theme because the author of the poem does not tell the reader how to act or behave. He simply describes a situation and leaves it up to the reader to infer the underlying meaning—that frequently more can be accomplished by serenity than by anger.

Statement (a) gives the plot of the poem rather than the theme. A plot is a pattern of events, the "what happens" in a poem or narrative. The theme is the underlying meaning, what the literary work is about. For ex-

---

1. Reprinted from OF CHINA AND HER WISDOM, by Paul Eldridge, by permission of the author.

ample, the plot of a story might concern a young soldier during his first battle. The events of the plot might include:

1. the man's thoughts before the battle
2. the battle itself and what the young man thinks, feels, and does during the battle
3. the outcome of the battle and the young man's new impressions of war

However, the theme of the story might be the idea that war is futile, that fighting solves nothing. This theme might not be stated anywhere in the story, but merely suggested through the events of the plot and the attitudes of the characters.

Not every literary work has a theme. Some are written purely to entertain the reader. A mystery story, for example, written primarily to keep the reader in suspense, may not have a theme.

> **THEME:** the underlying meaning of a literary work, a general truth about life or mankind. A theme may be stated or implied. Not every literary work contains a theme.

TONE

from **Song of the Open Road**
by Walt Whitman

Afoot and light-hearted I take to the open
   road,
Healthy, free, the world before me,
The long, brown path before me leading
   wherever I choose.
Henceforth I ask not good-fortune, I
   myself am good-fortune.
Henceforth I whimper no more, postpone
   no more, need nothing,
Done with indoor complaints, libraries,
   querulous criticisms.
Strong and content I travel the open
   road.

1. What is this poem about? What might the "open road" represent?
2. Does the speaker regret leaving the indoors? Explain.
3. What is the speaker's attitude as he sets forth? What words and phrases convey his attitude?

To achieve a complete understanding of most literary works, one must determine how the author feels about his subject. An author's attitude toward his subject is called *tone.* The tone of a literary work serves the same basic purpose as a tone of voice; it helps to indicate the speaker's attitude, whether it is one of anger, sadness, amusement, joy, defiance, or some other emotion. It may, in fact, be a combination of several different emotions, such as anger and pity.

Sometimes an author will state directly how he feels about a character, a situation, or an idea. The speaker in the poem, for example, states that he feels "light-hearted," "healthy," "free," "strong," and "content." The attitude, or tone of Whitman's poem, is one of enthusiasm, of joyful optimism.

It was Miss Murdstone who was arrived, and a gloomy-looking lady she was; dark, like her brother, whom she greatly resembled in face and

voice, and with very heavy eyebrows, nearly meeting over her large nose. She brought with her two
uncompromising hard black boxes, with her ini-
tials on the lids in hard brass nails. When she paid
the coachman she took her money out of a hard
steel purse, and she kept the purse in a very jail of
a bag which hung upon her arm by a heavy chain,
and shut up like a bite. It seemed that there had
never been such a metallic lady altogether as Miss
Murdstone was.

1. (a) What sort of woman is being described
in this paragraph? Cite specific words which
the author uses to describe her. (b) How do
the things she is carrying contribute to the
picture of this woman?
2. (a) What is the author's attitude toward
the woman? How do you know? (b) Is his
attitude stated or implied?

In most literary works, the author's attitude
will not be stated directly, as it is in the excerpt from Whitman's "Song of the Open
Road," but will be suggested through the
author's choice of words and details. In the
paragraph, for example, the author never
states that this character is to be disliked.
However, by describing her as "gloomy-
looking," "dark," "uncompromising," "metallic," he implies a certain feeling about her
and draws the reader into sharing his attitude.

> **TONE:** the stated or implied attitude
> of an author toward his subject in a
> particular literary work. The author
> reveals his attitude through his
> choice of words and details.

COMPOSITION GUIDE

Composition is not only writing; it is also getting ready to write. It is finding a subject and organizing your ideas about this subject in a way that will make your writing clear and understandable. It is finding appropriate details and examples to illustrate your ideas and make them concrete. Literature can help you in several of these areas by furnishing subject matter and ideas, and by providing material for support and illustration. The thirty-two lessons in this guide suggest subjects for writing based on your study of literature. The extra, optional assignments are for students who are especially interested in writing.

Always plan carefully before you begin writing, and always save enough time for a careful and thoughtful revision. In each case, write out a first draft; then revise and recopy it. Your language text can help you in each phase of your writing. Below are listed the unit titles and the composition lessons designed to accompany each unit.

UNIT 1: ENCOUNTER
1: Explanation
2: Description
3: Opinion
4: Evaluation

UNIT 2: TWO GENERATIONS
5: Opinion
6: Persuasion
7: Character Sketch
8: Persuasion
9: Personal Experience

UNIT 3: VALUES
10: Description
11: Persuasion
12: Ideas
13: Persuasion
14: Explanation

UNIT 4: POETRY
15: Description
16: Interpretation
17: Explanation

UNIT 5: THE AMERICAN ROMANCE
18: Narration
19: Personal Experience
20: Explanation
21: Explanation

UNIT 6: THE WELL-TOLD TALE
22: Opinion
23: Satire
24: Personal Experience
25: Ideas

UNIT 7: HEROES OF OLYMPUS
26: Research
27: Comparison and Contrast

UNIT 8: THE DIARY OF ANNE FRANK
28: Dialogue
29: Opinion
30: Review

GENERAL
31: Opinion
32: Evaluation

LESSON 1

Explanation

Based on "A Man of Peace" and "Fifteen," pages 4–23.

Most of the characters in these two selections have certain desires — things that they want — which lead them into conflict with others or within themselves.

Choose as the subject of your composition one of the characters in "A Man of Peace" — Mitchell, De Parma, or Lafleur — or the speaker in "Fifteen." Write a single paragraph on what you feel that character desires most.

First review in your language text the qualities that a good paragraph should have. Then before you begin writing, decide what is the greatest desire of the character you have chosen. Write a topic sentence which makes a statement about that character's desire; for example: "Ramon de Parma's greatest desire is for power and influence." Remember that a desire need not be for an object; it could be for happiness, or love, or simply to be left alone. (Is a motorcycle truly the thing that the speaker in "Fifteen" most desires, or something which the motorcycle represents?) You may have to read between the lines a bit in figuring out what a character really wants; characters don't always reveal their desires outright.

Develop your topic sentence by telling why you think your choice is right. Support your ideas by referring to specific details and events in the selection. After you have written a first draft of your paragraph, read it over carefully, checking for good organization, sentence structure, usage, and spelling. Revise, and rewrite, if necessary.

LESSON 2

Description

Based on "After the Anteater," "Top Man," and "The Highwayman," pages 24–59.

An important element — often a basic part — of many literary works is the setting. In "After the Anteater" the anteater's home, the savanna, proves both a help and a hindrance to the men who are there to capture the animal. In "Top Man" the mountain, K3, provides the basis for much of the conflict. Alfred Noyes tells in his description of "The Highwayman" on page 59 how the setting gave him the idea for his poem.

In this assignment you have the opportunity to describe a setting you are familiar with. Choose a scene you know well — a part of your neighborhood, perhaps, or that favorite spot you found on vacation or while traveling. (It need not be a "pretty" spot; you may be one who finds more fascination in a junkyard than in a flowery meadow.) In not more than one paragraph, describe the scene in detail. Your objective will be to describe it so accurately that your reader can visualize the scene for himself.

Before you begin writing, however, consider these questions: Where are you, the observer, standing when you describe what you see? (A different angle could give an entirely different picture.) What time of day is it? What sort of mood do you wish to create? (How does the scene make you feel: dreary, cold, relaxed, lively?) Will all the details you have chosen to include contribute toward creating the same mood in your reader? Since you are writing only one paragraph, you will have to choose these details carefully for their relative importance and for their contribution to the effect you wish to create.

Revise your first draft carefully. Can someone who is not familiar with the area described visualize it from your description?

OPTIONAL ASSIGNMENT

Try writing the first paragraph or two of a short story in which you picture the setting. Plan a situation in which the setting would be a major element; then, keeping in mind the directions given above, describe that setting in detail. Here, however, you will need to suggest a character and what is happening at the moment. For example, you might show your character performing some simple action, and describe what he sees as he looks around him. You will not be able to include a character description or develop a plot, but write your paragraphs as if you were going to finish the story.

When you have finished your description, add a single sentence explaining the kind of story for which your setting is intended (suspense, heroic adventure, humor, etc.).

LESSON 3

Opinion

Based on "Top Man," "The Highwayman," "The Turtle," and "Jail Breaks," pages 40–75.

Many of the encounters in this unit require the characters to make decisions, then to act upon them. Often these decisions influence greatly what is to happen to the character. Study the following list of decisions, all of which are found in the selections listed above:

1. Nace's decision to try to rescue Osborn from the ledge (page 53)
2. Osborn's decision to give up his claim as "top man" to Nace (page 54)
3. Bess' decision to sacrifice herself to warn the highwayman (page 58)
4. Jimmy's decision to spare the turtle (page 62)
5. Houdini's decision to go to Europe (page 69)

Do you feel strongly that any one of these decisions is a particularly wise or unwise one? Use the decision you feel most strongly about as the topic of a paragraph in which you express your opinion as to whether it was right or wrong, a wise or an unwise decision.

Before starting to write, reread the selection to find details which concern the decision. You may wish to take notes in answer to such questions as these: What factors influenced the decision? What were the alternatives? Would the character's personality have allowed him to act in any other way? Does the fact that the situation may have turned out badly for the character make this necessarily an unwise decision?

Now weigh the evidence you have collected. Did your rereading of the selection reinforce your opinion, or did it make you change your viewpoint? Once you are sure your opinion has a sound basis, you are ready to write your topic sentence and to choose details from your reading which will effectively support your statements.

Now write and revise. Your objective, if not to persuade your reader to change his opinion, should be to prove to him that your opinion is at least valid.

LESSON 4

Evaluation

Based on "Encounter," pages 2–77.

Several of the selections in this unit concern themselves to a large extent with leadership and raise the question, "What is a leader?" Write a paragraph on the qualities of a leader. You may use any of the unit selections in considering such questions as the following: Does a man become a leader because of his qualities, or does he develop certain qualities after becoming a leader? How does a leader behave? Is the one who leads always the best man? Is he always a good man?

From which characters did you draw the qualities you are discussing? Does any one character possess all the qualities of a leader? Are there any qualities you feel a leader should possess which are not expressed in any of these selections?

You may choose to consider any or all of the questions suggested above, but it would probably be best to concentrate on just a few—no more than you can successfully discuss in one paragraph.

Before you begin writing, choose and organize carefully the material you wish to present. Your language text will help you in organizing and outlining your material.

Check your first draft to make sure that you have presented your ideas clearly, that you have stuck to your topic, and that your statements are well supported by your examples. Now you are ready to rewrite.

LESSON 5

Opinion

Based on "The Scarlet Letter," "First Lesson," and "So Much Unfairness of Things," pages 80–123.

Emily Vanderpool and P. S. Wilkinson both seem to experience difficulties with the adult world. "Had anyone in the history of the world ever been so lamentably misunderstood?" wails Emily after a particularly difficult moment. P. S. had never managed to feel very close to his father: "He had given up their ever sharing anything. . . . And at fourteen respect and obedience had taken the place of love." Even the speaker in "First Lesson" speaks of a breaking apart, of a "journey to take" from which return will not be immediate.

What is the nature of the separation between generations in each of these selections? Is it truly as bad as the characters think? Following is a list of statements which disagree with the points of view of these characters. Choose one as the topic sentence for your composition:

1. The things that happen to Emily Vanderpool are really her own fault and no one else's.
2. Emily is unfair to Miss Holderness.
3. The speaker in "First Lesson" fails to appreciate a father's viewpoint.
4. Instead of Mr. Wilkinson's expecting too much of his son, P. S. expects too much of his father.
5. P. S. and his father will never really be able to come together after so long a separation.

Develop the topic sentence you have chosen into a composition of not more than 300 words. You may use the sentence as it stands, or you may choose to disagree with the attitude expressed and rewrite the sentence accordingly. Reread the selection, noting details which you can use to support your statements. Outline your material (your language text will help you here). As you write, take care to bring in your supporting details where they will be most effective. Be sure that you revise carefully.

OPTIONAL ASSIGNMENT

The speaker in "First Lesson" seems to suggest that this separation between generations is something which everyone must experience. Do you agree? What are your ideas on the separation between the younger generation and the older? What is the nature of the break? When does it happen? What are its causes? Is it a common situation? Is it necessary, or is it avoidable? How is it possible for people, once apart, to come back together again?

Discuss this topic in a composition of not more than 300 words. One of the above questions might provide a starting point. For support and illustration, draw upon your own experiences or upon the experiences of others you have known. If you wish, you may mention outside reading.

LESSON 6

Persuasion

Based on "So Much Unfairness of Things" and "Doc Marlowe," pages 98–129.

The main characters in the selections listed above are both cheaters: Doc Marlowe is a habitual cheat who is never caught, or at least never punished; P. S. Wilkinson cheats upon impulse only and is caught and punished, probably never to cheat again.

In this assignment you have an opportunity to try to persuade your reader to accept your ideas about cheating. Choose one of the sentences below as your topic sentence for a composition of one paragraph. You may use the sentence as it stands or if you wish you may rewrite it to express the opposite viewpoint:

1. Doc Marlowe is a worse cheat than P. S. Wilkinson.
2. A cheat should be more pitied than scorned.
3. Cheating is sometimes justified.
4. A cheater cheats only himself.

Develop your topic sentence into a paragraph by explaining your ideas. To persuade your reader that you are right, you will have to support your statements carefully. To give your arguments a sound basis, use material from your own experiences, from the experiences of others you have known, or from your reading.

LESSON 7

Character Sketch

Based on "Doc Marlowe" and "A Christmas Memory," pages 124–140.

Both of the selections named above are in effect fond recollections of persons who meant a great deal to the authors when they were young. Is there someone in your memory who meant a great deal to you—a relative, or close friend or acquaintance, perhaps—who is now gone, having either died or moved away? Share your memories of this person by writing a character sketch of one or two paragraphs. You may develop your sketch in any one of the following ways:

1. Describe the person, especially those character traits which made this person individual and special to you. Don't neglect physical traits, though, if they seem important.
2. Describe an incident you remember that you both participated in. Capote's description of flying kites and Thurber's recollection of matching for the drinks are examples of the type of incident you might include.
3. Characterize your subject by showing him or her in action. For this you could use narrative or dialogue, or a combination of both.

You may wish to use more than one of these approaches in your composition, but don't try to do too much. Your aim should be to make your reader feel as though he knows your character. If there is no one in your experience whom you wish to describe, use your imagination to create a memorable character.

LESSON 8

Persuasion

Based on "The Kitten," "Charles," and "The Colt," pages 141–160.

The selections listed above all illustrate conflicts and misunderstandings between the younger generation and the older. Sometimes these misunderstandings are deliberate, as when Richard Wright chooses to interpret literally his father's careless words. Sometimes they are due to lack of communication between the characters, or to lack of anyone's trying to communicate.

While you were reading these selections, did you find yourself wanting to tell something to one of the characters? Since you were outside of the conflict and able to view matters more objectively, did you feel that you could give a certain character advice or persuade him of the best thing to do? What would you have said, if you had had the opportunity?

Choose a character from one of these selections to direct your remarks to. In not more than one paragraph, give this character the advice you feel he needs. Address him by name, and if you wish, indicate early in your paragraph what the situation is at the time you are speaking. Be friendly; be yourself, not a superior being who knows everything. To some people, a word to the wise is sufficient, while others don't like to take advice from anyone about anything. How are you going to convince your character of the truth of what you are saying? What approach will be most effective?

OPTIONAL ASSIGNMENT

If you would prefer to attempt a more difficult approach to giving advice, write the kind of paragraph described above, but write it as if you were one of the characters in any selection in this unit. For example, you might choose to be Laurie's mother giving him advice about his father; or you might choose to imagine what Laurie's mother would have to say to the mother of Richard Wright. You will have to use your imagination here, as you will not be speaking from your own experience but from the experience of the character you are pretending to be. Be sure that you identify who you are and to whom you are speaking. It will still be necessary to plan your approach carefully in order to persuade the character to whom you are speaking of the soundness of your advice.

LESSON 9

Personal Experience

Based on "Two Generations," pages 78–163.

When a student once objected to a certain rule that had been established and asked why his teacher should want to enforce it so rigidly, the teacher tried to explain to him:

"Well, that's part of my job, you see, to help you understand that there are rules and limits which must be followed."

The student thought for a moment, then replied, "If that's true, then it's part of my job to try to break them. I mean, to test them—to see if we need new ones. I guess someday I'll be one of those who make the rules."

Have you ever learned something from trying to break a rule—perhaps succeeding? What you learned may have been simply that you'd better not try it again. Or you may have learned something important about why we have rules and limits in our society.

Write a composition of not more than 300 words about your experience with a certain rule. You will want to mention the rule and the specific situation, then tell about how (and perhaps why) you tried to break the rule and what happened because of it. Your approach can be humorous or serious. On the subject of "no talking," for example, a serious composition might be "The Importance of Not Talking During a Test"; while a humorous approach might be "What Happened When I Laughed Aloud in the Library."

What did you learn from your experience? Can it apply to someone else? (. . . And are you likely ever to try it again?)

LESSON 10

Description

Based on "The Flying Machine," "Flowers for Algernon," and "Nightmare Number Three," pages 166–197.

When Charlie Gordon's intelligence is increased, he feels he can do much to improve the world; his sadness when he realizes that his condition is only temporary is understandable. What do you think might have happened if the experiment had been successful and the process perfected? What if it were possible for everyone to have his intelligence permanently increased through an operation? Can you imagine a society in which everyone has an I.Q. of 200+? (It may not be as far away as it seems!) Use your imagination to write a paragraph or two describing such a society.

Since "society" is a very large topic, however, it will be necessary for you to limit your discussion to just a few aspects of this imaginary society: what schools would be like, for example, or what would happen to family relationships. You may wish to consider some of the following questions in writing your description: In what ways would such a society differ from ours? Would it be better, or worse? What problems would still exist? What new problems would be created? Would everyone be happy, since no one would be "different"? Your imagination is your only limit, but be sure that all aspects of your imaginary society are consistent with one another.

LESSON 11

Persuasion

Based on "Flowers for Algernon," "Nightmare Number Three," and "Children of the Harvest," pages 172–207.

Charlie Gordon in "Flowers for Algernon" and the narrator in "Children of the Harvest" both find that their popularity is influenced by their intelligence—but in different ways. Charlie believes himself popular when he has a low I.Q., but when his intelligence increases he finds himself unpopular with his fellow workers, who in fact manage to get him fired from the factory. In "Children of the Harvest," on the other hand, the narrator is not accepted by Barbara Baumann's circle of friends until the teacher moves her to the A class.

Choose as your topic for a one-paragraph composition one of the following statements about intelligence. You may choose to agree or disagree with the statement; rewrite it to suit your purpose.

1. People will hate and mistrust someone who has superior intelligence.
2. It's easy to make friends if you let people laugh at you.
3. Man should be very careful about the way in which he uses his intelligence.
4. People like to associate with someone who is very intelligent.

Develop your paragraph by explaining the statement you have chosen and supporting it. Your purpose here will be to persuade your reader to agree with you. Use supporting material from your own experience as much as possible.

LESSON 12

Ideas

Based on "Children of the Harvest," "No Boy. I'm a Girl!" and "The Parsley Garden," pages 198–222.

"Kids . . . are essentially what the human race just might be, at its best." (William Saroyan, biography, page 222.)

The quotation above presents one view of the younger generation which some people would strongly disagree with. How do you feel about the statement, after serious consideration? Do you agree that "kids" represent all the best aspects of the human race? If so, what do you mean by kids? Give an age span as an example, and explain in detail why people between these ages seem to represent the best of humanity. Or would you uphold some other age group—middle-aged or old-aged—as representing humanity's full potential?

Write a paragraph or two in which you present your ideas on this topic, using some variation of the statement below as a topic sentence: _____ are essentially what the human race can be, at its best.

After you have decided who is going to receive your praise or your blame, consider what tone you are going to use. Perhaps you will want to try a light, humorous approach, as in "No Boy. I'm a Girl!" Or perhaps you feel the subject is far too serious for humor. In either case, you will want to choose your statements and your details carefully so as to create the tone you desire. Now you are ready to write and revise.

LESSON 13

Persuasion

Based on "The Parsley Garden," "Taught Me Purple," and "The Kid Nobody Could Handle," pages 216–233.

One of the qualities which cause both Al Condraj and Jim Donnini to act as they do is pride. The speaker in "Taught Me Purple" also mentions pride as an important quality. Many other authors have felt pride worth writing about. Study the list of quotations below to be sure you understand what they say.

1. A man may be poor in purse, yet proud in spirit. (John Mason)
2. Pride goeth before destruction, and a haughty spirit before a fall.
                              (Proverbs)
3. Though pride is not a virtue, it is the parent of many virtues.
                        (Churton Collins)
4. He who would climb and soar aloft
   Must needs keep ever at his side
   The tonic of a wholesome pride.
                    (Arthur Hugh Clough)
5. In general, pride is at the bottom of all great mistakes. (John Ruskin)

You will notice that these quotations express various viewpoints. Is there one with which you agree wholeheartedly, or one with which you violently disagree? Does some experience you have had in the past affect your reaction?

Choose one of the quotations as the subject for a composition of a paragraph or two. Explain why you agree or disagree with the statement. Your argument will be far more convincing if you use a personal experience to prove your point.

LESSON 14

Explanation

Based on "Values," pages 164–235.

Because the Emperor of Ancient China wished his world to remain as it was, he saw the flying machine as a force for change and had the inventor executed. The actions of other characters in the unit also indicate the values they regard as important. Can you predict from considering the values he holds how one of these characters might act in another situation? Let your imagination work on one of the following:

1. Helmhotz is told that his school can no longer afford a band.
2. The narrator in "Children of the Harvest," when the family is no longer "tramping the fruit," meets a migrant child in the classroom.
3. Having escaped from his rooftop refuge, the narrator in "Nightmare Number Three" makes his way into the country.
4. The Emperor sees invaders in flying machines coming in over the Great Wall.
5. Charlie Gordon is asked whether he would like to have a new and improved version of the experiment tried on him.
6. Al Condraj is told by his mother that he must get a job to help support them.

Choose one of the situations described above and write a paragraph or two explaining what you think that particular character would do in the situation suggested. The character should act consistently, that is, in accord with the way he acts in the selection. Explain why you think he would act in the manner you describe.

LESSON 15

Description

Based on "Poetry," Sections 1 and 2, pages 238–265.

Poetry often gives us new ways of looking at familiar things. For their subjects, poets choose from the entire range of human experience—from smells of cooking, to dandelions, to cowboy movies, to death. To help make their impressions about these things clear and vivid, many poets make use of figurative language.

How keen is your vision? How closely do you look at the world about you? Do you observe the small details that give individuality to the people you see? Do you often see things in terms of comparisons; for instance, have you ever said something like, "The way he slouches when he sits makes him look like a pile of old clothes"? If so, you're using figurative language.

Choose an ordinary person, a commonplace object, or an everyday event. Write a paragraph, describing that person, object, or event in detail. If figurative language will help you to make your description vivid and interesting, use it. Remember, however, that your comparisons should be appropriate and should add color and meaning to whatever you're describing. Search for fresh images; avoid using trite, worn-out phrases. A good guide to follow is, if you've heard a descriptive phrase before, avoid using it.

OPTIONAL ASSIGNMENT

Perhaps you would like to write a poem about something or someone you know well. You can use basically the same method described above; but since poetry tends to be more concise than descriptive prose writing, every word must be carefully chosen to contribute to the desired effect. Your poem may rhyme or not, as you choose. Let your subject and the feelings you wish to create about it determine the form you use.

LESSON 16

Interpretation

Based on "Poetry," Sections 1, 2, and 3, pages 238–275.

In the first three sections of this unit you have read and discussed many poems. Do you have a favorite, one which you feel says something in particular to you? You may use that poem or any other poem in these sections as the basis for this assignment.

Write a composition of no more than 300 words in which you interpret the poem of your choice. Some of the aspects your interpretation might cover are: the general effect the poet intended; the methods he used in achieving this effect (the form of the poem, the use of rhyme, rhythm, imagery, figurative language, etc.); the kind of experience the poem is based on; the theme.

You probably will not be able to include in your composition a discussion of all of the aspects mentioned above. Some of them apply more to some poems than to others. In planning, however, consider all the aspects thoughtfully; then choose those which you think are most important in the poem you are writing about. Write about these few aspects in detail. You may wish to quote one or more lines from the poem to illustrate your points.

LESSON 17
Explanation

Based on "Poetry," pages 236–285.

The introduction to this unit states that "A poem can be many things," and the introductions to Sections 1, 2, and 3 elaborate somewhat on that statement:

1. The subjects they [the poets] observe are commonplace, but the ways in which they view them are not (Section 1, page 238).
2. Poetry is made from the things that concern all men (Section 2, page 248).
3. A poem is often a comment on life . . . (Section 3, page 266).

Choose one of the above statements as your topic sentence. Write a composition of one or two paragraphs in which you develop and explain the topic sentence. To illustrate and support your statements, refer specifically to poems in any section of the unit. Choose the poems carefully for the bearing they have on the idea you are developing. Quote one or more lines if you wish.

LESSON 18
Narration

Based on "Punch, Brothers, Punch" and "The Man Who Rode the Bear," pages 288–303.

The tall tale was a popular form of entertainment among frontiersmen in the early days of our country. Everyone could appreciate the tall tale, and anyone could join in a story-swapping session—provided he had imagination and a sense of humor.

Try your hand at writing a tall tale. Remember that a tall tale is simply a short, funny story or anecdote which gets most of its humor from exaggeration—often the wilder the exaggeration the funnier the story. But take a cue from master storytellers such as Hank Huggins and Mark Twain: they knew that a tall tale must be told with a straight face for the best effect. The more wildly exaggerated the story, the more it needs to be told as if there were nothing at all unusual about it. One other thing the master storytellers knew: a tall tale should be simple in form and told in conversational language—after all, the first tall tales were not written down, but told, often being made up on the spot.

Note that most tall tales are in reality a series of episodes. Keep your tall tale short; all you need to write is a single episode.

LESSON 19
Personal Experience

Based on "The Bride Comes to Yellow Sky," pages 304–326.

When Scratchy Wilson trudges away defeated in the final scene of "The Bride Comes to Yellow Sky," he seems almost a pathetic figure. He has finally come to realize that the old West, the West he once knew, is no more.

Have you ever been saddened (or cheered) by the passing of something familiar? It may have been a landmark in your town, a favorite play spot, a family tradition, or something that you could no longer do because you had grown older. How did this change affect you? Did you realize your loss immediately or not until later? Were you saddened or made glad by the realization? Was it something that could never be recaptured?

In a paragraph, describe something which was familiar to you but which no longer exists. Tell why it was important to you, how and why it passed, and your attitude about its passing. Try to make your reader understand your attitude. Can he be made to feel about this the way you do?

LESSON 20
Explanation

Based on "The First Day," "Music Inside My Head," and "Travels with Charley," pages 327–349.

When George Papashvily first came to America as an immigrant, he was confused by the language and bewildered by customs strange to him. He greatly appreciated the help given him by various citizens. Have you ever had the opportunity to help a confused immigrant or foreign visitor? Can you recall how he acted or what you said to him? How did you manage to get past the language barrier?

Imagine encountering such a visitor. Write a paragraph in which you explain to him some aspect of our culture which is very familiar to us but would not be to him. Be careful in your choice of words—you may have to avoid or explain certain terms or idiomatic expressions. Following are examples of aspects which you could write about:

1. Eating in a cafeteria (how to go through the line and choose food; where and when to pay; what to do with trays; whether or not to tip; etc.)
2. Attending a sports event—football, basketball, hockey, etc. (rules of play, sequence of events, types of people and their roles, etc.)
3. Riding public transportation (how to get information; where to get transportation; how to pay; how to transfer; etc.)

OPTIONAL ASSIGNMENT

If you have actually helped a foreigner in this country, or if you have traveled to another country and found yourself in the position of "bewildered foreigner," write instead a paragraph in which you describe your personal experiences. Focus on just one event or one brief span of time in order to be able to treat your explanation with sufficient detail. Did you have difficulty communicating? How did you make out, finally? Was your experience a humorous one? Did you find it funny at the time?

LESSON 21
Explanation

Based on "The American Romance," pages 286–353.

How well do you understand the concept of the American Romance? All of the selections in this unit were chosen to present various aspects of this concept. Can you sense the relationship of these selections to the unit theme? (The unit introduction on page 286 may provide some clues.)

Of course, there are many more works of literature, as well as many movies, which might illustrate this theme. Can you recall some that you have read or seen? Write a composition of not more than two paragraphs in which you express your understanding of the American Romance. You may develop it in any one of the following ways:

1. Write out your concept of the American Romance. Which aspects of it are applicable to America today, which are not? Explain.

2. Cite and describe a work of literature from your outside reading which you think fits the theme. Explain why your example could be considered part of the American Romance.

3. Relate a personal experience which made you aware of being an American.

LESSON 22

Opinion

Based on "The Tell-Tale Heart," "Dr. Heidegger's Experiment," and "Feathertop," pages 356–385.

Mother Rigby encourages Feathertop by telling him that he has a well-turned leg, a full chest, and an empty head, and that those qualities make a perfect natural endowment for any sort of career. Throughout the writings of Nathaniel Hawthorne, many characters make similar statements about the superficiality of people or the shallowness of their values and ideals. Do you agree that people are superficial, or foolish? Below are several statements from "Dr. Heidegger's Experiment" and Hawthorne's "Feathertop," the short story upon which the play was based. Choose one of them as the topic for a composition:

1. ". . . if the fountain gushed at my very doorstep, I would not stoop to bathe my lips in it—no, though its delirium were for years instead of moments." (Dr. Heidegger)

2. . . . the same ideas and phrases have been in vogue these fifty years. (Narrator, "Dr. Heidegger's Experiment")

3. . . . But the clothes . . . were to be the making of the man. (Narrator, "Feathertop")

4. "There are thousands upon thousands of vain and dishonest men in the world, made up of just such a jumble of wornout, forgotten, and good-for-nothing trash. . . . Yet they live in fair repute, and never see themselves for what they are." (Mother Rigby)

5. "A scarecrow . . . . is an innocent and useful vocation . . . and, if each of his human brethren had as fit a one, 'twould be the better for mankind." (Mother Rigby)

Write a paragraph in which you quote the statement and express your own ideas about it. Do you agree or disagree? What application can these words, written over a hundred years ago, have for our society today? What support or illustration from your own experience can you give for your viewpoint?

LESSON 23

Satire

Based on "The Ransom of Red Chief," pages 386–393.

O. Henry was a master at gently poking fun at our social attitudes. He applies his brand of satire to make the act of kidnapping seem harmful only to the kidnappers, and to ridicule the intellectual pretensions and weak will of Bill and the narrator. But behind the comedy there is implied criticism.

Write a composition of no more than 300 words in which you satirize a subject that you know something about from personal experience; for example, class elections, physical fitness, restaurant dining, music lessons, football practice, or any other subject that interests you. You may wish to write as if you were telling a personal experience, as O. Henry does.

Review the Handbook articles on satire (page 563) and on irony (page

551), which is widely used in satire, before you begin writing. The cutting by O. Henry in the article on irony will give you another example of O. Henry's methods of producing humor.

Remember, however, that satire is not always written merely to amuse; much satire has as its purpose a criticism or comment upon society or upon man's weaknesses, and sometimes it can be pretty grim humor. Do you wish to make your satire funny or biting? You will have to remain in careful control of your writing in order to achieve the effect you wish.

LESSON 24
Personal Experience

Based on "The Lady, or the Tiger?" pages 394–401.

Have you ever been in a dilemma? The princess in "The Lady, or the Tiger?" finds herself in a true dilemma: she must choose between two alternatives equally unpleasant to her. The part of the story on pages 399–400 describes the anguish she goes through before making her choice.

Most dilemmas are not as intense as that of the princess, but any situation can be uncomfortable when there is a choice to make that must bring about unpleasant results either way. Write a paragraph in which you describe a dilemma of your own. Explain how you found yourself in this situation in the first place. Describe each of your possible choices. Why were they unpleasant choices for you? Which did you finally choose? Why? How did you come to make your decision? What influenced your decision? Was the final outcome as bad as you had expected?

LESSON 25
Ideas

Based on "To Build a Fire," pages 402–415.

"The trouble with him was that he was without imagination. He was quick and alert in the things of life, but only in the things, not in the significances." So Jack London describes the main character in "To Build a Fire"—the character who is later to freeze to death in the snow. But what part exactly does the man's lack of imagination play in causing his death? Can a lack of imagination really be that dangerous? Perhaps you think instead that an imagination can in itself be harmful.

Write a paragraph in which you express your ideas on the importance of imagination. Following are some examples of topic sentences you might use:

1. A lack of imagination can be dangerous.
2. Having too much imagination can prove harmful.
3. Having no imagination is worse than having no money.
4. Misusing one's imagination is worse than having no imagination.

Develop your paragraph by explaining your ideas carefully and telling why you think as you do. Illustrate and support your statements from your own experience, if possible, or from outside reading.

LESSON 26
Research

Based on Introduction and "The Palace of Olympus," pages 418–431.

There are a great number of Greek myths, and any retelling of them must leave out many which may be equally interesting. In the introduction to this unit and in "The Palace of Olympus," many are hinted at, while others are mentioned only briefly. Each of the myths mentioned below is related in some way to one of the tales in this unit.

1. The creation of man by Prometheus and Epimetheus, and Prometheus' gift of fire
2. Theseus' killing of the Minotaur and escaping from the Labyrinth
3. The origin of the seasons with Persephone's return from Hades
4. Perseus' killing of Medusa
5. The theft of Apollo's cattle by the child Hermes
6. The nine Muses and their duties

Choose one of these myths as the subject for a composition. First look up the key names in the myth you have chosen and read the story. (Most libraries carry some books on Greek mythology, and encyclopedias also mention the major figures. You may find it necessary or desirable to try several sources.) Take brief notes to help you remember names and spellings and other details. Now retell the story in a paragraph or two, using your own words. Don't copy from your source. At the end of your composition, write the titles and authors of the books you used as sources. Share with your classmates the new story you know about the gods and heroes.

LESSON 27
Comparison and Contrast

Based on "The Labours of Heracles," pages 432–463.

Heracles was one of the most important and popular of the heroes of ancient Greece. Who are our heroes today? The U.S. astronauts, James Bond, Superman—all have been called heroes in one sense or another. If so, they represent various concepts of a hero. What do you feel to be our modern concept of a hero? What qualities must a character possess to be termed heroic? In what regard do we hold heroes in our society?

Write a paragraph or two in which you compare and contrast our modern concept of a hero with the ancient Greek concept. Describe the characteristics of each type of hero. What do you think might account for the differences between the ancient and the modern concepts of a hero? If you wish, you might illustrate your ideas by referring to specific characters who fit the descriptions you are setting forth.

LESSON 28
Dialogue

Based on "The Diary of Anne Frank," Act One, pages 466–506.

The feature article "Dramatic License" on pages 505–506 describes how the authors of the play chose certain entries from Anne's diary which they felt could be effectively dramatized. Many other entries were not used in the play; some were combined to form scenes which never actually happened.

Write a short scene of dialogue (two or three pages) using as your basis an incident which is only mentioned or hinted at in the play. Following are examples of incidents which could form the basis for your scene:

1. Mr. and Mrs. Frank, Anne, and Margot prepare to leave their home for the Annex.
2. Peter persuades his parents to allow him to bring his cat to the Annex.
3. Mr. Dussel and Mr. Kraler plan together to ask the Franks for help.
4. Anne puts a wet mop in Mr. Dussel's bed. (Anne mentions this incident on page 496.)

Use the play as a model to help you write the dialogue. (You may wish to review the Handbook article on page 539 for the ways in which dialogue is used.) Include stage directions and description as you find them necessary. Throughout your scene your purpose should be to capture the qualities which make each character individual and believable.

OPTIONAL ASSIGNMENT

Anne's actual diary, translated under the title *Anne Frank: The Diary of a Young Girl*, is available in most libraries. Read the diary; then dramatize a brief scene which actually is described by Anne. You may recognize throughout the book bits of scenes which were used in the play, but there will be many more which were not used. Your classmates will be interested in learning more about Anne and her family through the dialogue you have written.

LESSON 29
Opinion

Based on "The Diary of Anne Frank," Act Two, pages 507–532.

If Anne Frank could be characterized by a single line, it would probably be her well-known and often quoted words, "In spite of everything, I still believe that people are really good at heart." Does your own experience cause you to agree with Anne, or have you reason to believe that people are *not* good at heart?

Write a paragraph in which you comment from your own or others' real experiences upon Anne's statement. Why do you agree or disagree? Are you basing your opinion upon representative experiences, or upon a few rather special ones?

LESSON 30
Review

Based on "The Diary of Anne Frank," pages 466–534.

Soon after a new play or book appears, many magazines and newspapers carry reviews of the work. The reviewer gives a brief account of the subject of the play or book and then points out the strong and weak features of the work under discussion.

You have probably written book reviews in school; try your hand now at writing a play review. If you have seen *The Diary of Anne Frank* or any other play performed recently on a stage, use that performance as the subject of your review. If you have seen no stage productions, write about a movie or a television play which impressed you as being particularly good or bad.

Your review should be no longer than 300 words. Name the play and tell very briefly (in a sentence, if possible) what the play is about. Next tell whether or not you feel it is worth seeing, and why. Don't stop with a simple "I liked it," or "I thought it was awful"; go on to tell why you felt it was particularly good or bad. You may wish to consider some of the following questions: Was the plot believable? Did the characters seem real? Was the play well acted? Did it hold your interest? As you discuss each question, give examples to support your opinion.

A professional reviewer tries to be as objective as possible in his comments. Are you letting your personal likes and dislikes for certain actors or actresses, or for certain types of stories unduly influence your criticism?

LESSON 31

Opinion

Based on Counterpoint in Literature.

Of the selections you have read in this anthology, no doubt several will remain in your mind for one reason or another. Write a paragraph in which you name a selection that stands out in your memory and explain why it impressed you. You may remember one selection because it was the most exciting, another because it touched you deeply, or still another because it came closest to your personal experience. Use specific details from the selection to illustrate your statements.

LESSON 32

Evaluation

Based on Counterpoint in Literature.

Before being included in this anthology, many of the selections were read and commented upon by eighth-grade students throughout the country. Some of their comments are given below. Each one is, of course, simply one student's opinion. Choose the comment with which you agree or disagree most strongly. Write a paragraph in which you point out what you consider to be the faults or the strong points in the student's thinking.

1. The plot of "The Bride Comes to Yellow Sky" is not good enough. The characters are too drab except for Scratchy.
2. "Flowers for Algernon" leaves an effect that you won't forget—a feeling of anger, sadness, and thoughtfulness.
3. I think "A Man of Peace" was kind of gruesome and far-fetched.
4. The author's purpose in "Doc Marlowe" is to show how two-faced some people can be. He is telling us to watch out for people like this.
5. The play "Feathertop" seems to mirror man himself. Feathertop represents how man is continually bustling about, not caring or knowing what he himself looks like, or the effect he has on people, but just interested in getting his work done.
6. The author of "No Boy. I'm a Girl!" wrote easily and informally, much like high school students speak. This made the story funny and believable.
7. I feel that Mr. Vonnegut's story, "The Kid Nobody Could Handle," is a little far-fetched. I don't know a teacher who would act as Helmholtz did, or a boy who could be as negative as Jim.

Glossary

The pronunciation of each word is shown just after the word, in this way: **ab bre vi-ate** (ə brē′vē āt). The letters and signs used are pronounced as in the words below. The mark ′ is placed after a syllable with primary or strong accent, as in the example above. The mark ′ after a syllable shows a secondary or lighter accent, as in **ab bre vi-a tion** (ə brē′vē ā′shən).

Some words, taken from foreign languages, are spoken with sounds that otherwise do not occur in English. Symbols for these sounds are given at the end of the table as "Foreign Sounds."

a	hat, cap	o	hot, rock	ə represents:	
ã	age, face	ō	open, go	a in about	
ä	father, far	ô	order, all	e in taken	
		oi	oil, voice	i in pencil	
b	bad, rob	ou	house, out	o in lemon	
ch	child, much			u in circus	
d	did, red				
		p	paper, cup		
e	let, best	r	run, try	FOREIGN SOUNDS	
ē	equal, see	s	say, yes		
ėr	term, learn	sh	she, rush	Y as in French *du.* Pronounce (ē) with the lips rounded as for (ü).	
		t	tell, it		
f	fat, if	th	thin, both		
g	go, bag	ŦH	then, smooth		
h	he, how			œ as in French *peu.* Pronounce (ā) with the lips rounded as for (ō).	
		u	cup, butter		
i	it, pin	u̇	full, put		
ī	ice, five	ü	rule, move	N as in French *bon.* The N is not pronounced, but shows that the vowel before it is nasal.	
j	jam, enjoy				
k	kind, seek	v	very, save		
l	land, coal	w	will, woman		
m	me, am	y	young, yet	H as in German *ach.* Pronounce (k) without closing the breath passage.	
n	no, in	z	zero, breeze		
ng	long, bring	zh	measure, seizure		

<	from, derived from, taken from	*dial.*	dialect	*neut.*	neuter
?	possibly	*dim.*	diminutive	*pp.*	past participle
abl.	ablative	*fem.*	feminine	*ppr.*	present participle
accus.	accusative	*gen.*	genitive	*pt.*	past tense
cf.	compare	*lang.*	language	*ult.*	ultimately
		masc.	masculine	*var.*	variant

586

AF	Anglo-French (= Anglo-Norman, the dialect of French spoken by the Normans in England, esp. 1066–c. 1164)	Med.	Medieval
		Med.Gk.	Medieval Greek (700–1500)
		Med.L	Medieval Latin (700–1500)
		MF	Middle French (1400–1600)
Am.E.	American English (word originating in the United States)	MHG	Middle High German (1100–1450)
		MLG	Middle Low German (1100–1450)
Am.Ind.	American Indian	NL	New Latin (after 1500)
Am.Sp.	American Spanish	O	Old
E	English	OE	Old English (before 1100)
F	French	OF	Old French (before 1400)
G	German	OHG	Old High German (before 1100)
Gk.	Greek (from Homer to 300 A.D.)		
Gmc.	Germanic (parent language of Gothic, Scandinavian, English, Dutch, German)	Pg.	Portuguese
		Scand.	Scandinavian (one of the languages of Northern Europe before Middle English times; Old Norse unless otherwise specified)
HG	High German (speech of Central and Southern Germany)		
Hindu.	Hindustani (the commonest language of India)	Skt.	Sanskrit (the ancient literary language of India, from the same parent language as Persian, Greek, Latin, Germanic, Slavonic, and Celtic)
Ital.	Italian		
L	Latin (Classical Latin 200 B.C.–300 A.D.)		
		Sp.	Spanish
LG	Low German (speech of Northern Germany)	VL	Vulgar Latin (a popular form of Latin, the main source of French, Spanish, Italian, Portuguese, and Rumanian)
LGk.	Late Greek (300–700)		
LL	Late Latin (300–700)		
M	Middle		
ME	Middle English (1100–1500)		

OTHER ABBREVIATIONS

adj.	adjective	*E*	Eastern	*pron.*	pronoun
adv.	adverb	*esp.*	especially	*sing.*	singular
Anat.	anatomy	*interj.*	interjection	*SW*	Southwestern
Ant.	antonym	*n.*	noun	*Syn.*	synonym
Brit.	British	*pl.*	plural	*U.S.*	United States
conj.	conjunction	*prep.*	preposition	*v.*	verb

The pronunciation key is from the *Thorndike-Barnhart Advanced Dictionary,* copyright © 1973 by Scott, Foresman and Company.

a base (ə bās/), *v.*, **a based, a bas ing.** make lower in rank, condition, or character; humiliate; degrade: *A man who betrays a friend abases himself.* [< OF *abaissier* bring low < LL < L *ad-* + LL *bassus* low]

a bash (ə bash/), *v.* embarrass and confuse; make uneasy and somewhat ashamed: *The shy girl was abashed when she saw the room filled with strangers.* [< OF *esbaïss-*, stem of *esbaïr* be astonished < VL *batare* gape] —**a bash/ment,** *n.* **Syn.** disconcert, chagrin.

a bor tive (ə bôr/tiv), *adj.* **1.** coming to nothing; unsuccessful; fruitless: *The early attempts to make airplanes were abortive.* **2.** born before the right time; born prematurely. **3.** not developed properly; rudimentary —**a bor/tive ly,** *adv.* —**a bor/tive ness,** *n.*

a broad (ə brôd/), *adv.* **1.** outside one's country; to a foreign land; in foreign lands: *Go abroad.* **2.** out in the open air: *He walks abroad only at night.* **3.** going around; current: *A rumor is abroad that school will close.* **4.** far and wide; widely: *The news of his coming spread abroad.*

a brupt (ə brupt/), *adj.* **1.** sudden; hasty; unexpected: *an abrupt turn.* **2.** very steep. **3.** short or sudden in speech or manner; blunt. **4.** disconnected. [< L *abruptus,* pp. of *abrumpere* < *ab-* off + *rumpere* break] —**a brupt/ly,** *adv.* **a brupt/ness,** *n.* **Syn.** **2.** See **steep.** **3.** brusque, curt.

ab sorbed (ab sôrbd/, ab zôrbd/), *adj.* very much interested; completely occupied.

ab stract ed (ab strak/tid), *adj.* lost in thought; absentminded. —**ab stract/ed ly,** *adv.* **Syn.** preoccupied.

ab surd (ab sèrd/, ab zèrd/), *adj.* plainly not true or sensible; so contrary to reason that it is laughable; foolish; ridiculous. [< L *absurdus* out of tune, senseless] —**ab surd/ly,** *adv.* —**ab surd/ness,** *n.*

a bys mal (ə biz/məl), *adj.* too deep to be measured; bottomless. —**a bys/mal ly,** *adv.*

a byss (ə bis/), *n.* **1.** a bottomless or immeasurably deep space. **2.** anything too deep to be measured; lowest depth. **3.** the chaos before the Creation.

ac cede (ak sēd/), *v.,* **-ced ed, -ced ing.** **1.** give in; agree (*to*): *Please accede to my request.* **2.** come (*to*); attain (an office or dignity): *When the king died, his oldest son acceded to the throne.* **3.** become a party (*to*): *Our government acceded to the treaty.* [< L *accedere* < *ad-* to + *cedere* come]

ac claim (ə klām/), *v.* **1.** show satisfaction and approval of by words or sounds; shout welcome to; applaud: *The crowd acclaimed the fireman for rescuing two people from the burning house.* **2.** announce with signs of approval; hail: *The newspapers acclaimed the fireman a hero.* —*n.* shout or show of approval; applause; welcome. [< L *acclamare* < *ad-* to + *clamare* cry out]

ac cli mate (ə klī/mit, ak/lə māt), *v.,* **-mat ed, -mat ing.** *Esp. U.S.* accustom or become accustomed to a new climate, surroundings, or conditions. [< F *acclimater* < *à* to (< L *ad-*) + *climat* climate (< L *clima*)]

ac com plished (ə kom/plisht), *adj.* **1.** done; carried out; completed. **2.** expert; skilled. **3.** skilled in social arts and graces: *An accomplished lady has good manners.*

ac com mo date (ə kom/ə dāt), *v.,* **-dat ed, -dat ing.** **1.** have room for; hold comfortably: *This big bedroom will accommodate six beds.* **2.** help out; oblige: *He wanted change for a quarter, but I could not accommodate him.* **3.** furnish with lodging and sometimes with food as well. **4.** supply; furnish. **5.** provide (a person) with a loan of money. **6.** make fit; make suitable. The eye can accommodate itself to seeing objects at different distances. **7.** reconcile; adjust: *accommodate arguers.* [< L *accommodare* < *ad-* to + *commodare* make fit < *com-* with + *modus* measure]

ac cou ter ments (ə kü/tər mənts), *n.pl.* **1.** a soldier's equipment with the exception of his weapons and clothing. A belt, blanket, and knapsack are parts of a soldier's accouterments. **2.** personal equipment; outfit.

ac cou tre ments (ə kü/tər mənts), *n.pl. Esp. Brit.* accouterments.

a cute (ə kyüt/), *adj.* **1.** having a sharp point. **2.** sharp and severe: *A toothache can cause acute pain.* **3.** brief and severe. An acute disease like pneumonia reaches a crisis within a short time. **4.** keen: *Dogs have an acute sense of smell. An acute thinker is clever and shrewd.* **5.** high in pitch; shrill: *Some sounds are so acute that we cannot hear them.* **6.** having the mark (/) over it. **7.** less than a right angle. [< L *acutus,* pp. of *acuere* sharpen] —**a cute/ly,** *adv.* —**a cute/ness,** *n.*

ad dle (ad/l), *v.,* **-dled, -dling,** *adj.* —*v.* **1.** make or become muddled. **2.** make or become rotten. —*adj.* **1.** muddled; confused, as in **addlebrain, addleheaded,** etc. **2.** of eggs, rotten.

ad he sive (ad hē/siv, ad hē/ziv), *adj.* **1.** holding fast; adhering easily; sticky. **2.** smeared with a sticky substance for holding (something) fast: *adhesive tape.* —*n. U.S.* gummed tape used to hold bandages in place. —**ad he/sive ly,** *adv.* —**ad he/sive ness,** *n.*

ad min is ter (ad min/ə stər), *v.* **1.** manage the affairs of (a business, a city, etc.); control in behalf of others; direct: *The Secretary of the Interior administers a department of the government. A housekeeper administers a household.* **2.** give (to); apply; dispense: *A doctor administers medicine to sick people. Judges administer justice and punishment.* **3.** offer or tender (an oath). **4.** in law, settle or take charge of (an estate). **5.** act as administrator or executor. **6.** be helpful; add something; contribute: *administer to a person's comfort or pleasure.* [< L *administrare* < *ad-* to + *minister* servant]

ad vo cate (*v.* ad/və kāt; *n.* ad/və kit, ad/və kāt), *v.,* **-cat ed, -cat ing,** *n.* —*v.* speak in favor of; recommend publicly: *He advocates building more schools.* —*n.* **1.** person who pleads or argues for: *an advocate of peace.* **2.** lawyer who pleads in a law court. [< L *advocare* < *ad-* to + *vocare* call] —**ad/vo ca/tion,** *n.* —**ad/vo ca/tor,** *n.* **Syn.** *n.* **1.** champion; supporter.

Ae geus (ē/jüs).

aes thet ic (es thet/ik), *adj.* **1.** having to do with the beautiful, as distinguished from the useful, scientific, etc. **2.** (of persons) sensitive to beauty. **3.** (of things) pleasing; artistic. Also, **esthetic.**

aes thet i cal ly (es thet/ik lē), *adv.* **1.** in an aesthetic manner. **2.** according to aesthetics. Also, **esthetically.**

af fi da vit (af/ə dā/vit), *n.* statement written down and sworn to be true. An affidavit is usually made before a judge or notary public. [< Med.L *affidavit* he has stated on oath]

a gen da (ə jen/də), *n. pl. of* **a gen dum** (ə jen/dəm). **1.** things to be done. **2.** list of things to be done: *The chairman's agenda gave the members of the club an opportunity to acquaint themselves in advance with matters to be discussed or acted upon.* [< L *agenda* things to be done < *agere* do]

ag i tate (aj/ə tāt), *v.,* **-tat ed, -tat ing.** **1.** move or shake violently. **2.** disturb; excite (the feelings or the thoughts of): *She was much agitated by the news of her brother's illness.*

< = from, derived from, taken from;   cf., compare;   dial., dialect;   dim., diminutive;   lang., language; pp., past participle;   ppr., present participle;   pt., past tense;   ult., ultimately;   var., variant;   ? = possibly.

3. argue about; discuss vigorously.   4. keep arguing about and discussing a matter to arouse public interest: *agitate for a shorter working day.* [< L *agitare* move to and fro < *agere* drive, move]

a lac ri ty (ə lak′rə tē), *n.*   1. brisk and eager action; liveliness: *Although the man was very old, he still moved with alacrity.*   2. cheerful willingness. [< L *alacritas* < *alacer* brisk]   —**Ant.** 1. languor.

al ien (ā′lyən, ā′lē ən), *n.*   1. person who is not a citizen of the country in which he lives.   2. foreigner; stranger.   —*adj.* 1. of another country; foreign.   2. entirely different; not in agreement; strange: *Unkindness is alien to her nature.*

Al phe us (al fē′əs)

al ter ca tion (ôl′tər kā′shən, al′tər kā′shən), *n.*   an angry dispute; quarrel: *The two teams had an altercation over the umpire's decision.*

a lum ni (ə lum′nī), *n.* pl. of **alumnus.**

a lum nus (ə lum′nəs), *n.*, *pl.* **-ni.**   graduate or former student of a school, college, or university. [Am.E; < L *alumnus* foster child < *alere* nourish]

am bush (am′bush), *n.*   1. soldiers or other enemies hidden to make a surprise attack.   2. place where they are hidden. 3. an attack from an ambush.   4. act or condition of lying in wait: *Indians often trapped their enemies by ambush, instead of meeting them in open battle.* [< OF *embusche* < *embuscher.* See AMBUSH, v.]   —*v.* 1. attack from an ambush.   2. wait in hiding to make a surprise attack.   3. put (soldiers or other persons) in hiding for a surprise attack: *The general ambushed his troops in the woods on either side of the road.* [< OF *embuscher* < *en-* in (< L *in-*) + *busche* wood, bush < VL *busca* < Gmc.]

am ne sia (am nē′zhə), *n.*   loss of memory caused by injury to the brain, or by disease or shock. [< NL < Gk. *amnesia* < *a-* not + *mnasthai* remember]

am phib i an (am fib′ē ən), *n.*   1. animal that lives on land and in water.   2. plant that grows on land or in water. 3. aircraft that can take off from and alight on either land or water.   4. in military use, a tank for use on land and in water.

Am phi tri te (am′fə trī′tē)

a nach ro nism (ə nak′rə niz əm), *n.*   1. act of putting a person, thing, or event in some time where he or it does not belong: *It would be an anachronism to speak of George Washington riding in an automobile.*   2. something placed or occurring out of its proper time. [< F < Gk. *anachronismos* < *ana-* backwards + *chronos* time]

an ec do tal (an′ik dōt′l, an′ik dōt′l), *adj.*   of anecdotes; containing anecdotes.

an ec dote (an′ik dōt), *n.*   a short account of some interesting incident or event: *Many anecdotes are told about Abraham Lincoln.* [< Med.L. *anecdota* < Gk. *anekdota* (things) unpublished < *an-* not + *ek-* out + *didonai* give]

an es the sia (an′əs thē′zhə), *n.*   entire (**general**) or partial (**local**) loss of the feeling of pain, touch, cold, etc., produced by ether, chloroform, hypnotism, etc., or as the result of hysteria, paralysis, or disease. Also, **anaesthesia.** [Am.E; < NL < Gk. *anaisthesia* insensibility < *an-* without + *aisthesis* sensation]

an es thet ic (an′əs thet′ik), *n.*   substance that causes anesthesia. Chloroform and ether are anesthetics.   —*adj.* 1. causing anesthesia.   2. of or with anesthesia. Also, **anaesthetic.**

an gu lar (ang′gyə lər), *adj.*   1. having angles; sharp-cornered.   2. measured by an angle.   3. not plump; bony. 4. stiff and awkward.   —**an′gu lar ly,** *adv.*

an i mat ed (an′ə māt′id), *adj.*   1. lively; vigorous: *an*

animated discussion.   2. gay; joyful: *an animated smile.* 3. simulating life: *animated dolls.*   4. living; alive; animate. —**an′i mat′ed ly,** *adv.*

an i ma tion (an′ə mā′shən), *n.*   1. an animating or being animated.   2. life.   3. liveliness; spirit.

Anteater (total length 3½ feet)

An tae us (an tē′əs)

ant eat er (ant′ē′tər), *n.*   any of various toothless mammals with a long, slender, sticky tongue, that feed on ants and termites.

an ti phon (an′tə fon), *n.*   1. psalm, hymn, or prayer sung or chanted in alternate parts.   2. verses sung or chanted in response in a church service.

an tiph o nal (an tif′ə nəl), *adj.*   like an antiphon; sung or chanted alternately.   —*n.* book of antiphons.

an tiph o ny (an tif′ə nē), *n.*, *pl.* **-nies.**   1. antiphonal singing; antiphonal response.   2. an antiphon.

ap a thet ic (ap′ə thet′ik), *adj.*   1. with little interest or desire for action; indifferent.   2. lacking in feeling.   —**ap′a-thet′i cal ly,** *adv.*

a phid (ā′fid, af′id), *n.*   a very small insect that lives by sucking juices from plants; plant louse.

Aph ro di te (af′rə dī′tē)

ap pall or **ap pal** (ə pôl′), *v.,* **-palled, -pall ing.**   fill with horror; dismay; terrify: *We were appalled at the thought of another war. She was appalled when she saw the river had risen to the doorstep.* [< OF *apallir* become or make pale < *a-* to (< L *ad-*) + *pale* < L *pallidus*]

ap pall ing (ə pôl′ing), *adj.*   dismaying; terrifying; horrifying.   —**ap pall′ing ly,** *adv.*

ap pa ri tion (ap′ə rish′ən), *n.*   1. ghost; phantom. 2. something strange, remarkable, or unexpected which comes into view.   3. act of appearing; appearance.

ap pease (ə pēz′), *v.,* **-peased, -peas ing.**   1. satisfy (an appetite or desire): *A good dinner will appease your hunger.* 2. make calm; quiet.   3. give in to the demands of (especially those of a potential enemy): *Chamberlain appeased Hitler at Munich.* [< OF *apaisier* < *a-* to (< L *ad-*) + *pais* peace < L *pax*]   —**ap peas′er,** *n.*   —**ap peas′ing ly,** *adv.*

ap pli ca bil i ty (ap′lə kə bil′ə tē), *n.*   quality of being applicable.

ap pli ca ble (ap′lə kə bl, ə plik′ə bl), *adj.*   capable of being put to practical use; appropriate; suitable; fitting: *The rule "Look before you leap" is almost always applicable.*

ap pre hend (ap′ri hend′), *v.*   1. look forward to with fear; fear; dread: *A guilty man apprehends danger in every sound.*   2. arrest: *The thief was apprehended and put in jail.* 3. understand; grasp with the mind. [< L *apprehendere* < *ad-* upon + *prehendere* seize]

ap pre hen sion (ap′ri hen′shən), *n.*   1. expectation of evil; fear; dread.   2. a seizing; being seized; arrest. 3. understanding; grasp by the mind.

ap pre hen sive (ap′ri hen′siv), *adj.*   1. afraid; anxious; worried.   2. quick to understand; able to learn.   —**ap′pre-hen′sive ly,** *adv.*   —**ap′pre hen′sive ness,** *n.*

ap pren tice (ə pren′tis), *n.,* *v.,* **-ticed, -tic ing.**   —*n.* 1. person learning a trade or art. In return for instruction the apprentice agrees to work for his employer a certain length of time with little or no pay.   2. beginner; learner.   —*v.* bind or take as an apprentice. [< OF *aprentis* < *aprendre* learn < L *apprehendere*]

ap pren tice ship (ə pren′tis ship), *n.*   1. condition of

hat, āge, fär;   let, bē, tèrm;   it, īce;   hot, gō, ôrder;   oil, out;   cup, pùt, rüle;   ch, child;   ng, long; th, thin;   ŦH, then;   zh, measure;   ə represents *a* in about, *e* in taken, *i* in pencil, *o* in lemon, *u* in circus.

589

being an apprentice. **2.** time during which one is an apprentice.

ap pur te nance (ə pėr′tn əns), *n.* **1.** addition to something more important; added thing; accessory. **2.** a minor right or privilege belonging to another that is more important.

apt (apt), *adj.* **1.** fitted by nature; likely: *A careless person is apt to make mistakes.* **2.** suitable; fitting: *an apt reply.* **3.** quick to learn: *an apt to make mistakes.* **2.** suitable; fitting: *an apt reply.* **3.** quick to learn: *an apt pupil.* [< L *aptus* joined, fitted] —**apt′ly,** *adv.* —**apt′ness,** *n.*
Syn. **1.** prone, inclined, liable. **2.** apposite, appropriate. **3.** prompt, ready, clever, bright, intelligent.

aq ua ma rine (ak′wə mə rēn′), *n.* **1.** a transparent, bluish-green precious stone that is a variety of beryl. **2.** a light bluish green. —*adj.* light bluish-green. [< L *aqua marina* sea water]

A ra pou la o po lus (ä′rä pü′lä ō pō′lùs)

ar dor (är′dər), *n.* **1.** eagerness; warmth of emotion; great enthusiasm: *the ardor of a saint, patriotic ardor.* **2.** burning heat. Also, *Brit.,* **ardour.** [< L *ardor* < *ardere* burn]

ar du ous (är′jü əs), *adj.* **1.** hard to do; requiring much effort; difficult: *an arduous lesson.* **2.** using up much energy; strenuous: *an arduous effort to learn the lesson.* **3.** hard to climb; steep: *an arduous hill.* [< L *arduus* steep] —**ar′du ous ly,** *adv.* —**ar′du ous ness,** *n.*

Ar es (er′ēz, ar′ēz)

A re ti as (a rē′tē əs)

Ar gos (är′gos, är′gəs)

ar ma da (är mä′də), *n.* **1.** fleet of warships. **2.** fleet of airplanes. **3. the Armada,** the Spanish fleet that was sent to attack England in 1588. [< Sp. < L *armata* armed force, originally pp. neut. pl. of *armare* to arm. Doublet of ARMY.]

ar mor y (är′mər ē), *n., pl.* **-mor ies.** **1.** place where weapons are kept; arsenal. **2.** *U.S.* place where weapons are made. **3.** a building with a drill hall, etc., for militia.

ar mour y (är′mər ē), *n., pl.* **-mour ies.** *Esp. Brit.* armory.

ar range (ə rānj′), *v.,* **-ranged, -rang ing.** **1.** put in the proper order: *The army is arranged for battle.* **2.** settle (a dispute). **3.** come to an agreement. **4.** plan: *Can you arrange to meet me this evening?* **5.** adapt (a piece of music) to voices or instruments for which it was not written. —**ar rang′er,** *n.*

ar ro gant (ar′ə gənt), *adj.* too proud; haughty. —**ar′ro gant ly,** *adv.*
Syn. overbearing, presumptuous. —**Ant.** humble, meek.

ar ro gate (ar′ə gāt), *v.,* **-gat ed, -gat ing.** **1.** claim or take without right: *The despotic king arrogated to himself the power that belonged to the nobles.* **2.** claim for another without good reasons: *People are only too ready to arrogate kingly virtues to a king.*

Ar te mis (är′tə mis)

ar tic u late (*adj.* är tik′yə lit; *v.* är tik′yə lāt), *adj., v.,* **-lat ed, -lat ing.** —*adj.* **1.** uttered in distinct syllables or words: *A baby cries and gurgles, but does not use articulate speech.* **2.** able to put one's thoughts into words: *Julia is the most articulate of the sisters.* **3.** made up of distinct parts; distinct. **4.** jointed; segmented. —*v.* **1.** speak distinctly: *Be careful to articulate your words so that everyone in the room can understand you.* **2.** unite by joints. **3.** fit together in a joint: *After his knee was injured, he was lame because the bones did not articulate well.* —**ar tic′u late ly,** *adv.*

As cal a phus (as kal′ə fus)

as cot (as′kət, as′kot), *n.* necktie with broad ends, tied so that the ends may be laid flat, one across the other. [from *Ascot,* famous English race track]

as pen (as′pən), *n.* a poplar tree whose leaves tremble in the slightest breeze. —*adj.* **1.** of this tree. **2.** quivering; trembling.

as pire (ə spīr′), *v.,* **-pired, -pir ing.** **1.** have an ambition for something; desire earnestly: *Scholars aspire after knowledge. Tom aspired to be captain of the team.* **2.** rise high. [< L *aspirare* < *ad-* toward + *spirare* breathe] —**as pir′ing ly,** *adv.* —**Syn.** **1.** aim, long, crave.

as sim i late (ə sim′ə lāt), *v.,* **-lat ed, -lat ing.** **1.** absorb; digest: *The girl reads so much that she does not assimilate it all. The human body will not assimilate sawdust.* **2.** make or become like (people of a nation, etc.) in customs and viewpoint: *Swedes assimilate readily in this country. We have assimilated immigrants from many lands.* **3.** make like. *Consonants are frequently assimilated to the consonants which they precede; ads- becomes ass-; comr-, corr-; disf-, diff-;* etc. **4.** become like. [< L *assimilare* < *ad-* to + *similis* like]

asth ma (az′mə), *n.* a chronic disease that causes difficulty in breathing, a feeling of suffocation, and coughing.

asth mat ic (az mat′ik), *adj.* **1.** of or having to do with asthma. **2.** suffering from asthma. —*n.* person suffering from asthma.

as tro labe (as′trə lāb), *n.* an astronomical instrument formerly used for measuring the altitude of the sun or stars. [< OF *astrelabe* < Med.L < Gk. *astrolabon,* originally, star-taking < *astron* star + *lambanein* take]

A the na (ə thē′nə)

A the ne (ə thē′nē), *n.* Athena.

a tone (ə tōn′), *v.,* **-a toned, a ton ing.** make up; make amends (*for*): *Tom atoned for his unkindness to Dick by taking Dick to the movies.* [< *atonement*]

At ro pos (at′rə pos)

at tain (ə tān′), *v.* **1.** arrive at; reach: *attain years of discretion.* **2.** gain; accomplish. **3. attain to,** succeed in coming to or getting: *attain to a position of great influence.* [< OF *ataindre* < VL *attangere* < L *ad-* to + *tangere* touch] **Syn. 2.** achieve.

au da cious (ô dā′shəs), *adj.* **1.** bold; daring. **2.** too bold; impudent. —**au da′cious ly,** *adv.*

au dac i ty (ô das′ə tē), *n., pl.* **-ties.** **1.** boldness; reckless daring. **2.** rude boldness; impudence. [< L *audacia* < *audax* bold < *audere* dare]
Syn. 2. presumption.

Au ge us or **Au ge as** (ô gē′əs)

aug ment (ôg ment′), *v.* increase; enlarge: *The king augmented his power by taking over rights that had belonged to the nobles.* [< L *augmentare* < *augmentum* < *augere* increase]

aux il ia ry (ôg zil′yər ē, ôg zil′ər ē), *adj., n., pl.* **-ries.** —*adj.* **1.** helping; assisting. **2.** additional. —*n.* **1.** helper; aid. **2.** auxiliary verb. **3. auxiliaries,** *pl.* foreign or allied troops that help the army of a nation at war.

a vail (ə vāl′), *v.* **1.** be of use or value to: *Money will not avail you after you are dead.* **2.** help: *Talk will not avail without work.* **3. avail oneself of,** take advantage of; profit by; make use of. —*n.* use; help; benefit: *Crying is of no avail now.*

A ven tine (av′ən tin)

av id (av′id), *adj.* eager; greedy: *The miser was avid for gold.* [< L *avidus* < *avere* desire eagerly] —**av′id ly,** *adv.*

< = from, derived from, taken from;   cf., compare;   dial., dialect;   dim., diminutive;   lang., language; pp., past participle;   ppr., present participle;   pt., past tense;   ult., ultimately;   var., variant;   ? = possibly.

bach e lor's-but ton (bach/ə lərz but/n), *n.* 1. plant with a flower shaped somewhat like a button; cornflower. 2. the flower. 3. any similar flower.

bail (bāl), *n.* scoop or pail used to throw water out of a boat. —*v.* 1. throw (water) out of a boat with a pail, a dipper, or any other container. 2. dip water from. 3. **bail out**, drop from an airplane in a parachute. [< F *baille* < L *bajulus* carrier]

bale ful (bāl/fəl), *adj.* evil; harmful. —**bale/ful ly**, *adv.* —**bale/ful ness**, *n.*

ban tam (ban/təm), *n.* 1. Often, **Bantam**, a small-sized kind of fowl. 2. a small person who is fond of fighting. —*adj.* light in weight; small.

bar ba rous (bär/bər əs), *adj.* 1. not civilized; savage. 2. rough and rude; coarse; unrefined. 3. cruelly harsh; brutal. [< L < Gk. *barbaros* foreign, apparently originally, stammering] —**bar/bar ous ly**, *adv.* —**bar/bar ous ness**, *n.*

bar na cle (bär/nə kəl), *n.* animal with a shell that attaches itself to rocks, the bottoms of ships, the timbers of wharves, etc.

bar rage (bə räzh/), *n., v.,* **-raged, -rag ing.** —*n.* barrier of artillery fire to check the enemy or to protect one's own soldiers in advancing or retreating. —*v.* fire at with artillery; subject to a barrage. [< F *barrage* < *barrer* to bar]

barrel organ, a hand organ.

bas-re lief (bä/ri lēf/, bas/ri lēf/), *n.* carving or sculpture in which the figures project only slightly from the background. [< F < Ital. *bassorilievo* low relief]

bat tal ion (bə tal/yən), *n.* 1. two or more companies, usually commanded by a major and forming part of a regiment. 2. large part of an army organized to act together. 3. army. 4. organized group. 5. **battalions,** armies; military forces. [< F *bataillon* < Ital. *battaglione,* dim. of *battaglia* battle < LL *battalia.* See BATTLE.]

bat ten (bat/n), *v.* 1. grow fat. 2. fatten. 3. feed greedily. [< Scand. *batna* < *bati* improvement]

bat ter y (bat/ər ē), *n., pl.* **-ter ies.** 1. set of similar or connected things. 2. set of one or more electric cells that produce electric current. 3. set of guns or other weapons such as mortars, machine guns, and artillery pieces for combined action in attack or defense. 4. these guns together with the soldiers and equipment for them. 5. platform or fortification equipped with big guns. 6. in baseball, the pitcher and catcher together. 7. in law, the unlawful beating of another person; any threatening touch to the clothes or body of another. [< F *batterie* < *battre* beat < L *battuere.* Related to *battle.*]

bat tle (bat/l), *n., v.,* **-tled, -tling.** —*n.* 1. fight between armies or navies. 2. fighting; war: *wounds received in battle.* 3. fight; contest: *a battle of words.* —*v.* 1. take part in a battle. 2. fight; struggle; contend. [< OF *bataille* < LL *battalia* < L *battuere* beat. Related to *battery.*] —**bat/tler,** *n.*

battle fatigue, neurosis from anxiety during combat.

bay (bā), *n.* 1. a reddish brown. 2. a reddish-brown horse with black mane and tail. —*adj.* reddishbrown: *a bay horse.* [< OF *bai* < L *badius*]

bed lam (bed/ləm), *n.* 1. uproar; confusion. 2. insane asylum; madhouse. 3. **Bedlam,** insane asylum in London. [alteration of *Bethlehem* (for the Hospital of St. Mary of Bethlehem). See def. 3.]

be grudge (bi gruj/), *v.,* **-grudged, -grudg ing.** envy (somebody) the possession of; be reluctant to give (something); grudge: *She is so stingy that she begrudges her dog a bone.* —**be grudg/ing ly,** *adv.*

be lea guer (bi lē/gər), *v.* 1. besiege. 2. surround. [< Dutch *belegeren* < *leger* camp]

bel fry (bel/frē), *n., pl.* **-fries.** 1. tower for a bell or bells. 2. room, cupola, or turret in which a bell or bells may be hung. [< OF *berfrei* < Gmc.]

bel lows (bel/ōz, bel/əs), *n. sing. or pl.* 1. instrument for producing a strong current of air, used for blowing fires or sounding an organ. 2. the folding part of a camera, behind the lens. 3. the lungs.

bench (bench), *n.* 1. a long seat, usually of wood or stone. 2. worktable of a carpenter, or of any worker with tools and materials. 3. seat where judges sit in a law court. 4. judge or group of judges sitting in a law court. 5. position as a judge. 6. law court. 7. **on the bench, a.** sitting in a law court as a judge. **b.** sitting among the substitute players. 8. a raised level tract of land. —*v.* 1. furnish with benches. 2. assign a seat on a bench. 3. take (a player) out of a game.

be reft (bi reft/), *adj.* 1. bereaved; deprived. 2. left desolate.

ber yl (ber/əl), *n.* a very hard mineral, usually green or greenish-blue, a silicate of beryllium and aluminum. Emeralds and aquamarines are beryls.

be siege (bi sēj/), *v.,* **-sieged, -sieg ing.** 1. make a long-continued attempt to get possession of (a place) by armed force; surround and try to capture: *For ten years the Greeks besieged the city of Troy.* 2. crowd around: *Hundreds of admirers besieged the famous aviator.* 3. overwhelm with requests, questions, etc.: *During the flood, the Red Cross was besieged with calls for help.* —**be sieg/er,** *n.*

be troth al (bi trō/тнəl, bi trô/тнəl), *n.* promise in marriage; engagement.

bid dy (bid/ē), *n., pl.* **-dies.** hen. [origin uncertain]

big time, SLANG. the top level in arts, sports, politics, industry, etc.

bi jou (bē/ zhü), *n., pl.* **-joux** (-zhüz). 1. a jewel. 2. something small and fine. 3. a theater.

bilge (bilj), *n., v.,* **bilged, bilg ing.** —*n.* 1. the lowest part of a ship's hold; bottom of a ship's hull. 2. bilge water. 3. the bulging part of a barrel. 4. *Informal.* nonsense. —*v.* 1. break in (the bottom of a ship); spring a leak. 2. bulge; swell out.

bil lings gate (bil/ingz gāt/), *n.* vulgar, abusive language.

black guard (blag/ärd, blag/ərd), *n.* scoundrel. —*v.* abuse with vile language. [< *black* + *guard*]

black out (blak/out/), *n.* 1. a turning out or concealing of all the lights of a city, district, etc., as a protection against an air raid. 2. temporary blindness or unconsciousness experienced by a pilot, resulting from rapid changes in velocity or direction. 3. a turning off of all the lights on the stage of a theater.

blanch (blanch), *v.* 1. make white; bleach. Almonds are blanched by soaking off their skins in boiling water. 2. turn white or pale: *blanch with fear.*

bland (bland), *adj.* 1. smooth; mild; gentle; soothing: *A warm spring breeze is bland.* 2. agreeable; polite. **Syn.** 1. soft, balmy. 2. suave, urbane.

bloat (blōt), *v.* 1. swell up; puff up. 2. preserve (herring) by salting and smoking.

boarding house, house where meals, or room and meals, are provided for pay.

boot leg (büt/leg/), *v.,* **-legged, -leg ging,** *adj., n. U.S.* —*v.* sell, transport, or make unlawfully. —*adj.* made, transported, or sold unlawfully. —*n. Slang.* alcoholic liquor made, sold, or transported unlawfully. [modern use from practice of smuggling liquor in boot legs]

---

hat, āge, fär; let, bē, tèrm; it, īce; hot, gō, ôrder; oil, out; cup, pút, rüle; ch, child; ng, long; th, thin; ⊤н, then; zh, measure; ə represents *a* in about, *e* in taken, *i* in pencil, *o* in lemon, *u* in circus.

boot leg ger (büt/leg/ər), *n. Slang.* person who bootlegs.
bore (bôr, bōr), *v.*, **bored, bor ing,** *n.* —*v.* 1. make a hole by means of a tool that keeps turning, or as a worm does in fruit. 2. make (a hole, passage, entrance, etc.) by pushing through or digging out: *A mole has bored its way under the hedge.* 3. bore a hole in; hollow out evenly. —*n.* 1. hole made by a revolving tool. 2. a hollow space inside a pipe, tube, or gun barrel: *He cleaned the bore of his gun.* 3. distance across the inside of a hole or tube. [OE *borian*]
brake (brāk), *n.* thicket. [cf. MLG *brake*]
brand (brand), *n.* 1. a certain kind, grade, or make: *a brand of coffee.* 2. trademark. 3. mark made by burning the skin with a hot iron. Cattle and horses on big ranches are marked with brands to show who owns them. 4. an iron stamp for burning a mark. 5. mark of disgrace. 6. piece of wood that is burning or partly burned. 7. *Archaic and Poetic.* sword. —*v.* 1. mark by burning the skin with a hot iron. In former times criminals were often branded. 2. put a mark of disgrace on: *He has been branded as a traitor.* [OE]
bran.dish (bran/dish), *v.* wave or shake threateningly; flourish: *The knight drew his sword and brandished it at his enemy.* —*n.* a threatening shake; flourish.
bra va do (brə vä/dō), *n.* a great show of boldness without much real courage; boastful defiance without much real desire to fight. [< Sp. *bravada* < *bravo.* See BRAVE.]
brave (brāv), *adj.*, **brav er, brav est,** *n.*, *v.*, **braved, brav ing.** —*adj.* 1. without fear; having courage: *brave knights.* 2. making a fine appearance; showy: *The fair had brave displays.* 3. *Archaic.* fine; excellent. —*n.* 1. a brave person. 2. a North American Indian warrior. —*v.* 1. meet without fear: *Soldiers brave much danger.* 2. dare; defy: *He braved the king's anger.* [< F < Ital. *bravo* brave, bold < Sp. *bravo* vicious (as applied to bulls), ? < L *pravus*] —**brave/ly,** *adv.* —**brave/ness,** *n.*
Syn. *adj.* 1. **Brave, courageous** mean showing no fear. **Brave** suggests being able to face danger or trouble boldly and with determination, without giving in to fear: *The brave girl went into the burning house to save a baby.* **Courageous** suggests being fearless in the face of danger, having a strength and firmness of character that makes one able to endure any trial or even to welcome it: *The courageous pioneers were not stopped by the dangers of the journey westward.* —**Ant.** *adj.* 1. cowardly, fearful.
bra zen (brā/zn), *adj.* 1. made of brass. 2. like brass in color or strength. 3. loud and harsh. 4. shameless; impudent. —*v.* 1. make shameless or impudent. 2. **brazen a thing out** or **through,** act as if unashamed of it.
brim stone (brim/stōn/), *n.* sulfur.
buoy an cy (boi/ən sē, bü/yən sē), *n.* 1. power to float: *Wood has more buoyancy than iron.* 2. power to keep things afloat: *Salt water has more buoyancy than fresh water.* 3. tendency to rise. 4. light-heartedness; cheerfulness; hopefulness; ability to rise above to recover quickly from low spirits.
buoy ant (boi/ənt, bü/yənt), *adj.* 1. able to float: *Wood and cork are buoyant; iron and lead are not.* 2. able to keep things afloat: *Air is buoyant; balloons float in it.* 3. tending to rise. 4. light-hearted; cheerful; hopeful: *Children are usually more buoyant than old people.* —**buoy/ant ly,** *adv.*
bur nish (bėr/nish), *v.*, *n.* polish; shine.
burr (bėr), *n.* 1. a rough pronunciation of *r.* 2. a rough pronunciation: *a Scotch burr.* 3. a whirring sound. —*v.* 1. pronounce *r* roughly. 2. pronounce roughly. 3. make a whirring sound. [probably imitative]
Bu si ris (byü si/ris)

cache (kash), *n.*, *v.*, **cached, cach ing.** —*n.* 1. a hiding place to store food or supplies. 2. a hidden store of food or supplies. —*v.* put in a cache; hide. [< F *cache* < *cacher* hide]
ca coph o ny (kə kof/ə nē), *n.*, *pl.* **-nies.** a harsh, clashing sound; dissonance; discord. [< NL *cacophonia* < Gk. *kakophonia* < *kakos* bad + *phone* sound]
Ca cus (kā/kus)
ca den za (kə den/zə), *n.* an elaborate flourish or showy passage usually near the end of a section of a musical composition, such as an aria or a movement of a concerto.
cal li o pe (kə li/ə pē; *for 1, also* kal/ē ōp), *n.* 1. a musical instrument having a series of steam whistles played by pushing keys. 2. **Calliope,** in Greek mythology, the Muse of eloquence and heroic poetry. [< L < Gk. *kalliope* beautiful-voiced < *kallos* beauty + *ops* voice]
cam e o (kam/ē ō), *n.*, *pl.* **-e os.** a precious or semiprecious stone carved so that there is a raised part on a background.
cam ou flage (kam/ə fläzh), *n.*, *v.*, **-flaged, -flag ing.** —*n.* 1. disguise; deception. The white fur of a polar bear is a natural camouflage; it prevents the bear's being easily seen against the snow. 2. in warfare, giving things a false appearance to deceive the enemy. —*v.* give a false appearance in order to conceal; disguise. [< F *camouflage* < *camoufler* disguise]
can ni bal (kan/ə bəl), *n.* 1. person who eats human flesh. 2. animal that eats others of its own kind. —*adj.* of or like cannibals. [< Sp. *Caníbal* < *Caribe* Carib]
can ni bal is tic (kan/ə bə lis/tik), *adj.* of cannibals; characteristic of cannibals.
can ta ta (kən tä/tə), *n.* story or play set to music to be sung by a chorus, but not acted.
ca pit u late (kə pich/ə lāt), *v.*, **-lat ed, -lat ing.** surrender on certain terms or conditions: *The men in the fort capitulated upon the condition that they should be allowed to go away unharmed.*
ca pit u la tion (kə pich/ə lā/shən), *n.* 1. a surrender on certain terms or conditions. 2. agreement; condition. 3. statement of the main facts of a subject; summary.
cap ti vate (kap/tə vāt), *v.*, **-vat ed, -vat ing.** 1. hold captive by beauty or interest; charm; fascinate: *The children were captivated by the animal story.* 2. *Obsolete.* capture. —**cap/ti vat/ing ly,** *adv.* —**cap/ti va/tor,** *n.*
Syn. 1. enchant, entrance.
cap tive (kap/tiv), *n.* prisoner: *The army brought back a thousand captives.* —*adj.* 1. held as a prisoner; made a prisoner. 2. captivated. [< L *captivus* < *capere* take]
ca rafe (kə raf/), *n.* a glass water bottle.
ca ress (kə res/), *n.*, *v.* touch or stroke to show affection; embrace; kiss. [< F *caresse* < Ital. *carezza* < L *carus* dear]
car il lon (kar/ə lon, kar/ə lon, kə ril/yən), *n.* 1. set of bells arranged for playing melodies. 2. melody played on such bells. 3. part of an organ imitating the sound of bells. [< F, ult. < L *quattuor* four; originally consisted of four bells]
cas cade (ka skād/), *n.*, *v.*, **-cad ed, -cad ing.** —*n.* 1. a small waterfall. 2. anything like this. —*v.* fall in a cascade. [< F < Ital. *cascata* < L *cadere* fall]
case ment (kās/mənt), *n.* 1. window opening on hinges like a door. 2. *Poetic.* any window. 3. a casing; covering; frame.
cas ket (kas/kit), *n.* 1. a small box to hold jewels, letters, etc. 2. coffin. [origin uncertain]
cast (kast), *n.* 1. a throw; the distance a thing is thrown. 2. thing made by casting; thing that is molded. 3. mold used in casting; mold: *His broken arm is in a plaster cast.*

< = from, derived from, taken from;   cf., compare;   dial., dialect;   dim., diminutive;   lang., language; pp., past participle;   ppr., present participle;   pt., past tense;   ult., ultimately;   var., variant;   ? = possibly.

4. actors in a play. 5. form; look; appearance. 6. kind; sort. 7. a slight amount of color; tinge: *a white dress with a pink cast.* 8. a slight squint. —*adj.* made by casting.

cau ter ize (kô′tər īz), *v.,* **-ized, -iz ing.** burn with a hot iron or a caustic substance. Doctors sometimes cauterize wounds to prevent bleeding or infection.

cav i ar or **cav i are** (kav′ē är, kä′vē är), *n.* 1. a salty relish made from the eggs of sturgeon or other large fish. 2. **caviar to the general,** too good a thing to be appreciated by ordinary people.

ca vort (kə vôrt′), *v.* U.S. Informal. prance about; jump around: *The horses cavorted with excitement.* [Am.E; origin uncertain]

cay man (kā′mən), *n., pl.* **-mans.** a large alligator of tropical America. Also, **caiman.** [< Sp. *caimán* < Carib]

Cer ber us (sèr′bər əs)

Cer y ni tes (ker ə nī′tēz)

cess pool (ses′pül), *n.* 1. pool or pit for house drains to empty into. 2. any filthy place. [origin uncertain]

Ceu ta (sü′tə, syü′tə)

cha grin (shə grin′), *n.* a feeling of disappointment, failure, or humiliation. —*v.* cause to feel chagrin. [< F *chagrin* grained leather, vexation < Turkish *çāghrī* rump of a horse; shift of meaning comes from idea of being ruffled (cf. *gooseflesh*)]

Char on (ker′ən, kar′ən)

chase (chās), *v.,* **chased, chas ing.** engrave.

chasm (kaz′əm), *n.* 1. a deep opening or crack in the earth; gap. 2. a wide difference of feelings or interests between people or groups.

chas sis (chas′ē, shas′ē), *n., pl.* **chas sis** (shas′ēz or chas′ēz). 1. frame, wheels, and machinery of a motor vehicle that support the body. 2. the main landing gear that supports the body of an aircraft. 3. frame on which a gun carriage moves backward and forward. [< F < VL *capsiceum* < L *capsa* box]

chas ten (chā′sn), *v.* 1. punish to improve. 2. restrain from excess or crudeness. [< obsolete v. *chaste* < F < L *castigare* make pure < *castus* pure] —**chas′ten er,** *n.* Syn. 1. discipline.

chas tise (cha stīz′), *v.,* **-tised, -tis ing.** punish; beat. [< obsolete *chaste.* See CHASTEN.] —**chas tis′er,** *n.*

châ teau (sha tō′), *n., pl.* **-teaux** (tōz′). 1. a French castle. 2. a large country house in France. [< F *château* < L *castellum* castle. Doublet of CASTLE.]

che cha quo (chē chä′kō)

che mi don (chù mə don′), *n.* a suitcase.

chev y (chev′ē), *n., pl.* **chev ies,** *v.,* **chev ied, chev y ing.** Brit. —*n.* 1. a hunting cry. 2. a hunt; chase. —*v.* 1. hunt; chase. 2. scamper; race. 3. worry.

chic o ry (chik′ər ē), *n., pl.* **-ries.** 1. plant with bright-blue flowers whose leaves are used for salad. 2. its root, roasted and used as a substitute for coffee.

chid den (chid′n), *v.* a pp. of chide.

chide (chīd), *v.,* **chid ed** or **chid, chid ed, chid,** or **chid den, chid ing.** reproach; blame; scold.

chim ney (chim′nē), *n., pl.* **-neys.** 1. an upright structure to make a draft and carry away smoke. 2. part of this that rises above a roof. 3. a glass tube put around the flame of a lamp. 4. crack or opening in a rock, mountain, volcano, etc.

Chi ron (kī′ron)

chiv vy (chiv′ē), *v.,* **-vied, -vy ing,** *n., pl.* **-vies.** chevy.

cir cuit (sèr′kit), *n.* 1. a going around; a trip around: *It takes a year for the earth to make its circuit of the sun.* 2. way over which a person or group makes repeated

journeys at certain times. Some theater companies travel over regular circuits. Some judges make a circuit, stopping at certain places along the way to hold court. 3. part of the country through which such circuits are made. 4. district under the jurisdiction of a circuit court. 5. distance around any space. 6. line enclosing any space. 7. space enclosed. 8. the complete path or a part of it over which an electric current flows. —*v.* make a circuit of; go in a circuit. [< L *circuitus* a going around < *circum* around + *ire* go] Syn. *n.* 2. route, course.

cir cum spect (sèr′kəm spekt), *adj.* careful; cautious; prudent. [< L *circumspectus,* pp. of *circumspicere* < *circum* around + *specere* look] —**cir′cum spect′ly,** *adv.* Syn. watchful, wary, discreet.

cit a del (sit′ə dəl, sit′ə del), *n.* 1. fortress commanding a city. 2. a strongly fortified place; stronghold. 3. a strong, safe place; refuge.

Ci thae ron (si thē′ron)

clap board (klab′ərd, klap′bôrd, klap′bōrd), U.S. —*n.* a thin board, thicker along one edge than along the other, used to cover the outer walls of wooden buildings. —*v.* cover with clapboards. [Am.E]

clar et (klar′ət), *n.* 1. kind of red wine. 2. a dark, purplish red. —*adj.* dark purplish-red.

clique (klēk, klik), *n.* a small, exclusive set or snobbish group of people. [< F *clique* < *cliquer* click]

clock (klok), *n.* an ornamental pattern sewn or woven on the side of a stocking, extending up from the ankle. [origin uncertain]

clois ter (kloi′stər), *n.* 1. a covered walk along the wall of a building, with a row of pillars on the open side. A cloister is often built around the courtyard of a monastery, church, or college building. 2. place of

Cloister

religious retirement; convent or monastery. 3. a quiet place shut away from the world. —*v.* shut away in a quiet place. [< OF *cloistre* < L *claustrum* closed place, lock < *claudere* close]

Clo tho (klō′thō)

clutch¹ (kluch), *n.* 1. a tight grasp. 2. a grasping claw, paw, hand, etc.: *Quick shooting saved the hunter from the bear's clutches.* 3. Usually, **clutches,** *pl.* control; power: *in the clutches of the police.* 4. device in a machine for connecting or disconnecting the engine or motor that makes it go. 5. lever or pedal operating this device. [< v.] —*v.* 1. grasp tightly: *The girl clutched her doll to her breast.* 2. seize eagerly; snatch: *A drowning man will clutch at a straw.* [OE *clyccan* bend, clench]

clutch² (kluch), *n.* 1. nest of eggs. 2. brood of chickens. 3. group; bunch.

Cnos sos (nos′əs)

co-, *prefix.* 1. with; together: *Coöperate = act with or together.* 2. joint; fellow: *Coauthor = joint or fellow author.* 3. equally: *Coextensive = equally extensive.* [< L *co-,* var. of *com-*]

co da (kō′də), *n.* a final passage of a musical composition, which gives it a satisfactory ending. [< Ital. < L *cauda* tail]

co ed u ca tion al (kō′ej ə kā′shə nəl), *adj.* 1. educating boys and girls or men and women together in the same school or classes. 2. having to do with coeducation. [Am.E] —**co′ed u ca′tion al ly,** *adv.*

co gnac (kō′nyak, kon′yak), *n.* kind of French brandy.

---

hat, āge, fär;   let, bē, tèrm;   it, īce;   hot, gō, ôrder;   oil, out;   cup, pùt, rüle;   ch, child;   ng, long; th, thin;   ᴛʜ, then;   zh, measure;   ə represents *a* in about, *e* in taken, *i* in pencil, *o* in lemon, *u* in circus.

col ic (kol/ik), *n.* severe pains in the abdomen. [< LL < GK. *kolikos* of the colon]

col lab o rate (kə lab/ə rāt), *v.,* **-rat ed, -rat ing.** 1. work together: *Two authors collaborated on that book.* 2. aid or coöperate traitorously. [< L *collaborare* < *com-* with + *laborare* work]

col lat er al (kə lat/ər əl), *adj.* 1. parallel; side by side. 2. related but less important; secondary; indirect. 3. in a parallel line of descent; descended from the same ancestors, but in a different line: *Cousins are collateral relatives.* 4. additional. 5. secured by stocks, bonds, etc. —*n.* 1. a collateral relative. 2. stocks, bonds, etc., pledged as security for a loan. —**col lat/er al ly,** *adv.*

com-, *prefix.* with; together; altogether: *Commingle = mingle with one another. Compress = press together.* Also: **col-,** before *l;* **con-,** before *n* and before consonants except *b, h, l, m, p, r, w;* **cor-,** before *r.* [< L *com-* < *cum,* prep.]

com mem o rate (kə mem/ə rāt), *v.,* **-rat ed, -rat ing.** 1. preserve the memory of: *Roman emperors built arches to commemorate their victories.* 2. honor the memory of: *Christmas commemorates Christ's birth.*

com mence (kə mens/), *v.,* **-menced, -menc ing.** begin; start. [< OF *comencer* < VL < L *com-* + *initiare* begin (ult. < *inire* begin < *in-* in + *ire* go)] —**com menc/er,** *n.*

com mend (kə mend/), *v.* 1. praise. 2. mention favorably; recommend. 3. hand over for safekeeping.

com pas sion ate (kəm pash/ə nit), *adj.* desiring to relieve another's suffering; deeply sympathetic; pitying. —**com pas/sion ate ly,** *adv.*

com pen sate (kom/pən sāt), *v.,* **-sat ed, -sat ing.** 1. make an equal return to; give an equivalent to: *The hunters compensated the farmer for killing his cow.* 2. balance by equal weight, power, etc.; make up (*for*): *Industry and loyalty sometimes compensate for lack of ability.* 3. pay: *The company compensated her for extra work.* [< L *compensare* < *com-* with + *pensare* weigh < *pendere*] —**com/pen sa/tor,** *n.*

Syn. 1. recompense. 2. offset.

com pli ment (*n.* kom/plə mənt; *v.* kom/plə ment), *n.* 1. something good said about one; something said in praise of one's work. 2. a polite greeting: *In the box of flowers was a card saying "With the compliments of a friend."* —*v.* 1. pay a compliment to; congratulate: *The principal complimented the boy on his good grades.* 2. give something to (a person) as a polite attention.

con ces sion (kən sesh/ən), *n.* 1. a conceding; granting; yielding: *As a concession, Mother let me stay up an hour longer.* 2. anything conceded or yielded; admission; acknowledgment. 3. something conceded or granted by a government or controlling authority; grant. Land, privileges, etc., given by a government to a business company are called concessions. *A circus leases space for booths as concessions.*

conch (kongk, konch), *n., pl.* **conchs** (kongks), **conch es** (kon/chiz). a large, spiral sea shell.

con cus sion (kən kush/ən), *n.* 1. a sudden, violent shaking; shock: *The concussion caused by the explosion broke many windows.* 2. injury to the brain, spine, etc., caused by a blow, fall, or other shock. [< L *concussio, -onis* < *concutere* shake violently < *com-* (intensive) + *quatere* shake]

con de scen sion (kon/di sen/shən), *n.* 1. pleasantness to inferiors. 2. a patronizing attitude.

con firm (kən ferm/), *v.* 1. prove to be true or correct; make certain: *confirm a rumor.* 2. approve by formal consent; approve; consent to: *The Senate confirmed the treaty.* 3. strengthen; make firmer: *A sudden storm confirmed my decision not to leave.* 4. admit to full membership in a church after required study and preparation. [< OF < L *confirmare* < *com-* + *firmus* firm] —**con firm/a ble,** *adj.*

Syn. 1. **Confirm, corroborate** mean to prove to be true or genuine. **Confirm** means to make certain that something is true or correct, by facts or a statement that cannot be doubted: *The Mayor confirmed the report that he had resigned.* **Corroborate** means to make more certain that something suspected is true, by a statement or new evidence: *Finding the weapon corroborates the police theory.* 2. ratify, sanction.

con fla gra tion (kon/flə grā/shən), *n.* a big fire: *A conflagration destroyed most of the city.* [< L *conflagratio, -onis* < *conflagrare* < *com-* up + *flagrare* burn]

con i cal (kon/ə kəl), *adj.* 1. cone-shaped; like a cone. 2. a cone. —**con/i cal ly,** *adv.*

con jec tur al (kən jek/chər əl), *adj.* 1. involving conjecture. 2. inclined to conjecture.

con jec ture (kən jek/chər), *n., v.,* **-tured, -tur ing.** —*n.* 1. formation of an opinion admittedly without sufficient evidence for proof; guessing. 2. a guess. —*v.* guess. [< L *conjectura* < *conjicere* < *com-* together + *jacere* throw] —**con jec/tur a ble,** *adj.* —**con jec/tur er,** *n.*

Syn. *n.* 2. supposition. —*v.* suppose.

con jure (kon/jər, kun/jər *for 1-6;* kən jür/ *for 7*), *v.,* **-jured, -jur ing.** 1. **conjure up, a.** cause to appear in a magic way. **b.** cause to appear in the mind. 2. compel (a spirit, devil, etc.) to appear or disappear by magic words. 3. summon a devil, spirit, etc. 4. cause to be or happen by magic or as if by magic. 5. practice magic. 6. perform tricks by skill and quickness in moving the hands. 7. make a solemn appeal to; request earnestly; entreat: *I conjure you not to betray your country.* [< OF < L *conjurare* make a compact < *com-* together + *jurare* swear]

con jur er (kon/jər ər, kun/jər ər), *n.* 1. magician. 2. person who performs tricks with quick, deceiving movements of the hands; juggler.

con se quen tial (kon/sə kwen/shəl), *adj.* 1. following as an effect; resulting. 2. self-important; pompous. —**con/se quen/tial ly,** *adv.*

con serv a tive (kən ser/və tiv), *adj.* 1. inclined to keep things as they are; opposed to change. 2. Often, **Conservative.** of or belonging to a political party, especially the Conservative Party in Great Britain or Canada, that opposes changes in national institutions. 3. cautious; moderate: *conservative business methods.* 4. free from novelties and fads: *It is economy to choose suits of a conservative style.* 5. having the power to preserve from harm or decay; conserving; preserving. —*n.* 1. a conservative person. 2. Often, **Conservative.** member of a conservative political party, especially the Conservative Party in Great Britain or Canada. 3. means of preserving. —**con serv/a tive ly,** *adv.* —**con serv/a tive ness,** *n.*

con spic u ous (kən spik/yü əs), *adj.* 1. easily seen: *A traffic sign should be conspicuous.* 2. worthy of notice; remarkable: *Lincoln is a conspicuous example of a poor boy who succeeded.* [< L *conspicuus* visible < *conspicere* < *com-* + *specere* look at] —**con spic/u ous ly,** *adv.*

Syn. 1. noticeable. 2. notable, noteworthy. —**Ant.** 1. obscure.

con ster na tion (kon/stər nā/shən), *n.* great dismay; paralyzing terror: *To our consternation the train rushed on toward the burning bridge.* [< L *consternatio, -onis* < *con-*

< = from, derived from, taken from; cf., compare; dial., dialect; dim., diminutive; lang., language; pp., past participle; ppr., present participle; pt., past tense; ult., ultimately; var., variant; ? = possibly.

sternare terrify, var. of *consternere* lay low < *com-* + *sternere* strew]
Syn. See **dismay.**

con tempt (kən tempt′), *n.* 1. the feeling that a person, act, or thing is mean, low, or worthless; scorn; a despising: *We feel contempt for a liar.* 2. condition of being scorned or despised; disgrace: *A cowardly traitor is held in contempt.* 3. disobedience to or open disrespect for the rules or decisions of a law court, a lawmaking body, etc. A person can be put in jail for **contempt of court.** [< L *contemptus* < *contemnere*]
Syn. 1. disdain. See **scorn.**

con temp tu ous (kən temp′chü əs), *adj.* showing contempt; scornful: *a contemptuous look.* —**con temp′tu ous ly,** *adv.* —**con temp′tu ous ness,** *n.*

con tig u ous (kən tig′yü əs), *adj.* 1. in actual contact; touching: *A fence showed where the two farms were contiguous.* 2. adjoining; near. [< L *contiguus* < *com-* + *tag-,* root of *tangere* touch. Related to **contact.**] —**con tig′u ous ly,** *adv.* —**con tig′u ous ness,** *n.*

con tour (kon′tùr), *n.* outline of a figure: *The contour of the Atlantic coast of America is very irregular.* —*adj.* 1. showing the outlines of hills, valleys, etc.: *a contour map.* 2. following natural ridges and furrows to avoid erosion: *contour planting.*

con tri tion (kən trish′ən), *n.* 1. sorrow for one's sins or guilt; being contrite; sincere penitence. 2. deep regret.

con trive (kən triv′), *v.,* **-trived, -triv ing.** 1. invent; design: *contrive a new kind of engine.* 2. plan; scheme; plot: *contrive a robbery.* 3. manage; *I will contrive to be there by ten o'clock.* 4. bring about. [< OF *controver* < *con-* (< L *com-*) + *trover* find < L *turbare* stir up < *turba* commotion]
Syn. 1. devise.

con va les cence (kon′və les′ns), *n.* 1. a gradual recovery of health and strength after illness. 2. time during which one is convalescing.

con ven tion al (kən ven′shə nəl), *adj.* 1. depending on conventions; customary: *"Good morning" is a conventional greeting.* 2. formal; not natural; not original. 3. in art, following custom rather than nature. Flowers and leaves are used in a conventional design without any idea of making them look real.

con verge (kən vèrj′), *v.,* **-verged, -verg ing.** 1. tend to meet in a point. 2. turn toward each other: *If you look at the end of your nose, your eyes converge.* 3. come together; center: *The interest of all the students converged upon the celebration.* 4. cause to converge. [< LL *convergere* < L *com-* + *vergere* incline]

con vulse (kən vuls′), *v.,* **-vulsed, -vuls ing.** 1. shake violently: *An earthquake convulsed the island.* 2. cause violent disturbance in; disturb violently: *His face was convulsed with rage.* 3. throw into convulsions; shake with spasms of pain: *The sick child was convulsed before the doctor came.* 4. throw into a fit of laughter; cause to shake with laughter: *The clown convulsed the audience with his funny acts.*

con vul sion (kən vul′shən), *n.* 1. a violent, involuntary contracting and relaxing of the muscles; spasm: *The sick child's convulsions frightened its mother.* 2. fit of laughter. 3. a violent disturbance: *The country was undergoing a political convulsion.*

con vul sive (kən vul′siv), *adj.* 1. violently disturbing. 2. having convulsions. 3. producing convulsions.

co quet ry (kō′kə trē, kō ket′rē), *n., pl.* **-ries.** 1. flirting. 2. trifling.

cor net (kôr net′ *for 1;* kôr′nit, kôr net′ *for 2*), *n.* 1. a musical wind instrument somewhat like a trumpet, usually made of brass. It has three pistons that control the notes. 2. piece of paper rolled into a cone and twisted at one end, used to hold candy, nuts, etc.

cor nice (kôr′nis), *n., v.,* **-niced, -nic ing.** —*n.* 1. an ornamental molding that projects along the top of a wall, pillar, building, etc. 2. molding around the walls of a room just below the ceiling. —*v.* furnish or finish with a cornice.

cor re la tion (kôr′ə lā′shən, kor′ə lā′shən), *n.* 1. the mutual relation of two or more things: *There is a close correlation between climate and crops.* 2. a correlating or being correlated.

cor rob o rate (kə rob′ə rāt), *v.,* **-rat ed, -rat ing.** make more certain; confirm: *Witnesses corroborated the policeman's statement.* [< L *corroborare* strengthen < *com-* + *robur* oak] —**cor rob′o ra′tor,** *n.*
Syn. See **confirm.**

Cor te (kôr′tā)

cou die (kow′dyē), *n.* hat.

cow er (kou′ər), *v.* 1. crouch in fear or shame. 2. draw back tremblingly from another's threats, blows, etc. [< Scand. *kūra* sit moping]

crag gy (krag′ē), *adj.,* **-gi er, -gi est.** with many crags; rugged; rough. —**crag′gi ness,** *n.*

craw (krô), *n.* 1. crop of a bird or insect. 2. stomach of any animal. [ME *crawe*]

crest (krest), *n.* 1. comb, tuft, etc., on the head of a bird or animal. 2. decoration, plumes, etc., on the top of a helmet. 3. decoration at the top of a coat of arms. A family crest is sometimes put on silverware, dishes, letter paper, etc. 4. the top part; top of a hill, wave, etc.; ridge; peak; summit. [< OF *creste* < L *crista* tuft] —**crest′like′,** *adj.*

cre vasse (krə vas′), *n.* 1. a deep crack or crevice in the ice of a glacier. 2. *U.S.* break in the levee of a river, dike, or dam. [< F *crevasse* < OF *crevace.* Doublet of CREVICE.]

crev ice (krev′is), *n.* a narrow split or crack. [< OF *crevace* < VL *crepacia* < L *crepare* crack. Doublet of CREVASSE.]

crimp (krimp), *v.* press into small, narrow folds; make wavy: *The girl crimped her hair before going to the party.* —*n.* 1. a crimping. 2. something crimped; fold; wave. 3. a waved or curled lock of hair. 4. **put a crimp in,** *Slang.* interfere with; hinder. —**crimp′er,** *n.*

crop (krop), *n., v.,* **cropped, crop ping.** —*n.* 1. product grown or gathered for use, especially for use as food: *Wheat, corn, and cotton are three main crops of the United States.* 2. the whole amount (of wheat, corn, or the produce of any plant or tree) that is yielded in one season: *The potato crop was very small this year.* 3. anything like a crop; group; collection: *a crop of lies.* 4. clipped hair; a short haircut. 5. short whip with a loop instead of a lash. 6. handle of a whip. —*v.* 1. plant and cultivate a crop. 2. cut or bite off the top of: *Sheep crop grass very short.* 3. clip; cut short (the tail, ear, hair, edge of book, etc.). 4. **crop out** or **up, a.** appear; come to the surface. **b.** be shown unexpectedly. [OE *cropp* sprout, craw]

crypt (kript), *n.* an underground room or vault. The crypt beneath the main floor of a church was formerly often used as a burial place. [< L *crypta* < Gk. *krypte* vault < *kryptos* hidden]

crys tal lize (kris′tl īz), *v.,* **-lized, -liz ing.** 1. form into crystals; solidify into crystals: *Water crystallizes to form snow.* 2. form into definite shape: *His vague ideas crystallized into a clear plan.* 3. coat with sugar.

---

hat, āge, fär; let, bē, tèrm; it, īce; hot, gō, ôrder; oil, out; cup, pùt, rüle; ch, child; ng, long; th, thin; ͬH, then; zh, measure; ə represents *a* in about, *e* in taken, *i* in pencil, *o* in lemon, *u* in circus.

cu bi cle (kyü′bə kəl), *n.* a very small room or compartment. [< L *cubiculum* bedroom < *cubare* lie]

cull (kul), *v.* 1. pick out; select: *The lawyer culled important facts from the mass of evidence.* 2. pick over; make selections from. —*n.* something picked out as being inferior or worthless. Poor fruit, stale vegetables, and animals not up to standard are called culls.

Cu mae (kū′mē)

cur ry (kėr′ē), *v.*, **-ried, -ry ing.** 1. rub and clean (a horse, etc.) with a brush or currycomb. 2. prepare (tanned leather) for use by soaking, scraping, beating, coloring, etc. 3. curry favor, seek a person's favor by insincere flattery, constant attentions, etc.

curt (kėrt), *adj.* short; rudely brief; abrupt: *a curt way of talking.* [< L *curtus* cut short] —**curt′ly,** *adv.*

cut bank (kut′bangk′), *n.* the steep, overhanging wall of a meandering stream.

cut lass or **cut las** (kut′ləs), *n.* a short, heavy, slightly curved sword. [< F *coutelas* < L *culter* knife]

Cyc nus (sik′nus)

cyn i cal (sin′ə kəl), *adj.* 1. doubting the sincerity and goodness of others. 2. sneering; sarcastic. —**cyn′i cal ly,** *adv.* —**cyn′i cal ness,** *n.*
Syn. 1. **Cynical, pessimistic** means doubting and mistrustful. **Cynical** emphasizes the idea of doubting the honesty and sincerity of people and their motives for doing things: *People cannot make friends with a person who is cynical about friendship.* **Pessimistic** emphasizes the idea of always looking on the dark side of things and expecting the unpleasant or worst to happen: *He has a very pessimistic attitude toward the value of this work.*

dal ly (dal′ē), *v.*, **-lied, -ly ing.** 1. act in a playful manner: *The spring breeze dallies with the flowers.* 2. flirt (with danger, temptation, a person, etc.); trifle: *He dallied with the offer for days, but finally refused it.* 3. be idle; loiter. 4. waste (time).

Dan a us or **Dan a üs** (dan′ā əs)

Daph ne (daf′nē)

dap per (dap′ər), *adj.* 1. neat; trim; spruce. 2. small and active. [cf. MDutch *dapper* agile, strong]

deb o nair or **deb o naire** (deb′ə ner; deb′ə när′), *adj.* 1. gay; cheerful. 2. pleasant; courteous.

de bris or **dé bris** (də brē′, dä′brē; *esp. Brit.* deb′rē), *n.* 1. scattered fragments; ruins; rubbish: *The street was covered with debris from the explosion.* 2. in geology, a mass of fragments of rock, etc.: *the debris left by a glacier.*

de cease (di sēs′), *n.*, *v.*, **-ceased, -ceas ing.** —*n.* death. —*v.* die. [< F < L *decessus* < *decedere* < *de-* away + *cedere* go]

de cep tion (di sep′shən), *n.* 1. act of deceiving. 2. state of being deceived. 3. thing that deceives; illusion. 4. trick meant to deceive; fraud; sham.

dé cor (dā kôr′), *n.* 1. decoration. 2. scenery on a stage. [< F *décor* < *décorer* decorate]

de co rum (di kô′rəm, di kō′rəm), *n.* 1. propriety of action, speech, dress, etc.: *You behave with decorum when you do what is proper.* 2. observance or requirement of polite society. [< L *decorum* (that which is) seemly]

de crep it (di krep′it), *adj.* broken down or weakened by old age; old and feeble. [< L *decrepitus* broken down < *de- + crepare* creak] —**de crep′it ly,** *adv.*

de crep i tude (di krep′ə tüd, di krep′ə tyüd), *n.* fee-

bleness, usually from old age; decrepit condition; weakness.

def er ence (def′ər əns), *n.* 1. a yielding to the judgment or opinion of another; courteous submission. 2. great respect. 3. **in deference to,** out of respect for the wishes or authority of.

def er en tial (def′ə ren′shəl), *adj.* showing deference; respectful. —**def′e ren′tial ly,** *adv.*

de fin i tive (di fin′ə tiv), *adj.* 1. conclusive; final. 2. limiting; defining. —*n.* word that limits or defines a noun. *The, this, all, none,* etc., are definitives. —**de fin′i tive ly,** *adv.* —**de fin′i tive ness,** *n.*

deft (deft), *adj.* skillful; nimble: *The fingers of a violinist or surgeon are deft.* —**deft′ly,** *adv.*

deign (dān), *v.* 1. condescend; think fit: *So great a man would never deign to notice such petty criticisms.* 2. condescend to give (an answer, a reply, etc.).

de ject ed (di jek′tid), *adj.* in low spirits; sad; discouraged. —**de ject′ed ly,** *adv.* —**de ject′ed ness,** *n.*

de lib er ate (*adj.* di lib′ər it; *v.* di lib′ə rāt), *adj.*, *v.*, **-at ed, -at ing.** —*adj.* 1. carefully thought out; made or done on purpose: *His excuse was a deliberate lie.* 2. slow and careful in deciding what to do: *A deliberate person takes a long time to make up his mind.* 3. not hurried; slow: *The old man walked with deliberate steps.* —*v.* 1. think over carefully; consider. 2. discuss reasons for and against something; debate.

de lib er a tion (di lib′ə rā′shən), *n.* 1. careful thought. 2. discussion of reasons for and against something; debate: *the deliberations of Congress.* 3. slowness and care: *The hunter aimed his gun with great deliberation.* 4. slowness.

de lir i um (di lir′ē əm), *n.*, *pl.* **-lir i ums, -lir i a** (-lir′ē ə). 1. a temporary disorder of the mind that occurs during fevers, insanity, drunkenness, etc. Delirium is characterized by excitement, irrational talk, and hallucinations. 2. any wild excitement that cannot be controlled. [< L *delirium* < *delirare* rave, be crazy < *de lira* (*ire*) (go) out of the furrow (in plowing)]

de lude (di lüd′), *v.*, **-lud ed, -lud ing.** mislead; deceive. [< L *deludere* < *de-* (to the detriment of) + *ludere* play] —**de lud′er,** *n.*

de lu sion (di lü′zhən), *n.* 1. act of deluding. 2. state of being deluded. 3. a false notion or belief: *The insane man had a delusion that he was the king.* 4. a fixed belief maintained in spite of unquestionable evidence to the contrary. [< L *delusio, -onis* < *deludere.* See DELUDE.]
Syn. 1. deception. 3. See **illusion.**

de mean or (di mē′nər), *n.* way a person looks and acts; behavior; conduct; manner.

de mer it (dē mer′it), *n.* 1. fault; defect. 2. mark against a person's record for poor work or unsatisfactory behavior.

De me ter (di mē′tər)

de mor al ize (di môr′əl īz, di mor′əl īz), *v.*, **-ized, -iz ing.** 1. corrupt the morals of: *The drug habit demoralizes people.* 2. weaken the spirit, courage, or discipline of; dishearten: *Lack of food and ammunition demoralized the besieged soldiers.* 3. throw into confusion or disorder: *Threats of war demoralized the stock market.* [Am.E]

de mure (di myúr′), *adj.*, **-mur er, -mur est.** 1. artificially proper; assuming an air of modesty; coy: *the demure smile of a flirt.* 2. serious; thoughtful; sober: *The Puritan maid was demure.* —**de mure′ly,** *adv.*

de plete (di plēt′), *v.*, **-plet ed, -plet ing.** empty; exhaust: *Because the traveler's funds were depleted, he went home.* [< L *depletus,* pp. of *deplere* empty < *de- + -plere* fill]

de plore (di plôr′, di plōr′), *v.*, **-plored, -plor ing.** be

---

< = from, derived from, taken from;   cf., compare;   dial., dialect;   dim., diminutive;   lang., language; pp., past participle;   ppr., present participle;   pt., past tense;   ult., ultimately;   var., variant;   ? = possibly.

very sorry about; regret deeply; lament. [< L *deplorare* < *de-* + *plorare* weep]
Syn. bewail, bemoan.

de ploy (di ploi′), *v.* spread out (troops, military units, etc.) from a column into a long battle line. [< F *déployer* < *dé-* (< L *dis-*) + *ployer* < L *plicare* fold] **—de ploy′ment,** *n.*

de port (di pôrt′, di pōrt′), *v.* 1. banish; expel; remove. When an alien is deported, he is sent out of the country, usually back to his native land. 2. behave or conduct (oneself) in a particular manner: *The boys were trained to deport themselves like gentlemen.* [< F *déporter* < L *deportare* < *de-* away + *portare* carry]

dep o si tion (dep′ə zish′ən, dē′pə zish′ən), *n.* 1. act of putting out of office or a position of authority; removal from a throne. 2. testimony. 3. a sworn statement in writing: *A deposition made before the witness left town was used as evidence in the trial.* 4. act of depositing. 5. thing deposited; deposit.

dep re da tion (dep′rə dā′shən), *n.* act of plundering; robbery; a ravaging. [< L *depraedatio, -onis* < *depraedare* pillage < *de-* + *praeda* booty]

de prive (di priv′), *v.,* **-prived, -priv ing.** 1. take away from by force: *The people deprived the cruel king of his power.* 2. keep from having or doing: *Worrying deprived him of sleep.* [< OF *depriver* < *de-* (< L *de-*) + *priver* deprive < L *privare*, originally, exempt]
Syn. 1. dispossess, divest.

de pute (di pyüt′), *v.,* **-put ed, -put ing.** 1. appoint to do one's work or to act in one's place. 2. give (work, authority, etc.) to another.

de ri sion (di rizh′ən), *n.* 1. scornful laughter; ridicule; contempt. 2. an object of ridicule.

de ri sive (di rī′siv), *adj.* mocking; ridiculing. **—de ri′sive ly,** *adv.* **—de ri′sive ness,** *n.*

der ma tol o gist (dèr′mə tol′ə jist), *n.* expert in dermatology.

der ma tol o gy (dèr′mə tol′ə jē), *n.* science that deals with the skin and its diseases.

des pi ca ble (des′pi kə bəl, des pik′ə bəl), *adj.* to be despised; contemptible.

des ul to ry (des′əl tôr′ē, des′əl tōr′ē), *adj.* jumping from one thing to another; unconnected; without aim or method: *The careful study of a few books is better than the desultory reading of many.*

de te ri o rate (di tir′ē ə rāt), *v.,* **-rat ed, -rat ing.** 1. become worse; lessen in value; depreciate: *Machinery deteriorates if it is not given good care.* 2. make worse.

de te ri o ra tion (di tir′ē ə rā′shən), *n.* 1. a deteriorating. 2. condition of having deteriorated.

de ter mi nate (di tèr′mə nit), *adj.* 1. with exact limits; fixed; definite. 2. settled; positive. 3. determined; resolute.

de vi ous (dē′vē əs), *adj.* 1. winding; twisting; roundabout: *We took a devious route through side streets and alleys to avoid the crowded main streets.* 2. straying from the right course; not straightforward; going astray: *His devious nature was shown in half-lies and small dishonesties.* [< L *devius* < *de-* out of + *via* the way] **—de′vi ous ness,** *n.*

di a bol ic (dī′ə bol′ik), *adj.* 1. devilish; like the Devil; very cruel or wicked; fiendish. 2. having to do with the Devil or devils. **—di′a bol′i cal ly,** *adv.*

di a bol i cal (dī′ə bol′ə kəl), *adj.* diabolic.

di a tribe (dī′ə trīb), *n.* a bitter and violent denunciation of some person or thing. [< L *diatriba* < Gk. *diatribe* pastime, study, discourse < *dia-* away + *tribein* wear]

dic ta tor (dik′tā tər, dik tā′tər), *n.* 1. person exercising absolute authority; especially, a person who, without having any claim through inheritance or free popular election, seizes control of a government: *The dictator of the country had complete power over its people.* 2. person who says or reads words aloud to another who writes them down.

dic ta to ri al (dik′tə tôr′ē əl, dik′tə tōr′ē əl), *adj.* 1. of or like that of a dictator: *dictatorial government.* 2. imperious; domineering; overbearing: *The soldiers disliked the dictatorial manner of that officer.* **—dic′ta to′ri al ly,** *adv.*

dig ni fied (dig′nə fid), *adj.* having dignity; noble; stately. **—dig′ni fied′ly,** *adv.*

di lap i dat ed (də lap′ə dā′tid), *adj.* falling to pieces; partly ruined or decayed through neglect.

di min u tive (də min′yə tiv), *adj.* 1. small; little; tiny. 2. expressing smallness. **—***n.* 1. a small person or thing. 2. word or part of a word expressing smallness. The suffixes *-let* and *-kin* are diminutives.

Di o me des (dī′ə mē′dēz)

Di o ny sus or **Di o ny sos** (dī′ə nī′səs)

dire (dīr), *adj.,* **dir er, dir est.** causing great fear or suffering; dreadful. **—dire′ly,** *adv.* **—dire′ness,** *n.*

dis con cert (dis′kən sèrt′), *v.* 1. disturb the self-possession of; embarrass greatly; confuse: *His arrest of the wrong man disconcerted the policeman.* 2. upset; disorder: *The chairman's plans were disconcerted by the late arrival of the speaker.* **—dis′con cert′ing ly,** *adv.*

dis creet (dis krēt′), *adj.* careful and sensible in speech and action; wisely cautious; showing good sense. **—dis creet′ly,** *adv.* **—dis creet′ness,** *n.*
Syn. prudent, wary.

dis em bod y (dis′em bod′ē), *v.,* **-bod ied, -bod y ing.** separate (a soul, spirit, etc.) from the body: *Ghosts are usually thought of as disembodied spirits.*

dis em bow el (dis′em bou′əl), *v.,* **-eled, -el ing** or *esp.* Brit. **-elled, -el ling.** take or rip out the bowels of. **—dis′em bow′el ment,** *n.*

dis grun tled (dis grun′tld), *adj.* in bad humor; discontented; disgusted; displeased. [< *dis-* + obsolete *gruntle* to grunt, grumble]

dis may (dis mā′), *n.* loss of courage because of fear of what is about to happen. [< *v.*] **—***v.* trouble greatly; make afraid: *The thought that she might fail the history test dismayed her.* [ME *desmaye(n)* < OF (unrecorded) *desmaier* < VL *dismagare* deprive of strength < L *dis-* + Frankish (unrecorded) *magan* have strength]
Syn. *n.* Dismay, consternation mean a feeling of being unnerved or overwhelmed by the thought of what is going to happen next. **Dismay** suggests loss of ability to face or handle something frightening, baffling, or upsetting that comes as a surprise or shock: *The mother was filled with dismay when her son confessed he had robbed a store.* **Dismay** is often used in a weakened sense: *To my dismay, my son gave up literature for mathematics.* **Consternation** means dismay and dread so great that a person cannot think clearly, or sometimes, move: *To our consternation the child darted out in front of the speeding car.*

dis sec tion (di sek′shən, dī sek′shən), *n.* 1. act of separating or dividing an animal or plant into parts in order to examine or study the structure. 2. animal, plant, etc., that has been dissected. 3. analysis; consideration of something in detail or point by point.

dis sem ble (di sem′bəl), *v.,* **-bled, -bling.** 1. disguise or hide (one's real feelings, thoughts, plans, etc.): *She dissembled her anger with a smile.* 2. conceal one's motives, etc.;

---

hat, āge, fär;　let, bē, tèrm;　it, īce;　hot, gō, ôrder;　oil, out;　cup, pùt, rüle;　ch, child;　ng, long; th, thin;　ŦH, then;　zh, measure;　ə represents *a* in about, *e* in taken, *i* in pencil, *o* in lemon, *u* in circus.

be a hypocrite. **3.** pretend; feign: *The bored listener dissembled an interest he didn't feel.* **4.** pretend not to see or notice; disregard; ignore.

dis sim i lar (di sim′ə lər), *adj.* not similar; unlike; different. **—dis sim′i lar ly,** *adv.*

dis sim u la tion (di sim′yə lā′shən), *n.* act of dissembling; hypocrisy; pretense; deceit.

dis so ci ate (di sō′shē āt), *v.,* **-at ed, -at ing. 1.** break the connection or association with; separate: *When the honest man discovered that his companions were thieves he dissociated himself from them.* **2.** in chemistry, separate or decompose by dissociation. [< L *dissociare* < *dis-* apart + *socius* ally]

dis tem per (dis tem′pər), *n.* **1.** an infectious disease of dogs and other animals, accompanied by a short, dry cough and a loss of strength. **2.** sickness of the mind or body; disorder; disease. **3.** disturbance. [< v.] **—v.** make unbalanced; disturb; disorder. [< LL *distemperare* mix improperly < L *dis-* not + *temperare* mix in proper proportion]

dis tort (dis tôrt′), *v.* **1.** pull or twist out of shape; change the normal appearance of: *Rage distorted his face.* **2.** change from the truth: *The man distorted the facts of the accident to escape blame.*
Syn. 1. contort. **2.** misrepresent, falsify.

dis tor tion (dis tôr′shən), *n.* **1.** a distorting: *A lie is a distortion of the truth.* **2.** fact or state of being distorted. **3.** anything distorted.

di vers (dī′vərz), *adj.* several different; various. [< OF < L *diversus,* pp. of *divertere.* See DIVERT.]

di ver si ty (də vėr′sə tē, dī vėr′sə tē), *n., pl.* **-ties. 1.** complete difference; unlikeness. **2.** variety.

di vert (də vėrt′, dī vėrt′), *v.* **1.** turn aside: *A ditch diverted water from the stream into the fields.* **2.** amuse; entertain: *Music diverted him after a hard day's work.* [< F *divertir* < L *divertere* < *dis-* aside + *vertere* turn]

doc ile (dos′əl, *esp. Brit.* dō′sīl, dos′īl), *adj.* **1.** easily managed; obedient. **2.** easily taught; willing to learn. [< F < L *docilis* < *docere* teach] **—doc′ile ly,** *adv.*

dog wood (dôg′wůd′, dog′wůd′), *n.* **1.** tree with large white or pinkish flowers in the spring and red berries, called **dogwood berries,** in the fall. **2.** its hard wood. **3.** any tree of the same family as the dogwood.

dole ful (dōl′fəl), *adj.* sad; mournful; dreary; dismal. **—dole′ful ly,** *adv.* **—dole′ful ness,** *n.*
Syn. sorrowful, woeful, plaintive.

do min ion (də min′yən), *n.* **1.** supreme authority; rule; control. **2.** territory under the control of one ruler or government. **3.** a self-governing territory.

dot age (dō′tij), *n.* weak-minded and childish condition caused by old age. [< *dote*]

dour (důr, dour), *adj.* **1.** gloomy; sullen. **2.** *Scottish.* stern; severe. **3.** *Scottish.* stubborn. [< L *durus* hard, stern] **—dour′ly,** *adv.* **—dour′ness,** *n.*

drum mer (drum′ər), *n.* **1.** person who plays a drum. **2.** *U.S. Informal.* a traveling salesman.

du bi ous (dü′bē əs, dyü′bē əs), *adj.* **1.** doubtful; uncertain: *a dubious compliment, dubious authorship, a dubious friend.* **2.** of questionable character; probably bad: *a dubious scheme for making money.* [< L *dubiosus* < *dubius* doubtful < *du-* two] **—du′bi ous ly,** *adv.* **—du′bi ous ness,** *n.*

dun (dun), *n., adj.* dull, grayish brown. [OE *dunn,* ? < Celtic]

du o dec i mo (dü′ō des′ə mō, dyü′ō des′ə mō), *n., pl.* **-mos,** *adj.* **—n. 1.** the page size of a book in which each leaf is one twelfth of a whole sheet of paper, or about 5 by 7¹/₂ inches. **2.** book having pages of this size. **—adj.** having pages of this size. [< L *in duodecimo* in a twelfth]

dupe (düp, dyüp), *n., v.,* **duped, dup ing. —n. 1.** person easily deceived or tricked. **2.** one who is being deluded or tricked: *The young politician's inexperience is making him the dupe of some unscrupulous schemers.* **—v.** deceive; trick. [< F < L *upupa* hoopoe (a bird)] **—dup′er,** *n.*

du qua ni (dü kwä′ni), *n.* inn frequented by peasants.

ebb (eb), *n.* **1.** a flowing of the tide away from the shore; fall of the tide. **2.** a growing less or weaker; decline. **3.** point of decline: *His fortunes were at an ebb.* **—v. 1.** flow out; fall: *We waded farther out as the tide ebbed.* **2.** grow less or weaker; decline: *His courage began to ebb as he neared the haunted house.* [OE *ebba*]
Syn. *v.* **2.** wane, decrease.

ec cen tric i ty (ek′sen tris′ə tē), *n., pl.* **-ties. 1.** something queer or out of the ordinary; oddity; peculiarity. **2.** eccentric condition; being unusual or out of the ordinary.

ed dy (ed′ē), *n., pl.* **-dies.** water, air, etc., moving against the main current, especially when having a whirling motion; small whirlpool or whirlwind. [? < OE *ed-* turning + *ēa* stream]

ed i ble (ed′ə bəl), *adj.* fit to eat. **—n.** Usually, **edibles,** *pl.* things fit to eat.

ef face (ə fās′), *v.,* **-faced, -fac ing. 1.** rub out; blot out; do away with; destroy; wipe out: *The inscriptions on many ancient monuments have been effaced by time. It takes many years to efface the unpleasant memories of a war.* **2.** keep (oneself) from being noticed; make inconspicuous: *The shy boy effaced himself by staying in the background.* **—ef face′a ble,** *adj.*

ef fu sive (i fyü′siv), *adj.* showing too much feeling; too emotional in expression.

e go tism (ē′gə tiz əm, eg′ə tiz əm), *n.* **1.** excessive use of *I, my,* and *me;* habit of thinking, talking, or writing too much of oneself. **2.** self-conceit. **3.** selfishness.

e jac u late (i jak′yə lāt), *v.,* **-lat ed, -lat ing. 1.** say suddenly and briefly; exclaim. **2.** eject; discharge. [< L *ejaculari* < *ex-* out + *jaculum* javelin < *jacere* throw]

e lab o rate (*adj.* i lab′ər it; *v.* i lab′ə rāt), *adj., v.,* **-at ed, -at ing. —adj.** worked out with great care; having many details; complicated. **—v. 1.** work out with great care; add details to: *The inventor spent months in elaborating his plans for a new engine.* **2.** talk, write, etc., in great detail; give added details: *The witness was asked to elaborate upon one of his statements.* **3.** make with labor; produce. [< L *elaboratus,* pp. of *elaborare* < *ex-* out + *labor* work] **—e lab′or ate ly,** *adv.* **—e lab′or ate ness,** *n.*

e lic it (i lis′it), *v.* draw forth: *elicit a reply, elicit applause, elicit the truth.* [< L *elicitus,* pp. of *elicere* < *ex-* out + *lacere* entice]

em a nate (em′ə nāt), *v.,* **-nat ed, -nat ing.** come forth: *Fragrance emanated from the flowers. The rumor emanated from Chicago.* [< L *emanare* < *ex-* out + *manare* flow]

em i grate (em′ə grāt), *v.,* **-grat ed, -grat ing.** leave one's own country or region to settle in another. [< L *emigrare* < *ex-* out + *migrare* to move]

em i nent (em′ə nənt), *adj.* **1.** distinguished; exalted: *Washington was eminent both as general and as President.* **2.** conspicuous; noteworthy: *The judge was a man of eminent fairness.* **3.** high; lofty. **4.** prominent; projecting.

< = from, derived from, taken from; cf., compare; dial., dialect; dim., diminutive; lang., language; pp., past participle; ppr., present participle; pt., past tense; ult., ultimately; var., variant; ? = possibly.

en croach (en krōch′), v. 1. go beyond proper or usual limits: *The sea encroached upon the shore and submerged the beach.* 2. trespass upon the property or rights of another; intrude: *He is a good salesman and will not encroach upon his customer's time.*

en croach ment (en krōch′mənt), n. 1. an encroaching. 2. thing taken by encroaching.

en cum ber (en kum′bər), v. 1. hold back (from running, doing, etc.); hinder; hamper: *Heavy shoes encumber anybody in the water.* 2. make difficult to use; fill; obstruct: *Rubbish and old boxes encumbered the fire escape.* 3. weigh down; burden: *The farm was encumbered with a heavy mortgage.* Also, **incumber.**

end gate (end′ gāt′), n. *U.S.* tailgate; the movable board used to close the rear end of a wagon or truck.

en dow (en dou′), v. 1. give money or property to provide an income for: *The rich man endowed the college he had attended.* 2. furnish from birth; provide with some ability, quality, or talent: *Nature endowed her with both beauty and brains.* **Syn.** 2. furnish, equip, invest.

en dow ment (en dou′mənt), n. 1. an endowing. 2. money or property given to provide an income: *This college has a large endowment.* 3. gift from birth; ability; talent: *A good sense of rhythm is a natural endowment.*

en dur ance (en dūr′əns, en dyūr′əns), n. 1. power to last or keep on: *A man must have great endurance to run 30 miles in a day. Cheap, shoddy cloth has little endurance.* 2. power to put up with, bear, or stand: *His endurance of the pain was remarkable.* 3. act or instance of enduring pain, hardship, etc. 4. duration. **Syn.** 2. fortitude, patience, forbearance, tolerance.

en globe (en glōb′), v., **-globed, -glob ing.** 1. enclose in a globe or sphere. 2. form into a sphere.

en graft (en graft′), v. 1. insert or graft (a shoot from one tree or plant) into or on another: *Peach trees can be engrafted upon plum trees.* 2. add permanently; implant: *Honesty and thrift are engrafted in his character.* Also, **ingraft.**

en nui (än′wē), n. a feeling of weariness and discontent from lack of occupation or interest; boredom. [< F. Related to *annoy.*]

en sue (en sü′), v., **-sued, -su ing.** 1. come after; follow: *The ensuing year means the next year.* 2. happen as a result: *In his anger he hit the man, and a fight ensued.* **Syn.** succeed, result.

en tice (en tīs′), v., **-ticed, -tic ing.** tempt by arousing hopes or desires; attract by offering some pleasure or reward: *The robber enticed his victims into a cave by promising to show them a gold mine.*

en trails (en′trālz, en′trəlz), n. pl. 1. the inner parts of a man or animal. 2. intestines; bowels. 3. any inner parts.

en treat y (en trēt′ē), n., pl. **-treat ies.** an earnest request; prayer: *The savages paid no attention to their captives' entreaties for mercy.* **Syn.** supplication, appeal, solicitation, suit, petition.

é pée (ā pā′, e pā′), n. a fencing and dueling sword characterized by a thin, pointed blade without a cutting edge. [< F *épée* < OF *espee* < L *spatha* < Gk. *spáthē* blade, sword]

ep i logue (ep′ə lôg, ep′ə log), n. 1. concluding section added to a novel, poem, etc., which serves to round out or interpret the work. 2. speech or poem after the end of a play. It is addressed to the audience and is spoken by one of the actors. [< F *épilogue* < L < Gk. *epilogos*, ult. < *epi-* in addition + *legein* speak]

ep i taph (ep′ə taf), n. a short statement in memory of a dead person, usually put on his tombstone. [< L < Gk. *epitaphion* funeral oration < *epi-* at + *taphos* tomb]

ep i tha la mic (ep′ə thə lā′mik), adj. of marriage.

Er i gi nus (er i jī′nus)

E ros (ir′os, er′os)

E ry man thi a (er′i man′thē ə)

Er y thi a or **Er y the a** (er i thē′ə)

es o ter ic (es′ə ter′ik), adj. 1. understood only by the select few; intended for an inner circle of disciples, scholars, etc. 2. private; secret; confidential.

Eu boe a (yü bē′ə)

Eu sta chi an tube (yü stā′kē ən, yü stā′shən), a slender canal between the pharynx and the middle ear. It equalizes the air pressure on the two sides of the eardrum. [from Bartolommeo *Eustachio,* 16th c. Italian anatomist]

e vac u a tion (i vak′yü ā′shən), n. 1. a leaving empty; withdrawal from occupation or possession; act or process of evacuating. 2. removal.

e volve (i volv′), v., **e volved, e volv ing.** 1. develop gradually; work out: *The boys evolved a plan for earning money during their summer vacation.* 2. develop by a process of growth and change to a more highly organized condition. 3. release; give off; set free.

ex alt (eg zôlt′), v. 1. raise in rank, honor, power, character, quality, etc.: *We exalt a man when we elect him President of our country.* 2. fill with pride, joy, or noble feeling. 3. praise; honor; glorify.

ex e cu tion er (ek′sə kyü′shə nər), n. person who puts criminals to death according to law.

ex em pla ry (eg zem′plə rē, eg′zəm pler′ē), adj. 1. worth imitating; being a good model or pattern: *exemplary conduct.* 2. serving as a warning to others: *exemplary punishment of the ringleaders.* 3. serving as an example; typical. [< L *exemplaris* < *exemplum*]

ex hil a rate (eg zil′ə rāt), v. **-rat ed, -rat ing.** make merry or lively; put into high spirits; stimulate. [< L *exhilarare* < *ex-* thoroughly + *hilaris* merry]

ex hil a ra tion (eg zil′ə rā′shən), n. 1. an exhilarating. 2. a being or feeling exhilarated; high spirits; stimulation.

ex pend (ek spend′), v. spend; use up. [< L *expendere* < *ex-* out + *pendere* weigh, pay. Doublet of SPEND.] —**es pend′er,** n. **Syn.** disburse, consume.

ex ploit (n. ek′sploit, ek sploit′; v. ek sploit′), n. a bold, unusual act; daring deed: *Old stories tell about the exploits of famous heroes.* —v. 1. make use of; turn to practical account: *A mine is exploited for its minerals.* 2. make unfair use of; use selfishly for one's own advantage: *Nations sometimes exploit their colonies, taking as much wealth out of them as they can.* [< OF *esploit* < VL *explicitum* achievement < L *explicitum,* pp. neut. of *explicare* unfold, settle.] —**ex ploit′a ble,** adj. —**ex ploit′er,** n.

ex tinct (ek stingkt′), adj. 1. no longer in existence: *The dinosaur is an extinct animal.* 2. no longer active; extinguished: *an extinct volcano.* **Syn.** 1. dead.

ex trav a gant (ek strav′ə gənt), adj. 1. spending carelessly and lavishly; wasteful: *An extravagant person usually has extravagant tastes and habits.* 2. beyond the bounds of reason; excessive: *People laughed at the inventor's extravagant praise of his invention. He refused to buy the ring because of the extravagant price.*

ex trem i ty (ek strem′ə tē), n., pl. **-ties.** 1. the very end; farthest possible place; last part or point. 2. extreme need,

hat, āge, fär; let, bē, tèrm; it, īce; hot, gō, ôrder; oil, out; cup, pùt, rüle; ch, child; ng, long; th, thin; ᴛʜ, then; zh, measure; ə represents *a* in about, *e* in taken, *i* in pencil, *o* in lemon, *u* in circus.

danger, suffering, etc.: *In their extremity the people on the sinking ship bore themselves bravely.* **3.** an extreme degree. **4.** an extreme action: *The soldiers were forced to the extremity of firing their rifles to scatter the angry mob.* **5. extremities,** *pl.* **hands and feet.**
Syn. 1. termination.

ex tri cate (ek′strə kāt), *v.,* **-cat ed, -cat ing.** set free (from entanglements, difficulties, embarrassing situations, etc.); release: *Tom extricated his younger brother from the barbed-wire fence.* [< L *extricare* < *ex-* out of + *tricae* perplexities] —**ex′tri ca′tion,** *n.*

ex u ber ant (eg zü′bər ənt), *adj.* **1.** very abundant; overflowing; lavish: *exuberant health, good nature, or joy; an exuberant welcome.* **2.** profuse in growth; luxuriant: *the exuberant vegetation of the jungle.* —**ex u′ber ant ly,** *adv.*

ex ult (eg zult′), *v.* be very glad; rejoice greatly: *The winners exulted in their victory.*

ex ult ant (eg zult′nt), *adj.* rejoicing greatly; exulting; triumphant: *He gave an exultant shout.*

face (fās), *n., v.,* **faced, fac ing.** —*n.* **1.** the front part of the head. **2.** look; expression: *His face was sad.* **3.** an ugly or peculiar look made by distorting the face. **4.** outward appearance. **5.** the front part; right side; surface: *the face of a clock, the whole face of the earth.* **6.** *Informal.* boldness; impudence. **7.** personal importance; dignity; self-respect: *Face is very important to Oriental peoples.* **8.** the stated value: *The face of the note was $100, but $73 was all that anybody would pay for it.* —*v.* **1.** have the face (toward); be opposite (to). **2.** turn the face (toward). **3.** cause to face. **4.** meet face to face; stand before. **5.** meet bravely or boldly; oppose and resist: *The soldiers faced the enemy.* **6.** present itself to: *A crisis faced us.* **7.** cover or line with a different material: *a wooden house faced with brick.*

fain (fān), *Archaic* and *Poetic.* —*adv.* by choice; gladly. —*adj.* **1.** willing, but not eager; forced by circumstances. **2.** glad; willing. **3.** circumstances. **2.** glad; willing. **3.** eager; desirous. [OE *fægen*]

fast ness (fast′nis), *n.* **1.** a strong, safe place; stronghold. **2.** a being fast.

fa tal ism (fā′tl iz əm), *n.* **1.** belief that fate controls everything that happens. **2.** submission to everything that happens as inevitable.

fa tal ist (fā′tl ist), *n.* believer in fatalism.

fate (fāt), *n.* **1.** power supposed to fix beforehand and control everything that happens. Fate is beyond any person's control. **2.** what is caused by fate. **3.** one's lot or fortune. **4.** what becomes of a person or thing: *The jury settled the fate of the accused.* **5.** death; ruin. [< L *fatum* (thing) spoken (i.e., by the gods), pp. neut. of *fari* speak]

fate ful (fāt′fəl), *adj.* **1.** controlled by fate. **2.** determining what is to happen; important; decisive. **3.** showing what fate decrees; prophetic. **4.** causing death, destruction, or ruin; disastrous. —**fate′ful ly,** *adv.* —**fate′ful ness,** *n.*

fat u ous (fach′ü əs), *adj.* stupid but self-satisfied; foolish; silly. [< L *fatuus* foolish] —**fat′u ous ly,** *adv.* —**fat′u ous ness,** *n.*

fau na (fô′nə), *n.* animals of a given region or time: *the fauna of Australia, the fauna of the carboniferous age.* [< NL *fauna,* originally (in LL) name of a rural goddess]

feat (fēt), *n.* a great or unusual deed; act showing great skill, strength, etc.

feint (fānt), *n.* **1.** a false appearance; pretense: *The boy made a feint of studying hard, though actually he was*

listening to the radio. **2.** movement intended to deceive; pretended blow; sham attack. —*v.* make a pretended blow or sham attack: *The fighter feinted with his right hand and struck with his left.*

fer ret (fer′it), *n.* a white or yellowish-white weasel used for killing rats, hunting rabbits, etc. —*v.* **1.** hunt with ferrets. **2.** hunt; search: *The detectives ferreted out the criminal.* [< OF *fuiret,* ult < L *fur* thief]

fer vid (fer′vid), *adj.* **1.** showing great warmth of feeling; intensely emotional. **2.** intensely hot. [< L *fervidus* < *fervere* boil] —**fer′vid ly,** *adv.*

fes toon (fe stün′), *n.* **1.** a hanging curve of flowers, leaves, ribbons, etc.: *The flags were hung on the wall in colorful festoons.* **2.** a carved or molded ornament like this on furniture, pottery, etc. —*v.* **1.** decorate with festoons: *The Christmas tree was festooned with tinsel.* **2.** form into festoons; hang in curves: *Draperies were festooned over the window.*

fet lock (fet′lok), *n.* **1.** tuft of hair above a horse's hoof on the back part of the leg. **2.** part of a horse's leg where this tuft grows. [ME *fetlok*] See **pastern** for diagram.

fet ter (fet′ər), *n.* **1.** chain or shackle for the feet to prevent escape. **2.** Usually, **fetters,** *pl.* anything that shackles or binds; restraint. —*v.* **1.** bind with fetters; chain the feet of. **2.** bind; restrain. [OE *feter.* Related to *foot.*]
Syn. *v.* **2.** confine, hamper, impede.

fi as co (fē as′kō), *n., pl.* **-cos** or **-coes.** failure; breakdown.

fis sure (fish′ər), *n., v.,* **-sured, -sur ing.** —*n.* **1.** split or crack; long, narrow opening: *a fissure in a rock.* **2.** a splitting apart; division into parts. —*v.* split apart; divide into parts. [< F < L *fissura* < *findere* cleave]

flail (flāl), *n.* instrument for threshing grain by hand. A flail consists of a wooden handle with a short, heavy stick fastened at one end by a thong. —*v.* **1.** strike with a flail. **2.** beat; thrash. [OE *fligel*]

flaw less (flô′lis), *adj.* perfect; without a flaw. —**flaw′less ly,** *adv.* —**flaw′less ness,** *n.*

fledg ling or **fledge ling** (flej′ling), *n.* **1.** a young bird just able to fly. **2.** a young, inexperienced person.

flor id (flôr′id, flor′id), *adj.* **1.** highly colored; ruddy: *a florid complexion.* **2.** elaborately ornamented; flowery; showy; ornate. [< L *floridus* < *flos* flower]

flot sam (flot′səm), *n.* **1.** wreckage of a ship or its cargo found floating on the sea. **2. flotsam and jetsam, a.** wreckage or cargo found floating on the sea or washed ashore. **b.** odds and ends; useless things. **c.** people without steady work or permanent homes.

flu ent (flü′ənt), *adj.* **1.** flowing smoothly or easily: *Long practice enabled the American to speak fluent French.* **2.** speaking or writing easily and rapidly. [< L *fluens, -entis,* ppr. of *fluere* flow] —**flu′ent ly,** *adv.*

foal (fōl), *n.* a young horse, donkey, etc.; colt or filly.

foil¹ (foil), *v.* prevent from carrying out (plans, attempts, etc.); get the better of; turn aside or hinder: *The hero foiled the villain.* [< OF *fouler* trample, full (cloth) < VL *fullare* < L *fullo* a fuller; with reference to spoiling a trace or scent by crossing it]
Syn. frustrate.

foil² (foil), *n.* **1.** metal beaten, hammered, or rolled into a very thin sheet: *Candy is sometimes wrapped in tin foil to keep it fresh.* **2.** anything that makes something else look or seem better by contrast. **3.** a very thin layer of polished metal, placed under a gem to give it more color or sparkle. **4.** in architecture, a leaflike ornament; arc or rounded space between cusps. [< F < L *folia* leaves]

< = from, derived from, taken from;   cf., compare;   dial., dialect;   dim., diminutive;   lang., language; pp., past participle;   ppr., present participle;   pt., past tense;   ult., ultimately;   var., variant;   ? = possibly.

foil³ (foil), *n.* **1.** a long, narrow sword with a knob or button on the point to prevent injury, used in fencing. **2. foils,** *pl.* fencing. [origin uncertain]

fo li o (fō′lē ō), *n., pl.* **-li os,** *adj.* —*n.* **1.** a large sheet of paper folded once to make two leaves, or four pages, of a book, etc. **2.** book of the largest size, having pages made by folding large sheets of paper once; large volume. A folio is usually any book more than 11 inches in height. **3.** in printing, a page number of a book, etc. **4.** leaf of a book, manuscript, etc., numbered on the front side only. **5. in folio,** of folio size or form. —*adj.* of the largest size; made of large sheets of paper folded once: *The encyclopedia was in twenty volumes folio.*

fore bod ing (fôr bō′ding, fōr bō′ding), *n.* **1.** prediction; warning. **2.** a feeling that something bad is going to happen.

fore lock (fôr′lok′, fōr′lok′), *n.* **1.** lock of hair that grows just above the forehead. **2. take time by the forelock,** act promptly.

fraud (frôd), *n.* **1.** deceit; cheating; dishonesty: *Any intent to deceive is proof of fraud.* **2.** a dishonest act, statement, etc.; something done to deceive or cheat; trick. **3.** *Esp. U.S. Informal.* person who is not what he pretends to be. [< OF *fraude* < L *fraus* cheating]
Syn. **2.** dodge, sham, fake. **3.** cheat, impostor.

fraud u lent (frô′jə lənt, frô′dyə lənt), *adj.* **1.** deceitful; cheating; dishonest. **2.** intended to deceive. **3.** done by fraud; obtained by trickery. [< OF < L *fraudulentus*] —**fraud′u lent ly,** *adv.*

freight (frāt), *n.* **1.** load of goods carried on a train, ship, etc. **2.** the carrying of goods on a train, ship, etc. **3.** charge for this. **4.** train for carrying goods. **5.** load; burden. —*v.* **1.** load with freight. **2.** carry as freight. **3.** send as freight. **4.** load; burden.

fresh et (fresh′it), *n.* **1.** flood caused by heavy rains or melted snow. **2.** rush of fresh water flowing into the sea. [< *fresh* flood, stream or pool of fresh water + *-et*]

fruit less (früt′lis), *adj.* **1.** having no results; useless; unsuccessful. **2.** producing no fruit; barren. —**fruit′less ly,** *adv.* **Syn.** **1.** abortive, futile, vain.

frus trate (frus′trāt), *v.,* **-trat ed, -trat ing. 1.** bring to nothing; make useless or worthless; foil; defeat. **2.** thwart; oppose: *The great artist had never been frustrated in his ambition to paint.* [< L *frustrari* < *frustra* in vain]

fugue (fyüg), *n.* a musical composition based on one or more short themes in which different voices or instruments repeat the same melody with slight variations.

fun da men tal (fun′də men′tl), *adj.* **1.** of the foundation or basis; forming a foundation or basis; essential. **2.** having to do with the lowest note of a chord in music. —*n.* **1.** principle, rule, law, etc., that forms a foundation or basis; essential part. **2.** the lowest note of a chord in music. **3.** in physics, that component of a wave which has the greatest wave length. [< NL *fundamentalis* < L *fundamentum* foundation, ult. < *fundus* bottom] —**fun′da men′tal ly,** *adv.*
Syn. *adj.* **1.** basic, indispensable.

fu tu ri ty (fyü tùr′ə tē, fyü tyùr′ə tē), *n., pl.* **-ties. 1.** future. **2.** a future state or event. **3.** quality of being future.

gal le on (gal′ē ən, gal′yən), *n.* a large, high ship, usually with three or four decks, formerly used by the Spaniards and others. [< Sp. *galeón* < *galea* < Med. Gk.]

gal ley (gal′ē), *n., pl.* **-leys. 1.** a long, narrow ship of former times having oars and sails. Galleys were often rowed by slaves or convicts. **2.** a large rowboat. **3.** kitchen of a ship. **4.** in printing, a long, narrow tray for holding type that has been set. **5.** galley proof.

gant let¹ (gônt′lit, gant′lit, gänt′lit), *n.* **1.** a former military punishment in which the offender had to run between two rows of men who struck him with clubs or other weapons as he passed. **2. run the gantlet, a.** pass between two rows of men each of whom strikes the runner as he passes. **b.** be exposed to unfriendly attacks, criticism, etc. Also, **gauntlet.** [< Swedish *gatlopp* < *gata* lane + *lopp* course]

gant let² (gônt′lit, gant′lit, gänt′lit), *n.* gauntlet¹.

Gan y mede (gan′ə mēd)

gar ish (ger′ish, gar′ish), *adj.* unpleasantly bright; glaring; showy; gaudy. [ult. < obsolete *gaure* stare]

Gas coigne (gä skwän′)

gaunt (gônt, gänt), *adj.* **1.** very thin and bony; with hollow eyes and a starved look: *Hunger and suffering make people gaunt.* **2.** looking bare and gloomy; desolate; forbidding; grim. [origin uncertain] —**gaunt′ly,** *adv.* —**gaunt′ness,** *n.*
Syn. **1.** lean, spare, lank.

gaunt let¹ (gônt′lit, gänt′lit), *n.* **1.** a stout, heavy glove, usually of leather covered with plates of iron or steel, that was part of a knight's armor. **2.** a stout, heavy glove with a wide, flaring cuff. **3.** the wide, flaring cuff. **4. take up the gauntlet, a.** accept a challenge. **b.** take up the defense of a person, opinion, etc. **5. throw down the gauntlet,** challenge. Also, **gantlet.** [< OF *gantelet,* dim. of *gant* glove < Gmc.]

gaunt let² (gônt′lit, gänt′lit), *n.* gantlet¹.

gen ial (jē′nyəl), *adj.* **1.** smiling and pleasant; cheerful and friendly; kindly: *a genial welcome.* **2.** helping growth; pleasantly warming; comforting: *genial sunshine.* —**gen′ial ly,** *adv.* —**gen′ial ness,** *n.*

ge ol o gy (jē ol′ə jē), *n., pl.* **-gies. 1.** science that deals with the earth's crust, the layers of which it is composed, and their history. **2.** features of the earth's crust in a place or region; rocks, rock formation, etc., of a particular area. **3.** book about geology. [< NL *geologia* < Gk. *ge* earth + *-logos* treating of]

Ge ry on (gē′ri on)

ges tic u late (je stik′yə lāt), *v.,* **-lat ed, -lat ing. 1.** make or use gestures. **2.** make or use many vehement gestures. —**ges tic′u la′tor,** *n.*

ges tic u la tion (je stik′yə lā′shən), *n.* **1.** act of gesticulating. **2.** gesture.
Syn. 2. See **gesture.**

ges ture (jes′chər), *n., v.,* **-tured, -tur ing.** —*n.* **1.** movement of the hands, arms, or any part of the body, used instead of words or with words to help express an idea or feeling. **2.** any action for effect or to impress others: *Her refusal was merely a gesture; she wanted to go.* —*v.* make or use gestures.

gid dy (gid′ē), *adj.,* **-di er, -di est. 1.** having a confused, whirling feeling in one's head; dizzy. **2.** likely to make dizzy; causing dizziness: *The couples whirled and whirled in their giddy dance.* **3.** rarely or never serious; flighty; heedless: *Nobody can tell what that giddy girl will do next.* —*v.* make or become giddy. [OE *gydig* mad, possessed (by an evil spirit) < *god* a god] —**gid′di ly,** *adv.* —**gid′di ness,** *n.*
Syn. *adj.* **1.** light-headed. **3.** frivolous, fickle.

Gila monster (hē′lə), a large, poisonous lizard of Arizona and New Mexico having a short, stumpy tail and a

---

hat, āge, fär;   let, bē, tėrm;   it, īce;   hot, gō, ôrder;   oil, out;   cup, pùt, rüle;   ch, child;   ng, long;
th, thin;   ŦH, then;   zh, measure;   ə represents *a* in about, *e* in taken, *i* in pencil, *o* in lemon, *u* in circus.

heavy, clumsy body covered with beadlike orange-and-black scales. [Am.E; named after *Gila* River, Arizona]

glad i a tor (glad′ē ā′tər), *n.* 1. slave, captive, or paid fighter who fought at the public shows in ancient Rome. 2. person who argues, fights, wrestles, etc., with great skill. [< L *gladiator* < *gladius* sword]

glis sade (gli sād′), *v.,* **-ad ed, -ad ing.** slide or slip. —*n.* slope suitable for glissading.

glow er (glou′ər), *v.* stare angrily; scowl: *The fighters glowered at each other.* —*n.* an angry or sullen look. [? < obsolete *glow, v.,* stare]

glu ti nous (glüt′n əs), *adj.* sticky.

gorge (gôrj), *n., v.,* **gorged, gorg ing.** —*n.* 1. a deep, narrow valley, usually steep and rocky. 2. a gorging; gluttonous meal. 3. contents of a stomach. 4. feeling of disgust, indignation, resentment, or the like. 5. a narrow rear entrance from a fort into an outwork or outer part. 6. mass stopping up a narrow passage: *An ice gorge blocked the river.* 7. *Archaic.* throat; gullet. —*v.* 1. eat greedily until full; stuff with food. 2. fill full; stuff. [< OF *gorge* throat, ult. < LL *gurges* throat, jaws < L *gurges* abyss, whirlpool]

gout (gout), *n.* 1. a painful disease of the joints, often characterized by a painful swelling of the big toe. 2. drop; splash; clot: *gouts of blood.*

gout y (gou′tē), *adj.,* **gout i er, gout i est.** 1. diseased or swollen with gout. 2. of gout; caused by gout. 3. causing gout. —**gout′i ness,** *n.*

gran deur (gran′jər, gran′jür), *n.* greatness; majesty; nobility; dignity; splendor.

grat i fy (grat′ə fī), *v.,* **-fied, -fy ing.** 1. give pleasure or satisfaction to; please: *Flattery gratifies a vain person.* 2. satisfy; indulge: *A drunkard gratifies his craving for liquor.* 3. *Archaic.* give a fee to. [< F < L *gratificari* < *gratus* pleasing + *facere* make, do] —**grat′i fi′er,** *n.* —**grat′i fy′ing ly,** *adv.* Syn. 1. delight.

green horn (grēn′hôrn′), *n. Informal.* 1. person without experience. 2. person easy to trick or cheat.

griz zly (griz′lē), *adj.,* **-zli er, -zli est,** *n., pl.* **-zlies.** —*adj.* 1. grayish; gray. 2. gray-haired. —*n.* grizzly bear.

groin (groin), *n.* 1. the hollow on either side of the body where the thigh joins the abdomen. 2. a curved line where two vaults of a roof cross.

guer ril la (gə ril′ə), *n.* fighter in a war carried on by independent bands. Guerrillas harass the enemy by sudden raids, ambushes, plundering supply trains, etc. —*adj.* of or by guerrillas: *a guerrilla attack.* [< Sp. *guerrilla,* dim. of *guerra* war]

gut ta-per cha (gut′ə per′chə), *n.* substance resembling rubber, obtained from the thick, milky juice of certain tropical trees.

hab i ta tion (hab′ə tā′shən), *n.* 1. place to live in. 2. an inhabiting. Syn. 1. home, residence.

Ha des (hā′dēz′)

haft (haft), *n.* handle (of a knife, sword, dagger, etc.). —*v.* furnish with a handle or hilt; set in a haft. [OE *hæft*]

hag gard (hag′ərd), *adj.* looking worn from pain, fatigue, worry, hunger, etc.; gaunt; careworn.

ha rangue (hə rang′), *n., v.,* **-rangued, -rangu ing.** —*n.* 1. a noisy speech. 2. a long, pompous speech. —*v.* 1. address in a harangue. 2. deliver a harangue.

har ass (har′əs, hə ras′), *v.* 1. trouble by repeated attacks; harry: *Pirates harassed the villages along the coast.* 2. disturb; worry; torment. [< F *harasser* < OF *harer* set a dog on] Syn. 2. plague, bother.

har ry (har′ē), *v.,* **-ried, -ry ing.** 1. raid and rob with violence: *The pirates harried the towns along the coast.* 2. keep troubling; worry; torment: *Fear of losing his job harried the clerk.* [OE *hergian* < *here* army]

ha sai ka (hä sī′kə), *n.* a woman proprietor who acts as hostess.

hav oc (hav′ək), *n.* 1. very great destruction or injury: *Tornadoes, severe earthquakes, and plagues create widespread havoc.* 2. **play havoc with,** injure severely; ruin; destroy. [< AF var. of OF *havot* plundering, devastation (especially in phrase *crier havot* cry havoc) < Gmc.] Syn. 1. devastation, ruin.

heath (hēth), *n.* 1. *Brit.* open, waste land with heather or low bushes growing on it; moor. It has few or no trees. 2. a low bush growing on such land. 3. **one's native heath,** place where one was born or brought up. [OE *hæth*]

He be (hē′bē)

heft (heft), *n.* *Informal.* —*n.* 1. weight; heaviness. 2. *U.S.* the greater part; bulk. —*v.* 1. judge the weight or heaviness of by lifting. 2. lift; heave. [< *heave*]

He phaes tus (hi fes′təs)

Hes per us (hes′pər əs)

Him a la yas (him′ə lā′əz, hə mäl′yəz), *n.pl.* a mountain range extending for 1600 miles along the N borders of India and Pakistan. Their highest peak, Mt. Everest, 29,028 feet, is the highest mountain in the world.

Hip pol y ta (hi pol′i tə)

hoar (hôr, hōr), *adj.* hoary. [OE *hār*]

hoard (hôrd, hōrd), *n.* what is saved and stored away; things stored. —*v.* save and store away: *A squirrel hoards nuts for the winter.* [OE *hord*] —**hoard′er,** *n.* Syn. *v.* treasure, amass, accumulate.

hoard ing (hôr′ding, hōr′ding), *n.* 1. act of one who hoards. 2. something hoarded.

hoar y (hôr′ē, hōr′ē), *adj.,* **hoar i er, hoar i est.** 1. white or gray. 2. white or gray with age. 3. old; ancient. —**hoar′i ness,** *n.*

hob ble (hob′əl), *v.,* **-bled, -bling,** *n.* —*v.* 1. walk awkwardly; limp. 2. cause to walk awkwardly or limp. 3. move unsteadily. 4. tie the legs of (a horse, etc.) together. 5. hinder. —*n.* 1. an awkward walk; limp. 2. rope or strap used to hobble a horse, etc. 3. an awkward or difficult situation.

home stead (hōm′sted′), *n.* 1. house with its land and other buildings; farm with its buildings. 2. *U.S.* parcel of 160 acres of public land granted to a settler under certain conditions by the United States government. [Am.E]

hop (hop), *n., v.,* **hopped, hop ping.** —*n.* 1. vine having flower clusters that look like small, yellow pine cones. 2. **hops,** *pl.* the dried, ripe, flower clusters of the hop vine, used to flavor beer and other malt drinks. —*v.* 1. pick hops. 2. flavor with hops.

horde (hôrd, hōrd), *n.* 1. crowd; swarm. 2. a wandering tribe or troop: *Hordes of Mongols and Turks invaded Europe in the Middle Ages.*

horn y (hôr′nē), *adj.,* **horn i er, horn i est.** 1. made of horn or a substance like it. 2. hard like a horn: *A farmer's hands are horny from work.* 3. having a horn or horns.

hos pi ta ble (hos′pi tə bəl, ho spit′ə bəl), *adj.* 1. giving or liking to give a welcome, food and shelter, and friendly

---

< = from, derived from, taken from;   cf., compare;   dial., dialect;   dim., diminutive;   lang., language; pp., past participle;   ppr., present participle;   pt., past tense;   ult., ultimately;   var., variant;   ? = possibly.

treatment to guests or strangers: *a hospitable family, reception, etc.* **2.** willing and ready to entertain; favorably receptive or open: *a person hospitable to new ideas.* [< MF < L *hospitari* stay as a guest < *hospes* guest, host] —**hos′pi ta bly,** *adv.*

hos tel (hos′tl), *n.* a lodging place; especially, a supervised lodging place for young people on bicycle trips, hikes, etc.; inn; hotel. [< OF *hostel, ostel* < Med.L *hospitale* inn. Doublet of HOSPITAL, HOTEL.]

hos tler (os′lər, hos′lər), *n.* person who takes care of horses at an inn or stable. Also, **ostler.** [var. of *ostler* < OF *hostelier* < *hostel.* See HOSTEL.]

Hou di ni (hü dē′nē), *n.* **Harry,** pseudonym of Erick Weiss (1874-1926), American magician.

hov el (huv′əl, hov′əl), *n.* **1.** house that is small, mean, and unpleasant to live in. **2.** an open shed for sheltering cattle, tools, etc. [ME; origin uncertain]

hu mil i ate (hyü mil′ē āt), *v.,* **-at ed, -at ing.** lower the pride, dignity, or self-respect of. [< L *humiliare* < *humilis.*] —**hu mil′i at′ing ly,** *adv.*
Syn. humble, mortify, chagrin, disgrace, shame.

hu mil i ty (hyü mil′ə tē), *n., pl.* **-ties.** humbleness of mind; lack of pride; meekness. [< F *humilité* < L *humilitas*] **Syn.** lowliness, modesty.

hum mock .(hum′ək), *n.* **1.** a very small, rounded hill; knoll; hillock. **2.** bump or ridge in a field of ice. [origin unknown]

hy dra (hī′drə), *n., pl.* **-dras, -drae** (-drē). **1. Hydra,** in Greek mythology, a monstrous serpent having nine heads, each of which was replaced by two heads after being cut off unless the wound was cauterized. The Hydra was slain by Hercules. **2.** any persistent evil. **3.** kind of fresh-water polyp, so called because when the tubelike body is cut into pieces, each piece forms a new individual. **4. Hydra,** a southern constellation represented as a serpent. [< L < Gk. *hydra* water serpent < *hydor* water]

hyper-, *prefix.* over; above; beyond; exceedingly; to excess, as in *hyperacidity, hypersensitive.* [< Gk]

hypo-, *prefix.* under; beneath; below; less than; slightly; somewhat, as in *hypodermic.* [< Gk]

hy poc ri sy (hi pok′rə sē), *n., pl.* **-sies. 1.** act or fact of putting on a false appearance of goodness or religion. **2.** pretending to be what one is not; pretense. [< OF *ypocrisie* < LL < Gk. *hypokrisis* acting, dissimulation, ult. < *hypo-* under + *krinein* judge]

hyp o crite (hip′ə krit), *n.* **1.** person who puts on a false appearance of goodness or religion. **2.** person who pretends to be what he is not; pretender. [< OF *ypocrite* < L < Gk. *hypokrites* actor. Related to *hypocrisy.*]

hyp o crit i cal (hip′ə krit′ə kəl), *adj.* of or like a hypocrite; insincere. —**hyp′o crit′i cal ly,** *adv.*

hys ter i cal (hi ster′ə kəl), *adj.* **1.** unnaturally excited. **2.** showing an unnatural lack of control; unable to stop laughing, crying, etc.; suffering from hysteria. —**hys ter′i cal ly,** *adv.*

ice pan, *n.* a small piece of floating ice.

i de al ism (ī dē′ə liz′əm), *n.* **1.** an acting according to one's ideals of what ought to be, regardless of circumstances or of the approval or disapproval of others. **2.** a cherishing of fine ideals.

i de al ist (ī dē′ə list), *n.* **1.** person who acts according to his ideals; person who has fine ideals. **2.** person who neglects practical matters in following ideals.

ig no min y (ig′nə min′ē), *n., pl.* **-min ies. 1.** loss of one's good name; public shame and disgrace; dishonor. **2.** shameful action or conduct. [< L *ignominia* < *in-* not + *nomen* name; form influenced by OL *gnoscere* come to know]

il lu sion (i lü′zhən), *n.* **1.** appearance which is not real; misleading appearance. **2.** a false impression or perception. **3.** a false idea, notion, or belief. **4.** a delicate silk net or gauze, often used for veils and over wedding gowns. [< L *illusio, -onis* < *illudere* mock < *in-* at + *ludere* play]
Syn. 1. Illusion, delusion mean something mistakenly or falsely believed to be true or real. **Illusion** applies to something appearing to be real or true, but actually not existing or being quite different from what it seems: *Good motion pictures create an illusion of reality.* **Delusion** applies to a false and often harmful belief about something that does exist: *The old woman had the delusion that the butcher tried to cheat her.*
➤ **Illusion, allusion** are sometimes confused. An *illusion* is a misleading appearance: *an illusion of wealth.* An *allusion* is an indirect reference or slight mention: *He made allusions to recent events without recounting them.*

Il lyr i a (i lir′ē ə)

im bibe (im bīb′), *v.,* **-bibed, -bib ing. 1.** drink; drink in. **2.** absorb: *The roots of a plant imbibe moisture from the earth.* **3.** take into one's mind: *Children often imbibe superstitions that last all their lives.* [< L *imbibere* < *in-* in + *bibere* drink] —**im bib′er,** *n.*

im mi nent (im′ə nənt), *adj.* likely to happen soon; about to occur: *The black clouds, thunder, and lightning show that a storm is imminent.* [< L *imminens, -entis,* ppr. of *imminere* overhang] —**im′mi nent ly,** *adv.*
➤ See **eminent** for usage note.

im mor tal (i môr′tl), *adj.* **1.** living forever; never dying; everlasting. **2.** of or having to do with immortal beings or immortality; divine. **3.** remembered or famous forever. —*n.* **1.** an immortal being. **2.** Usually, **immortals,** *pl.* the gods of ancient Greek and Roman mythology. **3.** person remembered or famous forever: *Shakespeare is one of the immortals.* —**im mor′tal ly,** *adv.*
Syn. *adj.* **1.** eternal, endless.

im mor tal i ty (im′ôr tal′ə tē), *n.* **1.** endless life; living forever. **2.** fame that lasts forever.

im par tial (im pär′shəl), *adj.* showing no more favor to one side than to the other; fair; just. —**im par′tial ly,** *adv.*
Syn. unbiased, unprejudiced.

im pas sive (im pas′iv), *adj.* **1.** without feeling or emotion; unmoved: *He listened with an impassive face.* **2.** not feeling pain or injury; insensible: *The soldier lay as impassive as if he were dead.* **3.** incapable of being injured. —**im pas′sive ly,** *adv.*
Syn. 1. indifferent, apathetic, passive.

im pel (im pel′), *v.,* **-pelled, -pel ling. 1.** drive; force; cause: *Hunger impelled the lazy man to work.* **2.** cause to move; drive forward; push along: *The wind impelled the boat to shore.* [< L *impellere* < *in-* on + *pellere* push] —**im pel′ler,** *n.*

im per a tive (im per′ə tiv), *adj.* **1.** not to be avoided; urgent; necessary: *It is imperative that a very sick child stay in bed.* **2.** expressing a command. "Go!" and "Stop, look, listen!" are in the imperative mood. —*n.* **1.** a command: *The great imperative is "Love thy neighbor as thyself."* **2.** in grammar: **a.** the imperative mood. **b.** a verb form in this mood. [< L *imperativus* < *imperare* command] —**im per′a tive ly,** *adv.* —**im per′a tive ness,** *n.*

---

hat, āge, fär; let, bē, tèrm; it, īce; hot, gō, ôrder; oil, out; cup, pùt, rüle; ch, child; ng, long; th, thin; ŦH, then; zh, measure; ə represents *a* in about, *e* in taken, *i* in pencil, *o* in lemon, *u* in circus.

im per cep ti ble (im/pər sep/tə bəl), *adj.*
1. very slight; gradual. 2. that cannot be perceived or felt. —**im/per cep/ti bly,** *adv.*

im pe ri al (im pir/ē əl), *n.* a very small beard left growing beneath the lower lip.

im pe ri ous (im pir/ē əs), *adj.* 1. haughty; arrogant: domineering; overbearing. 2. imperative; necessary; urgent. —**im pe/ri ous ly,** *adv.*
Syn. 1. dictatorial.

Man wearing an imperial

im pet u ous (im pech/ü əs), *adj.* 1. moving with great force or speed: *the impetuous rush of water over Niagara Falls.* 2. acting hastily, rashly, or with sudden feeling: *Boys are more impetuous than old men.* —**im pet/u ous ly,** *adv.* —**im pet/u ous ness,** *n.*

im pos tor or **im pos ter** (im pos/tər), *n.* 1. person who assumes a false name or character. 2. deceiver; cheat. [< LL < L *imponere* impose < *in-* on + *ponere* place, put]

im pos ture (im pos/chər), *n.* deception; fraud. [< LL *impostura* < L *imponere* impose]

im preg nate (im preg/nāt), *v.,* **-nat ed, -nat ing,** *adj.* —*v.* 1. make pregnant; fertilize. 2. fill (with); saturate: *Sea water is impregnated with salt.* 3. instill into (the mind); inspire; imbue: *A great book impregnates the mind with new ideas.* —*adj.* impregnated.

im prob a ble (im prob/ə bəl), *adj.* not probable; not likely to happen; not likely to be true.

im promp tu (im promp/tü, im promp/tyü), *adv., adj.* without previous thought or preparation; offhand: *a speech made impromptu.* —*n.* something impromptu; improvisation.
Syn. *adj.* improvised.

im pro pri e ty (im/prə prī/ə tē), *n., pl.* **-ties.** 1. lack of propriety; quality of being improper. 2. improper conduct. 3. an improper act, expression, etc.: *Using "learn" to mean "teach" is an impropriety.*

im pro vise (im/prə vīz), *v.,* **-vised, -vis ing.** 1. compose or utter (verse, music, etc.) without preparation. 2. prepare or provide offhand; extemporize: *The boys improvised a tent out of two blankets and some long poles.* [< F < Ital. *improvvisare,* ult. < L *in-* not + *pro-* beforehand + *videre* see] —**im/pro vis/er,** *n.*

im pute (im pyüt/), *v.,* **-put ed, -put ing.** consider as belonging; attribute; charge (a fault, etc.) to a person; blame: *I impute his failure to laziness.*

in ar tic u late (in/är tik/yə lit), *adj.* 1. not distinct; not like regular speech: *an inarticulate mutter or groan.* 2. unable to speak in words; unable to say what one thinks; dumb: *Cats and dogs are inarticulate.* 3. not jointed: *A jellyfish's body is inarticulate.* —**in/ar tic/u late ly,** *adv.* —**in/ar tic/u late ness,** *n.*

in au di ble (in ô/də bəl), *adj.* that cannot be heard. —**in au/di bly,** *adv.*

in au gu rate (in ô/gyə rāt), *v.,* **-rat ed, -rat ing.** 1. install in office with a ceremony: *A President of the United States is inaugurated every four years.* 2. make a formal beginning of; begin: *The invention of the airplane inaugurated a new era in transportation.* 3. begin public use of with a ceremony or celebration.

in com pre hen si bil i ty (in/kom pri hen/sə bil/ə tē), *n.* fact or quality of being incomprehensible.

in com pre hen si ble (in/kom pri hen/sə bəl), *adj.* impossible to understand. —**in/com pre hen/si bly,** *adv.*

in con ti nent (in kon/tə nənt), *adj.* 1. without self-restraint. 2. not chaste; licentious. [< L *incontinens, -entis*]

in cor ri gi ble (in kôr/ə jə bəl, in kor/ə jə bəl), *adj.* 1. so firmly fixed (in bad ways, a bad habit, etc.) that nothing else can be expected: *an incorrigible liar.* 2. so fixed that it cannot be changed or cured: *an incorrigible habit of wrinkling one's nose.* —*n.* an incorrigible person. —**in cor/ri gi bly,** *adv.*

in cor rupt i ble (in/kə rup/tə bəl), *adj.* 1. not to be corrupted; honest: *The incorruptible man could not be bribed.* 2. not capable of decay: *Diamonds are incorruptible.* —**in/cor rupt/i bly,** *adv.*

in cred i ble (in kred/ə bəl), *adj.* seeming too extraordinary to be possible; unbelievable: *The hero fought with incredible bravery.* —**in cred/i bly,** *adv.*
➤ **incredible, incredulous.** *Incredible* means unbelievable; *incredulous* means not ready to believe or showing a lack of belief: *His story of having seen a ghost seemed incredible to his family. If they look incredulous, show them the evidence.*

in cre du li ty (in/krə dü/lə tē, in/krə dyü/lə tē), *n.* lack of belief; doubt.
Syn. unbelief, distrust.

in cred u lous (in krej/ə ləs), *adj.* 1. not ready to believe; not credulous; doubting: *People nowadays are incredulous about ghosts and witches.* 2. showing a lack of belief. —**in cred/u lous ly,** *adv.*
➤ See **incredible** for usage note.

in dig na tion (in/dig nā/shən), *n.* anger at something unworthy, unjust, or mean; anger mixed with scorn; righteous anger: *Cruelty to animals arouses indignation.*

in dis po si tion (in/dis pə zish/ən), *n.* 1. disturbance of health; slight illness. 2. unwillingness; disinclination; aversion.

in dis put a ble (in/dis pyü/tə bəl, in dis/pyə tə bəl), *adj.* not to be disputed; undoubtedly true; unquestionable. —**in/dis put/a bly,** *adv.*
Syn. undeniable, certain.

in dom i ta ble (in dom/ə tə bəl), *adj.* unconquerable; unyielding. [< LL *indomitabilis,* ult. < L *in-* not + *domare* tame] —**in dom/i ta bly,** *adv.*

in ef fa ble (in ef/ə bəl), *adj.* 1. not to be expressed in words; too great to be described in words. 2. that must not be spoken. [< L *ineffabili,* ult. < *in-* not + *ex-* out + *fari* speak] —**in ef/fa bly,** *adv.*

in ef fec tu al (in/ə fek/chü əl), *adj.* 1. without effect; useless. 2. not able to produce the effect wanted. —**in/ef fec/tu al ly,** *adv.*
Syn. 1. ineffective, futile, vain.

in ept (in ept/), *adj.* 1. not suitable; out of place. 2. absurd; foolish. [< L *ineptus* < *in-* not + *aptus* apt] —**in ept/ly,** *adv.* —**in ept/ness,** *n.*

in ert (in ért/), *adj.* 1. having no power to move or act; lifeless: *A stone is an inert mass of matter.* 2. inactive; slow; sluggish. 3. with few or no active properties: *Helium and neon are inert gases.* [< L *iners, inertis* idle, unskilled < *in-* without + *ars* art, skill] —**in ert/ly,** *adv.* —**in ert/ness,** *n.*

in ex haust i ble (in/ig zô/stə bəl), *adj.* 1. that cannot be exhausted; very abundant. 2. tireless. —**in/ex haust/i bly,** *adv.*

in fa mous (in/fə məs), *adj.* 1. deserving or causing a very bad reputation; shamefully bad; extremely wicked. 2. having a very bad reputation; in public disgrace: *A traitor's name is infamous.* —**in/fa mous ly,** *adv.*
Syn. 1. odious. 2. notorious, disreputable.

in fat u at ed (in fach/ü ā/tid), *adj.* extremely adoring; foolishly in love.

< = from, derived from, taken from;   cf., compare;   dial., dialect;   dim., diminutive;   lang., language; pp., past participle;   ppr., present participle;   pt., past tense;   ult., ultimately;   var., variant;   ? = possibly.

inferiority complex, an abnormal or morbid feeling of being inferior to other people.

in fest (in fest′), *v.* trouble or disturb frequently or in large numbers: *Mosquitoes infest swamps.* [< L *infestare* attack < *infestus* hostile]
Syn. overrun.

in fi nite (in′fə nit), *adj.* 1. without limits or bounds; endless. 2. extremely great: *Teaching little children takes infinite patience.* —*n.* 1. that which is infinite. 2. the **Infinite,** God. [< L *infinitus* < *in-* not + *finis* boundary]

in fir mi ty (in fèr′mə tē), *n., pl.* -ties. 1. weakness; feebleness. 2. sickness; illness. 3. a moral weakness or failing. **Syn.** 3. defect.

in graft (in graft′), *v.* engraft.

in iq ui ty (in ik′wə tē), *n., pl.* -ties. 1. very great injustice; wickedness. 2. a wicked or unjust act. [< L *iniquitas* < *iniquus* < *in-* not + *aequus* just]

in junc tion (in jungk′shən), *n.* 1. command; order: *Injunctions of secrecy did not prevent the news from leaking out.* 2. a formal order issued by a law court ordering a person or group to do, or refrain from doing, something.

in scru ta ble (in skrü′tə bəl), *adj.* that cannot be understood; so mysterious or obscure that one cannot make out its meaning; incomprehensible. —**in scru′ta bly,** *adv.*
Syn. unfathomable, impenetrable.

in sid i ous (in sid′ē əs), *adj.* 1. wily; sly; crafty; tricky; treacherous. 2. working secretly or subtly: *an insidious disease.* [< L *insidiosus* < *insidiae* ambush < *insidere* < *in-* in + *sedere* sit] —**in sid′i ous ly,** *adv.*

in sight (in′sit′), *n.* 1. a viewing of the inside or inner parts (of something) with understanding. 2. wisdom and understanding in dealing with people or with facts.

in sin u ate (in sin′yü āt), *v.,* -at ed, -at ing. 1. suggest indirectly; hint: *To say "Fred can't do it: no coward can" is to insinuate that Fred is a coward.* 2. push in or get in by an indirect, twisting way: *The spy insinuated himself into the confidence of important army officers.*

in so lence (in′sə ləns), *n.* bold rudeness; insulting behavior or speech.

in so lent (in′sə lənt), *adj.* boldly rude; insulting. —**in′so lent ly,** *adv.*
Syn. arrogant, impudent.

in sub or di na tion (in′sə bôrd′n ā′shən), *n.* resistance to authority; disobedience; unruly behavior.

in suf fer a ble (in suf′ər ə bəl, in suf′rə bəl), *adj.* intolerable; unbearable: *insufferable insolence.* —**in suf′fer a ble ness,** *n.* —**in suf′fer a bly,** *adv.*

in su per a ble (in sü′pər ə bəl), *adj.* that cannot be passed over or overcome: *an insuperable barrier.* —**in su′per a bly,** *adv.*
Syn. insurmountable, impassable.

in tan gi ble (in tan′jə bəl), *adj.* 1. not capable of being touched: *Sound and light are intangible.* 2. not easily grasped by the mind; vague: *She had that intangible something called charm.* —*n.* something intangible. —**in tan′gi bly,** *adv.*
Syn. *adj.* 1. insubstantial.

in ter mit tent (in′tər mit′nt), *adj.* stopping and beginning again; pausing at intervals. —**in′ter mit′tent ly,** *adv.*

in ter ur ban (in′tər ėr′bən), *adj.* between cities or towns. [Am.E]

in tim i date (in tim′ə dāt), *v.,* -dat ed, -dat ing. 1. frighten; make afraid. 2. influence or force by fear. [< Med.L *intimidare* < L *in-* + *timidus* fearful] —**in tim′i da′tion,** *n.* —**in tim′i da′tor,** *n.*

in tol er a ble (in tol′ər ə bəl), *adj.* unbearable; too much, too painful, etc., to be endured. [< L *intolerabilis*]
Syn. unendurable, insufferable.

in tol er ance (in tol′ər əns), *n.* 1. lack of tolerance; unwillingness to let others do and think as they choose, especially in matters of religion. 2. inability to endure; unwillingness to endure.

in tox i cate (in tok′sə kāt), *v.,* -cat ed, -cat ing. 1. make drunk: *Alcohol intoxicates people.* 2. excite beyond self-control. —**in tox′i cat′ing ly,** *adv.*

in trep id (in trep′id), *adj.* fearless; dauntless; courageous; very brave. [< L *intrepidus* < *in-* not + *trepidus* alarmed] —**in trep′id ly,** *adv.*
Syn. bold, daring.

in tro spec tive (in′trə spek′tiv), *adj.* inclined to examine one's own thoughts and feelings.

in tu i tion (in′tü ish′ən, in′tyü ish′ən), *n.* 1. perception of truths, facts, etc., without reasoning: *By experience with all kinds of people Mr. Jones had developed great powers of intuition.* 2. something so perceived. [< LL *intuitio, -onis* a gazing at < L *intueri* < *in-* at + *tueri* look]

in vin ci ble (in vin′sə bəl), *adj.* not to be overcome; unconquerable. [< L *invincibilis* < *in-* not + *vincere* conquer] —**in vin′ci bly,** *adv.*
Syn. indomitable.

in voice (in′vois), *n.* 1. list of goods sent to a purchaser showing prices, amounts, shipping charges, etc. 2. shipment of invoiced goods.

in vul ner a ble (in vul′nər ə bəl), *adj.* that cannot be wounded or injured; proof against attack: *Achilles was invulnerable except for his heel.* —**in vul′ner a bly,** *adv.*

I o la us (ī′ə lā′əs)

i ras ci ble (i ras′ə bəl), *adj.* 1. easily made angry; irritable. 2. showing anger. **Syn.** 1. touchy, testy.

ir i des cent (ir′ə des′nt), *adj.* 1. displaying colors like those of the rainbow. 2. changing colors according to position. [< L *iris, iridis* rainbow < Gk.] —**ir′i des′cent ly,** *adv.*

irk (ėrk), *v.* weary; disgust; annoy; trouble; bore: *It irks us to wait for people who are late.* [ME *irke(n)*]

ir ra tion al (i rash′ə nəl), *adj.* 1. not rational; unreasonable: *It is irrational to be afraid of the number 13.* 2. unable to think and reason clearly. 3. in mathematics, that cannot be expressed by a whole number or a common fraction. $\sqrt{3}$ is an irrational number. —**ir ra′tion al ly,** *adv.*
Syn. 1. illogical.

ir rel e vant (i rel′ə vənt), *adj.* not to the point; off the subject: *A question about arithmetic is irrelevant in a music lesson.* —**ir rel′e vant ly,** *adv.*

ir re place a ble (ir′i plā′sə bəl), *adj.* not replaceable; impossible to replace with another.

ir re sist i ble (ir′i zis′tə bəl), *adj.* that cannot be resisted; too great to be withstood. —**ir′re sist′i bly,** *adv.*

i sin glass (ī′zn glas′), *n.* a semi-transparent, whitish substance formerly used in place of glass.

Ix i on (ik sī′ən)

jave lin (jav′lən), *n.* a light spear thrown by hand. [< F *javeline*]

ju bi lant (jü′bə lənt), *adj.* 1. rejoicing; exulting. 2. expressing or showing joy. [< L *jubilans, -antis,* ppr. of *jubilare* shout with joy < *jubilum* wild shout] —**ju′bi lant ly,** *adv.*

hat, āge, fär;   let, bē, tèrm;   it, īce;   hot, gō, ôrder;   oil, out;   cup, pùt, rüle;   ch, child;   ng, long;
th, thin;   ᴛʜ, then;   zh, measure;   ə represents *a* in about, *e* in taken, *i* in pencil, *o* in lemon, *u* in circus.

kar a kul (kar′ə kəl), *n.* 1. variety of Russian or Asiatic sheep. 2. fur with flat, loose curls; caracul. [from *Kara Kul*, lake in Turkestan]

keel (kēl), *n.* 1. the main timber or steel piece that extends the whole length of the bottom of a ship or boat. 2. part in an airplane or airship resembling a ship's keel.

kink (kingk), *n.* 1. a twist or curl in thread, rope, hair, etc. 2. pain or stiffness in the muscles of the neck, back, etc.; crick. 3. *Informal.* a mental twist; queer idea; odd notion; eccentricity; whim. —*v.* form a kink; make kinks in. [probably < Dutch *kink* twist]

knot (not), *n.* 1. a fastening made by tying or twining together pieces of rope, cord, string, etc. 2. bow of ribbon, etc., worn as an ornament. 3. group; cluster: *A knot of people stood talking outside the door.* 4. a hard mass of wood formed where a branch grows out from a tree, which shows as a roundish, cross-grained piece in a board. 5. a hard lump. A knot sometimes forms in a tired muscle. 6. joint where leaves grow out on the stem of a plant. 7. unit of speed used on ships; one nautical mile per hour: *The ship averaged 12 knots.* 8. nautical mile, 6080.27 feet. 9. difficulty; problem. 10. thing that unites closely or intricately.

kow tow (kou′tou′), *v.* 1. kneel and touch the ground with the forehead to show deep respect, submission, or worship. 2. show slavish respect or obedience. —*n.* act of kowtowing. [< Chinese *k'o-t'ou,* literally, knock (the) head] —**kow′tow′er,** *n.*

Lach e sis (lak′ə sis)

la cu na (lə kyü′nə), *n., pl.* **-nas, -nae** (-nē). 1. an empty space; gap; blank: *There were several lacunas in her letter where words had been erased.* 2. a tiny cavity in bones or tissues.

La don (lā′don)

lam en ta ble (lam′ən tə bəl), *adj.* 1. to be regretted or pitied: *a lamentable accident, a lamentable failure.* 2. sorrowful; mournful. —**lam′en ta bly,** *adv.*

lap is laz u li (lap′is laz′yə li, lap′is laz′yə lē), 1. a deep blue, opaque semiprecious stone used for an ornament. 2. deep blue.

lapse (laps), *n.* 1. a slight mistake or error. A slip of the tongue, pen, or memory is a lapse. 2. a slipping or falling away from what is right: *a moral lapse.* 3. a slipping back; sinking down; slipping into a lower condition: *a lapse into savage ways.* 4. a slipping by; a passing away: *A minute is a short lapse of time.* 5. ending of a right or privilege because it was not renewed, not used, or otherwise neglected.

las civ i ous (lə siv′ē əs), *adj.* 1. feeling lust. 2. showing lust. 3. causing lust.

Lau sanne (lō zan′)

lee (lē), *n.* 1. shelter. 2. side or part sheltered from the wind. 3. side away from the wind. 4. direction toward which the wind is blowing. —*adj.* 1. sheltered from the wind. 2. on the side away from the wind. 3. in the direction toward which the wind is blowing. [OE *hlē o*]

Ler na (ler′nə)

le thal (lē′thəl), *adj.* causing death; deadly: *lethal weapons, a lethal dose.* [< L *let(h)alis* < *letum* death]

leth ar gy (leth′ər jē), *n., pl.* **-gies.** 1. drowsy dullness; lack of energy; sluggish inactivity. 2. an unnatural sleep.

Le to (lē′tō)

lev i ty (lev′ə tē), *n., pl.* **-ties.** lightness of mind, character,

or behavior; lack of proper seriousness or earnestness.

lib e rate (lib′ə rāt′), *v.,* **-rat ed, -rat ing.** set free. [< L *liberare* < *liber* free] —**lib′e ra′tor,** *n.*
Syn. emancipate, release.
Ant. enslave, subjugate.

lim bo (lim′bō), *n.* 1. Often, **Limbo.** in Catholic theology, a place for those who have not received the grace of Christ while living, and yet have not deserved the punishments of willful and impenitent sinners. 2. place for people and things forgotten, cast aside, or out of date: *The belief that the earth is flat belongs to the limbo of outworn ideas.* 3. prison; jail; confinement. [< L (*in*) *limbo* on the edge]

lin guist (ling′gwist), *n.* 1. person skilled in a number of languages besides his own. 2. person who studies the history and structure of language; philologist.

lin tel (lin′tl), *n.* a horizontal beam or stone over a door, window, etc., to support the structure above it.

lit er al (lit′ər əl), *adj.* 1. following the exact words of the original: *a literal translation.* 2. taking words in their usual meaning, without exaggeration or imagination; matter-of-fact: *the literal meaning of a word, a literal type of mind.* 3. true to fact: *a literal account.* 4. of the letters of the alphabet; expressed by letters. [< LL *lit(t)eralis* < L*lit(t) era* letter]

lit er al ly (lit′ər ə lē), *adv.* word for word; without exaggeration or imagination.

lithe (līŦH), *adj.* bending easily; supple. [OE *lī the* mild] —**lithe′ly,** *adv.* —**lithe′ness,** *n.*

liv id (liv′id), *adj.* 1. having a dull-bluish or leaden color. 2. discolored by a bruise.

loath (lōth, lōŦH), *adj.* unwilling; reluctant: *The little girl was loath to leave her mother.* Also, **loth.**
Syn. See **reluctant.**

loathe (lōŦH), *v.,* **loathed, loath ing.** feel strong dislike and disgust for; abhor; hate. [OE *lāthian* hate < *lāth* hostile]
Syn. abominate, detest.

-logy, *word element.* 1. account, doctrine, or science of, as in *biology, theology.* 2. speaking; discussion, as in *eulogy.* 3. special meanings, as in *analogy, anthology.* [< Gk. *-logia,* in a few cases < *logos* word, discourse, but usually < *-logos* treating of < *legein* speak (of), mention]

lope (lōp), *v.,* **loped, lop ing,** *n.* —*v.* run with a long, easy stride. —*n.* a long, easy stride. [< Scand. *hlaupa* leap] —**lop′er,** *n.*

love knot, an ornamental knot or bow of ribbon as a token of love.

lu di crous (lü′də krəs), *adj.* amusingly absurd; ridiculous. [< L *ludicrus* < *ludus* sport] —**lu′di crous ly,** *adv.*
Syn. laughable, droll, comical.

lu na tic (lü′nə tik), *n.* 1. an insane person. 2. an extremely foolish person. —*adj.* 1. insane. 2. for insane people. 3. extremely foolish.

lust (lust), *n.* 1. strong desire. 2. bad desire or appetite. —*v.* have a strong desire: *A miser lusts after gold.* [OE *lust* pleasure]

lyre (lir), *n.* an ancient stringed musical instrument somewhat like a small harp. [< OF < L < Gk. *lyra*]

lyr ic (lir′ik), *n.* 1. a short poem expressing personal emotion. A love poem, a patriotic song, a lament, and a hymn might all be lyrics. 2. *Informal.* words for a song. —*adj.* 1. having to do with lyric poems: *a lyric poet.* 2. characterized by a spontaneous expression of feeling. 3. of or suitable for singing. [< L *lyricus* < Gk. *lyrikos* of a lyre]

Lyre player

ma ca bre (mə kä′brə, mə kä′bər), *adj.* gruesome; horrible; ghastly. [< F]

Ma ca co (mə kä′kə)

Mac e do ni a (mas′ə dō′nē ə)

magic lantern, an early type of projector for showing photographic slides on a screen.

mag is te ri al (maj′ə stir′ē əl), *adj.* 1. of a magistrate; suited to a magistrate: *A judge has magisterial rank.* 2. showing authority: *The captain spoke with a magisterial voice.* 3. imperious; domineering; overbearing. **Syn.** 2. authoritative. 3. dictatorial, haughty, arrogant.

Ma ia (mā′yə)

mal a chite (mal′ə kīt), *n.* a green mineral used for ornamental articles.

mal e dic tion (mal′ə dik′shən), *n.* a curse.

mal ice (mal′is), *n.* active ill will; wish to hurt others; spite. [< OF < L *malitia* < *malus* evil] **Syn.** spitefulness, grudge, rancor. See **spite.**

ma li cious (mə lish′əs), *adj.* showing active ill will; wishing to hurt others; spiteful. **—mal li′cious ly,** *adv.*

ma lig nant (mə lig′nənt), *adj.* 1. very evil; very hateful; very malicious. 2. very harmful. 3. very infectious; very dangerous; causing death: *Cancer is a malignant growth.* [< LL *malignans, -antis* acting from malice < *malignus*] **—ma lig′nant ly,** *adv.*

ma lin ger (mə ling′gər), *v.* pretend to be sick in order to escape work or duty; shirk. [< F *malingre* sickly < *mal-* badly (< L *male*) + *heingre* sick (< Gmc.)]

man a cle (man′ə kəl), *n., v.,* **-cled, -cling.** *—n.* 1. Usually, **manacles,** *pl.* handcuff; fetter for the hands. 2. restraint. *—v.* 1. put manacles on: *The pirates manacled their prisoners.* 2. restrain. [< OF < L *manicula,* dim. of *manicae* sleeves, manacles < *manus* hand]

ma ni a (mā′nē ə), *n.* 1. kind of insanity characterized by great excitement and sometimes violence. 2. unusual fondness; craze. [< L < Gk. *mania* madness]

man ner ism (man′ə riz′əm), *n.* 1. too much use of some manner in speaking, writing, or behaving. 2. an odd little trick; queer habit; peculiar way of acting. **Syn.** 1. affectation. 2. peculiarity.

man tle (man′tl), *n.* 1. a loose cloak without sleeves. 2. anything that covers like a mantle: *The ground had a mantle of snow.* 3. a lacelike tube around a flame that gets so hot it glows and gives light.

mar row (mar′ō), *n.* 1. the soft tissue that fills the cavities of most bones. 2. the inmost or essential part.

Mar seille, usually **Mar seilles** (mär sā′)

mar shal (mär′shəl), *n., v.,* **-shaled, -shal ing** or *esp. Brit.* **-shalled, -shal ling.** *—n.* 1. officer of various kinds, especially a police officer. 2. a high officer in an army. 3. person arranging the order of march in a parade. 4. person in charge of events or ceremonies. *—v.* 1. arrange in order. 2. conduct with ceremony. [< OF *mareschal* < LL *mariscalcus* groom < Gmc., literally, horse servant]

mar tial (mär′shəl), *adj.* 1. of war; suitable for war: *martial music.* 2. fond of fighting; warlike; brave: *a boy of martial spirit.* [< L *Martialis* < *Mars* Mars]

mas tiff (mas′tif), *n.* a large, strong dog with drooping ears and hanging lips. [< OF *mastin,* ult. < L *mansuetus* tame; influenced by OF *mestif* mongrel]

me di a (mē′dē ə), *n.* pl. of **medium.** *Newspapers, magazines, billboards, and radio are important media for advertising.*

med i tate (med′ə tāt), *v.,* **-tat ed, -tat ing.** 1. think; reflect: *Monks and nuns meditate on holy things for hours at a time.* 2. think about; consider; plan; intend. [< L *meditari*] **Syn.** 1. ponder.

med i ta tion (med′ə tā′shən), *n.* continued thought; reflection, especially on sacred or solemn subjects. **Syn.** contemplation.

me di um (mē′dē əm), *adj., n., pl.* **-di ums** or **-di a.** *—adj.* having a middle position; moderate. *—n.* 1. that which is in the middle; neither one extreme nor the other; middle condition. 2. substance or agent through which anything acts; a means: *Radio is a medium of communication.* 3. substance in which something can live; environment: *Water is the medium in which fish live.* 4. liquid with which paints are mixed. 5. person through whom supposed messages from the world of spirits are sent.

Meg a ra (meg′ə rə)

mé lange (mā länzh′), *n.* mixture; medley.

Mel a nip pe (mel′ə nip′ē)

men di cant (men′də kənt), *adj.* begging. Mendicant friars ask alms for charity. *—n.* 1. beggar. 2. a mendicant friar.

mer cu ri al (mər kyur′ē əl), *adj.* 1. sprightly; quick. 2. changeable; fickle. 3. caused by the use of mercury: *mercurial poisoning.* 4. containing mercury: *a mercurial ointment.* *—n.* drug containing mercury. **—mer cu′ri al ly,** *adv.*

merg er (mėr′jər), *n.* a merging; absorption; combination: *One big company was formed by the merger of four small ones.*

me te or ol o gist (mē′tē ə rol′ə jist), *n.* person trained in meteorology.

me te or ol o gy (mē′tē ə rol′ə jē), *n.* science of the atmosphere and weather. [< Gk. *meteorologia* < *meteoron* (thing) in the air + *-logos* treating of]

me tic u lous (mə tik′yə ləs), *adj.* extremely or excessively careful about small details. [< L *meticulosus* < *metus* fear] **—me tic′u lous ly,** *adv.*

met tle (met′l), *n.* 1. disposition; spirit; courage. 2. **on one's mettle,** ready to do one's best.

mi li tia (mə lish′ə), *n.* military force; army of citizens trained for war or any other emergency. Every State has a militia called the National Guard. [< L *militia* < *miles* soldier]

mis con strue (mis′kən strü′), *v.,* **-strued, -stru ing.** take in a wrong sense; misunderstand.

mis cre ant (mis′krē ənt), *adj.* 1. having very bad morals; base. 2. *Archaic.* unbelieving; heretical. *—n.* 1. villain. 2. *Archaic.* unbeliever; heretic. **Syn.** *adj.* 1. depraved, vile, detestable.

mis de mean or (mis′di mē′nər), *n.* 1. a breaking of the law, not so serious as a felony. Disturbing the peace and breaking traffic laws are misdemeanors. 2. a wrong deed. 3. bad behavior.

moi e ty (moi′ə tē), *n., pl.* **-ties.** 1. half. 2. part: *Only a small moiety of high-school graduates go to college.*

mold ing (mōl′ding), *n.* 1. act of shaping: *the molding of dishes from clay.* 2. something molded. 3. strip, usually of wood, around the upper walls of a room, used to support pictures, to cover electric wires, etc. Also, *esp. Brit.* **moulding.**

mon ger (mung′gər, mong′gər), *n. Brit.* dealer in some article.

mon i tor (mon′ə tər), *n.* 1. pupil in school with special duties, such as helping to keep order and taking attendance. 2. person who gives advice or warning. 3. a low armoured warship having one or more turrets for guns. 4. a receiver

hat, āge, fär; let, bē, tėrm; it, īce; hot, gō, ôrder; oil, out; cup, pùt, rüle; ch, child; ng, long; th, thin; ᴛн, then; zh, measure; ə represents *a* in about, *e* in taken, *i* in pencil, *o* in lemon, *u* in circus.

used for checking radio transmissions. —*v.* check (a radio transmission) by listening in with a receiver. [< L *monitor* < *monere* admonish]

mo not o ny (mə not′n ē), *n.* 1. sameness of tone or pitch. 2. lack of variety. 3. wearisome sameness. [< Gk. *monotonia,* ult. < *monos* single + *tonos* tone]

mon sieur (mə syœ′), *n.,* *pl.* **mes sieurs** (mā syœ′). Mr.; sir. [< F *monsieur,* earlier *mon sieur* my lord]

moor (mür), *n.* Brit. open waste land, especially if heather grows on it. [OE *mōr*]

mor tal (môr′tl), *adj.* 1. sure to die sometime. 2. of man; of mortals. 3. of death. 4. causing death of the soul: *mortal sin.* 5. causing death: *a mortal wound.* 6. to the death: *a mortal battle.* 7. very great; deadly: *mortal terror.* —*n.* 1. a being that is sure to die sometime. 2. man; human being. [< L *mortalis* < *mors* death]
Syn. *adj.* 2. human. 5. lethal.

muse (myūz), *v.,* **mused, mus ing.** 1. think in a dreamy way; think; meditate. 2. look thoughtfully. 3. say thoughtfully. [< OF *muser* loiter] —**mus′er,** *n.*
Syn. 1. ponder, reflect, ruminate.

mute (myūt), *adj., n., v.,* **mut ed, mut ing.** —*adj.* 1. not making any sound; silent. 2. unable to speak; dumb. —*n.* 1. person who cannot speak. 2. clip or pad put on a musical instrument to soften the sound. 3. a silent letter. 4. *Archaic.* a hired mourner at a funeral. —*v.* put a clip or pad on (a musical instrument) to soften the sound. —**mute′ly,** *adv.* —**mute′ness,** *n.*

My ce nae (mī sē′nē)

my op ic (mī op′ik), *adj.* near-sighted.

na bob (nā′bob), *n.* a very rich man.

na ive or **na ïve** (nä ēv′), *adj.* simple in nature; like a child; artless; not sophisticated.

na ï ve té or **na i ve te** (nä ē′və tā′), *n.* 1. quality of being naïve; unspoiled freshness. 2. naïve action, remark, etc. [< F]

nat ty (nat′ē), *adj.,* **-ti er, -ti est.** trim and tidy; neatly smart in dress or appearance: *a natty uniform, a natty young officer.* —**nat′ti ly,** *adv.*

Nau pli a (nô′pli ə)

ne go ti ate (ni gō′shē āt), *v.,* **-at ed, -at ing.** 1. talk over and arrange terms: *The colonists negotiated for peace with the Indians.* 2. arrange for: *They finally negotiated a peace treaty.* 3. sell. 4. *Informal.* get past or over: *The car negotiated the curve by slowing down.*

Ne me a (ni mē′ə, ne′mē ə)

net tle (net′l), *n., v.,* **-tled, -tling.** —*n.* kind of plant having sharp leaf hairs that sting the skin when touched. —*v.* sting the mind of; irritate; provoke; vex.
Syn. *v.* exasperate, incense.

neu rone (nür′ōn, nyür′ōn), *n.* one of the conducting cells of which the brain, spinal cord, and nerves are composed. A neurone consists of a cell body containing the nucleus, and processes or fibers which may be very long. [< Gk. *neuron* nerve]

neu ro-sur geon (nü rō′sèr′jən), *n.* a doctor who specializes in neurosurgery.

neu ro sur ger y (nü rō′sèr′jər ē), *n.* surgery of the nervous system, especially of the brain.

nig ger head (nig′èr hed′), *n.* a dark-colored clump of vegetation found in regions of the far North.

no mad (nō′mad, nom′ad), *n.* 1. member of a tribe that moves from place to place to have pasture for its cattle.

2. wanderer. —*adj.* 1. wandering from place to place to find pasture. 2. wandering.

no mad ic (nō mad′ik), *adj.* of nomads or their life; wandering; roving. —**no mad′i cal ly,** *adv.*

non cha lant (non′shə lənt, non′shə länt′), *adj.* without enthusiasm; coolly unconcerned; indifferent. —**non′chalant ly,** *adv.*

non com mit tal (non′kə mit′l), *adj.* not committing oneself; not saying yes or no: *"I will think it over" is a noncommittal answer.* —**non′com mit′tal ly,** *adv.*

no to ri ous (nō tôr′ē əs, nō tōr′ē əs), *adj.* 1. well-known because of something bad; having a bad reputation: *The notorious thief was sent to prison for his many crimes.* 2. well-known. [< Med.L *notorius* < L *notus* known] —**no to′ri ous ly,** *adv.* —**no to′ri ous ness,** *n.*
→ **Notorious** means well-known for unsavory reasons: *a notorious cheat.* **Famous** means well-known for accomplishment or excellence: *a famous writer or aviator.*

nov el[1] (nov′əl), *adj.* of a new kind or nature; strange; new: *Red snow is a novel idea to us.* [< L *novellus,* dim. of *novus* new]
Syn. unfamiliar.

nov el[2] (nov′əl), *n.* story with characters and a plot, long enough to fill one or more volumes. [< Ital. *novella* < L *novella* new things, neut. pl. of *novellus* (see NOVEL[1]); intermediate meaning probably "a composition showing originality"]
Syn. **Novel, romance** mean a long fictitous story. **Novel** applies particularly to a long work of prose fiction dealing with characters, situations, and scenes that represent those of real life and setting forth the action in the form of a plot. **Romance** applies especially to a story, often a novel in form, presenting characters and situations not likely to be found in real life and emphasizing exciting or amazing adventures, love, etc., usually set in distant or unfamiliar times or places.

oar lock (ôr′lok′, ōr′lok′), *n.* a notch or U-shaped support in which the oar rests in rowing.

o bit u ar y (ō bich′ü er′ē), *n., pl.* **-ar ies,** *adj.* —*n.* a notice of death, often with a brief account of the person's life. —*adj.* of a death; recording a death.

ob lique (ə blēk′; *military* ə blik′), *adj., v.,* **-liqued, -liqu ing.** —*adj.* 1. not straight up and down; not straight across; slanting. 2. not straightforward; indirect: *She made an oblique reference to her illness, but did not mention it directly.* —*v.* advance in an oblique manner; slant.

ob strep er ous (əb strep′ər əs), *adj.* 1. noisy; boisterous. 2. unruly; disorderly.

o di ous (ō′dē əs), *adj.* very displeasing; hateful; offensive. [< L *odiosus* < *odium* odium] —**o′di ous ly,** *adv.* —**o′di ous ness,** *n.*
Syn. detestable, abominable, abhorrent, repulsive.

of fice (ô′fis, of′is), *n.* 1. place in which the work of a position is done; room or rooms for clerical work. 2. position, especially in the public service: *The President holds the highest public office in the United States.* 3. duty of one's position; task; job; work: *A teacher's office is teaching.* 4. staff of persons carrying on work in an office. 5. an administrative department of a governmental organization. 6. act of kindness or unkindness; attention; service; injury: *Through the good offices of a friend, he was able to get a job.* 7. a religious ceremony or prayer: *the communion office, last offices.* 8. **offices,** *pl.* parts of a house devoted to household

---

< = from, derived from, taken from;   cf., compare;   dial., dialect;   dim., diminutive;   lang., language; pp., past participle;   ppr., present participle;   pt., past tense;   ult., ultimately;   var., variant;   ? = possibly.

work, such as kitchen, pantry, laundry, etc., often also stables and buildings. [< OF < L *officium* service < *opus* work + *facere* do]
Syn. 2. post, situation. 3. function, charge.

o gre (ō′gər), *n.* giant or monster that supposedly eats people. [< F]

om i nous (om′ə nəs), *adj.* of bad omen; unfavorable; threatening: *Those clouds look ominous for our picnic.* **—om′i nous ly,** *adv.* **—om′i nous ness,** *n.*
Syn. inauspicious, foreboding.

on slaught (ôn′slôt′, on′slôt′), *n.* a vigorous attack: *The Indians made an onslaught on the fort.*

op por tun ist (op′ər tü′nist, op′ər tyü′nist), *n.* person influenced more by particular circumstances than by general principles.

op pres sive (ə pres′iv), *adj.* 1. harsh; severe; unjust. 2. hard to bear; burdensome. **—op pres′sive ly,** *adv.* **—op pres′sive ness,** *n.*

op u lence (op′yə ləns), *n.* 1. wealth; riches. 2. abundance; plenty.

orb (ôrb), *n.* 1. sphere; globe. 2. sun, moon, planet, or star. 3. *Esp. Poetic.* eyeball or eye. **—v.** 1. form into a circle or sphere. 2. *Poetic.* encircle; enclose. [< L *orbis* circle]
Syn. *n.* 1. ball.

or bit (ôr′bit), *n., v.,* **-bit ed, -bit ing. —n.** 1. path of the earth or any one of the planets about the sun. 2. path of any heavenly body about another heavenly body. 3. regular course of life or experience. 4. the bony cavity or socket in which the eyeball is set. **—v.** 1. travel around (a body in an orbit). 2. travel in an orbit. 3. place (a satellite) in an orbit. 4. of a satellite, etc., arrive in its orbit. [< L *orbita* wheel track < *orbis* wheel, circle] **—or′bit er,** *n.*

or ches trate (ôr′kə strāt), *v.,* **-trat ed, -trat ing.** arrange (music) for performance by an orchestra.

or ni thol o gy (ôr′nə thol′ə jē), *n.* study of birds. [< NL *ornithologia* < Gk. *ornis* bird + *-logos* treating of]

or tho don tia (ôr′thə don′chə, ôr′thə don′chē ə), *n.* branch of dentistry that deals with straightening and adjusting teeth. [< NL < Gk. *orthos* straight + *odon* tooth]

or tho don tist (ôr′thə don′tist), *n.* dentist who specializes in orthodontia.

os ten ta tious (os′ten tā′shəs), *adj.* 1. done for display; intended to attract notice. 2. showing off; liking to attract notice. **—os′ten ta′tious ly,** *adv.*
Syn. 1. showy, spectacular, pretentious, gaudy.

ost ler (os′lər), *n.* hostler.

os tra cize (os′trə sīz), *v.,* **-cized, -ciz ing.** 1. banish. 2. shut out from society, from favor, from privileges, etc.

pag eant (paj′ənt), *n.* 1. an elaborate spectacle; procession in costume; pomp; display: *The coronation of the new king was a splendid pageant.* 2. a public entertainment that represents scenes from history, legend, or the like. 3. empty show, not reality. [ME *pagent, pagen;* origin uncertain]

pal at a ble (pal′ə tə bəl), *adj.* agreeable to the taste; pleasing. **—pal′at a bly,** *adv.*

pall (pôl), *n.* 1. a heavy cloth of black, purple, or white velvet spread over a coffin, a hearse, or a tomb. 2. a dark, gloomy covering: *A pall of smoke shut out the sun from the city.* [OE *pæll* < L *pallium* cloak]

pal pa ble (pal′pə bəl), *adj.* 1. readily seen or heard and recognized; obvious: *a palpable error.* 2. that can be touched or felt. [< LL *palpabilis* < L *palpare* feel]
Syn. 1. perceptible, evident. 2. tangible.

pal sied (pôl′zēd), *adj.* 1. having the palsy; paralyzed. 2. shaking; trembling.

pan de mo ni um (pan′də mō′nē əm), *n.* 1. abode of all the demons. 2. place of wild disorder or lawless confusion. 3. wild uproar or lawlessness. 4. **Pandemonium,** hell's capital. [< NL < Gk. *pan-* all + *daimon* demon]

pan e gyr ic (pan′ə jir′ik), *n.* 1. speech or writing in praise of a person or thing. 2. enthusiastic or extravagant praise. [< L < Gk. *panegyrikos* < *pan-* all + *agyris* assembly]

pang (pang), *n.* a sudden, short, sharp pain or feeling: *the pangs of a toothache, a pang of pity.* [origin uncertain]

Pa phos (pā′fos)

par a pet (par′ə pet, par′ə pit), *n.* 1. a low wall or mound of stone, earth, etc., to protect soldiers. 2. a low wall at the edge of a balcony, roof, bridge, etc.

par a pher nal ia (par′ə fər nā′lyə), *n.pl.* 1. personal belongings. 2. equipment; outfit. [< Med.L *paraphernalia,* ult. < Gk. *parapherna* < *para-* besides + *pherne* dowry]

par a phrase (par′ə frāz), *v.,* **-phrased, -phras ing,** *n.* **—v.** state the meaning of (a passage) in other words. [< n.] **—n.** expression of the meaning of a passage in other words. [< F < L Gk. *paraphrasis* < *para-* alongside of + *phrazein* say]

parlor car, a railroad passenger car for day travel, more luxurious than ordinary cars.

par ox ysm (par′ok siz əm), *n.* 1. a severe, sudden attack: *a paroxysm of coughing.* 2. fit; convulsion: *a paroxysm of rage.*

par ry (par′ē), *v.,* **-ried, -ry ing,** *n., pl.* **-ries. —v.** ward off; turn aside; evade (a thrust, stroke, weapon, question, etc.). **—n.** act of parrying; avoiding. [< F *parez,* imperative of *parer* < Ital. *parare* ward off < L *parare* prepare]

par ti san (pär′tə zən), *n.* 1. a strong supporter of a person, party, or cause; one whose support is based on feeling rather than on reasoning. 2. member of light, irregular troops; guerrilla. **—adj.** of or like a partisan.
Syn. *n.* 1. follower, adherent, disciple.

pass port (pas′pôrt, pas′pōrt), *n.* 1. a paper or book giving official permission to travel in a certain country, under the protection of one's own government. 2. anything that gives one admission or acceptance: *An interest in gardening was a passport to my aunt's favor.* [< F *passeport* < *passer* pass + *port* harbor]

pas tern (pas′tərn), *n.* the part of a horse's foot between the fetlock and the hoof.

FETLOCK

PASTERN

HOOF →

pa thet ic (pə thet′ik), *adj.* 1. pitiful; arousing pity. 2. of the emotions. [< LL *patheticus* < Gk. *pathetikos,* ult. < *path-,* stem of *paschein* suffer] **—pa thet′i cal ly,** *adv.*
Syn. 1. pitiable, moving, touching, affecting.

pa thos (pā′thos), *n.* quality in speech, writing, music, events, or a scene that arouses a feeling of pity or sadness. [< Gk. *pathos* suffering, feeling]

pa tri arch (pā′trē ärk), *n.* 1. father and ruler of a family or tribe. In the Bible, Abraham, Isaac, and Jacob were patriarchs. 2. person thought of as the father or founder of something. 3. a venerable old man. 4. bishop of the highest rank in the early Christian church or in the Greek Church. [< L < Gk. *patriarches* < *patria* family + *archos* leader]

pa tron ize (pā′trə nīz, pat′rə nīz), *v.,* **-ized, -iz ing.** 1. be a regular customer of; give regular business to. 2. support or protect. 3. treat in a condescending way. **—pa′tron iz′ing ly,** *adv.*

hat, āge, fär; let, bē, tėrm; it, īce; hot, gō, ôrder; oil, out; cup, pût, rüle; ch, child; ng, long; th, thin; ŦH, then; zh, measure; ə represents *a* in about, *e* in taken, *i* in pencil, *o* in lemon, *u* in circus.

peak ed (pē′kid), *adj.* sickly in appearance; wan; thin. [< *peak*, v., look sick; origin uncertain]

Pe le us (pē′lē us)

Pe ne us (pē nē′us)

pen non (pen′ən), *n.* 1. a long, triangular flag, originally carried on the lance of a knight. 2. flag or banner.

pent-up (pent′up′), *adj.* shut up; closely confined.

per ceive (pər sēv′), *v.*, **-ceived, -ceiv ing.** 1. be aware of through the senses; see, hear, taste, smell, or feel. 2. take in with the mind; observe: *I perceived that I could not make him change his mind.* [< OF *perceivre* < L *percipere* < *per-* fully + *capere* grasp]

per cep tion (pər sep′shən), *n.* 1. act of perceiving: *His perception of the change came in a flash.* 2. power of perceiving: *a keen perception.* 3. percept. [< L *perceptio, -onis* < *percipere* perceive. See PERCEIVE.]
Syn. 1. insight, apprehension, discernment, comprehension.

pe remp tor y (pə remp′tər ē, per′əmp tôr′ē, per′əmp tōr′ē), *adj.* 1. imperious; positive: *a peremptory teacher.* 2. allowing no denial or refusal: *a peremptory command.* 3. leaving no choice; decisive; final; absolute: *a peremptory decree.* **—pe remp′tor i ly,** *adv.* **—pe remp′tor i ness,** *n.*
Syn. 1. arbitrary, dogmatic.

per jur er (pėr′jər ər), *n.* person who commits perjury.

per ju ry (pėr′jər ē), *n., pl.* **-ries.** act of swearing that something is true which one knows to be false.

per ni cious (pər nish′əs), *adj.* 1. that will destroy or ruin; causing great harm or damage: *Gambling is a pernicious habit.* 2. fatal. **—per ni′cious ly,** *adv.*
Syn. 1. injurious, noxious.

per pet u al ly (pər pech′ü əl ē), *adv.* forever.

Per seph o ne (pər sef′ə nē)

pes si mis tic (pes′ə mis′tik), *adj.* 1. disposed to take a gloomy view of things and to see the dark side of life. 2. believing that life holds more evil than good, and so is not worth while. **—pes′si mis′ti cal ly,** *adv.*
Syn. 1. See cynical.

pes ti lence (pes′tl əns), *n.* disease that spreads rapidly, causing many deaths. Smallpox, yellow fever, and the plague are pestilences.
Syn. epidemic, pest.

pet ty (pet′ē), *adj.,* **-ti er, -ti est.** 1. having little importance or value; small: *She insisted on telling me all her petty troubles.* 2. mean; narrow-minded. 3. lower; subordinate. **—pet′ti ly,** *adv.* **—pet′ti ness,** *n.*
Syn. 1. trivial, slight, insignificant. 3. minor.

phe nom e na (fə nom′ə nə), *n.* a pl. of **phenomenon.**

phe nom e non (fə nom′ə non), *n., pl.* **-na** or (*esp. for def. 2*) **-nons.** 1. fact, event, or circumstance that can be observed: *Lightning is an electrical phenomenon. Fever and inflammation are phenomena of disease.* 2. something or someone extraordinary or remarkable.

Phleg a thon (fleg′ə thon)

pho bi a (fō′bē ə), *n.* a morbid or insane fear. [< NL < Gk. *-phobia* < *phobos* fear]

Pho lus (fō′lus)

phos phate (fos′fāt), *n.* 1. salt or ester of an acid containing phosphorus. Bread contains phosphates. 2. fertilizer containing such salts. 3. drink of carbonated water flavored with fruit syrup, and containing a little phosphoric acid.

pho tot ro pism (fō to′trə piz əm), *n.* in botany, a tendency to turn in response to light. [< *photo-* + Gk. *-tropos* turning]

pho to stat (fō′tə stat), *n.* 1. **Photostat,** *Trademark.* a special camera for making copies of maps, drawings, pages of books, etc., directly on specially prepared paper. 2. photograph made with it. **—v.** make a photostat of.

piece meal (pēs′mēl′), *adv.* 1. piece by piece; a little at a time: *work done piecemeal.* 2. piece from piece; to pieces; into fragments. **—adj.** done piece by piece. [ME *pecemele*]

pi geon hole (pij′ən hōl′), *n.* 1. a small place built, usually as one of a series, for a pigeon to nest in. 2. one of a set of boxlike compartments for holding papers and other articles in a desk, a cabinet, etc.

pig nut (pig′nut′), *n.* 1. nut of the brown hickory of North America. 2. the tree itself. 3. the tuber of a certain European plant.

pike (pīk), *n.* a sharp point; spike. [OE *pīc* pick]

pike staff (pīk′staf′), *n., pl.* **-staves** (-stāvz′). 1. staff or shaft of a pike or spear. 2. staff with a metal point or spike, used by travelers.

pique (pēk), *n., v.,* **piqued, pi quing.** **—n.** a feeling of anger at being slighted; wounded pride: *In a pique, she left the party.* [< F *pique* < *piquer,* v. See PIQUE, v.] **—v.** 1. cause a feeling of anger in; wound the pride of: *It piqued her that they should have a secret she did not share.* 2. arouse; stir up: *The curiosity of the boys was piqued by the locked trunk.* 3. **pique oneself on** or **upon,** feel proud about. [< F *piquer* prick, sting < *pic* a pick (< Gmc.)]

pi rosh ki s (pē rush′kēz), *n.* meat or cheese pies.

pis ton (pis′tən), *n.* a short cylinder, or a flat, round piece of wood or metal, fitting closely inside a tube or hollow cylinder in which it is moved back and forth by some force (often the pressure of steam). A piston receives or transmits motion by means of a rod (**piston rod**) that is attached to it. [< F < Ital. *pistone* < *pistare* pound, ult. < L *pistus,* pp. of *pinsere* pound]

pitch (pich), *n.* 1. a throw; fling; hurl; toss. 2. point; position; degree: *The poor man has reached the lowest pitch of bad fortune.* 3. degree of highness or lowness of a sound. Notes in music with a low pitch have a slower rate of vibration than those with a high pitch. 4. height. 5. act or manner of pitching. 6. that which is pitched. 7. amount of slope. 8. distance between the successive teeth of a cogwheel. 9. distance between two things in a machine.

pit e ous (pit′ē əs), *adj.* to be pitied; moving the heart; deserving pity. **—pit′e ous ly,** *adv.*

piv ot (piv′ət), *n.* 1. shaft, pin, or point on which something turns. 2. that on which something turns, hinges, or depends; central point. **—v.** 1. mount on, attach by, or provide with a pivot. 2. turn on a pivot.

plac id (plas′id), *adj.* calm; peaceful; quiet: *a placid lake.* [< L *placidus* < *placere* please] **—plac′id ly,** *adv.* **—plac′id ness,** *n.*

plain tive (plān′tiv), *adj.* mournful; sad. **—plain′tive ly,** *adv.*

plait (plāt, plat *for 1;* plāt, plēt *for 2*), *n., v.* 1. braid. 2. pleat. [< OF *pleit,* ult. < L *plicare* to fold]

plume (plüm), *n.* 1. a large, long feather; feather. 2. a feather, bunch of feathers, or tuft of hair worn as an ornament on a hat, helmet, etc. 3. something resembling a plume. 4. the hollow cylinder of spray thrown up by an underwater atomic explosion.

po di um (pō′dē əm), *n., pl.* **-di ums, -di a** (-dē ə). 1. a raised platform. 2. an animal structure that serves as a foot. [< L < Gk. *podion,* dim. of *pous* foot]

poign ant (poi′nyənt), *adj.* 1. very painful; piercing: *poignant suffering.* 2. keen; intense: *a subject of poignant*

< = from, derived from, taken from;   cf., compare;   dial., dialect;   dim., diminutive;   lang., language; pp., past participle;   ppr., present participle;   pt., past tense;   ult., ultimately;   var., variant;   ? = possibly.

interest. **3.** sharp to the taste or smell: *poignant sauces.*
—poign′ant ly, *adv.*
Syn. 1. severe.

poise (poiz), *n., v.,* **poised, pois ing.** *—n.* mental balance,
composure, or self-possession: *She has perfect poise and
never seems embarrassed.* [< OF *pois* < L *pensum* weight]
—v. **1.** balance: *Poise yourself on your toes.* **2.** hold or carry
evenly or steadily: *The athlete poised the weight in the air
before throwing it.* [< OF *peser* weigh < L *pensare,* intensive
of *pendere* weigh]

poll (pōl), *n.* **1.** a voting; collection of votes. **2.** number of
votes cast. **3.** the results of these votes. **4.** list of persons;
especially, a list of voters. **5. polls,** *pl.* place where votes
are cast and counted. **6.** a survey of public opinion concerning a particular subject. **7.** the head, especially the part of it
on which the hair grows.

pol y glot (pol′ē glot), *adj.* **1.** knowing several languages.
2. written in several languages. *—n.* **1.** person who knows
several languages. **2.** book written in several languages.
[< Gk. *polyglottos* < *polys* many + *glotta* tongue]

pon der ous (pon′dər əs), *adj.* **1.** very heavy. **2.** heavy
and clumsy. **3.** dull; tiresome: *The speaker talked in a
ponderous way.* **—pon′der ous ly,** *adv.*
Syn. 1. weighty, massive. **2.** unwieldy, cumbersome.

por ter (pôr′tər, pōr′tər), *n.* **1.** man employed to carry
burdens or baggage. **2.** *U.S.* attendant in a parlor car or
sleeping car. [< OF *porteour,* ult. < L *portare* carry]

port ly (pôrt′lē, pōrt′lē), *adj.,* **-li er, -li est. 1.** stout; cor-
pulent. **2.** stately; dignified.

Po sei don (pə sīd′n)

po tent (pōt′nt), *adj.* **1.** powerful; having great power: *a
potent remedy for a disease.* **2.** exercising great moral
influence: *His good deeds had a potent effect on his com-
rades.* **—po′tent ly,** *adv.*
Syn. 1. mighty, strong.

pre am ble (prē′am′bəl), *n.* **1.** a preliminary statement;
introduction to a speech or a writing. The reasons for a law
and its general purpose are often stated in a preamble. **2.** a
preliminary or introductory fact or circumstance.

pre ar range (prē′ə rānj′), *v.,* **-ranged, -rang ing.** arrange beforehand. **—pre′ar range′ment,** *n.*

prec i pice (pres′ə pis), *n.* a very steep cliff; almost
vertical slope. [< F < L *praecipitium* < *praeceps* steep,
literally, headlong < *prae-* first + *caput* head]

pre cip i tous (pri sip′ə təs), *adj.* **1.** like a precipice; very
steep: *precipitous cliffs.* **2.** hasty; rash. **—pre cip′i tous-
ness,** *n.*
Syn. 1. See **steep.**

pre dic a ment (pri dik′ə mənt), *n.* **1.** an unpleasant,
difficult, or dangerous situation. **2.** any condition, state, or
situation.

pre dis pose (prē′dis pōz′), *v.,* **-posed, -pos ing.** give
an inclination or tendency to; make liable or susceptible: *A
cold predisposes a person to other diseases.*

pre dom i nance (pri dom′ə nəns), *n.* a being predominant.

pre dom i nant (pri dom′ə nənt), *adj.* **1.** having more
power, authority, or influence than others; superior.
2. prevailing; most noticeable. **—pre dom′i nant ly,** *adv.*
Syn. 1. controlling, ruling.
Ant. 1. subordinate, secondary.

pre em i nent or **pre-em i nent** (prē em′ə nənt),
adj. standing out above all others; superior to others.

preen (prēn), *v.* **1.** smooth or arrange (the feathers with the
beak, as a bird does. **2.** dress (oneself) carefully.

prel ude (prel′yüd, prā′lüd), *n., v.,* **-ud ed, -ud ing.** *—n.*
1. anything serving as an introduction: *the organ prelude to a
church service.* **2.** piece of music, or part of it, that introduces another piece or part. *—v.* **1.** be a prelude or
introduction to. **2.** introduce with a prelude. [< F < Med.L
praeludium, ult. < L *prae-* before + *ludere* play]

pre par a to ry (pri par′ə tôr′ē, pri par′ə tōr′ē), *adj.*
1. of or for preparation; preparing. Preparatory schools fit
pupils for college. **2.** as an introduction.

pre tend er (pri ten′dər), *n.* **1.** person who pretends.
2. person who makes claims to a throne without just right.

pre tense (prē′tens, pri tens′), *n.* **1.** make believe; pretending. **2.** a false appearance: *Under pretense of picking up
the handkerchief, she took the money.* **3.** a false claim: *The
girls made a pretense of knowing the boys' secret.* **4.** claim.
5. a showing off; display: *Her manner is free from pretense.*
6. anything done to show off.
Syn. 5. ostentation.

pre ter nat u ral (prē′tər nach′ər əl), *adj.* **1.** out of the
ordinary course of nature; abnormal. **2.** due to something
above or beyond nature; supernatural.

pro cliv i ty (prō kliv′ə tē), *n., pl.* **-ties.** tendency; inclination. [< L *proclivitas,* ult. < *pro-* forward + *clivus*
slope]
Syn. bias, bent.

proc tor (prok′tər), *n.* **1.** official in a university or school
who keeps order. **2.** person employed to manage another's
case in a law court. [short for *procurator*]

pro cure (prə kyür′), *v.,* **-cured, -cur ing. 1.** obtain by
care or effort; get: *A friend procured a position in the bank
for my big brother.* **2.** bring about; cause: *procure a person's
death.* **—pro cur′a ble,** *adj.* **—pro cur′er,** *n.*
Syn. 1. acquire, gain, win, secure.

pro found (prə found′), *adj.* **1.** very deep: *a profound
sigh, a profound sleep.* **2.** deeply felt; very great: *profound
despair, profound sympathy.* **3.** going far deeper than what
is easily understood; having or showing great knowledge or
understanding: *a profound book, a profound thinker, a
profound thought.* **4.** low; carried far down; going far down:
a profound bow. [< OF < L *profundus* < *pro-* at some
distance + *fundus* bottom] **—pro found′ly,** *adv.* **—pro-
found′ness,** *n.*
Syn. 3. abstruse, recondite.

pro gres sive (prə gres′iv), *adj.* **1.** making progress; advancing to something better; improving: *a progressive nation.* **2.** favoring progress; wanting improvement or reform
in government, business, etc. **3.** moving forward; going
ahead. **4.** going from one to the next; involving shifts of
players or guests from one table to another. **—pro-
gres′sive ly,** *adv.* **—pro gres′sive ness,** *n.*

proph e cy (prof′ə sē), *n., pl.* **-cies. 1.** telling what will
happen; foretelling future events. **2.** thing told about the
future. **3.** a divinely inspired utterance, revelation, writing,
etc. [< OF < L < Gk. *propheteia* < *prophētēs*]

proph e sy (prof′ə sī), *v.,* **-sied, -sy ing. 1.** tell what will
happen. **2.** foretell; predict: *The sailor prophesied a severe
storm.* **3.** speak when or as if divinely inspired. **4.** utter in
prophecy. **—proph′e si′er,** *n.*

pro pri e tar y (prə prī′ə ter′ē), *adj., n., pl.* **-tar ies.**
—adj. **1.** belonging to a proprietor. **2.** holding property.
3. owned by a private person or company; belonging to or
controlled by a private person as property. A proprietary
medicine is a patent medicine, that is, one which can be
made and sold only by some one person or certain persons.
—n. **1.** owner. **2.** group of owners. **3.** ownership; the

hat, āge, fär;   let, bē, tèrm;   it, īce;   hot, gō, ôrder;   oil, out;   cup, pùt, rüle;   ch, child;   ng, long;
th, thin;   ŦH, then;   zh, measure;   ə represents *a* in about, *e* in taken, *i* in pencil, *o* in lemon, *u* in circus.

holding of property. [< LL *proprietarius* < L *proprietas* ownership]

pro sa ic (prō zā′ik), *adj.* like prose; matter-of-fact; ordinary; not exciting. —**pro sa′i cal ly,** *adv.*
Syn. commonplace, humdrum, dull, tedious.

prov i den tial (prov′ə den′shəl), *adj.* 1. fortunate: *Our delay seemed providential, for the train we had planned to take was wrecked.* 2. of or proceeding from divine power or influence.

pro vin cial (prə vin′shəl), *adj.* 1. of a province. 2. belonging or peculiar to some particular province or provinces rather than to the whole country; local: *provincial English, provincial customs.* 3. having the manners, speech, dress, point of view, etc., of people living in a province. 4. lacking refinement or polish; narrow: *a provincial point of view.* —*n.* 1. person born or living in a province. 2. a provincial person. —**pro vin′cial ly,** *adv.*

prow (prou), *n.* 1. the pointed front part of a ship or boat; bow. 2. something like it: *the prow of an airship.* [< F *proue* < Ital. < L < Gk. *proira*]

pru dence (prüd′ns), *n.* 1. wise thought before acting; good judgment. 2. good management; economy.

pseu do (sü′dō), *adj.* 1. false; sham; pretended. 2. having only the appearance of. [< Gk. *pseudes* false]

psycho-, *word element.* mind, as in psychoanalysis. Also, **psych-** before some vowels. [< Gk. *psyche* soul, mind]

psy cho ex per i men tal ist (sī′kō ek sper′ə men′tl ist), *n.* one who conducts tests or experiments which have to do with the mind or behavior.

pum mel (pum′əl), *v.,* **-meled, -mel ing** or *esp. Brit.* **-melled, -mel ing.** beat; beat with the fists.

pur ga to ry (pèr′gə tôr′ē, pèr′gə tōr′ē), *n., pl.* **-ries.** 1. in the belief of the Roman Catholics, a temporary condition or place in which the souls of those who have died penitent are purified from venial sin or the effects of sin by punishment. 2. any condition or place of temporary suffering or punishment. [< Med.L *purgatorium*, originally neut. adj., purging < L *purgare*]

quaff (kwäf, kwaf, kwôf), *v.* drink in large draughts; drink freely. —*n.* a quaffing. [origin uncertain]

qualm (kwäm, kwälm), *n.* 1. a sudden disturbing feeling in the mind; uneasiness; misgiving; doubt: *I tried the test with some qualms.* 2. disturbance or scruple of conscience: *She felt some qualms at staying away from church.*

quar ry (kwôr′ē, kwor′ē), *n., pl.* **-ries.** 1. animal chased in a hunt; game; prey. 2. anything hunted or eagerly pursued. [< OF *cuirée* < *cuir* hide < L *corium*]

quar to (kwôr′tō), *n., pl.* **-tos,** *adj.* —*n.* 1. the page size (usually about 9 by 12 inches) of a book in which each leaf is one fourth of a whole sheet of paper. 2. book having this size. —*adj.* having this size. [< Med.L *in quarto* in the fourth (of a sheet)]

raf fish (raf′ish), *adj.* rowdy; disreputable.

rake (rāk), *n., v.,* **raked, rak ing.** slant; slope. A ship's smokestacks have a slight backward rake.

ram rod (ram′rod′), *n.* 1. rod for ramming down the charge in a gun that is loaded from the muzzle. 2. rod for cleaning the barrel of a gun.

ram shack le (ram′shak′əl), *adj.* loose and shaky; likely to come apart.
Syn. rickety, dilapidated.

rap scal lion (rap skal′yən), *n.* rascal; rogue; scamp. [earlier *rascallion* < *rascal*]

rap ture (rap′chər), *n., v.,* **-tured, -tur ing.** —*n.* 1. a strong feeling that absorbs the mind; very great joy. 2. Often, **raptures,** *pl.* expression of great joy. —*v.* to transport with rapture or joy. Also, **enrapture.** [< *rapt*]

rap tur ous (rap′chər əs), *adj.* full of rapture; expressing or feeling rapture. —**rap′tur ous ly,** *adv.*

rar e fy (rer′ə fi, rar′ə fi), *v.,* **-fied, -fy ing.** 1. make less dense: *The air on high mountains is rarefied.* 2. become less dense. 3. refine; purify.

ra tion al (rash′ə nəl), *adj.* 1. sensible; reasonable; reasoned out: *When very angry, people seldom act in a rational way.* 2. able to think and reason clearly: *As children grow older, they become more rational.* 3. of reason; based on reasoning. —**ra′tion al ly,** *adv.*
Syn. 1. sound, wise, sane.
Ant. 1. unreasonable.

rau cous (rô′kəs), *adj.* hoarse; harsh-sounding: *the raucous caw of a crow.* [< L *raucus*] —**rau′cous ly,** *adv.*

rav ish ing (rav′i shing), *adj.* very delightful; enchanting: *jewels of ravishing beauty.* —**rav′ish ing ly,** *adv.*

re as sure (rē′ə shúr′), *v.,* **-sured, -sur ing.** 1. restore to confidence: *The captain's confidence during the storm reassured the passengers.* 2. assure again or anew. 3. insure again. —**re′as sur′ing ly,** *adv.*

re con nais sance (ri kon′ə səns), *n.* examination or survey, especially for military purposes.

rec on noi ter (rek′ə noi′tər, rē′kə noi′tər), *v.,* **-tered, -ter ing.** approach and examine or observe in order to learn something; make a survey of (the enemy, the enemy's strength or position, a region, etc.) in order to gain information for military purposes. [< F *reconnoitre*, earlier form of *reconnaitre* (< OF *reconoistre*). —**rec′on noi′ter er,** *n.*

rec on noi tre (rek′ə noi′tər, rē′kə noi′tər), *v.,* **-tred, -tring.** reconnoiter. —**rec′on noi′trer,** *n.*

re fute (ri fyüt′), *v.,* **-fut ed, -fut ing.** prove (a claim, opinion, or argument) to be false or incorrent.

re gres sion (ri gresh′ən), *n.* act of going back; backward movement.

re gur gi tate (rē gèr′jə tāt), *v.,* **-tat ed -tat ing.** 1. of liquids, gases, undigested foods, etc., rush, surge, or flow back. 2. throw up: *The baby regurgitated food from his stomach.* [< Med.L *regurgitare*, ult. < L *re-* back + *gurges* whirlpool]

re it er ate (rē it′ə rāt′), *v.,* **-rat ed, -rat ing.** say or do several times; repeat (an action, demand, etc.) again and again: *The boy did not move though the teacher reiterated her command.* [< L *reiterare*, ult. < *re-* again + *iterum* again] —**re it′e ra′tion,** *n.*

re join (ri join′), *v.* answer; reply. [< F *rejoindre* < *re-* back + *joindre* join]

re ju ve nes cent (ri jü′və nes′ənt), *adj.* 1. becoming young again. 2. making young again.

re lent less (ri lent′lis), *adj.* without pity; unyielding; harsh: *The storm raged with relentless fury.* —**re lent′less- ly,** *adv.*
Syn. ruthless, implacable.

rel e van cy (rel′ə vən sē), *n.* being relevant.

rel e vant (rel′ə vənt), *adj.* bearing upon or connected with the matter in hand; to the point.
Syn. applicable, appropriate.

< = from, derived from, taken from;   cf., compare;   dial., dialect;   dim., diminutive;   lang., language; pp., past participle;   ppr., present participle;   pt., past tense;   ult., ultimately;   var., variant;   ? = possibly.

re luc tant (ri luk′tənt), *adj.* 1. unwilling; showing unwillingness. 2. slow to act because unwilling: *He was very reluctant to give his money away.* [< L *reluctans, -antis* struggling against, ppr. of *reluctari,* ult. < *re-* back + *lucta* wrestling] —**re luc′tant ly,** *adv.*
Syn. 1. **Reluctant, loath** mean unwilling to do something. **Reluctant** suggests struggling against doing something one finds disagreeable or unpleasant, disapproves of, is afraid of, etc.: *He was reluctant to leave her, but he had no choice.* **Loath** suggests unwillingness because one feels the thing to be done is extremely disagreeable or hateful: *His parents were loath to believe their son would steal.*
re morse (ri môrs′), *n.* deep, painful regret for having done wrong: *The thief felt remorse for his crime and confessed.* [< L *remorsus* tormented, ult. < *re-* back + *mordere* to bite]
Syn. contrition.
rend (rend), *v.,* **rent, rend ing.** 1. pull apart violently; tear: *Wolves will rend a lamb.* 2. split: *Lightning rent the tree.* 3. disturb violently: *His mind was rent by doubt.* 4. remove with force or violence.
Syn. 1. rip.
ren dez vous (rän′də vü), *n., pl.* **-vous** (-vüz), *v.,* **-voused** (-vüd), **-vous ing** (-vü′ing). —*n.* 1. an appointment or engagement to meet at a fixed place or time; meeting by agreement. 2. a meeting place; gathering place: *The family had two favorite rendezvous, the library and the garden.* 3. place agreed on for a meeting at a certain time, especially of troops or ships. —*v.* meet at a rendezvous. [< F *rendezvous* < *rendez-vous* betake yourself!]
ren e gade (ren′ə gād), *n.* deserter from a religious faith, a political party, etc.; traitor. —*adj.* deserting; disloyal; like a traitor. [< Sp. < Med.L *renegatus,* pp. of *renegare* deny]
Syn. *n.* recreant, backslider.
re nounce (ri nouns′), *v.,* **-nounced, -nounc ing.** 1. declare that one gives up; give up entirely; give up: *He renounces his claim to the money.* 2. make formal surrender. 3. cast off; refuse to recognize as one's own: *He renounced his wicked son.* [< F *renoncer* < L *renuntiare,* ult. < *re-* back + *nuntius* message] —**re nounce′ment,** *n.*
Syn. 1. forego, forsake, relinquish. 3. repudiate.
rep ri mand (rep′rə mand), *n.* a severe or formal reproof. —*v.* reprove severely or formally. [< F *réprimande* < L *reprimere* repress < L *reprimere*]
re served (ri zėrvd′), *adj.* 1. kept in reserve; kept by special arrangement. 2. set apart. 3. self-restrained in action or speech. 4. disposed to keep to one's self.
Syn. 1. withheld, retained. 3. restrained, reticent.
res pite (res′pit), *n., v.,* **-pit ed, -pit ing.** —*n.* 1. time of relief and rest; lull: *A thick cloud brought a respite from the glare of the sun.* 2. a putting off; delay, especially, in carrying out a sentence of death; reprieve. —*v.* give a respite to. [< OF < VL *respectus* delay < LL *respectus* expectation < L *respectare* wait for]
re tal i ate (ri tal′ē āt), *v.,* **-at ed, -at ing.** pay back wrong, injury, etc.; return like for like, usually to return evil for evil: *If we insult them, they will retaliate.* [< L *retaliare* < *re-* in return + *tal-* pay; influenced by *talis* such]
ret ri bu tion (ret′rə byü′shən), *n.* a deserved punishment; return for evil done, or sometimes for good done. [< L *retributio, -onis,* ult. < *re-* back + *tribuere* assign]
rev eil le (rev′ə lē), *n.* a signal on a bugle or drum to waken soldiers or sailors in the morning.
rev e la tion (rev′ə lā′shən), *n.* 1. act of making known: *The revelation of the thieves' hiding place by one of their own*

number caused their capture. 2. the thing made known: *Her true nature was a revelation to me.* 3. God's disclosure of Himself and of His will to His creatures. 4. **Revelation,** the last book of the New Testament. [< L *revelatio, -onis* < *revelare* reveal]
rev er ie (rev′ər ē), *n.* dreamy thoughts; dreamy thinking of pleasant things: *He loved to indulge in reveries about the future.* Also, **revery.** [< *rêverie* < *rêver* to dream]
ric o chet (rik′ə shā′; *esp. Brit.* rik′ə shet′), *n., v.,* **-cheted,** (-shād′), **-chet ing** (-shā′ing) or *esp. Brit.* **-chet ted** (-shet′id), **-chet ting** (-shet′ing). —*n.* the skipping or jumping motion of an object as it goes along a flat surface: *the ricochet of a cannon ball along the ground, the ricochet of a stone thrown along the surface of water.* —*v.* move with a skipping or jumping motion. [< F]
ridge (rij), *n., v.,* **ridged, ridg ing.** —*n.* 1. the long and narrow upper part of something: *the ridge of an animal's back.* 2. line where two sloping surfaces meet: *the ridge of a roof.* 3. a long, narrow chain of hills or mountains: *the Blue Ridge of the Appalachian Mountains.* 4. any raised narrow strip: *the ridges on corduroy cloth, the ridges in plowed ground.* —*v.* 1. form or make into ridges. 2. cover with ridges; mark with ridges. [OE *hrycg*]
rime (rīm), *n., v.,* **rimed, rim ing.** —*n.* white frost; hoarfrost. —*v.* cover with rime. [OE *hrīm*]
ri poste (rə pōst′), *n., v.,* **-post ed, -post ing.** —*n.* 1. in fencing, a quick thrust given after parrying a lunge. 2. a quick, sharp reply or return. —*v.* make a riposte; reply; retaliate. [< F < Ital. *risposta* reply, ult. < L *respondere* respond]
ro mance (*n.* rō mans′, rō′mans; *v.* rō mans′), *n., v.,* **-manced, -manc ing.** —*n.* 1. a love story. 2. story of adventure: *"Treasure Island" is a romance.* 3. story or poem telling of heroes: *romances about King Arthur.* 4. real events or conditions that are like such stories, full of love, excitement, or noble deeds; the character or quality of such events or conditions. 5. interest in adventure and love. 6. a love affair. 7. a made-up story: *Nobody believes her romances about the wonderful things that have happened to her.* —*v.* 1. make up romances. 2. think or talk in a romantic way. 3. exaggerate; lie. [ult. < OF *romanz,* ult. < VL *romanice* in a Romance language < L *Romanus* Roman < *Roma* Rome]
Syn. *n.* 1, 2. See **novel.**
ro man tic (rō man′tik), *adj.* 1. characterized by love, affection, or deep personal sentiment. 2. having no basis in fact; exaggerated; imaginary: *No one believes her romantic stories about the wonderful things that have happened to her.* 3. marked by the appeal of the heroic, adventurous, or mysterious characteristics of people, places, or things. *Treasure Island* is a romantic narrative. 4. fond of making up fanciful stories. [< F *romantique* < earlier *romant* a romance, var. of OF *romanz.* See **ROMANCE.**] —**ro man′ti cal ly,** *adv.*
Syn. 1. sentimental. 2. fanciful.
ro sette (rō zet′), *n.* ornament, object, or arrangement shaped like a rose. Rosettes are often made of ribbon. Carved or molded rosettes are used in architecture. [< F *rosette,* dim. of *rose* rose]
rounce (roun(t)s), *v.,* **-ed, -ing, -s.** to be agitated; flounce around; fuss.
ruck sack (ruk′sak′, rùk′sak′), *n.* a kind of knapsack.
ruf fi an (ruf′ē ən), *n.* a rough, brutal, or cruel person. —*adj.* rough; brutal; cruel. [< MF]
Syn. *n.* bully, rowdy, rough, hoodlum.

---

hat, āge, fär; let, bē, tėrm; it, īce; hot, gō, ôrder; oil, out; cup, pùt, rüle; ch, child; ng, long; th, thin; ₮H, then; zh, measure; ə represents *a* in about, *e* in taken, *i* in pencil, *o* in lemon, *u* in circus.

ru in ous (rü′ə nəs), *adj.* 1. bringing ruin; causing destruction. 2. fallen into ruins; in ruins. —**ru′in ous ly,** *adv.*

sac ri le gious (sak′rə lij′əs, sak′rə lē′jəs), *adj.* injurious or insulting to sacred persons or things. —**sac′ri le′gious ly,** *adv.*
Syn. impious, irreverent.

sa dism (sā′diz əm, sad′iz əm), *n.* 1. kind of insanity in which a person enjoys hurting someone else. 2. an unnatural love of cruelty. [< F; from the Count (or Marquis) de *Sade,* who wrote of it]

sa dist (sā′dist, sad′ist), *n.* one affected with sadism.

sa gac i ty (sə gas′ə tē), *n., pl.* **-ties.** keen, sound judgment; mental acuteness; shrewdness.
Syn. acumen, perspicacity.

sa hib (sä′ib, sä′hib), *n.* sir; master. Natives in colonial India called a European "sahib" when speaking to or of him. [< Hindu. < Arabic *çəhib* lord]

sa li ent (sā′lē ənt, sā′lyənt), *adj.* 1. standing out; easily seen or noticed; prominent; striking: *the salient features in a landscape, the salient points in a speech.* 2. pointing outward; projecting: *a salient angle.* —**sa′li ent ly,** *adv.*
Syn. 1. noticeable, conspicuous.

sal u tar y (sal′yə ter′ē), *adj.* 1. beneficial: *The teacher gave the boy salutary advice.* 2. good for the health; wholesome: *Walking is a salutary exercise.* [< L *salutaris* < *salus* good health]
Syn. 1. profitable, useful.

sal vage (sal′vij), *n., v.,* **-vaged, -vag ing.** —*n.* 1. act of saving a ship or its cargo from wreck, capture, etc. 2. payment for saving it. 3. rescue of property from fire, etc. 4. property salvaged: *the salvage from a shipwreck or a fire.* —*v.* save from fire, shipwreck, etc. [< F *salvage,* ult. < L *salvus* safe] —**sal′vag er,** *n.*

sanc ti mo ni ous (sangk′tə mō′nē əs), *adj.* making a show of holiness; putting on airs of sanctity.

sar casm (sär′kaz əm), *n.* 1. a sneering or cutting remark; ironical taunt. 2. act of making fun of a person to hurt his feelings; bitter irony: *"How unselfish you are!" said Ellen in sarcasm as Mary took the biggest piece of cake.* [< LL *sarcasmus* < Gk. *sarkasmos* < *sarkazein* sneer, strip off flesh < *sarx* flesh]

sar cas tic (sär kas′tik), *adj.* using sarcasm; sneering; cutting: *"Don't hurry!" was his sarcastic comment as I began to dress at my usual slow rate.* —**sar cas′ti cal ly,** *adv.* Syn. ironical, satirical, taunting, caustic.

sat u rate (sach′ə rāt), *v.,* **-rat ed, -rat ing.** 1. soak thoroughly; fill full: *During the fog, the air was saturated with moisture. Saturate the moss with water before planting the bulbs in it.* 2. cause (a substance) to unite with the greatest possible amount of another substance. A **saturated solution** (of sugar, salt, etc.) is one that cannot dissolve any more (sugar, salt, etc.). [< L *saturare* glut < *satur* full]
Syn. 1. steep, drench, imbue.

saun ter (sôn′tər, sän′tər), *v.* walk along slowly and happily; stroll: *saunter through the park.* —*n.* 1. a leisurely or careless gait. 2. a stroll. [origin uncertain] —**saun′ter er,** *n.*

sa van na or **sa van nah** (sə van′ə), *n.* a treeless plain, especially one in the S United States. [< earlier Sp. *zavana* < Carib]

scant ling (skant′ling), *n.* 1. a small beam or piece of timber, often used as an upright piece in the frame of a

building. 2. small beams or timbers collectively.

scav en ger (skav′ən jər), *n.* 1. person who cleans streets, etc., taking away the dirt and filth. 2. animal that feeds on decaying matter. Vultures are scavengers.

scep tic (skep′tik), *n., adj.* skeptic.

schism (siz′əm, skiz′əm), *n.* 1. division because of some difference of opinion about religion. 2. division into hostile groups. 3. offense of causing or trying to cause a religious schism. 4. sect or group formed by a schism within a church. [< L < Gk. *schisma* < *schizein* to split]

sci at i ca (sī at′ə kə), *n.* pain in a sciatic nerve and its branches; neuralgia of the hips, thighs, and legs.

sciatic nerve, a large nerve along the back part of the thigh and leg.

scoff (skôf, skof), *v.* make fun to show one does not believe something; mock. —*n.* 1. mocking words or acts. 2. something ridiculed or mocked. [< Scand. (Danish) *skuffe* deceive] —**scoff′er,** *n.* —**scoff′ing ly,** *adv.*

scope (skōp), *n.* 1. distance the mind can reach; extent of view: *Very hard words are not within the scope of a child's understanding.* 2. space; opportunity: *Football gives scope for courage and quick thinking.*

scorn (skôrn), *v.* 1. look down upon; think of as mean or low; despise: *Honest boys scorn sneaks and liars.* 2. reject or refuse as low or wrong: *The judge scorned to take a bribe.* —*n.* 1. a feeling that a person, animal, or act is mean or low; contempt: *We feel scorn for a traitor.* 2. person, animal, or thing that is scorned or despised. [< OF *escarnir* < Gmc.] —**scorn′er,** *n.*
Syn. *v.* 1. disdain, spurn. —*n.* 1. **Scorn, contempt** mean a feeling that a person or thing is mean, low, or worthless. **Scorn,** which expresses the strongest feeling, adds to this basic meaning the idea of feeling disgust mixed with anger, sometimes shown by unkind and bitter laughter. **Contempt** adds to the basic meaning the idea of disgust mixed with strong disapproval: *We feel contempt for a coward.*

scur vy (skėr′vē), *adj.,* **-vi er, -vi est.** —*n.* low; mean; contemptible: *a scurvy fellow, a scurvy trick.*

sea son al (sē′zn əl), *adj.* having to do with the seasons; depending on a season; happening at regular intervals. —**sea′son al ly,** *adv.*

sed i ment (sed′ə mənt), *n.* matter that settles to the bottom of a liquid: *Each year the Nile overflows and deposits sediment on the land.*

sed i men ta ry (sed′ə men′tər ē), *adj.* 1. of or having to do with sediment. 2. formed from sediment.

sem blance (sem′bləns), *n.* 1. outward appearance: *His story had the semblance of truth, but was really false.* 2. likeness: *These clouds have the semblance of a huge head.* [< OF *semblance* < *sembler* seem, ult. < L *similis* similar]

semi bar bar ic (sem′i bär bar′ik), *adj.* not completely barbaric; partly civilized.

se nil i ty (sə nil′ə tē), *n.* 1. old age. 2. weakness of old age; weakness of mind and body.

se pul chral (sə pul′krəl), *adj.* 1. of sepulchers or tombs. 2. of burial: *sepulchral ceremonies.* 3. deep and gloomy; dismal; suggesting a tomb.

se ra pe (sə rä′pē), *n.* shawl or blanket, often having bright colors, worn by Spanish American Indians. [Am.E.; < dialectal Sp.]

se rene (sə rēn′), *adj.* 1. peaceful; calm: *a serene smile.* 2. clear; bright; not cloudy: *a serene sky.* [< L *serenus*] —**se rene′ly,** *adv.*
Syn. 1. tranquil, placid.

< = from, derived from, taken from;　cf., compare;　dial., dialect;　dim., diminutive;　lang., language; pp., past participle;　ppr., present participle;　pt., past tense;　ult., ultimately;　var., variant;　? = possibly.

ser vi tude (sėr′və tüd, sėr′və tyüd), *n.* 1. slavery; bond-age. 2. forced labor as a punishment: *The criminal was sentenced to five years' servitude.* [< L *servitudo* < *servus* slave]

set tee (se tē′), *n.* sofa or long bench with a back and, usually, arms. [< *set*]

sev er (sev′ər), *v.* 1. cut apart; cut off: *sever a rope. The ax severed his head from his body.* 2. break off: *The two countries severed frinedly relations.* 3. part; divide; separate: *a church severed into two factions. The rope severed and the swing fell down.* [< OF *sevrer*, ult. < L *separare* separate] —**sev′er a ble,** *adj.*

shash lik (shä′shlik), *n.* slices of mutton roasted on sticks.

shelf (shelf), *n., pl.* **shelves.** 1. a thin, flat piece of wood, metal, stone, etc., fastened to a wall or frame to hold things, such as books, dishes, etc. 2. anything like a shelf. 3. **on the shelf,** put aside as no longer useful or desirable. [probably < LG *schelf*]

shoul der (shōl′dər), *n.* 1. the part of the body to which an arm or foreleg or wing is attached. 2. **shoulders,** *pl.* the two shoulders and the upper part of the back. 3. part of a garment covering this. 4. foreleg and adjoining parts of a slaughtered animal, used as meat for roasts, etc. 5. a shoulderlike part or projection: *Don't drive on the shoulder of the road.*

shrew (shrü), *n.* 1. a bad-tempered, quarrelsome woman. 2. a mouselike mammal with a long snout and brownish fur, that eats insects and worms.

si dle (sī′dl), *v.,* **-dled, -dling,** *n.* —*v.* 1. move sideways. 2. move sideways slowly so as not to attract attention: *The little boy shyly sidled up to the visitor.* —*n.* movement sideways. [< *sideling* sidelong]

sim per (sim′pər), *v.* 1. smile in a silly, affected way. 2. express by a simper; say with a simper. —*n.* a silly, affected smile. [cf. G *zimper* affected, coy]

sin gu lar (sing′gyə lər), *adj.* 1. extraordinary; unusual: *"Treasure Island" is a story of singular interest to boys.* 2. strange; queer; peculiar: *The detectives were greatly puz-zled by the singular nature of the crime.* 3. being the only one of its kind: *an event singular in history.* 4. one in number: *"Boy" is singular; "boys" is plural.* 5. separate; individual; private: *a singular matter.* —*n.* 1. the singular number in grammar. 2. a word in the singular number. [< L *singularis* < *singulus* single] —**sin′gu lar ly,** *adv.*
Syn. *adj.* 1. exceptional, uncommon, remarkable. 2. odd, curious, eccentric. 3. unique.

sire (sīr), *n.,v.,* **sired, sir ing.** —*n.* 1. a male ancestor; father. 2. the male parent: *Lightning was the sire of the race horse Danger.* 3. title of respect used formerly to a great noble and now to a king. —*v.* be the father of. [< OF < VL *seior* < L *senior,* nominative. Doublet of SENIOR.]

Sis y phus (sis′ə fəs)

skep tic (skept′tik), *n.* 1. person who questions the truth of theories or apparent facts; doubter. 2. person who doubts or questions the possibility or certainty of our knowledge of anything. 3. person who doubts the truth of religious doctrines. —*adj.* doubting; skeptical. Also, **sceptic.**
Syn. *n.* 3. unbeliever, disbeliever, agnostic.

skew er (skyü′ər), *n.* 1. a long pin of wood or metal stuck through meat to hold it together while it is cooking. 2. something shaped or used like a long pin.

skirt (skėrt), *n.* 1. the part of a dress that hangs from the waist. 2. a woman's or girl's garment that hangs from the waist. 3. something like a skirt: *the skirts of a man's long coat.* 4. border; edge. 5. the outer part of a place, group of

people, etc. 6. *Slang.* woman or girl. 7. one of the flaps hanging from the sides of a saddle. —*v.* 1. border or edge. 2. pass along the border or edge; pass along the border or edge of: *The boys skirted the forest because they did not want to go through it.* 3. be, lie, live, etc., along the border of.

sky light (skī′līt′), *n.* window in a roof or ceiling.

sleeve garter, a circular elastic band worn over a shirt sleeve to regulate its length.

slough (slou *for 1 and 3;* slü *for 2*), *n.* 1. a soft, deep muddy place; mud hole. 2. *U.S.* and *Canada.* slew. 3. hopeless discouragement; degradation.

snick er (snik′ər), *n.* a half-suppressed and usually dis-respectful laugh; sly or silly laugh; giggle. —*v.* laugh in this way. [imitative]

snig ger (snig′ər), *n., v.* snicker.

snip er (snī′pər), *n.* a hidden sharpshooter.

snuff (snuf), *v.* 1. draw in through the nose; draw up into the nose: *He snuffs up salt and water to cure a cold.* 2. sniff; smell: *The dog snuffed at the track of the fox.* 3. take powdered tobacco into the nose by snuffing; use snuff. —*n.* 1. powdered tobacco taken into the nose. 2. **up to snuff,** **a.** *Informal.* in perfect order or condition; as good as ex-pected. **b.** *Slang.* not easily deceived.

sol ace (sol′is), *n., v.,* **-aced, -ac ing.** —*n.* comfort; relief: *She found solace from her troubles in music.* —*v.* comfort; relieve: *He solaced himself with a book.* [< OF < L *solaci-um* < *solari* console]
Syn. *n.* consolation, cheer.

sol em nize (sol′əm nīz), *v.,* **-nized, -niz ing.** 1. observe with ceremonies: *Christian churches solemnize the resurrec-tion of Christ at Easter.* 2. hold or perform (a ceremony or service): *The marriage was solemnized in the cathedral.* 3. make serious or grave. —**sol′em ni za′tion,** *n.*

so lic i tude (sə lis′ə tüd, sə lis′ə tyüd), *n.* anxious care; anxiety; concern.

som ber (som′bər), *adj.* 1. dark; gloomy: *A cloudy winter day is somber.* 2. melancholy; dismal: *His losses made him very somber.* [< F *sombre,* probably ult. < L *sub-* under + *umbra* shade] —**som′ber ly,** *adv.* —**som′ber ness,** *n.*
Syn. 1. cloudy, murky. 2. depressing, sad.

som no lent (som′nə lənt), *adj.* sleepy; drowsy. [< L *somnolentus* < *somnus* sleep] —**som′no lent ly,** *adv.*

sor rel (sôr′əl, sor′əl), *adj.* reddish-brown. —*n.* 1. a reddish brown. 2. a reddish-brown horse with mane and tail of the same or a lighter color. [< OF *sorel* < *sor* yellowish-brown]

sor tie (sôr′tē), *n.* 1. a sudden attack by troops from a defensive position. 2. a single round trip of an aircraft against the enemy. [< F *sortie* < *sortir* go out]

sour dough (sour′dō′), *n.* *U.S. Informal.* prospector or pioneer in Alaska or Canada. [Am.E; so called from their practice of saving a lump of sour dough from each bread-making to start fermentation in subsequent baking]

sparse (spärs), *adj.,* **spars er, spars est.** 1. thinly scat-tered; occurring here and there: *a sparse population, sparse hair.* 2. scanty; meager. [< L *sparsus,* pp. of *spargere* scatter] —**sparse′ly,** *adv.* **-sparse′ness,** *n.*

spasm (spaz′əm), *n.* 1. a sudden, abnormal, involuntary contraction of a muscle or muscles. 2. any sudden, brief fit or spell of unusual energy or activity: *a spasm of temper, a spasm of industry.*

spas mod ic (spaz mod′ik), *adj.* 1. having to do with spasms; resembling a spasm: *a spasmodic cough.* 2. sudden and violent, but brief; occurring very irregularly. 3. having

hat, āge, fär; let, bē, tėrm; it, īce; hot, gō, ôrder; oil, out; cup, pùt, rüle; ch, child; ng, long; th, thin; ͲH, then; zh, measure; ə represents *a* in about, *e* in taken, *i* in pencil, *o* in lemon, *u* in circus.

or showing bursts of excitement. —**spas mod′i cal ly,** *adv.*
Syn. 2. jerky, fitful.

spawn (spôn), *n.* **1.** eggs of fish, frogs, shellfish, etc.
2. young newly hatched from such eggs. **3.** a swarming
brood; offspring. **4.** product; result. **5.** mass of white,
threadlike fibers from which mushrooms grow. —*v.*
1. produce eggs. **2.** bring forth; give birth to.

spec ter (spek′tər), *n.* **1.** ghost. **2.** thing causing terror or
dread. [< L *spectrum* appearance]

spec tral (spek′trəl), *adj.* of or like a specter; ghostly: *He
saw the spectral form of the headless horseman.*

spec tre (spek′tər), *n. esp. Brit.* specter.

spec u la tive (spek′yə lā′tiv, spek′yə lə tiv), *adj.*
1. thoughtful; reflective. **2.** theoretical rather than practical.
3. risky. **4.** of or involving speculation in land, stocks, etc.
—**spec′u la′tive ly,** *adv.*

spine (spin), *n.* **1.** series of small bones down the middle of
the back; backbone. **2.** anything like a backbone; long,
narrow ridge or support. **3.** a stiff, sharp-pointed growth on
plants, animals, etc.; thorn or something like it. A cactus has
spines; so has a porcupine. **4.** the supporting back portion of
a book cover. [< L *spina*, originally, thorn] —**spine′like′,**
adj.

spite (spit), *n., v.,* **spit ed, spit ing.** —*n.* **1.** ill will; grudge.
2. in spite of, not prevented by; notwithstanding. —*v.*
show ill will toward; annoy: *He left his yard dirty to spite the
people who lived next door.* [shortened from ME *despit*
despite] —**spite′less,** *adj.*

Syn. *n.* **1. Spite, malice** mean ill will against another.
Spite suggests envy or mean disposition, and applies to
active ill will shown by doing mean, petty things to hurt or
annoy: *She ruined his flowers out of spite.* **Malice** emphasizes actual wish or intention to injure, and suggests hatred
or, especially, a disposition delighting in doing harm or
seeing others hurt: *Gossips are motivated by malice.*

spit toon (spi tün′), *n.* container to spit into.

sprad dle (sprad′əl), *v.,* **-dled, -dling. 1.** to stretch the
legs wide apart. **2.** to stretch over or across; straddle.

sprint (sprint), *v.* run at full speed, especially for a short
distance. —*n.* a short race at full speed. [ME *sprente(n)*]
—**sprint′er,** *n.*

spu ri ous (spyur′ē əs), *adj.* **1.** not coming from the right
source; not genuine; false; sham: *a spurious document.*
2. illegitimate. [< L *spurius*]

stac ca to (stə kä′tō), in music: —*adj.* with breaks
between the successive tones; disconnected; abrupt. —*adv.*
in a staccato manner.

stag (stag), *n.* **1.** a full-grown male deer. **2.** the male of
various other animals. **3.** man who goes to a dance, party,
etc., alone or with other men. **4.** *U.S. Informal.* dinner,
party, etc., attended by men only. —*adj.* attended by, or for
men only. [OE *stagga*]

stam i na (stam′ə nə), *n.* strength; endurance. [< L *stamina* threads (of life, spun by the Fates)]

stealth y (stel′thē), *adj.,* **stealth i er, stealth i est.** done
in a secret manner; secret; sly: *The cat crept in a stealthy
way toward the bird.* —**stealth′i ly,** *adv.* —**stealth′i-
ness,**n.

Syn. furtive, sneaking, underhand, surreptitious.

steep (stēp), *adj.* **1.** having a sharp slope; almost straight up
and down: *The hill is steep.* **2.** *Informal.* unreasonable: *a
steep price.* —*n.* a steep slope. [OE *stēap*] —**steep′ly,** *adv.*
—**steep′ness,** *n.*

Syn. *adj.* **1. Steep, abrupt, precipitous** mean having a
slope almost straight up and down. **Steep** means having a

very sharp slope that is hard to go up: *I do not like to drive up
a steep hill.* **Abrupt** means very steep and sudden, with no
slope toward the sharp angle from which the surface goes up
or down: *From the rim they made their way down the abrupt
sides of the canyon.* **Precipitous** suggests something as
abrupt and straight up and down as a precipice: *The climbers
will attempt to scale the precipitous eastern slope of the peak.*

steer age (stir′ij), *n.* **1.** part of a passenger ship occupied
by passengers traveling at the cheapest rate. **2.** act of
steering.

ster e op ti con (ster′ē op′tə kən, stir′ē op′tə kən), *n.* an
improved form of magic lantern, having a powerful light that
projects pictures upon a screen.

stig ma (stig′mə), *n., pl.* **stig mas** or **stig ma ta. 1.** mark
of disgrace; stain or reproach on one's reputation. **2.** a
distinguishing mark or sign. **3.** a small spot or mark; spot in
the skin that bleeds or turns red. **4.** the part of the pistil of a
plant that receives the pollen. **5. stigmata,** *pl.* marks or
wounds like the five wounds on the crucified body of Christ,
said to appear supernaturally on the hands, feet, and side.
6. *Archaic.* a special mark burned on a slave or criminal.

sto i cal (stō′ə kəl), *adj.* self-controlled; indifferent to
pleasure and pain. —**sto′i cal ly,** *adv.*

strat e gy (strat′ə jē), *n., pl.* **-gies. 1.** science or art of war;
planning and directing of military movements and opera-
tions. **2.** plan based on this. **3.** the skillful planning and
management of anything. [< Gk. *strategia* < *strategos* general < *stratos* army + *agein* lead]

Stym phal us (stim fā′lus)

sua vi ty (swä′və tē, swav′ə tē), *n., pl.* **-ties.** smoothly
agreeable quality of behavior; blandness; smooth politeness.

sub due (səb dü′, səb dyü′), *v.,* **-dued, du ing. 1.** conquer;
overcome: *The Spaniards subdued the Indian tribes in
Mexico. We subdued a desire to laugh.* **2.** tone down; soften:
Pulling down the shades subdued the light in the room. [ult.
< *subducere* draw away < *sub-* from under + *ducere* lead;
influenced in meaning by L *subdere* subdue < *sub-* under +
dare put] —**sub du′a ble,** *adj.* —**sub du′er,** *n.*

Syn. 1. vanquish, subjugate, suppress.

sub ju gate (sub′jə gāt), *v.,* **-gat ed, -gat ing.** subdue;
conquer. [< L *subjugare* < *sub-* under + *jugum* yoke]

sub or di nate (*adj., n.* səb bôrd′n it; *v.* sə bôrd′n āt), *adj.,
n., v.,* **-nat ed, -nat ing.** —*adj.* **1.** inferior in rank: *In the
army, lieutenants are subordinate to captains.* **2.** inferior in
importance; secondary. **3.** under the control or influence of
something else; dependent. A complex sentence has one
main clause and one or more subordinate clauses.
4. subordinating. *Because, since, if, as,* and *whether* are
subordinate conjunctions. —*n.* a subordinate person or
thing. —*v.* make subordinate: *A polite host subordinates his
wishes to those of his guests.* [< Med.L *subordinatus,* pp. of
subordinare, ult. < L *sub-* under + *ordo* order]

Syn. *adj.* **3.** subject, subservient.

suf fer (suf′ər), *v.* **1.** have pain, grief, injury, etc.: *Sick
people suffer.* **2.** have or feel (pain, grief, etc.). **3.** experience
harm, loss, etc.: *His business suffered greatly during the war.*
4. allow; permit: *"Suffer the little children to come unto me."*
5. bear with patience; endure: *I will not suffer such insults.*
[< L *sufferre* < *sub-* up + *ferre* bear] —**suf′fer er,** *n.*

suf fuse (sə fyüz′), *v.,* **-fused, fus ing.** overspread (with a
liquid, dye, etc.): *At twilight the sky was suffused with color.
Her eyes were suffused with tears.*

suf fu sion (sə fyüz′zhən), *n.* **1.** a suffusing. **2.** a being
suffused. **3.** that with which anything is overspread. **4.** flush
of color.

< = from, derived from, taken from;   cf., compare;   dial., dialect;   dim., diminutive;   lang., language;
pp., past participle;   ppr., present participle;   pt., past tense;   ult., ultimately;   var., variant;   ? = possibly.

sun disk, *n.* an ancient symbol of the Near East consisting of a disk with conventionalized wings emblematic of the sun-god.

su perb (sù pèrb/), *adj.* 1. grand; stately; majestic; magnificent; splendid: *Mountain scenery is superb. The queen's jewels were superb.* 2. rich; elegant; sumptuous: *a superb dinner.* 3. very fine; first-rate; excellent: *The actor gave a superb performance.* [< L *superbus* < *super-* above] —**superb/ly**, *adv.*
Syn. 1. imposing.

su per cil i ous (sü/pər sil/ē əs), *adj.* haughty, proud, and contemptuous; disdainful; showing scorn or indifference because of a feeling of superiority: *The duchess looked down at the workman with a supercilious stare.* [< L *superciliosus* < *supercilium* eyebrow] —**su/per cil/i ous ly**, *adv.*

su per fi cial (sü/pər fish/əl), *adj.* 1. of the surface: *superficial measurement.* 2. on the surface; at the surface: *His burns were superficial and soon got well.* 3. concerned with or understanding only what is on the surface; not thorough; shallow: *Girls used to receive only a superficial education.* [< L *superficialis* < *superficies* surface < *super-* above + *facies* form]

su per im pose (sü/pər im pōz/), *v.,* **-posed, -pos ing.** 1. put on top of something else. 2. put or join as an addition.

su per in tend (sü/pər in tend/), *v.* oversee and direct (work or workers); manage (a place, institution, etc.). [< LL *superintendere* < L *super-* above + *intendere* direct]
Syn. supervise, administer.

su per nat u ral (sü/pər nach/ər əl), *adj.* above or beyond what is natural: *Angels and devils are supernatural beings.* —*n.* **the supernatural,** supernatural agencies, influences, or phenomena. —**su/per nat/ur al ly,** *adv.*

su per sede (sü/pər sēd/), *v.,* **-sed ed, -sed ing.** 1. take the place of; cause to be set aside; displace: *Electric lights have superseded gas lights in most homes.* 2. fill the place of; replace: *A new governor superseded the old one.* [< L *supersedere* be superior to, refrain from < *super-* above + *sedere* sit] —**su/per sed/er,** *n.*

sup po si tion (sup/ə zish/ən), *n.* 1. act of supposing. 2. thing supposed; belief; opinion: *The speaker planned his talk on the supposition that his hearers would be school children.*
Syn. 2. assumption, conjecture.

sur name (sèr/nām/), *n., v.,* **-named, -nam ing.** —*n.* 1. a last name; family name. 2. name added to a person's real name: *William I of England had the surname "the Conqueror."* —*v.* give an added name to; call by a surname: *Simon was surnamed Peter.* [< F *surnom* < *sur-* over < L *super-*) + *nom* name < L *nomen;* influence by E *name*]

sur rep ti tious (sèr/əp tish/əs), *adj.* 1. stealthy; secret. 2. secret and unauthorizea. [< L *surrepticius,* ult. < *sub-* secretly + *rapere* snatch] —**sur/rep ti/tious ly,** *adv.*

sus te nance (sus/tə nəns), *n.* 1. food: *He has gone for a week without sustenance.* 2. means of living; support: *He gave money for the sustenance of a poor family.*

swash buck ler (swosh/buk/lər), *n.* a swaggering swordsman, bully, or boaster. [< *swash* + *buckler*]

swas ti ka (swos/tə kə), *n.* an ancient symbol or ornament supposed to bring good luck. The swastika with arms turning clockwise was adopted as the symbol of the Nazis in Germany. [< Skt. *svastika* < *svasti* luck < *su* well + *asti,* n., being < *as* be]

Swastikas

swift (swift), *adj.* 1. moving very fast: *a swift automobile.* 2. coming or happening quickly: *a swift response.* 3. quick, rapid, or prompt to act, etc.: *swift to suspect.* —*adv.* in a swift manner. —*n.* a small bird with long wings. A swift looks somewhat like a swallow. [OE] —**swift/ly,** *adv.*
Syn. *adj.* 1. fleet, speedy, rapid.

swine (swin), *n., pl.* **swine.** 1. hogs; pigs. 2. a hog. 3. a coarse or beastly person. [OE *swīn*]

swiv el (swiv/əl), *n., v.,* **-eled, -el ing** or *esp. Brit.* **-elled, -el ling.** —*n.* 1. a fastening that allows the thing fastened to turn round freely upon it. 2. support on which a chair can revolve. 3. in a chain, a link having two parts, one of which turns freely in the other. 4. support on which a gun can turn round. 5. gun that turns on such a support; swivel gun. —*v.* 1. turn on a swivel. 2. fasten or support by a swivel. 3. swing round; rotate; turn. [ult. < OE *swīfan* move]

syl van (sil/vən), *adj.* of the woods; in the woods; consisting of woods; having woods: *They lived in a sylvan retreat.* Also, **silvan.** [< L *silvanus* < *silva* forest]

sym met ri cal (si met/rə kəl), *adj.* having symmetry; well-proportioned. —**sym met/ri cal ly,** *adv.*

sym me try (sim/ə trē), *n., pl.* **-tries.** 1. a regular, balanced arrangement on opposite sides of a line or plane, or around a center or axis: *A swollen cheek spoiled the symmetry of his face.* 2. pleasing proportions between the parts of a whole; well-balanced arrangement of parts; harmony.

syn drome (sin/drōm), *n.* a group of signs and symptoms characteristic of a particular disease. [< NL *syndrome* < Gk. *syndromē* < *syn-* with + *dramein* to run]

sys tem at i cal ly (sis/tə mat/ik lē), *adv.* with system; according to some plan or method.

tac i turn (tas/ə tèrn), *adj.* speaking very little; not fond of talking.
Syn. reserved.
Ant. talkative.

tack (tak), *n.* 1. a short, sharp-pointed nail or pin having a broad, flat head: *carpet tacks, thumbtacks.* 2. stitch used as a temporary fastening. 3. a zigzag course against the wind. 4. direction in which a ship moves in regard to the position of her sails. When on port tack, a ship has the wind on her left. 5. a zigzag movement; one of the movements in a zigzag course. 6. course of action or conduct: *He took the wrong tack to get what he wanted.* 7. **a.** rope to hold in place a corner of some sails. **b.** corner to which this is fastened.

tact (takt), *n.* ability to say and do the right things; skill in dealing with people or handling difficult situations. [< L *tactus* sense of feeling < *tangere* touch]

tact ful (takt/fəl), *adj.* 1. having tact. 2. showing tact. —**tact/ful ly,** *adv.* —**tact/ful ness,** *n.*

Tae na rum (tē/na rum)

tan gi ble (tan/jə bəl), *adj.* 1. capable of being touched or felt by touch: *A chair is a tangible object.* 2. real; actual; definite: *The good will of a business is not so tangible as its buildings and stock.* —*n.* **tangibles,** *pl.* things whose value is easily appraised; material assets. [< LL *tangibilis* < *tangere* touch] —**tan/gi bly,** *adv.*

Tan ta lus (tan/tl əs)

tan ta mount (tan/tə mount), *adj.* equivalent.

Tar ta rus (tär/tər əs)

taut (tôt), *adj.* 1. tightly drawn; tense: *a taut rope.* 2. in neat condition; tidy. [earlier *taught,* apparently var. of *tight*] —**taut/ly,** *adv.* —**taut/ness,** *n.*

Tel a mon (tel/ə mon/)

hat, āge, fär; let, bē, tèrm; it, īce; hot, gō, ôrder; oil, out; cup, pùt, rüle; ch, child; ng, long; th, thin; ᴛʜ, then; zh, measure; ə represents *a* in about, *e* in taken, *i* in pencil, *o* in lemon, *u* in circus.

Tem pe (tem′pē)

tem per (tem′pər), *n.* 1. state of mind; disposition; condition: *She was in a good temper.* 2. angry state of mind: *In her temper she broke a vase.* 3. calm state of mind: *He became angry and lost his temper.* 4. the hardness, toughness, etc., of a mixture given by tempering: *The temper of the clay was right for shaping.* 5. substance added to something to modify its properties or qualities. —*v.* 1. moderate; soften: *Temper justice with mercy.* 2. bring or be brought to a proper or desired condition by mixing or preparing. A painter tempers his colors by mixing them with oil. Steel is tempered by heating it and working it till it has the proper degree of hardness and toughness. 3. tune or adjust the pitch of (an instrument, a voice, etc.). **Syn.** *n.* 1. mood, humor. —*v.* 1. qualify, modify.

tem per a men tal (tem′pər ə men′tl), *adj.* 1. subject to moods and whims; easily irritated; sensitive. 2. showing a strongly marked individual temperament. 3. due to temperament; constitutional: *Cats have a temperamental dislike for water.*

ten dril (ten′drəl), *n.* 1. a threadlike part of a climbing plant that attaches itself to something and helps support the plant. 2. something similar: *tendrils of hair curling about a child's face.*

ten e ment (ten′ə mənt), *n.* 1. any house or building to live in; dwelling house. 2. part of a house or building occupied by a tenant as a separate dwelling. 3. a tenement house. 4. abode; habitation. [< OF *tenement*, ult. < L *tenere* hold]

tenement house, building divided into sets of rooms occupied by separate families, especially such a building in the poorer sections of large cities.

ten ta tive (ten′tə tiv), *adj.* done as a trial or experiment; experimental: *a tentative plan.* [< Med.L *tentativus* < L *tentare* try out, intensive of *tendere* stretch, aim; associated in L with *temptare* feel out] —**ten′ta tive ly,** *adv.* —**ten′ta tive ness,** *n.*

Ter ti ar y (tėr′shē er′ē, tėr′shər ē), *adj., n., pl.* **-ar ies.** —*adj.* 1. of or having to do with the Tertiary. 2. **tertiary,** of the third order, rank, formation, etc.; third. —*n.* 1. the third chief period of time in the formation of the earth's surface. During this period the great mountain systems, such as the Alps, Himalayas, Rockies, and Andes, appeared and rapid development of mammals occurred. 2. layer of rocks belonging to this period. 3. **tertiary,** one of a bird's flight feathers.

tes ti mo ni al (tes′tə mō′nē əl), *n.* 1. certificate of character, conduct, qualifications, value, etc.; recommendation: *The boy looking for a job has testimonials from his teachers and former employer. Advertisements of patent medicines often contain testimonials from people who have used them.* 2. something given or done to show esteem, admiration, gratitude, etc.: *The members of the church collected money for a testimonial to their retiring pastor.*

teth er (teⱦH′ər), *n.* 1. rope or chain for fastening an animal so that it can graze only within certain limits. 2. **at the end of one's tether,** at the end of one's resources or endurance. —*v.* fasten with a tether. [probably < Scand. *tjōthr*]

The mis (thē′mis)

Thes ti us (thes′ti us)

thick et (thik′it), *n.* shrubs, bushes, or small trees growing close together. [OE *thiccet* < *thicce* thick] **Syn.** shrubbery, copse, brake.

thith er ward (thiⱦH′ər wərd, ⱦHiⱦH′ər wərd), *adv.* toward that place; in that direction.

Thrace (thrās), *n.* region in the E part of the Balkan Peninsula. In ancient times it was first an independent country and later a Roman province. Today most of the region is in Bulgaria, and the rest of it in Greece.

thrust (thrust), *v.*, **thrust, thrust ing,** *n.* —*v.* 1. push with force: *He thrust his hands into his pockets.* —*n.* 1. a forcible push; drive. 2. a stab. 3. attack. 4. in mechanics, architecture, etc., the force of one thing pushing on another. 5. the endwise push exerted by the rotation of a propeller. 6. the force driving a rocket or a jet engine forward as a reaction to the discharge of gas or liquid through a nozzle or exhaust. [< Scand. *thrȳsta*] **Syn.** *n.* 1. shove, punch, lunge.

thwart (thwôrt), *v.* oppose and defeat; keep from doing something. [< adv.] —*n.* 1. seat across a boat, on which a rower sits. 2. brace in a canoe. [apparently < adj.] —*adj.* lying across. [< adv.] —*adv.* across; crosswise. [< Scand. *thvert,* adv., across, originally neut. of adj. *thverr* transverse] **Syn.** *v.* baffle, balk, foil.

tier (tir), *n.* one of a series of rows arranged one above another: *tiers of seats at a baseball game.* —*v.* arrange in tiers. [< F *tire,* originally, order < *tirer* draw]

tie wig (ti′wig′), *n.* a wig tied in back with ribbon.

Ti re si as (tī re′si əs)

Ti ryns (tī′rinz)

tol er a ble (tol′ər ə bəl), *adj.* 1. able to be borne or endured. 2. fairly good: *She is in tolerable health.* [< L *tolerabilis* < *tolerare* tolerate] —**tol′er a ble ness,** *n.* **Syn.** 1. bearable, endurable, sufferable, supportable. 2. passable, ordinary, indifferent.

tol er ance (tol′ər əns), *n.* 1. a willingness to be tolerant and patient toward people whose opinions or ways differ from one's own. 2. the power of enduring or resisting the action of a drug, poison, etc. 3. action of tolerating. 4. an allowed amount of variation from a standard, as in the weight of coins or the dimensions of a machine or part. **Syn.** 1. forbearance.

tongue (tung), *n.* 1. the movable piece of flesh in the mouth. The tongue is used in tasting and, by people, for talking. 2. an animal's tongue used as food. 3. power of speech: *Have you lost your tongue?* 4. way of speaking; speech; talk: *a flattering tongue.* 5. the language of a people: *the English tongue.* 6. something shaped or used like a tongue. 7. the strip of leather under the laces of a shoe. 8. a narrow strip of land running out into water.

top o graph i cal (top′ə graf′ə kəl), *adj.* of or having to do with topography. A topographical map shows mountains, rivers, etc.

to pog ra phy (tə pog′rə fē), *n., pl.* **-phies.** 1. the accurate and detailed description or drawing of places or their surface features. 2. the surface features of a place or region. The topography of a region includes hills, valleys, streams, lakes, bridges, tunnels, roads, etc. [< LL < Gk. *topographia* < *topos* place + *graphein* write]

tor tu ous (tôr′chü əs), *adj.* 1. full of twists, turns, or bends; twisting; winding; crooked. 2. mentally or morally crooked; not straightforward: *tortuous reasoning.* [< L *tortuosus,* ult. < *torquere* twist] —**tor′tu ous ly,** *adv.* —**tor′tu ous ness,** *n.* **Syn.** 1. sinuous, serpentine, zig-zag, circuitous. **Ant.** 1. direct.

trac ta ble (trak′tə bəl), *adj.* 1. easily managed or controlled; easy to deal with; docile: *Dogs are more tractable than mules.* 2. easily worked: *Copper and gold are tractable.*

tran quil (trang′kwəl), *adj.,* **-quil er, -quil est** or *esp.*

< = from, derived from, taken from;   cf., compare;   dial., dialect;   dim., diminutive;   lang., language;
pp., past participle;   ppr., present participle;   pt., past tense;   ult., ultimately;   var., variant;   ? = possibly.

Brit. **-quil ler, -quil lest.** calm; peaceful; quiet. [< L *tranquillus*] **—tran′quil ly,** *adv.*
Syn. placid, serene, undisturbed.

tran quil li ty or **tran quil i ty** (trang kwil′ə tē), *n.* calmness; peacefulness; quiet.

trans fix (tran sfiks′), *v.* 1. pierce through: *The hunter transfixed the lion with a spear.* 2. fasten by piercing through with something pointed. 3. make motionless (with amazement, terror, etc.). [< L *transfixus,* pp. of *transfigere* < *trans-* through + *figere* fix]

trans fuse (tran sfyüz′), *v.,* **-fused, -fus ing.** 1. pour from one container into another. 2. transfer (blood) from one person or animal to another. 3. inject (a solution) into a blood vessel. 4. infuse; instill: *The speaker transfused his enthusiasm into the audience.* [< L *transfusus,* pp. of *transfundere* < *trans-* across + *fundere* pour]

trans fu sion (tran sfyü′zhən), *n.* act or fact of transfusing.

tran sient (tran′shənt), *adj.* 1. passing soon; fleeting; not lasting. 2. passing through and not staying long: *a transient guest in a hotel.* —*n.* visitor or boarder who stays for a short time. **—tran′sient ly,** *adv.*
Syn. *adj.* 1. transitory, evanescent, momentary, ephemeral.
Ant. *adj.* 1. abiding.

trav erse (trav′ərs, trə vėrs′), *v.* 1. pass across, over, or through: *We traversed the desert.* 2. walk or move in a crosswise direction; move back and forth: *That horse traverses.* 3. go to and fro over or along (a place, etc.). 4. move sideways; turn from side to side.

trem u lous (trem′yə ləs), *adj.* 1. trembling; quivering. 2. timid; fearful. [< L *tremulus* < *tremere* tremble] **—trem′u lous ly,** *adv.* **—trem′u lous ness,** *n.*
Syn. 1. shaking, vibrating.

trep i da tion (trep′ə dā′shən), *n.* 1. nervous dread; fear; fright. 2. a trembling.

tri bu nal (tri byü′nl, trī byü′nl), *n.* 1. court of justice; place of judgment: *He was brought before the tribunal for trial.* 2. place where judges sit in a law court. [< L *tribunal* < *tribunus*]

trib ute (trib′yüt), *n.* 1. money paid by one nation to another for peace or protection or because of some agreement. 2. any forced payment. 3. an acknowledgement of thanks or respect; compliment: *Memorial Day is a tribute to our dead soldiers.* [< L *tributum* < *tribuere* allot < *tribus* tribe]

tri dent (trīd′nt), *n.* a three-pronged spear. —*adj.* three-pronged. [< L *tridens, -entis* < *tri-* three + *dens* tooth]

trite (trīt), *adj.,* **trit er, trit est.** worn out by use; no longer new or interesting; commonplace: *"Cheeks like roses" is a trite expression.* [< L *tritus,* pp. of *terere* rub away] **—trite′ly,** *adv.* **—trite′ness,** *n.*
Syn. hackneyed, stereotyped, banal, stale.
Ant. original, new, fresh.

Neptune
with a
trident

troll¹ (trōl), *v.* 1. sing in a full, rolling voice. 2. sing in succession. When three people troll a round or catch, the soprano sings one line, the alto comes in next with the same line, and then the bass sings it, and so on, while the others keep on singing. 3. fish (for) with a moving line. In trolling, a man usually trails the line behind his boat near the surface. 4. roll. —*n.* 1. song whose parts are sung in succession; round: *"Three Blind Mice" is a well-known troll.* 2. reel of a fishing rod. 3. lure or bait for fishing. 4. a trolling. [< OF *troller* wander < Gmc.] **—troll′er,** *n.*

troll² (trōl), *n.* in Scandinavian folklore, an ugly dwarf or giant living underground or in caves. [< Scand.]

tu ber cu lo sis (tü bėr′kyə lō′sis, tyü bėr′kyə lō′sis), *n.* an infectious disease affecting various tissues of the body, but most often the lungs. Tuberculosis of the lungs is often called consumption.

tur tle (tėr′tl), *n.* 1. any of certain marine reptiles having the body enclosed in a hard shell from which the head, tail, and four legs protrude. Turtles living on the land are often called tortoises. 2. **turn turtle,** turn bottom side up.

tus sock (tus′ək), *n.* a tuft of growing grass or the like. [origin uncertain]

ul cer (ul′sər), *n.* 1. an open sore that discharges pus. 2. a moral sore spot; corrupting influence.

un a bashed (un′ə basht′), *adj.* not embarrassed, ashamed, or awed.

un ap proach a ble (un′ə prō′chə bəl), *adj.* 1. very hard to approach; distant. 2. unrivaled; without an equal. **—un′ap proach′a ble ness,** *n.* **—un′ap proach′a bly,** *adv.*

un daunt ed (un dôn′tid, un dän′tid), *adj.* not afraid; not discouraged; fearless: *an undaunted leader.* **—un daunt′ed ly,** *adv.* **—un daunt′ed ness,** *n.*

un der class man (un′dər klas′mən), *n.,* *pl.* **-men.** *U.S.* freshman or sophomore. [Am.E]

un der grad u ate (un′dər graj′ü it), *n.* a student in a school, college, or university who has not received a degree for a course of study. —*adj.* of, for, or having to do with undergraduates.

un di min ish a ble (un′də min′ish ə bəl), *adj.* not capable of being diminished; unable to be made or become smaller in size, amount, or importance.

un du late (*v.* un′jə lāt, un′dyə lāt; *adj.* un′jə lit, un′jə lāt, un′dyə lit, un′dyə lāt), *v.,* **-lat ed, -lat ing,** *adj.* —*v.* 1. move in waves: *undulating water.* 2. have a wavy form or surface: *undulating hair.* 3. cause to move in waves. 4. give a wavy form or surface to. [< LL *undula* wavelet, dim. of L *unda* wave] —*adj.* wavy. [< L *undulatus* diversified as with waves < *unda* wave]

un du la tion (un′jə lā′shən, un′dyə lā′shən), *n.* 1. a waving motion. 2. wavy form. 3. one of a series of wavelike bends, curves, swellings, etc. 4. a sound wave. 5. vibration.

u ni son (yü′nə sən, yü′nə zən), *n.* 1. agreement: *The feet of marching soldiers move in unison.* 2. agreement in pitch of two or more tones, voices, etc.; a sounding together at the same pitch. [< Med.L *unisonus* sounding the same < LL *unisonus* < L *unus* one + *sonus* sound]

un per ceived (un′pər sēvd′), *adj.* not perceived; not noticed.

un set tle (un set′l), *v.,* **-tled, -tling.** make or become unstable; disturb; shake; weaken.
Syn. disorder, upset, disconcert.

un sheathe (un shēŦH′), *v.,* **-sheated, -sheath ing.** draw (a sword, knife, or the like) from a sheath.

un so lic i ted (un′sə lis′ə tid), *adj.* not solicited; not sought or asked for.

un tram meled (un tram′əld), *adj.* not hindered; not restrained; free.

un tram melled (un tram′əld), *adj.* *esp. Brit.* untrammeled.

un wont ed (un wun′tid, un wōn′tid), *adj.* 1. not customary; not usual. 2. not accustomed; not used. **—un wont′ed ly,** *adv.* **—un wont′ed ness,** *n.*

---

hat, āge, fär;   let, bē, tėrm;   it, īce;   hot, gō, ôrder;   oil, out;   cup, pút, rüle;   ch, child;   ng, long;
th, thin;   ŦH, then;   zh, measure;   ə represents *a* in about, *e* in taken, *i* in pencil, *o* in lemon, *u* in circus.

upright piano, a rectangular piano having vertical strings behind the keyboard.

u til i tar i an (yü til′ə ter′ē ən), *adj.* **1.** having to do with utility. **2.** aiming at usefulness rather than beauty, style, etc. —*n.* adherent of utilitarianism.

va can cy (vā′kən sē), *n., pl.* **-cies.** **1.** state of being vacant; emptiness. **2.** an unoccupied position: *Mr. Smith's death made a vacancy in the business.* **3.** state of being or becoming unoccupied. **4.** a room, space, or apartment for rent; empty space. **5.** lack of thought or intelligence.

vac u ous (vak′yü əs), *adj.* **1.** showing no thought or intelligence; foolish; stupid. **2.** empty. [< L *vacuus*] —**vac′u ous ly,** *adv.*

vague (vāg), *adj.,* **va guer, va guest.** **1.** not definitely or precisely expressed: *a vague statement.* **2.** indefinite; indistinct: *a vague feeling.* **3.** indistinctly seen or perceived; obscure; hazy: *In a fog everything looks vague.* **4.** lacking clarity or precision: *a vague personality.* [< O F < L *vagus* wandering] —**vague′ly,** *adv.* —**vague′ness,** *n.*

val e tu di nar i an (val′ə tü′də när′ē ən, val′ə tü′də-när′ē ən), *n.* **1.** an invalid. **2.** person who thinks he is ill when he is not.

va lise (və lēs′), *n.* a traveling bag to hold clothes, etc. [< F < Ital. *valigia*]

var ied (ver′ēd, var′ēd), *adj.* **1.** of different kinds; having variety: *a varied assortment of candies.* **2.** changed; altered. —**var′ied ly,** *adv.*

var si ty (vär′sə tē), *n., pl.* **-ties.** the most important team in a given sport in a university, college, or school. [< (*uni*)*versity*]

ve he ment (vē′ə mənt), *adj.* **1.** having or showing strong feeling; caused by strong feeling; eager; passionate. **2.** forceful; violent. —**ve′he ment ly,** *adv.* Syn. **1.** ardent, fervid.

ven er a ble (ven′ər ə bəl), *adj.* worthy of reverence; deserving respect because of age, character, or associations: *a venerable priest, venerable customs.* [< L *venerabilis* < *venerari* venerate] —**ven′er a bly,** *adv.*

ven om (ven′əm), *n.* **1.** the poison of snakes, spiders, etc. **2.** spite; malice: *Her enemies dreaded the venom of her tongue.* —**ven′om less,** *adj.* Syn. **2.** rancor, hate, malignity.

ven om ous (ven′əm əs), *adj.* **1.** poisonous: *Rattlesnakes are venomous.* **2.** spiteful; malicious. —**ven′om ous ly,** *adv.* —**ven′om ous ness,** *n.*

ve ra cious (və rā′shəs), *adj.* **1.** truthful. **2.** true. —**ve-ra′cious ly,** *adv.* —**ve ra′cious ness,** *n.*

ver i fy (ver′ə fī), *v.,* **-fied, -fy ing.** **1.** prove (something) to be true; confirm: *The driver's report of the accident was verified by eyewitnesses.* **2.** test the correctness of; check for accuracy: *Verify the spelling of a word by looking in a dictionary.* [< OF < Med.L *verificare* < L *verus* true + *facere* make] —**ver′i fi er,** *n.* Syn. **1.** substantiate, corroborate, authenticate.

vex (veks), *v.t.* **1.** anger by trifles; annoy; provoke. **2.** worry; trouble; harass. **3.** disturb by commotion; agitate: *The island was much vexed by storms.* [< L *vexare*]

Vic tro la (vik trō′lə), *n.* trademark for a kind of phonograph.

vict ual (vit′l), *n., v.,* **-ualed, -ual ing** or *esp. Brit.* **-ualled, -ual ling.** —*n.* Usually, *victuals, pl. Informal* or *Dialect.* food. —*v.* **1.** supply with food. **2.** take on a supply

of food: *The ship will victual before sailing.* [< OF *vitaille* < L *victualia*, pl., ult. < *vivere* live]

vil i fy (vil′ə fī), *v.,* **-fied, -fy ing.** speak evil of; revile; slander. —**vil′i fi er,** *n.* Syn. disparage.

vir ile (vir′əl), *adj.* **1.** manly; masculine. **2.** full of manly strength or masculine vigor. **3.** vigorous; forceful. [< L *virilis* < *vir* man]

vi sa (vē′zə), *n., v.,* **-saed, -sa ing.** —*n.* an official signature or endorsement upon a passport or document, showing that it has been examined and approved. —*v.* examine and sign. Also, **visé.**

vis age (viz′ij), *n.* **1.** face. **2.** appearance. [< OF *visage* < *vis* face < L *visus* a look < *videre* see] Syn. **1.** See **face.**

vis cer a (vis′ər ə), *n. pl. of* **vis cus** (vis′kəs). the soft inside parts of the body. The heart, stomach, liver, intestines, kidneys, etc., are viscera.

vo ca tion (vō kā′shən), *n.* **1.** occupation, business, profession, or trade: *Medicine is her vocation.* **2.** persons engaged in the same business or profession. **3.** an inner call or summons. [< L *vocationem*, literally, a calling < *vocare* to call < *vocem* voice]

voo doo (vü′dü), *n., pl.* **-doos,** *adj., v.* —*n.* **1.** religion that came from Africa, made up of mysterious rites and practices that include the use of sorcery, magic, and conjuration. Belief in voodoo still prevails in many parts of the West Indies and some parts of the southern United States. **2.** person who practices voodoo. **3.** a charm or fetish used in the practice of voodoo. —*adj.* of or having to do with voodoo. —*v.t.* affect by voodoo sorcery, magic, or conjuration. [< Creole; of African origin]

vo ra cious (və rā′shəs), *adj.* **1.** eating much; greedy in eating; ravenous. **2.** very eager; unable to be satisfied. [< L *vorax, -acis* greedy] —**vo ra′cious ly,** *adv.*

vo rac i ty (və ras′ə tē), *n.* being voracious.

vul ner a ble (vul′nər ə bəl), *adj.* **1.** capable of being wounded or injured; open to attack: *Achilles was vulnerable only in his heel.* **2.** sensitive to criticism, temptations, influences, etc.: *Most people are vulnerable to ridicule.* —**vul′ner a bly,** *adv.*

wage (wāj), *n., v.,* **waged, wag ing.** —*n.* **1.** Usually, **wages,** *pl.* **a** payment made periodically to a person, especially by the day or week, as compensation at a fixed rate for hours worked or services rendered. **b** something given in return: *"The wages of sin is death."* **2.** OBSOLETE. a pledge. —*v.t.* **1.** carry on: *Doctors wage war against disease.* **2.** OBSOLETE. pledge. [< Old North French; of Germanic origin] —**wage′less,** *adj.*

wa ger (wā′jər), *v.t., v.i.* make a bet; bet; gamble. —*n.* **1.** something staked on an uncertain event. **2.** act of betting; bet. [< A F *wageure* < Old North French *wage* pledge, wage] —**wa′ger er,** *n.*

wake (wāk), *n.* **1.** track left behind a moving ship. **2.** track left behind any moving body. **3. in the wake of,** following; behind; after. [< MDutch]

wane (wān), *v.,* **waned, wan ing,** *n.* —*v.* **1.** become smaller; become smaller gradually: *The moon wanes after it has become full.* **2.** decline in power, influence, importance, etc.: *Many great empires have waned.* **3.** decline in strength, intensity, etc.: *The light of day wanes in the evening.* **4.** draw to a close: *Summer wanes as autumn approaches.* —*n.* **1.** a

---

< = from, derived from, taken from;   cf., compare;   dial., dialect;   dim., diminutive;   lang., language; pp., past participle;   ppr., present participle;   pt., past tense;   ult., ultimately;   var., variant;   ? = possibly.

waning. **2. in** or **on the wane,** growing less; waning. [OE *wanian*]

war i ly (wer′ə lē, war′ə lē), *adv.* cautiously; carefully.

well-turned (wel′tėrnd′), *adj.* **1.** shaped well; well-formed. **2.** expressed happily or gracefully: *a well-turned compliment.*

wend (wend), *v.,* **wend ed** or **went, wend ing.** —*v.t.* **1.** direct (one's way): *We wended our way home.* —*v.i.* go. [O E *wendan*]

whelp (hwelp), *n.* **1.** puppy or cub; young dog, wolf, bear, lion, tiger, etc. **2.** a good-for-nothing boy or young man. —*v.* give birth to (whelps). [OE *hwelp*]

whip stock (hwip′stok′), *n.* handle of a whip.

wick er (wik′ər), *n.* **1.** a slender, easily bent branch or twig. **2.** twigs or branches woven together. Wicker is used in making baskets and furniture. **3.** something made of wicker. —*adj.* **1.** made of wicker. **2.** covered with wicker. [< Scand. (dialectal Swedish) *vikker* willow branch]

wick et (wik′it), *n.* **1.** a small door or gate: *The big door has a wicket in it.* **2.** a small window or opening: *Buy your tickets at this wicket.*

widow's peak, hair that grows to a point on the forehead, traditionally supposed to presage early widowhood.

will-o'-the-wisp (wil′ə ᴛʜə wisp′), *n.* **1.** a moving light appearing at night over marshy places, caused by combustion or marsh gas. **2.** thing that deceives or misleads by luring on.

wil y (wi′lē), *adj.,* **wil i er, wil i est.** using wiles or subtle tricks to deceive; crafty; cunning; sly: *a wily thief, a wily fox.* —**wil′i ly,** *adv.*

wind fall (wind′fôl′), *n.* **1.** fruit blown down by the wind. **2.** an unexpected piece of good luck.

wind ward (wind′wərd; *Nautical* win′dərd), *adv.* toward the wind. —*adj.* **1.** on the side toward the wind. **2.** in the direction from which the wind is blowing. —*n.* **1.** the side toward the wind. **2.** direction from which the wind is blowing.

wist ful (wist′fəl), *adj.* **1.** longing; yearning: *A child stood looking with wistful eyes at the toys in the window.* **2.** pensive; melancholy. [< obsolete *wist* attentive (< *wistly* intently, of uncertain origin) + *-ful*] —**wist′ful ly,** *adv.* —**wist′ful ness,** *n.*

with er (wiᴛʜ′ər), *v.* **1.** lose or cause to lose freshness, vigor, etc.; dry up; shrivel: *The grass withered in the hot sun. Age had withered the old lady's face.* **2.** cause to feel ashamed or confused: *She withered him with a scornful look.* [ME *wideren,* var. of *wederen* weather]

wont (wunt, wŏnt), *adj.* accustomed: *He was wont to read the paper at breakfast.* —*n.* custom; habit: *He rose early, as was his wont.* [originally pp., ult. < OE *wunian* be accustomed]

wood en (wud′n), *adj.* **1.** made of wood. **2.** stiff; awkward. **3.** dull; stupid. —**wood′en ly,** *adv.* —**wood′en ness,** *n.*

writhe (rīᴛʜ), *v.,* **writhed, writhed** or (*Obs. except Poetic*) **writh en** (riᴛʜ′ən), **writh ing.** **1.** twist and turn; twist: *The snake writhed along the branch. The wounded man writhed in agony.* **2.** suffer mentally; be very uncomfortable. [OE *wrīthan*]

wry (rī), *adj.,* **wri er, wri est.** turned to one side; twisted: *She made a wry face to show her disgust.* [ult. < OE *wrīgian* turn] —**wry′ly,** *adv.*

Wych er ly (wich′ər lē)

yeo man ry (yō′mən rē), *n.* **1.** yeoman. **2.** a British volunteer cavalry force, now a part of the Territorial Army.

yes treen (yes′trēn′), *n., adv. Scottish* or *Poetic.* yesterday evening.

Y saacs (ē′säks)

ze nith (zē′nith), *n.* **1.** the point in the heavens directly overhead. **2.** the highest point: *At the zenith of its power Rome ruled all of civilized Europe.* [< OF or Med.L *senit* < Arabic *samt* (*ar-rās*) the way (over the head)] **Syn. 2.** top, apex, summit.

Zu ra beg (zü′rä beg)

---

hat, āge, fär; let, bē, tėrm; it, īce; hot, gō, ôrder; oil, out; cup, pùt, rüle; ch, child; ng, long; th, thin; ᴛʜ, then; zh, measure; ə represents *a* in about, *e* in taken, *i* in pencil, *o* in lemon, *u* in circus.

INDEX OF LITERARY TYPES

INDEX OF AUTHORS AND TITLES

INDEX OF SKILLS

Interpretative Skills

ALLITERATION. Handbook: 536. *Application:* 262, 274, 284.

CHARACTERIZATION. Handbook: 537. *Application:* 95, 123, 129, 140, 160, 162, 170, 193, 326, 352, 370, 416, 440, 464, 492.

DIALOGUE. Handbook: 539. *Application:* 326, 352, 385, 492.

FACT AND FICTION. Handbook: 541. *Application:* 75, 76, 160, 207.

FIGURATIVE LANGUAGE. Handbook: 543. *Application:* 242, 244, 245, 247, 265, 267, 273, 277, 279, 284, 293, 339, 350.

FLASHBACK. Handbook: 545. *Application:* 339, 533.

FORESHADOWING. Handbook: 547. *Application:* 415, 497, 504, 514, 525, 533.

IMAGERY. Handbook: 549. *Application:* 140, 207, 239, 242, 245, 246, 250, 265, 267, 270, 272, 283, 284, 293.

INFERENCE. Handbook: 550. *Application:* 150, 161, 162, 170, 215, 222, 233, 361, 370.

IRONY. Handbook: 551. *Application:* 302, 352, 370, 393, 401.

PLOT. Handbook: 553. *Application:* 20, 54, 59, 63, 76, 170, 233, 252, 302.

POINT OF VIEW. Handbook: 558. *Application:* 123, 129, 140, 162, 222, 275, 415, 533.

RHYME. Handbook: 560. *Application:* 245, 246, 270, 273, 274, 279, 284.

RHYTHM. Handbook: 561. *Application:* 257, 258, 271, 284.

SATIRE. Handbook: 563. *Application:* 197, 215, 234, 370, 385, 393.

SETTING. Handbook: 564. *Application:* 54, 59, 63, 76, 96, 140, 160, 233, 239, 275, 361, 370, 415, 471, 478, 514, 530.

SYMBOL. Handbook: 565. *Application:* 222, 223, 234, 271, 273, 326, 431, 464.

THEME. Handbook: 566. *Application:* 170, 234, 326, 370, 385.

TONE. Handbook: 567. *Application:* 215, 239, 242, 245, 255, 262, 268, 271, 274, 352, 370, 385, 393, 401, 431, 464.

Vocabulary Skills

ACRONYMS. 479.

ANTONYMS. 207.

COMPOUND WORDS. 145.

CONTEXT. 37, 96, 333, 385, 520.

DICTIONARY. 75, 96, 129, 160, 193, 207, 233, 370, 401, 431, 449, 462, 479, 520.

ETYMOLOGY. 75, 129, 349, 370, 431, 449, 462, 520.

FIGURATIVE MEANINGS. 520.

HOMONYMS. 193.

IDIOMS. 385.

STRUCTURE. 55, 96, 145, 349, 370, 449, 462, 479.

SYNONYMS. 160, 233.